THE
Professional
WOMAN

Edited and Introduced by
ATHENA THEODORE

SCHENKMAN PUBLISHING COMPANY, INC.
Cambridge, Massachusetts

Copyright © 1971
SCHENKMAN PUBLISHING COMPANY, INC.
Cambridge, Massachusetts

This book is set in Linotype Melior.
Printed in the United States of America.

Library of Congress Catalog Card Number: 72-169697

Schenkman books are distributed by
GENERAL LEARNING PRESS
250 James Street
Morristown, New Jersey

Table of Contents

IV. Career Choice Processes

"The professions indeed supply the keystone to the arch of woman's liberty."

— Julia Ward Howe

Preface

In the recent past the American woman has received occasional but not too serious attention as a social "problem." This is particularly so with the well-educated married woman who does not utilize her talents and skills in the occupational system. Suddenly her dilemma has aroused a new appraisal in the public eye across the country as part of an expanding social movement. Now all women, both the married and the unmarried, are demanding a re-examination of the values of equality and freedom. Within this new ideological quest for "liberation," they are questioning their social and economic status and demanding that they be given the right to control their own destinies in occupational as well as in non-occupational directions. Political interest has also been moving in support of women's rights in such areas as discrimination in employment and constitutional reform. Less obvious, but also relevant, is the transition of the sexually segregated colleges to co-educational forms. Thus an atmosphere of greater openness appears to be generating in America, an atmosphere which questions the traditional institutions that have created and preserved the sexual imbalances and inequities in our society.

Most of the furor and attention addressed to the occupationally disadvantaged sex has not been directly concerned with the lot of the highly educated and trained professional woman. After all, she has had the advantages of an expensive education and a higher income than most non-professional males have. Yet female freedom and equality — the values which are being sought — may never materialize unless some attention is given to the socio-economic role of the highly educated professional woman. The need for information based on systematic studies in this crucial area appears particularly strong in the light of both present and future trends.

The aim of this book is to fill the gap, to bring together some of the recent research about the professional woman in America today, and to explore the various dimensions of this role within a sociological framework. The most desirable approach in accomplishing these objectives would be to outline the crucial variables concerning the professional woman and then to make selections from the research studies which fit neatly into this outline. Such an approach assumes a wealth of information from which the most appropriate choices could be made, but even a superficial search is sufficient to show that published sources fall far short of this ideal. In the exhaustive effort to survey the literature on professional women it was found that research output was heavily concentrated in two or three areas of the initial outline with a considerable dearth in the remaining areas. These gaps made it necessary to tailor the outline according to existing information. At best, the collected readings are a compromise between what a sociologist and other interested readers might like to see included and what actually was available. Also, despite any gaps and any overlap which might occur in the readings, each selection was made because it contributed in some important way towards a composite definition of the role of the professional woman. The effort was also made to ignore literature of an emotional and subjective nature with the hope of transcending some of the myths and misconceptions surrounding the role of the educated American female. The final collection of readings draws not only from the sociological and psycho-sociological literature but also from other sources in the various professions. Several hitherto unpublished articles are also included.

The book is divided into eight parts. Part I, written especially for this purpose, summarizes past and present trends concerning professional women based on the research whose outcome is the present volume. Part II is concerned with changes in the sexual structure of professions and with differences in professional roles according to sex status. The next three parts of the volume focus on the importance of the culture and the various institutions which define professional roles for women and either motivate or inhibit them in choosing careers, training for them, and practicing them. The unique career patterns of women are discussed in the selections in Part VI, especially as these relate to married women. Part VII takes a close look at the marginal position of the professional woman, especially with reference to discrimination. Finally, the last part explores several aspects of female professionalization according to the structure of the professions and social change.

The importance of the professions today cannot be overemphasized. They tell us much about our society. It is in the professions that liberal learning takes place, scientific ideas are pursued, and knowledge is applied. We live in a society teeming with rapid social and technological changes in which the professions play an increasingly greater part. In the face of continuing change in both the professions and the position of women in society, it becomes especially imperative to focus objectively on the role of the professional woman as she appears today and as she might appear in the foreseeable future.

Thus, the book is designed to appeal to a broad spectrum of individuals and groups in both an academic and decision-making setting, such as the college teacher, the administrator at all levels of the educational process, the employer of professionals, those who are in a position to counsel women, and, of course, professional women — and men — in every field. Moreover, the female college student, either undergraduate or graduate, will find great value in this book because of its immediate relevance to her own life and her place in society. Hopefully, her male counterpart will recognize its relevance to his life as well. In addition, the researcher should be able to recognize many inadequately covered or untapped areas of the subject which may stimulate further research.

I would like to acknowledge with thanks the cooperation of all those publishers and authors granting permission to use the selections included in this book.

Athena Theodore

Boston, Massachusetts

I

The Professional Woman:
Trends and Prospects

one

The Professional Woman:
Trends and Prospects

ATHENA THEODORE

Our knowledge about professional women is considerably limited and shrouded in misconceptions that have persisted over a century of time. Even with sophisticated methods of collecting and analyzing data about all forms of social life and the rapidly accumulating body of knowledge in the sociology of occupations, the sex variable has in the past been largely neglected. While the general area of female sex roles has received considerable attention by both sociologists and psychologists, sex roles have not been studied in relation to occupations. At most, the studies concerning professional women have tended to lump males together with females or to consider the female role mainly within the family subsystem, thus reinforcing the cultural bias that this is indeed where the female belongs.

A more recent direction taken in the research effort has been to study the socio-economic role of the female sex within its multi-role dimensions. However, this effort also limits itself to the general occupational structure. On the one hand, it focuses on the extension of the female role beyond the family system but, on the other, it concerns itself mainly with the various constraints imposed on all employed women and with the effects of such employment on the marital relationship and the child-rearing process. Although social class is often an important variable in this effort, the researcher fails to indicate whether the occupation is that of seamstress, nurse, or nuclear scientist.

A third and most recent trend involving research on women recognizes the specific occupation, or at least distinguishes between the broader categories of professional and non-profes-

1

sional women. It also compares males with females. Within this framework the professional woman begins to emerge as a distinctly different role. However, even here the research gaps are numerous, a fact which may explain the inability of many of the researchers to verify their own research conclusions. Furthermore, some of this effort does not go beyond the preliminary pilot stage.

The Professions

In attempting to define the role of the professional woman a problem arises which presently confounds many sociologists: which occupations are indeed professional? Because of the constantly changing nature of occupations, all of which strive to raise their status in the occupational hierarchy, a dynamic concept such as *professionalization* seems both useful and necessary for defining the role of the professional woman. The concept places occupations along a continuum according to certain criteria, with the non-professions at one pole and the most highly institutionalized professions at the other. In essence, the professions constitute an ideal type which all other occupations try to emulate. Since most professional women work in the semi-professions at a level below the highest professions, the use of the concept professionalization makes it possible to distinguish between these two levels; it also enables us to observe on a closer basis the processes by which female professional roles become institutionalized in the larger social structure even as the professions themselves change.

The professions are characterized by a theoretical body of knowledge, technical competence acquired through a protracted period of formal training, a strong service orientation, and a high degree of personal involvement. Social control is exerted in a professional "community" and through formal associations, and legitimacy is gained through both clientele and community sanctions. The central focus of the professional role lies in its rationality, functional specialization, and universalism. The professional acquires his social identity from his profession and derives considerable prestige and satisfaction from practicing it. Each profession develops its own subculture with a strong social and moral solidarity among the members. All occupations engage in professional group striving and attain professionalization to some degree.

Women in the Professions

In the American world of work, particularly in the high-level professional occupations, the female in relation to the male is both differentially involved and differentially patterned according to such factors as population distribution, type of profession, career choice processes, and degree of commitment to the profession. Furthermore, the career patterns of professional females differ distinctly from those of professional males.

We can begin with a few relevant facts. Since World War II the growth of gainfully employed females in all occupations has been continuous. About 41 percent of all women 16 years of age or over were employed in 1970, as compared with only 29 percent in 1940. Although participation rates for all age groups increased during this period, such growth is attributable mainly to the increase in the employment of married women, who today comprise about three-fifths of all fully employed females. Women now represent more than one-third of the employed labor force in America.

Despite such impressive gains, the relative position of professional women, both with respect to the total employed labor force in general and to employed females in particular, has consistently declined over the past few decades. This decline occurs at both the professional and semi-professional levels. For example, women held 45 percent of all professional and technical positions in 1940, but only about 40 percent in 1970. Furthermore, the relative position of professional women has also not improved with respect to the established professions. Today there are fewer women employed in these professions than at the turn of the century, comprising only about 10 percent of all professional workers as compared with about 12 percent in 1900. Not only have women failed to make any significant inroads into such traditionally male strongholds as law, medicine, college teaching, and the ministry, but they are not entering the newer fields in the natural sciences and engineering.

The relative decline of the position of professional women is further substantiated by data on earned professional degrees. Although the proportion of all bachelor's or first professional degrees earned by women was the same — about 40 percent — in the 1960's as in 1940, for the same years the proportion of master's degrees declined from 40 percent to 35 percent and that of doctor's degrees from 15 percent to about 12 percent.

How can we explain the relative decreasing involvement of females at the upper end of the occupational continuum? Why does occupational participation of females appear to have no upper limit in incompletely institutionalized occupations and a well defined upper limit in the highly institutionalized or most professionalized occupations? In other words, how can we account for the relative lack of change in the participation of women at the highest occupational levels in the professions and semi-professions despite their increasing involvement at the lower occupational levels? In the following summary an attempt will be made to focus on this important phenomenon.

Sex-Typing of Professions

As in most occupations, the process of sex-typing occurs in the professions, linking professional roles with sex roles. Medicine, law, science, engineering, dentistry, and the ministry are sex-typed as male occupations; and nursing, grade-school teaching, librarianship, and social work are sex-typed as female. Those professions in which males are concentrated are more highly professionalized than those in which females are concentrated and are therefore more prestigious. Thus, male and female professions are stratified on the occupational continuum according to how the sexes are ranked in the society. At the present time females comprise approximately two-thirds of all workers in the semi-professions and only one-tenth in the professions, indicating a considerably greater degree of sex-typing in the male-dominated professions. Both males and females are considered to be social deviates if they trespass into the territory that is typed for the opposite sex.

The male and female professions have historical derivations in which the two sexes have been segregated according to certain characteristics ascribed by the culture to masculine and feminine roles and to the degree of importance attached to their central role functions. In the early development of the male professions physical strength, endurance, and intellectual superiority were considered necessary attributes for the performance of these economic roles. Since females were rarely permitted the privilege of attending the appropriate training schools or working outside the home in paid employment, males were able to exclude females and maintain for themselves the segregated character of these professions. The cultural basis for sex-typing of professions is clearly supported by the fact that in Russia and other countries far greater proportions of females are engineers, dentists, doctors, and lawyers than in America, and in many instances they even surpass the number of males.

The female professions developed as extensions of the traditional role functions of the female in the family in tasks requiring nurturing, socializing, and helping. Interestingly enough, the married female, with her presumably greater expertise in these areas, was until recently completely excluded from employment. In their earlier development the female professions had some overlapping functions, and they shared a degree of meniality, drudgery, and negligible monetary reward. Later, however, they moved in different directions, with elementary teaching as the first to gain respectability in the last half of the nineteenth century. Today a wide variation continues to exist among the female professions with respect to standards and the competency required to practice them.

Although bureaucratization has helped to raise the prestige level of all the semi-professions, they continue to occupy a lower position than the established professions on the occupational continuum. They are less completely institutionalized than the male-dominated professions because they lack the distinct theoretical base and the autonomy to control themselves. Compared with the established professions, they are poorly integrated as professional communities outside the immediate boundaries of their own organizations. As such they are vulnerable not only to the male-dominated professions, but also to lay control and political influences in the larger society. Semi-professional females have a poor public image in their respective occupations: the community which helps support them believes that hospitals, libraries, and schools are important, not nurses, librarians, and teachers. Furthermore, the persistence of stereotypes concerning the professional role images of females in these semi-professions maintains barriers between them and the public: the old-maid schoolteacher, the pure and virtuous nurse, and the social worker as an outgrowth of the lady-bountiful volunteer are familiar examples.

Under these conditions a high degree of professional group striving expresses itself in a continuous search for public recognition. Such striving is manifested in the proliferation of professional associations, the lengthening of training periods, the establishment of more rigorous controls and standards, and constant attempts to expand the body of knowledge through research and other activities. Avoidance of work with the poor is another manifestation of professional group striving as, for example, recent efforts to shift the profession of social work from a bureaucratic setting serving the lower classes to private practice serving the middle classes. The semi-professions have also tried to raise their status through unionization: teachers have recently been joined in this effort by librarians who also engage in union activity to protect themselves from the growing threat of a managerial elite.

In recent decades the division of labor according to sex status has become less clear in the semi-professions. They are becoming less segregated. Males have invaded all the semi-professions except nursing to the degree that they now constitute the majority sex within some of the specialized areas of these professions such as secondary school teaching and community organization in social work. In addition, this invasion is of the stratificational type where males assume authority positions over females. More males than females are the superintendents and principals of schools and the directors of libraries and social work agencies. A variation of invasion occurs in the segmentation process when males usurp some of the specialized female areas and professionalize them as distinctly male strongholds: in the broad area of home economics, for example, teaching the subject remains in the firm possession of females, but design, fashion, and food and clothing management are now predominantly male domains.

The invasion of males into the semi-professions may be attributed to a variety of factors, among them the growing demand for social services by an expanding population in a period of rising living standards, the low supply of trained females to satisfy this demand, and the upgrading of these professions (including higher salaries and opportunities for "moonlighting") which makes them more attractive to males. Career openings in administrative positions counterbalance the stigma attached to identification with a "female" profession since sex identities are not culturally prescribed as relevant to the rational functions of large organizations and administrative roles. Sex barriers against male entry into the sacred female territory of elementary school teaching are also receding as both technical and pedagogical innovations such as computers, teaching machines, and team teaching approaches pose fewer identity threats to males. On the other hand, the feminization of the teaching role may account for different patterns of discipline and socialization in the schools, patterns which have serious implications for the education of children. Some indication exists that females encourage males to enter the semi-professions both because they prefer male supervision and because males raise the prestige and reward levels of these professions, especially with their concern for unionization. The field of nursing, where male invasion has been minimal, appears to be the last bastion of female dominance in the semi-professions.

While both the sex ratios and forms which sex-typing takes have been changing in the female professions, sex-typing in the established male professions has persisted almost unchanged since the turn of the century. This has occurred despite the increasing bureaucratization of these professions. Medicine, university teaching, law, and the ministry now all have their complex organizations. To these may be added the newer and even larger complexes of scientific research laboratories and business and government organizations (including the military), all of which employ high proportions of professionals compared to non-professionals. The newer scientific professions reflect the same patterns of sex distribution as do the older professions. In short, women have been unable to change these existing professional patterns.

In addition, males and females are segregated in the various specialities of each profession according to their sex-related tasks and prestige ranking. The ministry, which is a "sacredly" masculine profession with the clergyman as a father figure, traditionally eliminates the female as the appropriate sex. In medicine females are concentrated in pediatrics, psychiatry, and public health, while males dominate all the surgical specialities, including obstetrics and gynecology. Female lawyers have higher concentrations in law specialties which are sex-linked to the family and to clerical skills, such as trusts and estates, tax law, and domestic relations. In other areas as well they are more likely than males to do office-related tasks which do not utilize their training. The bureaucratization of professions has not only tended to reinforce sex-typing according to professional specialities, but has also institutionalized stratification patterns in ways similar to the semi-professions, that is, on the basis of male authority and influence. Males thus dominate the entire professional and bureaucratic structure, including the professional associations and the decision-making staffs of the professional training schools.

Stratificational sex-typing also occurs between the professions and semi-professions within the same organization according to their rank on the occupational continuum. Doctors have authority over social workers and nurses in the hospital, academicians have authority over librarians in the university, and various professionals in administrative positions have authority over teachers in the public school system. Stratificational sex-typing in complex organizations thus reinforces male-female dominance patterns in the larger society. It also results in the emergence of adaptive structures through role deviation and avoidance rituals among both female professionals and semi-professionals. The authority vested in the male professional role also carries over to the student or apprentice in the organization who has not yet acquired full professional status, often resulting in conflict situations.

Cultural Determinants of the Professional Role

Differential sex involvement in the occupational structure has deep roots in the cultural values shared by the society. These values prescribe the appropriate role behavior for each sex and are rooted in a division of labor which assigns the care of children and the home to the female and responsibility for the economic support of the family to the male. The institutionalized role of the male lies in the occupational system from which he derives his chief source of status. The male's occupation positions him in the class structure of the society according to both its prestige and income. At marriage the male shares his social status with his wife and children, and the professional male confers an especially high status on his wife. Thus, it is not uncommon for the wives of professional males to establish organizations such as lawyers' wives' clubs when they are not themselves professionals.

But the wife also has a key status of her own, that which she derives from her role combination of wife, mother, and homemaker. She is expected to receive her main gratifications in the home on a primary level of person-centered and expressively-oriented relationships revolving around her husband and children. Marriage is thus considered to be the principal goal of the

female, even the professionally trained female; and the unmarried female is considered a social deviate if she outwardly
rejects marriage for a "career." As an ideal type, the female role
appears opposite to the rational, functionally specific, and universalistic role of the professional person in the occupational
system.

In addition, the female role in relation to the male is differently
evaluated by the society. Female status is essentially regarded as
inferior and subordinate to male status, and this value is shared
by both males and females, with males supporting a considerably stronger view. Females are usually considered lacking in
the intellectual ability needed to pursue abstract and theoretical
disciplines; and all females, no matter what their educational
attainments, tend to be judged first on the basis of physical
attractiveness rather than on intelligence, a criterion which
affects their bargaining position in both the marriage market and
the economy. Even when females achieve professional status,
lay attitudes of distrust, based on these perceptions of females
as both the inferior and less intelligent sex, force professional
women to avoid relating directly to the public except within
culturally approved situations.

It is in the early socialization period that self-concepts regarding sex-roles are formed and occupations first selected. Girls and
boys internalize their sex roles differently according to the cultural definitions of what is considered appropriate male and
female behavior. Girls learn that their central role obligation is
in procreation and that their other role obligations are preferably
confined to family and community. Within these boundaries the
sex-role images acquired by young females are of a nurturant,
helping, and empathizing nature. These images affect their
notions about probable future occupational involvement, and
they select occupational roles according to these sex-related

qualities. Parents, teachers, peers, and communication media all
reinforce the occupational images and stereotypes throughout
the socialization process. Institutional structures such as sexually segregated schools and colleges further emphasize distinctions between the sexes and affect occupational images and
aspirations.

Despite the gradual lowering of barriers to the economic
participation of women, cultural values and attitudes concerning
such participation have been far slower to change. Full approval

for involvement in the occupational system is granted only to the female who lacks the economic support of a male provider, and even she is permitted only temporary status. For the single female education beyond high school and subsequent employment constitute a dalliance period before marriage. The modern, educated woman, no matter how professionally skilled she may be, is expected to stop short of complete involvement in the labor market at the time of marriage, particularly when children arrive. A notable exception is the Negro professional woman who finds marriage to be far less constraining than does her white counterpart. But for all women the variations which occur in the degree of approval or disapproval focus largely on the maternal function. Even those colleges and graduate schools which educate females and admit them for professional training subscribe to the norm that employment for women is conditional or expendable, and they plan their admissions and educational programs on that basis.

Progression through the various stages of socialization introduces sex-role dilemmas for females which are not experienced by males. In the school especially girls internalize norms of achievement and universalism in relation to the occupational system. The strength of the role conflicts which they experience depends on how they define their roles according to masculinity and femininity and on the degree to which they perceive any incompatibility between the two normative systems of home and work. That sex-role dilemmas do in fact occur for highly educated females is amply illustrated in the research. Even the trained professional already engaged in actual practice is no exception. Cultural values which position females in the home conflict with educational structures which prepare and condition them to anticipate careers and with occupational structures which seek to recruit them. At the same time, females are placed in a relatively disadvantaged position compared with males in the mate-selection process, and they cannot plan with certainty the extent of their occupational involvement until the question of marriage is resolved. Family and peer group pressures to date and marry by the time of college graduation are especially strong during the college years when the greatest supply of prospective mates is available; and female involvement in the dating and courtship system during the undergraduate years usually undermines serious plans for graduate study. The intensity of the dating experience in college among females may also indicate latent motives to resolve present or anticipated sex-role conflicts rather than to marry merely for financial security or even for personal or sexual fulfillment.

In the face of institutional and status inconsistencies, the costs to personality structure, although not easily isolated, are high. Unclear role expectations and uncertainty about the future affect the self-concepts and achievement needs of young females. Disillusionment and frustration appear to be especially strong for the college girl who must lower aspirations below her level of intellectual competence and skills to satisfy a "deference need." Indeed, with the realization of marital ambitions, the rewards of occupational achievement may be rejected overnight even as they are almost within reach. Females internalize failure as they proceed through the socialization process and prepare for work, and this sense of failure carries over into family role images and performances after marriage. Ambition is not clearly recognized, specifically set, or as actively pursued by females as by males; in most females it is almost non-existent or, at most relatively weak. Yet ambition is a necessary condition for both the pursuit of high professional training and continuous achievement throughout the professional career.

Weak self-concepts are especially apparent in the expressions of guilt and rationalization, especially among those highly educated females who retreat either temporarily or permanently from occupational life. Young married wives who contemplate a return to work after their maternal and homemaking responsibilities have declined tend to underestimate their own abilities and lack the confidence to make the necessary decisions for re-entry. The self-defacing image of "only a housewife" is often internalized to the point where satisfactory adjustment to the new system, if it is entered at all, is difficult or even impossible to make. It is also suggested that the failure of educated females to insist on greater equality for their sex derives from the weak self-concepts which they develop over their lifetimes. Lack of ambition is also manifested in the actual work involvement of highly educated women. Only about 15 percent of female graduate students prefer a full-time professional career for the first five years after completing their education. And even before they enter college, almost half of exceptionally talented females anticipate no career at all, a deferred career, or are uncertain.

Within the ambiguous value system in which college-educated females find themselves today they define success, work, and career in vastly different ways than do college-educated males. In the first place, males judge success in terms of occupational achievement: they are compelled to work, and the amount of their income determines the standard of living and the style of life they will be able to enjoy. Success in work is thus judged on the basis of monetary gain as well as on the satisfactions gained through professional tasks and activities. Even the most honorific rewards are sometimes equated with financial benefits. The legitimate channels for the achievement of both recognition and the accompanying monetary rewards usually lie in the career pattern. For males the concept of career involves a continuous progression of commitment by stages over a period of years, a progression whereby the professional person moves from a subordinate to a superordinate position in the organizational and professional structure and receives additional rewards as he assumes a more responsible or prestigious position. Career thus implies vertical mobility, and in the professions this often means movement towards added administrative responsibility.

The different role definitions that professional females have of work derive both from their dependency on males for social status and economic support and from their own role images as females. Most college-educated females judge their own success first in terms of marriage-related achievements such as "finding" a husband, rearing "successful" children, and contributing to the husband's occupational goals and emotional needs. Although today most females in college profess to the belief in the equal importance of marriage and career in their lives, they establish priorities which give work a subordinate position to marriage. The importance of work acquires a range of changeable emphasis at various periods of the life cycle according to any single circumstance or combination of circumstances present at any one time. In effect, marriage is the only path to social mobility for most women. After marriage the importance of work for the female depends upon the presence and ages of children, the husband's attitude, financial needs, the extent of her professional skills, and the availability of appropriate work.

The evidence strongly suggests that the college-educated woman, and especially the professionally trained woman, marries within the higher socio-economic levels and thus does not work primarily for financial goals. Unlike her non-college counterpart, she considers the acquisition of money as secondary to the achievement of individual gratifications, to the fulfillment of personal and social needs, to being a helpmate to her husband's career. Moreover, the gratifications sought are of an immediate rather than a deferred nature, a fact which may help explain why professional women are, in general, more satisfied with their work than are professional men. Extrinsic rewards are sought through the husband's career, and income is important only insofar as it fills a temporary financial exigency or covers a period of family crisis. Escape from the monotony of the home and the achievement of recognition outside the traditional female role are in themselves goals for the married woman, irrespective of the kind of work performed. This is one reason why professional women prefer employment in organizations rather than on a completely independent basis. The occupational role is viewed as working for someone else, not oneself. The female artist, musician, and writer are examples of professional roles in the creative arts which are performed in either the home or in a completely isolated setting, and such structural constraints may help to account for the smaller proportion of females, compared with males, who practice these professions and for their lesser productivity.

Work and career are thus usually indistinguishable in the perceptions of women. Although males are often aware of the processes involved in moving from one career stage to another, females think of their work more as a "job" without reference to its future development. Since their own position in the larger society is ascribed to them at both birth and marriage, they do not view a career of their own as a means for raising their social status or exerting influence on others. Unlike males, females do not choose an organization for the career prospects it presents, such as salary, future research opportunities, and promotions. They not only have short-range work goals, but they also tend to see themselves only within certain limited kinds of social systems, such as schools or hospitals, rather than within a vast industrial complex. Professional females who work in large organizations lack the occupational reference groups needed in the career pattern both within the organization and in the wider professional community of peers. It may well be that females have a different loyalty structure than males. Support for this view also derives from the fact that females prefer employment in small work groups while at the same time avoiding situations of extreme isolation such as may occur in scientific research. Finally, it is suggested that different clique structures occur within the organization for the married female compared with both her unmarried counterpart and the professional male.

For many reasons, including her relatively weak ambition and her short-ranged goals, the professional woman often does not manifest the kind of individuality, self-reliance, and opportunism that is stressed in business. Independent practice entails business acumen and even competition with other practicing professionals in the community; the entrepreneurship of the doctor's or dentist's private practice is thus usually avoided by the woman. Whatever the form the employment takes, the values sought are generally of a helping and empathetic nature having person-centered tasks. But aesthetic and intellectual values are also present, and possession of these values may indicate different degrees of goal-directedness. This possibility has yet to be put to empirical test.

Career Choice Processes

The processes by which people select professions and become committed to them differ both from one individual to the next and between the two sexes. Cultural values are strong and pervasive: for women they prescribe not only appropriate sex roles within professions but also which occupations should be selected and practiced. The social sanctions for deviance are manifested in societal disapproval and discrimination. At the same time, female personality is affected by varying degrees of role strain.

As indicated above, females are continuously confronted with a dual set of interrelated choice patterns, the first of which is broad and determines the relative weight to assign work versus marriage, and the second of which forms the basis for making more narrow and instrumental decisions, particularly those which affect commitment to a profession. Both kinds of decisions are made according to marital status and other situational circumstances at any one period in the life cycle. In this respect females have the choice of a life style, a luxury not afforded the American male. On the other hand, within this conditional framework females are not the decision-makers about their place in the occupational system, and they do not "choose" an occupation as do males. They usually wait for signals from others, whether these signals consist of outright approval or disapproval, encouragement or discouragement.

Thus, universalistic norms related to intellectual ability and academic performance are less operative in the selection of professions by females than by males. For women education beyond the bachelor's degree is an uncalculated risk, and no certainty exists that the time put into an extensive period of training will reach fruition in professional practice worthy of the time and money spent in its preparation. Major decisions for advance training are thus usually made *after* the bachelor's degree is obtained. Much of the shifting of career fields during the college years by females derives from a mounting reluctance to pursue an extended period of academic commitment beyond the four-year college span. The deeper involvement in the dating and courtship system during the college years contributes to the recognition of realities which make the serious pursuit of a career a questionable process or at least a decision worth postponing. Advanced degrees requiring extended training are often easily sacrificed. The established professions of medicine, law, the ministry, and college teaching all require graduate work beyond the bachelor's degree of at least three years' duration; yet, despite the fact that these professions involve central task functions which emphasize humanitarian values and which might be expected to attract females, women reject these professions for the less time-consuming preparation required by their sister areas in the semi-professions, such as grade-school teaching, nursing, or social work.

Comparison with males also reveals some striking differences in respect to career shifting and second-choice careers. College males shift career choices to be like other students, but they also lower their occupational goals because of the highly selective admission process to the graduate and professional schools. Most college females, however, shift career choices according to their own individual circumstances in relation to marriage and because of direct and indirect social pressures to avoid advanced educational training that might limit marriage prospects. Those professions in which entrance skills may be obtained at the undergraduate level such as teaching and nursing gain adherents among females even though they may not constitute first choices. However, terminal degrees in education or advanced degrees for teaching in collegiate programs of nursing are rarely contemplated by females who specialize in these programs at the undergraduate levels.

Teaching at the secondary-school level thus often becomes a second-choice profession in the liberal arts college for the female who avoids the specialized teacher-training college either because she is not genuinely interested in becoming a teacher at the time of high school graduation or because lower prestige is attached to such a college. However, teaching in the pre-college grades is also a second-choice occupation for many college males. Whatever the differences in motives may be between the sexes for choosing teaching as a second-choice occupation, it is highly likely to be more dissatisfying than the first choice and affects both the motivation to practice and performance on the job. However, females who choose pre-college teaching either as a first- or second-choice profession are likely to be more academically talented than their male counterparts.

The process of career hedging emphasizes even more the persistent dilemmas of occupational choices for females created by uncertainties concerning the future. Although males are also known to be undecided about their future professions, even up to and following graduation from college, more procrastination in occupational decisions takes place among college females. They are therefore less likely than males to enter the pre-professional curricula required for medicine, law, and scientific research. The liberal arts curriculum is more often selected because it offers enjoyment, cultural enrichment, and intellectual values; it also does not threaten the social identity of the female student. At the same time, selection of the liberal arts curriculum leaves the door open for graduate education in several fields, should circumstances make this an appropriate goal. Shifts from various subject areas to the broad area of the humanities and the creative arts constitute a common pattern of career hedging for females.

Again, although the proportion of females in college and university teaching has been declining compared with males, more females are in this profession than in any of the others requiring three years or more of extended training beyond the bachelor's degree. Career hedging accounts for this distribution pattern to a considerable degree, but the flexibility of the free elective system in the liberal arts program is also a facilitating factor. In this respect it has been suggested that those females in college teaching are there more by default than by design, although the same is undoubtedly true for a smaller proportion of males. However, women in college do not make comparable moves into the natural or social sciences where advanced degrees might also entitle them to teach at the college level. Such avoidance substantiates the point that female choices in college are more a function of social class and marital status than they are of either interest or aptitude; the images which college females have of their future roles are oriented towards leisure and balancing the more specialized roles of their husbands with their own more diffusely oriented cultural and intellectual interests.

Whether or not females pursue extended study in the graduate or professional schools is also dependent on factors other than motivation and accident. In the first place, for the few females who do aspire to such study, the financial costs of such education constitute deterrents which are applicable also to males. But females are less favored than males to elicit financial support through scholarships and fellowships. Similarly, females compete with male siblings for financial support, and if priorities must be set, the education of the son is favored over that of the daughter. Thus, although a sizeable proportion of males from low socio-economic backgrounds succeed in attaining terminal degrees, usually only the females from the upper socio-economic strata can afford the advanced study. But even in the upper classes the norm for the female's education is the bachelor's degree, so that even when family financial support is available, it may be reluctantly offered as well as reluctantly sought. The relatively homogamous marriages which occur in the upper classes assure not only financial security but also satisfying involvement in a subculture of complex and time-consuming social relationships and economically non-productive activities concerned with the husband's occupation, with leisure pursuits, and with voluntary involvement in community social services.

Among women who study beyond the bachelor's degree it is the female who is single at the time of graduation from college who is more likely to pursue extended graduate study, although the number of married females has been increasing. The high cost of graduate training constitutes a strong deterrent for the young married female to enter or even complete graduate study, since for females marriage usually means financial emancipation from the family of orientation. However, married males may continue to receive parental support until completion of the terminal degree. The young wife is also likely to work to contribute to the financial support of her husband's graduate education. Although males also lower their aspirational levels for advanced study after marriage, early marriage appears to be more dysfunctional for the female than for the male in respect to achieving terminal-degree status. The long period of training ahead is in itself a deterrent to entering a professional school, and only rarely does the married female begin extensive graduate study after marriage. However, married females in substantial numbers do enter and complete semi-professional training programs which are limited to one or two years of graduate study; in this respect social work and librarianship are late but frequent choices for young married women. Age and educational level at marriage thus become closely linked with the financial resources which are available for the pursuit of graduate work beyond the bachelor's degree and constitute crucial variables in the decision to pursue a career in those professions requiring protracted study.

What emerges from this brief view of the complex processes by which females choose and enter professions is that they are less likely than males to choose and study professions which interest them most and in which they might have satisfying careers, and they are far less likely than males to practice those professions for which they actually prepare. Financial barriers and cultural definitions of female roles not only affect female motivation to pursue careers but also determine the specific professional choices that will be made. Females not only avoid entering those professions which require extended periods of formal socialization in the graduate and professional schools but also avoid professions which stress stereotyped "male" qualities and dominant values antithetical to their own sex-role images. The intellectual challenges of discovery and creativity in science may appear highly desirable on the one hand; but, on the other hand, femininity and female beauty are seen as incompatible with science. Two-thirds of all females having some professional skills with at least five years of education beyond high school graduation, and about one-tenth with terminal degrees requiring three or more years of professional training beyond the bachelor's degrees are not in the labor force. As such, females constitute the largest category of an unemployed, underemployed, and overtrained work force, perhaps the largest pool of economically wasted talent in the United States.

Adult Socialization and Career Commitment

Commitment to work and to a specific profession increases with the amount of higher education beyond the college degree. If commitment is measured as the length of time in which the female plans to work, those females with a master's degree show greater commitment than those with a bachelor's degree, and those with a terminal degree show greater commitment than those with a master's degree. The higher the educational attainment among married women, the greater likelihood of labor force participation. A higher proportion of married women work on a full-time, rather than a part-time, basis as their educational achievements are raised. Educational attainment is also a more significant factor for females than for males when the level reached is the bachelor's degree: employed females who have acquired this degree are concentrated in the semi-professional areas, whereas relatively fewer males have semi-professional competence. However, the same does not apply at the higher degree level.

Many of the conditions which create a weak work orientation have already been mentioned. To these may be added other factors which also influence the female's choice of a specific career. Positive family influences in the early socialization period of girls appear to affect significantly the degree of female commitment to work. The mother's involvement in work, regardless of profession, appears to be an important variable in the transmission of occupational values to the daughter, and the young girl may also find other female models to emulate in school. The father's educational attainment is also a significant variable in the level of professional aspiration the daughter sets for herself: females who choose non-traditional professions are likely to have highly educated fathers, a pattern which is less true among males. But encouragement by other professional relatives and by college professors also constitutes the initial impetus for many female students, like male students, to pursue professional careers in a particular discipline. Negro college women, though far fewer in number than white women, are known to have a stronger work orientation. However, recent evidence indicates that some change is beginning to take place in the direction of preferences for family roles by educated Negro women similar to educated white women. Finally, the favorable attitude of the spouse or intended spouse is the single most significant factor in the woman's pursuit of a professional career. College women who receive such support are far more likely to develop a stronger career orientation than those who do not receive this support.

Whatever the motivating and facilitating factors might be in the decision to seek a professional career, it is not until entrance into the graduate or professional training school that the first important step in a person's commitment to a profession takes place. Here again, an important difference occurs between males and females. For females the establishment of a new self-identity takes place at two levels instead of one: internalization of the occupational role and identification with a specific profession. The male's concern is with the latter only. Although the two levels are not easily separated for females, they are nevertheless distinct processes, involving a complexity of factors related to both sex identity and achievement values. The preponderance of males with strong achievement orientations in the professional training schools provides a testing environment for the resolution of sex-role dilemmas at this critical point in the lives of female students. Not surprisingly, females in graduate programs have a far higher attrition rate than their male counterparts, with the highest female attrition taking place in the first year. Compared with males, the length of time females spend in the professional training school is more significant for both identification with a profession and commitment to work: the longer the period of socialization into the professional culture, the stronger the work orientation becomes. Females who complete the rigorous training programs in the high professions and receive their degrees are more likely to practice their professions than those females who train in the semi-professional areas requiring the bachelor's or master's degree only. They are also more likely to practice their professions on a full-time basis.

The Multi-Roled Professional Woman

Even as adult socialization in the professional training program strengthens work commitment, a minority of females who complete their degree requirements nonetheless retreat from professional life early in their careers on either a temporary or permanent basis. For both professional and semi-professional women, marriage immediately defines the boundaries of occupational involvement. New obstacles are encountered which may make it either undesirable or impossible to pursue a profession; among these are the occupation and income of the husband, the residential location of the family, and the presence of children. One career disruption at this stage of the life cycle may be sufficient to change the career plans of the wife in an accommodating direction which was not previously planned.

.The necessity to integrate the wife's role into the husband's occupation is a barrier which often obliterates her professional involvement from the very beginning of the marriage: social entertaining, travel, and assisting with the husband's occupational role are all examples of deterrents to her own professional goals. Differences in the relative prestige of the husband's and wife's occupations, such as marriage between a doctor and a nurse, may also result in permanent withdrawal for the wife. The neolocal and virilocal structure of the American family restrains the mobility of the wife with children, limiting her employment opportunities and interrupting any already established career pattern. Since higher mobility rates occur during the earlier stages of male careers, the wife of either a professional or a business executive is at a particular disadvantage. For married women in certain professions satisfactory employment opportunities may not be available in the area of residence, suburban locations being especially restrictive. Independent practice requires even greater stability in residential location, and when wives do enter such practice, it is often through partnership with the husband in a similar professional role rather than on a solo basis.

The arrival of children into the family, an occurrence which rarely affects the occupational involvement of the father, has a decided effect on that of the professional mother. As with non-professional mothers, the greatest number of both temporary absences and complete withdrawals from work occur during the stage of early marriage; professional mothers, however, do have lower withdrawal rates than do non-professional mothers. In all cases the additional obligations of the maternal role necessitate the allocation of time and energy among several roles. Although the middle-class father tends to assist more in the child-care process than does the father in the lower classes, the professional wife continues to assume the major responsibilities of the home and care of children; thus, even the dual-professional marriage does not insure an egalitarian family. Despite the proliferation of labor-saving devices, domestic and child-care obligations are both fatiguing and distracting from full professional involvement. The inadequacy or unavailability of child-care substitutes and day-care facilities are additional deterrents, even for part-time employment. Professional mothers usually have fewer children than do non-professional mothers, but the period of responsibility for children nevertheless covers a span of approximately twenty years, a period of time which seriously affects the career commitment of professional women.

Some aspects of the structure of professions also inhibit the multi-roled professional woman from practicing her profession. In this respect the professions make greater demands on the professional than on the semi-professional role. Professions such as the ministry and private practice of medicine often require that the professional be available to parishioners and patients on an almost unlimited time basis. College and university teaching includes not only the required teaching and other related tasks but also independent research for publication — tasks performed largely on one's own time. The necessity to exchange knowledge in the scientific professions, particularly in the area of research, requires extensive participation in the formal and informal networks of the scientific community, while the desirability of exchanging services through referrals and consultations in professions like law and medicine require involvement in informal social networks beyond those occurring during office hours. All professions require keeping up with a rapidly expanding body of knowledge. A higher degree of flexibility is possible with certain professions than with others, such as summer vacations and sabbatical leaves for professors and the opportunity to arrange office hours in private practice for dentists, doctors, and other health specialists. Although professional women, like all employed women, devote less time to housekeeping tasks than do unemployed women, complete fulfillment of even the central role tasks necessitate long hours devoted to the professional role. The lesser productivity of married females compared to males in some professions appears to be attributable more to the lack of time than to either motivation or interest.

The necessity to allocate time among several roles has more serious implications for the professional role itself. Fully employed professional mothers tend to discard the more marginal professional tasks such as attendance at professional meetings and participation in the social networks outside the work organization. They also spend fewer hours at their work than do male professionals even when such work is considered to be full-time. The professional role for the female is thus defined more narrowly than it is for the male, and the same professional role may even entail a different time allocation between tasks or even consist of different tasks altogether for the two sexes. Indications that male professionals have been increasing the number of hours which they devote to work raises the possibility that further changes and distortions will occur in the definition of professional roles for women who must divide their time between home and work.

The question has frequently been raised as to whether or not the employment of the mother is harmful to the child or threatens the stability of the family. The research on this subject focuses on maternal role performance mainly as a function of social class. In the absence of distinct occupational categories, we can only infer that middle-class mothers are either professionals or semi-professionals. The available evidence does not indicate any clear relationship between middle-class maternal employment and the emotional adjustment of children, regardless of their ages. Work satisfaction is positively correlated with both the child-rearing process and with spouse relationships. Less guilt is associated with the fully employed mother than with the mother who is employed part-time, and the presence of guilt is known to have an effect on the mother's relationship with her children. Although conclusive evidence is lacking, it appears that less guilt is experienced by professional women than by non-professional women. Moreover, female college students are less inclined today than ten years ago to consider the presence of children as an obstacle to their involvement in careers. The professional mother defines her maternal role obligations differently than does the non-professional, and she raises her children differently.

Preoccupation in the research effort with the broad stratum of the "middle class" leaves us with scant information concerning the marital stability of the spouses when the wife is a professional. In order to minimize conflict the professional woman must be married to the "right" husband. It has already been pointed out that the husband's favorable attitude toward the wife's employment is significant for her career ambitions and plans, and it might be inferred from this that such approval contributes to the stability of the marriage. However, approval may be more likely to be given when the husband is secure in his own occupation and does not feel threatened by his wife's professional status and achievements. It also appears that the husband's occupation and the mode of integrating family and work in his own life is crucial for the wife's successful participation in a career and the marital satisfaction of both spouses. No evidence is available which would support the conclusion that wives and husbands are in basic competition with each other when both are professionals at the same prestige levels. On the contrary, since a high percentage of marriages occur between spouses having similar or related professions of equal prestige, it may be that the common interests and activities centering around their professions often provide a basis for a more stable marriage. The older age of marriage among professional women (median age 27) also suggests a greater degree of maturity brought to the marital relationship. Finally, as with all married women who are employed, professional wives contribute to the financial security of the family, thus providing husbands with more freedom to pursue their own careers without the strains imposed by mounting financial burdens, especially those created by the children's educational needs. As indicated earlier, it is not unusual for semi-professional males, especially teachers, to engage in additional occupational pursuits beyond the regular employment in order to increase their incomes. However, the practice of "moonlighting" also appears among professional males, and in such cases financial motives are perhaps as strong as are the challenges and interest provided by the added activities.

Career Discontinuity

The barriers imposed on professional women necessitate the allocation of roles between two different systems, both requiring a considerable amount of time and energy. This duality has resulted in a highly individualistic pattern of work or "career" for married women at all occupational levels. The pattern may be described as discontinuity between work and leisure, leisure being defined as either disguised unemployment or the "non-work" of household tasks. In this pattern short-termness and intermittency are the essential characteristics. Discontinuity comprises a new life style in which females enter and withdraw from employment according to various situational factors occurring in the life cycle, such as the presence and ages of children, child care and household help, the availability of appropriate work, financial pressures, and the emotional needs of the woman herself. Considerable variation occurs in both the time of entry and re-entry into the occupation and in the length of the work period, with the longest period of withdrawal occurring at the birth of the first child and the greatest re-entry period occurring after the children have left home. Another pattern is the maintenance of a part-time position through a longer period on both a regular and irregular basis. At present about one-fourth of all employed women work on a part-time basis, including a substantial proportion of semi-professional women and a smaller proportion of professional women.

Discontinuity between work and leisure for females trained in the professional areas has been institutionalized both out of their own needs and those of labor. Specialization and the segmentation of tasks in bureaucratic organizations have created conditions whereby employers are able to mobilize a highly skilled and scarce source of labor in a flexible and convenient arrangement based on the married woman's part-time availability. For the woman who is either unwilling or unable to work on a full-time basis, the financial pressures of maintaining a high standard of living and educating children is perhaps as strong an incentive for part-time employment as is the necessity to care for children, maintain skills, relieve boredom, and serve society.

Although a small proportion of professional women do make the transition from discontinuous work patterns to full-time continuous employment, the majority of those who accept part-time employment and those who withdraw completely run the risk of jeopardizing their future careers. In part-time employment choices tend to be based more on expediency and situational factors than on interests and competency. Part-time employment is more likely to be looked upon as a source of additional income rather than as a stage in a professional career. Often the "job" is more of a non-professional or quasi-professional nature in which the professional or semi-professional role is segmented into certain chores or tasks which may not even be relevant to the profession. Females employed on a part-time basis are likely to be placed in the lower and more undesirable positions in the organization when they are employed, and they often receive salaries which are below their level of intelligence and competence. In this respect they are highly vulnerable to exploitation by employers. Thus, discontinuity helps to support a system of social inequality. Moreover, part-time employment often results in disillusionment with the assigned tasks and the emergence of unfavorable occupational images which may discourage the transition to full-time employment.

In the case of complete withdrawal with the anticipation of return, the risks are high that the future career may either not eventuate or may prove unsatisfactory. This is especially true in the leading professions. Once the decision to withdraw is made, continuous postponement is likely to occur from loss of confidence in one's ability during the inactive period: the longer the postponement, the more difficult the return. It has been suggested that the peak of creativity appears in the ages of the late twenties and throughout the thirties, years in which married women are likely to be most deeply involved in maternal role obligations. But prolonged withdrawal takes its toll on productivity and performance both in regard to isolation from professional colleagues and the obsolescence of skills. The necessity for re-training in the professions may not always be financially feasible when children are still dependents, and, moreover, re-training opportunities are seldom available. For these and other reasons females in the highest professions, who comprise the most committed category of female workers, are extremely reluctant to withdraw even temporarily from work or to accept employment on a part-time basis. Those who do encounter barriers and are forced to withdraw experience the greatest degree of frustration and dissatisfaction, a fact which may also affect their roles as wives and mothers.

For the professional woman the stage of early marriage constitutes a crucial period for the continuation of the career by women who have completed their professional training and who may have already practiced their professions. Early in the marriage the "seriatim" approach to work minimizes emotional strains for the work-oriented mother who can continue to anticipate full occupational involvement in the future. In this respect discontinuity serves an important function in forestalling conflict in the marital relationship, especially when the husband does not approve of the wife's work involvement. What actually occurs with part-time employment, however, is that the prospects afforded by occasional and convenient employment patterns also provide young college women with rationalizations to postpone serious decisions about their own professional roles and involvement in careers. The emergence of "continuing education" programs designed to lure inactive married women back to the classrooms, laboratories, and eventual practice also serve as an additional source of rationalization to young college women that postponed career plans may be resumed at some indefinite time in the future.

Whether eventual return to full-time employment is anticipated or not, the pattern of discontinuity between such diversely structured social roles as professional woman and homemaker has serious implications for personality integration. An erratic and inconsistent work pattern may result in a greater degree of emotional instability than that caused by full retreat from professional work. Women who repeatedly enter the occupational male world are confronted anew each time with problems of sex identity. In addition, part-time middle-class women have been shown to be less satisfied with their work than those employed on a full-time basis. Both inconsistency and the greater degree of guilt associated with the part-time mother's employment have further implications for maternal role performance and its effects on children.

Sex Discrimination

Discrimination against female professionals occurs when females of equivalent qualifications, experience, and performance as males do not share equally in the decision-making process nor receive equal rewards. These rewards consist of money, promotions, prestige, professional recognition, and honors. In addition, lack of normative patterns to facilitate normal entry into the profession and the imposition of barriers which limit access to both the organization and to professional colleagues also constitute discrimination when such barriers are based on sex.

Discrimination against professional females has deep roots in the American past. Exploitation of females at all occupational levels is amply recorded in the descriptive literature. The historical accounts of mid-nineteenth century America, when females first attempted to enter the professional schools of the ministry, law, and medicine, provide dramatic evidence of the severe exclusion policies practiced against women. One aspect of the earlier feminist movement consisted of attempts to receive recognition for the possession of intellectual competence and to gain admission into the professional schools. Even today different salary schedules for the two sexes are maintained in various work organizations, despite the illegality of such practices.

In both the professions and the semi-professions females have continued to remain in a disadvantageous position compared with males. (An exception occurs among Negroes where a discriminating environment has had a different impact on the two sexes.) Even in the semi-professions where females have traditionally comprised the majority sex, males have usually held the positions of authority. In the established professions where males are the dominant sex, they have retained their strong control over females. This occurs through the elaborate structure of both the formal and informal networks of tightly knit professional communities that stretch across the entire country. Male professionals exert tremendous power over every aspect of professional life, from recruitment into the professional schools, the curriculum, residencies and apprenticeships, grants for scientific research, and even the income of professionals through consultations, referrals, and the disposition of honorific rewards. In the ministry recruitment is also controlled by a non-occupational organization consisting of lay people. Because females comprise only a small minority of the professional population, they are in an especially disadvantageous position in terms of both entrance into the professions and in the distribution of the rewards.

The argument that females do not enter certain professions or that they become sex-typed because of either direct or indirect discriminatory practices has already been shown to be weak. A considerable amount of self-imposed exclusion from the traditionally male professions does occur. Females avoid choosing some professions for a variety of reasons and they choose some for other reasons, but fear of discrimination is not the crucial motivating factor in their initial avoidance and selection of professions. As indicated earlier, those females who have been sufficiently motivated to reach professional status have demonstrated a willingness to occupy subservient positions in organizations and they have been relatively less concerned with mobility and rewards than males. In the semi-professions where females are clearly not excluded, they are known to avoid the problems of the organization by showing no interest in policy positions and allowing males to take the initiative in professional group striving, and they are also known to display negligible ambition in reaching high levels of individual achievement. Furthermore, they have indicated almost no resistance to male invasion of their professions.

Thus, it would be fallacious to state unconditionally that deliberate attempts are made by males in authority positions to exclude females from the established professions and to restrain them from occupying the higher positions in work organizations. In the male-dominated professional schools formal barriers based on sex are alleged to have been largely eliminated in the admission policies, although the numbers of entering females continue to be based on male-female ratios of applicants, and in some areas, such as medical residencies, specialty admissions are virtually closed to women. While discrimination may or may not take subtle forms in such admissions, the fact is that female college graduates having the required academic competence simply do not apply to these schools in the same proportions as do males. Even after admission to the professional school the attrition rate is far higher for females than for males throughout the period of training and extremely high during the first year. Actual or perceived threats of discrimination do not appear to be the important reasons for this attrition during the training period. The risks of training females, who are less likely than males either to reach terminal degree status or to practice their professions on a full-time basis, are not considered to be worth the costs of subsidizing a substantial portion of an expensive training period, particularly when the supply of professionals is scarce. An especially selective system of recruitment occurs for scientific study, and since only a fraction of college graduates qualify for and enter basic research in the exact sciences, there is often justifiable resistance shown by admission boards to female applicants for this highly socialized and elite group.

However, discriminatory practices against female professionals clearly occur at the level of recruitment into the work organization and throughout the employment period. Professional females who have comparable performance records with males are concentrated in the lower-status and less visible specialties and, in proportion to their numbers, are negligibly represented in the most prestigious and more visible positions in the organization. The practice of discrimination with respect to the distribution of the most coveted rewards appears to be more widespread in some professions than others. For example, female lawyers do not have partner status in the large law firms; female professors do not sit in the professorial chairs of the universities; and female artists do not have their paintings displayed in major galleries. Granted that many of the most coveted rewards are scarce commodities for which all the professionals will enter into sharp competition, females who have demonstrated equal competence in both performance and productivity do not even begin to share in the rewards proportionally to males. While lack of precedence in the employment of professional females may in fact make it difficult to "place" females in the system, and while male professionals themselves experience ambivalence in making distinctions between the various contradictory roles of women, the result is that females are discouraged from seeking both employment and advancement when they perceive the opportunity structure within a profession as being limited for them. The concentration of female professionals in government bureaucracies occurs to a considerable extent because of the discrimination felt by these women when they are employed by privately controlled organizations. Nepotism rules impose further constraints on married females where employment opportunities are already limited through residential immobility.

Discrimination of a more subtle nature is also evidenced in the exclusion of females from the informal networks of cliques, clubs, and other peer relationships where professional decisions are made, knowledge shared, and favors exchanged in terms of clients, consultantships, grants, and research collaborations. Sex status operates strongly against their involvement in these "inner" circles, including their socialization as neophytes into professions having male sponsorship.

Rationalizations by employers for paying lower salaries to females center around the point that females constitute a costlier source of labor than do males through their higher turnover and absenteeism rates. However, these employers make little or no distinction between married and unmarried female professionals. In effect, married females may even comprise a more stable labor source than do males in the same positions: they are older and, as indicated earlier, more loyal to the organization and more satisfied with their work. In terms of publishing and serving clients, they perform as well as males in similar positions. In addition, they are an easily available and highly skilled source of labor which can be utilized on a part-time basis, a fact which compensates the employer in large part for any financial losses attributable to complete withdrawal. However, it is also true that female professionals with deep career orientations constitute a highly select category of exceptionally talented and motivated women who must perform "better" than their male counterparts in the same positions. They therefore pose a threat both to their professional male colleagues and to their employers, some of whom may be competing for the same rewards.

Both the fear of discrimination and its actual occurrence affect the direction which the female career pattern will take. Females choose professional specialties not only because of sex-role dilemmas, but also because of perceived discrimination in those specialties labeled as male. Furthermore, they are either openly encouraged by males to choose the female specialties in the professional training schools or they are denied access to the specialty training as, for example, in medical residencies. Discrimination thus reinforces old patterns of sex-typing even when there is no longer any support in public attitudes, and it creates new patterns of sex-typing according to both the prestige of the specialty and that of the tasks involved. In this way it sets limits to the range of opportunities for employment, usually entailing acceptance of positions below the level of the female's intelligence and skills. Competition for professional positions, even during periods of temporary unemployment, might also be expected to limit opportunities to qualified females.

Finally, discrimination distorts the normative structure of the professional role and threatens the professional identity. This occurs through processes of modification, hybridization, and degradation, resulting in different roles for the two sexes. It encourages the creation of accommodative structures such as discontinuous work patterns and separate professional associations which widen the breech between male and female professionals whatever other functions they may perform. It results in female behavior which is deviant from the institutional pattern, and which places considerable strain on the professional self-image. Female professionals not only experience the need to seek invisible identities in large organizations from both the public and from other professional reference groups, but they also feel the need to keep proving themselves and reinforcing their positions in the professional structure.

Concluding Remarks

What does the future hold for the professional woman in America? Evidence suggests that despite the rapid increase of women in the general labor force, female participation at the professional levels has not kept up with this trend and has, instead, been declining over a substantial period. Does this evidence suggest that the immediate outlook for the professional woman is less than bright?

There are, of course, one or two encouraging signs which may be mentioned from the events of the very recent past. It is significant that the greatest increase in the female labor force occurs among married women in non-professional, white-collar occupations who still have children living at home and who work for reasons other than financial necessity alone. If their upward mobility into the middle classes has been too recent to have allowed them the benefit of a college education, it at least suggests changing role images which will be more clearly reflected in the occupational aspirations of their daughters. As a matter of fact, such a trend may be already present among today's young female college population who consider career roles as more compatible with family roles than did college females of ten years ago. Inceasing societal concern with such moral issues as war and race also portends greater preoccupation with the issue of sex equality. Already, a deliberate and vocal effort to "liberate" women through political and social pressures include attempts to raise their socio-economic levels.

However, all these changes are too recent to be clearly reflected in present statistics on professional women. As part of an occupational minority to begin with, females in the professional areas constitute an especially disadvantaged category. In varying degrees social, cultural, and structural barriers have prevented a completely open system of communication by which females can enter and leave the professions in ways and under conditions which are similar to males. These barriers have tended to perpetuate the marginal position of the female in the highest professions and to relegate the more central position of the semi-professional female to a marginal place in the semi-professional structure. If present trends in both the professions and semi-professions continue, the participation of semi-professional women in full-time employment may eventually stabilize at a fixed percentage similar to that of women in the professions.

A great deal of attention has been given in the research to the amount of role strain experienced by highly educated females in varying degrees through inability to overcome those barriers which keep them from expanding their roles beyond traditionally female boundaries. The evidence that considerable female role strain exists is based on studies of cross-sex differences rather than on the female sex alone and may present some bias in the conclusions reached. It appears, however, that the degree of combined frustration is not yet sufficient to threaten the stability of society or even any of its major institutions. Most highly educated women do not internalize occupational values to the point where they will attempt, either individually or on a collective basis, to remove the barriers which stand in the way of professional careers. Despite educational supports which motivate them to anticipate and plan careers, they continue to receive their major gratifications within the family, and they are relatively well satisfied with their marginal position in the occupational system. While there may be boredom at home, lack of strong financial motives and the norm of procrastination do not induce enthusiasm for instituting active reforms which would involve them more deeply in professional life. Serious commitment to work is also a threat to their expanding definition of leisure and freedom; and overworked male professionals constitute important reference groups which females may not be particularly anxious to emulate.

Additional research concerning the husbands of achieving women might also shed some light on the dynamics of female motivation to change the present state of affairs. At any rate, those few highly educated females who fall to a point of deep dissatisfaction with present arrangements are too few and too powerless to create the degree of tension in the larger social system needed to bring about economic equality with males at the professional levels where such equality would be more clearly demonstrated than at the lower levels of occupations. The very small minority of professional women who consider work to be as important, or more important, in their lives than the family lack the power to effect even those changes which would eliminate the discrimination they encounter in the daily practice of their professions. The social organization of the family weakens the possibility of fostering group cohesion and building power through organization as a sex collectivity: the very males whom married females would oppose as the group denying them their right to equality also provide them with a high degree of personal gratification as their husbands. Females identify males first as males and then as professionals or employers. Finally, attempts to organize through segregated professional associations based on sex are themselves self-defeating since they emphasize sex differences and reinforce prevailing attitudes about working women.

Any significant changes which would substantially increase the female professional labor force cannot occur as long as basic values and attitudes concerning the sexual division of labor in the society remain unchanged. As in all societies, the American labor force is patterned by both the organization of the economy and the prevailing family system. But while the economy has both needed and encouraged the participation of a highly skilled labor force such as that provided by professional women, the family system has remained relatively unchanged throughout the period of industrial expansion. Today the principal responsibility for children is still assigned to the female. Males and females continue to be distributed in a supersystem-subsystem arrangement in which energy is becoming more unequally distributed as the technology expands. Highly educated married women are finding themselves with increasingly diminishing role responsibilities in the home, while their husbands are spending increasingly more time at their own occupational pursuits.

Such an imbalanced system of role allocation between the sexes establishes clear upper limits against the further full-time participation of professional women in the labor force. Unless both sex roles and major social institutions are re-structured in the direction of a more equitable distribution of energy, talent, and leisure, any efforts to both increase and facilitate female participation in all occupations on an equal basis with males will do little more than treat the symptoms rather than the sources of the problem. Part-time work, maternity leaves, child-care centers, continuing education, co-education, and anti-discriminatory legislation all fail to confront the crucial problem that women can contribute perceptibly to economic goals only insofar as other changes occur which will restore the balance between economic and family structures. The future of the professional woman thus depends to a large extent on the redefinition of sex roles in the society in general and in the family in particular. This means that women themselves will need to contribute substantially to such redefinitions and become the important catalysts for change. In this respect the educational system may in the future be forced to play a more crucial role in the socialization (or re-socialization) process of females, to recruit professional women from a wider range of social strata, and to pay far greater attention to motivational approaches at every educational level, all of which will insure a higher degree of full professional participation for women. But it also goes without saying that in order to break down the existing and seemingly inflexible power structure in the professions, a concerted effort will be required on the part of both sexes, along with the continued support of government, to press for sexual equality in employment practices.

All told, we have observed, on the one hand, a number of forces which inhibit greater participation of professional women commensurate with their education and competence. On the other hand, the relatively recent resurgence of a social movement concerned with the establishment of equality between the sexes offers considerable hope for improving the position of professional women.

II

The Sexual Structure of Professions

two

Plus Ça Change . . . ? The Sexual Structure of Occupations Over Time

EDWARD GROSS

One of the most heavily documented and frequently referred to trends in the United States is the increase in female employment. It is hardly necessary to repeat again the familiar figures. It will be enough to recall that the ratio of women to men working increased from a figure of one woman to 4.5 men in 1900 to one woman to every 1.8 men at the present time. Various analysts have also shown that this change has been accompanied by increased participation rates and by participation of women in employment for a greater part of their lives, to the point where an increasing proportion of women regard working as normal. Any interruptions for child-bearing or other family needs are considered episodes between jobs.[1]

These great changes have been accompanied by over half-a-century of feminist agitation for equal opportunities, and for equal pay for equal work. There are some who regard the increases in employment, just mentioned, as consequences of this feminist effort. Certainly much of the literature on women at work has a strong note of advocacy in it, as illustrated in an authoritative collection of articles in a special issue of *Daedalus*,[2] and even straightforward Census-based studies exhibit this tone, as in the following:[3]

> The extent to which the United States depends on the presence of more than 22 million women in the labor force is not always appreciated. One way of illustrating the importance of the part they play in the production of goods and services is to ask what would

From SOCIAL PROBLEMS, Vol. 16, No. 2 (1968), pp. 198-208. Reprinted by permission of the author and The Society for the Study of Social Problems.

happen to the operation of the nation's schools and hospitals if there were no women workers; how many offices and stores would be able to function without women secretaries and salesgirls; and where the textile and clothing industries — to mention only two — would find an adequate labor supply if they could not hire women.

Such arguments themselves raise the question they are presumed to answer for one wonders immediately why it is that the contribution of women is "not always appreciated," and hence why we have to be reminded. One might think that the true test of acceptance is being taken for granted. Recent controversy on legislation and constitutional revisions designed to ensure women equal treatment suggests that the battle — if indeed there be one — has not quite been won.

Hauser's[4] discussion of labor force participation trends raises further doubts that increases in female employment can be regarded as "triumphs" in the battle between the sexes. Referring to Long's[5] conclusion that labor force participation rates show remarkable stability over time, he holds that the result is the net effect of conflicting trends in specific age and sex labor force rates. On the one hand there has been a decline in the work participation of young persons and of older males, and on the other an increase in that of women. For males 25 to 64 years of age there has been very little change. The increase in labor force participation of females, then, has almost exactly balanced the decreased labor force participation of younger persons and older males. Hauser concludes:[6]

> The explanation lies in the fact that intermediate aged females, by reason of higher education than older males, pushed them out of the labor force. With the increased family income resulting from female employment, it became increasingly possible for younger persons to prolong their schooling and thus to decrease their work activity.

The spectacle of middle-aged females (with superior education, it is true) pushing out the poor, uneducated elderly men is hardly an accomplishment that most feminists will take pride in. Apart from such shifts in age specific participation rates, much of the remaining growth in female employment may, perhaps, be related to the overall growth of the economy and the labor force. That is, women employees are increasing because the opportunities have increased.

With uncertainty as to the significance of trends in female employment, the question that still remains unanswered may be stated as follows: is sexual segregation in fact changing? If there has been an actual decline in segregation then those working for women's rights may take pleasure (if not credit). Unfortunately, existing discussions provide no clear answer. Some refer to the fact that before 1880 almost all clerical and sales workers were men. In a very short time, however, women took over and they have dominated these occupations ever since. It is doubtful whether such examples, even if multiplied, proved anything one way or the other for if an occupation once dominated by men has now become dominated by women, then we have as much sexual segregation as before. The situation is similar to that of an urban census tract which was once all-white and is now all-black. Evidence of a basic structural change would be that of an occupation which was once all-male or all-female but which became equally accessible to both sexes.

The designation of such occupations requires information on the total proportion of female employees in the employed population. In 1960 there were about twice as many men as women employed. Hence, if only chance were operating in distributing men and women in occupations, then all occupations would be expected to have an excess of men. A "normal" proportion would be a ratio of two to one, a situation we find in 1960 for such occupations as: artists and art teachers, editors and reporters, personnel and labor relations workers, managers (etc.) apparel and accessories stores and in personal services, foremen in textiles and apparel manufacturing, and elevator operators. If we examine the trends for this last occupation, we find a genuine shift from a segregated occupation to one that is not segregated (at least as far as may be judged from census data). The data are provided in Table 1. As can be seen this occupation started out as an overwhelmingly male one, dropped rather soon to one which only slightly favored men, and continued doing so until

Table 1 / Example: Sexual Segregation Trends in Number of Elevator Operators

	1900	1910	1920	1930	1940	1950	1960
Males	12,660	25,010	33,376	55,255	72,612	67,477	48,882
Females Elev. Op.	30	25	7,337	12,359	14,491	29,380	23,000
M/F Ratio	400/1	1000/1	4.5/1	4.5/1	5/1	2.3/1	2.1/1
Total Employed M/F Ratio	4.5/1	4/1	4/1	3.5/1	3.2/1	2.6/1	2/1

World War II when the numbers of men dropped and women increased to a point where the ratio was about the same as that in the total population of employed persons. Note that men still, of course, greatly outnumbered women. Insofar as figures show, there is no evidence here for sexual segregation.

However many such illustrations one might provide (and there are not many), they still do not answer the question of whether there have been any changes throughout the occupational distribution. A measure provided by Duncan and Duncan[7] enables us to answer this question.

Calculation of the measure (called the Index of Dissimilarity) may be illustrated by the following hypothetical data (presented by Duncan and Duncan[8] but adapted to the case being discussed here):

Occupation	Males	Females	Absolute Difference
1	10%	15%	5%
2	20	15	5
3	40	25	15
4	30	45	15
Sum:	100%	100%	40%

Index = Sum of Absolute Differences/2 = 40%/2 = 20%

The result of 20 percent may be interpreted as meaning that 20 percent of the females would have to change occupations in order to have the percentage distribution of females correspond to that of males (or vice versa).

It is necessary to calculate such Indices of Dissimilarity (more properly, for the case of only two categories, these are Indices of Segregation) for occupations in each Census year for which reliable trend occupational data are available. It is possible to do this with broad occupation groups, such as Professional, Technical and Kindred, Operative, etc., and the ease of securing such data makes it tempting to do so. Such broad categories, however, tend to mask the amount of segregation that exists. For example, any calculation for Professional, Technical and Kindred as a whole would submerge the fact that engineers are overwhelmingly male, while nurses and teachers are overwhelmingly female. Hence it is desirable to use occupational categories as detailed as the Census provides.

What was done, therefore, was to take the detailed occupations provided by the Census for each census year from 1900 to 1960, and calculate the Index of Segregation for the approximately 300-400 occupations in each year. Occupations with very small numbers were treated as zero categories. The results are presented in Table 2.

Table 2 / Sexual Segregation in Occupations: United States, 1900-1960*

	1900	1910	1920	1930	1940	1950	1960
Index of Segregation	66.9	69.0	65.7	68.4	69.0	65.6	68.4

* Indices are read as percentages and may be interpreted as the percentage of females (or males) who would have to change occupation in order that the distribution of sexes in occupations should be the same.

The immediate conclusion is that there is as much sexual segregation now as there was some sixty years ago. Further, the closeness of all figures to each other over the years suggests that this phenomenon is very persistent, being seemingly unaffected by the vast changes (wars, depressions) which have affected labor market behavior in so many ways. Those concerned with sexual segregation as a social problem can take small comfort from these figures. They suggest that the movement of women into the labor market has not meant the disappearance of sexual typing in occupation. Rather, the great expansion in female employment has been accomplished through the expansion of occupations that were already heavily female, through the emergence of wholly new occupations (such as that of key punch operator) which were defined as female from the start, and through females taking over previously male occupations. This last may be compared to the process of racial invasion in American cities. From the groups point of view, such invasion provides new opportunities but still in a segregated context.

There is also a second impression one gets from the data in Table 2; namely, that the indices are very large. In effect, these data say that some two-thirds of the women in any census year would have to change occupations in order that their distribution would approximate that of men. Intuitively this seems like a very large proportion indeed. Some sense of its enormity can be secured by a rough comparison of such sexual segregation with racial segregation in occupations. Taking the data for 1960 as an example, the corresponding figure for racial segregation is 46.8 percent. In sum, sexual segregation in occupations is considerably more severe than racial segregation.

Attempts to explain sexual segregation in occupations (apart from outright prejudice and other special conditions)[9] have generally taken the form of an examination of the motives for female employment. These include five major groups of motives: the desire to earn money, the preference for paid work over unpaid housework, the search for meaningful activity when children no longer need much care, the desire to utilize education or training, and the desire to "keep busy." Various analysts have noted that none of these motives necessarily involves a rejection of the roles of wife and mother, and hence the picture tends to support that offered by Parsons[10] on the functional significance of sexual role segregation in the American family. Whereas the husband is expected to have a job and be the family breadwinner, the wife's situation is described as follows:[11]

> In the case of the feminine role the situation is radically different. The majority of married women, of course, are not employed, but even of those that are a very large proportion do not have jobs which are in basic competition for status with those of their husbands. . . . In . . . [the] urban situation the primary status-carrying role is in a sense that of housewife. The woman's fundamental status is that of her husband's wife, the mother of his children, and traditionally the person responsible for a complex of activities in connection with the management of the household, care of the children, etc.

Parsons further calls attention to the alternative roles a wife might assume: "common humanistic" role (art, community welfare, "serious" interests), "glamor" role, and careerist. Since housewife and "common humanistic" roles are not satisfying to many wives, and since the latter two roles threaten the stability of the family, the married woman role is, in sum, unstable. The data on sexual segregation, however, suggest a way of resolving such instability: the case of the woman who regards her role as wife and mother as her major role (for the single woman as the future major role), but who works when that work does not threaten her major role. She is able to accomplish this by limiting herself to a distinct set of occupations (which may, however, change over time) rather than trying to enter into direct competition with men, for this course would lead her to give primary attention to her job rather than to her family. In turn, the cost of such segregation has been lower wages and a reluctance of employers to promote or encourage persons who regard their jobs to be of secondary significance.

This conclusion, while providing support for a functional analysis, left me feeling unsatisfied since it seemed to provide a strong case for making women themselves rather too willing partners in their own segregation. In a manner similar to that of the real-estate agent who discourages a Jewish family from buying a house in Mayflower Acres on the grounds that "you wouldn't be happy there," women are seen as themselves recognizing that they really would not be happy if they were in direct competition, and that the feminine mystique is really their destiny. Further, data presented by Barth and Watson[12] cast doubt on the traditional assumption that the family can be treated as a single unit for purposes of stratification analysis. They report that 78 percent of working-wife families have a difference of at least one occupational level between spouses and that when a difference does exist, the wife is more apt than the husband to hold the position with greater occupational prestige. They also offer suggestive data that such differences may have important implications not only for income but also for life-style, socialization, and other family behavior.

These considerations suggested the possibility that the consistency of my findings on sexual segregation might be masking trends that would require a rather different theory. A paper by Gibbs[13] offers an alternative. In a discussion of inter-state comparisons of racial segregation, Gibbs made use of the Duncans' index with puzzling results. For example, higher amounts of discrimination were found in Iowa, North Dakota, Nebraska, Kansas, Wyoming, and Nevada than was found in Mississippi. Gibbs was led to speculate that structural differences might account for such apparent discrepancies. Shifting to my data, the argument is as follows: My data appear to show no difference in sexual segregation over the years. Is it possible that the labor force as a whole might perhaps be less segregative but that those occupations that do segregate are those that are growing the fastest? The fact that it is the white collar occupations which are both growing the fastest and are also among the heaviest employers of women lends support to this possibility. Gibbs presented a measure (called Standardized Measure of Differentiation) which provides a means of controlling for such differences. Essentially it consists of preserving the proportions male and female in a given occupation, but treating all occupations as being of equal size. The results are presented in Table 3.

Table 3 / Standardized Measure of Differentiation:*
United States, 1900-1960

	1900	1910	1920	1930	1940	1950	1960
Standardized Measure of Differentiation	70.3	68.1	65.9	66.6	63.8	59.3	62.2

* Measure described in Jack P. Gibbs, "Occupational Differentiation of Negroes and Whites in the United States," *Social Forces*, 44 (Dec., 1965), pp. 159-165. The measure is based on the Duncans' Index used in Table 2 and described in the body of the paper. It is designed to control for changes in size of occupational categories.

As can be seen, the figures while remaining high show a small, but definite, drop. They support the claim that there has been a reduction in sexual segregation in occupations but that reduction does not show up because those occupations that segregate more have been growing faster than those that segregate less.

In Table 4, a set of data is presented which supports this claim and enables us to draw certain conclusions. For each detailed occupation I compared the sex distribution to what would be expected if chance were operating. As I said above, most occupations were either male or female in the sense that the proportion of either was beyond chance expectations. When this was the case, I characterized it as "male" or "female" and then calculated the extent of divergence from chance. For example, if it were estimated that there would be 4 times as many men as women by chance alone when in fact there were six times as many, then I would divide the six by four to obtain a figure of 1.5 times expectation. On the other hand, if there were more women than expected, I called it a female occupation and made a similar calculation. In Table 4 are contained the means of the detailed occupations, calculated for the occupation group. For example, the first figure in the upper left hand corner may be read: In 1900 those professional occupations which had more men than one would expect on the basis of chance, had, on the average, 1.30 times as many men as chance would lead one to expect.

First, it is the most rapidly increasing occupations, namely those in clerical, professional, sales, and service that also contain the higher averages. However, there is a second finding which is more interesting. If one reads across the years, holding sex constant, a striking difference emerges. The male occupational groups tend to remain as segregative as they were or to become even more segregative. Of these two tendencies, the

Table 4 / Mean Amount of Sexual Segregation in Major
Occupational Groups: United States, 1900-1960*

	1900		1910		1920		1930		1940		1950		1960	
	M	F	M	F	M	F	M	F	M	F	M	F	M	F
Professional, Tech. and Kindred	1.30	4.06	1.28	3.58	1.34	3.64	1.36	3.87	1.30	3.31	1.30	2.78	1.32	2.28
Farmers and Farm Managers	1.12	0.00	1.10	0.00	1.11	0.00	1.24	0.00	1.29	0.00	1.32	0.00	1.43	0.00
Managers, Officials and Prop. (exc. farm)	1.24	0.00	1.24	0.00	1.24	0.00	1.23	0.00	1.24	0.00	1.25	0.00	1.30	0.00
Clerical and Kindred	1.23	4.21	1.27	4.20	1.19	3.67	1.21	3.81	1.27	3.56	1.29	3.11	1.29	2.54
Sales Workers	1.19	3.61	1.23	3.58	1.26	3.23	1.25	3.45	1.25	3.34	1.25	2.94	1.32	2.08
Craftsmen, Foremen and Kindred	1.20	2.83	1.22	3.08	1.23	2.96	1.26	2.47	1.29	0.00	1.32	2.02	1.43	1.70
Operatives and Kindred	1.42	4.08	1.37	3.42	1.33	3.25	1.31	2.97	1.32	2.82	1.31	2.39	1.34	2.09
Private Household	0.00	5.33	0.00	4.87	0.00	4.76	0.00	4.40	0.00	3.98	0.00	3.44	0.00	2.98
Service	1.44	4.57	1.38	3.79	1.32	3.57	1.28	3.15	1.35	2.94	1.33	2.49	1.35	2.40
Farm Laborers and Foremen	1.15	0.00	1.14	0.00	1.19	0.00	1.26	0.00	1.24	0.00	1.26	0.00	1.40	0.00
Laborers, exc. farm and mine	1.21	3.28	1.26	2.72	1.24	2.57	1.24	0.00	1.24	0.00	1.28	0.00	1.37	0.00

* The figures "0.00" mean that there were no occupations that fell in that category.

second is more marked. The averages show little change for professional occupations and, except for 1900, for Operatives. Segregation is more extreme, over time, for Farmers and Farm Managers; Managers, Officials, and Proprietors, Clerical and Kindred; Sales Workers; Craftsmen, Foremen and Kindred; and Farm Laborers and Foremen.

On the other hand, for women, with the exception of Craftsmen, Foremen and Kindred (those figures are based on a very small number of occupations), which showed little change, all others having any significant number of women show declining amounts of segregation.

Roughly speaking, then, male occupations have become rather more segregative, or resistant to female entry, whereas female occupations have become less segregative, or more permissive, if one likes, about including males.[14]

It is impossible to draw final conclusions on the amount of segregation from sheer numbers in any occupational category.[15] The finer the distinctions, the more segregation one will "catch." Further, a major form that segregation takes is stratificational, where men become the supervisors, or take over the more prestigious forms of the occupation which may have the same name for males or females. Caplow,[16] describing sexual segregation in retail selling, says:

> The prevailing pattern is that salesmen serve male customers, and saleswomen serve female customers. Where the customers are mixed in gender, the sales force follows the majority. An exception is made for very heavy or very valuable commodities, which are commonly sold by men. A whole set of folkways is developed on the basis of these principles. Thus, in a normally organized department store, there will be men in the sportsgoods department, women to sell curtains and dishware, men to sell hardware, women to sell books, but men to sell wedding silver and furniture.

In teaching, although the census figures show a heavy proportion of men,

> ... most men teach in high schools while most women teach in elementary schools. In high schools the physical sciences and some of the social sciences are usually taught by men, while languages and literature are usually taught by women. In vocational, commercial, and industrial arts classes, and physical education, men generally instruct boys, while women teach girls.[17]

Similarly, school principals and other administrators tend to be

men, and in social work, promotion to supervisory status for men is practically automatic.

Insofar as our data enable us to generalize, however, they suggest there are signs of some reduction in segregation, which seems to be accomplished by men entering the female occupations, rather than the reverse. A term paper by Helen Warfield, a former student of mine, reported an interesting finding on male nurses. She found a new attitude among female nurses, especially the leadership, to such male nurses. Rather than seeing them in a segregated way, as persons who do the dirty work of handling heavy bodies, or controlling overenergetic male patients, they are being sought as colleagues, to do substantially the same work, if possible. In the words of one Dean of a school of nursing:

> We want men because we think they will upgrade the profession. Men will never put up with the miserable hours and rotten wages that we are forced to take. But they can only do this if they are peers, neither subordinate, nor superior. Then they will lift us up with them.

I cannot say that this is a trend, but it suggests a new lead for research. On the whole, the trend data suggest that when women invade a male occupation they take it over, with the result that there is as much segregation as before, perhaps because the men leave or take over the better jobs. This is something like the case of Negroes invading a white block, as was suggested above. However, when men enter a female occupation, the women seem much less likely to leave. Therein, perhaps, may lie a direction toward which feminists might turn. Instead of expressing their resentment of the number of areas "off limits" to women, they might ask how to attract men in the areas now "off limits" to men.[18] This strategy may also have implications for the reduction of racial segregation.

NOTES

1. The literature on female employment is voluminous, much of it going over the same ground. Comprehensive summaries and references are available in F. Ivan Nye and Lois Wladis Hoffman, editors, *The Employed Mother in America,* Chicago: Rand McNally, 1963; Janet M. Hooks, *Women's Occupations Through Seven Decades,* Women's Bureau Bull. No. 218, U.S. Dept. of Labor, U.S. Government Printing Office, 1947; Murray Gendell, *Swedish Working Wives,*

Totowa, N.J.: Bedminster, 1963; and Dale L. Hiestand, *Economic Growth and Employment Opportunities for Minorities*, New York: Columbia U., 1964.

2. *Daedalus*, 93 (Spring, 1964), entire issue. The papers have been reprinted in Robert Jay Lifton, editor, *The Woman in America*, Boston: Beacon, 1967.

3. National Manpower Council, *Womanpower*, New York: Columbia U., 1957, p. 46.

4. Philip M. Hauser, "Labor Force," in Robert E. L. Faris, editor, *Handbook of Modern Sociology*, Chicago: Rand McNally, 1964, Chap. 5.

5. C. D. Long, *The Labor Force under Changing Income and Employment*, National Bureau of Economic Research, Princeton, N.J.: Princeton U., 1958.

6. Hauser, *op. cit.*, p. 171. A different explanation for the shift in age and marital status structure of employed women is offered by Oppenheimer. Examining the relative strength of demand (job opportunities) and supply (availability of employable women) factors on such participation, she concludes that a rising demand for female labor met a declining supply of those who traditionally worked. As a consequence, a new class of women (the older, married) was drawn into the labor force. She assigns no weight to "change of heart" on the part of employers, suggesting instead that they had little choice. Valerie K. Oppenheimer, "The Interaction of Demand and Supply and Its Effect on the Female Labour Force in the United States," *Population Studies*, 21 (Nov., 1967), pp. 239-259.

7. Otis Dudley Duncan and Beverly Duncan, "Residential Distribution and Occupational Stratification," *American Journal of Sociology*, 60 (March, 1955), pp. 493-503. See also the general discussion and critique of segregation indices in Otis Dudley Duncan and Beverly Duncan, "A Methodological Analysis of Segregation Indexes," *American Sociological Review*, 20 (April, 1955), pp. 210-217.

8. Duncan and Duncan, "Residential Distribution and Occupational Stratification," *op. cit.*, p. 494.

9. See, for example, Cynthia F. Epstein, "Woman's Place: The Salience of Sex Status in the Professional Setting," paper presented at the 62nd Annual Meeting of the American Sociological Association, August 29, 1967, mimeo.

10. Talcott Parsons, "Age and Sex in the Social Structure of the United States," *American Sociological Review*, 7 (Oct., 1942), pp. 604-616.

11. *Ibid.*, pp. 608-609.

12. Ernest A. T. Barth and Walter B. Watson, "Social Stratification and the Family in Mass Society," *Social Forces*, 45 (March, 1967),

pp. 392-402. The particular statistics are found in Walter B. Watson and Ernest A. T. Barth, "Questionable Assumptions in the Theory of Social Stratification," *Pacific Sociological Review*, 7 (Spring, 1964), pp. 10-16.

13. Jack P. Gibbs, "Occupational Differentiation of Negroes and Whites in the United States," *Social Forces*, 44 (Dec., 1965), pp. 159-165.

14. In private conversations, Stanley Lieberson raised the question of a possible artifact in Table 4. Since the proportion of males exceeds that of females, then the distribution of males will affect the overall average to a greater extent. The effect will be that the figures for males will be closer to one (in the ratios) than the figures for females, and that this effect will become less marked as the proportion of females increases. Whether this would account for all of the reduction in ratios of the females is, however, unknown. Unfortunately, there is no easy way to test the hypothesis of decreasing female segregativeness directly, except by treating all occupations as equivalent (that is, a change in an occupation with small numbers as having the same weight as one with large numbers).

15. In their discussion of mobility measures, Peter M. Blau and Otis Dudley Duncan (*The American Occupational Structure*, New York: Wiley, 1967, pp. 90 ff.) point to a serious problem in the use of such contingency measures for examination of trends in mobility. A given matrix of such measures implies a unique set of marginals and hence cannot be said to "hold marginals constant" for temporal comparisons. However, we use these ratios with no intent of holding opportunity (marginals) constant but to observe how, in a given year, there is departure from "perfect mobility" (that is, equal opportunity irrespective of sex). Blau and Duncan suggest (p. 97) that these ratios have "some attraction" for such a purpose.

In the light of these methodological considerations, it is necessary to emphasize that the findings offered in Table 4 are only suggestive. These problems do not arise in the data presented in Tables 1-3.

16. Theodore Caplow, *The Sociology of Work*, Minneapolis: U. of Minnesota, 1954, p. 232.

17. National Manpower Council, *op. cit.*, p. 60.

18. In a paper which came out too late for fuller discussion here, Wilensky suggests, by using several examples (secondary school teaching, social work, librarianship, hospital, and perhaps nursing administration), that when men do enter female domains, they tend to take control of them. Even if true (and I suspect that it is), the net result may be an upgrading of the whole occupation. L. Wilensky, "Women's Work: Economic Growth, Ideology, Structure," *Industrial Relations*, 7 (May, 1968), pp. 235-258. The discussion to which I refer is on pp. 241.

three

Encountering the Male Establishment: Sex-Status Limits on Women's Careers in the Professions[1]

CYNTHIA F. EPSTEIN

During the past half-century women have entered many upper-level occupations and positions from which they were once excluded, and their general level of involvement in the labor force has risen. But their participation in the occupations of highest rank — among them the professions of law, medicine, teaching in higher education, and the sciences — has not kept pace with these developments nor has their access to the elite levels of the professions been greatly improved. Further, despite pressures to implement the equalitarian values in American culture and impressive extensions of women's social and political rights, there have been no accompanying extensions of the sex-linked boundaries existing in the occupations of high prestige in this society.

The processes which undermine women's motivations for professional careers and work against their completion of the necessary education, their entry into practice after training, and their aiming at the highest levels of performance in professional practice have been described in various works. (Rossi 1965; Bernard 1964; Friedan 1963; Komarovsky 1953; Epstein 1970). Here I wish to focus on one set of these processes; those anchored in the structures of the professions and having the consequence of causing women's sex status to become salient[2] in the professional role, equal to or above the occupational status. We will also draw attention to the consequences of "sex-typing"[3] and of "status-set typing"[4] in the professions which

From AMERICAN JOURNAL OF SOCIOLOGY, Vol. 75, No. 6 (1970), pp. 965-982. Reprinted by permission of the author and The University of Chicago Press.

have made the professions almost exclusively male. The important processes which underlie these questions are: (1) the colleague system of the professions, especially at the upper levels; (2) the sponsor-protégé relationship, which determines access to the highest levels of most levels of most professions; (3) the demands of the specific professions' "inner" structure and its attendant patterns of social interaction which are, under most circumstances, incompatible with the sex-role expectation repertory of even those women engaged in professional careers; and (4) the sex-typing of occupations, which reinforces these processes in linking occupational roles and sex roles.

This analysis applies not alone to women, but to others who possess statuses (such as age or race) which are culturally defined as "inappropriate" when held in conjunction with certain occupational statuses. That is, those persons whose status-sets do not conform to the expected and preferred configuration cause discordant impressions on members of the occupational network and the society at large: the black physician, the Jewish Wall Street lawyer, and the football-hero philosophy professor all generate such discordance.

Sex-Typing of Occupations

One element of "status-set typing" is the sex-typing of occupations. The typing of certain occupations as male or female has consequences for entry to them and performance within them by persons who possess the "wrong sex." Those occupations defined as male provide a social context uncomfortable for women. Those who seek entry to them are regarded as deviants and are subjected to social sanctions. As a result, few women attempt to enter such fields, and those who do often are blocked from the opportunity structure.[5]

As Table 1 shows, women lawyers have increased from 1 percent of the profession in 1910 to 3.5 percent in 1950, but there has been no change in this percentage for the past ten years. Women now form 6.8 percent of the medical profession, an all-time high, but not a striking increase over the 6.1 percent of ten years before or since 1910, when women constituted 6 percent of the profession. The percentage of women college teachers has gone down steadily since 1930 from 32 percent to 19 percent today. Although the U.S. census figures are now almost ten years old, and there are certain indicators of increasing participation by women in some fields such as law,[6] it is doubtful that a really new trend is emerging.

Table 1 / Women as Percentage of All Workers in Selected Professional Occupations (USA, 1900-1960)

Occupation	1960	1950	1940	1930	1920	1910	1900
College professors, president, instruction ..	19.0	23.0	27.0	32.0	30.0	19.0	...
Doctors	6.8	6.1	4.6	4.0	5.0	6.0	...
Lawyers*	3.5	3.5	2.4	2.1	1.4	1.0	...
Engineers	0.8	1.2	0.3	...	...	...	...
Dentists	2.1	2.7	1.5	1.8	3.2	3.1	...
Scientists	9.9	11.4	...	...	...	...	...
Biologists	28.0	27.0	...	...	...	...	...
Chemists	8.6	10.0	...	...	...	...	...
Mathematicians	26.4	38.0	...	...	...	...	...
Physicists	4.2	6.5	...	...	...	...	...
Nurses	97.0	98.0	98.0	98.0	96.0	93.0	94.0
Social workers	57.0	66.0	67.0	68.0	62.0	52.0	...
Librarians	85.0	89.0	89.0	91.0	88.0	79.0	...
Clergy	5.8	8.5	2.2	4.3	2.6	1.0	4.4

Source — U.S. Bureau of the Census of 1963, vol. 1, table 202, pp. 528-33. 1900-50 statistics from U.S. Department of Labor 1954, p. 57.

a The lack of change in the percentage of women lawyers is even more striking if one use the adjusted figures of Hankin and Krohnke (1965):

1963	1960	1957	1954	1951	1946
2.7	2.6	2.7	2.3	2.5	1.8

Some occupations which have remained predominantly male in the United States are, in other countries (most notably the Communist-block nations), regarded as female occupations. In the Soviet Union, women constitute 75 percent of the medical profession, 30-40 percent of the judges, and 28 percent of the engineers; in Denmark, they make up 70 percent of the dental profession.

Yet even in these countries women's share of the leading positions in the professions is meager. While social definitions regarding the "proper" sex of a practitioner are important in determining the sex-composition of an occupation, the sex-ranking of occupations provides an added inhibitor of women's advancement. High-ranking occupations in all societies are typically male (Goode 1964, p. 70). Medicine does not rank low in the Soviet Union, but it does not rank nearly as high as in the United States. For all occupations in all societies, as one approaches the top, the proportion of men increases and the proportion of women decreases. In the Soviet Union, for example, only the tiniest proportion of professors of surgery within the great teaching universities and research institutes are women (Dodge 1966) in the United States, although women constitute close to 20 percent of the academic ranks of higher education, few women attain the rank of full professor in the institutions of highest prestige.

It is evident that the dynamics of recruitment and involvement at the higher echelons of professions are different than they are at the lower levels and that they militate against the participation of women. Further, these processes are integral to the "culture" of the professions as we know them and may not be intentionally exclusionary. Of course, cultural attitudes tied to women's roles and women's biologically linked characteristics interweave with these processes in making the woman professional's sex-status salient in the course of her career.

Characteristics of Professions

Professions share many characteristics of communities (Goode 1957; Merton, Reader, and Kendall 1957). They tend toward homogeneity and are characterized by shared norms and attitudes. The work of the professions depends greatly on mutual understanding between practitioners and common standards of behavior which permit them control of their share without much intervention from the state or lay public.

Interaction in professions, especially in their top echelons, is characterized by a high degree of informality, much of it within an exclusive, club-like context. As Hughes (1962) describes these qualities, professionalism "indicates a strong solidarity of those in an occupation. . . . The very word 'profession' implies a certain social and moral solidarity, a strong dependence of one colleague upon the opinions and judgments of others" (Hughes 1962, pp. 124-25).

Thus, it is difficult for someone not equipped with a status-set of appropriate statuses to enter the exclusive society, to participate in its informal interactions, to understand the unstated norms,[7] and to be included in the casual exchanges.

Entry to the upper echelons of many professions is commonly gained through the protégé system. This system, linked to the colleague system, operates both to train personnel for certain specialties (special areas of surgery or corporate law, for example), and to assure continuity of leadership. These fields are marked by the interplay between the formal and informal relationships of the practitioners. At certain levels one must be "in" to learn the job. Becker and Strauss (1956) point out that "until a newcomer is accepted [in these fields] he will not be taught crucial trade secrets," much less advance in the field.[8]

The sponsor-protégé (or master-apprentice) relationship may inhibit feminine advancement. The sponsor is apt to be a man and will tend to have mixed feelings about accepting a woman as protégé. Although the professional man might not object to a female assistant — and might even prefer her — he cannot easily identify her (as he might a male assistant) as someone who will eventually be his successor. He may therefore prefer a male candidate to a female in the belief that she has less commitment to the profession. When the woman is accepted as a protégé, her other role-partners — husband, father, child, etc. — may be jealous and suspicious of her loyalty to the sponsor and her dependence on him. The sponsor's wife may also resent the intimacy of the relationship between the sponsor and his female protégé and object to it.[9]

If the sponsor wants to minimize his risks in adopting recruits, the collegial group will not favor an unsuitable member likely to weaken its intimacy and solidarity and it may exert pressure on the sponsor to pick the protégé with whom it will be comfortable (see Etzioni 1961, p. 260).

For a sponsor, a protégé (1) eases the transition to retirement (Hall 1948; Hughes 1945); (2) gives him a sense of continuity of his work, and (3) gives some assurance that his intellectual offspring will build on his work. It is considered unwise to depend on a woman for these.

Even if she serves an apprenticeship, the female professional may not get the sponsor's support in gaining entry to the inner circles of the profession — support which a male neophyte would expect as a matter of course. The sponsor may exert less effort in promoting a female student for career-line jobs. First, he may believe that she is financially less dependent on a career position than a man might be.[10] Second, because of her presumably highly contingent commitment and drive (she might forego all for marriage, after all), he might only reluctantly introduce her or recommend her to colleagues.

However, it is often true that a protégé relationship may be more important to the woman than a man, and that a male sponsor may make an extra effort to promote a female protégé because he is aware of the difficulties she faces. In fact, she may only be able to rise or gain notice in a field because she is a protégé, although this form of entry is not as important for others. I have suggested elsewhere (Epstein, in press) that women in professional life seem to find jobs and feel most comfortable in situations which are highly particularistic and are considered a unique exception to the general rule excluding women (e.g., because a particular woman is brilliant, or is in partnership with her husband), or in highly bureaucratized situations, such as government service, where strictly universalistic criteria, such as standing on competitive examinations, are applied. In fact, as Table 2 shows, women professionals go into government service

Table 2 / Percentage of Professional Workers in Selected
Occupations in Government Service by Sex (1960)

Occupation	Male	Female
Dentists	0.03	10.0
Lawyers	14.0	27.0
Doctors	14.0	30.0
Engineers	17.0	32.0

Source — U.S. Bureau of the Census 1963, p. 277.

in far greater proportions to their number than do men. In this respect, they are much like other minority groups, such as Negroes.[11]

This pattern tends to be self-perpetuating. Women tend to select these two kinds of work situations because they know they will meet least opposition. Placement offices in professional schools often fit women students to government work and counsel them to avoid high-prestige firms or research centers. This means that many women never even enter environments where contacts are made for protégé relationships essential to entering the elite corps of their professions. Even within these environments, it is often true that women are guided into peripheral or low-ranking specialties where their work is not likely to draw the elite's attention.[12]

Later progress in a woman's career may be inhibited by similarly limited access to fellow practitioners and peers and their clubs and associations — the circle in which job opportunities are made known and informal recommendations are made. Hall (1948) illustrates the interdependence of career advancement and sponsorship by specifying the channels through which younger doctors of proper class and acceptable ethnic origins are absorbed into the inner fraternity of the medical profession. He notes that perpetuation of this fraternity depends on a steady flow of suitable recruits.

The collegial relationship is also important in the assessment of the performance of professionals. Although adequacy of performance may be simple to judge at lower levels of a profession, the fine distinctions between good and superior performance require subtle judgments. Members of professions affirm that only peers can adequately judge performance at these levels (as opposed to the lay public or outside agencies); they know the standards, they know the men, and they can maintain control. And the professions typically close ranks to maintain control when their autonomy is threatened. At higher levels, high stakes are often involved: legal decisions can affect people's lives or huge sums of money; medical decisions can assure a patient's life or death. Although there are gross guidelines for the behavior of professionals at these levels, formal scrutiny is minimal and the social controls exercised by peers act most effectively to prevent deviance. The professions depend on intense socialization of their members, much of it by immersion in the norms of professional culture even before entry; and later by the professional's sensitivity to his peers. These controls depend on a strong network cemented by bonds of common background, continual association, and affinity of interests.

Not only do contacts with professional colleagues act as a control system, they also provide the wherewithal by which the professional may become equipped to meet the highest standards of professional behavior. As we know, the learning of a profession is not completed with graduation from the professional school. Techniques and experience must still be acquired in interaction with established practitioners. This is true also for acquiring new knowledge.[13]

Evidence suggests that women professionals are not involved in the collegial networks to the extent that men are.[14] Thus they are excluded from the situations in which they can learn and are also excluded from the social control system which lets them know how well they perform (Epstein 1969).

The judgment of whether a professional is "top" rank is contingent on a number of elements linked to the collegial system:

Contributions. — Definitions of "contributions" vary from field to field but each profession has norms regarding quality and quantity of contributions deemed adequate for consideration as high-level performance. Women probably do make proportionately fewer contributions to their professions than do men (in male-dominated professions) although there is some evidence to the contrary (Simon, Clark, and Galway 1967). Few women have achieved fame for discoveries in science, designing great architectural structures, devising new surgical techniques, or the triumphant argument of cases before the Supreme Court. If publication in the academic professions is used as a criterion, it is probably true that women are responsible for proportionately fewer books and articles considered important to their fields. Even if one does not use standards of "greatness," it is not commonly believed that women do very much publishing at all.[15] The colleague and network systems are probably important in assessing these "facts." These are some of the dynamics involved:

a) Contributions must be visible to be noted; work from the larger and more prestigious institutions probably has a greater chance of being noticed than work performed at lesser-known institutions.[16] Women are less likely to be affiliated with large and prestigious institutions.[17]

b) Contributions are also made visible by the activity of senior men in the field to promote them or by joint publications with those in eminent positions.[18] I tentatively suppose that women's contributions are not promoted as much as men's and that they less often collaborate with those in eminent positions.

On the other hand, women professionals in male-dominated professions have greater visibility than men simply because they are a small minority. At professional meetings they are physically more visible (as are Negroes), and their written work identifies their sex by name. When their work is good, it may get even greater notice than that of men who perform at the same level of competence.

Performance. — Not only are written or material works assessed in considering a person for a place at the top, but also the quality of his general performance. Colleagues "get to know" a man by their exposure to his work in the courtroom, at the operating table, in the laboratory. Performances bearing the labels of well-known institutions are more apt to attract public notice; further, the great men who will make the judgments are at the great institutions and are likely to be in a better position to judge the potential of the young who are already in their midst.

The relative invisibility of the woman professional's performance stems directly from women's disadvantageous position in the structure of the professions. They are not only routed into less visible positions, such as library research, but the specialities in which they predominate are typically regarded as the less important and less demanding ones, and their skills in them count for less.

Incomes are lower in the professional specialities in which women predominate. Women lawyers in a relatively unlucrative field, such as matrimonial law, are less apt to gain distinction and advance in a firm because they are unable to contribute substantially to the firm's total profits. Women are also seldom given the accounts of important clients; their comparatively unimportant clients cannot effectively press for their promotion.[19]

Women also tend less than men to be in positions where they can exercise the greatest autonomy. Figure 1 indicates that women who work in the male-dominated professions are self-employed to a far lesser degree than are men. They are also less likely to be in high-ranking, decision-making positions if they are on the staffs of institutions, or in professional or business firms.

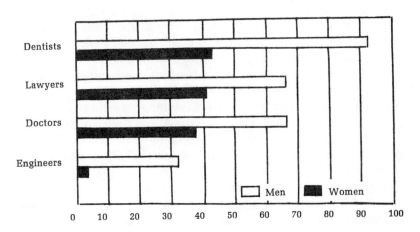

Figure 1. Proportion of males and females in selected professions who are self-employed. Source: U.S. Bureau of the Census 1963, table 21, p. 277.

Associations. — Membership and participation in profession-al associations characterizes the active professional and rein-forces his ties to colleagues and work. At professional meetings information is traded about new techniques and theories, and informal judgments are exchanged about the profession's rising "stars." Professional friendships develop into personal relation-ships at the cocktail hours, and at committee and dinner meet-ings. The appointment of members to special committees may publicize their achievements to their colleagues.

Women are less active in professional organizations than are men, particularly at the decision-making levels. It is generally believed, but not generally proven, that proportionately fewer women than men join professional organizations (see Fava 1960, pp. 171-72; Bernard 1964, p. 152; Simon et al., 1967, p. 234; Ep-stein 1970, p. 185 ff.) Certainly, however, women's past partici-pation and performance in professional organizations has been limited.

Women's reticence to participate in these associations is due in part to past discrimination against women in some cases in the recent past, although no professional organization today ex-cludes women from membership. In cases where there were no legal barriers based on sex (or where they were removed), wom-en were nevertheless made to feel unwelcome. Women have been barred particularly from full participation at decision-making levels. They are seldom elected to prestigious commit-tees or to executive posts. In the field of sociology, out of a total of 57 presidents, only one woman has been elected to serve as president of the American Sociological Association. In the American Psychological Association too, they have been con-tinuously underrepresented in posts of distinction.[20] In law, they tend to serve disproportionately on bar association com-mittees concerned with family law[21] (reflecting their high repre-sentation in the specialities of matrimonial law, custody, adop-tion, etc.) and not on the committees of high rank.

To some extent the establishment of women's professional organizations has served to deflect woman's participation in the general professional groups. Some women's organizations were formed because the general organizations had formal or infor-mal bans on female membership.[22] Following the removal of these barriers, they have generally managed to keep their inner sanctums free of women.[23]

Male clubs which recruit members cross-occupationally and which are also centers of informal contacts between those at the top, by their very definition exclude women. Prestigious clubs, such as the Harvard and Princeton Clubs, permit women entry only on ludicrously limited bases, and their resistance to full integration is dramatized to the women by certain symbolic devices; among them are separate women's entrances and restaurants limited to male patronage during lunch hours. Of course, there is no shortage of places for male and female colleagues to lunch together but many men seem to favor the club setting, and when women go along, they must use "the back entrance" (the Harvard Club), if they are admitted at all.

Dedication to the profession. — The ideal professional is one whose work dominates the other parts of his life. As his professional associations blend into personal friendships, so his working and leisure hours may merge. Although styles of work differ, the professional's involvement with his craft is generally expressed by the long hours he puts in. Because women professionals do not or cannot work the same number of hours as their male colleagues (Table 3), their commitment is suspect and they are not deemed colleagues in the full sense of the word.

Exclusivity of the elite. — The collegial system has the further consequence of creating an image of exclusivity which reinforces professional boundaries. Even if inner circles do not act to explicitly exclude "inappropriate" members, outsiders are loath to place themselves in a situation which they anticipate would be embarrassing or uncomfortable. Women, as members of an inappropriate category often practice self-exclusion and limit their professional interactions. Although they might or might not be rebuffed if they initiated contact, the situation is often never put to the test.[24] The woman's self-imposed limits on professional interaction often complete the self-fulfilling prophecy of her ineptitude. To a large extent, this behavior results in her acceptance of the prevailing image of professions as societies of men.

Women often not only exclude themselves, but favor exclusion of other women. They accept the image and definitions of this behavior as appropriate. The more informal the professional context, the more willing women seem to concede the "rightness" of their exclusion.[25]

Table 3 / Weekly Hours Worked by Employed Engineers
Scientists, and Technicians, by Sex, 1960

Occupation	Mean No. Hours		No. Hours Worked (%)					
			Men			Women		
	Men	Wo-men	1-34	35-40	41+	1-34	35-40	41+
Engineers	42.8	38.6	1	67	32	9	82	9
Scientists	42.1	38.6	5	68	27	11	75	14
Biologists	43.0	39.1	6	58	36	12	66	21
Chemists	41.6	38.8	4	72	24	9	80	11
Mathematicians	41.4	38.6	3	74	23	6	87	7
Physicists	41.6	*	5	72	23	18	59	23
Professors-instructors:								
Biological sciences	43.6	33.8	17	28	54	37	28	35
Chemistry	40.8	*	25	25	50	41	26	33
Engineering	42.5	*	15	32	53	60	20	20
Mathematics	36.4	35.4	34	30	36	37	31	32
Physics	40.5	*	26	26	48	54	..	46
Technicians:								
Medical and dental	42.2	38.5	10	51	39	15	61	24
Electrical and electronic ..	42.2	39.8	3	70	27	5	81	14
Other engineering and phys-ical science technicians ..	41.5	38.7	4	71	25	8	80	12
Lawyers and judges	46.7	38.9	6	33	59	22	47	28

Source — U.S. Bureau of the Census 1963, table 13. Statistics (except for lawyers) cited in Rossi (1965).
*Mean not shown when the case base is less than 1,000.

The Interactional Setting

Because women don't "fit" well in the professional structure just described, their appearance in the collegial networks as legitimate coprofessionals often causes a considerable amount of role-confusion. Male colleagues typically are unable to engage in the normal collegial relationship with them and instead fall back on the traditional norms governing male-female interaction.

Performance of the professional task may be seriously inhibited, when not only colleagues but clients focus on the sex-status instead of the occupational status of women. This occurs, for example, when a patient responds to a woman physician first as a woman and only second as a doctor, instead of as a doctor primarily and perhaps exclusively — the appropriate response in a professional relationship. This kind of social response colors both the attitude and behavior of the woman practitioner and forces her to work out ways to counter violations of the norms of professional relationships by her role partners. The following consequences may occur:

1. Women in professional life feel self-conscious[26] about being women, with the result that they are unsure of how they will be received.[27] They may overreact to conceal or inhibit "womanly attributes," and overconform or overproduce in an attempt to make up for their situationally downgraded status.[28] Women lawyers may, as noted earlier, try to be unobtrusive and not create "trouble" or attract attention by holding back in conversation or by accepting work which keeps them in "invisible" positions where they do not have individual clients.[29] They thereby accept and reinforce the common definitions about the inappropriateness of their presence in the field in which they have chosen to work.

2. Similarly the role partner — colleague, supervisor, client — may try to compensate[30] by being overly solicitous, congenial, courtly, underdemanding,[31] or overdemanding in the professional interaction.

3. Status discrepancies make continuous role definition necessary during interactions which should be routine. Thus, all group members are sensitized to problems of ambiguity and are forced to form new ground rules (i.e., establish norms) for the situation. When the inappropriate status of the person's status set is activated in the professional context, refocusing of the interaction to the appropriate status must occur so that the professional task may be accomplished.

Situations Where Focusing on Sex-Status Will be Minimized

In view of the difficulties which are apt to be encountered by the woman professional in the course of her working life, I interviewed successful women professionals at length about the factors that had helped them in their careers. They described situations and patterns of professional life which helped to avoid or minimize the problems commonly faced by professional women. These were of the following types:

Formality in the professional context. — Where the working environment was formal and the tasks well defined, role partners were not unsure about the norms of governing the interactions. For example, where authority patterns and the division of labor were clearly laid out, men would not feel disturbed by a woman giving instructions.

Defined standards of performance. — If there was no indecision about how to rate performance because the outcome could be measured and lead to a specific result, relationships with role partners were easier. For example, although it is difficult to evaluate the enduring quality of philosophical ideas, it is less difficult to evaluate the efficiency of a newly designed motor for a given piece of equipment. In cases where ability had been clearly demonstrated, other criteria for inclusion in the team become less important. Women in professional life counsel neophytes to make an effort to become experts in some speciality, because their special talents will then be sought out regardless of attitudes concerning women "in general."

Correlatively, where role partners in the professional encounter have a high stake in the task at hand and are dependent on each other for performance and information, women experience little difficulty. For example, an industrial engineer will show respect for the female patent lawyer who is charging him $60 an hour for consultation services, and she, in turn, is motivated to keep the relationship professional if she wishes to keep him as a client.

Flexibility of role-playing. — Where the woman wins acceptance of her sex status as natural and unobtrusive, she has fewer professional difficulties. Collegial relationships demand that role partners shift easily from formal roles to informal ones, from professional colleague to "one of the boys." Women must perform the functional equivalent of this flexibility in role-switching, but not imitate it. Women who act "professional" but not especially formal or aggressive, who try to be gracious as women and not to be one of the boys, are said to be able to make the best impression on men and gain their acceptance. Often sex status intrudes less when it is permitted expression in normal sex-role behavior. For example, women who work in top law firms or hospitals report that male colleagues are used to treating women in a courtly manner and can work best with women who respond graciously. Women who tell off-color jokes or demand always to be treated just like the men cause their colleagues discomfort. Attempts to suppress sex-role behavior in such contexts only succeed in making it obtrusive.

Supervision of the professional interaction. — It was easier for professional women where third parties supported the professional interaction. The professor of medicine instructing a male and a female medical student in a laboratory, for example, ensures that the relationship is task directed (see Goode 1960).

Length of career and length of professional relationships. — In time, men and women in professional relationships usually establish ground rules to govern behavior and eliminate awkwardness which flows from being unsure of whether to focus on the norms governing interaction between men and women or those which govern the relationship between colleagues. For example, women lawyers who had worked in a firm for a number of years and who had early set a precedent of paying their own way, were not reticent in inviting colleagues to lunch. Of course, age itself gives the woman a certain amount of authority and if she has gained eminence, problems are further reduced. Not only do many of the feminine role components attached to the female sex status become less intrusive in professional interactions as the woman grows older (it is probably safe to say that in most cases as the woman ages, her sexual appeal becomes less an object of focus), but her position is bolstered by the rank derived from her experience and her age.

High rank of institution. — When the firm or organization is of high rank and good reputation, it is probably more likely that a woman can expect fair and open treatment than if she were at an institution of lower rank. One encounters more adherence to norms at the top and, once a member of an elite group, the woman professional may count on being treated by the universalistic criteria appropriate to the situation. In low-ranking institutions, practitioners tend to be relatively insecure about their own abilities and financial security, and the woman may become a scapegoat. Perhaps this is simply a case where once the woman is "in," she is truly "in."

Women, like others with statuses which do not conform to cultural preferences, must learn the dynamics of handling inappropriate responses to them as well as the skills of their trade. Some are protected by social structure more than others; some have greater personal skill in handling people and ambiguities. The more a woman can depend on the environment filtering out responses to her sex status which intrude on accomplishing the professional task, and the more she has perfected techniques for handling responses, the more likely she is to continue at her work and proceed along a "normal" career sequence. American women may leave professional careers at almost any point, no matter how high the investment in it or the amount of talent shown for it, with a high degree of cultural approval (Epstein 1969). We suspect that those who enter professional life and who remain within it are from environments in which obstacles are minimal, or they have, for idiosyncratic reasons, been able to define the obstacles as minimal.

Changes in the Structure of Professions

I have examined some of the causes of the woman professional's failure to fulfill her career potential. I have also noted some of the factors which can, depending on the case, mitigate this failure. It would be well to close by drawing attention to some of the changes in American society and in the professions, which may have consequence for women's career patterns.

At this time, the most important change seems to be the loss of prestige of traditional elite centers to new foci of professional interest, notably those in the spheres of public welfare and service. Whether or not it proves to be temporary, many of today's gifted young professionals are no longer eager to enter the traditional inner corps of the professions, and are instead being drawn to the new fields of professional opportunity. This seems to be particularly so in law and medicine, where there are signs of a breakdown in the collegial structure and an increasing challenge to the traditional insistence on recruits of particular types.

This disruption of traditional processes, coupled with the recently renewed movement toward women's occupational equality, should bring some important changes in the direction of women's greater participation in the professions. But probably far more radical changes than these, both in the institutions of the economy and the family, will be necessary to eliminate the peculiar problems of professional women, along with the cultural and occupational views of them as deviants.

NOTES

1. This is publication A-575 of the Bureau of Applied Social Research, Columbia University. Permission has been granted by the

University of California Press to publish a revised version of sections of *Woman's Place: Options and Limits in Professional Careers,* issued in April 1970. The paper is based on research performed for a study of women lawyers in the New York City area in 1966-67. It was prepared with the support of NIMH grant no. F1 MH-22, 158-03 and grant no. 91-34-68-26 from the Manpower Administration, U.S. Department of Labor. The author is indebted to Howard M. Epstein and William J. Goode for critical assistance and to Robert K. Merton for his extensive comments on an earlier version. Harriet Zuckerman also offered valuable suggestions.

2. Part of the analysis which follows draws on Robert K. Merton's conceptualization of the dynamics of status-sets, presented in lectures at Columbia University over the past years, but as yet unpublished. According to Merton, the "salient" status is the one that is focused upon—made salient—in the interaction under analysis. The salient status may be the one that is most germane to the interaction but it may be one that is inappropriate to the situation. The black teacher who is invited to join a faculty because he is black, not because his professional status merits the offer, has had his racial status made salient.

3. According to Merton, "occupations can be described as 'sex-typed' when a very large majority of those in them are of one sex and when there is an associated normative expectation that this is as it should be."

4. Thus I have labeled it "status-set typing" when a class of persons who share a key status (e.g., lawyer) also share other matching statuses (e.g., white, Protestant) and when it is considered appropriate that this be so.

5. In fields which are not sex-typed or have not yet become sex-typed, or where there are few expectations concerning what would constitute an appropriate status-set to complement the occupational status, opportunities for women are great. As far as I know, computer programming in an occupation which has not become typed and many bright women and minority group members have been drawn to the field.

6. The enrollment of women in some law schools has increased in recent years. The University of Notre Dame Law School admitted women for the first time in the fall of 1969. The 20 women comprised 12 percent of the entering class, an unusually high proportion for law school classes (*New York Times,* September 14, 1969).

7. Goffman (1963, p. 129) points out that "more is involved than norms regarding somewhat static status attributes . . . that failure to sustain the many minor norms important in the etiquette of face-to-face communication can have a very pervasive effect upon the defaulter's acceptability in social situations."

8. The work of Hall (1948) illustrates this for medicine. See also Smigel (1964, pp. 100-102).

9. A number of placement officers in law schools report that it is difficult to place female graduates with solo practitioners. The reason offered, evidently considered as legitimate, is that the men complain that their wives would object.

10. A dramatic example of this is the Ruth Benedict-Franz Boas relationship in the Columbia University Anthropology Department. Boas regarded Ruth Benedict, as the wife of Stanley Benedict, "amply supported and with the obligation of a wife, someone for whose talents he must find work and a little money, someone on whom he could not make extreme demands and for whom he need not be responsible" (Mead 1959 pp. 342-43). Later, when Ruth Benedict separated from her husband and pressed for professional standing, Boas got her an assistant professorship. (The illustration is cited in Bernard [1964, pp. 105-6].)

11. A larger proportion of nonwhites than whites are employed by the government in practically every occupational category in the professional and technical group in the census. For example, 20.1 percent of Negro lawyers and judges go into government work as contrasted with 14 percent of whites; 24.7 percent of Negro physicians contrasted with 14.8 percent of whites (U.S. Bureau of the Census 1963, p. 284).

12. A disproportionate number of women lawyers specialize in the low-ranking speciality of matrimonial law and a disproportionate percentage of women doctors practice psychiatry, a relatively low-ranking medical speciality. For a further analysis see Epstein (1970, chap. 4).

13. Sir Alfred Egerton has noted, in fast-moving sciences, "of the total information extant, only part is in the literature. Much of it is stored in the many brains of scientists and technologists. We are as dependent on biological storage as on mechanical or library storage." It is to this source of unpublished information that access may be more limited for women than for men (cited by Bernard 1964, p. 303).

14. Bernard's (1964, p. 152) study of women zoologists showed that women faculty members at colleges had less contact with fellow scientists than did the men there. They were less likely than other scientists to attend meetings of professional societies. They were also less likely than male scientists to be on regular mailing lists for reprints of researchers. Women on the staffs of universities seemed to do better in becoming part of the communications network.

15. For a review of some surveys on women's productivity see Epstein (1970, p. 171).

16. This is an example of the "halo" effect of the institution on the author of a piece of work where his identity is not commonly known.

Cole and Cole (1968) have found that the visibility of physicists, for example, is highly correlated with the rank of department in which they work.

17. In 1963, 82 percent of women faculty members, contrasted with 74 percent of the men, worked in colleges and technical institutions with a faculty numbering under 200; 18 percent of the women as contrasted with 26 percent of the men teaching in colleges were in institutions with more than 200 faculty.

Women faculty members were also affiliated with smaller universities to a greater extent than were men (Dunham, Wright, and Chandler 1966, pp. 64-65).

18. Zuckerman (1967, p. 393) finds, for example, that Nobel laureates who themselves had laureate "masters" received the prize, on the average, nine years earlier than scientists who had not studied with a prize winner.

19. See Smigel's evaluation of client sponsorship as a path to partnership in a large firm (1964, pp. 100-102).

20. Mitchell (1951, p. 200) reported that women had not become fellows, officers, committee chairmen, committee members, editors, representatives to other organizations, members of the Council of Representatives, members-at-large, on the Executive Committee, or division presidents of the American Psychological Association in proportion to their numbers and qualifications. Only as secretaries have they served in proportion to their numbers. In 1968 no women held major offices.

21. For example, in a listing of the principal committees and members of the New York County Lawyers' Association for 1967-68, women served on fourteen of thirty-seven committees, and some appeared on more than one (*New York Times*, August 6, 1967, p. 37). Of a total of 1,103 members of the State Bar of California serving on committees, only eighteen are women (letter from Karl E. Zellman, Assistant Secretary, State Bar of California, March 21, 1967).

22. For example, the National Council of Women Psychologists was established in 1942, after it became clear that the Emergency Committee in Psychology of the National Research Council was continuing to omit women from its plans for the wartime use of psychologists (Mitchell 1951, p. 193). The National Association of Women Lawyers and other women's bar associations were also formed in response to exclusion by the men. There are also separate professional associations for women in the fields of medicine (founded 1915), dentistry (founded 1921), engineering (founded 1950), geography (founded 1925), and certified public accounting (founded 1933). It is interesting to note that in professions typed as female, there are no separate men's organizations, nor have men been legally excluded from membership at any time.

23. New York attorney Doris Sassower, former president of the New York Women's Bar Association, tells of the experience of Florence Allen, Chief Judge of the U.S. Court of Appeals, Sixth Circuit, who, when appointed as a federal judge, found the resistance of fellow judges so great that they refused to look at her or speak to her, except when forced to by the business at hand (speech delivered at the Waldorf Astoria Hotel, May 13, 1967, on the occasion of the first Florence E. Allen Award).

24. Some of the women lawyers I interviewed, for example, avoided joining colleagues at lunch. One commented, "Sometimes when the natural thing to do would be to join an associate and a client at lunch if you were a man, you feel, well, maybe I'd better not. It might be awkward for them. They might want to talk about something and might feel constrained."

25. A lawyer described her feelings in this way: "There was a camaraderie in the County (Law) Association — a terrific spirit. In other associations the members are very staid . . . but there everybody knows one another and they joke. They were prejudiced against admitting women but I think they were justified. It's not the same with a woman around. They aren't free to express themselves, to tell off-color stories — they should have that."

26. There is considerable congruence here between women professionals and other individuals who have some highly visible objectionable characteristic, trait, or status. Like them, during contacts with "normals" the woman may feel that she is "on," having to be self-conscious and calculating about the impressions she is making, to a degree and in areas of conduct which she assumes others are not (Goffman 1963, pp. 13-14, 33).

27. This problem is identified by Barker (1948, p. 34) in pointing to the uncertainty of status for the disabled person over a wide range of social interactions, including employment. "The blind, the ill, the deaf, the cripples, can never be sure what the attitude of a new acquaintance will be, whether it will be rejective or accepting, until the contact has been made. This is exactly the position of the adolescent, the light-skinned Negro, the second generation immigrant, the socially mobile person and the woman who has entered a predominantly masculine occupation."

28. These two types of behavior are, of course, examples of "compulsive" behavior or overconformity (identified by Merton 1957, pp. 131-60), whereby adherence to norm prescriptions in spite of the situational context may weaken role relationships and in addition impede the accomplishment of the goal.

29. White's data showed that women see fewer clients than do men (1967, p. 1093).

30. Compensation may be a consequence of the discomfort per-

sons feel in interaction with a stigmatized person, or, in our case, the person with a deviant status. Since he doesn't know how to act, because he feels sorry for the person with the stigma, or because he resents him for causing an awkwardness, the role partner tries to assuage his guilt by being extra-nice (Goffman 1963).

31. As with the cripple, the woman professional's accomplishments are often judged by a different set of standards than the man's. Thus minor accomplishments may be assessed as signs of remarkable and noteworthy capacities "in the circumstances." This may well be interpreted as a "put down" on the part of whoever is judging the accomplishment.

REFERENCES

Barker, Roger. 1948. "The Social Psychology of Physical Disability." *Journal of Social Issues* 4:22-54.

Becker, Howard, and Anselm Strauss. 1956. "Careers, Personality and Adult Socialization." *American Journal of Sociology* 62:253-63.

Bernard, Jessie. 1964. *Academic Women*. University Park: Pennsylvania State University Press.

Cole, Jonathan, and Stephen Cole. 1968. "The Visibility and the Structural Bases of Awareness of Scientific Research." *American Sociological Review* 33:397-413.

Dodge, Norton T. 1966. *Women in the Soviet Economy*. Baltimore: Johns Hopkins Press.

Dunham, Ralph E., Patricia Wright, and Marjorie O. Chandler. 1966. *Teaching Faculty in Universities and Four-Year Colleges*. Washington, D.C.: Office of Education.

Epstein, Cynthia Fuchs. 1969. "Women Lawyers and Their Profession: Inconsistency of Social Controls and Their Consequences for Professional Performance." Paper presented at 64th Annual Meeting of American Sociological Association, September 4, San Francisco, Calif. Mimeographed.

————. In press. *The Woman Lawyer*. Chicago: University of Chicago Press.

Etzioni, Amitai. 1961. *A Comparative Analysis of Complex Organizations*. New York: Free Press.

Fava, Sylvia Fleis. 1960. "Women in Professional Sociology." *American Sociological Review* 25:271-72.

Friedan, Betty. 1963. *The Feminine Mystique*. New York: Norton.

Goffman, Erving. 1963. *Stigma: Notes on the Management of Spoiled Identity*. Englewood Cliffs, N.J.: Prentice-Hall.

Goode, William J. 1957. "Community within a Community: The Professions." *American Sociological Review* 22:194-200.

————. 1960. "Norm Commitment and Conformity to Role-Status

Obligations." *American Journal of Sociology* 66:246-58.

————. 1963. *World Revolution and Family Patterns.* New York: Free Press.

————. 1964. *The Family.* Englewood Cliffs, N.J.: Prentice-Hall.

Hall, Oswald. 1948. "The Stages of a Medical Career." *American Journal of Sociology* 53:327-36.

Hankin, F., and D. Krohnke. 1965. *The American Lawyer.* 1964 Statistical Report 29. Chicago: American Bar Association.

Hughes, Everett. 1945. "Dilemmas and Contradictions of Status." *American Journal of Sociology* 50:353-59.

————. 1962. "What Other." In *Human Behavior and Social Processes,* edited by Arnold Rose. Boston: Houghton Mifflin.

Komarovsky, Mirra. 1953. *Women in the Modern World: Their Education and Their Dilemmas.* Boston: Houghton Mifflin.

Mead, Margaret, ed. 1959. *Anthropologist at Work: The Writing of Ruth Benedict.* Boston: Houghton Mifflin.

Mead, Margaret, and Frances Kaplan, eds. 1965. *American Women.* New York: Scribner's.

Merton, Robert K. 1957. *Social Theory and Social Structure.* Glencoe, Ill.: Free Press.

Merton, Robert K., George Reader, and Patricia L. Kendall, eds. 1957. *The Student-Physician.* Cambridge, Mass.: Harvard University Press.

Mitchell, Mildred B. 1951. "Status of Women in the American Psychological Association." *American Psychologist* 6:193-201.

New York Times. 1969. "20 Women to Study Law at Notre Dame." September 14.

Rossi, Alice S. 1965. "Barriers to the Career Choice of Engineering, Medicine or Science among American Women." In *Women and the Scientific Professions,* edited by Jacquelyn A. Mattfeld and Carol G. Van Aken. Cambridge, Mass.: M.I.T. Press.

Simon, Rita James, Shirley Merritt Clark, and Kathleen Galway. 1967. "The Woman Ph.D.: A Recent Profile." *Social Problems* 15:221-36.

Smigel, Erwin O. 1964. *The Wall Street Lawyer.* New York: Free Press.

U.S. Bureau of the Census. 1963. *1960 Subject Reports. Occupational Characteristics.*Final Report PC (2)-7A. Washington, D.C.: Government Printing Office.

U.S. Department of Labor. 1954. *Changes in Women's Occupations, 1940-1950.* Women's Bureau Bulletin No. 253. Washington, D.C.: Government Printing Office.

White, James J. 1967. "Women in the Law." *Michigan Law Review* 65:1051-1122.

Zuckerman, Harriet A. 1967. "Nobel Laureates in Science: Patterns of Productivity, Collaboration and Authorship." *American Sociological Review* 32:391-403.

four

Male and Female: Differing Perceptions of the Teaching Experience

HARMON ZIEGLER

The differential roles of men and women in politics have not been studied very extensively, and among those studies which have been made the main focus is upon voting behaviors in elections. The general conclusions of these limited studies suggest quite strongly that men take a more active role in politics than do women. Explanations of this phenomenon center upon the concept of sexually differentiable roles. The argument is that the society assigns a dominant power-wielding role to men and a submissive receptive role to women.

No matter how one might want to quarrel about niceties of definition, politics is an arena for the exercise of power and control, and equation of the political role with the masculine role accordingly is not illogical. Yet, gross classification of political roles according to sex overlooks many of the subtleties of being a man or a woman. In political life, economic and social modernization is gradually eroding sex differences in political roles, but this does not mean that popular perceptions of masculine and feminine roles have changed. For instance, if the popular stereotype defines the masculine role as one of power and dominance, what can we say of men who hold an occupation that is perceived as feminine?

From Harmon Ziegler, THE POLITICAL LIFE OF AMERICAN TEACHERS © 1967. Reprinted by permission of Prentice-Hall, Inc., Englewood Cliffs, New Jersey.

This study is based mainly on interviews with 803 high school teachers living in Oregon in 1965, three fifths of whom were male and two-fifths female. In addition, another study which served as a national "central group" and information from comparative sources were also utilized. See Ziegler's introduction to *The Political Life of American Teachers* for further details.

The Feminization of the Teaching Role

Secondary school teachers, males not less than females, are playing just such a feminine role. At the elementary level, teaching is almost exclusively a woman's occupation; in higher education, men predominate. At the secondary level, however, there is a relatively even balance of male and female teachers. About two out of three male teachers are in high schools, and at the high school level today males are a slight majority of the teaching population. This numerical balance of the sexes, however, does not diminish the primarily female dominance of the educational establishment.

The numerical dominance of males in high school teaching is relatively new. In 1950 males made up only about 40 per cent of the high school teaching population; by 1960 males made up the majority. The rapid increase in the male teaching population at the high school level is the result of elaborate inducements offered both in colleges of education and in public schools to diminish female dominance of the teaching profession. The reasons for these efforts are not based on an assumption that men are better teachers than women; rather, they stem from the concept of authority.

The teacher's first task in the classroom is to establish authority over the pupils. Educational psychologists believe that the child's need to identify with a father figure offers a good way through which to establish the teacher's classroom authority and to improve the pupil's learning experience. The identification problems of girls are not very severe. However, if a boy establishes an emotional contact primarily with women teachers, it is believed the school can offer him little help in learning a male role, for women represent the values of mothers and homemakers and can hardly be expected to provide male guidelines. So the effort to recruit males was begun, and it has been successful. However, I maintain that, far from converting the secondary school establishment from a feminine into a masculine enterprise, the recruitment of male teachers into secondary teaching has led to the playing of a feminine role by men.

It must be clearly understood that by *feminine role* I do not mean an *effete role*. I mean, rather, that laymen *look upon* teaching traditionally as a woman's job; insofar as high school teaching is thus interpreted to be a feminine role, those who play that role conform to society's expectations for it; and that it is consequently difficult for a male teacher to establish male authority in this role. I further intend to argue that males who play this feminine role behave politically much as do women, although it cannot be argued that they do this solely *because* they are high school teachers.

The feminization of teaching is primarily an American phenomenon. In most other countries men have always assumed a major role in secondary education. Richard Hofstadter has succinctly described the position of the male teacher in America:

> But in America, where teaching has been identified as a feminine profession, it does not offer men the stature of a fully legitimate male role. The American masculine conviction that education and culture are feminine concerns is thus confirmed, and no doubt partly shaped, by the experiences of boys in school. . . . The boys grow up thinking of men teachers as somewhat effeminate and treat them with a curious mixture of genteel deference (of the sort due to women) and hearty male condescension. In a certain constricted sense, the male teacher may be respected, but he is not "one of the boys."[1]

Most of the formal teachers' organizations do not provide for separate organizations for high school teachers. Consequently, assuming an equal attendance at professional meetings by elementary and high school teachers, male teachers are still outnumbered by female teachers. Even more important, it takes a long time for popular stereotypes to be erased. Males now comprise the majority of the high school teaching population, but the image of the schoolmarm still plagues them. In 1932, Willard Waller published a book that has since become a classic, *The Sociology of Teaching.*[2] In an anecdote about a high school principal's experience in a barbershop, Waller describes the stereotypic treatment of teachers. As the man enters, the barber, who apparently has been telling off-color stories, hushes his clients. Recognizing the artificiality of the situation, the principal encourages resumption of normal conversation, but to no avail. After the principal leaves the shop the conversation resumes, but the barber admonishes his clients to be on their guard whenever a teacher or principal enters because, he says, "I have many women customers." As Waller comments:

> The assimilation of the teachers of the feminine character ideal, the suppression of normal activity when the teacher entered the

room — all these things make the above stand out as an interesting and significant incident. It has been said that no woman and no Negro is ever fully admitted to the white man's world. Possibly we should add men teachers to the list of the excluded.[3]

I have discussed Waller's decades-old comments with many educators, and most of them believe that the situation is still much the same today. High school teachers throughout the country are sensitive to the fact that the pronoun *she* is almost invariably used in discussions about teachers and most of the literature about teachers uses this pronoun. In a Supreme Court decision [Adler v. Board of Education, 342 U.S. 485 (1952)] involving plaintiffs all of whom were made high school teachers, the opinion handed down by the Court uses the pronoun *she*. Recruitment of males into the high school teaching population did not really get started until the middle 1950's, long after most of the adults in today's society were high school students. It is perhaps only natural, then, that when people think back upon a high school teacher, they think in terms of *her*.

It may well be that the tenacity of the stereotype will be reduced in a few generations. Teachers and administrators certainly hope so. A popular series of TV dramas, "Mr. Novak," produced with the approval of the National Education Association, is a clear example of the vigorous efforts being made to change the stereotype.[4] However, sociologists have learned that stereotypes are not accurate reflections of reality and that stereotypes persist long after their counterpart realities have changed, or disappeared. For example, an occupation that, like high school teaching, is burdened with the stereotype problem is that of the lobbyist. Popular press exposés condemn lobbyists as subverters of the public interest. Lobbyists, supposed to be the evil power behind the scenes, the manipulators of practically all legislative decisions, are often depicted as smoking long, black cigars while lavishly distributing money in an attempt to buy the vote of legislators. In fact, lobbyists, at least those who make lobbying a full-time career, are generally well-educated advocates of a particular point of view and spend most of their time transmitting information, not money, to legislators. Most legislators regard lobbyists as very useful in the legislative process precisely because lobbyists can provide information that might not otherwise be readily available. It is probably true, especially at the state level, that at one time lobbyists did engage in corrupt practices. Today lobbyists are trying desperately to live down this stereotyped image and are extremely sensitive to public criticism. Many are reluctant to be called lobbyists, preferring to be known as *legislative representatives* or some other such innocuous term.

Male high school teachers, like lobbyists, are struggling to overcome a stereotype. Doing what is popularly regarded as women's work has both tangible and relatively intangible consequences for male teachers. They not only suffer degradation of status by working in a feminine occupation, they also incur considerable degradation of financial rewards. Financial discrimination against male teachers exists relative to males in other occupations and relative to female teachers. It is true that male and female teachers are paid according to the same salary scales (it is also true that various under-the-table inducements are made to male teachers). However, the salaries of most married female teachers merely augment the husbands' income, whereas married male teachers must use the entirety of their salary to support their families. Female high school teachers are better paid than are most women working at other jobs. This is decidedly not the case with male teachers. Thus, not only are male teachers doing women's work, they are only getting paid women's wages for doing it. Men who become high school teachers may not expect to make as much money as they might were they to enter another occupation, it is nonetheless damage to the male ego for a man to be on a financial par with women. In practically every other occupation, the financial discrimination is against women. The failure of high school teaching to follow suit clearly makes the position of the male teacher somewhat unique.

Another way of analyzing the male and female roles in high school teaching is to examine the differing career orientations of the sexes. For both men and women, teaching is an unstable occupation, a contingent role rather than a dominant one. The turnover rate in high school teaching is exceptionally high. The reasons for this instability differ markedly as between men and women, however. Female teachers intend to teach only until they get married or until a bit later when they begin a family. The female perception of the teaching occupation is thus *in and* out. For males, however, the orientation is *up or out.* Males regard high school teaching as women's work, a stepping-stone into either educational administration, which is almost entirely dominated by males, or into another profession altogether. Here is one of the frustrations of the male high school teacher: only about a third of the male beginning teachers anticipate remaining in that occupation until retirement, yet in actual practice, more males than females remain career teachers.

Insofar as teaching is a feminized occupation, and if it is assumed that teaching is a middle-class occupation, then for males teaching becomes a mechanism of status change while for females it is a mechanism of status maintenance. The majority of males who become high school teachers come from lower-class backgrounds, whereas the majority of females who become high school teachers come from middle- and upper-class backgrounds. For males entering teaching, then, a change in status comes about as they move up into a subsystem with a female ethos. Significantly, women rank public school teaching substantially higher in occupational status than men do.

Robert Lane observed that "A person's work life is certain to color his outlook on society, to structure his attitudes, and to affect his behavior."[5] This is to say that it is not necessarily a person's occupation as such but rather his perception of his occupation that colors his attitudes. To some persons, occupation is clearly a major component of personal identity, but others look upon occupation in a much more casual fashion, viewing it primarily as a money-making device that is not a major determinant of one's total life style. Teaching appears less likely to elicit total commitment than other professions, hence it might be expected that the teaching experience would not operate to produce in the teacher a cohesive set of values. Actually, different types of people react to the teaching experience in different ways, but there is evidence that the teaching experience does operate to amalgamate the need structures of varying types of people to produce a pattern common to all teaching groups. There is also evidence suggesting that the teaching experience molds a characteristic set of personality traits. To illustrate, a person has many identities. In addition to such given identities as sex and race, one is further identified by his occupation, income, education, place of residence, and so forth. Consider the forces at work in the Southern judge striving to reach a decision on a question of racial integration. Will he react primarily as a Southerner reared in the traditions of segregation, or as a judge required by law and the judicial tradition to enforce impartially the decisions of the legislature or a higher court?

The way a person will react in a decision-making situation depends upon the relative strengths of the identities at work in him. It is questionable that one can talk about teachers as a whole on the assumption that personality variables are eroded by the teaching experience. It is the argument of this book that the teaching experience has greatly diverse impacts upon recruits into the profession according to what combination of personality and social variables each recruit brings into the teaching career, but that the basic variable — hence the key to understanding individual reactions to the teaching career — is sex. In short, men teachers and women teachers are different animals, and the remarkable political behavior of men teachers can be understood as a masculine reaction to their feminine occupational role.

What Teaching Does to Teachers

Waller has described the teacher as being inflexible, conservative, and as having an abnormal concern about status. Waller believes that if one does not have these traits when he starts teaching, he develops them before long.[6] His argument is that these traits flow naturally out of the relations of teachers with their students: The first order of business on the agenda of the high school teacher is to establish who is boss. The teacher must define the teacher-student situation for the students: discipline must be maintained. For the male high school teacher, paradoxically, this can be difficult, although the argument in favor of recruitment of more males into the teaching profession rests upon the assumption that males can impose authority more easily and can readily establish a father image (at least for male students). The method of establishing authority most frequently relied on by teachers involves performance of some rather dramatic act during the first session of a class. For example, a teacher is usually able to locate the one or two students in the class who are most likely to lead a minor revolt, primarily because they are looked upon by the other students as leaders. Having located the potential troublemakers, the teacher's task is to put them in their place. This confrontation occasionally takes the form of actual physical combat. In a sense, then, the teacher is acting somewhat like an officer in the Army but without the status or sanctioning power available to an officer. The maintenance of the superordinate-subordinate relationship leads to personal rigidity, and the teacher's dominant need, based upon fear of loss of authority, is for security. Hence, security is exaggerated in the need structure of teachers in comparison to other values. Whether the characteristics of conservatism, rigidity, and the need for security that teachers display are personality characteristics which influence one to choose teaching rather than some riskier calling or whether these characteristics are a product of teaching has not been established. Roger's view that "It is likely that the people who enter the teaching profession *are* conservative . . . because individualists fear the regimentation imposed on teachers . . ." is provocative but speculative.[7] The portrait of the teacher nonetheless is of one who is not likely to do unconventional things or to engage in unconventional behavior. It is my belief, however, that as a portrait of the teacher, it is far more one of the male than of the female teacher. To advance this argument, let us examine the relative impacts that three variables — sex, income, and teaching experience — may have upon teacher behaviors and attitudes. There are three possible relationships among the three variables: first, males and females may have largely different characteristics of income and teaching experience; second, people at a given income level may have different characteristics irrespective of teaching experience and sex; and third, the teaching experience may operate to minimize differences based upon income or sex. If the third relationship proves true, then we may conclude that teaching is a role overwhelming male-female role differentials.

Let us see how sex, income, and teaching experience mold certain factors that may be presumed to be central to the life style of the individual. The factors are:

1. Job satisfaction,
2. Political values,
3. Educational values, and
4. Personal orientations toward life.

Job Satisfaction

Research has produced clear and unequivocal evidence indicating there is substantial job dissatisfaction among male teachers.[8]

One measure of a person's job satisfaction is whether or not he would choose the same occupation were he given the opportunity to start life over again. A substantial majority of the female teachers polled said they would choose teaching again, whereas only about one third of the male teachers indicated that they would again choose to become teachers. Males begin teaching with the expectation of moving up to a different, better job. What happens when these expectations are shattered? Money is important for males in our society, which measures success by material yardsticks, but do males with high incomes exhibit more satisfaction with their jobs than males with low incomes, or does it really matter? Is making a fairly high income a satisfactory compensation for doing women's work, or is good pay a poor reward for such denigration?

Among low-income teachers (those with an annual family income of less than $10,000) about one third of the males are satisfied, compared to more than half the females. For teachers in this group an increase in teaching experience makes neither males nor females either more or less satisfied with their positions. In other words, the attitudes which they brought into the profession remain unchanged by the teaching experience. By contrast, the male teacher starting his career at a high income level is considerably more satisfied than his low-income counterpart. Thus, at least among *beginning male* teachers, money seems to be conducive to job satisfaction. Curiously enough, relatively inexperienced low-income female teachers are no less satisfied with their jobs than are relatively inexperienced high-income female teachers. The male who started out relatively satisfied and happy becomes dissatisfied. Presumably his dreams of moving on to a better job have been shattered and he is left with the unpleasant task of facing the truth: he has been teaching for years, he is not an administrator, he has not left teaching; he has been treading water. There is a decline in the job satisfaction of high-income males down to the point where, at the more experienced level, all males (irrespective of income) have roughly the same extent of satisfaction with their jobs. For females, a remarkably dissimilar pattern develops. For them, the cumulative effects of increasing income and increasing teaching experience operate to increase dramatically their satisfaction. What this means is that the teaching experience is beneficial to the job satisfaction of females, but is harmful for males.

It seems reasonable to suppose that financial reward is a basic ingredient in inducing job satisfaction. Why is this not the case among male high school teachers? The answer is simple. Relative to other occupations requiring similar education, male teachers are underpaid; perhaps more important, they receive the same compensation as female teachers. In every school district in the country school boards are gradually raising the salaries of teachers, under considerable pressure from educational associations and, occasionally, the threat of teacher walkouts. However, teaching is an occupation to which men and women have equal access, and it therefore may be that a basic cause of dissatisfaction among men may never be corrected. That is to say, no matter how high teacher salaries go, as long as men and women are paid equally job dissatisfaction among men teachers will not be reduced. The obvious if unconventional remedy for improving the self-esteem of the male teacher, then, is to introduce some sort of male-female salary scale differential. In an informal way this is already being done in many school districts. Increments to salaries can be earned for various extraclass duties, such as serving as advisor for student organizations, coaching, and supervision of extracurricular student affairs. The practice is to make these opportunities more available to men than to women.

Political Conservatism

Citizens who concern themselves with public education often are anxious about how teacher values may affect the nature of the curriculum, and, through personal contacts, the students. Seeking to categorize the political values of teachers, laymen usually describe a teacher as holding either liberal or conservative beliefs. Indeed, in the literature about teacher politics these words occur time and time again, although there is rarely any accompanying clear definition of *liberal* and *conservative* mean. Conservatism is a difficult idea to define with objectivity, and opinion polls are not necessarily the most reliable guide to a definition of conservatism in terms of overt ideology. An instrument called the Domestic Conservatism Scale, developed by political scientists, is an interesting attempt to establish a standard of conservatism by measuring individuals' attitudes toward such government activities as federal aid to education, integration of public schools, equalization of job opportunities, medical care for the aged, and so forth.[9] To educational sociologists, teachers appear to be conservative in the sense of being creatures of habit, not experimentalists by professional nature. The conservatism apparent in teachers is best understood, perhaps, by considering them as advocates of the interests of the middle class. Teachers prefer to do regular rather than radical things, and they do not encourage their students to participate in politics other than in the most accepted and established fashions. This interpretation is based upon the assumption that teachers, charged with the responsibility of injecting system maintenance values into the educational subculture, encourage their students to become good citizens and in so doing do not offer students an alternative to acceptance of the *status quo.*

For our purposes, *conservatism* is perhaps best defined as a personal reluctance to take risks, an inclination to and dependence upon the established order and patterns of behavior. Conservatism thus defined is an expression of middle-class values. In terms of this definition, teachers themselves think they are conservative, to judge by a recent National Education Association[10] poll of high school teachers in which 56 per cent of those who responded to a question asking them to classify themselves as either liberal or conservative chose the conservative alternative. Several findings of the NEA study are of relevance to our inquiry. The responses indicated that an overwhelming majority of teachers regard themselves as moderate conservatives or liberals; only about one fourth of the sample described themselves as ultraconservative or ultraliberal. Most of the moderates, however, lean toward the conservative end of the spectrum. Also of significance is the finding that about one third of the women but almost one half of the men indicated that they regard themselves as liberals. It is, of course, generally true that women irrespective of occupation, are considered somewhat more conservative than men, and so this finding is not surprising.

Conservatism is often equated with conformity to middle-class values. Beyond question, it is a difficult matter to establish exactly what middle-class values are, even more difficult to measure them. In the literature that attempts to catalog the presumed values of the middle class, however, thrift, frugality, individual initiative, self-reliance, hard work, and respect for authority seem to occur most frequently.

There is yet another yardstick of conservatism, one that has become very much a part of the American vocabulary since the end of World War II. This archconservatism emphasizes morality and patriotism as its chief values. People who subscribe to this philosophy avow profound love of country. They believe, for example, that American history should be taught so as to instill within the child a love of country. They believe they have discovered a fundamental breakdown in moral standards in this country (which perhaps can be traced to a decline in the acceptance of middle-class values). They argue that most of the basic evils of modern American society would be eradicated if Americans would return to something called old-fashioned patriotism. One intuitively suspects that all three interpretations of conservatism are somehow related, but it is possible that people who appear to be conservatives in their current postures on domestic public policy might not turn out to be conservatives if their attitudes were measured against middle-class values or arch-conservative dogmas.

Older people tend to be more conservative than younger people. Teachers become *more* conservative as their teaching experience increases. Is this tendency of teachers to become more conservative a specific function of the teaching experience, or is it a general function of the aging process? The answer to this is that among teachers of the same age those who have taught the longest tend to be the most conservative. What effect does the teaching experience have on the viability of middle-class values among teachers? Does teaching shape teachers into loyal volunteers of the middle class, faithful advocates of the *status quo*, stern repressors of radicalism? Is this kind of conservatism more characteristic of female teachers than of male teachers? The evidence strongly suggests that teachers' allegiance to middle-class values increases with teaching experience. It appears, however, that there is no relationship between age and allegiance to middle-class values. Why is it that the teaching experience boosts the stock of the *status quo*? Is it because of community pressures demanding conformity from teachers? Is it because of teacher *perception* of community pressures demanding conformity? Or is it a consquence of teachers' desire to avoid threats to authority in the classroom? Children with strongly imbued middle-class values are likely to be well-behaved in the classroom.

There is a curious ambivalence attaching to the role of education as a transmitter of the values of culture. In schools of education the future teacher is taught that it is the job of the schools to build good democratic citizens. Accordingly, it is taught, students should be encouraged to express themselves to the end of developing in them a healthy interest in participating in the affairs of society, and the best forum for such expression is within the school itself. But there is the problem of discipline: student activism must not disrupt the smooth flow of the classroom situation. Sociologists of education maintain that the classroom authority of the teacher is slipping and that respect for teachers is diminishing among students. It is therefore quite possible that the necessity for maintaining discipline overrides the textbook obligation of teachers to encourage student self-expression.

Teachers' allegiance to middle-class values increases with teaching experience, but among low-income teachers (irrespective of sex) that allegiance becomes extremely tenacious. When asked about their experiences with the maintenance of proper discipline, the majority of teachers responding to the NEA study answered that maintaining classroom discipline had become progressively more difficult than it was when they first started teaching, and the longer the experience the greater the perceived increase in the difficulty of maintaining discipline. Only about one fourth of the relatively inexperienced teachers but a majority of the more experienced teachers, claimed that discipline seemed to be increasingly difficult to maintain.

It appears that the high-income female teachers, who are politically conservative, have very low allegiance to middle-class values. Male teachers, on the other hand, even those who are political liberals, demonstrate high allegiance to middle-class values in comparison with women. These findings may relate to the fact that maintaining discipline is much more of a problem for male teachers than for female teachers; indeed, one suspects that the crisis in authority is related to the recruitment of male teachers. Male teachers tend to seek out the comfort and security of a disciplined, middle-class conformist world. Paradoxically, however, the recruitment of males into the high school teaching profession has brought male teachers into the majority, but has not brought about the concomitant learning situation that one would expect. It appears that the mere existence of males does not automatically produce discipline, perhaps because the desired creation of a strongly masculine figure has not occurred.[11]

My-country-right-or-wrong conservatism, the radical right, which received an enthusiastic if somewhat unclear articulation by the Republican Party in the 1964 Presidential election, seems to appeal less to female teachers than to male teachers, especially to those making low income relative to length of teaching experience. Among such males, the longer their teaching experience the more conservative they tend to be. There are probably more moderate than radical conservatives among the teaching population.

Conservatism among male teachers seems to be related to the fact that most male teachers do not like their work. It appears that one method of creating an advocate of the Radical Right is to take a male, place him in the incongruously feminine teaching role, keep him there for years and at low income, and allow his hopes for advancement to fade as his experience increases but his situation does not change. Male teachers are a disadvantaged segment, and their attitudes reflect a correlation between job satisfaction and conservatism. By contrast, the moderate conservatism typically espoused by female teachers, on the other hand, seems to be essentially the traditional conservatism of the middle and upper classes, a conservatism which reflects, not anxiety, but rather an essential satisfaction with one's society and his or her position in it.

Attitudes Toward Education: A Progressive Orthodoxy?

Conservatism, whatever its mode of expression, bespeaks a disposition to maintain things as they are. If it is true that teaching tends to confirm teachers in political conservatism, it is therefore reasonable to suppose that the teaching experience tends to confirm them in educational conservatism also. Educational conservatives are those who do not like progressive education. Whereas the roots of the political conservatism of the high school teacher are somewhat ambiguous, the educational establishment, as it is represented in schools of education, vigorously fosters the cause of educational progressivism. Progressivism is the establishment's orthodoxy. Certainly the recent attacks upon American education, critical of the emphasis on techniques rather than subject matter, whether or not one agrees with them, have correctly described the dominant theme of the training of public secondary school teachers. An occasional revolt, principally in the form of public candidates running for the school board on a platform of returning to the three R's, does not diminish very much the firm control that educational progressives have over the training of public school teachers. Progressive teachers would prefer to abandon the traditional discipline and learning that had little regard for individual needs, and to substitute for them a program in which the student is in essence allowed to set his own pace. One envisions a confrontation, for example, between teachers who prefer to return to the practice of administering a good spanking when other methods fail and teachers who would like to see psychiatric services made available in the public schools from kindergarten up.

These comments about the orthodoxy of educational progressivism are offered primarily to prepare the reader for the finding that, unlike political conservatism, educational conservatism *decreases* with teaching experience. As teachers are becoming politically more conservative, they are simultaneously becoming educationally more progressive. Moderate political conservatism and educational progressivism are values which conform to the expectations of the educational system, and are values which are held by those who have derived the most benefits from the system. On the other hand, radical conservatism and lack of belief in the methods of progressive education are deviant attitudes held by those who have derived the least benefit from the system. The pattern of conformity is typical of females; the pattern of deviance is typical of males. For example, high-income females, politically the most conservative, are educationally the most progressive. It is hardly coincidental that teachers in this group are also the most satisfied with their jobs and hence can be assumed to be deriving the most psychological benefits from the educational system.

Corroborative evidence is provided by the NEA survey, which showed that about 60 per cent of the male high school teachers would use physical punishment as a disciplinary measure, as compared to about 40 per cent of the female high school teachers. Approximately 25 per cent of the female teachers but only about 13 per cent of the male teachers reported that they never have any disciplinary problems, which perhaps explains the greater readiness of the men to resort to physical punishment.[12]

The real problem here is, not the disposition of males to radical conservatism and lack of educational progressivism, but that these attitudes may be related to the crisis of authority, a situation that in turn can be related to the incursion of men into what had been almost exclusively a feminine occupation. That male teachers should develop anti-establishment attitudes is understandable, but has resulted in high schools staffed with teachers who do not like their work, who espouse an ideology of discontent, and who reject the educational orthodoxy of the educational establishment. Whether one judges this to be good or bad depends entirely upon his own values. One might predict that this dissident element would ultimately become absorbed and conform. This is the established pattern of deviant movements in the political world. On the other hand, the extent to which males are able to increase their benefits from the educational system and reduce their nonconformity depends, paradoxically, less upon the educational system itself than upon the general society. For male teachers to become more satisfied with their jobs, they will first have to be accorded more legitimacy by society itself.

Personal Rigidity

The position of the male teacher should become especially perilous in the classroom, for it is the classroom that provides the greatest threat to a teacher's authority. The classroom situation is supposed to contribute to the development of an unusually high concern with status and authority among teachers. Facing a crisis of authority, teachers can be expected to emphasize superior-subordinate relationships and to be suspicious of change, for they prefer that their professional world be structured so as to minimize risk-taking and to maximize established authority.

Two indices — tolerance of change and need for respect — of these dimensions of personality were used in the Oregon study. The expectation was that these measures would discriminate distinctive male-female attitude differences. The tolerance-of-change index measured the willingness of individuals to try something new without prior knowledge of the consequences. Those willing to accept change are, in a sense, risk-takers. Those unwilling to accept change are typified by the person who fits himself into a routine and sticks to it, who prefers the security of established procedures to the insecurity of new ideas.

Teachers are presumed to have a high need for respect. The use in the Oregon study of an index to measure these dimensions of teacher personality rests largely upon the theoretical contributions of Waller, who observed that:

> Inflexibility or unbendingness of personality, which we have mentioned as characterizing the school teacher, flows naturally out of his relations with his students. The teacher must maintain a constant pose in the presence of students. . . . The teacher must not accept the definition of situations which students work out but must impose his own definition upon the students. . . . The teacher lives much by the authority role. . . . Those who live by one role must learn to defend its ultimate implications. . . . On the objective side, this dignity which arises in the classroom is an exaggerated

concern over all the ramifications of respect and the formal amenities due to one who occupies a narrow but well-defined social
status. . . . In the life of every teacher there is significant long-term
change in the psychic weight of these roles, a not unusual result
being that role number one, the authority role, eats up the friendly
role or absorbs so much of the personality that nothing is left for
friendliness to fatten upon.[13]

Waller made these observations at a time when two-thirds of
the nation's high school teachers were women. It now appears,
however, that the syndrome he observed — rigid personality,
exaggerated concern for authority, and a deep need for respect
— is more pronouncedly characteristic of male teachers than of
female teachers. Male teachers are substantially more routinized
than female teachers. This relationship is especially pronounced
among high-income teachers. Nearly 60 per cent of the high-
income female teachers are *not* opposed to change, whereas
nearly 60 per cent of the males in this category *are* opposed to
change. If as Waller suggests the classroom situation produces
a deep need for respect, then those who have the most experience in the classroom should have the deepest need for respect.
But experienced teachers demonstrated no greater need for
respect than did less experienced teachers, even though the more
experienced teachers indicated that the maintenance of classroom discipline was a major problem, whereas the less experienced teachers indicated it was not. It develops, however, that
the teaching experience produces a differential need for respect
upon male and female teachers: men have a higher need for
respect than women do. The differential reaches its most extreme proportions among the higher income groups, where about
30 per cent of the male teachers have a depth of need for respect
that is equalled by only about 15 per cent of the female teachers.
Just as the job satisfaction of the male teacher does not depend
solely upon income, neither does his need for respect. Low income males and high income males have about the same depth
of need for respect.

The deep need for respect felt by males suggests that the
teaching experience threatens their authority, for the respect accorded a teacher is a gauge of his authority. Women do not seem
to have as great a concern for authority when they begin teaching and apparently are not as bothered by challenges to authority as men are. It is not just being a high school teacher that contributes to an exaggerated concern for authority, it is being a

male teacher. The fact that male teachers have more trouble than women do in maintaining classroom discipline feeds this need for respect. An unusual paradox of status may be developing: as men they should be able to command respect, but apparently they cannot.

Emergent Patterns in Male and Female Values

This chapter undertook to discover if male and female teachers react to the teaching experience in markedly different patterns. The evidence is that they do, and that the patterns are typified in the behaviors respectively of high-income females and low-income males. The high-income females have the greater satisfaction with their jobs, the lesser need for respect, the lesser opposition to change, the more conservative political opinions, not the lesser tendency to radical conservatism. They are also the more educationally progressive. The low income males are the less satisfied with their jobs, have the greater need for respect, and are more likely to oppose change. They are more liberal politically than females, but the most radically conservative of teachers are in this group. They are less educationally progressive than women.

Between these two extreme patterns fall the behavior of high-income males, who seem to have more in common with low-income males than with high-income females, and of low-income females, whose values seem at times closer to low-income males and at other times closer to high-income females. That is to say, for male teachers the clearest congruence of values is with those of other males, whereas females have a less exclusive tendency to adopt the values of other females. Granted that income is important for the males, it does not seem to provide a set of identifications as viable and permanent as simply being a male. Maleness emerges as the essential variable and the male high school teacher is, in a sense, the underclass of the teaching profession, a rebel in a female system.

NOTES

1. Richard Hofstadter, *Anti-Intellectualism in American Life* (New York: Vintage Books, 1963), p. 320. Italics supplied. See also Margaret Mead, *The School in American Culture* (Cambridge: Harvard University Press, 1951), pp. 5-6.

2. New York: John Wiley & Sons, Inc., 1965. Recently reissued in

paperback, this book has been widely used in courses dealing with the sociology of education.

3. *Ibid.*, p. 50.

4. In spite of the fact that this program's hero was a male high school teacher, male teachers had a less positive reaction to the program than did female teachers. In a survey of teachers, conducted by the National Education Association, 60 per cent of the female teachers but only 49 per cent of the male teachers who viewed "Mr. Novak" felt that the program had a good effect on their own morale and self-esteem. Perhaps this result is related to the fact that fewer male than female teachers believed that the dramatizations were reasonable portrayals of the real problems of real high school teachers.

5. Robert Lane, *Political Life* (New York: The Free Press of Glencoe, Inc., 1965), p. 331.

6. Waller, pp. 386-400.

7. Dorothy Rogers, "Implications of Views Concerning the 'Typical' School Teacher," *Journal of Educational Sociology*, 59 (September 1953), 484.

8. Ward S. Mason, *The Beginning Teacher: Status and Career Orientations* (Washington: U.S. Department of Health, Education, and Welfare, 1961), pp. 81-83; National Education Association, *The American Public School Teacher, 1960-1961* (Washington: National Education Association, 1963), p. 67; National Education Association *Research Bulletin*, 35 (1957), p. 38.

9. V. O. Key, Jr., *Public Opinion and American Democracy* (New York: Alfred A. Knopf, 1961), p. 561.

10. National Education Association, *What Teachers Think: A Summary of Teacher Opinion Poll Findings, 1960-1965* (Washington: National Education Association, 1965), p. 51.

11. Leo J. Cronback, *Educational Psychology* (New York: Harcourt, Brace and Co., 1954), p. 318.

12. National Education Association, *Student Behavior in Secondary Schools, 1964* (NEA, August, 1965).

13. Waller, *op. cit.*, pp. 386-400.

five

Head Librarians: How Many Men?
How Many Women?

W. C. BLANKENSHIP

It is possible that many men hesitate to enter college library work because they feel that the profession is over-feminized and that most of the administrative jobs are held by women. Conversely, it is possible that many women believe that most head librarians' positions are filled by men and that administration-minded women have few opportunities to enter this area of librarianship. Accordingly, the purpose of this paper is to present some data which may help to form some tentative conclusions concerning the frequency that men and women may be found serving as head librarians in various types and sizes of colleges. Therefore, the central problem may be stated in the form of this question: Is there a difference in the percentages of men and women who are head librarians of colleges, when the institutions are grouped according to the nature of their financial support and by the size of their enrollments?

In order to collect the data, 660 questionnaires were mailed to selected head librarians of colleges of the United States.[1] Of this number, 414 were returned. This number of returns was above average, being 62.727 per cent of the total number. Among the items included on the schedules were the following questions, which will serve as the bases for this report.

A. How long have you been the head librarian of your institution?

   (1) 1-5 yrs.?_____ (2) 6-10 yrs.?_____ (3) 11-15 yrs.?_____ (4) 16 or more?_____

From COLLEGE AND RESEARCH LIBRARIES, Vol. 28, No. 1 (1967), pp. 41-48. Reprinted by permission.

B. Please check the total length of time that you have been a head librarian in all academic libraries with which you have been associated.
(1) 1-5 yrs.?——— (2) 6-10 yrs.?——— (3) 11-15 yrs.?——— (4) 16 or more?———
C. Is your age (1) 20-30?——— (2) 31-40?——— (3) 41-50?——— (4) Over 50?———
D. Sex: Male——— Female———
E. Please check the percentage of the institutional budget that is allotted to your library. Please estimate the figure if you do not know exactly. (1) Under 2 per cent——— (2) 2-4 per cent ——— (3) 4-6 per cent——— (4) Over 6 per cent———

The data were coded and placed upon punched cards, which were verified for accuracy by a key-punch operator, and most of the information was abstracted by use of the card sorting machine.

Of the 414 head librarians who returned the questionnaire, the number of men and women was almost equally divided. The number and per cent of male and female respondents is listed in Table 1.

Table 1 / Responses According to the Sex of College Head Librarians

College Head Labrarians	Number	Per Cent
Males	201	48.55
Females	213	51.45
Total	414	100.00

In analyzing the data by comparing the returns from men and women head librarians when their colleges are classified according to type and size, the institutions were divided into five groups, which may be described in this manner:

Group 1 consists of publicly supported colleges which have enrollments ranging from 1,501 to 5,000 students.

Group 2 consists of publicly supported colleges which have enrollments ranging from 500 to 1,500 students. One college having an enrollment of less than 500 students is included in this group.

Group 3 consists of privately supported colleges which have enrollments ranging from 1,501 to 5,000 students.

Group 4 consists of privately supported colleges which have enrollments ranging from 500 to 1,500 students.

Group 5 consists of privately supported colleges which have enrollments of fewer than 500 students.

Table 2 indicates the number and per cent of the respondents according to groups in which the colleges were placed.

Table 2 / Responses According to the Type and Size of the Colleges With Which the Head Librarians Are Associated

Number of the Group	Number of Male Head Librarians	Per Cent of Male Head Librarians	Number of Female Head Librarians	Per Cent of Female Head Librarians	Total Number of Head Librarians
1	50	66.67	25	33.33	75
2	32	47.06	36	52.94	68
3	22	58.72	17	41.28	39
4	71	44.375	89	55.625	160
5	26	36.11	46	63.89	72
Total	201	48.55	213	51.45	414

From the figures included in Table 2, it would appear that the majority of college head librarians are women; however, the difference is only 2.90 per cent. The figures would indicate also that men are more likely to be heads of publicly supported libraries than are women, since Table 2 indicates that from a total of 143 head librarians, 82 men (57.34 per cent) and 61 women (42.66 per cent) are the respondents which compose Groups 1 and 2. On the other hand, from the total of 271 head librarians included in Groups 3, 4, and 5, 119 men (43.91 per cent) and 152 women (56.09 per cent) are associated with privately supported colleges.

A further inspection of this table reveals that men are more likely to be head librarians of the larger colleges. For example, Groups 1 and 3 are composed of 114 head librarians who are associated with colleges having enrollments ranging from 1,501 to 5,000 students. Of this number, 72 (63.16 per cent) are men and 42 (36.84 per cent) are women. Conversely, the table indicates that the majority of the head librarians of the colleges having enrollments of 500 to 1,500 students are women. Groups 2 and 4 include 228 librarians; of these, 103 (45.175 per cent) are men and 125 (54.825 per cent) are women. The percentage of women is even larger in Group 5, which includes a total of 72 head librarians, who are associated with colleges having enrollments of fewer than 500 students. Of the 72 head librarians, 26 (36.11 per cent) are men and 46 (63.89 per cent) are women.

From the analysis of the information reported by the head librarians the following generalizations may be derived:

There is very little difference in the percentages of men and women who serve as head librarians in colleges of the United States.

There is a considerable difference in the percentages of men and women who serve as head librarians when the colleges are divided into groups according to the nature of financial support.

There is a considerable difference in the percentages of men and women who serve as head librarians when the colleges are divided into groups according to the size of the enrollment.

In the paragraphs above, the central question of this study has been answered. Additional questions concerned with head librarians were included on the schedules, and in the following pages these data are analyzed when the respondents are grouped according to sex and (a) the length of time that they have served as head librarian in their present colleges, (b) the total length of time that they have been a head librarian in all academic libraries with which they have been associated, (c) their approximate ages, (d) the geographical location of their colleges, and (e) the per cent of the collegiate budgets which are allotted to their libraries. The above topics will be examined in the order in which they are listed. Therefore, Table 3 indicates the tenure of the head librarians in their present positions.

From examining the data presented in Table 3 it appears that women tend to move less often than men since we notice that the number and per cent of male respondents steadily decreases as the number of years increases, whereas the opposite is true for women. When tenure is examined from the viewpoint of the total length of time that the respondents have been head librarians of all institutions with which they have been associated, however, the results are slightly different.

Table 4 indicates that there is a rising percentage of men in the six-ten year length-of-time group and a sharp drop in the percentage of women in this same group. Perhaps marriage and/or age have something to do with this. In any case, men who have been head librarians for ten years or less number 110 (58.33 per cent) from a total of 192 respondents. On the other hand, 126 (58.33 per cent) women are found in a total of 216 head librarians who have served in that capacity for eleven years. Percentages for the other periods of service may readily be determined from inspecting the table.

Table 3 / Length of Time That the Respondents Have Been in Their Present Positions As Head Librarians

Length of Time (Yrs.)	Number of Male Head Librarians	Per Cent of Male Head Librarians	Number of Female Head Librarians	Per Cent of Female Head Librarians	Total Number of Head Librarians
1-5	96	60.76	62	39.24	158
6-10	40	51.28	38	48.72	78
11-15	39	42.87	52	57.13	91
16+	25	30.49	60	69.51	82
No Answer	1	..	1	..	2
Total	201	48.55	213	51.45	414

Table 4 / Total Length of Time the Respondents Have Served As Head Librarians in All Institutions

Length of Time (Yrs.)	Number of Male Head Librarians	Per Cent of Male Head Librarians	Number of Female Head Librarians	Per Cent of Female Head Librarians	Total Number of Head Librarians
1-5	59	54.62	49	45.38	108
6-10	51	60.71	33	39.29	84
11-15	43	53.75	37	46.25	80
16+	47	34.56	89	65.44	136
No Answer	1	..	5	..	6
Total	201	48.55	213	51.45	414

From an inspection of Table 5, it would seem that men become heads of college libraries at a younger age than do women, since the number and percentage of women who are head librarians rises sharply after they reach forty years of age.

Table 5 / Approximate Ages of the Head Librarians

Ages of the Head Librarians	Number of Male Head Librarians	Per Cent of Male Head Librarians	Number of Female Head Librarians	Per Cent of Female Head Librarians	Total Number of Head Librarians
20-30 yrs.	8	72.73	3	27.27	11
31-40 yrs.	57	77.03	17	22.97	74
41-50 yrs.	76	55.88	60	44.12	136
50+ yrs.	60	31.58	130	68.42	190
No Answer	0	..	3	..	3
Total	201	48.55	213	51.45	414

It was noted earlier that women tend to remain in a position for longer periods than men. Thus, it may be true that some women inherit the job of head librarian by virtue of a combination of capability and seniority rather than by actively seeking the position.

It seems to be well known in the library profession that if one wishes to become a supervisory or administrative librarian more quickly than might otherwise be the case, he must move. Thus, since women apparently do not change jobs as often as men, they do not become heads of libraries as quickly as men.

Table 6 is a more detailed presentation of the data. In this table, the respondents are grouped: (1) by the total length of time that they have been college head librarians, (2) by approximate ages, and (3) by sex.

In almost every age group there is a steady rise in the percentage of women head librarians; however, the correlation between men and women does not appear to be a perfect —1.00. For instance, in the 16+ years group, the percentage of men head librarians is 50 per cent, whereas in the 50+ years group, the percentage drops to 32.1 per cent. It is true that there is a great deal of difference in the actual numbers of head librarians in the two age groups, but nevertheless the drop in percentage seems to be a sharp one.

What happens to these men? Do they tend to retire earlier than women? Do some of them leave college libraries to become associated with university libraries? Presumably, the life span of men and women engaged in library work does not vary from the national norm; therefore, is it possible that this is the cause for the lowered percentage of men in this age bracket? These are interesting questions, but these data cannot answer them.

In most age groups, however, within the four total length-of-service divisions of the table, there is a drop in the percentage of men who are librarians, which, as was mentioned previously, may indicate that men become head librarians at earlier ages than women.

It is also interesting to note the curve that is formed by the "Total Length of Time as Head Librarian" groups. The 1-5 years group includes 106 head librarians; the 6-10 years group includes 83 head librarians; the 11-15 years group includes 79 head librarians; and the 16+ years group includes 135 of the total of 414 head librarians.

Table 6 / Number and Per Cent of Head Librarians When Grouped by Total Length of Time Served as Head Librarian, Sex, and Age

Total Length of Time as Head Librarians (Yrs.)	Ages of the Head Librarians	Number of Male Head Librarians	Per Cent of Male Head Librarians	Number of Female Head Librarians	Per Cent of Female Head Librarians	Total Number of Head Librarians
1-5	20-30 years	7	70.0	3	30.0	10
	31-40 years	28	73.6	10	26.4	38
	41-50 years	19	47.5	21	59.5	40
	50+ years	5	27.8	13	62.2	18
	Total	59	..	47	..	106
6-10	20-30 years	0	00.0	0	00.0	0
	31-40 years	25	86.2	4	23.8	29
	41-50 years	17	63.0	10	37.0	27
	50+ years	8	29.7	19	70.3	27
	Total	50	..	33	..	83
11-15	20-30 years	0	00.0	0	00.0	0
	31-40 years	4	66.7	2	33.3	6
	41-50 years	26	61.9	16	39.1	42
	50+ years	13	41.9	18	58.1	31
	Total	43	..	36	..	79
16+	20-30 years	0	00.0	0	00.0	0
	31-40 years	0	00.0	0	00.0	0
	41-50 years	13	50.0	13	50.0	26
	50+ years	35	32.1	74	67.9	109
	Total	48	..	87	..	135
No Answer	..	1	..	10	..	11
Total	..	201	..	213	..	414

The punched cards representing each college were coded according to type, size, and regional accrediting body. Therefore, when it was decided to determine the number of the respondents reporting from various geographical locations, it was a simple matter to do so. Table 7 contains this information.

Table 7 / Responses from Men and Women Head Librarians According to the Location of the College

Accrediting Body of the College	Number of Male Head Librarians	Per Cent of Male Head Librarians	Number of Female Head Librarians	Per Cent of Female Head Librarians	Total Number of Head Librarians
North Central	87	52.09	80	47.91	167
Southern	52	45.61	62	54.39	114
Middle States	32	45.07	39	54.93	71
New England	14	53.85	12	46.15	26
Northwest	9	50.00	9	50.00	18
Western	7	38.89	11	61.11	18
Total	201	48.55	213	51.45	414

Because of the wide range in numbers (although the percentage of returns according to regional accrediting associations did not vary excessively), it is difficult to make assumptions from these data. One observation that might be made is that since the South has many of the smaller private colleges, and since women are more likely to be head librarians in such colleges, this might account for the higher percentage of women in this group. No attempt will be made, however, to explain the difference in the percentages of men and women head librarians in the New England and Middle States, respectively, other than to say that, perhaps, the number of respondents may not be large enough to present a true picture.

Since one of the more important duties of a head librarian is getting an appropriation large enough so that a "quality" library may be provided to aid the college in achieving its educational objectives, the respondents were also grouped according to the percentages of the institutional budgets which were allotted to their libraries.

It would appear that the ladies are slightly better at getting the money than are the men, as Table 8 indicates. One hundred and twenty-seven (53.37 per cent) of the 238 colleges which report receiving over 4 per cent of the institutional budget are headed by women. Conversely, 87 (56.86 per cent) of the 153 colleges which receive less than 4 per cent of the total college budget are headed by men. On the other hand, twenty of the women did not know, or did not have access to information concerning the amount of the college budget; whereas, only three men lacked this information.

Table 8 / Per Cent of Institutional Budgets Allotted to the Libraries

Per Cent of Institutional Budget	Number of Male Head Librarians	Per Cent of Male Head Librarians	Number of Female Head Librarians	Per Cent of Female Head Librarians	Total Number of Head Librarians
Under 2 per cent	9	60.00	6	40.00	15
2-4 per cent	78	56.52	60	43.48	138
4-6 per cent	92	45.87	109	54.13	201
Over 6 per cent	19	51.35	18	48.65	37
No Answer	3	. .	20	. .	23
Total	201	48.55	213	51.45	414

Some of the more obvious generalizations, which according to the data appear to have a factual basis are summarized below:

1. *There are opportunities for administration minded people of either sex in librarianship.* Responses to 660 questionnaires totaled 414. Of this number, 201 (48.55 per cent) of the head librarians were men and 213 (51.45 per cent) were women.

2. *Men are more likely to be head librarians of publicly supported colleges.* Even though the percentage of head librarians of colleges is nearly equal, men are more likely to be head librarians of tax-supported colleges. There are 143 head librarians in the study that are associated with these institutions, and 82 (57.34 per cent) of this number are men.

3. *Men are more likely to be head librarians of larger colleges.* Included in this study are 114 head librarians associated with colleges having enrollments ranging from 1,500 to 5,000 students. Of these librarians, 72 (63.16 per cent) are men. The percentage of men head librarians decreases as the enrollments of the colleges decrease.

4. *Women head librarians tend to change positions less often than men.* Of 173 head librarians, who had been in their present positions for over ten years, 112 (64.80 per cent) were women. Of the 82 librarians, who had been in their present positions for over sixteen years, 60 (73.17 per cent) were women.

5. Men tend to become head librarians at an earlier age than women. Of the 85 librarians in the study who are under forty years of age, 65 (76.46 per cent) are men. If the age limit is raised to fifty, of 221 head librarians who range from twenty to fifty years of age, 141 (63.80 per cent) are men.

6. Women appear equally as capable, as if not more capable than, men in getting funds for the library. Two hundred and forty colleges reported receiving over 4 per cent of the institutional budget as the library appropriation, and of this number 127 (52.92 per cent) were colleges which had libraries headed by women. This is a very small difference, but it does raise the question: Are women more adept at getting library appropriations than men? Equally important, however, is the fact that 153 (36.96 per cent) of the 414 college libraries receive less than 4 per cent of the institutional budget for the library and that 23 (5.5 per cent) of the respondents cannot ascertain the amount of the institutional budget.

Perhaps the chief value of this report lies in its indication that there are opportunities for both men and women, who want to be administrators, to be appointed as head librarians of colleges in the United States.

NOTE

1. The term "colleges" is used in this report as it is defined in the "Standards for College Libraries," *College and Research Libraries*, XX (July 1959), 274 — except that institutions were not included in the population, which: (a) do not pay their head librarians a salary, and/or (b) have enrollments exceeding five thousand students.

six

Predominance of Male Authors in Social Work Publications

AARON ROSENBLATT,
EILEEN M. TURNER,
ADALENE R. PATTERSON,
and CLARE K. ROLLESSON

The predominance of male authors in social work publications has been given relatively little attention. In this study the writings of social workers published in five professional social work journals from 1964 to 1968 are examined. Following the presentation of the findings, a theory is proposed that seeks to account for the greater intellectual productivity of men.

Social work is usually thought of as a woman's profession. The 1968 survey of the National Association of Social Workers (NASW) showed that about two-thirds of its members were women.[1] Furthermore, social work generally has been equated with casework, and caseworkers are more likely to be women.[2] This fact is particularly true in such fields as counseling and child welfare. In 1957, for example, approximately four of every five caseworkers employed by member agencies of Family Service Association of America (FSAA) were women.[3]

The qualities needed for excellence in social work practice are often thought of as feminine qualities. According to sociologist Ferdinand Lundberg and psychiatrist Marynia Farnham, "the psychically balanced woman finds greatest satisfaction for her ego in nurturing activities. Teaching, nursing, doctoring, social service work . . . are all entirely feminine nurturing functions. . . ."[4]

Most of social work's founding "fathers" were women: Zilpha

From SOCIAL CASEWORK, Vol. 51, No. 7 (1970), pp. 421-430. Reprinted by permission of the authors and SOCIAL CASEWORK.

Smith and Beatrice Webb, Mary Richmond and Jane Addams, Lillian Wald and Florence Kelley. Social work began when feminists were struggling to win equality. It was the first profession requiring graduate training that welcomed large numbers of women students.[5]

Although one might, therefore, expect women to be the dominent sex in the social work profession, distribution of honorific positions in social work shows a relative absence of women. The following facts merit consideration.

1. Of fifty-two candidates running for national office in the 1969 NASW election, 65 percent were men.[6]

2. Among NASW members, men are twice as likely as women to hold general administrative jobs.[7] This is also true of FSAA agencies although three of every four professional staff members were women. (The proportion of women executives is decreasing. From 1957 to 1967 the percentage of women executives fell from 60 to 34.) Furthermore, women are likely to be executives of small agencies. In 1957 "the proportion of women [executives] decreased as size of community and size of agency increased. In communities of under 100,000, 72 percent of the executives were women. In contrast, only 42 percent of executives were women in communities of 500,000 and over."[8]

3. In 1968-69 only 11 percent of the deans and directors of accredited graduate schools of social work in the United States and Canada were women. Not one dean or director of ten new schools, either open and working toward accreditation or planning to open in 1968-69, was a woman.[9]

4. In 1969 the top executive officer of each of the following major national social work organizations was a man: Council on Social Work Education, Child Welfare League of America, Family Service Association of America, National Social Welfare Assembly, National Association of Social Workers, National Conference on Social Welfare, National Urban League, and United Community Funds and Councils of America.

Prominence in social work is often associated with the occupancy of leadership or administrative positions in large social agencies. Theoretically it should be possible to achieve prominence within the profession through excellence in two other areas — direct practice and intellectual affairs. With evaluation of social work practice still in an early stage of development, validity in this area is often problematic.[10] Consequently, under present conditions it is not known if women are better practitioners than men.[11]

Contributions to intellectual affairs can be determined more readily. The publication record of social work journals offers a strategic site for studying one type of intellectual contribution. It is assumed that articles selected for publication are intellectually superior to those that are rejected although an editor may occasionally use another standard. The topicality of a subject or the prominence of an author may receive undue weight. On occasion an editor may reject a manuscript because its ideas are either too advanced or too radical. These occasions, like the appearance of true genius, are undoubtedly rare. It is also assumed that the sex of both the author and the editor has no effect whatsoever on the decision to publish a manuscript.

Primarily, then, this article presents the publication record of social work journals as an index, albeit an imperfect one, of the contributions of men and women to intellectual matters. It also offers findings that touch upon other aspects of the sociology of social work publication. This subject, which in itself is of substantive interest, has received little systematic attention.[12]

Methodology

Twelve first-year students enrolled in a reseach course at the University of Arkansas Graduate School of Social Work collected and coded all of the information reported in this study.[13] The study included articles, book reviews, and books reviewed that had been published during the five-year period from 1964-1968 in the following major social work journals: *Child Welfare, Smith College Studies in Social Work, Social Casework, Social Service Review,* and *Social Work.*[14] To be able to make comparisons with a journal from an allied field, the students also collected information about authors and book reviewers whose work was published in the *American Journal of Orthopsychiatry* during the same five-year period.

Each journal provides relatively standardized information about authors and book reviewers although there were some minor variations. The *Social Service Review* does not list an author's academic degree but notes only medical degrees. The *Smith College Studies in Social Work* does not publish book reviews. With the exceptions noted, the following standard information was available for authors: name, academic degree, position, employer, and place of employment (city and state). The information available for book reviewers usually was limited to name, employer, and location of employer. The students coded the number of authors and sequence of authorship for both journal articles and books reviewed. (The first author is referred to as the senior author.) Because of multiple authorship, the number of authors is different from the number of articles and the number of books that were reviewed.

The given name of an author or a book reviewer was used to determine sex. In the same way the students also determined the sex of the authors of books that were reviewed in these journals. A five percent reliability check of all information coded amounted to an error rate of less than 1 percent.[15]

Findings

From 1964-1968 the five social work journals in this study published 938 articles by 1,173 authors. In addition, 827 books were reviewed. (Some books, however, were reviewed in more than one journal.)

Authors were more likely to collaborate in writing books than in writing journal articles. This finding was consistently noted in the four journals publishing both articles and book reviews. The extent of collaboration appears in Table 1. Among the books reviewed, the extent of collaboration ranged from 26 percent in *Child Welfare* to 44 percent in *Social Work*. Among the articles

Table 1 / Extent of author collaboration, 1964-1968*

Journal in which book reviews and articles appear	Books (Percent of collaboration)	Articles (Percent of collaboration)
	—	5
Smith College Studies in Social Work	(—)	(43)
	26	14
Child Welfare	(136)	(247)
	39	20
Social Casework	(173)	(247)
	38	16
Social Service Review	(289)	(133)
	44	25
Social Work	(229)	(268)
	52	50
American Journal of Orthopsychiatry	(172)	(351)

* Number of books and articles in parentheses.

published, the comparable range is 5 percent in *Smith College Studies* to 25 percent in *Social Work*.

Collaboration is more common among the authors of articles published by and among the authors of books reviewed in the *American Journal of Orthopsychiatry;* 50 percent of the articles and 52 percent of the books reviewed were collaborative efforts. This journal, it should be noted, serves the professions of psychiatry and psychology as well as that of social work.

Although, as already indicated, the most recent NASW survey showed that two-thirds of its members were women, Table 2

Table 2 / Percent of male authors of books, book reviews, and articles 1964-1968*

	Books (Percent of male authors)	Book Reviews (Percent of male reviewers)	Articles (Percent of male authors)
Smith College Studies in Social Work	— (—)	— (—)	33 (45)
Child Welfare	66 (162)	52 (136)	52 (293)
Social Casework	74 (223)	67 (173)	50 (322)
Social Service Review	78 (369)	64 (289)	71 (160)
Social Work	81 (331)	74 (229)	75 (353)
Total Male	—a (—)	65 (827)	60 (1,173)
American Journal of Orthopsychiatry	84 (256)	87 (172)	76 (603)

* Number of books, books reviewed, and articles appear in parentheses.

† This percentage was not calculated because of the bias introduced by multiple reviews of the same book in several journals.

shows that more than two-thirds of the authors of books reviewed in journals are men. In addition, 65 percent of the book reviewers and 60 percent of the authors of journal articles are men.

The percentages in Table 2 can be read both horizontally and vertically. Horizontally, the comparisons show that, in all journals, men are more likely to have written books than to have written book reviews. The differences in percentage points are

Child Welfare, +14; *Social Casework,* +7; *Social Service Review,* +14; and *Social Work,* +7.

The same general pattern is also apparent when authors of books are compared with authors of journal articles. Men are more likely to write books than journal articles. The differences in percentage points are *Child Welfare,* +14; *Social Casework,* +24; *Social Service Review,* +7; and *Social Work,* +6.

When percentages are compared vertically we learn that journals show considerable variation in the following respects: (1) the extent to which authors of books are men; (2) the extent to which book reviewers are men; and (3) the extent to which authors of articles are men. The percentage of male authors increases from 66 percent in *Child Welfare* to 74 percent in *Social Casework,* 78 percent in *Social Service Review,* and 81 percent in *Social Work.* The percentage of male book reviewers also increases from 52 percent in *Child Welfare* to 67 percent in *Social Casework,* 64 percent in *Social Service Review,* and 74 percent in *Social Work. Smith College Studies* published the fewest articles by men. Only 33 percent of these articles were written by men as compared with 75 percent of those in *Social Work.*

Table 2 also shows that the *American Journal of Orthopsychiatry* makes greater use of men than does any of the social work journals in each of three categories: books reviewed, book reviewers, and authors of articles. The percentage of men in these three categories of the *American Journal of Orthopsychiatry* soars to 84, 87, and 76 respectively.

To determine the degree to which the various social work journals were "dominated" by men, scores ranging from 4 to 1 were assigned. A score of 4 indicated the journal with the largest percent of male authors of books, and a score of 1 indicated the journal with the smallest percent. The same procedures were followed with the authors of book reviews and articles. Differences of four percentage points or less were considered ties. The results were then totaled, the possible range extending from a low of 3 to a high of 12. The results are as follows: *Child Welfare,* 3.5; *Social Casework,* 6.0; *Social Service Review,* 9.5; *Social Work,* 11.0. *Child Welfare* was the least "male-dominated" journal and *Social Work* was the most "male-dominated" journal. (*Smith College Studies* was excluded from this analysis because it did not review books.)

When two or three authors collaborate in writing articles, the senior author is more likely to be a man than a woman. Of the 180 articles written by two or three authors, 117 or 65 percent were written by men: *Table 3* shows that the modal pattern was

Table 3 / Pattern of author collaboration for articles and books reviewed, 1964-1968*

	Articles published				Books reviewed		
Sex composition of authors	In social work journals (N=180)	In AJO[a] (N=157)	Child Welfare (N=28)	Social Casework (N=40)	Social Service Review (N=82)	Social Work (N=62)	AJO (N=63)
All-male team	38%	47%	50%	55%	57%	68%	70%
Mixed team (senior author a male)	27	31	21	20	27	16	18
Mixed team (senior author a female)	14	16	21	17	11	8	8
All-female team	21	6	7	8	5	8	4
Total	100	100	99	100	100	100	100

* Includes articles and books written by two or three authors.
[a] *American Journal of Orthopsychiatry.*

for an all-male team to write an article; 38 percent of the articles were written by all-male teams. In contrast, 21 percent of the articles were written by all-female teams. When the writing teams comprised men and women, men were almost twice as likely as women to be the senior author. Of these articles written by mixed teams, men were the senior authors of 48 (27 percent) and women were the senior authors of only 26 (14 percent). Thus, the least likely pattern was for a woman to be the senior author of a team that included at least one male.

The same general pattern, with minor variations, is maintained when the authorship of books reviewed in the four social work journals is examined. Men are more likely than women to be the senior authors of books representing collaborative efforts. The percentage of male senior authors for the four journals is as follows: *Child Welfare,* 71 percent; *Social Casework,* 75 percent; *Social Service Review,* 84 percent; *Social Work,* 84 percent. Once again the modal pattern is for an all-male writing team to collaborate. The least likely pattern in the four journals, however, is for an all-female team to write a book.

When men and women do collaborate, however, women are as likely as men to be the senior authors of books reviewed in *Child Welfare* and *Social Casework.* Of the books reviewed in *Social Service Review* and *Social Work,* men are twice as likely as women to be the senior authors. The latter journals publish more reviews, which, in all likelihood, include books from related fields of knowledge.

The percentage of male senior authors is higher in the *American Journal of Orthopsychiatry* than it is in the social work journals; 78 percent of the journal articles and 88 percent of the books reviewed were written by senior authors who are men. As in social work, men are even more likely to be the senior authors of books than of journal articles.

Further analysis of the data reveals that when occupational positions are considered, faculty and researchers are the most productive writers. They are a small group, accounting for less than one of every ten employed members of NASW. Yet they write almost half of the articles published in social work journals. Men in these occupations are even more productive than are the women. Of the articles published, men write almost one-third and women, one-seventh.

Supervisors and direct service personnel, who represent approximately 55 percent of all employed NASW members, have been found least likely to write articles. Only 19 percent of the articles were written by them. Men in these positions are more likely than women to write articles, but the differences are much less pronounced than those noted among the faculty.

Sex shows no effect on the intellectual productivity of administrators. Male and female administrators constitute 18 and 13 percent of the employed NASW members and their productivity percentages are equal.

Discussion

This study, as measured by our indicators, shows that men are more likely than women to be productive in publications activities. Men write more journal articles. They are even more likely to write books than journal articles.[16] When men and women collaborate, men are much more likely than women to be the senior authors of both articles and books. In addition, editors more frequently select men to review books. These facts suggest that the movement to secure equal rights and opportunities for women has not fully achieved its objectives. This unequal treatment of the sexes is characteristic of social work circles and the larger society, in both of which women either are barred from certain positions or must overcome barriers to attain them.[17]

Different treatment of the sexes in society begins literally at birth. Certain given names, various baby toys, baby clothes — even colors — are differentiated by sex. Sex-typing widens and intensifies in adolescence. Boys are steered into competitive athletics. In these contests they compete against others of their sex. Girls witness these encounters; however, they do not compete on the same field. In high school and college the tomboy becomes an obsolete role. Girls who wish to attract boys also learn not to compete with them intellectually.[18]

College women acknowledge that they are not expected to be "as dominant or aggressive as men. . . ." An anxious mother, as reported in one study, advised her daughter "not to be too intellectual on dates. . . ." A helpful brother told his sister to "cover up that high forehead and act a little dumb once in a while. . . ." About 40 percent of the girls acknowledged "that they have occasionally 'played dumb' on dates, that is, [either they] concealed some academic honor, pretended ignorance of some subject, or allowed the man the last word in an intellectual discussion."[19]

One girl made this confession about the strains she felt at college: "I am a good student; my family expects me to get good marks. At the same time I am normal enough to want to be invited to the Saturday night dance. Well, everyone knew that on that campus a reputation of a 'brain' killed a girl socially. I was always fearful lest I say too much in class or answer a question which the boys I dated couldn't answer."[20] These constraints reduce the number of Mary McCarthy's and Susan Sontag's produced in the United States.

There are additional constraints upon career aspirations of women. Child rearing comes to be the primary role desired by young women. As they move through college most coeds become more interested in becoming mothers than in pursuing full-time vocational careers. At the end of college, according to one study, only one-third as many women as men expect their careers to represent a major life satisfaction.[21] In another study, fewer than half the women wanted to work all or most of their lives and less than one-fourth wanted to continue working after they became mothers.[22]

The average middle-class woman works for a few years after graduation and then gives up her job either when she marries or when her first child is born.[23] Most women willingly come to prefer this primary attachment to their families to the attachment to their career. They have been taught to seek fulfillment as mothers and homemakers.[24] They become "less intrinsically committed to work than men and less likely to maintain a high level of specialized knowledge . . . their work motives are more utilitarian and less intrinsically task-oriented than those of men."[25]

In short, by the time most girls become women they have learned not to march in lockstep with men. Indeed, by that time, most prefer to dance than to march. The same event comes to evoke quite different responses. When a husband becomes a father, he usually tries to work harder at his profession. He recognizes an increased responsibility to provide for his wife and child. In contrast, becoming a mother is often a signal for a wife to withdraw from her profession.

Her abandonment of a career is thought to have positive consequences for the marriage. It minimizes rivalry and promotes solidarity.[26] Starting a family thus results in lengthy discontinuous work histories for many women who enter the social work profession. "While men are being promoted or gaining experience that will equip them for promotion, many women are at home tending babies, their skills growing rusty and their knowledge lagging behind new developments in their fields."[27] The NASW survey shows that 29 percent of married women with children below the ages of five are unemployed as social workers for long periods of time.[28]

Graduates of doctoral programs are, in a sense, charged with responsibility for the dissemination of new knowledge and developments. A recent study reports that seven of every ten doctoral students and recent graduates of doctoral programs are men.[29] After their doctoral studies, 72 percent of the students from 1965-1968 were employed in teaching or research.[30] Teachers and researchers are much more likely to write articles than are other social workers. They account for less than 10 percent of all social workers. Yet almost one-half of all authors of articles are teachers and researchers.

Men are more likely than women to become teachers and researchers.[31] And male teachers and researchers are more likely to write articles than are women in similar positions. This difference in intellectual productivity may reflect not only difference in doctoral study among the sexes but also differences in faculty assignments. Men are much more likely to be classroom teachers; women are more frequently field instructors.[32] Generally these male teachers are also more likely than field instructors to write more articles.

The thesis of this discussion is not that men are smarter than women and that therefore they are intellectually preeminent even in a woman's profession. The argument, in brief, is that women are constrained before they enter social work not to compete with men intellectually. Furthermore, many women in social work become attached to a set of career goals based on the home rather than on their profession. Even within the profession, sharp differences persist in the percentage of men and women who seek doctoral study and of men and women administrators, teachers, researchers, and direct service personnel. Even among those who teach, differences are manifest in the types of teaching assignment. In all instances the effect of these differentials is to increase the likelihood that men rather than women will be intellectually preeminent in social work.

Primarily we have described one ideal type of social worker — the married woman whose major career is that of homemaker. Another ideal group comprises spinsters, divorcées, and women who quickly return to work full time after becoming mothers. At present little is known about such women for the necessary data are not available.[33] Further research, however, may prove careerists to be intellectually more productive than homemakers.

Indeed, the intellectual achievements of women careerists may equal or even exceed those of men. Such women often may be more heavily invested in their professional careers than are married men, because they are not distracted by husbands or children from wholeheartedly pursuing their careers.

In time they may modify, or perhaps discard, many components of the sex-linked roles they learned in childhood and adolescence and they may become more competitive. They may even come to relish the challenge of entering into direct competition with men.

The intellectual contribution of these women, however, has not been ascertained. It is only hypothesized. Further study with suitable controls for marriage and family are required. If the careerists are found to make a sizable intellectual contribution, admissions officers at schools of social work may wish to give special consideration to such applicants.

In the meantime, on the basis of the present study, social workers may wish to consider whether or not they wish to introduce other changes to increase the intellectual contribution of women. The problem concerns not only the social work profession but other professions in the United States. After examining the plight of women as a minority group in higher academic settings, Ann Davis concludes, "good intellectual ability among women is being wasted as a social and national resource."[34]

Other observers are aware that this nation "make[s] less use of talented women in the labor force than do some rival nations (notably Russia). In fact, although the greatest disregard of talent is commonly assumed to arise from class and racial inequality, this source of loss is probably less than that involving women."[35]

The yoke of inequality may be unduly difficult to remove from women's shoulders. Everyone does not consider inequality a burden. For many, men and women alike, the present arrangement is preferred because it serves to remove or limit competition between the sexes. If few women are appointed to high administrative and honorific posts, few tears are shed because many women prefer not to seek such appointments. Other advantages accrue to women who accept limited career goals. They need not drive themselves as hard as ambitious men do. They can enjoy the intrinsic merits of their social work efforts. They fret less about their position and their salary. Once granted a license for intellectual underachievement, they may feel free of the need to publish merely for the sake of publishing.

Many women may be spoiled by their special, protected status in social work and in other professions. Before they can begin to produce at their full intellectual capacity, we will have to devise a program calling for more incentives and retraining programs. Perhaps even more essential is that men come to welcome full competition from women. If that is so, we suspect that the prospects for change are poor.

NOTES

1. Alfred M. Stamm, NASW Membership: Characteristics, Deployment, and Salaries, *Personnel Information,* 12:34 (May, 1969).
2. Ibid., p. 40.
3. Livia Lowy, *Characteristics of the Professional Staff of Family Service Agencies, January 1, 1967* (New York: Family Service Association of America, 1968), p. 4; see also William B. McCurdy, *Characteristics of the Professional Staff of Family Service Agencies* (New York: Family Service Association of America, 1960), p. 4.
4. Ferdinand Lundberg and Marynia F. Farnham, *Modern Woman: The Lost Sex* (New York: Harper & Brothers, 1947), p. 366.
5. For a view of the restricted choices among women of Jane Addams's generation, see Christopher Lasch, *The New Radicalism in America [1889-1963]: The Intellectual as a Social Type* (New York: Alfred A. Knopf, 1965), pp. 3-37. "Another, on the face of it totally independent, factor in bringing about establishment of the new professional association was the growing momentum in the economic emancipation of women. While probably no profession was legally closed to women in this country, not even that of the ministry, there were few of that sex in medicine, law, finance, or the ministry. Woman's occupations, other than factory jobs and domestic participation in family farming, were chiefly teaching, secretarial work, and nursing. Social work suddenly came over the horizon as another, although not yet very large, area of occupation particularly suitable for and favored by women" (Philip Klein, *From Philanthropy to Social Welfare: An American Cultural Perspective* [San Francisco: Jossey-Bass, 1968], p. 203).
6. *Biographical Information for 1969 Election* (New York: National Association of Social Workers, 1969), pp. 3-31.
7. Stamm, NASW Membership, p. 40.
8. Lowy, *Characteristics of the Professional Staff,* p. 4; and McCurdy, *Characteristics of the Professional Staff,* p. 4.
9. *Graduate Professional Schools of Social Work in Canada and the U.S.A.* (New York: Council on Social Work Education, 1968), pp. 2-12; see also the supplement entitled *New Schools of Social Work, 1968-1969.*
10. For further discussion see Aaron Rosenblatt, Critique, in *Modes of Professional Education: Functions of Field Learning in the Curriculum,* ed. Helen Cassidy, *Tulane Studies in Social Welfare,* vol. II (New Orleans, 1969), pp. 235-43; and Aaron Rosenblatt, Reputation of Effectiveness in Social Agencies (Paper delivered at the American Public Welfare Association Conference, Little Rock, Ark., 1968).
11. One can argue, on the one hand, that women are better practi-

tioners than men because they are more likely to possess such essential qualities as nurturance, succorance, and intuitiveness. These are all expressive qualities. On the other hand, excellence in social work practice may depend more on instrumental qualities, such as ability to evaluate, to plan, and to implement plans. And men, rather than women, may be more likely to possess these and other instrumental qualities.

12. For example, Marvin Silverman, Knowledge in Social Group Work: A Review of the Literature, *Social Work*, 11:56-62 (July, 1966).

13. The principles of data collection were first discussed in class meetings. The students then received additional training in two small seminars. Six students collected information on book reviewers and the authors of books reviewed, and the other six, on authors of journal articles. The instructor supervised students and they received course credit for their efforts. The students' names are Dorothy Ahring, Veronica Dopierala, Mary Farrell, Jessie Foster, Lois Mackey, Polly McQuade, Beth Nelson, Adalene R. Patterson, Clare K. Rollosson, Eileen M. Turner, Elizabeth Vaught, and John Whitehead.

14. Every article published in these journals is automatically abstracted by *Abstracts for Social Workers*. This is not true of other social work journals.

15. All of the coded information was punched onto IBM cards by keypunch operators and there was 100 percent verification of the keypunch operation. The data were tabulated by the electronic data processing unit of a Little Rock bank. We wish to express our appreciation to David Frantz of the Worthen Bank and Trust Company for providing the keypunching and tabulation without cost.

16. Jessie S. Bernard reports that in general women are more interested in teaching and that they write less than do male faculty members (*Academic Women* [University Park: Pennsylvania State University Press, 1964]).

17. Last year women won the right to be jockeys and to join males in the press box of a football stadium. A recent plea for equal opportunities for women is made by Patricia Cayo Sexton, who hopes that equality of opportunity will free women from the need to stay at home and tyrannize over the men and boys in the household (*The Feminized Male* [New York: Random House, 1969]).

18. The argument can be made that sexual mores are changing rapidly in high school and college. This may be so. But those who are not writing for social work journals attended school before the advent of the pill.

19. Mirra Komarovsky, Cultural Contradictions and Sex Roles, *American Journal of Sociology*, 52:185, 187 (November 1946).

20. Ibid., p. 187.

21. Morris Rosenberg et al., *Occupations and Values* (New York:

Free Press, 1958), pp. 48-49.

22. Mirra Komarovsky, *Women in the Modern World: Their Education and Their Dilemmas* (Boston: Little, Brown and Company, 1953), pp. 92-97.

23. Esther Peterson, Working Women, *Daedalus*, 93:674 (Spring 1964).

24. Lundberg and Farnham promulgate this "rule": "The less a woman's desire to have children and the greater her desire to emulate the male in seeking a sense of personal value by objective exploit, the less will be her enjoyment of the sex act and the greater her general neuroticism" (*Modern Woman*, p. 265). This hypothesis remains to be tested.

25. Richard L. Simpson and Ida Simpson, Women and Bureaucracy in the Semi-Professions, in *The Semi-Professions and Their Organization: Teachers, Nurses, Social Workers*, ed. Amitai Etzioni (New York: Free Press, 1969), p. 199.

26. Talcott Parsons, *Social Structure and Personality* (New York: Free Press, 1964), p. 242.

27. Ibid., p. 229. Single women and married women without children advance in the nursing profession more rapidly than those who marry and have children. In a study of nurses in Arkansas only 32 percent of nursing supervisors were married compared with 58 percent of general duty nurses (Donald Stewart and Christine E. Needham, The General Duty Nurse, in *Twenty Thousand Nurses Tell Their Story*, ed. Everett C. Hughes, Helen M. Hughes, and Irwin Deutscher [Philadelphia: Lippincott, 1958], p. 21).

28. An additional 42 percent of these mothers work less than full time (Stamm, NASW Membership, Table 4, p. 37).

29. Frank M. Lowenberg and Eugene B. Shinn, *Special Study of Doctoral Students In Schools of Social Work*, mimeographed (New York: Council of Social Work Education, 1969), p. 28.

30. *Social Work Education Reporter*, 17:3 (September 1969).

31. Stamm, NASW Membership, Table 6, p. 40.

32. The study shows that 55.3 percent of full-time classroom faculty and 68.1 percent of part-time classroom faculty were men. The comparable percentages for full-time and part-time field faculty are 30.5 and 38.2 (Richard Onken, *A Survey of Faculty in Graduate Schools of Social Work* [New York: Council on Social Work Education, 1968]).

33. In FSAA agencies, almost three-quarters of the women who are executive directors are either single or widowed. One may say the relationship between position and marital status is inverse for women: the higher the position, the less likely the woman is married (see Lowy, *Characteristics of the Professional Staff*, Table 7, p. 7).

34. Ann E. Davis, Women as a Minority Group in Higher Academ-

ics, *American Sociologist,* 4:98 (May 1969); see also Alice S. Rossi, Status of Women in Graduate Departments of Sociology, 1968-69, *American Sociologist,* 5:1-14 (February 1970).

35. Kingsley Davis, The Sociology of Demographic Behavior, in *Sociology Today: Problems and Prospects,* ed. Robert K. Merton, Leonard Broom, and Leonard S. Cottrell, Jr. (New York: Basic Books. 1959), pp. 328-29.

seven

Farmer's Daughter Effect: The Case of the Negro Female Professionals

E. WILBUR BOCK

There have been numerous studies on the recent advances in occupational status among Negroes. Most of these studies have concentrated on data regarding males, with the assumption that only racial comparisons of males would provide any real meaning.[1] Research on racial comparisons in occupational changes have thus neglected the ways in which females have participated in occupational changes. This study is directly concerned with racial comparisons of the participation of women in the labor force, particularly at the professional level.

Most professions in the United States have been defined traditionally as open only to males and have been male dominated and male controlled. It has been suggested that the percentage of individuals in a given occupation that is female is an indication of the degree to which that occupation is professionalized.[2] The professions have also been dominated and controlled by the white population.[3] There is still some debate regarding whether the amount of discrimination against Negro occupational incumbents is greater or less among the professions than at lower levels of the occupational structure,[4] however, as in the case of the female, the percentage of individuals in a given occupation that are Negroes could be used as an indication of the degree to which that occupation is professionalized.

Professional occupations have long played an important part in the occupational aspirations of Negroes. Numerous factors have helped focus sharply the occupational orientation of Negroes on the professions: discrimination in lower levels of work,

From PHYLON, Vol. 30, No. 1 (1969), pp. 17-26. Reprinted by permission of PHYLON.

the lack of business know-how, a poor history of businesses owned by Negroes, as well as the opportunities for Negroes to become professionals serving the Negro communities.[5] These factors have helped produce an occupational mobility pattern among Negroes that is different from that obtaining among whites. The common pattern of generational mobility among whites has been from manual labor to business, and from business to the professions. Although relatively more and more Negro professionals may come from the professional class, the pattern of generational mobility among Negroes has often involved using clerical work rather than business as a springboard into the professions.[6]

The higher occupational aspirations of Negroes, however, have often been frustrated. It has been noted, for example, that between 1940 and 1960, Negro males, relative to white, lost ground at the professional and managerial levels,[7] moreover, due to various circumstances, Negroes who aspire to professional occupations often find themselves trapped in such occupations as teaching, since avenues to training for, and practice in, other professions are blocked.[8] Thus, although a larger representation of Negroes in professional occupations might add to the prestige of the Negro community, data regarding Negro males do not point to such improvement.

The lack of any substantial growth in the number of professional Negroes has been attributed to the long history of discrimination and its effects, rather than the present number of professional opportunities.[9] In comparison with whites, Negroes have been characterized by low levels of education, high dropout rates in public schools, and low educational and occupational aspirations. In spite of the many new professional opportunities now being opened to Negroes, there are not enough Negro males to take advantage of these educational and occupational avenues. If they are aware of professional opportunities, Negro males have generally lacked educational qualifications and financial resources to enter and remain in graduate school. The great majority of Negro males, however, probably has lacked even the awareness of professional opportunities and the motivation to work against such odds.

The discriminating environment of the dominant society, however, has had a differential impact on Negroes of the two sexes. The history of Negroes, in fact, has created what Jessie Bernard has called the "unnatural superiority" of Negro women. In comparison with Negro males, females belong to a higher class, as measured by education, acculturation, income and familiarity with the white world. It has been suggested that more contacts with the dominant society have been available to Negro women because they have been less feared sexually and less threatening occupationally.[10]

The unnatural superiority of Negro females has also been related to the Negro family. Female hypogamy has been well documented among Negroes. Although Negro parents have high occupational aspirations for their sons and daughters, they apparently have had a clearer picture of occupational opportunities for their daughters than for their sons, and greater assurance that aspirations for their daughters will be realized.[1] Thus, many Negro parents have considered an education, including a college education, to be a better investment for their daughters than for their sons, and have been more willing to sacrifice for the education of daughters than for that of sons.[12] School enrollment at all levels of education has reflected this differential evaluation by Negro parents.[13] Broom and Glenn have stated that "The maternal Negro family tends to be perpetuated by the fact that Negro females are, on the average, better educated and therefore more able to find secure employment than males."[14] Moreover, they reported that, compared with males, well-educated females have faced less discrimination and have been able to find employment more nearly equal to their educational attainment.[15]

These differential experiences of Negro males and females have produced what might be called a "farmer's daughter effect." There seems to be a parallel between the occupational mobility of farm youth and that of the youth of low-income groups generally, particularly regarding crossing from blue-collar into white-collar occupations. The daughters rather than the sons of the farm family were likely to stay in school through high school and likely to acquire a conscious value of education. When migration to the urban areas occurred, daughters were better prepared than sons to acquire additional education and training, obtain white-collar work, and perhaps even enter a profession. One profession that was available to her was public school teaching. Both the length and the type of public school education that the sons received in the farm areas were likely to prepare them for farm work, factory employment and manual labor. Much of this differential in mobility patterns of the two sexes might be construed as spurious, particularly the comparison of the sons of farmers moving into manual labor and the daughters moving into low-paying white-collar work. However, the differences in educational background have perhaps prepared farm daughters for a greater chance of actual mobility than was true for the sons. Similar to farm parents, then, Negro parents seem to have made the assumption that daughters will be more successful than sons in attending school, acquiring occupational training, obtaining a job equal to their education, and generally improving themselves.

These considerations led to the formulation of the following general proposition which guided the present research:

In comparison with Negro males, Negro females have a greater chance of entering and remaining in professional occupations. Although Negro females have two characteristics which may hinder their entrance into the professions, sex and color, this differential opportunity is to be expected because of the "unnaturally" superior population of Negro females.

Data for the present study were drawn from tabulations published by the United States Bureau of the Census. Whenever possible, the analysis was limited to those persons employed in 1950 and 1960. Racial and sex comparisons were made regarding the percentage of the labor force that was professional, and regarding the percentage of the professionals who were in the various professional occupations. The percentage of each occupational category that was female was also calculated and racial comparisons made. Available information on some of the characteristics (e.g., age, education, and marital status) of these professionals was also utilized.

Census data lend support to the proposition that Negro females have a greater chance of entering professional occupations than have Negro men. In 1960, for example, 7.2 percent of the Negro female labor force was in professional occupations, compared with 3.1 percent of the Negro male labor force in the professions. This sex differential was true for the white labor force as well, with 13.8 percent of the female labor force and 10.9 percent of the white male labor force in professional occupations. The differential, thus, was greater for the Negro than for the white population. In fact, the number of professional Negro women was larger than that of professional Negro men; in the white population, the male professionals outnumbered the women.

It might be argued that the visibility of the females among

Negro professionals is large because Negro females participate in the labor force in a relatively greater number than white females participate. This argument does not explain the situation entirely, however, since the proportion of the Negro professionals that is female is greater than the proportion of the Negro labor force that is female (60.8 percent compared to 40.2 percent). Moreover, the difference between whites and Negroes in female visibility is greater at the professional level (60.8 percent compared to 37.2 percent) than for the total labor force (40.2 percent compared to 31.9 percent) (see Table 1). These

Table 1 / Percentage of the Employed Professional, Technical, and Kindred Workers that is Female, by Race, 1950 and 1960*

Year	Race			
	White		Negro	
	Number	Percent	Number	Percent
1950	1,841,040	39.4	102,090	58.4
1960	2,553,417	37.2	175,223	60.8

* Sources: United States Bureau of the Census, *U.S. Census of Population: 1950*, Vol. IV, *Special Reports*, Part 1, Chap. B, *Occupational Characteristics* (Washington, D. C.: Government Printing Office, 1956), Table 3, p. 29; United States Bureau of the Census, *U.S. Census of Population: 1960*, Subject Reports, Occupational Characteristics, Final Report, PC (2)-7A (Washington, D. C.: Government Printing Office, 1963), Table 3, pp. 21-22.

comparisons hold true for 1950 and 1960 in every region (see Table 2). The only occupational level at which the percentage of Negroes who are females is as high as, or higher than, that found among professionals, is that of private household workers.

As one might expect, female visibility varied tremendously among the various professional occupations, and these variations supposedly reflect the sex appropriateness of the occupations. It has been shown repeatedly that there are far fewer professional opportunities for Negroes than for whites. Census data for 1960, for example, displayed a wider distribution of white male professionals among the various professional occupations than was true for Negro males, white females and Negro females. Negro male professionals, in turn, were more widely distributed than Negro female professionals. Female professionals were highly concentrated in a few occupations, such as teaching, and Negro females appeared to be the most highly concentrated of all.

Thus, if Negro female teachers, social workers, and others in typically feminine occupations were to be removed from the

Table 2 / Percentage of the Employed Professional, Technical, and Kindred Workers that is Female, by Race and Region, 1950 and 1960*

Year by Region	Race			
	White		Negro	
	Number	Percent	Number	Percent
1950				
Northeast	551,826	37.4	13,736	51.9
North Central	550,331	39.1	12,230	49.0
South	449,464	40.4	74,480	61.5
West	278,819	38.6	3,282	48.5
1960				
Northeast	706,419	35.6	31,192	57.3
North Central	741,441	38.0	28,147	35.7
South	667,948	39.5	105,458	63.9
West	440,524	35.0	10,511	52.8

* Sources: United States Bureau of the Census, *U.S. Census of Population: 1950*, Vol. II, *Characteristics of the Population, Part 1, United States Summary*, Chap. C (Washington, D. C.: Government Printing Office, 1953), Table 159, pp. 397-402; United States Bureau of the Census, *U.S. Census of Population: 1960, Detailed Characteristics, United States Summary*, Final Report. PC (1)-1D (Washington, D. C.: Government Printing Office, 1963), Table 257, pp. 717-19.

total number of Negro female professionals, the total number of Negro professional men would appear in a more favorable light. However, it must be noted that the differences between the distributions of white and Negro male professionals is greater than the differences shown by racial comparisons of female professionals. In fact, it appears that, in many ways, the distribution of Negro male professionals is closer to that of females, both white and Negro, than it is to that of white males. For example, in 1960, 28.3 percent of the Negro male professionals were teachers, compared to 10.3 percent of the white males, 42.7 percent of the white females, and 57.2 percent of Negro females. Moreover, between 1950 and 1960 the concentration of Negro male professionals in teaching appeared to increase more than was true of Negro female professionals.

The data suggest a restatement of the general proposition which guided the present study:

Negro females have a greater chance of entering professional occupations designated as open to women than Negro men have of entering professions open to men. In fact, it might also be hypothesized that Negro men have a greater chance of entering professional occupations open to women than they have of entering professions open to men.

The propositions are inferred from a number of observations regarding census data: (1) the difference between the white and Negro male labor forces that is professional was greater than was true of the white and Negro female labor forces; (2) the Negro professionals tended to be concentrated in a few occupations, e.g., teaching and clergy; and (3) although Negro female professionals were even more concentrated in a few occupations, the social base from which professional Negro females are drawn was larger than the social base of professional Negro males. The number of Negro men who enter and remain in the majority of professional occupations is so small that the presence of Negro females in these occupations becomes significant. Thus, in the majority of professional occupations the percentage of Negroes that is female is greater than that of the whites. This differential appears to be more conspicuous for "masculine" than for "feminine" professions (see Table 3).

Table 3 / Percentage of the Employed Individuals in Selected Professions that is Female, by Race, 1960*

Selected Professions	Race			
	White		Negro	
	Number	Percent	Number	Percent
Accountants and Auditors	75,578	16.3	1,217	33.7
Clergymen	3,859	2.1	508	3.7
College Staff	35,225	21.0	2,302	39.2
Designers	11,466	17.0	222	31.3
Dietitians and Nutritionists	20,967	93.8	3,325	88.6
Funeral Directors and Embalmers	1,919	5.6	341	10.2
Lawyers and Judges	6,898	3.3	222	9.1
Librarians	68,489	86.0	3,274	86.5
Musicians and Music Teachers	105,263	58.0	3,750	42.6
Natural Scientists	13,261	9.3	730	23.2
Professional Nurses	531,482	97.8	31,112	94.8
Physicians and Surgeons	14,031	6.4	487	9.7
Social and Welfare Workers	53,399	63.8	6,489	62.6
Elementary School Teachers	778,288	86.0	76,314	84.5
Secondary School Teachers	225,209	46.6	18,292	54.5
Medical and Dental Technicians	79,885	62.9	5,756	58.0

* Source: Same for Table 1 for the year 1960.

Changes that are occurring in the occupational composition of the Negro professionals appear to show a continued, if not increasing, visibility of females.[16] For example, the number of Negro male teachers increased more rapidly than the number of other Negro professional males in every region between 1950 and 1960. This did not hold true for Negro females. At the same time, the number of Negro male teachers increased more rapidly than the number of Negro female teachers, whereas the reverse was true for all professionals other than teachers. Thus, while Negro professional males may be concentrating more in teaching, Negro females are concentrating less. Nursing appears to be slowly becoming an alternative to teaching for Negro professionals; however, these changes are very gradual. The net results of changes in the numerical contributions by Negro males and females to the professions indicate a lingering, if not increasing, greater visibility of females among Negro professionals than is true for the white population in a large number of professional occupations.

The present data point to a differential pattern of professional opportunities for Negro males and females. Although Negro females, relative to white females, contribute less than their proportionate share to the number of professionals and tend to be more concentrated in a limited number of professional occupations, the most invidious comparisons are those between white and Negro males. Whether these differential opportunities are the results of the pull of attractive positions or the push of the necessity of working remains conjecture.

On the one hand, the opportunities for Negro females to contribute disproportionately to the number of Negro professionals may simply reflect the tremendously small number of qualified Negro men. It has been suggested, however, that because Negro women may be less feared sexually and less threatening occupationally, they are more likely to be hired in a biracial economy. This argument says nothing about the position of Negro female professionals within the Negro community. It has yet to be determined whether the amount of masculine discrimination against women in the professions is as strong among Negroes as among whites. The greater visibility of females among Negro professionals may reflect and/or encourage greater acceptance of female professionals and provide them with more opportunities to perform professional roles.

On the other hand, the number of Negro female professionals results perhaps from the necessity of employment. Negro women, whether married or not, are more likely to work than white women. If married, their employment is intimately related to the low income of their husbands, and they have to work in order to increase the family income to a level more comparable to that of white families. Their employment and income, in turn, often place a great strain on marital and family relations, particularly when their positions and incomes approach those of their husbands who perceive these as threats to their "masculinity."[17] This type of marital strain is probably more likely to occur among Negroes than among whites. For example, census data for 1960 disclose that the median annual income of white female professionals was approximately one half that of white male professionals, whereas the median annual income of nonwhite female professionals was three fourths that of nonwhite male professionals.

The practical significance of the noted racial differential in female visibility among professionals is related to both discrimination against females and against Negroes in the professions. It might be suggested, for example, that the data provide clues to the improvement of the occupational status of Negroes. There may be sex differences in status ascription and these differences may affect the competition threat perceived by whites. If the number of Negro males in the professions is a result of racial discrimination, then it might be inferred that the sex component of Negro females lessens this discrimination and provides them with relatively more occupational opportunities. Negro females may also be more tractable to the requirements of routine professional training than their male colleagues, and be more willing to work under inimical conditions for less money.

However, the situation is perhaps not due simply to the variable of sex but rather to the differential impact of the dominant society on the two sexes. As a result of the "farmer's daughter effect," there is a relatively large number of educated females from which professionals are drawn, while the pool of educated males remains small.

There are thus two variables which may be used to explain the present situation: sex and education. The first argument is: Given the same level of education and training, sex makes a difference in the amount of discrimination and the number of opportunities. The second argument is: Regardless of sex, education makes the difference. Which of these two variables is the principal explanatory factor and under what conditions each contributes to the present picture remain unknowns. Probably both sex and education are interacting, but in ways that have yet to be determined.

Whatever factors produce the present picture, it might be proposed that, for the quickest tangible results, programs oriented toward improvement of the educational and occupational status of Negroes be intensified for Negro women. This proposal assumes that female-oriented training programs for Negroes promise greater yields and fewer frustrations than the training programs oriented toward Negro males. Negro females have a greater chance than Negro men of entering professions, and this line of least resistance should be exploited. The success of Negro females would act as models for others, and they would be contributing, in fact, toward an improvement in the occupational status of Negroes generally. Their success, even if they are primarily in relatively low-paying semi-professions, would encourage their offspring to advance toward higher levels of professional occupations.

A dilemma is noted in such a proposal. Intensification of programs for improvement of Negro females would increase their disproportionate contributions to the professions and possibly magnify the unnatural superiority of Negro women. It has been pointed out that the progress of Negro females is closely related to the improvement of Negro males.[18] Any efforts to intensify training programs and provide opportunities for Negroes must concentrate on Negro males. Under the present cultural demands that males be the primary if not sole breadwinners, to do otherwise would aggravate strain which already exists between Negro males and females. This argument does not imply ignoring the possibility of differential professional opportunities for Negro males and females. Under present conditions, however, programs for Negro males must be intensified to a far greater extent than those for females.

Improvement of the occupational status of Negroes must take into account the general pattern of generational mobility noted among Negroes. In light of previous research and the present study, the pattern has frequently been mobility from manual labor to clerical work, from clerical work to low-paying semi-professions, and from semi-professions to higher-paying full professions.[19] The present concentration of Negro males in low-paying semi-professions may indicate that the advancement of the occupational status of Negroes has just reached what might be called the "semi-professional stage." If this be true, then perhaps the present generation of Negro males who aspire to enter professions should be encouraged to focus on those avenues most open to them — the semi-professions. Subsequent generations of sons of these Negro semi-professional men would, in turn, be encouraged by the success of their fathers and be supported by them to enter the higher-paying professions.

A great deal more information is necessary before the noted visibility of females among Negro professionals can be utilized. Very little is known about Negro professionals in general, and even less is known about Negro female professionals in particular. Research is required on both Negro males and females regarding occupational motivations, financial resources, educational experiences, experiences during professional training, and actual performance of professional roles. For example, census data indicate that female professionals are more likely than male professionals to be governmental workers, and Negro professionals are more likely than white professionals to be governmental workers. This suggests that, although Negro females have a greater chance than Negro males to enter professions, their opportunities are more narrowly confined in various social structures. Their experiences in employment may reflect as well as influence their attitudes toward the norm of open competition with their white and Negro colleagues. It has been shown recently that Negro male professionals do not heartily accept the idea of open competition with their white male colleagues,[20] but it has yet to be determined whether the acceptance by Negro female professionals is greater or less than the acceptance by Negro males.

In the majority of occupations listed in the United States Census as "professional" occupations, the proportion of Negroes that is female is greater than the proportion of whites that is female. The relatively greater visibility of females among Negro professionals suggests that, although sex discrimination has long existed in the professions, this discrimination may be relatively less for Negro than for white females. The relatively greater opportunity for Negro females to serve in professional roles is probably related to the fact that Negro males, compared to white males, have long been handicapped educationally and occupationally. In fact, Negro females appear to be superior generally to Negro males in terms of education, occupation, "acculturating contacts with the outside world," and earning power. These advantages of Negro females have helped them make relatively greater contributions to the total number of Negro professionals than would be expected by taking the sex composition of the white professionals as a model.

It was suggested that the relatively low sex ratio among Negro professionals may have practical significance for programs related to improvement of the occupational status of Negroes. Although a great deal more information is necessary for such programs, this study indicates that more attention should be given to those women who may be participating to a significant degree in the advancement of Negroes of both sexes.

NOTES

1. See, for example, Elwood Guernsey, "Nonwhite Occupational Status, by Region, as Related to Per Cent Nonwhite," *Research Reports in Social Science,* VII (August, 1964), 37.

2. Howard M. Vollmer and Donald L. Mills (eds.), *Professionalization* (Englewood Cliffs, 1966), p. 340.

3. Guernsey, along with others, has suggested that not only the professions but the entire occupational structure is determined primarily by whites. See Guernsey, *op. cit.,* pp. 42-43.

4. See, for example, Leonard Broom and Norval D. Glenn, *Transformation of the Negro American* (New York, 1965), p. 187; and Vollmer and Mills, *op. cit.,* p. 332.

5. See, for example, Broom and Glenn, *op. cit.,* p. 143ff; and Dan Cordtz, "The Negro Middle Class Is Right in the Middle," *Fortune,* LXXIV (November, 1966), 228-31.

6. See Broom and Glenn, *op. cit.,* pp. 146-47.

7. Guernsey, *op. cit.,* p. 38.

8. G. Franklin Edwards, *The Negro Professional Class* (New York, 1959), pp. 138-39; and Daniel C. Thompson, "Career Patterns of Teachers in Negro Colleges," *Social Forces,* XXXVI (March, 1958), 272.

9. Eli Ginzberg, *The Negro Potential* (New York, 1956), pp. 108-09; and Broom and Glenn, *op. cit.,* p. 146.

10. Jesse Bernard, *Marriage and Family Among Negroes* (Englewood Cliffs, New Jersey, 1966), pp. 68-70.

11. *Ibid.,* pp. 136-37.

12. Broom and Glenn, *op. cit.,* pp. 20, 89.

13. See Ginzberg, *op. cit.,* pp. 48-50; Daniel C. Thompson, *The Negro Leadership Class* (Englewood Cliffs, New Jersey, 1963), p. 145; and Margaret Mead and Frances Balgley Kaplan (eds.), *American Women* (New York, 1965), p. 221.

14. Broom and Glenn, *op. cit.,* p. 20; cf. John H. Rohrer and Munro S. Edmonson (eds.), *The Eighth Generation Grows Up* (New York, 1964), p. 31.

15. Broom and Glenn, *op. cit.,* p. 89.

16. Cf. Joseph R. Houchins, "The Negro in Professional Occupations in the United States," *The Journal of Negro Education,* XXII (Summer, 1953), 406.

17. Bernard, *op. cit.,* pp. 90ff.; and Mead and Kaplan, *op. cit.,* pp. 220-21.

18. Mead and Kaplan, *op. cit.,* p. 221.

19. Cf. Edwards, *op. cit.,* pp. 64, 70.

20. David H. Howard, "An Exploratory Study of Attitudes of Negro Professionals toward Competition with Whites," *Social Forces,* XLV (September, 1966), 20-27.

III

Cultural Definitions of the
Female Professional

eight

The Clash Between Beautiful Women and Science

DAVID P. CAMPBELL

When the archeologists of the 25th century resurrect us, they are bound to comment on at least two dominant themes in our society — the first is our reverence toward science, demonstrated by the fact that one-fourth of our national government's discretionary expenditures go to support some form of scientific research or development. The second is our idolization of beautiful young women. Facts to document this are hardly necessary; one only has to look at the output of the mass media to see what a large role these women play in our lives, and our economy. One statistic will suffice — the combined monthly circulation of the magazines designed for the physical and spiritual beautification of young women, magazines such as Glamour, Seventeen, Redbook, Vogue, Harper's Bazaar, and Cosmopolitan, exceeds 10 million, which is at least 100 times as large as the combined circulation of all of our psychological journals. (Curiously, there are a few parallels to these magazines for young men — they are left to flounder between Boy's Life and Playboy.)

While these two themes, science and beautiful women, are among the dominant ones in our society, no one, as far as I am aware, has studied their relationship, for it is not obvious that there is any link. Indeed, I did not set out to study their interaction; my data led me to it.

At our research institute at Minnesota, we are continually collecting information on the vocational interests of men and women in a wide variety of occupations. In the past few years, we have asked several hundred women in each of about 50 occupations to fill in the Strong Vocational Interest Blank, and this

Paper presented at the annual meeting of the American Psychological Association, San Francisco, August, 1968. Printed by permission.

paper came from those data. We have strived for diversity in our occupational coverage and have collected information from groups ranging from women PhD mathematicians to power sewing machine operators, from fashion models to licensed practical nurses, from simultaneous translators at the UN to physical education teachers.

In working over the responses of these groups to the Strong Blank I noticed that three occupations were frequently clustered together. They were airline stewardesses, fashion models, and nightclub-TV entertainers, and the items where they clustered together tended to be the livelier ones — "Be a professional dancer," "Thrilling, dangerous activities." (An earlier paper reported on this trend among one of the samples, the fashion models. Campbell, 1967.) When one looks for common characteristics among these groups to explain this clustering, the most immediately apparent one is that all of the women in these occupations must, as an occupational requirement, be physically attractive. Now and then a Phyllis Diller may come along but even she is, for my purposes, psychometrically beautiful.

As this clustering seemed to be a lead worth following, those items that the three groups answered differently from other women were isolated and used as a scoring scale. The selected items are listed in Table 1. Some of them are worded strangely because they have been taken out of the context of the Strong booklet, but they are all concerned with the sparkling part of life.

The scale was normed by using the fashion models as a standardization group and their raw score mean and standard deviation are used in the usual T-score conversion formula. This converts each respondent's answers into a scale where the fashion models have an average of 50 and a standard deviation of 10.

Naming this scale has been something of a problem. While a title such as Cathexis for Hedonistic Cyclothymia might be suitably academic, I have never been very enthusiastic about social science jargon. Around our office, the scale is known as the "Swinger" scale. While that may be too popularized, it does capture the flavor. Of course, it will quickly become dated, for one essential ingredient of this entire syndrome is the necessity for being up to date and the vocabulary changes rapidly — today's swinger was yesterday's hubba-hubba girl. Still, even with these problems, the title "Swinger" is the best condensation I know to describe the contents of this scale.

Table 1 / Selected Items and Their Weights*

Item Number	Item	Weights		
1	Actress	1	0	—1
7	Artist's Model	1	0	—1
15	Beauty Specialist	1	0	—1
57	Criminal Lawyer	1	0	—1
62	Fashion Model	1	0	—1
86	Professional Dancer	1	0	—1
114	Dancing Teacher	1	0	—1
171	Being the first to wear the very latest fashions	1	0	—1
202	Entertaining others	1	0	—1
210	Continually changing activities	1	0	—1
310	Taking a chance (vs Playing safe)	1	0	—1
317	Work in which you move from place to place (vs Work where you stay in one place)	1	0	—1
318	Great variety of work (vs similarity in work)	1	0	—1
331	Thrilling, dangerous activities (vs Quieter, safer activities)	1	0	—1
339	Usually liven up the group on a dull day	1	0	—1

* These items from the SVIB have been reproduced here with the permission of Stanford University Press.

After the scale was standardized, all of the women's occupational samples were scored; their mean scores are rank-ordered in Table 2. After each occupation, in parentheses, is a number in that sample, and the year tested. The women included here have all had three years experience in their job (with the exception of a few occupations such as stewardess where the turnover is too rapid to hold to that criterion), all have said they enjoy their work, and, where it has been possible to obtain the necessary information, all have achieved some minimum level of proficiency such as licensing, certification, or earning of an advanced degree. In general, each sample represents the successful, satisfied women in that occupation.

The occupations scoring high on this scale are the ones we have been discussing; there are no surprises there. Lower down in the table, roughly between scores of 30 and 40, are the majority of the women's occupations — this also is to be expected.

The startling results are at the bottom of the table. There, with mean scores two standard deviations below the norm group, are the women scientists along with, curiously, the power sewing machine operators. Three of the bottom four occupations, the chemists, mathematicians, and math-science teachers, have sur-

Table 2 / Mean Scores for 46 Occupations (First number in parentheses is number in sample; second is year tested)

Mean
Score

55	Top Fashion Models — NYC (17, 1967)
54	Airline Stewardesses (443, 1967)
53	
52	
51	
50	Fashion Models (70, 1964-65)
49	Nightclub-TV Entertainers (104, 1966-67)
48	
47	
46	
45	
44	Recreation Leaders (205, 1968)
43	
42	
41	News Photographers (30, 1966), Newswomen (189, 1966)
40	Beauticians (262, 1967), YWCA Staff Members (282, 1967)
39	Interior Decorators (172, 1966), Secretaries (366, 1967)
38	WAC Officers (307, 1967), Art Teachers (359, 1967) Language Translators (130, 1966-67), Registered Nurses (193, 1967), P. E. Teachers (310, 1967), Radiologic Technologists (307, 1967)
37	Dental Assistants (418, 1966), Life Underwriters (188, 1967), English Teachers (352, 1967), Guidance Counselors (287, 1967)
36	Occupational Therapists (607, 1966), Psychologists (275, 1966), Directors, Christian Education (434, 1967), Language Teachers (287, 1967)
35	Saleswomen (243, 1966), Telephone Operators (129, 1966), Instrument Assemblers (89, 1966), Lawyers (235, 1967), Home Economics Teachers (373, 1967)
34	WAC Enlisted (218, 1967), Physical Therapists (267, 1966), Social Science Teachers (183, 1967), Speech Pathologists (353, 1965)
33	Business Education Teachers (300, 1967), Executive Housekeepers (281, 1967), Librarians (410, 1967), Dietitians (327, 1967)
32	Physicians (329, 1967), Artists (297, 1967), Medical Technologists (345, 1967)
31	Elementary Teachers (325, 1966), Licensed Practical Nurses (222, 1967)
30	
29	PhD Chemists (173, 1966), Math-Science Teachers (308, 1967)
28	PhD Mathematicians (119, 1966), Power Sewing Machine Operators (295, 1967)

vived rigorous training in the sciences, are all employed in some educational or scientific setting, and now a substantial majority of them reject the activities listed in Table 1. Whether there is any cause and effect relationship here is impossible to determine but the correlational relationship is clear — scientific interests and beauty in women are antagonistic.

Of course, there are exceptions. Somewhere there must be a fashion model, or a few airline stewardesses, who enjoy mathematics, who like to be responsible for precision instruments, who occasionally browse through technical handbooks. And in the research laboratories across the country, there must be a few attractive women who enjoy zesty activities. Still, the conclusion stands — women scientists do not enjoy the same things as do women who are in occupations where beauty is an essential asset.

Some confirmatory data for this proposition can be found elsewhere. When Playboy magazine presents their monthly Playmate, the girl in the centerfold, they usually comment on her occupational aspirations. Of the last 78 Playmates over a span of 7 years, only three of these spectacularly displayed women have expressed any interest in scientific activities — one reported a secret ambition to be a mathematician, another was a medical technician who was, however, thinking of switching to interior decorating, and the last was a mathematics major who aspired to be a future astronaut.

Although I don't have time to discuss it further here, one of the more interesting discoveries in this project was the trend of increasing scores over time among all occupations. Table 3 shows the mean scores of 14 occupational samples tested in the 1930's versus comparable samples tested in the 1960's. Clearly, there has been a definite increase over time among all of these samples. One might note especially that the YWCA is apparently not what it used to be. The statistics strongly suggest that the women in our society are becoming more vivacious.

To return to the main point — the low scores of women scientists — the interpretation of these data must be tentative, for we have no further information to help us decide between several possible alternatives.

One is that scientific training, such as these women have had, may dampen one's livelier instincts. Science prides itself on being proper and precise, and any type of flamboyantness is looked upon with distrust. As a timely example, the study of

Table 3 / Mean Scores for Samples Tested in the 1930's versus
Comparable Samples Tested in the 1960's

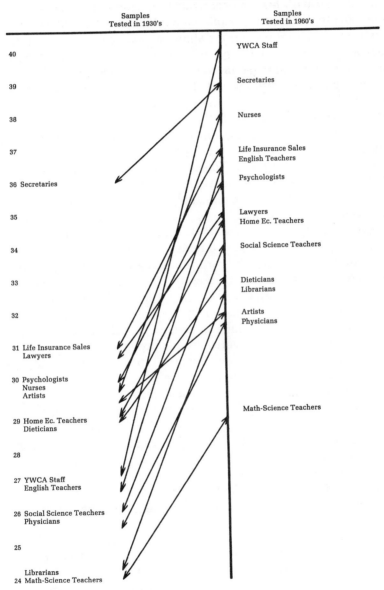

Table 3

Mean Scores for Samples Tested in the 1930's versus Comparable Samples
Tested in the 1960's

beautiful women is viewed very suspiciously by some of my hard-headed colleagues. Apparently it is more "scientific" to study schizophrenics or stutterers than models and stewardesses.

A second possible explanation for these findings is that somehow women with these interests are selected out of the educational ladder before they reach the graduate level. An attractive, lively coed will have many options as to how she wishes to spend her evenings, and a good many of those will lead to marriage, which usually means an end to her education. Those women who persist to the PhD in science have frequently had to give up a large share of their social life during their young adult years.

A third explanation is that there really is some basic antagonism between these two modes of life, the beautiful woman and the scientist. In earlier research with vocational interests, a similar dichotomy has frequently been identified — interests in people versus interest in things. The same split has appeared in other research areas under the terms of introversion and extroversion. This dichotomy may be the simplest explanation for the findings here — it certainly is related.

I would like to close with a partially whimsical, but partially serious, comment on this schism between beauty and science. It is only a mild exaggeration to say that these are the two basic forces in our society. On the one hand, young, curving sensuality central to our system of merchandising, on the other, the scientific expertise which is the very core of our technological culture. If the two were ever rolled up together into a single force, the total power would be awesome.

Can it be that the standoff between them has evolved as some sort of protective "survival of the fittest" mechanism for the total society? A flamboyant and wild-eyed conclusion — just the proper thing with which to end this scientific paper.

REFERENCE

Campbell, D. P., The vocational interests of beautiful women. *Personnel and Guidance Journal*, 1967, 45, 968-972.

nine

A Study of Occupational Advice
for Women in Magazines

PETER CLARKE and VIRGINIA ESPOSITO

One of the functions served by the mass media is to reveal how objects in the environment may be used to satisfy motivational needs. Examples are numerous. Anxious housewives learn that a hair tint will help them secure affection from their husbands, children discover outlets for power and aggression by observing adventure programs and young men find that their chances for achievement are enhanced by a careful selection of ties and footwear.

Much of this learning from television, magazines and the like is incidental. The illustration involving children is such a case; objects like guns and 007 paraphernalia are linked with violent behavior in order to develop a plot and not to teach aggressive behavior.

This paper concerns a kind of media content that is overtly instructional — magazine articles describing occupational opportunities available to women. Our interest in this magazine fare has been stimulated by the intensified debate about "feminine mystique."

Betty Friedan, Marya Mannes and other essayists have been strenuous in their efforts to liberate women from a role assignment that condemns them to babies and brooms.[1] Their proposed restructuring of feminine behavior relies heavily on the revolutionary impact of occupation on self-esteem. This renewed interest in careers for women has come at a time, and perhaps as a consequence, of increased college enrollment among women and an expansion of the economy to include more working wives.

From JOURNALISM QUARTERLY, Vol. 43, No. 3 (1966), pp. 477-485. Reprinted by permission.

While there has been much debate concerning why women work, or should work, scant attention has been devoted to the ways in which occupations are represented to women. There are many sources of such information, including formal counseling services in schools, employment agencies and the like. However, our concern for the social impact of the mass media led us to examine the content of women's magazines like *Cosmopolitan* and *Mademoiselle*. These publications are a source of articles designed to reveal the vistas of occupational choice.[2]

We have analyzed this content for two kinds of statements about jobs for women — inputs and outputs. These two categories of information present: 1) the personal characteristics, like motives and abilities, women need in order to consider entering a particular occupation, and 2) the rewards, in terms of motive satisfaction, they can expect to derive from the occupation.

This paper pursues four goals. *First*, a system of content analysis categories, derived partly from motivation theory, is explicated to analyze the inputs and outputs described in occupational advice articles. *Second*, these categories are applied to a sample of contemporary content and contingencies among content characteristics are analyzed. *Third*, data are presented from a sample of young women who were asked to Q-sort output statements according to how rewarding the motive satisfaction was to them. And *fourth*, content findings and Q-sort findings are compared in order to make inferences about the effects of magazine treatment on women's perceptions of the occupational world.

Content Categories

The concept of motive is a convenient way to systematize the analysis of goal-directed behavior. A motive is a state of tension antecedent to reward-seeking; occupations are means of seeking rewards. Hence, this study of career articles in magazines began with a review of the research literature on motivation in the hope that this work would suggest the relevant features of media content.

Four motivational variables were found that have helped other researchers explain a variety of behaviors. The first was the *achievement* motive, which McClelland and his colleagues have studied to predict task performance and to account for some of the variability in rates of national economic growth.

among other things.[3] McClelland also has employed variables of *affiliation* need and *power* need in cross-cultural studies of business and government executives.[4]

To this list we added a fourth variable that has received some attention in research on attitude structure and change; the factor is *cognitive need*, or the desire to seek out information preparatory to problem solving.[5] From previous evidence it was concluded that these motivational states are among the dominant reasons people enter occupations, and that the gratification of these motive states yields substantial rewards.

A preliminary look at magazine articles not included in the final sample revealed that these four motivational categories did not exhaust the content. For example, we found statements that seemed to express a raw need for kinetic outlet; these were labeled *diffuse energy*.

Other statements seemed to describe quite specific requirements or characteristics of a job without relating the aspects overtly to a need satisfaction. Rather than force these statements into existing categories, they were treated separately under the heading, *terminal values*.

Finally, some statements seemed representative of the *feminine mystique* dialog. These were phrases that portrayed occupational advantages in instrumental terms — e.g., the job is useful for putting a husband through school.

The seven coding categories describing inputs and outputs are illustrated with examples below. A copy of the coding manual with a more complete explication of each category may be obtained from the authors. The coding of the first three types of themes followed closely the work by McClelland.

a) *Achievement.* Statements that referred to the need for ambition or to the opportunities to prove oneself, meet challenges, face competition, gain respect, advance up the status ladder or enter male-dominated realms of work.

b) *Power.* Statements that promised personal autonomy on a job or chances to train others, make major decisions, change existing conditions or have one's voice heard on issues of social importance.

c) *Affiliation.* Statements that associated a job with opportunities to help others, meet new people, meet interesting men or attend parties and other convivial events. Input statements described the need for a warm personality and the ability to empathize with others' problems.

d) *Cognitive need.* Statements that suggested job applicants must be of an inquiring mind or that promised jobs would provide chances to exchange ideas with other people, explore frontiers of knowledge, analyze data or develop new products.

e) *Diffuse energy.* Statements that associated activity with no specific reward. Examples included being on the go or where the action is, feeling involved, enjoying adventure or engaging in unpredictable work.

f) *Terminal values.* A catchall category of statements that described narrow aspects of work, such as long hours, or inputs unrelated to other themes, such as a need for versatility, reliable behavior or persistence.

g) *Feminine mystique.* Statements that suggested a job was ideal for women, prepared one for marriage, could be combined with marriage and family or permitted easy entry and exit later in life.

It can be seen that the major coding categories reflect familiar variables used by occupational sociologists to study worker mobility and morale.[6] These researchers frequently ask respondents to indicate important satisfactions derived from their work, including the chance to help others (affiliation), to manage the activities of others (power), to demonstrate abilities (achievement), and to learn new things (cognitive need).

Studies of occupational values have found wide differences between the motives and interests of men and women. The principal difference involves affiliation. As McClelland has expressed it:

> ... female occupational interests show only one major pattern (as contrasted with several for males) which covers whatever it is that housewives, office workers, stenographers, nurses and teachers have in common ... (This is) the *interdependence* category we have been using to describe one of the main dimensions of female interests and actions. To summarize, women are quicker to recognize their own interdependence; they are more interested in situations where interdependence is important; they enter jobs where this characteristic is salient ...[7]

This emphasis on affiliation needs has been underscored by laboratory studies of group problem solving, where it has been found that women quickly seek interpersonal, as opposed to instrumental roles. These findings are a measure of sex-typing during early socialization when boys are taught to be assertive and demanding and girls are encouraged to be accommodating and sensitive to the needs of others.[8]

The content analysis was designed to reveal the extent to which female as opposed to male motivational themes were associated with occupations. A large number of popular women's magazines were scanned to find articles about occupations. This content appeared with frequency in only three publications during 1963-64: *Cosmopolitan*, *Mademoiselle* and *Glamour*. This study includes all 19 articles published in these three magazines during this period, which was chosen in order to represent current magazine perspectives on women's work.

The articles embraced an array of job opportunities, including oceanography, political staff work, fashion modeling, teaching, television research, psychiatric social work, urban planning and film making. The apparent diversity of these careers hides an underlying similarity: for the most part the jobs were somewhat esoteric. The magazines seemed averse to discussing ordinary jobs that are more accessible to women. This preference for the unusual, the romantic and the exciting careers, must be kept in mind as we explore characteristics of the article content, and as we speculate on the social functions performed by these media offerings.

For purposes of content analysis the coding unit was a statement, the linking of any attribute with either of two subjects, a job or someone holding (or anticipating entering) a job. Articles were first scanned and statements underlined; coding of statements into appropriate categories followed.[9]

Content Characteristics

Table 1 shows proportions of themes that were coded into each of the seven categories, and the within-theme breakdowns

Table 1 / Use of Themes to Describe Inputs and Outputs of Occupations for Women

	Per cent of total	Per cent of statements that were:	
		Inputs	Outputs
Achievement	26%	13%	87%
Power	19	7%	93%
Affiliation	17	29%	71%
Cognitive need	12	36%	64%
Diffuse energy	11	39%	61%
Terminal values	10	70%	30%
Feminine mystique	5	36%	64%

N = 453

for inputs and outputs. The most frequently stressed motive for working women was achievement (26%), the chance to advance up the occupational and social ladder or engage in competitive activities. The second most popular theme was power. Almost half (45%) of these magazines' statements outlining the requirements and rewards of work referred to these two characteristically male values.

Affiliation, the chance to make friends, be with people and help others, ranked third in use, followed by cognitive need, diffuse energy, terminal values and, finally, feminine mystique. This last theme accounted for just 5% of the content; opportunities to mix marriage and career were infrequently cited during 1963-64 as rationales for women to join the workaday world.

One of the threads of this inquiry concerned how much descriptions of careers for women are a function of the jobs, or the articles' topics, and to what extent the descriptions reflect a consistent world view shared by writers and editors of the articles. It is plain that this research design is inadequate to resolve the question, but the analysis will suggest some of the complexities involved in finding an answer.

A crude way of studying this issue is to imagine that each of the 19 authors of the career articles had a "vocabulary" of seven themes at his disposal. If these authors' descriptions of careers open to women were highly consistent, and not related to aspects of the different jobs being described, the authors might always have given achievement gratifications first prominence, power needs second importance, chances for affiliation third rank, etc. The concordance coefficient between articles would be 1.0. Actually, the coefficient was .20, which was statistically significant, but indicative of considerable variation.

Magazine treatment of female work roles probably is prepared within some constraints that originate outside of specific content. These constraints may result from the writers' and editors' perceptions of what work is like, or an anticipation of what their reading audience prefers or needs to be told about occupations.

To some extent the constraints may reflect the narrow range of occupations featured. Several of the work roles described in science, business and politics have traditionally been male preserves; indeed, one type of achievement reward frequently portrayed was the opportunity to succeed in a role considered out-of-bounds for women.

The articles differed widely in length, ranging from a six-statement item about TV casting directors to a 76-statement feature about a political administrative assistant. The long pieces naturally contained greater detail and more information and probably offered readers a more interesting view of women in occupational roles. We asked: is there a relationship between the length of an occupational article and the choice of motivational themes used to describe the occupation? From the viewpoint of the writer, this amounts to learning whether increased space availability results in the increased use of some themes but not others.

To study this question, correlations were computed between 1) the number of each type of theme, and 2) the total number of themes, minus the number contributed by the independent variable. The highest correlation between theme use and article length was .73 for achievement motivation. This means that when the writer described women's occupations in considerable detail, he was likely to mention repeatedly the opportunities for achievement gratification, i.e., competitive activity, meeting performance criteria and working up to higher positions. When the writer was brief, the number of these themes declined.

The correlation for affiliation was .47, which is not significantly smaller than that for achievement ($p < .20$). Other themes that varied in use with the length of articles were terminal values (.61) and diffuse energy (.50). There was no significant tendency for the use of power, cognitive need or feminine mystique themes to be a function of the length or detail with which an occupation was described.

The importance of article length as a variable fades if it is highly related to the kind of occupation described, since the correlations just reported would reflect associations between motive satisfaction and type of work. As mentioned earlier, the jobs portrayed in these magazine articles were generally atypical. Within the limitations of this sample of 19 articles, however, it is hard to discern any relationship between kind of occupation and the extent of editorial attention it received. Long articles included ones about oceanography and financial counseling. Least space was devoted to somewhat similar careers, such as engineering, television research and banquet management.

Hence correlations between theme use and length seem to reflect the perspectives of writers and editors on the world of careers for women. Given the chance to publish detailed descriptions of work, the magazines chose to focus on accomplishment, activity and friendship, but not the gratifications of power, cognitive outlet or feminine mystique.

Contingencies between frequency of motive-theme use were analyzed by computing partial correlations between each pair of themes; the effect was to hold length of article constant (through the use of correlations reported above). Table 2 presents the four coefficients that were statistically significant.[10]

Table 2 / Significant Correlations* Between Motive-Theme Use

	r
Affiliation x Power	.66
Achievement x Cognitive need	.58
Power x Feminine mystique	—.43
Power x Diffuse energy	.46

* Partial coefficients, holding article length constant.

In light of earlier findings, the correlation of .66 between frequency of affiliation and power motives is especially noteworthy. It was shown that friendship and social intercourse were less commonly pictured as career motives for women than achievement and striving (17% of the themes were affiliation; 26% were achievement). Now it is clear that when opportunities for affiliation did appear, they were likely to be coupled with power gratifications. This suggests that the magazines' conception of social contact on the job leans heavily on opportunities to influence others, to control their actions, to instruct and to maintain a superordinate status.

A "natural" for combining affiliation and power was the role of political assistant, according to *Mademoiselle*. Their heroine was in the "VIP whirl," served as liaison between a governor and legislators and assisted lawyers in the governor's office; she also *managed* county campaigns, *ran* testimonial dinners and *clarified* political issues and politics to the voters. A busy girl, she.

A closer look at the data reveals a second aspect of this link between affiliation and power. When the two motive themes were broken down into inputs and outputs (see Table 1), we found that 71% of the affiliation statements described work rewards, or outputs, compared with 93% of the power statements (Chi-square equals 13.3). The figure for affiliation was about the average for all categories, but power was much higher.

Thus when the magazines touted social skills as a requirement for *entering* an occupation, they were likely to show power over others as a *reward*. In many other cases, opportunities for affiliation and power appeared jointly as work rewards.

The frequency of achievement motive satisfaction was strongly correlated (.58) with cognitive need. Apparently the jobs that require a commitment to knowledge and offer outlets for intellectual inquisitiveness are also the jobs that enable women to meet performance demands and move up the status ladder. Cognitive behavior and success go together.

An article about medical secretaries illustrated the mixture of cognitive need and achievement. The ability to assemble charts and check recordings of necessary information was an important input for the job; a prominently featured reward was the chance that girls with ability could move into more responsible medical jobs.

It should be emphasized that formal educational requirements for a job were not coded as a cognitive need input, only curiosity, skill at handling information and an interest in the unknown. Consequently, these articles were not simply reinforcing the cultural expectation that a B.A. degree equals success or social mobility.

Cognitive need was more likely to be described as a work requirement than was achievement motivation; 36% of the cognitive need themes were coded as characteristics women must bring to their jobs, compared to 13% for achievement (Chi-square equals 11.5).[11]

Two other correlations between motive-theme use are worth attention. First is the negative relationship (—.43) between power and feminine mystique, which is not surprising. Jobs that were described as enabling the exercise of authority were not also likely to be shown as satisfying a need for outside interests, helpful for putting husband through school or desirable because a woman with such skills could move in and out of the employment world at will.

The remaining significant coefficient was between power and diffuse energy (.46). Women who wanted to be "on the go" and who sought to work in exciting or crisis-ridden atmospheres were rewarded by chances to wield social influence.

What are the most salient of these findings? Occupational articles written for women made an extraordinarily heavy use of male motivational themes. Statements bearing on affiliation needs were far less frequent than those oriented toward achievement and power. To a modest extent this pattern of theme emphasis was consistent between articles.

When detailed job descriptions were separated from the synopses, achievement statements correlated most highly with article length. The more career information supplied the female reader, the more likely it was to stress competition and success.

Correlations between the frequencies of theme use revealed that when affiliation motives did appear, they were likely to be coupled with power gratifications. Even the goal of companionship was tinged with a flavor of social control.

This discrimination against feminine interests might be attributed to at least three factors; these explanations are, of course, speculative. First and most simply, the writers and editors responsible for these articles may be men. This is not a very intriguing explanation and not even true, if bylines and mastheads can be trusted.

Second, the magazines may be attempting to reach an atypical audience that is unlike the usual subjects available to psychologists and anthropologists who have studied female values and occupational goals. These target readers may be more "mannish" in the rewards they seek from careers.

The general content of these magazines should appeal to an audience of women concerned with fashion, makeup, travel and urban life. These dimensions of "sophistication" may extend to the goal-seeking that motivates women to enter occupations. At the least, this extension may be *perceived* by the editors.

Third, and least appealing, the harsh world of magazine publishing may attract a peculiarly competitive and power-hungry female — an "iron butterfly" to adopt a label recently applied to Helen Gurley Brown, editor of *Cosmopolitan*.[12] These editors and writers may report the occupational world by projecting their own needs and aspirations onto career situations where they may be less applicable.

Firm evidence is not available concerning any of these speculations. However, something may be said about the second explanation and about the probable impact of these magazine articles.

The Q-Sort Study

To make inferences about impact, we studied women 1) who are potential recruits to the occupations featured by the magazines, and 2) who also are likely to have relatively little information about such jobs, and thus could make use of the magazine content. Forty upper-division girls at the University of Washington were asked to Q-sort a sample of 30 typical output statements according to "how appealing or desirable" the job characteristics were to them. The statements represented all of the content categories except terminal values.[13] The packet of five statements from each category was sorted into five equal-numbered stacks. The statements were presented in random order, and none of the girls was aware the statements represented any system of categories.

The 40 girls were selected from a sample of 95 respondents who completed a career-orientation questionnaire. Selection for the Q-sort task was based on responses to two items: 1) whether or not the girl expected that a career or job would be an important source of her life satisfactions, and 2) whether or not the girl definitely expected to hold a full-time job after marriage. Twenty-seven girls indicated high career orientation, and 31 girls were low.[14] Twenty respondents from each group were given the Q-sort task; respondents with intermediate career orientation scores were discarded.

Despite this use of extreme groups, no differences were found between career girls and non-career girls. The means for all 40 subjects are reported in Table 3, and they show that the job char-

Table 3 / Girls' Mean Ratings for Job Characteristics
(low score indicates high desirability)

Affil.	Diff. En.	Cog. Nd.	Fem. Mys.	Power	Achiev.
2.00	2.33	2.68	3.32	3.58	4.08

acteristics were rated for desirability in the following order: affiliation, diffuse energy, cognitive need, feminine mystique, power and achievement. All means were significantly different from each other by t-test.[15]

Content vs. Q Data

Comparisons between the data in Tables 1 and 3 illustrate the lack of congruence between these girls' preferences for job characteristics and the career aspects featured by magazines aimed at a young audience. Affiliation and diffuse energy (being "active" and "on the go") were clearly the most prized rewards offered by jobs, although these two values accounted for only 28 per cent of the content. Even more striking is the girls' rejection of achievement rewards, which ranked first in magazine content.

On one point the girls and the magazine writers agreed, however. This was the relationship between affiliation and power. The magazines tended to use these themes in conjunction, or to avoid them both ($r = .66$). Similarly, the girls' ratings of affiliation and power statements correlated significantly, at .31, even though the nature of the sorting task made positive correlations difficult to obtain. Girls who liked being with other people and helping them also were attracted by the reward of supervising others and guiding their activities.

Conclusion

Girls were sampled by separating them into career-orientation groups in order to test whether high interest in occupations was related to reward expectations similar to those stressed by the magazines. Instead of differences in motivational needs, we found homogeneity, although research using employed women or women working in esoteric or glamorous jobs might reveal a different picture.[16]

It would seem that if occupational articles are directed at young, college-educated women, the motivational language employed fails to meet the audience's interests. As a consequence, the articles may have two effects. They may be avoided by readers as a source of helpful insights into rewards women may gain from careers. Also, it is possible that the articles are read as entertainment. A woman may scan this magazine content as a window on an occupational world remote from her experience, much as one reads accounts of missionaries in Africa.

Use of these occupational articles as vicarious entertainment might be functional, rather than self-alienating. Identification with achievement and power-oriented girls in the magazines might serve as a catharsis for motivational needs that female readers are unlikely to satisfy in real life.[17]

In any event, it is doubtful that the articles are taken seriously as advice. Magazine editors and writers should be alert to the therapeutic possibilities of this content and to the possibility that there is a wide gulf between their own perspectives on work and the values shared by many of their readers.

NOTES

1. A casual sample of this literature includes the following: Betty Friedan, *The Feminine Mystique* (New York: Norton, 1963); Marya Mannes, *But Will It Sell?* (Philadelphia: Lippincott, 1964); Marya Mannes, "The Problems of Creative Women," in Seymour Farber (editor), *Man and Civilization: The Potential of Woman* (New York: McGraw-Hill, 1963); Simone deBeauvoir, *The Second Sex* (New York: Knopf, 1952); Helene Deutsch, *The Psychology of Women* (New York: Grune and Stratton, 1944); and Alva Myrdal, *Women's Two Roles, Home and Work* (London: Routledge and Keegan Paul, 1962).

2. For a sensitive study of career portrayals on television, see Melvin L. DeFleur, "Occupational Roles as Portrayed on Television," *Public Opinion Quarterly,* 28:57-74 (1964).

3. David C. McClelland, *The Achievement Motive* (New York: Appleton-Century-Crofts, 1953); and *The Achieving Society* (Princeton: Van Nostrand, 1961).

4. See *The Achieving Society, ibid.,* Ch. 7.

5. H. C. Kelman and Jonas Cohler, "Reactions to Persuasive Communications as a Function of Cognitive Needs and Styles," paper read at the 30th annual meeting of the Eastern Psychological Association, 1959. Also see Arthur R. Cohen, *Attitude Change and Social Influence* (New York: Basic Books, 1964).

6. Morris Rosenberg, *Occupations and Values* (Glencoe: Free Press, 1957).

7. See McClelland's paper in Robert J. Lifton (editor), *The Woman in America* (Boston: Houghton Mifflin, 1965).

8. For discussions of early socialization practices, see Robert R. Sears, Eleanor Maccoby and Harry Levin, *Patterns of Child Rearing* (Evanston: Row, Peterson, 1957).

9. Unless otherwise stated, tests for statistical significance reported in this paper met the .05 level (two-tailed).

Inter-coder reliabilities for the content variables were estimated by William Scott's formula (see "Reliability of Content Analysis: The Case of Nominal Scale Coding," *Public Opinion Quarterly,* 19:321-25 (1955). The between-theme reliability was .77. Within each theme, reliabilities were computed for distinctions between inputs and outputs. These values were:

Achievement	.41
Affiliation	.72
Power	.86
Cognitive need	.24
Feminine mystique	.72
Terminal values	.34
Diffuse energy	.75

A total of 453 statements were coded from the 19 articles. This excludes a miscellaneous category, which was seldom used, and categories of *negative* inputs and outputs. These statements described attributes women should not bring to their careers, and rewards they should not count on receiving. Thirty-eight of these were coded, but they have been excluded from the analysis since 21 were found in one article.

10. These four coefficients have been drawn from a matrix of 21 intercorrelations. Use of the .05 level of significance means that one of these values may be spuriously significant.

11. Despite the significance of this difference, one must note the modest coding reliabilities for distinguishing between inputs and outputs within each of these themes. See footnote 9.

12. *Life,* Nov. 19, 1965, pp. 65-84.

13. Q methodology is discussed in detail in William Stephenson, *The Study of Behavior* (Chicago: University of Chicago Press, 1953). Statements describing terminal values were excluded because of their vague and heterogeneous content.

14. The two questionnaire items correlated at beyond the .01 level.

15. These significant differences between output categories provide some validation for the content analysis variables. One may conclude that the magazine study analyzed content into categories that have meaning — at least for college girls in the reading audience.

16. Although few of the 40 girls were currently employed, all had held full-time jobs, and a majority had worked for two or three different employers.

17. A drive-reduction hypothesis analogous to this has been a central concern of research on aggressive behavior and mass media exposure. For a comprehensive discussion, see Leonard Berkowitz, Ronald Corwin and Mark Hieronimus, "Film Violence and Subsequent Aggressive Tendencies," *Public Opinion Quarterly,* 27:217-29 (1963).

ten

Masculinity or Femininity?
Differentiating Career-Oriented and
Homemaking-Oriented College Freshman Women

LORRAINE RAND

This study examines a major difference between college women with extreme vocational orientations. Masculinity-femininity is the proposed dimension along which career- and homemaking-oriented college women differ. That the majority of modern college coeds plan to play roles of both homemaker and wage earner in the future is a well-known fact conclusively established by many studies (Berry, 1955; Empey, 1958). By contrast, girls who seek the role of homemaker exclusively or to enter high professional levels after extensive graduate training are atypical in vocational orientation. College women, therefore, who deviate from the typical pattern, choosing either postcollege role primarily, are the focus of this study.

Previous studies have established differences between career- and homemaking-oriented college women in interests, personality, ability, and values. Implied in the findings of these studies is that career-oriented women are more masculine in the studied characteristics and the homemaking-oriented more feminine, that is, they differ on characteristics generally considered by our culture to be more appropriate to one sex than the other. More specifically, the greater achievement, dominance, endurance, and independence found to typify career-oriented women are generally considered masculine personality characteristics while the nurturance, succorance, empathy, understanding, sociality, and heterosexuality found to typify homemaking-oriented women are generally considered feminine personality characteristics

From JOURNAL OF COUNSELING PSYCHOLOGY, Vol. 15, No. 5 (1968), pp. 444-450. Reprinted by permission.

by our culture. Similarly, the social dimensions of friendliness, sociability, interpersonal competency, heterosexuality, and closer family relationships found to characterize homemaking-oriented women and the achievement orientation, intraception, material awards for grades, later dating, phantasy work roles, and earlier vocational choices found among career-oriented women further suggest a basic difference in motivational patterns (Hoyt & Kennedy, 1958; Vetter & Lewis, 1964; White, 1957; Zissis, 1962). Whereas the homemaking-oriented women may derive satisfaction from social relationships (both with the same and the opposite sex), career-oriented women may receive satisfaction from achieving competency and recognition in school subjects, activities, and hobbies. This object-process tendency in career-oriented women and the people-language orientation in marriage-oriented women is generally referred to as more typical of males or more typical of females in our culture and called masculine or feminine respectively.

Further support for the masculine-feminine dichotomy exists in the findings on measured vocational interests by Hoyt and Kennedy (1958) and Zissis (1962), which suggest that homemaking-oriented women have extrinsic job motivation and interests similar to women in occupations requiring little educational training. Career girls, on the other hand, seem to have intrinsic job motivation and interests similar to women in occupations generally dominated by men and which require educational training beyond the 4-year level.

Finally, the tendency for the career sample in the Wagman study (1965) to score higher on the AVL Theoretical scale and the tendency for the homemaking-oriented sample to excel on the AVL Religious scale lends further support to the masculinity-femininity dichotomy. Consistent sex differences have been demonstrated not only on these value measures but for most of the personality and interest characteristics that have been found to differentiate career- and homemaking-oriented women samples.

Hypotheses

This investigation will consider the masculinity-femininity scheme a basic dimension on which these extreme groups differ. The major hypothesis of this study is that career- and homemaking-oriented college freshman women will differ on psychological and behavioral characteristics culturally defined as masculine or feminine, the career-oriented woman being more masculine and the homemaking-oriented more feminine.

It can be assumed that substantiating this hypothesis would confirm other expectations about basic differences between these two groups; namely, that they differ in their perception of their sex roles. A typical definition of the feminine role would include those model characteristics and behaviors which are typically ascribed to the female in our society. Apparently, homemaking-oriented women more frequently reflect characteristics considered feminine in our society, thereby adopting the traditional feminine role. Career-oriented women, on the other hand, possessing more masculine characteristics, have deviated from the traditional sex-role expectations and have redefined their sex role to include characteristics and behavior appropriate to both sexes in our culture. Indeed, confirmation of the masculine-feminine dichotomy would strengthen the vocational-orientation theory regarding career- and homemaking-oriented women and encourage further investigation of sex-role perceptions.

As a by-product of this study, the validity of the masculine-feminine dimension was examined further by comparing scores made by the two groups with those made by all college males and females in the parent sample. If the dimension has wider applicability, then the career-oriented women should score more like college males and homemaking-oriented women more like college females.

Method

Survey and Sample. The data for the study were responses of college freshmen women enrolled in 28 colleges to the American College Survey (ACS), a descriptive inventory of ideas, attitudes, and experiences. This survey was designed by the American College Testing Program (ACT) for its nation-wide study of the typical freshman in the fall of 1964 (Abe, Holland, Lutz, & Richards, 1965). Of the 6,132 female participants in the ACT study, 848 were selected for this investigation on the basis of their responses to two questions of the ACS. The homemaking sample were defined as the 548 freshmen women who "agreed strongly" or "agreed" that finding a husband in college was more important than finding a suitable field of training after college. The career-oriented sample were 300 freshmen women who chose MD, LLB, DDS, or PhD as their highest expected level of education and who "disagreed" or "disagreed strongly" to the homemaking criterion question. Thus, "marriage-fixated" women were inferred to be homemaking-oriented and "ambitious" professionally-motivated women to be career-oriented. (The reader should recognize that the two criterion groups were chosen on the basis of their expressed attitudes and future expectations while they were freshmen. To what extent college women implement their freshman choices upon graduation is presently unknown. This issue is one which the author plans to research.)

Procedure. Responses of the two extreme groups to other questions of the ACS were compared. The study variables were interests and personality, achievement, competency, potential, vocational and life goals, and self-perceptions, and were classified as masculine or feminine if two criteria were met: (a) if previous research by Terman and Miles (1936), Strong (1943), Allport, Vernon, and Lindzey (1960), and Tyler (1947), had established sex differences on the relevant variables; and (b) if the responses of college males and females in the ACT study were consistent with sex differences revealed by research. For example, previous research by Terman and Miles had revealed aggressiveness to be a masculine characteristic. And since males in the ACT 1965 study more frequently gave high self-ratings on this trait, it was therefore classified as masculine.

Seven research hypotheses were advanced concerning differences between the career- and homemaking-oriented samples on characteristics culturally regarded as appropriate to the male and female sex. The career-oriented women in this sample were predicted to score higher on masculine (a) interest and personality, (b) achievement, (c) competency, (d) potential, (e) vocational goal, (f) life goal, and (g) self-perception characteristics than the homemaking-oriented women, who in turn would score higher on more feminine measures of these characteristics.

The *t* test and chi-square were used to determine the significance of the difference between the two groups on scale and item variables, respectively. Although predictions were made that the career- and homemaking-oriented samples would score higher or lower on certain scales, two-tailed tests were employed throughout. This approach was considered appropriate to account for possible opposite findings in a theoretical area which has so few guidelines. Since the present study was involved in an area which had not been explored in any great depth, the .05 level of confidence was chosen to indicate an area worthy of further study, and the .01 level was chosen to indicate a conclusive difference.

Results and Discussion

The results by and large substantiate masculinity-femininity as a dimension along with career- and homemaking-oriented women differ. All seven research hypotheses specifying that the career-oriented sample would score higher on masculine variables were supported. More specifically, the career sample scored significantly higher on 9 out of 10 masculine interest and personality, potential, achievement, and competency scales (see Table 1). On the tenth scale, the difference was non-significant.

Table 1 / Test Comparisons for Career and Homemaking Samples on Masculine and Feminine Interest and Personality, Potential, Achievement, and Competency Measures

Scales	Career		Homemaking		
	M	SD	M	SD	t
Interest and personality					
Realistic (M)	1.81	2.49	1.18	1.66	4.33**
Intellectual (M)	5.75	4.37	3.00	3.63	9.77**
Enterprising (M)	3.47	3.07	3.88	2.98	—1.89
Masculinity (M)	4.97	2.51	3.83	2.07	7.06**
Social (F)	7.43	3.81	7.96	3.67	—1.99**
Self Control (F)	9.35	3.50	10.49	3.18	4.80**
Conventional (F)	2.10	2.90	2.73	3.07	—2.94**
Potential					
Leadership (M)	21.00	5.96	18.89	5.77	5.01**
Scientific (M)	16.00	6.66	12.50	5.72	8.00**
Musical (F)	18.41	5.68	17.49	5.64	2.26*
Dramatic Arts (F)	20.77	6.73	17.66	6.67	6.39**
Achievement					
Dramatic Arts (F)	2.79	2.69	2.10	2.19	4.02**
Artistic (F)	1.19	1.89	1.00	1.88	1.37
Literary (F)	2.11	1.92	1.09	1.39	8.91**
Competencies					
Scientific (M)	3.90	2.41	2.69	2.08	7.61**
Technical (M)	6.04	3.71	4.64	2.96	6.01**
Social and Educational (F)	7.17	2.74	7.68	2.52	.13
Homemaking (F)	17.06	5.22	17.82	4.27	—2.26*
Arts (F)	12.46	6.49	10.76	5.96	3.83**

Note: Abbreviated: M = masculine variable, F = feminine variable.
* p ≤ .05.
** p ≤ .01.

In addition, on 15 out of 15 masculine self-perceptions, life and

Table 2 / Chi-Square Tests of Masculine and Feminine
Self-Perception Ratings Given by Career ($N = 300$)
and Homemaking ($N = 548$) Groups

Self-perception item	Criterion Groups	Below Av.	Average	Above Av.	Top 10%	Chi-Square value
Leadership (M)	Career	12.7	41.3	34.7	11.3	20.51**
	Homemaking	14.1	52.7	28.6	4.6	
Athletic Ability (M)	Career	23.8	40.6	26.2	9.4	18.97**
	Homemaking	22.8	52.4	21.1	3.6	
Drive to Achieve (M)	Career	2.3	21.3	49.0	27.3	96.05**
	Homemaking	7.3	48.3	35.5	9.0	
Mathematical Ability (M)	Career	26.0	37.3	26.7	10.0	14.64**
	Homemaking	35.8	38.7	19.7	5.8	
Aggressiveness (M)	Career	12.0	56.3	24.0	7.7	16.48**
	Homemaking	18.2	60.0	18.6	3.1	
Independence (M)	Career	1.0	25.1	44.8	29.1	47.14**
	Homemaking	5.3	39.6	41.8	13.3	
Scientific Ability (M)	Career	27.7	42.0	22.7	7.7	69.35**
	Homemaking	48.5	41.4	8.6	1.5	
Intellectual Self-Confidence (M)	Career	6.4	43.5	40.5	9.7	54.50**
	Homemaking	13.9	59.1	24.5	2.6	
Perseverance (M)	Career	3.3	50.0	34.8	11.7	22.07
	Homemaking	4.8	63.9	25.9	5.5	
Research Ability (M)	Career	16.4	53.8	24.7	5.0	47.39**
	Homemaking	28.3	59.4	11.4	0.9	
Understanding of Others (F)	Career	2.3	21.3	56.3	20.0	15.29**
	Homemaking	0.4	31.0	50.5	18.0	
Sociability (F)	Career	9.3	44.7	35.3	10.7	9.59**
	Homemaking	4.4	46.2	40.3	9.1	
Artistic Ability (F)	Career	38.1	36.8	17.7	7.4	8.38*
	Homemaking	42.0	37.7	17.2	3.1	
Self-Control (F)	Career	7.0	41.5	40.1	11.4	4.25
	Homemaking	4.9	47.1	39.2	8.8	
Conservatism (F)	Career	18.0	51.7	25.7	4.7	15.69**
	Homemaking	10.0	63.0	21.2	5.7	
Writing Ability (F)	Career	6.3	44.3	35.7	13.7	38.97**
	Homemaking	15.3	52.7	27.0	4.9	
Social Self-Confidence (F)	Career	19.1	46.8	25.4	8.7	5.32
	Homemaking	18.8	52.4	23.7	5.1	
Sensitivity to Needs of Others (F)	Career	3.3	31.1	48.5	17.1	1.91
	Homemaking	2.4	35.1	46.8	15.7	

Note: M = masculine variable, F = feminine variable.
* $p \leq .05$.
** $p \leq .01$.

vocational goal items, the career-oriented group gave relatively
more high ratings than the homemaking-oriented group. These

data, with the exception of vocational goal items, are shown in Tables 2 and 3.[1]

Table 3 / Chi-Square Tests of Masculine and Feminine Life-Goal Ratings Given by Career ($N = 300$) and Homemaking ($N = 548$) Groups

Goal item	Criterion groups	Importance rating				Chi-square value
		Not im-portant	Some-what im-portant	Very im-portant	Essen-tial	
Becoming an authority in a special vocational area (M)	Career	5.7	15.0	33.3	46.0	132.77**
	Homemaking	23.5	28.5	34.5	13.5	
Obtaining awards or recognition (M)	Career	24.1	38.5	30.4	7.0	18.34**
	Homemaking	35.8	38.9	21.3	4.0	
Having executive responsibility for the work of others (M)	Career	35.3	30.0	27.7	7.0	10.52*
	Homemaking	37.5	37.5	18.9	6.0	
Helping others in difficulty (F)	Career	2.3	24.7	33.4	39.5	20.00**
	Homemaking	2.4	29.4	43.3	24.9	
Making sacrifices for others' happiness (F)	Career	3.3	31.0	35.7	30.0	3.31
	Homemaking	6.0	29.8	36.6	27.6	
Being well liked (F)	Career	4.3	20.7	41.0	34.0	40.16**
	Homemaking	1.1	10.4	35.6	52.9	
Being a good wife (F)	Career	4.3	4.3	12.7	78.7	51.31**
	Homemaking	0.9	1.3	3.1	94.7	
Being a good parent (F)	Career	4.3	2.0	8.0	85.6	28.13**
	Homemaking	1.1	0.7	2.4	95.8	

* $p \leq .05$.
** $p \leq .01$.

By contrast, four out of six major predictions that the home-making-oriented sample would score higher on feminine interest and personality, achievement, competency, potential, life goals, and self-perception items, were rejected. In fact, on some of the feminine variables, the homemaking-oriented sample was significantly exceeded by the career-oriented group. These results indicate a significant tendency for the career-oriented women in this study to score higher not only on masculine characteristics but on many feminine characteristics as well.

This count of the number of masculine or feminine characteristics on which the criterion groups excelled justifies certain interpretations. For example, the career-oriented women in this sample reflect more masculine characteristics and behaviors than the homemaking-oriented women. However, the reverse interpretation, that the homemaking-oriented sample are more feminine, as measured by the variables in this study, than the career-oriented sample, is not justified by this simple count. Do the results of this study, therefore, appear to support only the masculine dimension as a differentiating one? Are the two groups equally as "feminine"?

Examination of the feminine scales and items on which the career-oriented sample scored higher or gave more frequently high ratings reveals that 7 out of 10 are related to competencies, potentials, and achievements in the performing arts. Of the eight potential, competency, and achievement scales classified as feminine, the career-oriented sample obtained significantly higher mean scores on five scales: Arts Competency, Musical Potential, Dramatic Arts Potential and Achievement, and Literary Achievement. And on two of the feminine self-perception items, Artistic and Writing Abilities, more of the career sample gave high self-ratings more frequently than the homemaking-oriented sample.

Inspection of the feminine scales and items on which the homemaking-oriented sample scored higher, or more frequently gave high ratings to, shows that seven out of eight are personality and social characteristics. They scored higher than the career group on the Social and Self-Control scales of the Vocational Preference Inventory (VPI) and lower on the masculinity VPI scale. Further, they gave high ratings more frequently to items concerning being well liked, being sociable, and being good wives and parents. The results of this study suggest then that, with the measures used, the career-oriented sample has higher masculine personality and ability characteristics and higher feminine ability characteristics compared to homemaking-oriented women, while the homemaking-oriented sample has higher feminine personality and social-interest characteristics.

Since this is a rather narrow comparison, the career and homemaking groups were compared with college males and females in general. The masculine-feminine concept can be extended if, on masculine variables, the following descending trend of scores is observed among four groups: college males, career-oriented women, college females, and homemaking-oriented women. Responses made by the career- and homemaking-oriented samples were compared with those made by the parent ACT sample of 6,132 female freshmen, and 6,289 male freshmen. Since the career and homemaking groups were a part of the college female sample, and thus contraindicating statistical tests, observation of the data was employed in this by-product phase of the study (see Footnote 1).

When the four groups were compared on the nine interest and personality, potential, competency, and achievement scales classified as masculine, the descending pattern was evidenced on six scales — Realistic, Masculinity, Leadership and Scientific Potential, and Scientific and Technical Competency. And on two other scales, the Intellectual VPI and Science Achievement scales — the career group scored higher than college males themselves. Similarly, when the self-ratings of the four groups were compared on masculine self-perceptions, the data revealed three important observations. First, on all 10 personality items, the career-oriented sample chose "above average" and "top 10%" ratings relatively more frequently than both the college female and the homemaking-oriented samples. Second, the self-ratings given by the career-oriented sample were remarkably more similar to those of college males than they were to those of college females. In fact, on half of the items (i.e., the personality and ability characteristics, Drive to Achieve, Independence, Perseverance, Intellectual Self-Confidence, and Research Ability), the career-oriented sample gave high self-ratings more frequently than college males. Third, the ratings given by the homemaking-oriented sample to the masculine self-perception items are strikingly similar to those of the college female sample. (Further comparison of importance ratings given by the four groups to achieving masculine life-goal items supports the same three observations.)

These data demonstrate not only the applicability of the masculine-feminine concept to career-oriented and homemaking-oriented women in this sample but the validity of applying these constructs to the general college population. The career-oriented woman studied is masculine on some characteristics, since she resembles the college male, and the homemaking-oriented woman is feminine, since she resembles more closely the college female on certain masculine characteristics. It is reasonable to conclude from this study that the career-oriented freshman woman deviates from the traditional feminine role and has redefined her role to include behaviors appropriate to both sexes. The homemaking-oriented freshman woman, by contrast, appears to adhere closely to the traditional feminine role.

Counselors and researchers might examine developmental correlates of masculinity-femininity between career- and home-making-oriented women. Attitudes toward sex roles as learned in the home, school, and community seems a fruitful avenue. Similarly, a semantic search should be made for words other than masculine or feminine because of the stereotyped negative emotions attached to these concepts, which should be viewed in a more objective manner.

NOTES

1. Tables A and B, presenting typescript with variables marked, and Tables C, D, and E, presenting separate factor matrices have been deposited with the American Documentation Institute. Order Document No. 10056 from ADI Auxiliary Publications Project, Photoduplication Service, Library of Congress, Washington, D.C. 20540. Remit in advance $1.25 for microfilm, or $1.25 for photocopies, and make checks payable to: Chief, Photoduplication Service, Library of Congress.

REFERENCES

Abe, C., Holland, J. L., Lutz, S., & Richards, J. M., *A description of American college freshmen.* Iowa City. American College Testing Program, 1965.

Allport, G. W., Vernon, P.E., & Lindzey, G., *A study of values.* Boston: Houghton Mifflin, 1960.

Berry J., Life plans of college women. *Journal of the National Association of Women Deans and Counselors,* 1955, 18, 76-80.

Empey, L. T., Role expectations of young women regarding marriage and a career. *Marriage and Family Living,* 1958, 20, 152-155.

Hoyt, D., & Kennedy, C., Interest and personality correlates of career-motivated and homemaking-motivated college women. *Journal of Counseling Psychology,* 1958, 5, 44-49.

Strong, E. K., Jr., *Vocational interests of men and women.* Stanford, Calif.: Stanford University Press, 1943.

Terman, L. M., & Miles, C. C., *Sex and personality.* New York: McGraw Hill, 1963.

Tyler, L.E., *The psychology of human differences.* New York: Appleton-Century, 1947.

Vetter, L., & Lewis, E. C., Some correlates of homemaking vs. career preference among college home economics students. *Personnel and Guidance Journal,* 1964, 42, 593-598.

Wagman, M., Interests and values of career and homemaking oriented women. *Personnel and Guidance Journal,* 1965, 44, 794-801

White, B., The relationship of self-concept and parental identification to women's vocational interests. Unpublished doctoral dissertation, University of California, 1957.

Zissis, C., The relationship of selected variables to the career-marriage plans of university freshman women. Unpublished doctoral dissertation, University of Michigan, 1962.

eleven

Are Women Prejudiced Against Women?

PHILIP GOLDBERG

"Woman," advised Aristotle, "may be said to be an inferior man."

Because he was a man, Aristotle was probably biased. But what do women themselves think? Do they, consciously or unconsciously, consider their own sex inferior? And if so, does this belief prejudice them against other women — that is, make them view women, simply because they *are* women, as less competent than men?

According to a study conducted by myself and my associates, the answer to both questions is Yes. Women *do* consider their own sex inferior, And even when the facts give no support to this belief, they will persist in downgrading the competence — in particular, the intellectual and professional competence — of their fellow females.

Over the years, psychologists and psychiatrists have shown that both sexes consistently value men more highly than women. Characteristics considered male are usually praised; those considered female are usually criticized. In 1957 A. C. Sheriffs and J. P. McKee noted that "women are regarded as guilty of snobbery and irrational and unpleasant emotionality." Consistent with this report, E. G. French and G. S. Lesser found in 1964 that "women who value intellectual attainment feel they must reject the woman's role" — intellectual accomplishment apparently being considered, even among intellectual women, a masculine preserve. In addition, ardent feminists like Simone de Beauvoir and Betty Friedan believe that men, in important ways, are superior to women.

From TRANS-action, Vol. 5, No. 5 (1968), pp. 28-30. Reprinted by permission of TRANS-action.

Now, is this belief simply prejudice, or are the characteristics and achievements of women really inferior to those of men? In answering this question, we need to draw some careful distinctions.

Different or Inferior?

Most important, we need to recognize that there are two distinct dimensions to the issue of sex differences. The first question is whether sex differences exist at all, apart from the obvious physical ones. The answer to this question seems to be a unanimous Yes — men, women, and social scientists agree that, psychologically and emotionally as well as physically, women *are* different from men.

But is being different the same as being inferior? It is quite possible to perceive a difference accurately but to value it inaccurately. Do women automatically view their differences from men as *deficiencies*? The evidence is that they do, and that this value judgment opens the door to anti-female prejudice. For if someone (male or female) concludes that women are inferior, his perceptions of women — their personalities, behavior, abilities, and accomplishments — will tend to be colored by his low expectations of women.

As Gordon W. Allport has pointed out in *The Nature of Prejudice*, whatever the facts about sex differences, anti-feminism — like any other prejudice — *distorts perception and experience.* What defines anti-feminism is not so much believing that women are inferior, as allowing that belief to distort one's perceptions of women. More generally, it is not the partiality itself, but the distortion born of that partiality, that defines prejudice.

Thus, an anti-Semite watching a Jew may see devious or sneaky behavior. But, in a Christian, he would regard such behavior only as quiet, reserved, or perhaps even shy. Prejudice is self-sustaining: It continually distorts the "evidence" on which the prejudiced person claims to base his beliefs. Allport makes it clear that anti-feminism, like anti-Semitism or any other prejudice, consistently twists the "evidence" of experience. We see not what is there, but what we *expect* to see.

The purpose of our study was to investigate whether there is real prejudice by women against women — whether perception itself is distorted unfavorably. Specifically, will women evaluate a professional article with a jaundiced eye when they think it is the work of a woman, but praise the same article when they think its author is a man? Our hypotheses were:

■ Even when the work is identical, women value the professional work of men more highly than that of women.

■ But when the professional field happens to be one traditionally reserved for women (nursing, dietetics), this tendency will be reversed, or at least greatly diminished.

Some 140 college girls, selected at random, were our subjects. One hundred were used for the preliminary work; 40 participated in the experiment proper.

To test the second hypothesis, we gave the 100 girls a list of 50 occupations and asked them to rate "the degree to which you associate the field with men or with women." We found that law and city planning were fields strongly associated with men, elementary-school teaching and dietetics were fields strongly associated with women, and two fields — linguistics and art history — were chosen as neutrals, not strongly associated with either sex.

Now we were ready for the main experiment. From the professional literature of each of these six fields, we took one article. The articles were edited and abridged to about 1500 words, then combined into two equal sets of booklets. The crucial manipulation had to do with the authors' names — the same article bore a male name in one set of booklets, a female name in the other set. An example: If, in set one, the first article bore the name John T. McKay, in set two the same article would appear under the name Joan T. McKay. Each booklet contained three articles by "men" and three articles by "women."

The girls, seated together in a large lecture hall, were told to read the articles in their booklets and given these instructions: "In this booklet you will find excerpts of six articles, written by six different authors in six different professional fields. At the end of each article you will find several questions. . . . You are not presumed to be sophisticated or knowledgeable in all the fields. We are interested in the ability of college students to make critical evaluations. . . ."

Note that no mention at all was made of the authors' sexes. That information was contained — apparently only by coincidence — in the authors' names. The girls could not know, therefore, what we were really looking for.

At the end of each article were nine questions asking the girls

to rate the articles for value, persuasiveness, and profundity —
and to rate the authors for writing style, professional competence, professional status, and ability to sway the reader. On
each item, the girls gave a rating of from 1 (highly favorable) to
5 (highly unfavorable).

Results

Generally, the results were in line with our expectations —
but not completely. In analyzing these results, we used three
different methods: We compared the amount of anti-female bias
in the different occupational fields (would men be rated as better city planners, but women as better dieticians?); we compared
the amount of bias shown on the nine questions that followed
each article (would men be rated as more competent, but women
as more persuasive?); and we ran an overall comparison, including both fields and rating questions.

Starting with the analysis of bias by occupational field, we
immediately ran into a major surprise.(See box below).That there
is a general bias by women against women, and that it is strong-
est in traditionally masculine fields, was clearly borne out. But

---

Law: A Strong Masculine Preserve

These are the total scores the college girls gave to the six
pairs of articles they read. The lowest possible score—9—
would be the most favorable; the highest possible score—
54—the most critical. While male authors received more
favorable ratings in all occupational fields, the differences
were statistically significant only in city planning, linguistics, and—especially—law.

Field of Article	Mean	
	Male	Female
Art History	23.35	23.10
Dietetics	22.05	23.45
Education	20.20	21.75
City Planning	23.10	27.30
Linguistics	26.95	30.70
Law	21.20	25.60

in other fields the situation seemed rather confused. We had expected the anti-female trend to be reversed in traditionally feminine fields. But it appears that, even here, women consider themselves inferior to men. Women seem to think that men are better at *everything* — including elementary-school teaching and dietetics!

Scrutiny of the nine rating questions yielded similar results. On all nine questions, regardless of the author's occupational field, the girls consistently found an article more valuable — and its author more competent — when the article bore a male name. Though the articles themselves were exactly the same, the girls felt that those written by the John T. McKays were definitely more impressive, and reflected more glory on their authors, than did the mediocre offerings of the Joan T. McKays. Perhaps because the world has accepted female authors for a long time, the girls were willing to concede that the female professionals' writing styles were not *far* inferior to those of the men. But such a concession to female competence was rare indeed.

Statistical analysis confirms these impressions and makes them more definite. With a total of six articles, and with nine questions after each one, there were 54 points at which comparisons could be drawn between the male authors and the female authors. Out of these 54 comparisons, three were tied, seven favored the female authors — and the number favoring the male authors was 44!

Clearly, there is a tendency among women to downgrade the work of professionals of their own sex. But the hypothesis that this tendency would decrease as the "femaleness" of the professional field increased was not supported. Even in traditionally female fields, anti-feminism holds sway.

Since the articles supposedly written by men were exactly the same as those supposedly written by women, the perception that the men's articles were superior was obviously a distortion. For reasons of their own, the female subjects were sensitive to the sex of the author, and this apparently irrelevant information biased their judgments. Both the distortion and the sensitivity that precedes it are characteristic of prejudice. Women — at least these young college women — are prejudiced against female professionals and, regardless of the actual accomplishments of these professionals, will firmly refuse to recognize them as the equals of their male colleagues.

Is the intellectual double-standard really dead? Not at all — and if the college girls in this study are typical of the educated and presumably progressive segments of the population, it may not even be dying. Whatever lip service these girls pay to modern ideas of equality between men and women, their beliefs are staunchly traditional. Their real coach in the battle of the sexes is not Simone de Beauvoir or Bety Friedan. Their coach is Aristotle.

twelve

Occupational Aspects of Social Work

REBA M. BUCKLEW and VERNON J. PARENTON

This study in the sociology of professions is concerned with occupational ideologies in the field of social work. The importance of occupations as a means of social classification and differentiation has been recognized for some time by sociologists. Social work is one of the twentieth century occupations which is emerging as a profession. The use of the term emerging is an indication that social work is not a fully-matured profession but one experiencing the gradual and painful process of professionalization. Public attitudes toward the profession of social work cover a wide range, and to a considerable degree they reflect the self-image and stereotypes of the profession. An examination of the papers presented before the National Conference of Social Work and social work literature in general demonstrates that social workers hold many images of their roles, and these images are sometimes even contradictory.[1] It is not surprising that the public image of the social work profession is confused and clouded when social workers themselves cannot clearly define their own area of competence and feel threatened by a status dilemma. This social work image is further complicated by the conflict in norms and ideologies of its own subculture and those of the general culture. The concept of image is simply a picture which the public holds of social workers as people and of social work as a profession. At this time, social work's responsibility for shaping public attitudes and public images of the profession is highly controversial.

From SOCIAL FORCES, Vol. 41, No. 1 (1962), pp. 39-43. Reprinted by permission of the University of North Carolina Press.

This paper is primarily interested in certain occupational aspects which influence the self-image of social work as a profession. The comparative analysis is based upon information obtained from social workers and university students by means of a questionnaire. The responses of the social workers represent a section of a more extended questionnaire concerning the professional aspects of social work, and were obtained in 1959 from two groups of social workers in a North Texas city. The same questions were given to a group of university students enrolled in sociology classes at three North Texas universities and colleges in the summer of 1960.

In the past social work has been dominated generally by women and while young as a profession (in comparison to the traditional professions), social workers have never been considered as a young age group. The social workers included in this study bear out the two assumptions stated above. Of the 132 social workers participating in the study, only 30 or 23 percent were men and 102 or 77 percent were women. The median age of the entire group was 48 years. Not only were there more women in the field, but the women were older in general. The age and sex characteristics of the social workers in this sample population fully support the association made by the general public of social work with women's occupations.

Of the 226 students responding to the questionnaire, 49 or 22 percent were male students and 177 or 78 percent were female. The median age was 21 years even though there was an age range from 17 to 55 years in the student group. The students were residents of 21 states and three foreign countries. However, 174 or 77 percent were from Texas.

This paper is limited to the consideration of three aspects of an occupation: (1) the type of occupation from the standpoint of authority and sanction, (2) the prestige of social work as a profession, and (3) work satisfactions derived from social work as a profession.

Social Work: A Helping Profession

A profession is endowed with authority because of the competence and skill it has developed through education in the systematic theory of the profession. The professional possesses types of knowledge and techniques that accentuate the comparative lack of such on the part of the layman. Professional authority expresses itself in the client-professional relationship and establishes a monopoly granted by the community.[2] The client's subordination to professional authority invests the worker with a kind of monopoly of judgment, and the client derives a sense of security from the assumption of authority.

Social work is classified as one of the helping professions, and for social workers, one might assume that placing one's self in a position to help others would be an important source of satisfaction and perceived as highly valued. One author has referred to social work as belonging to the *helping* and *healing* professions.[3] Social workers do feel that social work as a profession is service-oriented and the specific aspect of man with which social work deals is man in his interdependence with his human and social environment. Increasingly social work recognizes that since it deals directly with but one part of the whole it must collaborate with other competencies if its service is to be effective and productive. Since there are other helping professions, the question here is, how does social work rank in comparison to other helping professions? The respondents, both social workers and students, were asked to rank ten professions and/or service-oriented occupations pertaining to their respective abilities to help others. (See Table 1.)

Table 1 / Professions and Occupations Ranked According to Helping Power by Social Workers and Students 1959-1960

Occupation	N = 132 Social Workers		N = 236 Students	
	Mean Rank	Rank	Mean Rank	Rank
Medicine	2.3	1	2.3	1
Social Work	3.6	2	4.3	3
Ministry	3.7	3	3.5	2
Teaching	4.2	4	4.9	4
Psychoanalysis	5.0	5	5.2	5
Law	5.8	6	6.4	7
Nursing	6.3	7	5.3	6
Occupational Therapy	7.5	8	7.0	8
Dentistry	7.6	9	7.1	9
Public Relations	8.8	10	8.2	10

The ten professions and occupations were medicine, ministry, teaching, social work, law, nursing, occupational therapy, dentistry, psychoanalysis, and public relations. Medicine, one of the traditional professions, ranked first with both social workers and students while public relations was tenth in both groups. The extent of agreement in ranking these ten service-oriented professions is worth some consideration. Both social workers and students agreed upon the rank order of all the professions with the exception of social work and ministry. The social workers placed their own field of service second in power to help people while the students moved social work to third place giving the ministry second place in this hierarchy. The other seven occupations ranked as follows: teaching, psychoanalysis, law, nursing, occupational therapy, dentistry, and public relations. Although both groups placed social work high in the helping professions, students showed less agreement in this ranking than did social workers. The standard deviation of the students' ranking of social work was 2.4, but the social workers' standard deviation was 1.7.

Since this listing was presented to the participants, the authors recognized that the respondents were limited to the ten occupations listed for them. Therefore, two other questions were included in the questionnaire following the one discussed above. These two categories were designed to allow the respondent to name three occupations which he felt were similar to social work and three which were dissimilar. A few interesting observations can be drawn from this type of response in contrast to the perceived relative ranking of the ten helping professions listed. Social workers granted that medicine was endowed with the greatest power to help people, but it was not considered to be the most similar profession to social work. Responses to this question showed that medicine came third and was in the same position as counseling when it was considered from the standpoint of similarity to social work. Students also placed medicine in third place in their response to this question. Both social workers and students felt that the ministry was most similar to social work and that teaching was second in order. There is no doubt that both social workers and students believe that the ministry, teaching and medicine are the professions most similar to social work. Those who define social work as both therapeutic and educational in the services rendered might find comfort in this response. The other seven professions most similar to social work listed by social workers were: counseling, psychiatry, psychology, nursing, psychoanalysis, occupational therapy, and law. Only three students made the association of sociology with social work. Associations with charitable connotations were rescue mission, charity, volunteer work, and missionary societies.

Social workers and students appear to be more agreed on the professions which they consider similar to social work than on the occupations which are dissimilar. The occupations considered most dissimilar by social workers were engineering, salesmanship, farming, and the sciences. The students regarded secretarial and clerical positions, carpentry, salesmanship, and law as occupations most unlike social work.

It is apparent that social workers tend to identify their work situation in terms of service, which is in agreement with the first finding, that social work provides them with the power to help others. This same attitude is reflected by the evaluation of college and university students.

Occupational Prestige of Social Work

Occupational prestige is a specific kind of prestige indicating the rank in the hierarchy of invidious value which any occupation holds relative to other occupations. Prestige, in other words, is the enviable value attached to a status or office independently of who occupies it. However, the prestige of the occupation reflects on the prestige of the person identified with the occupational title. The question of the prestige of social work is a matter of importance to the social worker, to the social work client, and the social work profession. Occupational prestige is of importance to the profession of social work because of its consequences for recruitment. One researcher stated that on the basis of available research it would appear that, in the image of the public, social work is a minor, if not a marginal profession.[4]

This study employed a ranking device which has been used by others to determine relative prestige. Respondents were asked to number a group of occupations in the order of their social standing and prestige. Thirteen occupations were listed including professions, business, and skilled work.

All of the traditional professionals in the group were assigned greater prestige than the social worker. These include the doctor, the highest on the list; the minister, third; the lawyer, fourth;

and the teacher, sixth. The banker was second, and the social workers agreed that the salesman, the plant foreman, the secretary, the clerical worker, and the carpenter all came at the lower end of the scale and in that order. Social workers ranked themselves as eighth on the scale of 13 occupations. Students agreed in ranking social work as eighth with very few differences in the relative prestige of the other 12 occupations. (See Table 2).

Table 2 / Ranking of Occupational Prestige by Social Workers and Students 1959-1960

Occupation	N = 132 Social Workers		N = 236 Students	
	Mean Rank	Rank	Mean Rank	Rank
Doctor	1.6	1	1.6	1
Banker	3.1	2	3.8	4
Minister	3.4	3	3.4	3
Lawyer	3.8	4	3.1	2
Plant Executive	4.8	5	4.9	5
Teacher	6.1	6	6.2	6
Store Owner	6.4	7	6.8	7
Social Worker	7.1	8	7.8	8
Salesman	9.3	9	11.3	12
Plant Foreman	9.4	10	9.5	9
Secretary	10.2	11	9.8	10
Clerical Worker	11.5	12	10.8	11
Carpenter	11.8	13	12.6	13

Social workers and students ranked the doctor as having highest prestige. According to both social workers and students, the carpenter was least prestigeful, and secretarial and clerical workers were not much above the carpenter. The students thought the lawyer, whom they ranked second, was more prestigeful than the banker who was fourth. Social workers reversed this order. The important thing is that the position of social work prestige is the same for students and social workers, and the prestige of social work based upon the social workers' self-ranking and the evaluation of students is middle range in the general occupational scene and low in the professions.

The respondents in this study showed more variation in the ranking of social work than in most of the other occupations. Individual variations ranged all the way from one to 13 with a standard deviation of 2.0 for social worker's own self-ranking, which was ninth in order of the deviation scores. The standard deviation of students' ranking of social work was 2.2 and the greatest of all 13 occupations. The implication from these findings indicates that social work prestige is less positioned than most of the professions included in this study. Students are less agreed upon this prestige status than social workers.

Work Satisfactions Derived From Social Work

It has been fairly well established that social work is a service-oriented profession, but both the self-image and public image of the profession indicate that social work ranks low in prestige among the professions and middle range in the general occupational hierarchy. Are there some satisfactions in the practice of social work which compensate for the imbalance of prestige factors discussed above? The respondents were asked the simple question: What do you consider the greatest satisfactions derived from social work? They were directed to number the 11 items suggested on the questionnaire in the order of importance as work satisfactions offered by social work. Both social workers and students agreed that services to troubled people ranked first. (See Table 3). This was then the greatest satisfaction of an

Table 3 / Listing of Satisfactions Derived from Social Work in Order of Preference by Social Workers and Students

Satisfaction	N = 132 Social Workers		N = 236 Students	
	Mean Rank	Rank	Mean Rank	Rank
Services to Troubled People	2.8	1	2.1	1
Prevention of Individual and Social Breakdown	2.9	2	2.9	2
Contact with Clients	4.2	3	5.3	6
Personal Growth as an Outgrowth of Development in the Field	4.4	4	4.7	4
Contributions to Society	4.5	5	3.1	3
Continuing Progress of the Profession	5.4	6	5.2	5
Association with Colleagues	6.2	7	6.9	7
Training and Supervising	6.6	8	7.3	8
Security in Employment	8.0	9	8.5	9
Financial Returns	8.5	10	9.4	10
Physical Setting	9.5	11	9.5	11

occupational group with only a medium range prestige. The ideal of service has long been associated with the professions, and even Flexner as early as 1915 agreed that social work qualified at least on this criterion of professionalism.[5] Social work had its beginnings in the concern for troubled persons, and it has retained principles and practices firmly rooted in humanitarianism. The self-image and public image (represented here by the students) were closely paralleled on the concept of social work as a service to troubled people. This was indicated by mean, rank, and standard deviation scores on this item.

The prevention of individual and social breakdown was the second greatest satisfaction received by social workers in their practice. Students agreed with this ranking. Work satisfactions upon which the two groups did not agree were contact with clients, which was third with social workers and sixth with students; contributions to society, which was fifth with social workers and third with students; continuing progress of the profession, which was sixth with social workers and fifth with students. There was agreement between both social workers and students on the factors which gave the least satisfaction. Association with colleagues, training and supervising workers, financial returns, and physical setting were the lower levels of work satisfactions.

The standard deviation of ranking of the satisfactions by social workers indicated that there was closer agreement on such items as physical setting, service to troubled people, and prevention of individual and social breakdown. The students displayed less variation in service to troubled people, physical setting, and contribution to society. One interesting observation was that students were more in agreement on some items of work satisfaction than the social workers.

In general, social workers felt that the rewards for services to troubled people and prevention of social breakdown were not well-balanced with security in employment, financial returns and physical setting for work. The students reflected the same general picture of social work satisfactions. Social workers are then people-oriented in their practice.

Summary — Conclusions

A primary factor in any profession is its concept of itself — the image it hopes to project to its members, to those it hopes to recruit as future practitioners, and to the community. This study has been an attempt to analyze some aspects of this image and was based upon the empirical data furnished by social workers and university students. The public image of the student group is of importance to social work from the standpoint of recruitment. The self image and public image of the respondents in this study reveal that both groups have a healthy and lofty respect for social work as a helping profession. Social workers ranked themselves second among the helping professions; students ranked social work third. This segment of the image of the profession does not seem to be in agreement with the relative prestige of social work in the general occupational scene. Social work was ranked eighth in a group of 13 occupations. Both social workers and students seemed more agreed upon the professions which are similar to social work than those which are dissimilar. The ministry, medicine, and teaching are occupational groupings most similar to social work. A long list of occupations was considered dissimilar, but those listed with the greatest frequency were engineering, salesmanship, clerical, farming, carpentry, dentistry, and science.

The satisfactions offered by the practice of social work indicated that social workers are people-oriented rather than money-oriented in their service.

The elements of the self-image of social work considered in this paper appear to have been transmitted to the college students who represent a most fertile field of recruitment for social workers. If this "status dilemma" in which social work is now trapped is to ever be improved, social workers must present to the public a field of service based upon professional competence and supported by a confident self-image.

NOTES

1. Melvin A. Glasser, "Public Attitudes Toward the Profession: What Shall They Be?" *NASW News* (August 1958), p. 7.

2. Ernest Greenwood, "Attributes of a Profession," *Social Work,* II (July 1957), pp. 45-55.

3. Swithun Bowers, "Social Work as a Helping and Healing Profession." *Social Work,* II (January 1957), p. 57-62.

4. Alfred Kadushin, "Prestige and Social Work — Facts and Factors" *Social Work,* III (April 1958), pp. 37-41.

5. Abraham Flexner, "Is Social Work a Profession?", *Proceedings of the National Conference of Charities and Correction* (Chicago: University of Chicago Press, 1915), pp. 578-581.

thirteen

Social Influence and the Social-Psychological Function of Deference: A Study of Psychiatric Nursing*

WILLIAM A. RUSHING

In recent years sociologists and social psychologists have shown an active interest in the phenomena of influence attempts[1] and deference behavior.[2] Researchers and writers interested in each of these phenomena, however, have not turned their attention to the connection between the two — that is, deference as social influence. The first objective of this paper will be to redress this omission by pointing out, with empirical illustrations, how deference behavior may be viewed as an influence attempt.

A second objective is to conceptualize these two phenomena — influence attempts and deference behavior — within the context of an institutionalized or normative social order. Most studies of influence attempts have been conducted in the laboratory and *ad hoc* experimental groups — groups lacking in a tradition of established social norms and ties and, therefore, lacking in a stable, crystallized group structure.[3] Consequently, the relationship of influence attempts to the normative social structure is not clear. On the other hand, there is the tendency to assume that deference behavior *is* institutional behavior. That is to say, an individual is deferential toward another because of the status or role relationships between him and another actor; deference behavior tends to be viewed as a component of one's social role and the result of social norms which define the role.[4] No doubt this normative assumption is a valid one in many instances. However, data will be presented in this

From SOCIAL FORCES, Vol. 41, No. 2 (1962), pp. 142-148. Reprinted by permission of The University of North Carolina Press. (A version of this paper was read at the twenty-fifth annual meeting of the Southern Sociological Society, Louisville, Kentucky, April 13, 1962.)

paper which reveal that under at least some circumstances deference behavior is more accurately described in terms other than institutionalized (role) behavior. Nevertheless, deference behavior, like all social behavior, takes place only within a normative context, the description of which is necessary if social behavior is to be understood. The conceptualization of deference behavior in terms of the functions it performs for the psychiatric nurse in her relationship with the psychiatrist will uncover certain empirical linkages between deference behavior as an influence attempt and the normative order.

In achieving these two objectives I will present empirical illustrations of the concept of power strategy and then indicate the function these behaviors perform for the psychiatric nurse in her relationship with her superior, the psychiatrist.

Data are based on interviews with 16 psychiatric nurses who work on the inpatient service of a teaching mental institution, where strong emphasis is placed on the nurse-patient relationship as an important aspect of the patient's therapeutic milieu.[5]

Normative Components of the Nurse Role

The performance of the psychiatric nurse role involves two moral principles or commitments. (1) The nurse, like the doctor, is morally obligated to help the patient recover from his illness. The present group of nurses indicate their acceptance ("internalization") of this commitment in two different ways. First, 14 of 15 nurses state that they are trying to help the patient "get well," to "return to normal," to "return to society," or to "get back on their feet and be socially accepted again."[6] This moral commitment is also revealed by the responses nurses give to the question of how they feel about a drug research project. Doctors are supposed to place all patients requiring day-time sedation on a project where they will receive one of three drugs or an inert placebo. The project is so designed that no one, including the patient's doctor, knows what drug the patient is receiving, or if indeed he is receiving a drug at all. (Such procedure is necessary to control for possible contaminating effects due to patients responding in terms of their knowledge of the drug's alleged effects, and effects due to ward personnel interacting with patients in terms of their expectations of the drug's effects.) Of 16 nurses 13 express disapproval of placing patients on this project. Reasons given for this objection are: the patient may be given a placebo which will not help him; the drugs are administered by random placement and not according to the patient's needs; and the project drugs are slow acting, thus leading to unnecessary expense to the patient. The nurse's moral obligation to the patient rather than to the objective of scientific research is aptly summed up by the following nurse:

> It's the drug that happens to come up that the patient gets. I disagree very strongly with this. If it's not helping the patient, we have no right to keep him on it. It's okay for people wanting to know about drugs — they want to know about them and that's all right, but what about the patient? *It's the patient's welfare that is utmost, not knowing about some drug.*[7]

(2) Although all nurses were not asked specific questions regarding the doctor's authority over them, it was assumed that the nurse is the subordinate in the doctor-nurse relationship: she is subordinate to the doctor relative to the responsibility for the patient and the doctor's authority (i.e., she carries out the doctor's "orders"). This assumption is consistent with findings regarding the doctor-nurse relationship in other mental hospital settings, as well as previous studies conducted in the present setting.[8] Therefore, the nurse's function may be described as the responsibility to carry out the doctor's orders. A head nurse expresses this the following way:

> As I see it, the function of the psychiatric nurse, the major function, is to carry out the doctor's care and treatment plan. The doctor is head of the team and it is the nurse's responsibility to carry out his treatment plan . . . She is the go-between the doctor and the patient. She relates to the patient so as to support him when he needs it and so on. [But] she relates to him in terms of the doctor's care plan.

These two normative components of the nurse's role are clear enough. The interesting question arises, what does the nurse do when these two principles are in conflict? For example, what does she do when she thinks the orders prescribed by the doctor are unsuitable for meeting the patient's therapeutic needs. Such situations are especially likely in a hospital setting which emphasizes the nurse-patient relationship as an adjunct to therapy because the nurse is with the patient eight hours of the day while the doctor is with him only during the therapeutic hour. Also, most doctors on the inpatient service of this hospital are first-year residents and, therefore, are lacking in psychiatric experience.[9] For these reasons the nurse may come to think she knows more than the doctor about the proper treatment procedure for particular patients.

The existence of a conflict between these two moral commitments — responsibility for the patient and his welfare and responsibility to carry out the doctor's order — can be seen from the fact that 15 of 16 nurses replied in the affirmative when asked if doctors ever gave them an order which they thought was contrary to the patient's welfare. Data reveal two types of reactions to this conflict: conforming to the doctor's authority and attempts to influence the doctor's treatment decision.

Four nurses report that they usually continue to carry out the order as stated by the doctor. When questioned why they did this although they felt the order was an incorrect one, the general response was that it was the doctor's decision to make and the nurse's responsibility was to carry out his decision. For example, one states, "If he gives an order that I disagree with, I go along with it because that's supposed to be his decision. The nurse is supposed to carry out his decision." Another says, "It's sort of an unwritten law . . . The nurse accepts it that way. She takes her orders from the doctor and carries them out. It may be that I do not agree with him, but it's his decision and, so, I go on and carry it out the way he thinks it should be." Certainly these repsonses are explicit manifestations of the internalization of the doctor-nurse authority relationship which implies that the doctor possesses superior knowledge and competence to that of the nurse.

Power Strategies

More interesting, for purposes of this paper, are the 11 nurses who report that, rather than conforming to the doctor's orders, they try to *influence* the doctor to modify or change his order. Three different types of influence attempts were reported.

Influence through the Doctor's Superior. Nine nurses report that they go to the chief resident or ward chief and let them take the matter up with the resident in an effort to elicit a change in the treatment plan.

Reporting Observations that are Contrary to the Doctor's Order. Because nurses are with the patients on the ward eight hours a day, they have an opportunity to observe many aspects of the patient's behavior. Consequently, in an attempt to get the doctor to change his treatment decision, eight nurses confront him with aspects of the patient's behavior that suggest some other treatment plan is indicated. For example:

> I will tell him things about the patient that are contrary to the order given. I just let him know about these things in hopes that he will change the order. I will merely tell him things about the patient that are contrary to the order.

Asking Questions. Finally, four nurses state they ask the doctor questions about the order indicating they do not understand it.

> I will ask if this was intended in the order or should it be something else. Or I might say that I thought it would be thus-and-so. If he puts something in the order that I disagree with, I will sometimes say, "I've never seen it like this before." Work around it this way . . . without coming right out and telling him. You have to do it this way — you have to be more tactful. I can't come right out and tell him what I think the order should be.

A pertinent question is: are these three influence attempts conforming behavior or deviant behavior? To the extent that they are actions which call into question the legitimacy of the doctor's order they might be considered deviant actions. At the same time, however, they are carried out in the interest of the patient; in this sense they are actions which conform to one of the major normative principles of the nurse's role.

Correctly viewed, these actions are neither a form of conformity nor a form of deviancy. Rather, they are actions that are caused by conflict between two normative principles of the nurse's role: the patient's welfare and the doctor's authority. Both principles are components of the definition of the nurse role, but the influence attempts are *not* actions specified in that definition. The definition does not say that the nurse should try to influence the doctor's decision, nor how she should go about this when she does try. Therefore, they are not role behaviors.[10]

Greater understanding of these influence attempts can be obtained by viewing them as *power strategies:* behaviors designed to influence the behavior of another, but behaviors that are oriented *to*, rather than in conformity *with*, institutionalized normative orders.[11] The nurse's influence attempts are efforts to get the doctor to change his order; therefore, they are not in conformity *with* the legitimate order — the doctor's authority. This is not to say that they are expressions of disrespect for the doctor's authority and competence; the contrary is the case because they are *oriented* to his greater authority and competence.

An example will illuminate. A nurse thinks doctors often prescribe drugs when they are not indicated. She tries to influence doctors to revoke their decision by asking questions, e.g., "I would say that I *wonder* if this drug is helping the patient. I may think that the drug isn't helping the patient but I wouldn't tell him that." She does not tell the doctor what she thinks —

> Because I respect him. If I don't respect him as a person, I respect his title . . . because he's a doctor and I'm a nurse. (That) means that he's more educated and knows more and is more able to handle the situation than I, or at least he's supposed to.

We therefore have the situation in which the doctor is defined as possessing greater knowledge than the nurse, but where the nurse thinks she knows more about the needs of specific patients than the doctor. In her attempts to influence his decision, however, the nurse does not openly indicate that she *thinks* she knows more about the patient than the doctor. Clearly, the nurse's power strategies are types of deference behavior, if by deference we mean expression of "regard," "respect," and "appreciation" for another and his role responsibilities.[12] For example, a nurse who says: "I have to be careful. I can't let it look like I am trying to tell him what to do. I have to approach him in a manner so it looks like I am not telling him."

It is true that the influence attempts originate with the nurse thinking she is better informed than the doctor. At the same time they are expressions of respect and regard for the doctor's superiority and greater competence. In being "careful" the nurse orients her actions to the doctor's superior status. Such "careful" actions may also be viewed as "avoidance rituals"[13] — taking care not to infringe upon the duties and responsibilities of another role performer. It is important to keep in mind that although the nurse engages in the above described deference behaviors, she is doing so with the intention of influencing the doctor's treatment orders. Her power strategies then are influence at the price of deference: she attempts to exchange[14] her deference behavior for a change in the doctor's treatment plan.

Not only are these actions oriented to the normative authority structure, they are oriented to a power structure as well. To understand the nature of the doctor's power over the nurse, it is necessary to realize that the role of the psychiatric nurse involves an interpersonal relationship with patients.[15] Nevertheless her background and training may not have prepared her for this role. Her task is to meet the emotional needs of patients, but she has received little training in the skills necessary to recognize, identify, and meet these needs. Consequently, she must turn to the doctor for direction and guidance to determine how she shall "relate to" patients. Nurses are quite explicit in expressing their dependence on the doctor.[16] One states, for example:

> He's the one who has to tell us how to handle the patient. We don't want to overdo, or underdo, something with the patient, and we look to him for direction . . . Everything comes from him. He tells us how we should treat the patient. He's our guide, the one we look to in order to know whether what we are doing is right.

What the nurse does in her relationship with the patient is thus dependent on what the doctor instructs her to do. Accordingly, the doctor has a high degree of power over her.[17] It should be noted that directives and guidance are not given solely through the medium of written instruction. Verbal instructions are issued during team meetings and ward rounds,[18] and in response to questions nurses have throughout the day. Several nurses volunteer that instructions given through face-to-face contacts are more useful than written orders.[19] A head nurse says, for example, "there's not much in the form of written orders" since most directions come through face-to-face contact by "sitting down and talking to (the doctor), and in team meetings." Therefore, the nurse's interpersonal relationship with the patient is dependent on a face-to-face relationship with the doctor, a relationship in which the patient's illness and methods of treatment are discussed. With this in mind we can begin to understand the function performed by the nurses' deferential power strategies.

First, however, the distinction between the power and the authority of the doctor should be made explicit. Regarding power, the nurse is dependent on the directions and orders of the doctor — directions are needed to determine how she shall perform her interpersonal role with the patient. In reference to authority, the nurse is responsible for conforming to the doctor's directives and "orders." Otherwise stated, authority is a normative phenomenon; power is not. The nurse is ethically obligated to carry out the doctor's orders because of the nature of the general norms of medicine: the doctor is defined as the superior, and it is on the basis of his greater knowledge and competence that decisions should be made. On the other hand, the doctor has power over the nurse because of the nature of their work: with his superior knowledge and competence, the doctor is the source to whom the nurse must turn to determine how she shall relate to patients. In any concrete course of action (a particular nurse-patient relationship), the nurse does, of course, respond to both orders. The distinction is, then, an analytic one: it refers to different aspects or properties of the nurse's action in her relationship with the patient. Nevertheless, the distinction is crucial for understanding the function of the nurse's power strategies.

Function of Deference

Goffman has stated that deference behavior serves to confirm the conception of selves.[20] In a recent analysis, Coser observes that deference also functions to "maintain the relational system."[21] According to the latter formulation, the nurses' power strategies should function to maintain the nurse-doctor relationship. As I have indicated, the relational system between nurse and doctor is a continuous face-to-face one. The continuity of this relational system is made difficult if the nurse-doctor relationship is strained. A nurse says, for example:

> I think that there should be a good relationship between the nurse and the doctor because if there are hard feelings neither one will want to help each other with the patient ... You should be able to talk to him, (and) I think he should discuss with the nurse why he does something.

One method of creating strain (e.g., "hard feelings") in this relationship is for the nurse to try to invert the status differences (e.g., to question the doctor's superior knowledge and competence by questioning his order). In a previous study of the nurse-doctor relationship in this setting, it was found that doctors withdrew from their relationship with nurses when the latter questioned their orders.[22] This, however, deprives the nurse of something she *values* — a close relationship with the doctor. Consequently, by questioning the doctor's order the nurse runs the risk of incurring unpleasant *costs* — having to forego the value of doctor-nurse relationship.[23] Such costs are illustrated by two nurses who speak of the doctor putting the nurse in a "bad position" and making her "insecure": When he fails to instruct the nurses in how they should handle his patients, "We don't know if we are doing the right thing. We might even be doing something to hurt the patient. We don't know."

Therefore, to prevent this costly situation from occurring, the nurse must maintain her relationship with the doctor. Her strategies of deference are to be viewed in these terms. By refusing openly to question the doctor's orders she does not alienate him, thereby maintaining her relationship with him; the function of this is to prevent the cost of having to "relate to" patients without knowing what to do — that is, without sufficient direction from the doctor. Support for this inference is provided by comments from nurses regarding the use of each of the three previously described power strategies.[24]

One nurse goes to the ward chief rather than express her opinion to the doctor, so she will not "threaten" the doctor. If she openly questions his order, he is threatened and becomes angry. She also says that she must have "good interpersonal relationships" with the doctor so she can talk to him. If she "threatens" the doctor by questioning his order, her relationship with him is strained — "I can't talk to him." Consequently, "I go to the ward chief and tell him what the situation is," rather than openly questioning the doctor's order. Another states that she has openly questioned doctors about their orders, but that this "ruined" her relationship — a relationship in which she "would feel comfortable in talking to the doctor about the patient's problems, and he would feel the same way about talking to me; he would listen to me when I have something to say . . . Our relationship was ruined when I went directly to him." This nurse states that now she always goes to the ward chief and lets him handle the matter.

A nurse who reports that she confronts the doctor with observations that are contrary to the order he has given says she does so because, upon voicing her disagreement to the doctor in the past, "He would get angry and I would get hostile. The whole relationship would blow up — he would get so mad." Another reports the following as reasons for confronting the doctor with a report of the patient's behavior, rather than expressing her opinion to him.

> Well, I guess a nurse in talking to a doctor has to be a little more diplomatic . . . Our observations are important, but we can't tell the doctor what to do. We aren't doctors. They are the ones who are supposed to be right; but a lot of times they aren't. But when they are not right, we can't tell them. It's a matter of interpersonal relations . . . he's the doctor and it's his decision to make, not mine. When you tell him, then . . . He has to take the position that whether you like it or not, I am right. He can't let you tell him what to do. If you do, he has to put you in your place and then your interpersonal relationship with him is destroyed. I have to be careful not to do this. The nurse and the doctor have to have a good interpersonal relationship in order to work as a team.

Obviously, this nurse's power strategy is determined by the doctor's power over her, as well as by his normative authority.

Finally, a nurse who says that she is "insecure" when the doctor does not provide her with orders is quite explicit about the function of asking questions; it enables her to maintain her relationship with the doctor and so prevents her from incurring the cost of foregoing the value of the doctor's orders and directives. If she expressed her opinion rather than utilize this strategy,

> The doctor wouldn't like it and this would make me insecure. He would get mad and wouldn't discuss the patient with me at all then. It works out better if we just ask him; work around it this way. If I told him (what I think), it would make me feel insecure — I wouldn't be able to find out anything about the patient then.

Conclusion

The above data indicates that the concept of power strategy is a useful one for describing actions which are sociologically relevant. They are actions an actor performs in reference to another actor, but they do not fit the category of institutionalized role behavior. The concept also enables us to conceptualize noninstitutionalized behavior — influence attempts — in terms of the institutionalized order. Power strategies are not institutionalized in the sense that they are actions which are in conformity with the prescriptions of a social order; however, they cannot be understood unless seen in terms of the institutionalized order within which they are enacted — they are actions which are *oriented to* (rather than in *conformity with*) the legitimate (institutionalized) order.[25] For example, the nurse's deferential influence attempts are oriented to the legitimate order (doctor's authority): the nurse thinks she knows more than the doctor, but she is "careful" not to act as if she thinks she does. When these behaviors are considered *only* as actions which are oriented to a normative order — that is, only in terms of the property of deference involved, the important property of influence attempt is ignored. The nurse not only "respects" the doctor's authority, she also attempts to elicit a change in his order. Only when the doctor's power over the nurse is considered, and its analytic distinction from his authority made explicit, is the function of nurse's power strategies revealed. The conceptualization of power in terms of dependency and of authority in terms of the responsibility to comply with the orders of another allows us, in turn, to conceptualize influence attempts in terms of their relationship to the normative order.

NOTES

This paper reports on one phase of a broader study of the mental health professions. See William A. Rushing, "Professional Adaptive Problems on a Psychiatric Service," (unpublished dissertation, Department of Sociology and Anthropology, University of North Carolina, 1961). The author would like to express thanks to Harvey L. Smith, who directed the research, for his suggestions and guidance throughout the course of the study.

1. See, for example, Kurt Back, "Influence through Social Communication," *Journal of Abnormal and Social Psychology,* XLVI (1951), 2-23; Leon Festinger, *et al.,* "The Influence Process in the Presence of Extreme Deviates," *Human Relations,* V (1952), 327-46; and Stanley Schachter, "Deviation, Rejection and Communication," *Journal of Abnormal and Social Psychology,* XLVI (1951), 190-207. For reviews of recent research on influence, see George C. Homans, *Social Behavior: Its Elementary Forms* (New York: Harcourt, Brace and World, Inc., 1961), pp. 83-111 and James G. March, "An Introduction to the Theory and Measurement of Influence," *The American Political Science Review,* XLIX (1955), 439-51.

2. See Erving Goffman, "The Nature of Deference and Demeanor,"

The American Anthropologist, LVIII (1956), 473-502; see also, Rose Laub Coser, "Insulation from Observability and Types of Social Conformity," *American Sociological Review,* XXVI (1961), 28-39.

3. Homans, *op. cit.,* p. 84.

4. Goffman, for example, regards deference behavior as behavior guided by ceremonial *rules. Op. cit.*

5. Material for the present paper may be found in more extended form in Rushing, *op. cit.,* Chapter XII, "Psychiatric Nursing: Role Conflict and Maintaining Power Strategies," pp. 388-434.

6. These responses are replies to the question: "What specifically are you — as a psychiatric nurse — trying to accomplish in the performance of your nursing duties?" The fifteenth — who states that the objective of the nurse is "to carry out the doctor's care and treatment plan" — implies a similar objective since it is the doctor's ethical obligation to do what he can to facilitate the recovery of the patient. Although 16 nurses were interviewed, only 15 were asked the above question.

7. These data are based on the nurses' response to the question: "How do you feel about the drug project?" If the answer was not unambiguous, the respondent was asked, "Are you for it or against it?" Reasons for the nurse's position were probed in all cases.

8. See, for example, Ivan Belknap, *Human Problems of a State Mental Hospital* (New York: The Blakiston Division, McGraw-Hill Book Co., 1956); Robert G. Brown, "Problems of Social Organization of a New York Psychiatric Inpatient Service" (unpublished Ph.D. dissertation, Department of Sociology and Anthropology, University of North Carolina, 1960); William Caudill, *The Psychiatric Hospital as a Small Society* (Cambridge: Harvard University Press, 1958); and Dorothea Scott, "The Relation of the Uniform to the Professional Self-Image of the Psychiatric Nurse" (unpublished Master's thesis, Department of Sociology and Anthropology, University of North Carolina, 1960).

9. For a discussion of this problem, see Harvey L. Smith, "Professional Strains and the Hospital Context," in Milton Greenblatt, Daniel J. Levinson, and Richard H. Williams (eds.), *The Patient and the Mental Hospital* (Glencoe: The Free Press, 1957), pp. 3-9.

10. The author is aware of the lack of agreement among sociologists and social psychologists regarding the definition of the concept of role; see Neal Gross, S. Mason, and Alexander W. McEachern, *Explorations in Role Analysis* (New York: John Wiley and Sons, Inc., 1958), pp. 11-18. The concept is used in this paper to refer to behaviors that are the enactment of positions or statuses in a social structure, or to the "dynamic aspect of status." See Ralph Linton, *The Study of Man* (New York: D. Appleton-Century Company, 1936), p. 114. Linton's formulation — as well as the formulations of Parsons,

Merton, and Kingsley Davis — views "role behavior" as *institutional-ized* behavior.

11. A discussion of this concept and its relevance to general socio-logical theory can be found in Rushing, *op. cit.*, pp. 3-4, 22-25, 28-29, and 30-34. The concept power strategy is borrowed from John W. Thibaut and Harold H. Kelley, *The Social Psychology of Groups* (New York: John Wiley and Sons, 1959), 119-122; however, the exact formu-lation of power strategy in this paper and in the author's above work are the author's.

12. Goffman, *op. cit.*

13. *Ibid.*

14. George C. Homans, "Social Behavior as Exchange," *American Sociological Review*, LXIII (1958), 597-606.

15. See Rushing, *op. cit.*, esp. pp. 397-401.

16. *Ibid.*, esp. pp. 401-03.

17. For similar formulations of power and its relationship to de-pendency, see Thibaut and Kelley, *op. cit.*, Chapter 7; Robert Dubin, *The World of Work* (Englewood Cliffs, N. J.: Prentice-Hall, Inc., 1958), pp. 29, 48; and Richard M. Emerson, "Power-Dependence Relations," *American Sociological Review*, XXVII (1962), 31-41.

18. Ward rounds are held each morning and are attended by the chief ward psychiatrist, chief resident, psychiatric residents, nurses, psychologist, occupational therapist, recreator, and aides and order-lies. Each resident has his own individual team meetings which are attended by the "ancillary professions" (psychology, social work, etc.) and nurses. Both ward rounds and team meetings are devoted to a discussion of patients, their problems, and how the "team" might best cope with them.

19. See Rushing, *op. cit.*, p. 390.

20. Goffman, *op. cit.*

21. Rose Laub Coser, *op. cit.* p. 29.

22. See Brown, *op. cit.*, p. 90.

23. George C. Homans defines cost as a "value forgone." See his *Social Behavior: Its Elementary Forms, op. cit.*, p. 59. For a study of power strategies, their relationship to social norms and to different stages of the institutionalization process, and the use of the concept of cost to conceptualize these relationships, see Rushing. *op. cit.*

24. For additional data and elaboration, see *ibid.*, pp. 425-429.

25. Max Weber has recognized this distinction between actions that are in conformity with an institutionalized social order and actions which are oriented to that order. "It is possible for action to be oriented to an order in other ways that through conformity with its prescriptions . . ." Max Weber, *The Theory of Social and Economic Organization*, trans., A. M. Henderson and Talcott Parsons (Glencoe: The Free Press, 1947), p. 125.

fourteen

The Female Physician in Public Health: Conflict and Reconciliation of the Sex and Professional Roles

JOHN KOSA and
ROBERT E. COKER, JR.

The professions show a sex-based division; some of them, such as law and medicine, are predominantly for males, while others, such as nursing and teaching, are predominantly for females. Any attempt to explain this division has to take into consideration the relationship of sex roles and professional roles as they are defined by our social norms.[1] Since both roles prescribe duties as well as other socially required tasks, one may contend that the compatibility of the two roles is an important factor associated with the predominance of males or females in any of the professional fields. One study suggested that in nursing and teaching the professional and female roles can be reconciled with relative ease because they prescribe compatible duties to such an extent that the professional duties are, in fact, but sublimated forms of the female task.[2] If this finding can be generalized, one may assume that in some professions (1) members of one sex tend to become predominant because the congruence of the two roles delineate for them suitable places of work, and, on the other hand (2) practitioners of the minority sex find the twofold roles more or less incompatible, experience a conflict between the professional and sex roles and have to employ specific means to reduce the conflict to a tolerable level.

Medicine, being one of the oldest professions, has a tradition of being a male occupation, and particularly so in the United States where the proportion of women doctors has been

From SOCIOLOGY AND SOCIAL RESEARCH, Vol. 49, No. 3 (April, 1965), pp. 294-305. Reprinted by permission.

consistently smaller than in many other comparable countries of the western world. The American Medical Directory of 1958 enumerated in the U.S. and dependencies 13,233 female physicians who represented 5.7 percent of all physicians listed. The ratio of 19 males for every female seems to be a stable feature of the American medical profession. For example, in the ten year period of 1951 to 1960, females constituted 5.5 percent of all the graduates of the country's medical schools. Evidently, women represent a small minority in medicine, and, within their ranks, signs of a role conflict have been repeatedly noted.[3]

Previous studies pointed out that the female physician is not fully accepted by the public which, in case of need, tends to prefer a male to a female doctor of similar qualifications.[4] She is not fully accepted by her male colleagues either who are apt to ask for a stricter selection among women than among men applicants to medical schools; and indeed, the traditional quota of 5 per cent allotted to women medical students suggests that the policy of the professional governing boards complies with this pattern of reasoning.[5] The incomplete acceptance of female physicians has not changed over the last few decades although conspicuous changes have taken place in the tasks generally assigned to females and to professionals.[6] For example, a few decades ago, when the practice of midwifery was still general, obstetrics appeared as a task appropriate to women and attracted many female doctors; subsequently, however, midwifery declined; help given at delivery became a more professional task, and obstetrics turned out to be a field of medicine for males.

If we consider the problem of females as the minority sex in medicine, we may theoretically outline three main areas of role conflict as well as a professional procedure to cope with those conflicts. It is reasonable to assume that (1) the professional role tends to impose limitations upon the full realization of the female role; (2) the female role tends to limit the full realization of the professional role; and, in addition, (3) female practitioners face particular difficulties in assuming those professional duties which are more or less incompatible with female tasks. While the three areas of conflict, are, to a great extent, overlapping and make it difficult, or impossible, to restrict the role conflict to one area only, women doctors tend to manage their professional career by selecting for work those fields of medicine and that type of practice which are least likely to offer work duties incompatible with the female task.

This paper attempts to investigate these assumptions in a nationwide sample of 525 physicians who at one point of their career worked in public health. The sample, taken in the course of a more extensive study of medical career patterns, included doctors with short and long service in public health as well as doctors who worked in, but subsequently left, the field of public health.[7] The male and female respondents were rather similar in their socioeconomic origin, religion, medical education, age, etc., but differed on those variables of career patterns which are affected by sex roles.

As a general rule, the norms of our society greatly influence young people to assume their full sex roles in marriage at a rather early age, females doing so earlier than males.[8] The professional role, on the other hand, counters this tendency since professional training, and higher education in general, lead to frequent deferment of marriage.[9] In the present sample, for example, late marriages were common. At the time of graduation from medical school which took place at a median age of 25 years, 35 per cent of all respondents were married, while 49 per cent of them were single, not engaged. Within this general pattern, however, females were more likely than males to defer marriage: 37 per cent of the males but only 18 per cent of the females were married, and, on the other hand 46 per cent of the males but 72 per cent of the females were single, not engaged. (The proportion of single, engaged people was pretty much the same among males as well as females.) What the data suggest is that preparation for the professional role is more compatible with the male role of breadwinner and father (as this role is posed for the medical student) than with the female role of homemaker and mother. Such a difference in the compatibility of two roles leads to a more frequent deferment of marriage among females.

After graduation and licensing comes the practice of the professional role and females are again at a disadvantage. This time the sex role tends to restrict the female physician in her full assumption of the professional role, and especially, in her continuous performance of medical duties.

In every comparable position of the medical career, women work on the average for a shorter time than men. For example, male doctors were working in their "present" position on the average for 7.3 years, while their female colleagues for only 5.2 years. Table 1 compares the work career of men and women in

Table 1 / Physicians' Work Career in Public Health by Sex

	Male	Female
Mean of years worked in public health:		
on full-time basis*	6.53	5.62
on part-time basis	6.60	6.35
Mean number of positions in public health:		
on full-time basis	1.70	1.69
on part-time basis**	1.29	1.80
Mean length of one position in public health (years):		
on full-time basis	3.84	3.33
on part-time basis**	5.12	3.53

* $p < .05$
** $p < .01$ (Two-tailed t test)

public health and indicates that females stay in any of the public health positions for a shorter period and have a shorter total service in the field of public health than males. The differences are especially conspicuous in part-time positions. Females accept on the average more part-time positions, but stay in each of them for a shorter time than men. In the medical career of women, part-time work has a special importance. One-fourth of the women held at one point of their career a part-time position as the only medical position, while none of the male physicians reported such a case. For the male physician, part-time work is an additional duty to a full-time position, but for a sizable proportion of the female doctors there is a stage in the career when a part-time position represents the total work commitment.

When interpreting this difference, it should be pointed out that the demands of motherhood and home making become particularly pressing at certain stages of the life cycle. At such stages a part-time position appears preferable; hence, women take part-time positions more frequently than men. However, the combined duties of the sex and the professional roles may often turn out to be more burdensome than anticipated and, accordingly, there is a tendency to relinquish the part-time position after a short service.

An important part of the physician's professional role might be called entrepreneurship, and this term refers to such features of medical practice as self-employment, independence in work, preference for money as the main reward of work, as well as willingness for hard work and competitiveness in matters of career. According to our generally accepted social norms, entrepreneurship is associated with the male role and has a conspicuous place in male, but not in female, professions. Thus, one can expect that female physicians are less likely than their male colleagues to realize the entrepreneurial role as the latter is posited in the various situations of medical practice.

Self-employment is less important in the career of women than in that of men physicians. At the time of the survey, 73 per cent of the females but only 56 per cent of the males worked in salaried positions; moreover, women spent on the average about seven-tenths of their total full-time work career in salaried positions in contrast to four-tenths of the men. The differences associated with the early assumption of the full sex role in marriage are even more conspicuous. Forty-five per cent of the males who assumed the full sex role relatively early and were married or engaged at the time of their graduation from medical school had salaried positions at the time of the research, while 82 per cent of the females of the same category had salaried positions. On the other hand, sex did not differentiate among those who were single, not engaged at the time of graduation from medical school, 68 per cent of such males and 66 per cent of the females were working in salaried positions. In other words, early marriage or engagement is among males associated with a tendency of selecting private practice with its generally higher income, but among females it is associated with an opposite tendency of taking salaried positions. Accordingly, deferment of marriage (as shown by those who were single, not engaged at the time of graduation) is associated with a frequent selection of salaried positions among males, but with a relatively frequent selection of private practice among females.

The matter of money marks again noteworthy differences. Women on the whole have less professional income than men of comparable positions. (See Table 2) In the first position after graduation, females earn somewhat more than males since more men than women take an interim position after graduation in order to discharge military obligations or obtain advance training. After that, however, men establish their greater earning

Table 2 / Mean Professional Income in Various Positions by
Sex, in Dollars

	Male	Female
Mean income of respondents in the . . .		
first position after graduation	10,494	10,888
first position in public health	10,493	9,790
last position in public health	12,586	11,053
first position after leaving public health*	17,672	14,676

* p < .05 (Two-tailed t test)

power, and in each of the subsequent positions the difference in
income increases. A more detailed examination of the data indicates that women are unlikely to reach the high income
brackets. For example, in the last position in public health 46
men but only one woman earned more than $15,000, that is, one
out of every 5 men, but only one in 22 women, had a chance to
reach the high income bracket.

To be sure, women are less likely than men to attribute importance to money as a reward of work. As the data in Table 3

Table 3 / Attitudes Toward the Entrepreneurial Role by
Sex, in Percentages

	Male (481)	Female (44)
Percent saying that they . . .		
. . . prefer close relationships with patients to large income	24	45
. . . prefer new problems to large income	29	50
. . . regard good income as of no importance in a job	19	32
. . . regard regular and not extremely long working hours indispensable	3	32
. . . prefer close relationships with patients to independence in work	33	59
. . . dislike competition with other people when the stakes are high	24	50
. . . regard the aid of experienced persons as important in a job	35	55

For all items listed the difference is significant on the 5 per cent level or better.
(Chi-square test)

show, more women than men prefer relationships with patients
and new problems in work to good income, and more women
say that good income is of no importance in a job. If we com-

bine the questions, it appears that more than two-thirds of the women regard patient relationships and challenging problems as the main rewards of work, but less than one-third of the men do so with the rest naming money as the main reward of work.

In addition, more women than men express a preference for short working hours, a dislike for competition with other people, a willingness to renounce independence in work for close patient relationships, and a preference for the aid of experienced persons. The value preferences expressed in these statements might rightly be interpreted as signaling the females' perception of the role conflict. For example, when one-third of the female doctors state that "regular and not extremely long working hours" are indispensable in a position (see Table 3), they indicate, not their unwillingness to work hard, but their realization that a position requiring long hours of work is likely to interfere with discharging the duties of the female role.

In view of such differences between the sexes, one may ask how female physicians manage to reduce the role conflict and find their place within the profession. Table 4, which sums up the choice of medical fields at the successive stages of career, furnishes some information on this point. As it appears, females show a consistent preference for selecting pediatrics, a preference accompanying their career from early times on to the "present" position. At the time of the first decision to become a physician (and the majority of the respondents made this decision before or during high school) proportionally more women than men were most interested in pediatrics, and from this stage on the differential selection of pediatrics (or maternal and child health in public health service) was a constant characteristic of female physicians.

At the subsequent stages of career two additional fields appeared as preferential choices of women. In the first position after graduation both males and females selected public health frequently, but females were more likely to stay with that field through the following stages of career, including the present position. In the career stage following the work in public health, psychiatry appeared as a field attracting a fairly large proportion of females. In the "present" position, 80 per cent of the females were concentrated in those three fields of medicine where only 36 per cent of the male physicians worked; on the other hand, females were greatly underrepresented in those

Table 4 / Interest in Medical Fields at the Successive Stages of Career by Sex, in Percentages

	Male (481)	Female (44)
Per cent who, at the time of the first decision to become a physician, were most interested in:		
Pediatrics**	3	14
Public health and preventive medicine	5	2
Psychiatry	3	9
All other fields*	89	75
Per cent who, as seniors in medical school, were most interested in:		
Pediatrics**	11	36
Public health and preventive medicine	7	5
Psychiatry	5	2
All other fields**	77	57
Per cent who, in the first position after graduation, worked in:		
Maternal and child health**	10	34
Mental health	5	9
Per cent who, in their last full-time position in public health, worked in:		
Maternal and child health**	5	27
Mental health	4	5
Per cent who, at present, work in:		
Pediatrics**	7	23
Public health and preventive medicine*	22	39
Psychiatry**	7	18
All other fields**	64	20

* p < .02
** p < .01 (Chi-square test)

many fields where the majority of males found their proper places of work. The proportion of females selecting those "other" fields gradually declined from 75 per cent at the time of the first decision to 20 per cent at the time of the present position.

The career patterns that we have just examined suggest that within medicine there exists a sex-based division of fields comparable to the division existing within the professions generally.[10] In other words, men and women doctors are not engaged in the various types of medical duties proportionally; rather, we may speak of male and female fields of medicine in a sense as we speak of male and female professions. Moreover, the females' concentration in the three preferred fields seems to be a process evolving gradually through the progressive stages of career. As the female physician progresses in her professional career, she gradually perceives the role conflict as well as the structure of the profession and, accordingly, tends to decide for one of those fields where she can reasonably expect a reduction of the conflict.

The preference for pediatrics shown by females hardly needs further comments, and the preference for psychiatry might be interpreted, although not fully explained, by pointing to the predominance of females among such ancillary therapists as psychiatric social workers and nurses. In the present context we wish to deal with the preference for public health and, in particular, with the question whether female physicians are attracted to public health by a special liking for the field itself or rather by the compatibility of the sex and professional role that is offered within the institutional setting of public health.

The respondents completed a Public Health Evaluation Scale[11] on which males reached a mean score of 28.8 and fe-

Table 5 / Attractive Features of Public Health by
Sex, in Percentages

	Male (481)	Female (44)
Per cent naming the following reasons for entering public health:		
it provided an immediate source of income	25	50
it did not require building a practice	12	32
it meant regular and not extremely long working hours	17	59
it enabled me to simplify work and keep work load manageable	7	30
Per cent who . . .		
. . . name the working hours as the most liked aspect of public health	13	34
. . . name low salary as the least liked aspect of public health	20	9

For all items listed the difference is significant on the 1 per cent level or better. (Chi-square test)

males, a mean of 28.7. This almost perfect agreement indicates that women did not tend to evaluate the field of public health

204 / *The Professional Woman*

per se in more favorable terms than men. However, significantly more women than men were attracted to public health by such considerations as immediate income, freedom from building a practice, regular working hours and manageable work load; in addition, more females than males claimed to like the working hours and accept the relatively low salary offered by public health (see Table 5). Such differences suggest that the liberation from the entrepreneurial role and the possible discharge of the female role were important considerations on the mind of female physicians in their selection of public health.

An examination of the value preferences by sex and medical field, as presented in Table 6, gives further support to this sug-

Table 6 / Professional Attitudes by Sex and
Medical Field, in Percentages

	FEMALES		MALES	
	in public health and prev. med.	in other fields	in public health and prev. med.	in other fields
Per cent saying that they ...	(17)	(27)	(106)	(375)
... prefer close relationships with patients to large income	47	44	38*	20*
... prefer new problems to large income	53	44	47*	24*
... regard good income as of no importance in a job	29	33	25	17
Per cent naming the following reasons for entering public health				
... it provided an immediate source of income	47	52	32	23
... it did not require building a practice	35	30	20*	10*
... it meant regular and no extremely long working hours	59	59	25*	10*

* The difference between the two groups of males is significant on the 5 per cent level or better. (Chi-square test)

gestion. Female physicians, whether their present medical field is public health or another field of medicine, agree among themselves on professional attitudes and are equally likely to reject the entrepreneurial values. Male physicians, however, differ according to their field: those who name public health as their medical field are more likely than the rest to underrate the importance of money as the main reward of work and to name nonentrepreneurial reasons for entering public health. Male physicians in public health, when compared to male physicians in other fields, tend to reject the entrepreneurial role, and the female physician entering public health can expect to find there male colleagues who hold value preferences similar to those of hers.

Altogether it appears that female physicians are attracted not by the whole field but only by one aspect of public health — the elimination, or restriction, of entrepreneurial competitiveness that prevails there as a contrast to what prevails in fields emphasizing the private practice of medicine. At the same time, male physicians who identify themselves with public health sufficiently enough to name it as their medical field, also tend to reject the same competitiveness. If this is so, then we may assume that women doctors tend to regard as incompatible with their sex role work situations where they would be set up in free entrepreneurial competition with their male colleagues and tend to move into fields and work situations where the institutional setting and the attitude of the male colleagues are likely to eliminate competition between professionals of different sex. Such an explanation needs further corroboration, if possible from different fields and work situations, before fully accepted, but even in a tentative form it helps to explain many facets of the occupational cooperation of males and females.

To sum it up, this paper has attempted to outline three main areas of role conflict that female physicians as the minority sex in the medical profession may face. It has presented evidence to the effect that the existing specialization of the profession offers institutionalized procedures for reducing the role conflict and, accordingly, female physicians tend to select medical fields where the sex and professional roles are relatively compatible. When selecting the field of public health, for example, the female physician expects an alleviation of those limitations that the sex role puts upon the full performance of the professional role and, at the same time, a reduction of the possible conflict centering around the entrepreneurial role and free competition with members of the opposite sex.

NOTES

1. Talcott Parsons, *Essay in Sociological Theory Pure and Applied.* (New York: The Free Press of Glencoe), 185-99, 218-32; and *The Social System.* (New York: The Free Press of Glencoe, 1951), 466-73.

2. Rose K. Goldsen and John Kosa, "Women's Roles and the Female Professionals." (Paper presented at the 25th Annual Meeting of the Southern Sociological Society, 1963).

3. For a popularly worded statement on the role conflict, see M. Louise Gloeckner, "The Challenge of Medicine for Women Today," Journal of the American Medical Women's Association, 15 (March, 1960), 271-74.

4. Josephine J. Williams, "Patients and Prejudice: Lay Attitudes Toward Women Physicians," American Journal of Sociology, 51 (January, 1964), 282-87.

5. Josephine J. Williams, "The Woman Physician's Dilemma," Journal of Social Issues, (1950), No. 3, 38-44; Roscoe A. Dykman and John M. Stalnaker, "Survey of Women Physicians Graduating from Medical School 1925-1940, "Journal of Medical Education, 32 (March, 1957), Part 2, 3-38; Anon., "Women in Medicine," Journal of Medical Education, 38 (June, 1963), 518-19.

6. Carla A. Pullum, "Women, Medicine and Misconceptions, Journal of the American Medical Women's Association, 18 (July, 1963), 563-65; Edward J. Van Liere and Gideon S. Dodds, "Women in Medicine in West Virginia University," Journal of Medical Education, 34 (September, 1959), 911-15. For some interesting comparative data see A.H.T. Robb-Smith, "The Fate of Oxford Medical Women," The Lancet, December 1, 1962, 1158-61.

7. Concerning the details of sampling see Robert E. Coker, Jr., John Kosa and Bernard G. Greenberg, "Medical Careers in Public Health," Milbank Memorial Fund Quarterly, 44 (April, 1966), 149-152.

8. John Kosa, Leo D. Rachiele and Cyril O. Schommer,, "Marriage, Career and Religiousness," Marriage and Family Living, 24 (November, 1962), 376-80; Dykman and Stalnaker, "Survey of Women Physicians," 14-15.

9. See John Kosa, Robert E. Coker, Jr., and Bernard G. Greenberg, "Deferment of Marriage and Professional Training: Study of a Group of Physicians." (Paper presented at the meeting of the Society for the Study of Social Problems, 1964).

10. Dykman and Stalnaker ("Survey of Women Physicians," 20) list anesthesiology as a fourth field preferred by females.

11. The six-item scale asked for the respondent's agreement or disagreement with such statements as "Public Health is going to become more and more important," "Public Health is as challenging a field of medicine as any other specialty."

fifteen

Women in the Soviet Economy

NORTON DODGE

Although the focus of this study has been on the role of women in Soviet science and technology, it has been necessary to discuss women in a much broader context. The complexity of the interrelationship of the roles of woman, as wife, mother, consumer, and producer, makes it difficult simply to summarize or to characterize Soviet policy toward women in the Russian economy as a whole or in any part of it. These varied roles so interact that Soviet policy in one area may have unintended repercussions on the way in which women perform in other areas. There is still little evidence that Soviet planners have managed to achieve a single, coherent, over-all policy with respect to the economic utilization of women but, rather, that they have several imperfectly co-ordinated and sometimes contradictory policies. An attempt will now be made, nevertheless, to summarize, interpret, and evaluate Soviet experience in the utilization of women in the economy, particularly in the fields of science and technology.

To begin with, war, revolution, and political repression over the past five decades drastically altered the sex ratio in the Soviet Union in favor of women. In 1897, with a sex ratio of 99 males per 100 females, there was near balance between the sexes in the Russian population. But in 1926, as a result of World War I and the Civil War, there were 5 million fewer males than females, and the sex ratio was 94. The census of 1939 reported 7 million fewer males than females and a further

From *Women in the Soviet Economy* by Norton T. Dodge, 1966, pp. 238-247. Reprinted by permission of The Johns Hopkins Press.

decline in the sex ratio to 92. These changes reflected the impact of collectivization and the purges, in which more men than women were killed. But by far the most drastic change came with World War II, which decimated the adult male population. The 1959 census reported 114.8 million females and 94 million males, a deficit of 20.8 million males. By calculating backward, with published birth rates and certain assumptions about the distribution of mortality by sex, it can be estimated that in 1946 there were 26 million fewer males than females in the adult population and that the sex ratio for the entire population was only 74 males per 100 females. The tremendous imbalance of the late 40's and early 50's was moderated by time, and by 1959 the sex ratio had risen to 83. At the present time the imbalance in the sexes is confined to the age groups over 35, but it is estimated that not until 1980 will the sex ratio be 92, or at the level prior to the outbreak of World War II.

Irregularities in the Soviet population pyramid caused by war and other vicissitudes are so great that many decades will be required to moderate them. Although the male deficit is now confined to the older age groups, the manpower shortage continues for other reasons. Most important, the birth rate during and immediately after the war was unusually low. As a result, during the past half dozen years additions to the labor force have been small and the pressure to utilize women, which was so insistent in the decade following the war, has continued up to the present. Furthermore, the shrunken generation of war babies is now entering the childbearing age, and, therefore, the annual number of births is significantly reduced. In another generation, these small numbers will in turn keep additions to the labor force and to the population below the normal level. Thus, irregularities in the population pyramid will be perpetuated through several generations.

The present population policy of the government is aimed at maintaining or increasing the rate of growth in population, because a large and rapidly growing population is viewed as an asset rather than a liability. Certain programs, such as family allowances and medals for mothers of large families, are designed to increase the birth rate. On the other hand, in 1955, the government felt obliged once again to legalize abortion because of pressures from women and from the medical profession which was concerned with the large number of illegal abortions performed under unsafe circumstances. Continuing concern over the high rate of abortion has led to increased efforts to develop and distribute effective contraceptive devices. The combined effect of legalized abortions and more effective contraception will be, of course, to reduce the birth rate at the same time other measures are being taken to increase it. Nevertheless, in spite of these contradictions in Soviet population policy, the intent of the government is to increase fertility. Thus far, however, the results are not impressive.

Demographic factors have played, and will continue to play, an important part in determining the role of women in the Soviet economy. The present high rate of participation of women in the Soviet labor force is not without precedent, however. In 1926, when the country was largely agricultural, almost every woman participated in economic activity outside the home for a part of the year. What is unique in the Soviet situation today is the very high rate of participation by women in the economy of a country so industrially advanced. At the present time, the Soviet participation rate of close to 70 per cent in the working ages is almost twice as high as the rate in the United States. This high rate has been maintained despite a major structural shift in the population away from rural areas, where the participation rate has always been very high, into urban areas where the participation rate initially was much lower. Since 1926, however, the participation rate of urban women age 16 to 59 has increased from 40 to 67 per cent. This increase has almost completely offset the decline in the average participation rate which would otherwise have occurred as the industrialization process proceeded.

Although rates of female participation in the labor force are high in all regions of the U.S.S.R., variations occur which are usually related to the degree of urbanization, the influence of Moslem traditions, and the size of the male deficit. Since urbanization and Moslem traditions tend to lower the rate, while the shortage of men tends to raise it, the rate reaches its extreme high in largely rural and traditionally Christian republics which were badly hit by the war, such as Belorussia, and its extreme low in the more urbanized of the traditionally Moslem republics, such as Azerbaidzhan. Another factor which affects the local rates of female participation, but about which little statistical information is available, is the lack of employment opportunity near women's homes or in particular specialties.

The continuance of a high rate of female participation at all ages, even through the childbearing and child-rearing ages, is another distinctive Soviet characteristic. In the age group 20 to 39, which encompasses the most important childbearing and child-rearing ages, approximately 80 per cent of the women are employed, a remarkably high rate for a country as advanced industrially as the Soviet Union. Women begin to withdraw from employment in the socialized sector of the economy as they approach the retirement age, but many older women continue to work on private agricultural plots.

In the United States and other highly developed countries the pattern is quite different. Although in the United States 45 per cent of the women in their early twenties are employed, many of these women withdraw from the labor force when they begin to have children. Only 33 per cent remain employed in their late twenties. The participation rate then climbs to a second peak for women in their forties and early fifties when their children are able to fend for themselves. In the age groups under 40 and over 65, the participation rate of Soviet women is approximately double that of American women. In the age group 40 to 65 it exceeds the American by a little more than 50 per cent.

The male population deficit in the older age groups, coupled with high female participation rates, has resulted in a substantial majority of women in the Soviet labor force age 35 and older. This is a crucial age group for any economy, since it is from this group that the leadership of an economy and of a society is normally drawn. This special circumstance has made the effective utilization of women since World War II even more vital for the Soviet Union than numbers alone would suggest.

If the present high proportion of working women in the Soviet Union is examined in terms of the gradual restoration of a normal male-female ratio in the population, the share of women in the total employment of the future is not likely to increase above the present 52 per cent. In the United States and other developed countries, on the other hand, there is still ample room for growth in the employment of women. The President's Commission on the Status of Women projects a level of 34 per cent for the United States in 1970.[1] Given circumstances more favorable to working women, still further increases would be a possibility.

In the Soviet Union economic pressures compelling women to work to make ends meet play a major role in keeping women in the labor force. The shortage of men has left many women without husbands, and they must work to support themselves and their families. Furthermore, for many families a single pay check provides only a bare subsistence, and many married women feel they must work in order to maintain an acceptable standard of living. Also, government and party action has altered social custom and public attitudes toward the employment of women. At the present time, few fields are considered inaccessible, and a woman is actually likely to feel defensive if she does not have a job. The regime has been particularly successful in opening the fields of science and technology to women. Attitudes toward women participating in these fields have so radically changed that they are freely accepted everywhere — except in work considered detrimental to their health.

The policies of the Soviet regime on the employment of women, protection on the job and maternity benefits have been embodied in extensive legislation and executive orders issued since the Revolution. Often the legislation has not been enforced, particularly during the war emergency when women were in fact employed in many occupations from which by the existing law they were excluded for reasons of health. At the present time, however, the legal provisions concerning Soviet women are generally enforced, and in this respect the Soviet Union is among the more enlightened countries of the world.

Another factor affecting the participation of women in the labor force is the burden of family responsibilities. Although adequate data are lacking, the participation rate of Soviet women appears to decline, as is normally the case everywhere, as the number of their children increases. We have seen, however, that the Soviet participation rate holds up remarkably well, even in the face of this burden, throughout the childbearing and child-rearing ages. This is possible partly because the varied child-care facilities provided in the Soviet Union free several millions of women with young children for employment outside the home. As has been pointed out, the demand for the services of these institutions continues to outrun the supply. According to estimates, approximately 12 per cent of the children of nursery age and 20 per cent of the children of kindergarten age can be accommodated in permanent child-care facilities. Substantially more can be accommodated in seasonal summer facilities. Most of the permanent facilities are concentrated in urban centers, and the seasonal facilities in the countryside. In a major city such as Moscow, almost half the children of nursery and kindergarten age are cared for in child-care centers, but in most communities there are long lists of children waiting to be admitted.

Although the government has allocated substantial investment funds over the years to the expansion of child-care facilities, it has been unwilling to assign to this program sufficient resources to satisfy demand. On the contrary, it has chosen to compel most working women to make their own arrangements — with members of their families or outside help — for the care of their young children. This policy can hardly be considered beneficial to the working mothers. From the standpoint of the regime's overriding goal of economic growth, however, the imposition of hardship on the working mother and a slightly lower rate of participation of women in the labor force have apparently been considered preferable to the diversion of investment funds and other resources to additional child-care facilities.

More information than is presently available would be required to judge whether the government's policy has struck the correct balance, given its schedule of priorities. It is equally difficult to pass judgment on party and governmental thinking with respect to housing, consumers' goods, and the provision of services, to relieve women of some of the burden of housework. Such a judgment would require an assessment of whether or not a larger investment in labor-saving devices for the home would encourage a sufficiently larger number of women to enter the labor force, or would sufficiently increase the productivity of those already in the labor force, to offset the negative effect on the rate of growth which a diversion of resources to the consumer sector would entail. One would also need to assess the effect of such improvements on fertility rates and the long-run supply of labor. Until more data are available, these questions cannot be conclusively answered.

As the Soviet economy has passed through successive stages of development, there have, of course, been changes in the pattern of priorities. What was conceived as correct strategy during the period of forced industrialization under Stalin does not appear applicable today, at a higher stage of economic development when emphasis on producers' goods production is no longer so important. As a result, conditions in the Soviet Union are now favorable to greater investments in housing, production of consumers' goods, and child-care facilities with the aim of lightening the burden on women. Apparently the government expects to sustain or to increase the participation rate of women in this fashion rather than through the more Draconic policies pursued in the past.

Education was the first step by which Soviet women were enabled to equip themselves for a broader and more productive participation in the Soviet economy. Dramatic progress has been made in raising the educational levels of the population, and women have been, perhaps, the principal beneficiaries of this process. For all practical purposes, illiteracy among women has been wiped out except among the older generation and in some of the more stubbornly backward areas of the country. The most striking improvements have been realized by women in rural areas and in some of the less developed republics where, in the past, Moslem traditions barred women from acquiring an education. It should not be overlooked, however, that a third of the persons in prime working ages still have less than a four-year education, and that two-thirds of this group are women. It appears that the government has never intended to provide the bulk of the older female population with more than the minimal educational requirements for "functional" literacy. These older women apparently were written off at the start as prospects for the development of special skills.

By concentrating its efforts on the younger age groups during the past four decades, the Soviet government has succeeded in raising substantially the level of educational attainment of millions of young men and women in those occupational fields critical for economic growth and development. Great numbers of younger women have been given on-the-job training in industry and have become an important element in the industrial labor force. Similarly, many young women have been afforded a specialized secondary or higher educational training in science and technology and in other key fields for economic development. Girls have been as well prepared as boys for admission to the scientific or technical faculties of specialized secondary and higher educational institutions because the curricula at the lower educational levels were made uniform for both sexes. Initially, minimum quotas were set for women to encourage their enrollment, and other efforts were made to increase female matriculation, especially in scientific and technical disciplines. As a result, women have had opened to them many of the more interesting and attractive occupations from which they had previously been excluded. This has been a major positive accomplishment of the Soviet regime.

The remarkable success of the Soviet Union in attracting women to the fields of science and technology is apparent from the statistics on education which we have surveyed. The great demand for women with scientific and technological training which arose in the 1930's initiated the impressive increase in the proportion of women enrolled in these fields. Although comprehensive statistics on the proportion of women enrolled in specific fields of science and technology are not available, such data as we do have show that women make up approximately three quarters of the enrollment in courses in the technology of food and consumers' goods production and approximately three fifths of those studying chemical engineering, hydrology, meteorology, geodesy, and cartography. In fields such as mining engineering, transportation, and machine building, on the other hand, only a fifth to a sixth of the students are women. But 53 per cent of the medical students and 25 per cent of the agricultural students are women, both percentages having dropped sharply in recent years. It is estimated that at Soviet universities three fourths to four fifths of the students enrolled in biology, more than two thirds of those in chemistry, two fifths to a half in mathematics, and a quarter to two fifths in physics, geology, and the agricultural sciences are women. In comparison with other countries of the world, these are strikingly high percentages.

It should be emphasized that the choice of a specific field of study by young Soviet men and women is not decided by the state. The percentage of men and women enrolled in each discipline is a fairly faithful reflection of the relative attraction of a field. Initially, the proportion of women grew in all fields, but by no means to the same degree. Certain disciplines, such as medicine, came to be dominated by women; others, such as architecture, by men. In recent years, however, more men have been attracted to medicine — a tendency which has been reinforced by the fact that today men seem to be given admission preference. There have, then, been shifts in the attitudes of young men and women toward certain fields, with resulting shifts over the years in the proportion of women enrolled. To what extent these shifts are a function of altered admission policies and to what extent they depend on changes in individual preferences are matters for conjecture.

There has been a major shift in the overall proportion of women enrolled in specialized secondary and higher education since World War II. During and immediately after the war, the proportion of women enrolled reached its peak. In the past decade, however, the proportion of women has declined — slightly in specialized secondary education and sharply in higher education. This decline has occurred in every field, but is particularly pronounced in medicine, agriculture, and the socioeconomic disciplines. The immediate causes limiting the proportion of women in higher education have been changes in the organization of the secondary school system and more especially in the regulations governing admission to higher educational institutions. Although equality of the sexes remains the stated policy of the Soviet regime, actual admission policies indicate an increasing departure from this principle. Although we cannot be certain that the reduction in the proportion of female enrollment has in fact stemmed from considerations of efficiency, such a reduction does admit of justification on economic grounds. In fields such as medicine, an excessively high proportion of women (from the standpoint of efficient utilization) was permitted to receive training. The government is now eager to restore a more desirable balance of the sexes. In other fields also, where the proportion of women was always lower, the proportion is being further reduced in the interest of efficiency, since the productivity of professional women in most fields tends to be less than that of men.

Even though education has prepared many Soviet women for professional careers, most Soviet women are still engaged in heavy, unskilled work. According to 1959 census data, four fifths of the total 56 million women employed in the labor force were engaged in what is officially termed "physical" labor, and of these the majority were employed in agricultural occupations. Nonspecialized agricultural work alone accounts for one third of the women engaged in physical labor. Typically, women are the field workers and livestock tenders, while men handle the skilled mechanical and construction work and serve as administrators. When the other more skilled agricultural occupations are included, agriculture accounts for 63 per cent of all women employed in physical labor. The large number of women still working in the fields, in spite of Soviet industrial advances, is one of the distinctive features of the Soviet economy.

Women have also come to play an important role in the non-agricultural sectors of the economy — particularly in industry and in the service sector. Throughout a wide range of occupations the percentage of women is substantially higher than that in the United States. Only in such traditional areas of female employment as secretarial, sales, and clerical work and nursing are the American percentages equally high. A high percentage of women is employed in communal and household services and in public dining, and women are relatively well represented in the garment trades and in various occupations in the textile and food industries. Large numbers of women may also be found in metalwork, construction, and transportation. Although most of the industrial and unskilled occupations have little intrinsic appeal for women, for those who lack training or talent for professional work they offer an opportunity to supplement the family income. Also, the high percentage of Soviet women in such occupations dramatically reflects the shortage of males of working age and the determination of the regime to maintain high rates of economic growth at the cost, if necessary, of individual welfare.

Perhaps even more distinctive than the high over-all participation rate of Soviet women, and the vital role they play in the older age groups of the labor force, is their heavy representation in white-collar occupations and the professions. This is the bright side of the employment picture for Soviet women. The role of women in white-collar occupations has increased greatly since the Revolution and has assumed proportions unequaled elsewhere in the world. Today, women comprise more than half the labor force employed in "mental" work. About half of the 11 million women in this category have had a specialized secondary or higher education. The proportion of

women among specialists with a specialized secondary education is very high, amounting to 63 per cent in recent years.
Among professionals with a higher education, the proportion is
53 per cent. Thus, women form a clear majority of the semiprofessional and professional labor force in the Soviet Union. The
woman physician, engineer, research worker, or technician is a
commonplace. American women, in contrast, make up very
small minorities in most professions, the only exception being
teaching; and in such fields as engineering, physics, and medicine, the professional woman is a rarity. For example, while
women comprise only 7 per cent of the physicians in the United
States, they make up 75 per cent of the total in the Soviet Union.
In engineering, the contrast is even more striking; over a quarter of a million Soviet women are engineers, and make up a
third of the profession,[2] while in the United States, female engineers account for less than 1 per cent of the total.[3] The number
of women in the natural sciences in the Soviet Union is also substantial, although the proportion of women varies considerably
from field to field, tending to be higher in the biological sciences
and chemistry and lower in a field such as physics.

In 1947, the only year for which data are available, women
made up 35 per cent of the staffs of Soviet higher educational institutions, while in the United States they constituted 22 per
cent in 1954-55.[4] In the Soviet Union, 68 per cent of the philolo-
gists were women, 48 per cent of the teachers of medicine
and biology, 45 per cent of the chemists, and 40 per cent of the
education teachers. In the remaining fields, the proportion of
women lay below the average of 35 per cent for all fields combined. For example, 34 per cent of the staffs in the arts were
women, 30 per cent of the historians, 29 per cent of the ge-
ographers, 23 per cent of the geologists, 21 per cent of the physicists and mathematicians, 16 per cent of the economists, and 11
per cent of the engineers. U.S. statistics, while they do not follow exactly the Soviet classification of occupations, nevertheless present interesting comparisons. In 1954-55, 40 per cent of
education teachers in colleges and universities were women; 28
per cent of those in English, journalism, and foreign languages;
27 per cent in the fine arts; 20 per cent in business and commerce; 14 per cent in mathematics; 11 per cent in the social sciences; 10 per cent in agriculture and the biological sciences; 6
per cent in the physical sciences; and less than 1 per cent in en-

gineering and architecture.[6] As these figures reveal, only in education, and to a lesser degree in the arts, are the percentages of women at all comparable in the two countries. In all other corresponding fields, the Soviet percentages are substantially higher, evincing the success of the Soviets in utilizing the talents of women in fields which in the United States and other western countries remain almost exclusively male domains.

Although the prospects for a woman's embarking upon a professional career in the Soviet Union are much more favorable than in the United States or other Western countries, the prospects for her professional advancement are not so happy; for the proportion of Soviet women in the higher professional echelons tends to decrease as the rank advances. This phenomenon can be observed even in fields, such as education and health, where women predominate. In the former the proportion of women primary school directors in the Soviet Union is almost identical to the percentage of women teachers, but the percentage declines sharply from 72 per cent for primary school directors to 24 per cent for eight-year school directors and 20 per cent for secondary school directors. A similar attrition occurs in higher education, where in 1960 women comprised 41 per cent of the assistant professors and other lower-level professionals, 24 per cent of the associate professors, 11 per cent of the professors, 12 per cent of the department heads, 9 per cent of the deans, and only 5 per cent of the deputy directors and directors. In medicine and health, although women make up 75 per cent of the medical profession, they account for only 57 per cent of the directors, deputy directors, and chief physicians of medical establishments. In research institutions where women make up half the scientific workers (*nauchnye rabotniki*), they account for about a third of heads and deputy heads of branches, 21 per cent of the division heads and their deputies, and 16 per cent of the directors and their deputies and other top administrative personnel. This pattern of declining representation of women as rank increases is repeated in all other fields for which data are available.

The lodging of a disproportionate share of women in the lower and intermediate professional levels suggests that the Soviet government is not receiving so high a return on its educational investment in women as in men, since Soviet professional women with comparable educational training show, on the whole, a lower level of achievement than men. Further evidence of this is provided by various indexes of scholarly productivity. For example, among the top Soviet scientists — full and corresponding members of the Academies of Sciences — very few women are to be found. Women also make up a very small proportion of the recipients of Lenin prizes. An extensive survey of scholarly publications gives further unmistakable evidence that the scholarly productivity of women is lower than that of men. In a comparison of the proportion of women in various specialties on the staffs of higher educational institutions with the proportion of scholarly articles contributed in each field by women, it was found that on the average women contributed about half as many articles as would be expected from their numbers.

The Soviets have done little or no research on the possible effects of various social or environmental factors on the achievement of women. To what extent their lower productivity and their smaller proportions at the higher administrative and professional levels may be due to innate rather than to socially or culturally determined factors is a question that cannot be easily answered. Unlike the woman farmer or factory worker doing a routine job, the Soviet professional woman is likely to derive considerable satisfaction from her work and to be seriously interested in it. But even though her motivation is high, the obstacles to achievement are considerable. Some of the important factors inhibiting a woman's productivity are lost work time and distractions due to family responsibilities, the interruption of a career because of childbearing, and job assignment difficulties. Such factors cannot, of course, readily be eradicated. Other conditions which involve the intellectual development of girls and their career motivations can perhaps be improved. Great progress has already been made in altering the image of a woman's role in society. The intellectual, career-oriented girl in the Soviet Union today can find much support and social approval compared with the girl of only a few decades ago. It appears, however, that conflicts between career and marriage and motherhood will remain for some time to come, since the greater involvement of a woman with her family is not susceptible of drastic change even in Soviet society. If the regime should choose to divert a greater proportion of its investment funds toward the provision of child-care facilities and consumers' goods to lighten the burden of housework, women would be thereby relieved of some of the drain on their creative energies caused by family responsibilities, and their productivity should increase accordingly.

It is evident from this survey that the Soviet regime has a very different attitude toward women from that of a largely unplanned, individualistic society such as our own. Reflecting a philosophy which conceives of the individual's welfare as the basic social goal, our society views the education of women, as well as that of men, to be desirable as an end in itself. Although much of our education is career-oriented, the failure of a young woman after her marriage to pursue a career for which she has been trained does not mean that her education is considered wasted. The raising of a family is considered in itself a sufficient contribution to the welfare of society and is not normally viewed as a distraction from which a woman should, if possible, be relieved so that she can pursue a "productive" career. In contrast, the Soviets see women as an economic asset or resource, to be developed and exploited as effectively as possible. This attitude reflects, of course, the regime's overriding goal of promoting economic development, a goal which has governed Soviet economic policies since the late 1920's. Concurrently, the regime has been concerned with the enlargement of women's rights and with freeing women from all forms of repression and discrimination. This idealistic motif in Soviet policy cannot be denied, but it must be viewed in the proper perspective.

As we have seen, Soviet policy toward women is complex and sometimes contradictory. However, if the predominance of the economic motive in determining Soviet policies toward women is recognized and borne in mind, many of the apparent contradictions can be better understood. It is true that, on occasion, policies inspired by idealism have coincided with those motivated by strictly material considerations, but wherever they diverge, the Soviets have consistently chosen to pursue the economic rather than the idealistic goal. In the first years following the Revolution, for example, the regime was altruistically concerned with securing women's rights and bringing about a greater equality of the sexes. A great deal of legislation was passed to these ends, and the percentage of women in specialized secondary and higher educational institutions, as well as the percentage employed in industry and other branches of the economy, increased significantly during the 1920's and 1930's. But women were perhaps too successful in securing "equality." Too much equality can become a burden to women whose physiological function of motherhood makes impossible their avoidance of heavy responsibilities over and above those imposed by their work. Soviet time-use studies show clearly that the total burden of employment in the labor force and in the home falls much more heavily upon women than upon men. Although Soviet legislation recognizes that physiological differences necessitate certain safeguards to a woman's health and welfare, the laxity of enforcement and even the suspension of some of these safeguards during various periods of Soviet history suggest that the goal of greater production has more often than not overridden the altruistic concern for protection. Naturally, even under the most extreme pressures, the regime cannot afford a complete abandonment of safeguards and protective measures, since the effective utilization of women as producers depends to a considerable degree upon the reduction of the conflicts which arise from woman's competing roles as wife and mother. But if the regime had consistently placed women's welfare ahead of production in its scale of priorities, there would be concrete evidence of this in a greater abundance of child-care facilities and a more conscientious enforcement of protective legislation. Similarly, if equality of educational opportunity between the sexes had been of primary concern, admissions regulations and other factors which have contributed to the decline over the past decade in the proportion of women among students in higher education would have been altered when the decline first became evident. Failure to alter them until recently is evidence that the regime in fact preferred the efficient use of its limited higher educational facilities to the social ideal of equality. Apparently realizing that a woman is not likely to be so economically productive as a man in the course of a lifetime, Soviet planners opted for productivity as a social goal and chose accordingly to restrict access to higher education to a smaller proportion of women. It remains to be seen whether the recent modifications in admission requirements are sufficient to redress the balance between the

sexes and to permit the percentage of women in higher education to rise to a level proportionate with the percentage of
women in the college age population as a whole.

In a totalitarian society such as the Soviet Union, many options are open to the regime in purusing its policies which are
not available to a government responsive to the public will. The
party, both directly and through the government, exercises a
decisive influence on almost every aspect of economic and
social behavior. As we have seen, certain of the policies
adopted may be mutually counter-productive — as are, for instance, those aimed simultaneously at the achievement of a
higher birth rate and a greater participation of women in the
labor force. Others may be in conflict with deep-seated beliefs
and customs and may make slow headway — as, for example,
the higher education of women in Central Asia, where the traditional subservience of women leads to the early withdrawal of
girls from school. For the most part, however, through its control of the means of mass communication and education, the
regime has succeeded in achieving acceptance of the new attitudes toward female participation in the labor force, particularly in sectors and occupations which had previously been all
but closed to women.

To a society such as our own, which does not tap more than
a fraction of the full economic potential of its women, both a
lesson and a challenge are implied in the success of the Soviets
in developing skilled and capable professional women, particularly in the fields of science and technology. Indeed, Soviet
numerical superiority in certain scientific and technological
fields is due entirely to the employment of a large number of
women in these fields. Although it has been pointed out that the
achievement of Soviet women, on the average, falls short of
that of men, there can be no doubt that many talents and skills
which would have been neglected in another society have been
developed and utilized in the Soviet Union and that Soviet
policies have made of women one of the major sources of economic strength. Indeed, the imbalance of the sexes in the Soviet
population, particularly in the mature age groups, has made the
effective participation of women in all sectors of the economy
essential to its development. In other, more advanced, societies,
this urgent need for the services of women does not arise. The
Soviet example proves, however, that a large reservoir of fe-

male talent in the United States and other Western countries remains untapped or underdeveloped. Although the tools and mechanisms required to exploit this potential may not be so readily available to our governments, nor the motivation to exploit it so pressing, it is clear that our own society could go much farther than it presently does toward a full utilization of its womanpower. Indeed, the question might be raised whether we can really afford — not only from the standpoint of the national interest, but also from that of the welfare of women as individuals — to neglect their potential contribution of talent and intellect and to leave them so largely at the margin of our economic life.

NOTES

The sources on which this data is based derive mainly from published Soviet materials. Additional first-hand information was gathered in 1955, 1962, and 1965, including both formal and informal conferences and interviews with Soviet officials, administrators, and professionals. Many of those interviewed were women. See p. viii of the preface to *Women in the Soviet Economy.*

1. President's Commission on the Status of Women, *American Women* (Washington, D.C., 1963), p. 28.

2. Tsentral'noe statisticheskoe upravlenie pri Sovete ministrov SSSR, *Zhenshchiny i deti v SSSR* (Moscow, 1961), p. 109.

3. National Science Foundation, *Women in Scientific Careers* (Washington, D.C., 1961), p. 9.

4. *Ibid.* and Sinetskii, *op. cit.,* p. 130.

5. "Philologist" is the common Soviet term for a teacher of languages and literature.

6. National Science Foundation, *op. cit.,* p. 9.

IV

Career Choice Processes

Career Choice Processes

sixteen

Some Aspects of Women's Ambition[1]

RALPH H. TURNER

Sociological thinking about the nature of ambition has generally been geared to the situation of men rather than women. A man works toward some goal that the sociologist can locate on the stratification grid; it can be related to his starting point in order to measure mobility; and its components such as education, money, and occupation can be tested for consistency. The term "ambition" is appropriately used because many features of his life are focused about an active pursuit of a particular station in society. Because of this focus, specific measures of ambition can be used interchangeably for many purposes.

When women's ambition is discussed or measured, it is usually by direct but questionable analogy. Most frequently, women are asked about their educational and occupational goals. But the relative concentration of women college students in majors which are not markedly vocation-related makes the interpretation of gradations in educational ambition in the same terms as for men a doubtful procedure.[2] And the applicability of serious career patterns to only a fraction of all women makes occupational ambition plainly non-comparable between men and women.[3]

Our objective in this paper is to shed some light on the character of women's ambitions, by making use of data regarding 1,441 high-school senior women in Los Angeles. Measures of several types of ambition were secured for both women and

From AMERICAN JOURNAL OF SOCIOLOGY, Vol. 70, No. 3 (1964), pp. 271-285. Reprinted by permission of the author and The University of Chicago Press.

men students, and gross frequencies and relationships with socioeconomic background have been reported elsewhere.[4] The data were secured in questionnaires administered by the investigator and his assistants under carefully controlled classroom conditions. Ten high schools were selected so as to provide a sample which would be socioeconomically representative of the central metropolis.

The Problem of Women's Ambition

There are two broad ways in which women's ambition can pose a different problem in measurement from men's ambition. First, the nature of ambition may be different in women, perhaps in degree, in goal, and in means to the goal. Second, women's ambition may be more differentiated or segmented, so that a typical individual simultaneously pursues different ambitions which have little relationship to one another. An exploration of these two kinds of distinctiveness will set the stage for the consideration of data.

The nature of ambition — There is recurring evidence that sex of respondent is a pervasive variable affecting behavior and attitudes of many sorts. Carlson and Carlson observed that twenty-two out of thirty-two studies in the *Journal of Abnormal and Social Psychology* from 1958 to 1960 showed significant differences in response for males and females.[5] They warn investigators against the danger of using only male subjects in experiments, and of failing to keep separate the responses of males and females.

W. E. Vinacke and his associates have called attention to the different patterns of performance by men and women subjects in competitive game experiments.[6] From a series of experiments has come the formulation of an ideal-typical *accommodative* strategy for women, contrasted to *exploitative* strategy for men. Applied to coalition formation in a three-person group, accommodative strategy involves offers to form triple coalitions when two-person coalitions are needed to win, division of prizes equally rather than according to bargaining strength, altruistic offers in which one player suggests that the other two form a coalition to her disadvantage, and similar steps. Procedures of this sort serve to modify the character of the game away from the masculine strategy of exploiting others in order to win.

There is consistent evidence that the ambition of women in the socioeconomic realm is lower than that of men. Although women make better records in high school, fewer aim to graduate from college and still fewer to earn graduate degrees.[7] The ambitions of women are constricted to a few occupational categories, with few aspiring to the highest professions and business positions.[8]

Evidence from the Los Angeles high-school study, reported elsewhere, suggests a distinctive pattern of values associated with high ambition in women.[9] Indorsement of deferred gratification is associated with high ambition in men but not in women; indorsement of individuality is associated with high ambition in women but not in men. Deferred gratification suggests an active stance, with the individual shepherding his resources for the sake of achievement. Individuality suggests the concern with being conspicuous by being different, which in turn is necessary if the individual wishes to be noticed and selected by others. If the woman's ambitions depend upon her being selected by the right man, individuality plays a key part in the woman's ambition configuration.

The same study also showed that most of the values which were found to distinguish ambitious from unambitious boys also distinguished men from women. Association of "feminine" values with low ambition and "masculine" values with high ambition suggests the extension of Vinacke's *accommodative* and *exploitative* strategies from the game situation into the world of socioeconomic stratification.

It is not easy to say, however, whether women aspire less highly in the socioeconomic realm than men, or whether their lower scores on conventional indicators merely reflect somewhat different emphases in their ambition or the use of different means in the pursuit of similar goals. The evidence which makes individuality the feminine value counterpart to deferred gratification suggests a difference in means, though nothing is said about goals. It is also disquieting to find, in Vinacke's work, that the women's *accommodative* strategy actually led to victory over the male players in certain game situations.

Diversification of ambition — In a recent paper, French and Lesser reviewed differences in findings regarding achievement motivation in men and women.[10] When male subjects are placed in situations which ostensibly test their intelligence and leadership, they consistently show heightened achievement-motivation scores. Results for women, on the other hand, are inconsistent, a finding which French and Lesser ascribed to the alternative goals available to women. A man's "one primary goal is almost universally success in his job area . . . What spells achievement for a woman is somewhat less universal." The authors then present experimental evidence in which they initially distinguished women according to their *intellectual* and *women's role* value orientations, and employed corresponding arousal cues in the experimental treatment. Their findings are that the heightened achievement-motive scores occur for women when arousal cues correspond to their own value orientations. Women high in intellectual role orientation respond with heightened indications of achievement motivation when stimulated by intellectual cues; women high in the traditional homemaker role orientation exhibit heightened achievement motive when the cue is relevant to that role.

The problem of women's ambition is inherently more complex than that of men. First, there are some areas in which the girl normally sets and pursues an ambition in much the same fashion as a boy. Such is the case with education. Second, there are those areas in which a woman may or may not choose to set and pursue an ambition of her own. When girls are asked for statements of occupational ambition there will always be some who have career goals in the same manner as boys, some who have occupational goals which are quite secondary in importance to their other goals, and some who genuinely have no such goal. And third, there are areas in which a woman may set goals which can be realized only through the efforts and achievement of a husband. Each of these areas poses difficult problems in the conceptualization and measurement of ambition.

In the case of education the women's ambitions can be measured in exactly the same fashion as men's, but the result is not necessarily interpretable in the same manner. A man's educational ambition should be viewed in two ways, as a goal desired for itself and for the achievement of a "cultured" style of life, and as a means toward high occupational and material status. The former aspect of education can be the same for the two sexes. But the latter aspect for some women will be the means to their own occupations and for others the means to securing husbands through whom to realize their other ambitions.

In dealing with women's own career ambitions we not only confront the problem that many have no such ambitions, but we must deal with the existence of pseudo-career or secondary career objectives. Talcott Parsons has remarked on the frequency with which women have careers that would place them much lower than their husbands if their own careers did in fact determine their social stations.[11] The wife of a professional man who herself works as a secretary, a laboratory technician, or in some other modest white-collar occupation thinks of her "career" in a rather different sense from her husband's career. The career in this sense supplies a supplementary rather than essential income, and is a serious diversion or a way of remaining alert and useful rather than the major determinant of either the woman's socioeconomic station or her style of life. While the decision to have a career is a component of ambition, and while the choice of career is likewise one facet of ambition, it appears unreasonable to treat either as the central goal about which other goals are arrayed. In E. T. Hiller's terms, occupation is the American male's key status,[12] but her own occupation is not usually the key status for a woman.

If the key status for most women lies in the husband's occupation, we might seek the core of women's ambition by examining the qualifications they seek in their husbands. However, the nature of marriage in American society and the cultural sentiment of love support a social norm opposing mate selection which is governed primarily by considerations of ambition. Mate selection primarily on the instrumental grounds of socioeconomic ambition which is realizable through the husband's successes is improper when marriage is viewed as an intimate relationship in which social-emotional[13] interaction supplies the crucial criterion of adequacy. The additional pattern of romantic love in courtship leads many girls to deny that marriage is in any sense a vehicle for their ambitions and to insist that they will marry entirely for love.[14] Hence, while the husband's occupation may be the principal medium through which a woman achieves whatever ambitions she has, the ambitions are not likely to be either so clearly recognized, so specifically set, or so actively pursued as those of the men. As ambitions they are stifled to varying degrees by the attitude that a woman should passively accept the station in life her husband brings her rather than actively striving for a given station as a man is urged to do.

If the husband's occupation is woman's key status, then it should be the primary vehicle through which a material level of living is sought. But it is appropriate to ask whether her other ambitions are for more of the same, or for different goals. Is her educational ambition both a direct and indirect means toward high socioeconomic status, or is it aimed at satisfactions of a different kind? In seeking a career does the woman hope to add to the scale of living which her husband's occupation can bring her, or does she seek something else?

Questions such as these will be difficult to answer. But hints can be sought through two sorts of operation. First, a search for pattern in the intercorrelations of women's various forms of ambition should help to show whether their various ambitions apply to the same goals as their husband's occupations, or whether they point toward alternative satisfactions. Second, examination of the patterns of ambitions which characterize girls who choose to have careers, as compared with girls who do not, will shed some light on what goals are to be realized through a career.

Distributions of Ambition

The measure of ambition employed, the levels observed, and comparative data for men will be briefly reviewed as a prelude to the main analysis. In most instances the levels are not directly comparable between men and women. Previous experience had led us to doubt the usefulness of questions directed toward high-school and college women which asked for positive statements of intention or expectation regarding husband's occupation, education, and material standard of living. Hence the expedient of asking for acceptable minimums was employed — with good success as judged by obtained correlates of ambition.

Two measures of educational ambition were secured. Each woman answered the same question as the men: "Eventually, how much more schooling do you expect to get after you finish high school?" In addition, she answered the question, "Would you be a little disappointed if your future husband didn't have a certain amount of education? Check either 'yes' or 'no' for every item." There followed seven items, from no schooling to college graduate. These measures, with educational expectations for the males, are summarized in Figure 1. The percentage of respondents endorsing a given level of ambition is indicated on the vertical axis, with levels of ambition along the horizontal axis.

Level of material aspiration was stated in the same form for men and women, to permit comparison (Fig. 1). "Will you feel

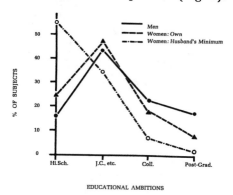

Figure 1. Educational and material ambitions

a little disappointed if — in your whole life — the best you can afford is — ?" Eight alternatives followed, ranging from "a one-room house and a fifteen-year-old car," to "several large houses and several new top-priced cars."

Occupation of the husband was asked both as a minimum and as an ideal. "Would you feel a little disappointed to have your husband spend his life as a —— ?" was followed by a representative set of ten occupations. There followed an open-ended question, "What kind of occupation would you *like* your future *husband* to have?" Nearly a third of the women offered no codable reply to the latter question, so the tabulation in Figure 2 is based on nearly all cases for *minimum* level and

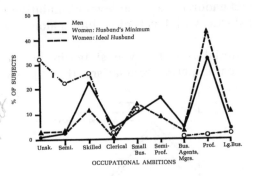

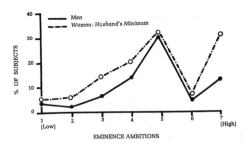

Figure 2. Occupational and eminence ambitions

about two-thirds of the cases for *ideal* level. For males, the data are statements of expected life work.

A question regarding *eminence* ambition had been used for the men, with some interesting results. The aim was to measure concern for standing and accomplishment within the occupational category, as an alternative to striving for identification with a high-ranking occupation or class. Men were asked, "After you are in the occupation which will be your life work, when will you consider yourself successful enough that you can relax and stop trying so hard to get ahead?" The multiple-choice replies ranged from "when I am doing well enough to stay in the occupation" to "when doing better than everyone else in my occupation" and "never." The same question was reworded for women, to refer to their husbands: "After your husband is in the occupation that will be his life work, when will you consider him successful enough that he should relax and stop trying so hard to get ahead?"

Two tentative observations can be made regarding the distributions of ambition. First, women's ambition is lower than men's in the two respects which are directly comparable (education and material level). A rough measure of difference in level of ambition can be secured by dividing the graph in two at the point where two distributions cross, and summing the differences in percentages on either the right or the left of the dividing point. If there were no overlap in the distributions, the measure would reach the maximum of 1.00. By this measure, female educational ambition is less than male educational ambition to almost the same degree as female and male material ambitions differ (0.15, 0.16, respectively). Since, as we shall see later, the relationship of own educational to material ambition is different for men and women, the finding has some special interest.

Second, in three instances the women's statements of an acceptable minimum for their husbands can be compared with the actual ambitions of the male students in the same classrooms. Here we find the greatest difference in the case of occupational ambition (0.58), the least difference for eminence (0.20), and an intermediate difference for education (0.40). If these fairly substantial differences can be taken seriously, they support the view that women are less concerned with the specific occupation or even with the placement in a particular occupation-based stratum of society than men. Their greatest relative emphasis is on standing and accomplishment within strata. In the technical sense suggested by Kingsley Davis, it may be that the balance of concern between prestige and esteem[15] is different for men and women, the latter placing relatively less emphasis on prestige. The intermediate position of education is to be expected, since it is an instrumentality in the attainment of both prestige and esteem.

The latter relationship can be stated in another fashion. Although the class system consists of more or less separable ranked strata, there is a great deal of overlapping with respect to style of life, scale of living, reputation, etc. Thus the lowest members of a given stratum will normally fall below the highest members of the next lower stratum in all important respects except for the stratum designation. These limited findings are consistent with a view that, relatively speaking, women are more concerned with standing on the attributes of station in life which constitute a continuum than they are with specific stratum.

The Interrelationship of Ambitions

The most general procedure for examining the extent of differentiation among the forms of ambition and for locating clues to the meanings of specific types of ambition is to look for patterns in a matrix of intercorrelations. The pattern of interrelationships could suggest a relatively unitary ambition, measured with varying accuracy by each specific index, or a few major types of ambition, or that each index constituted a form of ambition that is relatively unrelated to any other.

Seven ambition measures have been intercorrelated. Because of the lack of cardinal numbers, the ρ or Spearman rank-order coefficient was used throughout.[16] Because the *eminence* measure does not correlate to an appreciable degree with any of the other measures, it has been omitted from Table 1. Separate matrices are presented for the women who choose to have careers and for those who do not.

The problem at hand might best be resolved by factor analysis, except that the number of variables and the ordinal correlations would magnify errors in the use of such procedures to an excessive degree. Hence we have followed the simpler procedure of rearranging columns and rows in a search for pattern. With the exception of *ideal* husband occupation, the matrix for career-seekers fits perfectly a pattern suggesting that two distinct underlying types of ambition are being measured. The variables have been arranged in Table 1 according to this pattern.

The principle underlying this pattern is simply that coefficients should decrease in size as their distance from the diagonal increases. The attainment of such a pattern indicates that adjacent variables are relatively similar to one another and distant variables are dissimilar. Variables falling toward the ends describe best the underlying types of ambition. The pattern can be achieved in a two-dimensional matrix only if placement along a single axis will suffice to describe the major relationships among the variables.[17]

In this case, we find that material ambition is near one pole

Table 1 / Rank Correlations Among Six Types of
Ambition, for Women

Type of Ambition	Material	Mini- mum Husband Occupa- tion	Mini- mum Husband Educa- tion	Own Educa- tion	Own Career	Preferred Husband Occupa- tion
Women Planning To Have Careers						
Material (N=546)	..	0.41	0.39	0.17	0.08	0.08
Minimum husband occupation (N=546)	0.41	..	.51	.29	.27	.21
Minimum husband education (N=546)	.39	.51	..	.43	.33	.22
Own education (N=546)	.17	.29	.43	..	.65	.22
Own career (N=484)	.08	.27	.33	.65	..	.20
Preferred husband occupation (N=339)	0.08	0.21	0.22	0.22	0.20	..
Women Not Planning To Have Careers						
Material (N=563)	..	0.42	0.46	0.22	..	0.27
Minimum husband occupation (N=563)	0.42	..	.49	.33	..	.33
Minimum husband education (N=563)	.46	.49	..	.47	..	.42
Own education (N=563)	.22	.33	.47	..	..	0.30
Preferred husband occupation (N=374)	0.27	0.33	0.42	0.30	..	..

and the specific choice of career near the other. Thus the level
of material ambition and the level of career ambition have
nothing in common. The girl's own educational ambition has
much in common with her choice of career, but is not quite so
far removed from her material ambition. The minimum husband
occupation has most in common with material ambition, but is
not quite so far removed from the girl's choice of career. The
girl's designation of a minimum acceptable education for her
husband is something of a bridge between the extreme foci of
female ambition. This pattern demonstrates in comprehensive
fashion the bifurcation of women's ambition. And it shows
clearly that the differentiation between material and non-
material goals corresponds with a difference between values
sought through the husband and by the girl's own effort.

The girl's designation of an ideal husband occupation bears

a uniform modest relationship with all but material ambition. Perhaps the introduction of an ideal or fantasy element removes it from the polar continuum which orders the remaining forms of ambition.

The girls who choose only to be homemakers lack one of the polar measures of ambition, and it will be crucial for interpretation to see whether the remaining variables assume the same pattern as before.[18] It might be supposed that women's educational ambition is "pulled away" from the more strictly socioeconomic goals only because it must serve as a means toward attainment of a career goal, in which case it should not be so sharply differentiated from the minimum husband occupation and material level among the non-career girls. On the other hand, if the pattern persists, the idea of an underlying polar continuum of ambition will be more impressive.

While the fit is not quite so perfect as for the career-choosers, the best-fitting pattern maintains exactly the same ordering of the four measures of ambition, with material aspiration and the girl's own education at the poles. The *ideal* husband occupation remains outside of the main pattern but is substantially more highly correlated with the other measures than it was among the career-choosers. Ideal husband occupation cannot be fitted into the correlation matrix in the place of the girl's own career. But the suggestion that more of what a girl values is vested in her *ideal* husband occupation when she herself does not elect to have a career may warrant further notice.

Although the patterning of women's ambitions is intrinsically interesting, it takes on full significance for our purposes when compared with the patterning for men (Table 2). Comparison

Table 2 / Rank Correlations among Four Types of Ambition, for Men*

Type of Ambition	Material	Occupation	Education	Eminence
Material	..	0.42	0.48	0.35
Occupation	0.42	..	.72	.55
Education	.48	.72	..	0.66
Eminence	0.35	0.55	0.66	..

* All coefficients are based on 1,000 cases. Twenty cases were removed from the full sample of 1,057 native white "Anglo" men because 1 or more of the forms of ambition were coded "not answered," and the remaining 37 were eliminated with the use of a table of random numbers so as to stay within the capacity of the available computer program.

will supply evidence bearing on the hypothesis that men's ambition is less differentiated than women's. In addition, similarities and differences of other sorts may afford clues to the interpretation of female patterns.

The various forms of ambition have much more in common for men, as demonstrated by the generally higher correlations in Table 2. The most crucial difference lies in the correlations between education and material ambition. For women, education is not an important instrumentality in securing an expected material level of living ($\rho = 0.17$); for men there is a substantial relationship ($\rho = 0.48$).

This difference cannot be discounted as an artifact of poorer measurement in the case of women, because the magnitudes of certain crucial relationships are quite comparable. Thus the relationship between a man's educational and occupational ambitions ($\rho = 0.72$) is similar to the corresponding relationship between the career-choosing woman's educational and career ambitions ($\rho = 0.65$). The same is true of the man's occupational and material ambitions ($\rho = 0.42$) as compared with the woman's minimum husband occupation and material ambitions ($\rho = 0.41$).

Although the range in magnitude of correlations is not so great for men, an effort was made to discover a pattern by the same procedures applied to the matrix for women. The best arrangement of the four variables produces a pattern marred only by a single trivial reversal. This order has been followed in Table 2.

Two features of the arrangement of variables are striking. First, the order corresponds with the order for women — material level, the man's occupation, and educational ambition. Second, the position in the arrangement which is occupied by the woman's career ambition is filled by eminence ambition for men. In spite of the closer clustering for men, apparently the same latent dimension organizes the forms of ambition for men and women. If career and eminence ambition are female and male counterparts in the pattern, consideration of the nature of eminence ambition may shed light on the nature of the woman's career.

Eminence may be coupled with an ambition to rise in the socioeconomic scale, or it may be an alternative to mobility. It is not primarily a preoccupation with material reward, as indicated by the polarization. It is more closely related with education than with other types of ambition. The man's ambition normally combines a desire to achieve high status with a desire to achieve some recognition for the quality of role performance within his status. For many men the mere achievement of a high station in life and its translation into a high material level of living are empty without the complementary satisfaction of a job well done. In the same way, the woman's satisfaction with her station in life and corresponding level of living which are anchored to her husband's occupation, are often empty by themselves. But she is not usually involved in the performance aspects of her husband's occupation except in peripheral ways; and the separation is even more marked for the girl who is not yet married. For a considerable proportion of these girls, the career may convey a promise of the same complementary type of achievement which the man attains by striving incessantly to perform his occupational role with excellence.

The Career Goal

More light can be shed on the differentiation in women's ambition by a specific examination of the career goal, and some comparisons of women who wish to have careers with women who do not.

Career or homemaker? — If we are to determine whether the goals these high school girls seek through careers are different from those they seek through husband status, it is important not to confuse career with the casual and temporary jobs which the majority of women hold at some time in their adult lives. The term, "life-time career," was selected as a simple way of designating the serious occupational goal. The term "homemaker" was used in case any of the women had an aversion to the word "housewife." Expectation rather than wish or desire was requested because such wording had generally been found more satisfactory in aspiration research. The actual wording of the question was as follows:

Do you expect to

_____ (1) Have a life-time career?

_____ (2) Be a homemaker?

_____ (3) Both have a life-time career and be a homemaker?

The distribution of responses to the question appears in Table 3.

From the very small number naming a "career only" it is clear that very few of these girls think in terms of a choice

Table 3 / Career-Homemaker Choice for Women

Choice	Per Cent
Lifetime career	3.6
Homemaker	48.4
Both	47.9
Total	99.9
Total No	(1,437)
No. Not Answering	(4)

between career and homemaker roles. The choice, on which they are evenly divided, is between having or not having a serious career *in addition to* their home role. Forty-eight per cent of the girls are undeterred by frequent discussions of the supposed difficulties in combining the two major roles.

Career in relation to educational and material ambition — Does the girl's decision to seek a career reflect aspiration to higher social station or socioeconomic status than the choice of homemaking alone? Is the motivation described by Smuts applicable to high-school career aspirants, when he says: "Most of today's working wives show no strong internal commitment to work . . . they work mainly in order to earn money they don't absolutely have to have"?[19] The most direct way to answer this question is to see whether there are relationships between electing a career and measures of educational and material ambition. Chi-squares based upon cross-tabulation with the three career-homemaker categories show a highly significant association ($p < .001$) of career only with high educational ambition (career-plus-homemaker in intermediate position), but no relationship with material ambition. A result of this sort undermines the view that women choose the career role in order to achieve socioeconomic status.

A difference in emphasis can be measured by use of the *material-education polarization index* (MEPI). Material ambition and educational ambition were each converted to standard scores, the score for education was subtracted from the score for material ambition, and a constant was added to make all scores positive. The χ^2 indicates a highly significant ($p < .001$) relationship between MEPI and career choice, and when career-only and career-plus-homemaker categories are combined for comparison with homemaker-only, a biserial coefficient of —0.29 is secured. Women who want careers are likely to stress educational ambition more than material ambition; women who wish only to be homemakers are likely to stress material ambition more than educational ambition.

The irrelevance of material ambition for the choice between career and homemaking can be documented in an even more specific fashion. If women choose to have careers because of their ambitions for higher material standards than husbands alone can provide them, then the relationship of husband's and own occupational ambition to material ambition should be cumulative. Families in which the wife has a career are two-income families, and the total income should be higher than in a one-income family with the same husband occupation. If the prospect of this double income is important in deciding to have both career and homemaker roles, the girls who choose both should report higher material ambitions than girls who name similar minimum husband occupations but choose only the homemaker role. A glance at Table 4 reveals that this is not the case. There

Table 4 / Effect of Combining Career and Homemaker Roles on Women's Material Ambition

Minimum Husband Occupation*	Mean Material Ambition	
	Homemaker Only	Career and Homemaker
Unskilled labor	2.95 (238)	3.01 (197)
Semiskilled labor	3.21 (179)	3.33 (159)
Skilled labor	3.67 (186)	3.67 (203)
Clerical and sales clerks	[4.00] (10)	[3.63] (24)
Small business owners — managers and salesmen	4.14 (76)	4.10 (86)

* Higher-level occupations are not included in the table because the number of women specifying them was too small to produce stable means. The clerical and sales clerk category is included only to avoid a break in the table.

is a clear relation between minimum husband occupation and material ambition, but girls who choose both career and homemaker roles do not reflect the double income in setting their own material ambitions.

Values and career-homemaker choice. — Included in the questionnaire were thirty-one value items, selected to reflect several of the major sorts of values often thought to distinguish respondents from high and low socioeconomic backgrounds.[20] Comparison of those items associated with the career choice and those associated with level of ambition may shed further light on what is distinctive about the goals of girls who wish to pursue careers.

In Table 5 all items which were significantly associated with either career choice or ambition level are reported. The ambition index is a composite measure, based upon a score of 0-3 for minimum husband occupation, 0-3 for material ambition, 0-2 for own educational ambition, and 0-2 for minimum husband education. A smaller number of items are related to the career-homemaker choice as compared with general socioeconomically relevant ambition. To the extent to which the items used in this study can be taken as a sample of socioeconomically relevant values, the choice to have a career is less a reflection of class values than are ambitions which do not center on the career.[21]

The similarities and differences with respect to individual items fit a pattern of similar goal and dissimilar means. The career girls are not set apart by the use of individuality (items 14, 24, 25) as an adjunct to ambition through the traditional female role, as the ambitious girls are. But they also do not place emphasis on the more masculine virtue of self-reliance (items 22, 28). Likewise they do not share the moral opportunism (items 15, 21, 30) of the ambitious girls. However, they do place the same emphasis on the pursuit of secular success (items 13, 21, 34, 37).

At the same time, the career girls do significantly more often state that they would prefer enjoyment of music, art, and books to making a very good living (item 9), suggesting a difference in the hierarchy of goals as well as means. It is notable that the career girls and ambitious girls choose business success over family (item 13) with equally great significance. It is only when the choice is for a "cultured" way of life that the career girls depreciate secular success.

This limited evidence suggests, in summary, that there are differences in both goal and means that set the career girl apart. The career girls place the "cultured" way of life higher in their value hierarchy. What means they favor for the pursuit of their goals is not clear; we see only that they do not distinctly employ the values of individuality, self-reliance, and moral opportunism, as the ambitious women seem to do.

Sociometric correlates of career-homemaker choice — Al-

Table 5 / Values Associated with Ambition Index and
Career-Homemaker Choice

Value Item*	Ambition Index	Career-Homemaker Choice
8. Can do a few things perfectly vs. can do many things fairly well	0.05†	0.01
9. Enjoys art, music, books vs. makes very good living	..	.01
12. Spends extra money on friends vs. saves extra money for future	.01	..
13. Real success in business vs. real family man	.001	.001
14. Shows people how to argue intelligently vs. smooths over disagreements	.001	..
15. Will tell small lie to help friend vs. sticks by truth	.001	..
17. Rather be own boss vs. will take orders to get ahead	.001	..
21. Smooth operator always comes out on top vs. too kind to take unfair advantage ..	.001	.05
22. Prides self on doing things on his own vs. likes advice and help from others ..	.02	..
24. Does many things better than friends vs. does most things as well as friends	.001	..
25. Tries to get group to do things his way vs. quick to go along with group	.001	..
28. Neither a borrower nor a lender be vs. often borrows-lends with friends	.01	..
29. Talks foreign policy and politics vs. talks popular music and sports	.001	.02
30. Laughs off his failures and mistakes vs. takes full blame for own failures	.05	..
31. Laughs off insult to his honor vs. never lets insult to honor go by	..	.05
34. Risks what he has to get ahead vs. prefers small but secure position	.001	.001
37. Always looking for something better vs. satisfied with what he has	0.001	0.01

* The alternative associated with higher ambition or choice of career has been listed first in each instance. There are no reversals of relationship.
† The probability that the observed associations could have occurred by chance in a random sample is less than the figure indicated in each instance. Associations were tested by chi-square, using two degrees of freedom.

though it is less directly relevant to assessing the character of ambition, sociometric evidence may add to the picture of the career girl. Students were asked to name three other students in their classroom whom they would like as long-term close friends, to identify two students as "big wheels," and to name two students who were best in their school work. Indexes based on proportion of possible choices *received*, adjusted and equated by schools, were computed. The indexes will be called "friend rating," "brain rating," and "wheel rating." Percentage analysis is summarized in Table 6.

Table 6 / Sociometric Indexes and Career-Homemaker Choice (Per Cent)

Index Value	Percentages		
	Career Only	Homemaker Only	Both
Friend rating			
1, 2 (low)	36	27	33
3	42	38	32
4	12	24	20
5, 6 (high)	9	12	15
Total	99	101	100
Wheel rating			
1 (not wheels)	85	83	79
2-4 (wheels)	15	17	21
Total	100	100	100
Brain rating			
1 (not brains)	70	77	70
2-4 (brains)	30	23	30
Total	100	100	100
Total No	(33)	(558)	(512)

Wheel rating appears to be unrelated to career-homemaker choice. If the girls who choose careers were thereby seeking social prominence, we should have expected that they would have converted such aspirations into social prominence in their own schools.

Brain rating, on the other hand, shows a small but significant relationship with career preference ($p < .02$, 2 degrees of freedom; $p < .01$ when "career only" and "both" are combined,

1 degree of freedom). This finding fits the interpretation already placed on the relative preference for a "cultured" style of life, suggesting that the career girl has accepted academic values more fully than the girl who chooses only homemaking.

The relationship with friend rating is more complex. Girls who eschew the homemaking role altogether are the least desired as friends. Girls who are satisfied with homemaking alone are disproportionately a middle group — neither the most nor the least chosen as friends. The girls who wish to combine roles include disproportionately both extremes, the most and the least desired. The over-all relationship is of moderate significance ($p < .05$, 6 degrees of freedom), but the contrast between the homemaker-only group and the other girls is more firmly significant ($p < .02$, 3 degrees of freedom).

Type of career — The specific careers intended by the 52 per cent of girls who expressed such ambition were identified in response to the following question: "If you plan on a lifetime career, what occupation do you think you will make your life work?" The responses are summarized in Table 7. Nearly 14

Table 7 / Occupational Ambition of Career Women

Occupational Category	Per Cent
Unskilled labor	0.2
Semiskilled labor	1.3
Skilled labor	6.4
Clerical and sales clerks	26.4
Small business owners-managers and salesmen	0.6
Semiprofessionals	35.0
Business agents and managers	0.9
Professionals	29.1
Large business owners and officials	0.2
Total	100.1
Total No	(640)
No. not answering	(101)

per cent of those who said they planned on a lifetime career were unable to name a specific occupation. Considering that these students are approaching graduation, and that the combined non-response and unclassifiable responses by men total only 1 per cent, it is clear that many of the girls who state that they plan to have a career have not taken their plans as seriously as have the men.[22]

The occupations named by women are concentrated in three categories the semi-professions, the professions, and clerical work. Business management and ownership are almost entirely lacking, with women choosing almost exclusively the clerical phase of business. The three most popular groups of occupations are similar to those named by the men, except that the clerical category takes the place of skilled labor as the peak of ambition in the lower portions of the scale. Nearly two-thirds named one of the professions or semiprofessional occupations. The largest single group, about 24 per cent, named occupations in the education-scientific professions. The other major groups were in the semi-professions related to medicine and in the entertainment, art, and literature group. The choices correspond with the present concentrations of "women's occupations."

Concluding Reflections

The investigation into women's ambition began with several queries. But the same answer crops up in reply to each. The fundamental differentiation of women's ambition, related to *direct* and *indirect* pursuit of goals imposed by the married woman's role, appears to be the key to the data at hand. The differentiated elements in women's ambition seem to be present in men's ambition; but because men pursue the entire range of ambitions directly, there is less structurally imposed separation among the forms of ambition.

Specific measures of ambition convey rather different meanings for men and women: educational and occupational ambitions are substantially related to material ambitions for men, but women's own educational and career aspirations bear little relationship to their material expectations. This observation should be an immediate warning to investigators never to attempt to compare the level of men's with women's socioeconomic goals or ambition by comparing levels of educational and career aspirations. Likewise, there are probably differences between career-and non-career-choosers, especially in the significance of an ideal husband occupation as a reflection of ambition. But the supervening observation is the uniform latent structure of ambition in men and in women, and in career- and non-career-choosers.

The underlying pattern of differentiation suggests — but does not exactly fit — the standard sociological distinction between prestige and esteem. Occupational level and *eminence* correspond well to prestige and esteem; but material rather than occupational level is the polar category opposite eminence in our data. *Extrinsic* and *intrinsic* rewards may supply a closer fit. Material reward reflects least the interest in effort and work for its own sake; eminence points most strongly toward striving for excellence within the occupation; educational ambition may be a better indication of dedication to achievement or accomplishment for its own sake than mere choice of occupation. The pole of intrinsic reward suggests an *achievement motive*, though no measure of this variable was included in the investigation.

A woman cannot seek both types of reward through the same activities, so long as she employs the traditional perspective in relating herself to the socioeconomic system — as these women do. With few exceptions, these women choose to *add* a special role rather than substitute for the traditional homemaker role. In adding this role they leave the extrinsic reward of material level of living entirely in its traditional place, as a function of the husband's efforts. But so long as they accept this traditional assignment, women cannot reap the intrinsic rewards of accomplishment that their husbands will in association with extrinsic returns.[23]

The general pattern which emerges is one in which educational ambition becomes more preponderantly a vehicle for the pursuit of intrinsic reward in women than in men. For girls who choose careers, the career carries this tendency even further.

A man's occupation normally offers both the intrinsic enjoyment of specific forms of activity and the extrinsic rewards, such as material comfort and social standing, which belong principally to level of occupation. But if the former is not part of the woman's perspective toward her husband's work and accomplishments, it is not surprising that she is willing to consider marriage to a man whose occupational level is low. Her *fantasy* about a husband's occupation seems to mean little when she invests intrinsic ambitions in her own career, but reflects some of her non-material ambitions when she does not have a career goal of her own.

If women plan to leave the extrinsic goal of high socioeconomic status to their husbands, it is not surprising that career-choosers are not set apart from other women with respect to some of the attitudes normally associated with high socioeconomic ambition. "Ambitious" men and women are likely to be identified as "big wheels" by their peers; but career-choosers show no such distinguishing evidence of interest in social climbing or influence. Nor do career-choosers differentially indorse values which correspond to the *means* for attaining high socioeconomic status, such as individuality and self-reliance. They do resemble the "ambitious" in valuing "success," especially when the choice is with security and adjusting to one's current situation. Thus, while the decision to have a career does not incorporate more of the same kind of ambition as the desire for high socioeconomic status, it does reflect concern with success — by different means and of a different sort.

The difference in kind of success sought through career is suggested by two kinds of evidence. Career-choosers are distinguished by their reputation for doing well in their school-work, though "ambitious" women are similarly distinguished. But they alone are distinguished by a preference for aesthetic and intellectual values in contrast with good living. If aesthetic and intellectual goals are more in the nature of intrinsic than extrinsic rewards from activity, then the two kinds of evidence point toward the same conclusion: (a) extrinsic rewards are sought through the husband's occupation and intrinsic rewards through the woman's own career; (b) women who value intrinsic rewards more highly are more likely to seek careers.

These conclusions can, of course, be offered only as plausible inferences. And they refer only to girls seventeen to eighteen years of age, looking in most cases toward a future which they are as yet in no position to see clearly. What transformations of motive and attitude will accompany experience in marriage and career are not indicated. But the decisions made in this Senior year of high school have far-reaching consequences. To the extent that the interpretations have been correct, they describe a structure which is likely to enter into the choice process and the initial experiences in marriage and career.

NOTES

1. These data were collected under a grant from the Social Science Research Council and analyzed with assistance from the U.C.L.A.

Research Committee and National Science Foundation, using facilities of the Western Data Processing Center. David Chandler assisted in the statistical computations and made valuable substantive suggestions. Melvin Seeman painstakingly read and criticized a draft.

2. Subject-matter fields in which degrees were awarded in 1961-62 are reported, by sex, in U.S. Office of Education, *Digest of Educational Statistics* (Washington, D.C.: Government Printing Office, 1963), p. 70.

3. See, e.g., Rose K. Goldsen, Morris Rosenberg, Robin M. Williams, Jr., and Edward A. Suchman, *What College Students Think* (Princeton, N.J.: D. Van Nostrand Co., 1960). pp. 46-59.

4. Ralph H. Turner, *The Social Context of Ambition: A Study of High School Seniors in Los Angeles* (San Francisco: Chandler Publishing Co., 1964).

5. Earl R. Carlson and Rae Carlson, "Male and Female Subjects in Personality Research," *Journal of Abnormal and Social Psychology,* LXI (February, 1960), 482-83.

6. Thomas K. Uesugi and W. Edgar Vinacke, "Strategy in a Feminine Game," *Sociometry,* XXVI (March, 1963), 75-88.

7. On superior secondary-school performance of girls, see G. R. Johnson, "Girls Lead in Progress through School," *American School Board Journal,* CXV (1937), 25-26; and Robert S. Carter, "How Invalid Are Marks Assigned by Teacher," *Journal of Educational Psychology,* XLIII (April, 1952), 218-28. Only 38 per cent of degree-credit enrolments in U.S. institutions of higher learning in the fall of 1962 were women, as compared with 51 per cent of high-school graduates for 1961-62 (see U.S. Office of Education, *op. cit.,* pp. 41, 58). Sixty-two per cent of girls who graduated from Los Angeles high schools in 1963, as compared with 70 per cent of boys, were attending college or junior college in the fall of the year (see *After High School* [Los Angeles: City School Districts, Evaluation and Research Section, 1964], p. 4). The 51 per cent of high-school graduates who are women constitute further evidence of the superiority of women in secondary schools, when compared with the 49.6 per cent of the population 15-24 years of age who are females (see U.S. Bureau of the Census, *Statistical Abstract of the United States: 1963* [Washington, D.C.: Government Printing Office, 1963], p. 24).

8. Robert W. Smuts, *Women and Work in America* (New York: Columbia University Press, 1959), pp. 35-36 and *passim* concerning the occupational distribution of women.

9. Turner, *op. cit.,* pp. 98-99. Suggestively similar are the implications of a finding that whereas Machiavellianism contributes to good grades in college for certain men, it is physical attractiveness which does so for certain women (Jerome E. Singer, "The Use of Manipulative Strategies: Machiavellianism and Attractiveness," *Sociometry,* XXVII [June, 1964], 128-50.

10. Elizabeth G. French and Gerald S. Lesser, "Some Characteristics of the Achievement Motive in Women," *Journal of Abnormal and Social Psychology*, LXVIII (February, 1964), 119-28.

11. "The Social Structure of the Family," in Ruth N. Anshen (ed.), *The Family: Its Future and Destiny* (rev. ed.; New York: Harper & Bros., 1959), p. 265.

12. *Social Relations and Structures* (New York: Harper & Bros., 1947), pp. 339-43.

13. Robert F. Bales, *Interaction Process Analysis* (Cambridge, Mass.: Addison-Wesley, 1950).

14. In an earlier pilot interview study with college girls, a large number objected to the direct question, "What occupation do you want your husband to have?" indignantly insisting that they would marry for love, not for their husband's occupation.

15. Kingsley Davis, *Human Society* (New York: Macmillan Co., 1949), pp. 93-94.

16. Sidney Siegel, *Nonparametric Statistics for the Behavioral Sciences* (New York: McGraw-Hill Book Co., 1956, pp. 202 ff. This analysis applies to the native white "anglo" subjects only, though spot checks indicate similar patterns for the whole sample.

17. The procedure is an adaptation from a method developed for use in archeological research (see William S. Robinson, "A Method for Chronologically Ordering Archaeological Deposits," *American Antiquity*, XVI [April, 1951], 293-301).

18. The choice between career and homemaker roles is explained in the following section of this paper.

19. Smuts, *op. cit.*, p. 148.

20. Each value item was worded, "Which kind of person would you rather be . . .," followed by two alternatives and a second question for intensity. The number of cases is reduced by about one-fifth, because some questionnaires were distributed with an alternative formulation of the value questions.

21. It is consistent that the career-homemaker choice is also uncorrelated with measures of paternal socioeconomic level.

22. For evidence suggesting that girls lack realistic knowledge of the occupations they have chosen, see Therese M. Rauner, "Occupational Information and Occupational Choice," *Personnel and Guidance Journal*, XLI (December, 1962), 311-17.

23. The evidence in this paper may offer a little support for the common assumption in stratification theory that "the family is the solidary unit of equivalent evaluation and that the husband's occupation is the principal unit of equivalent evaluation . . .," which has been so ably challenged by Walter B. Watson and Ernest A. T. Barth (see "Questionable Assumptions in the Theory of Social Stratification," *Pacific Sociological Review*, VII (Spring, 1964), 10-16).

seventeen

FAIL: Bright Women

MATINA HORNER

Consider Phil, a bright young college sophomore. He has always done well in school, he is in the honors program, he has wanted to be a doctor as long as he can remember. We ask him to tell us a story based on one clue: *"After first-term finals, John finds himself at the top of his medical-school class.* Phil writes:

> John is a conscientious young man who worked hard. He is pleased with himself. John has always wanted to go into medicine and is very dedicated . . . John continues working hard and eventually graduates at the top of his class.

Now consider Monica, another honors student. She too has always done well and she too has visions of a flourishing career. We give her the same clue, but with "Anne" as the successful student — *after first-term finals, Anne finds herself at the top of her medical-school class.* Instead of identifying with Anne's triumph, Monica tells a bizarre tale:

> Anne starts proclaiming her surprise and joy. Her fellow classmates are so disgusted with her behavior that they jump on her in a body and beat her. She is maimed for life.

Next we ask Monica and Phil to work on a series of achievement tests by themselves. Monica scores higher than Phil. Finally we get them together, competing against each other on the same kind of tests. Phil performs magnificently, but Monica dissolves into a bundle of nerves.

Reprinted with permission from PSYCHOLOGY TODAY, Volume 3, No. 6 (1969), pp. 36, 38, 62. Copyright © Communications/Research/Machines Inc.

The glaring contrast between the two stories and the dramatic changes in performance in competitive situations illustrate important differences between men and women in reacting to achievement.

In 1953, David McClelland, John Atkinson and colleagues published the first major work on the "achievement motive." Through the use of the Thematic Apperception Test (TAT), they were able to isolate the psychological characteristic of a *need to acheive.* This seemed to be an internalized standard of excellence, motivating the individual to do well in any achievement-oriented situation involving intelligence and leadership ability. Subsequent investigators studied innumerable facets of achievement motivation: how it is instilled in children, how it is expressed, how it relates to social class, even how it is connected to the rise and fall of civilizations [see *Evan Davies, page 42*]. The result of all this research is an impressive and a theoretically consistent body of data about the achievement motive — in men.

Women, however, are conspicuously absent from almost all of the studies. In the few cases where the ladies were included, the results were contradictory or confusing. So women were eventually left out together. The predominantly male researchers apparently decided, as Freud had before them, that the only way to understand women was to turn to the poets. Atkinson's 1958 book, *Motives in Fantasy, Action and Society,* is an 800-page compilation of all of the theories and facts on achievement motivation in men. Women got a footnote, reflecting the state of the science.

To help remedy this lopsided state of affairs, I undertook to explore the basis for sex differences in achievement motivation. But where to begin?

My first clue came from the one consistent finding on the women: they get higher test-anxiety scores than do the men. Eleanor Maccoby has suggested that the girl who is motivated to achieve is defying conventions of what girls "should" do. As a result, the intellectual woman pays a price in anxiety. Margaret Mead concurs, noting that intense intellectual striving can be viewed as "competitively aggressive behavior." And of course Freud thought that the whole essence of femininity lay in repressing aggressiveness (and hence intellectuality).

Thus consciously or unconsciously the girl equates intellectual achievement with loss of femininity. A bright woman is caught in a double bind. In testing and other achievement-oriented situations she worries not only about failure, but also about success. If she fails, she is not living up to her own standards of performance; if she succeeds she is not living up to societal expectations about the female role. Men in our society do not experience this kind of ambivalence, because they ,are not only permitted but actively encouraged to do well.

For women, then, the desire to achieve is often contaminated by what I call the *motive to avoid success*. I define it as the fear that success in competitive achievement situations will lead to negative consequences, such as unpopularity and loss of femininity. This motive, like the achievement motive itself, is a stable disposition within the person, acquired early in life along with other sex-role standards. When fear of success conflicts with a desire to be successful, the result is an inhibition of achievement motivation.

I began my study with several hypotheses about the motive to avoid success:

1) Of course, it would be far more characteristic of women than of men.

2) It would be more characteristic of women who are capable of success and who are career-oriented than of women not so motivated. Women who are not seeking success should not, after all, be threatened by it.

3) I anticipated that the anxiety over success would be greater in competitive situations (when one's intellectual performance is evaluated against someone else's) than in noncompetitive ones (when one works alone). The aggressive, masculine aspects of achievement striving are certainly more pronounced in competitive settings, particularly when the opponent is male. Women's anxiety should therefore be greatest when they compete with men.

I administered the standard TAT achievement motivation measures to a sample of 90 girls and 88 boys, all undergraduates at the University of Michigan. In addition, I asked each to tell a story based on the clue described before: *After first-term finals, John (Anne) finds himself (herself) at the top of his (her) medical-school class.* The girls wrote about Anne, the boys about John.

Their stories were scored for "motive to avoid success" if

they expressed any negative imagery that reflected concern about doing well. Generally, such imagery fell into three categories:

1) The most frequent Anne story reflected strong fears of social rejection as a result of success. The girls in this group showed anxiety about becoming unpopular, unmarriageable and lonely.

Anne is an acne-faced bookworm. She runs to the bulletin board and finds she's at the top. As usual she smarts off. A chorus of groans is the rest of the class's reply. . . . She studies 12 hours a day, and lives at home to save money. "Well it certainly paid off. All the Friday and Saturday nights without dates, fun — I'll be the best woman doctor alive." And yet a twinge of sadness comes thru — she wonders what she really has . . .

Although Anne is happy with her success she fears what will happen to her social life. The male med. students don't seem to think very highly of a female who has beaten them in their field . . . She will be a proud and successful but alas a very *lonely* doctor.

Anne doesn't want to be number one in her class . . . she feels she shouldn't rank so high because of social reasons. She drops down to ninth in the class and then marries the boy who graduates number one.

Anne is pretty darn proud of herself, but everyone hates and envies her.

2) Girls in the second category were less concerned with issues of social approval or disapproval; they were more worried about definitions of womanhood. Their stories expressed guilt and despair over success, and doubts about their femininity or normality.

Unfortunately Anne no longer feels so certain that she really wants to be a doctor. She is worried about herself and wonders if perhaps she isn't normal . . . Anne decides not to continue with her medical work but to take courses that have a deeper personal meaning for her.

Anne feels guilty . . . She will finally have a nervous breakdown and quit medical school and marry a successful young doctor.

Anne is pleased. She had worked extraordinarily hard and her grades showed it. "It is not enough," Anne thinks. "I am not happy." She didn't even want to be a doctor. She is not sure what she wants. Anne says to hell with the whole business and goes into social work — not hardly as glamorous, prestigious or lucrative; but she is happy.

3) The third group of stories did not even try to confront the ambivalence about doing well. Girls in this category simply denied the possibility that any mere woman could be so successful. Some of them completely changed the content of the clue, or distorted it, or refused to believe it, or absolved Anne of responsibility for her success. These stories were remarkable for their psychological ingenuity:

Anne is a *code name* for a nonexistent person created by a group of med. students. They take turns writing exams for Anne . . .

Anne is really happy she's on top, though *Tom is higher than she* — though that's as it should be . . . Anne doesn't mind Tom winning.

Anne is talking to her counselor. Counselor says she will make a fine *nurse.*

It was *luck* that Anne came out on top because she didn't want to go to medical school anyway.

Fifty-nine girls — over 65 per cent — told stories that fell into one or another of the above categories. But only eight boys, fewer than 10 per cent, showed evidence of the motive to avoid success. (These differences are significant at better than the .0005 level.) In fact, sometimes I think that most of the young men in the sample were incipient Horatio Algers. They expressed unequivocal delight at John's success (clearly John had worked hard for it), and projected a grand and glorious future for him. There was none of the hostility, bitterness and ambivalence that the girls felt for Anne. In short, the differences between male and female stories based on essentially the same clue were enormous.

Two of the stories are particularly revealing examples of this male-female contrast. The girls insisted that Anne give up her career for marriage:

Anne has a boyfriend, Carl, in the same class and they are quite serious . . . She wants him to be scholastically higher than she is. Anne will deliberately lower her academic standing the next term, while she does all she subtly can to help Carl. His grades come up and Anne soon drops out of medical school. They marry and he goes on in school while she raises their family.

But of course the boys would ask John to do no such thing:

John has worked very hard and his long hours of study have paid off . . . He is thinking about his girl, Cheri, whom he will marry at the end of med. school. He realizes he can give her all the things she desires after he becomes established. He will go on in med. school and be successful in the long run.

Success inhibits social life for the girls; it enhances social life for the boys.

Earlier I suggested that the motive to avoid success is especially aroused in competitive situations. In the second part of this study I wanted to see whether the aggressive overtones of competition against men scared the girls away. Would competition raise their anxiety about success and thus lower their performance?

First I put all of the students together in a large competitive group, and gave them a series of achievement tests (verbal and arithmetic). I then assigned them randomly to one of three other experimental conditions. One-third worked on a similar set of tests, each in competition with a member of the same sex. One-third competed against a member of the opposite sex. The last third worked by themselves, a non-competitive condition.

Ability is an important factor in achievement motivation research. If you want to compare two persons on the strength of their *motivation* to succeed, how do you know that any differences in performance are not due to initial differences in *ability* to succeed? One way of avoiding this problem is to use each subject as his own control; that is, the performance of an individual working alone can be compared with his score in competition. Ability thus remains constant; any change in score must be due to motivational factors. This control over ability was, of course, possible only for the last third of my subjects: the 30 girls and 30 boys who had worked alone *and* in the large group competition. I decided to look at their scores first.

Performance changed dramatically over the two situations. A large number of the men did far better when they were in competition than when they worked alone. For the women the reverse was true. Fewer than one-third of the women, but more than two-thirds of the men, got significantly higher scores in competition.

When we looked at just the girls in terms of the motive to avoid success, the comparisons were even more striking. As predicted, the students who felt ambivalent or anxious about doing well turned in their best scores when they worked by themselves. Seventy-seven per cent of the girls who feared success did better alone than in competition. Women who were low on the motive, however, behaved more like the men: 93 per cent of them got higher scores in competition. (Results significant at the .005.)

| | Female Fear of Success and Performance | |
	Perform better working alone	Perform better in competition
High fear of success	13	4
Low fear of success	1	12

As a final test of motivational differences, I asked the students to indicate on a scale from 1 to 100 "How important was it for you to do well in this situation?" The high-fear-of-success girls said that it was much more important for them to do well when they worked alone than when they worked in either kind of competition. For the low-fear girls, such differences were not statistically significant. Their test scores were higher in competition, as we saw, and they thought that it was important to succeed no matter what the setting. And in all experimental conditions — working alone, or in competition against males or females — high-fear women consistently lagged behind their fearless comrades on the importance of doing well.

These findings suggest that most women will fully explore their intellectual potential only when they do not need to compete — and least of all when they are competing with men. This was most true of women with a strong anxiety about success. Unfortunately, these are often the same women who could be very successful if they were free from that anxiety. The girls in my sample who feared success also tended to have high intellectual ability and histories of academic success. (It is interesting to note that all but two of these girls were majoring in the humanities and in spite of very high grade points aspired to traditional female careers: housewife, mother, nurse, schoolteacher. Girls who did not fear success, however, were aspiring to graduate degrees and careers in such scientific areas as math, physics and chemistry.)

We can see from this small study that achievement motivation in women is much more complex than the same drive in men. Most men do not find many inhibiting forces in their path if they are able and motivated to succeed. As a result, they are not threatened by competition; in fact, surpassing an opponent is a source of pride and enhanced masculinity.

If a woman sets out to do well, however, she bumps into a number of obstacles. She learns that it really isn't ladylike to be too intellectual. She is warned that men will treat her with distrustful tolerance at best, and outright prejudice at worst, if she pursues a career. She learns the truth of Samuel Johnson's comment, "A man is in general better pleased when he has a good dinner upon his table, than when his wife talks Greek." So she doesn't learn Greek, and the motive to avoid success is born.

In recent years many legal and educational barriers to female achievement have been removed; but it is clear that a psychological barrier remains. The motive to avoid success has an all-too-important influence on the intellectual and professional lives of women in our society. But perhaps there is cause for optimism. Monica may have seen Anne maimed for life, but a few of the girls forecast a happier future for our medical student. Said one:

> Anne is quite a lady — not only is she tops academically, but she is liked and admired by her fellow students — quite a trick in a man-dominated field. She is brilliant — but she is also a woman. She will continue to be at or near the top. And . . . always a lady.

eighteen

Career or Marriage?:
A Longitudinal Study of Able Young Women

DONIVAN J. WATLEY

Highly intelligent women in our society generally go to college, do well academically, and develop considerable knowledge and skill in many different areas. It has not been traditional, however, for women, as it has been for men, to move from college into productive and satisfying career roles.

Even at the highest levels of intelligence, most women do not pursue careers. Terman's well-known longitudinal study, started in the early 1920's, included 671 women with an average IQ of 150; when these women were in their mid-forties Terman and Oden (1959) reported that: fewer than one-half are employed outside the home and "for most, a career is not of primary importance." They also observed that:

"the accomplishments of the gifted women do not compare with those of the men. This is not surprising since it follows the cultural pattern to which most of the gifted women as well as women in general have succumbed. Not only may job success interfere with marriage success, but women who do seek a career outside the home have to break through many more barriers and overcome many more obstacles than do men on the road to success. Although the gifted women equalled or excelled the men in school achievement from the first grade through college, after school days were over the great majority ceased to compete with men in the world's work. This characteristic appears to be due to lack of motivation and opportunity rather than to lack of ability" (Terman and Oden, 1959, p. 106).

National Merit Scholarship Corporation, Research Report, Vol. 5, No. 7 (1969). Reprinted by permission.

In reviewing research on gifted women reported by Ginzberg, et al. (1966) and Mattfield and Van Aken (1967), McCormack (1967) reached conclusions similar to those of Terman and Oden. Commenting on the general life patterns found among talented women, she stated that:

"the overall impression is of a group of women who are intelligent, rarely intellectual; competent, rarely creative; performing necessary and useful services, rarely critical. They are in every sense of the word — socially, intellectually, and economically — underemployed"(McCormack, 1967, p. 118).

This study focused on the marriage and career plans of able women who were winners of National Merit Scholarships. Since 1956 the National Merit Scholarship Corporation has conducted an annual talent search to identify and honor the nation's most intellectually able high school graduates. Selected without regard to sex, these students generally score within the top one percent on tested scholastic aptitude. The primary aim of a Merit Scholarship is to enable its recipient to obtain an undergraduate education.

Women scholarship winners during the years 1956 to 1960 were followed up in 1965 to determine their marriage and/or career plans. Therefore, five to nine years had elapsed when the followup was conducted, depending on the year college was initially entered. Women with plans of different types were asked to indicate the highest level of education they sought; and of those seeking careers, an attempt was made to learn which fields they planned to enter. All Scholars were asked to indicate major conflicts they had encountered in making and implementing their marriage and/or career plans. They were also asked to reveal problems experienced *because* they were women.

Method

The National Merit Scholarship Qualifying Test (NMSQT) is administered on a voluntary basis to juniors in high schools that enroll approximately 95 percent of all eleventh-grade students in the United States. Students who score in approximately the top one percent of each state are selected as Semifinalists. The Semifinalists who are endorsed by their schools and whose high scores are verified by a second test — the Scholastic Aptitude Test (SAT) of the College Entrance Examination Board — become Merit Finalists. Finally, a selection committee and scholarship sponsors use high school records, recommendations, and test scores to select the Merit Scholars for each state.

Women who obtained Merit Scholarships during 1956 to 1960 were included in this study. A total of 1,079 received scholarships during this period; 152 were given in 1956, 216 in 1957, 278 in 1958, 219 in 1959, and 214 in 1960.

A questionnaire was mailed during the summer of 1965 to recipients of Merit Scholarships during 1956 to 1960. Of the 1,079 women who were sent questionnaires, usable responses were obtained from 883 (about 82 percent). Usable information was not obtained, however, for all items.

Concerning the marriage and/or career plans of women Scholars, the following question was asked:

"There has been much concern recently about the proper role for talented women. Some contributors to the discussion emphasize the importance of being a mother and homemaker, others stress work and a career, and still others maintain that these aspects of life need not conflict. What are your own plans for family life, work, or both?"

Based on the responses obtained, each woman Scholar was placed into one of five categories: marriage only, marriage with deferred career, marriage with immediate career, career only, or uncertain.

In attempting to learn about the problems encountered in making and implementing their marriage and/or career plans, this question was asked:

"Have you had difficulty in making your marriage or career plans, or in carrying them out? What, if any, relevant special problems or satisfactions do you anticipate? Please be as specific as you can in your answers."

The information obtained was coded and classified into the following major problem types: (1) not aiming high enough, (2) difficulty finding a husband, (3) hindered because of husband's job location, (4) decreased or lack of career ambition, (5) frustration from being pulled in several directions, (6) difficulty in obtaining part-time employment or part-time graduate work, (7) unfair competition with males, (8) keeping up with knowledge in major area or career field. The problems reported here are those which were either described as "major" by the woman Scholar or appeared to independent readers to be highly important to the person describing it. A distinction was necessary between "major" and "minor" problems because some of the women described only their "major" problems while others mentioned problems they considered both "major" or "minor." To be consistent, only the "major" problems are reported here. This information has relevance only to the extent that it provides clues about some of the more important problems they have encountered that they are willing to reveal.

This question was asked to get information about the problems experienced because of being a woman:

"In pursuing your intellectual goals have you encountered any special problems, advantages, or disadvantages because you are a woman?"

The responses were coded into problems of these types: discrimination because of sex, internal conflict over feminine-masculine role, and insufficient time — drawn in too many directions; a separate category was made to include the comments of those who attributed advantages to being a woman. Only those responses were coded that appeared to be of major importance.

The Scholars were asked to indicate their career field plans. Because of the relatively small number of women involved, Scholars' plans were classified into these broad career fields: (1) physics, (2) other physical sciences (e.g., astronomy, chemistry, geology, metallurgy, meteorology); (3) mathematics; (4) biological sciences (e.g., anatomy, biology, botany, pharmacology, physiology, zoology); (5) social sciences (e.g., anthropology, economics); (6) sociology, social work, psychology; (7) humanities and fine arts; (8) education — elementary and secondary; (9) English; (10) medicine; (11) law; (12) business; (13) other (i.e., those not classified in another career field); (14) housewife; and (15) undecided.

Scholar's precollege career plans were also available. This information was collected as part of the Merit Scholar selection process. Thus it was possible to compare Scholars' initial career choices with their plans at the time of the followup.

In addition to initial career plans, each Scholar was asked to indicate any changes in her choice after entering college. A rough validity check was possible for the responses obtained.

During their undergraduate years, Scholars are annually asked to provide information about their educational progress, and whether there were changes in their career objectives. The information obtained on the followup questionnaire was compared with the "changes in career objective" data already in the National Merit files for a five percent sample. The information provided on the followup questionnaire was generally quite similar to that listed on the annual reports. The number of career field choices were counted for each Scholar.

In addition, they were asked:

"If you had to do it over, would you choose a different career field from the one you now see yourself pursuing?" (yes or no)

The following information was obtained from the married Scholars: age at marriage, number of children (including current pregnancy) and husband's education.

Results

Each woman's plans was classified into one of these groups: marriage only, marriage with career deferred, marriage with immediate career, career only, or uncertain. Table 1 shows the proportions of women in each category.

Table 1 / Marriage and/or Career Plans of 1956-1960
Female National Merit Scholars

Plans	Number	Percent
Marriage Only	76	8.6
Marriage and Deferred Career	289	32.8
Marriage and Immediate Career	410	46.4
Career Only	53	6.0
Uncertain	55	6.2
Total Number	883	100.0

Almost one-half (46 percent) planned marriage and an immediate career. Altogether, 85 percent indicated that they planned to pursue a career.

The emphasis here is on plans and not on Scholars' actual status. Although many were already actively carrying out their stated plans, some were not. Thus, *planned* status should provide a clearer picture of their intentions than *actual* status.

It is worthwhile to consider information for those married by the time this followup was conducted. For example, 95 percent of those with "marriage only" plans were already married. In contrast, fewer proportions of those planning to combine marriage and career were married: 80 percent with marriage and deferred career plans were married, and 65 percent desiring marriage and an immediate career were already married. Thus, plans were related to their actual marital status.

Of those who expressed uncertainty about their plans, only 27 percent were already married. Thus, "uncertainty" seemed to include both the marriage only versus career only question as well as the question of whether or not a combination of marriage and career might work better.

The median age at marriage was 22 for women in the "marriage only," "marriage with career deferred," and "uncertain" groups. For those combining marriage with an immediate career, the median age at marriage was 23.

The number of children belonging to women in the various groups are given in Table 2. Many of the married women in each group had no children. Almost 50 percent of those in the "marriage only" and "marriage with deferred careers" groups reported having no children. Thus, in many cases, plans were not affected by the presence of children. Almost one-third of the married Scholars in the marriage-immediate career group planned immediate career employment despite the presence of children in their homes.

Table 2 / Percentages of Married Women with Various Marriage and/or Career Plans who have Different Numbers of Children

| Number of Children | Plans | | | | % of Total |
	Marriage Only	Marriage & Deferred Career	Marriage & Immediate Career	Un-certain	
None	48.6	47.8	68.2	80.0	58.0
1	20.8	25.7	20.6	13.3	22.4
2	25.0	20.9	9.0	6.7	15.6
3	2.8	3.9	1.1	..	2.4
4	..	0.4	..	..	0.2
No Response	2.8	1.3	1.1	..	1.4
Total Married	72	230	267	15	584

Husbands' education of women with different plans is shown in Table 3. The conclusion suggested is that husband's educa-

Table 3 / Percentage of Married Women Scholars with Various Marriage and/or Career Plans whose Husbands have Completed Different Levels of Education

| Husband's Education | Plans | | | | % of Total |
	Marriage Only	Marriage & Deferred Career	Marriage & Immediate Career	Uncertain	
Grade School	..	..	0.4	..	0.2
Some High School	2.7	..	0.7	6.7	0.9
High School Graduate	4.1	0.4	2.6	6.7	2.1
Voc./Bus. College	..	0.4	0.4	..	0.3
College, No Degree	8.2	9.1	9.0	6.7	8.9
Bachelor's Degree	19.2	20.0	11.0	6.6	15.4
Some Graduate Work	27.4	21.3	22.4	33.3	22.9
Master's Degree	19.2	26.7	27.7	20.0	25.6
PhD. or Equivalent	17.8	21.3	22.8	20.0	21.5
No response	1.4	1.8	3.0	..	2.2
Total Married	73	230	267	15	585

tion is not differentially related to the plans of women Scholars. For example, 65 to 75 percent of the women in each of the four groups had husbands with more than a baccalaureate degree.

Although the process by which these women were selected insured considerable homogeneity on tested scholastic ability, it is relevant to determine whether mean test score differences existed among those with different plans. The mean SAT-Verbal and SAT-Mathematic scores for the various groups are shown in Table 4. The means for each ability measure differed among those with different plans. Most notable perhaps are the differences between women who planned marriage only or marriage with a deferred career versus those who planned a career only or marriage with an immediate career; those planning an immediate career scored higher on the average than those who either planned no career or who planned to delay

Table 4 / SAT-Verbal and SAT-Mathematics Means and Standard Deviations for Women with Different Marriage and/or Career Plans

Plans	SAT-Verbal			SAT-Mathematics	
	N	M	S.D.	M	S.D.
Marriage Only	76	693.4	51.4	670.4	77.2
Marriage & Deferred Career	288	695.3	48.5	678.2	65.2
Marriage & Immediate Career	408	711.3	44.9	687.7	69.3
Career Only	53	706.7	42.4	685.7	64.1
Uncertain	55	718.4	41.2	700.1	63.1

entering them. The mean difference of 15.4 between these combined groups on SAT-Verbal is highly significant ($<.001$), and the 10.9 mean difference on SAT-Mathematics is significant at the .05 level.

Results for the highest degree planned by women in the various groups are given in Table 5.

Table 5 / Percentages of Women Scholars with Various Marriage and/or Career Plans who Aspire to Different Educational Degrees

Plans	N	Highest Level of Education Aspired						
		Less than Bachelors	Bachelor's	Masters	PhD	LLB	MD	Other
Marriage Only	76	8.2	40.8	46.9	4.1	..	..	..
Marriage & Deferred Career	289	1.1	20.6	51.1	22.8	2.8	1.1	0.6
Marriage & Immediate Career	410	1.1	11.2	37.1	38.2	1.5	6.7	4.1
Career Only	53	..	9.0	33.3	54.5	..	..	3.0
Uncertain	55	3.4	10.3	34.5	48.3	..	..	3.4

These results suggest that amount of education desired is related to marriage and/or career plans. In general, those who wanted careers sought more education than those who planned no career, and those who planned immediate careers sought more education than those planning to delay them. For example, whereas 51 percent of the women who planned marriage but no career sought a Master's degree or higher, 91 percent desiring careers only sought at least a Master's degree. Since many of those planning careers, particularly those desiring to begin them immediately, sought doctoral level training, it may be inferred that they expected to enter the job market seeking jobs commensurate with their intellectual capabilities.

The career fields selected when these women entered college and the ones they actually entered or expected to enter are shown in Table 6. Considerable shifting occurred among the various fields. Education and "other" professions were the biggest losers from initial to final choices, regardless of group. With the exception of the "marriage only" group, where "housewife" gained from all the career fields, the humanities and fine arts field was the biggest gainer of talent in the other four marriage and/or career groups.

Almost one-half (49 percent) of those who planned a "career only" wanted careers in the humanities-fine arts and "other" fields. Almost none sought careers in the social sciences, medicine, law, business, and education fields.

The humanities-fine arts field was the most frequently chosen "final" career field by women who planned to combine marriage with an immediate career; and, in contrast with the "career only" group 22 percent sought careers in the education, medicine, law, and business fields. Thus, their career preferences tended slightly more toward the traditional types than women who planned a career only.

About one-fourth of the women planning to defer their careers indicated that they expected to enter the field of education. This is a considerably larger proportion than was found for women planning immediate careers.

The number of career field choices after entering college was counted for each woman. In making this count, "undecided" or "housewife" was not included. Interpretative confusion would have resulted from counting "housewife" as an occupational field, particularly for those combining marriage with a career.

It might be expected that women in the "marriage only" and "marriage with deferred career" groups changed their career plans more frequently than those planning to go into careers

Table 6 / Percentages of Women Scholars with Various Marriage and/or Career Plans who had Initial and Final Career Field Plans

Career Field	Plans									
	Marriage Only		Marriage & Deferred Career		Marriage & Immediate Career		Career Only		Uncertain	
	Initial	Final	Initial	Final	Initial	Final	Initial	Final	Initial	Final
Physical Science	9.3	..	8.3	6.6	11.2	4.5	7.5	7.5	21.8	3.6
Physics	1.3	..	4.2	1.0	4.7	1.7	5.7	5.7	3.6	3.6
Mathematics	6.7	..	4.5	5.6	7.0	9.2	1.9	3.8	7.3	5.5
Biological Science	2.7	..	1.0	3.1	2.7	5.2	3.8	5.7	1.8	12.7
Social Science	..	..	1.0	0.7	0.5	3.5	..	..	..	..
Sociology, Social work, Psychology	1.3	..	3.5	4.2	2.7	8.0	3.8	7.5	1.8	1.8
Humanities, Fine Arts	6.7	..	2.8	13.5	6.0	27.4	5.7	24.5	..	16.4
Education	37.3	..	37.5	24.0	31.1	11.2	41.5	3.8	21.8	5.5
English	1.3	..	1.4	..	1.5	0.2	..	1.9	1.8	..
Medicine	4.1	..	6.3	1.4	7.5	7.2	7.5	1.9	7.3	..
Law	1.3	..	1.0	2.1	1.0	1.7	..	..	..	1.8
Business	1.3	..	1.4	0.7	2.5	1.7	1.9	..	..	1.8
Other professions	21.4	..	21.9	9.4	16.6	8.5	17.0	24.5	18.2	7.3
Housewife	..	100.0	0.3	16.3	0.8	2.5	..	..	..	3.6
Undecided	5.3	..	4.9	11.4	4.2	7.5	3.8	13.2	14.5	36.4
Total number	75		288		402		53		55	

immediately. This expectation could be justified on the grounds that women in these two groups have to adjust their plans more frequently than the others in order to find workable solutions to include both marriage and their initial (precollege) career ambitions. Table 7 shows, however, that this result did not occur. About 53 percent in each group had only one career choice, and about 37 percent in each group had two. Only five of the 874 women for whom information was available indicated that they did have at least one career choice after entering college.

Table 7 / Percentage of Women Scholars with Various Marriage and/or Career Plans Who Have Made Different Numbers of Career Choices

Number of Career Choices	Plans				
	Marriage Only	Marriage & Deferred Career	Marriage & Immediate Career	Career Only	Uncertain
None	. .	0.7	0.2	2.0	1.9
1	51.3	55.7	51.4	56.9	47.2
2	42.1	36.3	37.3	33.3	37.7
3	5.3	6.3	10.6	7.8	13.2
4	1.3	0.7	0.5	. .	. .
5	. .	0.3	. .	. .	. .
Total N	76	287	407	51	53

Only 37 of 870 said they would choose a different career field if they had to do it over again. Whereas 11 percent of the "uncertain" women said they would change, the percentages in the other four groups that said "yes" ranged from 2 to 4 percent.

The results presented above suggest that both the level of education sought and the type of career planned are related to the marriage and career plans of these highly intelligent women. Although it is impossible to determine from these data the extent to which marriage and career plans affected the career fields selected, an attempt was made to determine some of the major problems encountered in making and implementing their plans.

Of those who sought a "career only," 98 percent expressed no major problems; 91 percent with "marriage only" plans indicated no major problems. On the other hand, 78 percent, 82 percent, and 84 percent in the "marriage with deferred career," "uncertain," and "marriage with immediate career" groups, respectively, indicated no problems. Thus, those who made definite decisions regarding marriage *or* career were more likely to have expressed no problems.

As shown in Table 8, the most frequent problem (12.2 percent) expressed by women planning marriage with deferred

Table 8 / Percentages of Women Scholars who Expressed having Experienced these Major Problems in Carrying Out their Marriage and/or Career Plans

Major Problems	Plans				
	Marriage Only	Marriage & Deferred Career	Marriage & Immediate Career	Career Only	Un-certain
Not aiming high enough	..	1.0	..	..	..
Difficulty finding mate	..	0.3	3.2	1.9	10.9
Husband's job location	1.3	2.8	2.9	..	..
Decreased career ambition	5.3	1.7	0.7	..	..
Frustration — pulled in many directions	2.6	12.2	3.2	..	3.7
Lack part time employment	..	0.3	2.0	..	..
Unfair competition with males	..	0.7	1.4	..	1.8
Keeping up with field	..	3.5	1.7	..	..
Total N	76	289	410	53	55

careers was one of being pulled in too many directions. One may be surprised that more of them did not express this problem. However, it is incorrect to assume that, with no family obligations, most of these women would have begun their careers immediately; note from Table 2 that 48 percent of them had no children.

The most frequent problem expressed by women uncertain about their plans was one of difficulty finding a mate.

Many more women, regardless of their plans, expressed problems related to their gender than expressed problems that interfered with making and implementing their plans.

As Table 9 shows, the problem of discrimination was cited most frequently by women in each of the five groups. Interest-

Table 9 / Percentages of Women Scholars with Various Marriage and/or Career Plans Who Expressed Having Encountered These Problems *Because* of Being Female

Major Problems	Plans				
	Marriage Only	Marriage & Deferred Career	Marriage & Immediate Career	Career Only	Un-certain
Discrimination because of sex	14.5	12.8	22.9	13.2	21.8
Internal Conflict	1.3	4.8	7.3	..	10.9
Insufficient time	7.9	10.7	5.4	..	3.6
Total N	76	289	410	53	55

ingly, women who were "uncertain" or who wanted marriage with an immediate career expressed this problem proportionally more frequently than women in the other groups.

Women composing the "career only" group were least likely to express major problems related to being a female. In fact, six percent reported *advantages* to being a woman. Only 13 percent of them revealed any problem related to being a woman, and all of these involved discrimination.

Discussion

In contrast to Terman and Oden's (1959) finding that most of the gifted women in their sample did not pursue careers, 85 percent of the women Merit Scholars who participated in this study reported that they planned a career. An important difference, however, is that the women in Terman's sample were in their mid-forties and reported *actual* behavior; the Merit Scholars were in their mid-twenties and reported their *plans*. About 52 percent of the woman Scholars reported, however, that they were either already working in their career fields or planned to begin as soon as their educational programs would permit.

A woman Scholar's actual marital status at the time of this followup was related to her career and/or marriage plans. This result is hardly surprising. It was surprising, however, that the marriage and career plans of many Scholars were apparently not strongly affected by whether or not they had children.

Whereas about 50 percent of the married Scholars who planned a combination marriage-*deferred* career reported having no children, about one-third of the marriage-*immediate* career group had children in their homes. Although traditionally the "place of the young mother is in the home," many of these talented women clearly planned to depart from that tradition.

Although the Merit Scholar selection process insures considerable homogeneity on scholastic ability, it was found nevertheless that the woman Scholars who planned to pursue a career immediately, included those planning a marriage-career combination, scored slightly higher on the SAT-Verbal and SAT-Mathematics tests than those who either planned no career or who planned to delay beginning them.

In addition to these slight ability differences, it was observed that, in general, women who planned careers sought more education than those who did not plan a career; and those who planned to begin their careers immediately wanted more education than those who planned to delay them. Thus, the career ambitions of those seeking immediate careers seem clear: they expect to waste no time getting started and they plan to enter the job market well-equipped educationally.

Although considerable shifting occurred from initial to final career choices, the intentions of these women can be seen in the "final" career fields they selected. In general, they chose high-level professions. Some interesting differences were noted, however, among those who planned a "career only" or a marriage-immediate career combination. Whereas only three of the former group chose careers in the social sciences, medicine, law, business, and education fields, almost one-fourth of the latter group selected these same fields. Almost one-half of the "career only" women were attracted by the humanities-fine arts and "other" fields. Few women said they would choose a different career if they had to make the choice over again.

Most women did not reveal major problems encountered in making and implementing their plans. Those with clear cut "marriage only" or "career only" decisions seldom spoke of major problems.

Many women felt, however, that they had encountered problems pursuing their intellectual goals because of their sex. Although discrimination because of sex was the problem mentioned most frequently, internal conflict over feminine-masculine role and insufficient time were other problems frequently expressed.

A number of women were keenly perturbed because of problems they traced directly to their sex. One described her sex-role conflict in this way:

> "I think intelligent women have a hell of a time, because they read great books and aspire to imitate great deeds of the past. The trouble is, the great books were written by men and the great deeds done by men. This is probably one of the main reasons why women never write great books or do great deeds; we're much too frustrated trying to decide whether to act like men or like women, never succeeding in doing either properly."

About six percent of the "career only" Scholars saw advantages to being a woman in pursuing their intellectual objectives. However, few of her colleagues with different plans shared this view. For example, as an afterthought, one noted sarcastically: "Oh yes, the *advantage* — the ladies room is seldom crowded in the math building."

Although traditionally women, even the most intelligent ones, seldom pursue professional careers, most female Scholars give every indication that they have no intention of maintaining this tradition. In addition to being very able, these women are generally highly motivated to excel, and they have been given the financial assistance they needed to achieve a college education. Perhaps these are some of the reasons they reject the typical feminine role. How successful they will be in fulfilling their ambitions of course remains to be seen.

REFERENCES

Ginzberg, E., Berg, I. E., Brown, C. A., Herma, J. L., Yohalem, A. M., and Gorelick, S., *Life Styles of Educated Women*. New York and London: Columbia University Press, 1966.

McCormack, T., Styles in educated females. *Nation*, January 23, 1967, 204, 117-118.

Mattfeld, J. A., and Van Aken, C. G. (Eds), *Women and the Scientific Professions*. Cambridge: Massachusetts Institute of Technology Press, 1967.

Terman, L.M., and Oden, M. H., *The Gifted at Mid-Life*. California and London: Stanford University and Oxford University Press, 1959.

nineteen

Female Identity and Career
Choice: The Nursing Case

Commitment
to career

RODNEY F. WHITE

A development which is of increasing interest to students of occupations and of work in general is the growing and changing participation of women in the work world. The general importance of this development is reflected in the studies which have been conducted on this subject at top governmental levels in a number of countries[1] and the increasing volume of research which has been carried out in this area in the last few years.[2] The changes which are occurring have become a topic of considerable interest, and best-sellers concerned with this question continue to be heatedly debated on all sides.[3]

An important theoretical problem which is posed by these developments is the determination of the influences which lead women to adopt various different conceptions of their work roles as conditions change. Since the generally accepted sexual division of labor in this society places the major responsibility for the family's economic support on the father, most women can still choose to stop work after marriage, and then return to work later — or not — as they decide. However, women today actually select a wide range of alternatives from lifetime careers in established professions like medicine to being full-time homemakers and devoting any additional energy which is left over from their family responsibilities to non-income-producing projects in the home or the community. The question then arises as to what factors are operating to produce one kind of decision as opposed to another.

The proposition advanced in this paper is that identity is a

Paper read at the annual meeting of the American Sociological Association, Montreal, Canada, August, 1964.

275

major determinant of both occupational and career choice. It will be argued that the strengths or weaknesses of certain key components of identity will influence the kind of occupation a woman selects and the extent to which she views her role in her chosen occupation in career terms. These decisions are particularly complex ones for women since they must always choose what they consider to be an appropriate balance between career and family responsibilities, and may experience a certain amount of identity conflict in so doing.[4] In the remainder of the paper the concept of identity will be explored and its effects on career choice will be examined.

The Process of Identity Formation

A major result of the socialization process for the members of any society is the development of an identity or series of identities — responses to the question, "Who am I?", which incorporate the person's values, attitudes and motivations. The type of identity which a person develops then becomes a key factor in determining his or her orientation to the different roles which he or she is called upon to play.

The concept of identity is useful in sociology because it combines elements of both personality and social structure. Its definition for purposes of this study is the person as she is viewed by herself and others. One's identity is a product of social interaction, and to become stabilized it must be ratified by significant others.[5]

As the individual's identity develops she forms images of herself as possessing certain characteristics to a greater or lesser degree, and these affect her orientations to her various social roles. Three components of this developing identity seem particularly important: the "instrumental" component — the extent to which she views herself as a competent, productive person; the "expressive" component — the extent to which she views herself as an emphatic, helpful, nurturant person; and the commitment component — the extent to which she is dedicated to a particular set of values and objectives.[6] It is the strengths of these components that are proposed as having a critical influence on occupational and career choice.[7]

Career Choice for Women

For purposes of this paper, careers are defined as work-life patterns — those portions of peoples lives which are devoted to their occupational responsibilities as opposed to activities related to the family, the community and other institutional areas.

If one compares the generally accepted stereotypes of male and female careers they present a direct contrast. The male tends to be portrayed as putting his career first, even if it interferes with family life; as striving to be successful and consequently expecting, in time, to rise in his organization; and as hard-headed and aggressive, preferring manipulation of people and things to the subtler area of human relations. The female, on the other hand, is viewed as building her career around her family obligations; is considered only as temporary in any position; and is expected to play a dependent, supportive role in which she looks after details and takes care of "people" problems.

If this were a fairly realistic picture, the analysis of women's careers would be relatively simple. However, a number of other societal factors make feminine career choices much more complex than this would suggest. Two of the more important of these are the pressures in American society on persons, regardless of sex, to develop and achieve on their own,[8] and the increasing assumption by other institutions of many functions formerly performed within the family. Still another is the rising standard of living — including the increased cost of educating children — which encourages wives to contribute to the family income by working.

The process of career choice for women would appear to be somewhat similar to that for men, except that they frequently have the alternative of not working outside the home — a pattern which is becoming less frequent. The choice process is viewed as a "progressive delineation of alternatives," and people with varying backgrounds and experiences will generally have differing images of the various occupations and will be choosing from a different set of alternatives.[9]

The position taken here is that the choice involves a matching of the perceived characteristics of various occupational roles with those of the individual's evolving identity. However, since individuals appear to vary in the strengths of the several components of identity, and since occupational roles vary in the opportunities which they present and in the rewards that they offer, this matching process is an extremely complex one. Also, some occupations are known to people early in life and others are not discovered until later, and the knowledge which people have of the actual characteristics of different occupations varies considerably.

As an oversimplification, the girl who sees herself as a competent, creative person will seek out occupations which provide opportunities for playing this kind of role and similarly for the individual who sees herself as an empathic and nurturant person. Those who view themselves as possessing both sets of characteristics will seek roles which offer both kinds of opportunities.

As Becker has pointed out in a recent article, once a person selects an identity and presents herself to others in a fashion appropriate to that identity, she has, in large part, committed herself to it.[10] Thus, in later discussions, commitment to an occupation will be taken to be equivalent to identification with that occupation. This needs to be distinguished, of course, from "investment" in an occupation, where the person has no intrinsic involvement in a particular occupational role, but feels that she stands to lose more than she is willing to give up by leaving it for another. It is, of course, possible that, after a person is tied to an occupation by virtue of an investment in it, an identification with it will develop.

The position advanced earlier can now be further elaborated by proposing that the degree of commitment which a person has to a particular occupation will be a major factor in determining whether she defines her role in it in career terms. Some data which seems to lend support to this contention is presented later in the paper.

Methods Employed in this Study

Three populations were surveyed during the course of the study: 4,000 freshman nursing students in all nursing schools in New York state; comparison group of 1,677 freshman girls in eleven institutions in the state which provide post high school education for a variety of occupations; and a sample of 1,000 registered nurses in the state, most of whom were working at the time of the study.

The data were gathered using self-administered, largely precoded questionnaires in which there was a high proportion of matched items among the three questionnaires. Additional corroboratory material was obtained through interviews. The items included questions related to occupational role and the respondent's present identity. The strength of commitment was measured by the use of a Guttman-type scale for each group (C. of R. 's = >.90 in each case).

Results of this Research

The Choice of Specific Occupations — In line with the propositions stated earlier, one would expect that the perceptions of an occupation held by those who select it would differ from those of persons who have chosen another field of work. To get some idea of the extent of both the similarities and the differences in the ways in which occupations are perceived, the descriptions of nursing as provided by the nursing students were compared with those obtained from the girls preparing for other occupations. On some of the characteristics there is very close agreement. Both groups agree that nursing has high prestige with the public; that nurses are looked up to; and that the kind of women going into nursing would appeal to them as colleagues. Most of them would place considerable trust in a nurse within her own field of competence, and believe that nurses follow a high code of ethics.

The major differences appear to lie in the perceived extent of the restrictions which are considered to affect the nursing field (see Table 1).

Table 1 / Contrasting Descriptions of Nursing by Nursing Students and Others

(figures shown are %'s of respondents who agree with statement indicated)		
	Nursing Students	Other Students
Nurses' jobs usually require longer hours	59%	79%
Nurses' jobs give you less chance to get ahead	6	25
Nurses have less chance to be their own boss	31	65
Nurses' jobs are less stimulating intellectually	6	29

Those girls who are training to be nurses seem to appreciate the demands which are placed on nurses in terms of hard work, responsibility and long hours but they generally deny the importance of other restrictions. Those who have rejected nursing (or not considered it), on the other hand, in addition to viewing the nurse's lot as even tougher than the nurse views it herself, also believe that nurses are over-bossed, have little chance for advancement and have most of their thinking done for them. Thus, to the extent that they are women who are seeking outlets for their own abilities and initiative, they reject nursing as a potential field of work.

The influence of identity on final choice is demonstrated most effectively when the self-images of persons who have selected different occupations are compared. This relationship is demonstrated dramatically when the views of those who are now in nursing, and those who are not, are contrasted regarding both what they believe to be essential characteristics of nursing, and the conceptions which they have of themselves (see Table 2).

Table 2/ Some Characteristics of Occupational Role and Self
as Viewed by Students and Practitioners

	(figures are %'s of respondents checking each item)					
	Essential for Nursing			Essential for my chosen field	I am above average in . . .	
Qualities described	According to			According to	According to	
	Nursing Students	Registered Nurses	Others	Entrants to this Field	Nursing Students	Other Students
Being respectful	97%	89%	93%	78%	79%	70%
Willing to take orders	97	93	94	68	76	55
Willing to do dirty work	84	(Not asked)	92	32	61	25
Putting work first	82	84	83	58	50	31
Willing to sacrifice self for others	77	(Not asked)	80	46	41	28
Willing to do drudgery	57	50	80	32	33	12
Leadership ability	72	70	36	61	21	35
Ability to express ideas	78	68	27	77	34	37
Originality	41	43	17	57	20	46

The first thing which is apparent is that there is fairly general agreement between those who have chosen nursing and those who picked some other field of work as to the characteristics which are essential for a good nurse. The responses of the non-nurses may be somewhat stereotyped,[11] and those of the nurses overly idealistic, but they show surprising similarity. Nursing is viewed as an occupation which calls for hard work, sacrifice and even drudgery, and the nurse is seen as being very much subordinated to her supervisors and to physicians. Although nurses themselves see their occupation as calling for more leadership and ability to express ideas than do outsiders, both groups rate the occupation low on originality.

If one now examines the self-ratings of the nursing students, the majority see themselves as above average on most of the characteristics viewed as essential to a good nurse and much lower on those which are seen as less important. Also, their self-ratings on the hard working, submissive characteristics are significantly *above* those of the girls going into other occupations, and their ratings on the leadership and originality factors are significantly *lower* than those of the other girls.

The picture is completed when the views which the non-nurses have of the occupations that they are preparing for are contrasted with that which they have of nursing. Here, again, the differences are in the same direction as the differences in the self-ratings, with the other occupations being viewed as requiring more originality, leadership qualities, and ability to express ideas than does nursing; and calling for a lesser degree of hard and dirty work, and less self-sacrifice.[12]

The same correspondence between role-images and self-pictures is observable when the responses of girls preparing for other occupations such as medicine and teaching are examined (see Table 3). For example, those girls who are planning to enter medicine are more likely than those who are going into other occupations to demand high qualifications in almost every area (including a 100% agreement as to the necessity of High I.Q.) as essential for the person to do a good job in her field. They are also the ones in the group who are most likely to rate *themselves* high on most of these same qualities.

In contrast to the prospective physicians, the girls who are training for secretarial work are least likely to make high demands regarding the necessary qualifications of persons to do good work in their field, and a low proportion of these girls view themselves as above average on most of the characteristics under study.

Table 3 / Role Images and Self Conceptions of Students
in Various Occupations

(figures shown are %'s of respondents in category indicated)

Job Requirements	Medicine (27)	Grade School Teaching (375)	Nursing (4004)	Dental Hygiene (71)	Secretarial Work (156)
Essential quality for good work is . . .					
High IQ	100%	60%	63%	52%	54%
Analytical ability	93	60	73	49	42
Express ideas	37	93	78	68	57
Originality	33	79	41	21	25
Willing to sacrifice self	85	62	77	31	29
Sympathy	85	85	90	85	54
Being objective	78	74	76	56	51
Being unemotional	78	48	52	75	55
Attention to details	96	73	93	93	86
Self Image					
I am above average in . . .					
High IQ	70	28	20	16	28
Analytical ability	70	30	30	16	21
Originality	30	42	20	24	24
Putting work first	44	32	50	37	32
Willing to do dirty work	33	20	61	32	19
Willing to sacrifice self	59	33	41	14	23
Sympathy	70	71	68	51	54
Doing things with hands	41	37	42	51	21
Leadership ability	30	44	21	10	20

This generalization continues to hold true when specific qualities thought necessary for a particular occupation are considered. To illustrate, the only occupation, of those considered here, in which a high proportion of entrants view originality as an essential quality, is teaching. This is also the only occupation in which nearly half of the members rate themselves as above average on originality.

Identity and Career Stages — For most women their major career problem is how best to combine work and family responsibilities in such a way that the former do not interfere too drastically with the latter. When it comes to a question of family versus career, there is little doubt about which takes precedence. Although ninety-four per cent of the nursing students and eighty per cent of the girls preparing for other occupations claimed that a career was important to them, only a small proportion of either group selected career in preference to family as their most important satisfaction in life.[13] In addition, only a quarter of the practicing nurses stated that they considered their work in nursing to be their principal career or life work (as opposed to being secondary to family considerations), even though more than that number were still single.

One would expect that those persons who have incorporated a particular occupational role into their identity, and so are committed to this occupation, will also manifest a much greater interest in following a long-term career in this field than those whose attachment is not as close. This certainly appears likely for males, where, as Everett Hughes has stated, "career is his ultimate enterprise . . ." and "contains a set of projections of himself into the future."[14] But does this also hold for women for whom career is less salient, and who tend to express themselves through their relations with others rather than through their work?[15]

It would seem that the only circumstances under which the relationship between career plans and identity development is likely to be problematical is where there is direct conflict between the person's occupational identity and sex identity. This is not a frequent occurrence for males,[16] but is much more likely to be true for females[17] until there is a substantial change in their sex-role expectations.

One can say, however, that if a girl is already identified with an occupation and has consolidated her occupational "we" feeling by continual association with future colleagues in a training situation, that it is probably more difficult for her to transfer this identification to the housewife role. Thus, she is likely to have a strong desire either to continue practicing, or to work part-time and return wherever she can do so without undue burden on her family. There will, of course, be some strains involved in re-entry to the work-world for those committed women who have taken time off from work to rear their families.[18]

Analysing the responses of the two student groups in this study to questions related to their careers strongly confirms this proposed link between commitment and career plans. The highly committed girls (as indicated by their scale scores) are much more likely to state that having a career of their own is very important to them (see Table 4) and this group also includes a larger proportion who expect that their career will provide the most satisfaction of any of their lifetime activities, including family life. It should, of course, be noted that the responses on both these items among the comparison group girls varied greatly according to the occupation that they plan to enter. Over half of those training for medicine, nursing and dental hygiene say that career is very important to them, and more than one third name it as the activity from which they expect the most satisfaction. On the other hand, relatively small proportions of those preparing for dietetics, nursery school teaching and public relations take this position.

Table 4 / Relationship of Commitment to Emphasis on Career

	Nursing Students Commitment				Comparison Group Commitment					
	Hi		Lo		Hi		Med		Lo	
	#	%	#	%	#	%	#	%	#	%
How Important Own Career										
Very Important	368	65	204	47	286	53	194	33	117	21
Other	196	35	232	53	252	47	385	67	443	79
Total	564		436		538		579		560	
	$X^2 =$	$p = <$			$X^2 =$	$p = <$				
Stop School If Marry										
Def'ly Go on	409	72	211	48	354	66	304	53	229	41
Other	155	28	225	52	184	34	275	47	331	59
Total	504		436		538		579		560	
	$X^2 =$	$p = <$			$X^2 =$	$p = <$				
Displeased If Marry — No Career										
Very or Some	333	59	206	47	334	62	296	51	242	43
Other	231	41	230	53	204	38	283	49	218	57
Total	564		436		538		579		560	
	$X^2 =$	$p = <$			$X^2 =$	$p = <$				
Go on For Advanced Degree										
Yes	298	53	171	39	288	54	264	46	180	32
Other	266	47	265	61	250	46	315	54	380	68
Total	564		436		538		579		560	
	$X^2 =$	$p = <$			$X^2 =$	$p = <$				

In addition, the strongly committed in both groups studied were much more likely to state that they were sure that they would practice in their chosen field. In confirmation of this, those nursing students who later were reported in correspondence with their schools to have dropped out of their programs were checked and found to be lower on the commitment scale than their classmates.

A second indication of the importance which commitment has for career decisions comes in the responses of the girls to questions related to the effect of marriage on their career plans. When asked if they anticipated stopping their education if they should marry before finishing, from two-thirds to three-quarters of the strongly committed girls checked that they would definitely continue their education in this event, as compared to less than half of the less committed girls. Finally, more than half of the strongly committed girls expect to go on for an advanced degree as compared to only about a third of their fellow students.

In order to see clearly how commitment affects those women who have completed their education and are out in the field, it is necessary to separate the practicing nurse sample according to their marital status. Only then is the need to find a satisfactory balance between family and career demands brought into perspective.

Looking now at the effective commitment within different marital status groups (see Table 5) it can be seen that most single nurses of all degrees of commitment are employed full-time, but their satisfaction with their work decreases with decreased commitment and so does the importance which they place on their career in their general scheme of things. The married nurses, on the other hand, include a majority who are either unemployed or employed only part-time, except in the case of the most highly committed women. As in the case of the single nurses, their satisfaction in nursing is directly related to their degree of commitment but their careers almost always take second place to their family responsibilities.

The nurses who are on their own by virtue of widowhood or divorce resemble the single nurses in most cases, but many still indicate a strong tie to their families — presumably their growing or grown-up children.

Finally, as has already been indicated, the primary goal of most women is to marry and rear a family. As a result, their career decisions tend to be contingent on their marital and family plans. As time passes, however, two types of development may occur. Those who haven't married may come to accept this state as a permanent one and direct all their energies into their careers. In addition, some of those who have married may be

Table 5 / Relationship of Commitment to Career Orientation for Single versus other Nurses

(Figures shown are %'s for each category indicated)

	Degree of Commitment								
	High			Medium			Low		
	Marital Status			Marital Status			Marital Status		
	S* (75)	W/D (36)	M (158)	S (139)	W/D (42)	M (287)	S (58)	W/D (25)	M (180)
Present Employment Status									
Employed Full-Time	94	70	58	89	99	43	81	76	39
Employed Part-Time	1	11	24	2	5	25	9	12	29
Other	5	19	18	9	7	32	10	12	32
How long worked as nurse									
Over 10 years	84	94	60	66	72	46	52	54	43
Other	16	6	40	34	28	54	48	36	57
View present work in nursing as . . .									
Career	81	58	9	63	52	8	38	12	3
Career, but Secondary to Family	16	28	87	23	36	78	24	40	68
Job	3	14	4	13	12	14	38	48	29
How satisfied with nursing compared with expectation									
More than expected	87	92	90	74	74	79	38	48	53
Other	13	8	10	26	26	21	62	52	47
How important own career									
Very	55	69	30	37	57	24	38	36	15
Other	45	31	70	63	43	76	62	64	85
First Satisfaction in Life									
Career	47	22	8	48	26	6	22	24	3
Family	19	33	78	21	45	83	21	48	91
Other	34	45	14	31	29	11	57	28	6

* S = Single; M= Married; W/D = Widowed or Divorced

forced to support themselves because of divorce or widowhood, and others, once their families are partially grown and in school may be ready to return to work either part or full-time.

Any of these developments are likely to change the way that the persons affected regard their work-life, and may lead to greater occupational commitment and career activity among older women — particularly those who already have some kind of professional affiliation.

The effects of these developments are evident in this study. For example, if a comparison is made of the way in which single nurses of differing age groups regard their current work in nursing (see Table 6), the transition from relatively little interest in career to a great deal is revealed quite dramatically. Whereas only fifteen per cent of those nurses who are 25 years-of-age and under view their present work in nursing as their career or life-work, nearly half of those between twenty-six and thirty-five have this view, and this increases to almost eighty per cent for those over age thirty-five.

Table 6 / Changing View of Nursing with Age for Single Nurses

| | Age Group | | | | | |
| | 25 or under | | 26-35 | | Over 35 | |
	#	%	#	%	#	%
Career	4	15	33	44	134	79
View present Work in Nursing as ... but secondary						
to family	8	55	24	32	15	9
Other	15	30	18	24	21	12
Total	27		75		170	

Summary

The findings of this study appear to support the proposition that identity has an important influence on both occupational choice and career plans for women. As the opportunities for women in various parts of the work world increase and as even more married women enter the labor force, there should be still further changes in female roles in our society and a greater diversity of role models to influence girls' identity formation in the future. Career girls have always been in the minority, and the female image may have moved in the direction of the passive homemaker role since World War II as Betty Friedan claims, but as both parents and educators continue to stress creativity and productivity for girls as well as boys there would seem to be a reversal in the offing if it hasn't already occurred.

Suggestions for Further Research

Two kinds of research appear to be needed in order to test further the ideas developed in the present paper.

(a) Other women's occupations should be investigated to determine whether the approach developed in this research is

see p. 289

useful in predicting career orientations in other fields. One group which the writer has considered are female administrators. Another obvious occupation would be teachers.

(b) Since identities are a result of socialization, it would be helpful to be able to relate identity development and its effects on work-role conceptions to family background, and particularly to patterns of interaction between parents and children.[19]

NOTES

This paper derives from a larger study which investigated why girls select nursing as a career. This larger project was conducted by the Department of Sociology and Anthropology at Cornell University under the direction of Professors Robin Williams and Rose K. Goldsen, and the author served for a year as assistant study director. The field research for the project was supported by grant #GN-4465-C from the U.S. Public Health Service. The author also wishes to acknowledge support received from the Sloan Foundation during the period of analysis which preceded the writing of this paper.

1. For instance: President's Commission on the Status of Women, *American Women*, (Washington, D.C., U.S. Gov't Printing Office, 1963); and Royal Commission on Population, *Report*, (London; H.M. S.O. Cmd. 7695, 1949).

2. For example: F. Ivan Nye and Lois Hoffman, *The Employed Mother in America*, (Chicago: Rand McNally, 1963); National Manpower Council, *Work in the Lives of Married Women*, (New York; Columbia University Press, 1958; and Alva Myndal and Viola Klein, *Women's Two Roles: Home and Work*, (London: Routledge and Kegan Paul, 1956).

3. One which has been receiving considerable attention recently is Betty Friedan, *The Feminine Mystique* (New York, W. W. Norton, 1963). Since the publication of her book the author has been on T.V., written articles in the popular press and so on.

4. For a discussion of this, see Fred Davis and Virginia Oleson, "Initiation into a Women's Profession: Identity Problems in the Status Transition of Coed to Student Nurse," *Sociometry*, Vol. 26, No. 1, March, 1963.

5. The approach taken in this paper follows that developed by Everett Hughes in his work on occupations. For example, see *Men and Their Work* (Glencoe, Ill.: Free Press, 1958). See also Nelson Foote, "Identification as the Basis for a Theory of Motivation," *American Sociological Review* Vol. XVI, No. 1 (February, 1951).

6. The terms "instrumental" and "expressive" derive from the work of Talcott Parsons and R. F. Bales, *Family, Socialization and Interaction Process* (Glencoe, Ill.: Free Press, 1955).

7. It is possible to develop a typology of identities based on the strengths of these three components which can be used to predict work-role orientations. This has been presented by the writer in another paper. See Rodney F. White, "Toward a Typology of Work Oriented Identities" (mimeographed).

8. For a recent discussion of this see Talcott Parsons and Winston White, "The Link Between Character and Society," Chapter 6 in Seymour Lipset and Leo Lowenthal *Culture and Social Character* (Glencoe, Ill.: Free Press, 1961) pp. 118-19.

9. The dynamics of this process are described in Morris Rosenberg et al, *Occupations and Values* (Glencoe, Ill.: Free Press, 1957).

10. Howard S. Becker, "Notes on the Concept of Commitment," *American Journal of Sociology* LXVI, No. 1 (July, 1960).

11. A considerable proportion of the comparison group girls answer "don't know" to a number of the questions which ask about nursing.

12. All of the responses on items like "respectfulness," "taking orders," etc., may seem high, but it is probably due to the fact that the respondents are all female and that most of them are preparing for service-type occupations.

13. It should be noted, of course, that some studies have suggested that only a minority of men view their work as their major satisfaction in life also, but it is a larger minority. See, for example Morris Rosenberg, et al, *op cit.* p. 48. Also, one might well argue that people, both males and females, do not regard satisfactions from family life and occupation (or avocation) in "either/or" terms, but desire and expect both.

14. Everett Hughes, "The Making of a Physician," *Human Organization* 14, (Winter, 1956).

15. See, for example, the comparison presented in Talcott Parsons, "Age and Sex in the Social Structure of the United States," Chapter X in *Essays in Sociological Theory, Pure and Applied,* (Glencoe, Ill.: Free Press, 1949).

16. See, for example, Bernard Segal, "Male Nurses — A Case Study in Status Contradiction and Prestige Loss," *Social Forces,* 41, #1, (October 1962).

17. For a discussion of this, see Fred Davis and Virginia Olesen, "Initiation into a Women's Profession: Identity Problems in the Status Transition of Coed to Student Nurse," *Sociometry,* 26 #1, (March, 1963).

18. For a discussion of this process for nurses, see Marcella Davis, "The Return Phenomenon — The Process of Becoming a Working Mother," *Nursing Forum,* II, #3, (1963).

19. A start in this has already been made by Miriam Johnson. See her "Instrumental and Expressive Components in the Personalities of Women," (unpublished Ph.D. dissertation, Radcliffe College, 1955).

twenty

Career Choice Processes

FRED E. KATZ and HARRY W. MARTIN

This paper investigates career choices among student nurses. It explores the possibility that entry upon an occupational career, such as nursing, may be predicated less upon a deliberate choice of nursing than upon a series of limited decisions focused upon immediate problems encountered at the stage of the life cycle in which the adolescent girl finds herself. The view which is here adopted is that the process of entry into an occupation may be looked upon as the cumulative product of a series of specific acts, which may or may not be directly focused upon a deliberate career choice. In the present paper the emphasis is primarily upon non-career oriented acts. It is not suggested that such acts characterize all types of career choice.

Eli Ginzberg has done pioneering work in the study of decision-making processes involved in career choice. In his *Occupational Choice*[1] he took as his point of departure Lazarsfeld's admonition to seek a genetic approach to the topic.[2] Ginzberg and his colleagues build a theory based on an evolution of increasing self-determination as well as increasingly realistic attunement of the individual to his environment as he matures. The individual is thought to go through a period of fantasy (when he cannot assess his capacities), a tentative period (when he weighs various satisfactions), and finally, a realistic period (when he makes compromises between his individual wants and the actual opportunities which exist for him). We are in broad

From SOCIAL FORCES, Vol. 41, No. 2 (1962), pp. 149-154. Reprinted by permission of The University of North Carolina Press.

agreement with Ginzberg's basic thesis that "occupational choice is a process," that "the process is largely irreversible" (that is, decisions once made cannot be "unmade," and that they affect the subsequent career life), and that the process "ends in a compromise." Our main divergence from Ginzberg is one of emphasis. Whereas his focus is upon career choices as seen in the context of the individual's maturation, we suggest conceiving career choices as courses of action which are composites of adaptations — by individuals, to be sure — to meet the exigencies of particular, immediate situations.

Our study deals with students at the School of Nursing of a southern university. The study spanned a four-year period. It was possible, therefore, to obtain data on one class from the time of admission to the time of graduation. The questionnaires on which the present paper is largely based included some questions which Columbia University researchers asked medical students;[3] this provides an opportunity of comparing career choice behavior of student nurses with that of student physicians.

The thesis of this paper is as follows: The decisions which underlie embarkation on a nursing career *for at least some persons* revolve around limited, situational contingencies — in which the matter of nursing-as-career enters only tangentially or not at all. Such "situationally delimited" decisions, we are suggesting, do not involve definite career decisions in terms of a subjective career commitment[4] but nonetheless these decisions constitute the active steps toward entry upon a career.

We first began to formulate the thesis when a perusal of answers to open-ended questions suggested that the student nurses exhibited much vagueness as to the time and occasion when they first began to consider becoming nurses. In response to the open-ended question "In your own words, what were the main reasons that let you to choose nursing for your career?" We received such answers as: "I really don't know exactly, but for a long time I wanted to be a nurse. . . ."[5] and, "As do many little girls, I had an early childhood ambition of becoming a nurse — I never became disinterested (sic) in this field although I had no specific reasons for entering nursing. . . ." It is conceivable, of course, that the events which are crucial in the "decisions" have been forgotten or repressed. This is the customary explanation of answers of this kind. It is supported by the fact that when we posed the question "When did you definitely decide on nursing?"[6] over 99 percent of the nurses did indicate that they had made a "definite decision." Unfortunately this type of question assumes that there was a "definite decision" — that it is only a question of finding out when it occurred. The real question, we suggest, is to what extent were there *actually* definite decisions or, conversely, to what extent are the *"decisions"* artifacts of the research procedure?[7] Do we not have to reckon with the likelihood that a student — or any individual for that matter — is inclined to give a reply within the scope of the framework provided for him? And, more pointedly, we are inclined to ask to what extent and in what manner are the "decisions" related to a desire for a career of nursing, or are they merely decisions relating to the solutions of problems which may be quite removed from the notion of a career of nursing?

Support for the thesis comes from statements by girls concerning uncertainty and vagueness as to when they first thought of nursing as a career for themselves. We combined answers to the two open-ended questions: "Which occupations or professions did you consider (before deciding on nursing), and why did you decide against them?" and "In your own words, what were the main reasons that led you to choose nursing for your career?" from a class of freshman students. Twenty-six percent (17 out of 65) made statements to the effect that they did not know when they began to be interested in nursing, or that they "had always" wanted to do the sort of work which they felt nursing entailed (helping the sick, alleviating suffering, being around hospitals, etc.). We were persuaded to think that students' statements to the effect that they could not recall specific occasions on which they first entertained the idea of becoming nurses might point to an absence of specific career decisions. We asked ourselves whether it is not likely that for some of the students, the expressions of vagueness about career decisions constitute *relatively accurate descriptions of a series of unplanned, situation-bound acts* — acts which were not specifically and explicitly tied to a conception of a career of nursing but which, in their totality, added up to the girl's entering a nursing training program.

This is amplified by responses to the question: "At what age did you *definitely* decide to study nursing?" The following results emerged:

Group 1	Number	Percent
Before 14	7	10.6
At 14 or 15	8	12.1
At 16 or 17	41	62.1
Between 18 and 20	10	15.2
Since 21	..	..
Total	66	100.0
Group 2	Number	Percent
Before 14	17	13.0
At 14 or 15	27	20.6
At 16 or 17	72	54.9
Between 18 and 20	14	10.7
Since 21	1	.8
Total	131	100.0

The first group is comprised of a freshman class. The second is made up of a freshman, a sophomore, and a junior class. (The members of the first freshman class are not included in the second group.) It is apparent that in both groups the responses concentrate heavily in the period immediately preceding entrance to college and during the early years in college. On the basis of our conceptualization, we propose that persons who have made only situationally-delimited decisions will be more likely to place themselves in the "16 or 17 years of age" or "18 to 20 years of age" categories of the above question than any other category. Our thinking is based on the notion that even though they have not definitely decided that they wish to become nurses, they must, at this stage of their life, make decisions about their occupational future (including the type of course they wish to follow in college). We are suggesting that what many of these persons reported as "definite" career decisions were really decisions revolving around such things as the choice of college education — rather than a definite desire to be a nurse. (The corollary to this postulate is that persons who have made definite career decisions are no more likely to place themselves in the "16 to 17" and "18 to 20" age categories than in any other category of the above question.) We would then expect a greater proportion of the persons with definite commitment to nursing to fall in the "under 16" age category. If we can take successful completion of nursing school as an index of "commitment" to nursing,[8] we would expect that a greater proportion of the persons stating that they made a definite career decision before the age of 16 will complete the nursing program than persons placing themselves in the "16 and over" categories. This is, indeed, borne out by the data in Table 1.[9]

Table 1 / Relation between Graduating from Nursing School and Age when Definitely decided to Study Nursing*

	Age at time of "definite decision"		
	Under 16	16 or over	Total
Graduated	12	24	36†
	80%	47%	
Not Graduated	3	27	30
	20%	53%	
Total	15	51	66

X2=3.8352, corrected for continuity; significant at the .025 level for a one-tail test: 1 d.f.
* We have graduation data only for the first group.
† We do not know what proportion of the 36 graduates are persons who have made definite subjective career commitments. The practical importance of discovering the proportion of subjectively committed graduates need hardly be elaborated.

The question regarding age of definite decisions was asked of medical students by the Columbia researchers.[10] The findings were quite similar to ours: 67 percent of the students reported that they made their definite decisions between the ages of 16 and 20.[11] However, the explanation offered by the Columbia researchers differs markedly from ours. They state:

> For the modal student — the definite career choice is keyed to the institutional requirements of the educational system. He does not prolong his choice much *beyond* the point when he must select courses appropriate to medical school prerequisites, nor does he arrive at the decision before the socially prescribed time.[12]

We may ask, to what extent do the requirements of the institutional system make it *seem* (to the medical student himself as well as to the behavioral researcher) that there have been definite career decisions? As far as the institutional system goes, signing up for pre-medical course work at a time when the medical school program requires it means that the individual has empirically demonstrated compliance with the system. He has, indeed, made a decision. But is it *necessarily* a decision involving a definite desire for a medical career?[13] To what extent can one accept the responses of "definite decisions" at face value? We are not suggesting that the students are deliberately making false statements. But we are suggesting that those students who have not made definite career commitments are likely to place themselves in the 16 to 20 year age group because at this period, our system of education dictates taking certain definite steps in the direction of a career. These steps may be perceived, in the absence of other commitments, as definite career choices. Rogoff's explanation of the clustering of responses in the 16 to 20 age category is that the time of "definite career choice is geared to the institutional requirements of the educational system."[14] While *some* students may make their definite decisions at this time — and may be encouraged to do so by the character of the system — we would voice an element of caution as to the adequacy of this explanation in view of our previous considerations.

It might seem that persons who have given longest consideration to a nurse career are most likely to graduate. This gains some support from our finding that early "definite deciders" are more likely to graduate than late "definite deciders."[15] In order to examine this further we consider responses to the question "At what age did you first think of becoming a nurse?" This yielded the following results:

Before 10	35	53.0
Between 10 and 13	12	18.2
At 14 or 15	10	15.2
At 16 or 17	8	12.1
Since 18	1	1.5
Total	66	100.00

A large proportion of the answers fall into the "before 10" age category. This led us to investigate whether a preponderant proportion of these "before 10" persons are "committed" to nursing. We shall again use graduation from nursing school as an index of commitment. The present question, it must be emphasized, does not purport to deal with *definite decisions* — but merely with "thinking about" studying nursing. It is our contention that this difference is crucial in career commitments. The latter, we suspect, may frequently connote little more than cultural exposure to "playing nurse" — a childhood experience to which almost every girl in our society is exposed. On the basis of this consideration we would expect no significant difference in the proportion of graduates from those who first state they thought of nursing before the age of 10 and those who first thought of nursing at 10 or later. The results are in line with this expectation.

We may carry this a step further. It seemed to us that many of the persons who claimed they thought of becoming nurses before the age of 10 were quite vague and unclear about the occasion when they first thought of becoming nurses. To check whether such "vagueness" might also connote an absence of definite commitment to a nursing career we investigated whether persons placing themselves in the "under 10" category of the question concerning first thinking about nursing also placed themselves in the "16 and over" category on the question dealing with definite decision about nursing.

Table 2 / Relation between Graduation from Nursing School and Age when first thought of becoming a Nurse

	Age at time of first thinking of becoming a nurse		
	Under 10	10 and over	Total
Graduated	20	16	36
	57.1%	50%	
Not Graduated	15	16	31
	42.9%	50%	
Total	35	32	67

$X^2 = .167$, corrected for continuity; not significant at 0.05 level; 1 d.f.
When using the same age breadown as in Table 1 — "under 16" and "16 and over" — the X^2 is .087.

Table 3 / Relation between Early Consideration of Nursing and Definite Decision to Study Nursing

	Definite decisions to study nursing		
	Under 16	16 or over	Total
First thought of becoming a nurse before age 10	11	24	35
	31.4%	68.6%	

$X^2 = 4.114$, corrected for continuity; significant at .05 level; 1 d.f.

A significantly high proportion of those who first thought of nursing before age 10 regard their definite decisions as having been made at age 16 or later. The latter age category has been postulated to have a high proportion of non-committed persons (in comparison with the "under 16" age category). On this basis it would seem that the "vagueness" regarding the occasion of initial interest in nursing bespeaks an absence of commitment. But the evidence cannot be claimed to be conclusive.

An inspection of the distribution of students by age of "definite decisions" and "first thinking" about nursing yields further insights.

Table 4 / Distribution of Age of Definite Decision to Study Nursing by Age of First Thinking about Nursing

Age at time of first thinking of becoming a nurse	Age at time of definite decision			
	Before Age 14	At 14 or 15	At 16 or 17	Between 18-20
Before age of 10	7	4	19	5
Between 10-13	..	3	7	2
At 14 or 15	..	1	9	..
At 16 or 17	..	..	6	2
Since 18	..	..	..	1

Those who report that they first thought of nursing before the age of 10 tend to fall into a bimodal pattern: One cluster of "definite decisions" comes before the age of 14, and another at 16 or 17 years of age. On the basis of our thesis and data already presented we hold that early "definite decisions" are positively related to definite commitment, as indicated by graduation from the nursing program. We found that five of the seven persons who "first thought" of nursing before the age of 10 and "definitely decided" before 14, graduated (71 percent). Only nine of 19 (47 percent) persons who "first thought" of nursing before 10 and "definitely decided" at 16 or 17, graduated from nursing school. We suggest that one cluster of the bimodal distribution consists of persons who made primarily "situationally-delimited" decisions, whereas the other cluster consists of persons who made relatively explicit "career" decisions.

In summary, data has been presented in support of the thesis that is possible to demonstrate the existence of a type of career choice process which does not involve subjective career-oriented decisions. This formulation involved the postulation of being able to distinguish between subjective career commitment and compliance with the institutionalized process leading to embarkation upon a career.[16] It also involved postulation of a form of sequential process, where embarkation on a course of action — in the present case, entry upon a particular occupational career — may be the end result of a series of steps which, individually, are not teleologically oriented to that course of action. (Thus, for a particular young woman, the decision to enter a nursing school and, subsequently, to be a nurse may rest primarily upon following her immediate desire to be in the proximity of young, eligible physicians, or to remain close to a friend of her own sex who has chosen nursing training.) Such "situationally delimited" actions are deemed to be basic ingredients in this process. It is felt that this conceptualization might fruitfully be applied to areas other than career choice.

The data for our formulations are based on a small sample — one professional school. Hence, it is probable that refinements in the thesis will need to be made as data from broader samples become available. In practical terms, understanding career commitments[17] has obvious importance. Ultimately, one would wish to be able to correlate patterns of commitment which develop in the course of actual career choice behavior with patterns of performance by occupational practitioners. Also, a clear understanding of occupational commitments might enable streamlining of career training procedures.

NOTES

This investigation was supported by a grant, 2M-6157, from the National Institute of Mental Health, United States Public Health Service.

1. Eli Ginzberg and Associates, *Occupational Choice: An Approach to a General Theory* (New York: Columbia University Press. 1951).

2. Paul Lazarsfeld, *Jugend und Beruf* (Jena: G. Fischer, 1931). Cited in R. K. Merton, G. G. Reader, P.L. Kendall, Editors, *The Student Physician* (Cambridge: Harvard University Press, 1957), p. 110.

3. R. K. Merton, G. G. Reader, P. L. Kendall, Editors. *The Student Physician, op. cit.* We are particularly referring to N. Rogoff's article entitled, "The Decision to Study Medicine."

4. By "subjective commitment to a career" we refer to an individual's incorporating conceptions about practicing the career into himself; we do not know, at this stage what conceptions are in-

volved, and we do not wish to make statements about the degree of "depth" of personality and emotional involvement.

Although there may be no subjective *career* commitment, the situationally-delimited decisions are likely to involve action commitments for the individual. For example, enrolling in nursing school carries a degree of commitment to complete nursing education — the third year student may feel that she has "invested" in nursing education and, if lacking other motivations, she may continue in nursing because of this investment alone. In Ginzberg's terms we might say that the situationally-delimited decisions are not "realistic" in terms of a career.

5. This is the type of response which is often discarded in the analysis of data.

6. This question is a replica of the question asked by the Columbia researchers (Merton, et. al. *op. cit.*, p. 14 ff). The question is worded thus:

"At what age did you definitely decide to study nursing?

_____Before the age of 14

_____At 14 or 15 years of age

_____At 16 or 17 years of age

_____Between 18 or 20 years of age

_____Since the age of 21"

7. The senior author's present thinking was affected by another study on which he has been engaged. This involves case studies of practicing physicians. One of the subjects of that study stated that it was only in his second year of medical school that he discovered that he *really* wanted to become a physician. We would venture the opinion that if the above question concerning a definite career decision had been asked of this man in his *first* year in medical school he would probably have indicated a "definite decision" in his past. One must of course reckon with retrospective bias here. The older man may feel that his basic decision was made after he entered medical school — on the basis of his current perspective. To the young man, however, an earlier decision may have appeared crucial and definitive (rationalization may or may not have been involved). But another explanation, the one we are here exploring, is that there was no definite career decision before the person entered professional school, and that this can be objectively demonstrated.

8. This is an admittedly crude yardstick.

9. We would also expect drop-out rates during the school program to reflect this differential rate of graduation. The questionnaire was administered to the first group at the beginning of their freshman year when no students had yet dropped out of the program. When the second group took the questionnaire there had been a drop-out of 27.5 percent — based on the initial freshman enrollment of the respective

classes. As we compare the responses of the two groups we note that in the second group the "under 16" age categories make up 33.6 percent of the responses (as against 22.7 percent of the first group) and the "16 and over" categories account for the remaining 66.4 percent of the responses of that group (as against 77.3 percent in the first group). This would seem to suggest that more of the "under 16" persons are remaining in the program — that is, "drop-outs" of the second group seem to follow the same pattern as the "non-graduates" in the first group. Our conclusions must be tentative, however, since we do not have the distribution of responses from the second group at an earlier period of time.

10. *The Student Physician, op. cit.* See N. Rogoff's "The Decision to Study Medicine."

11. *Ibid.,* p. 115.

12. *Ibid.*

13. We are making a distinction between a subjective commitment and an overt compliance with a system. The two may proceed with varying degree of interdependence; but we postulate that they need not be identical.

14. Rogoff, *loc. cit.*

15. We might add, parenthetically, that psychoanalytic theory leads us to expect that *definite* career decisions are quite likely to occur in the early part of life, and that definite commitments may have occurred even when there is no explicit recollection of the occasion when they came into being.

16. In this study, completion of professional training has been used as an index of subjective commitment — and non-completion as an index of absence of such commitment. Yet it must be pointed out that it is by no means claimed that all persons who lack subjective commitment are likely to fail to complete their professional training, and thus be excluded from the ranks of professional practitioners. What is claimed — and used in the present study — is that there is a greater likelihood, statistically, that those who lack a subjective commitment will not complete their professional training.

17. We hope that our paper, an essentially theoretical discussion, will not lead to exaggerated notions as to the actual proportion of non-committed persons in occupations. We make no claim to have assessed what this proportion is in the nursing profession. There is also indication that some nursing students may lose commitment in the course of the experience in nursing school. See Ida Harper Simpson, "The Development of Professional Self-Images among Student Nurses" (Unpublished doctoral dissertation, University of North Carolina, 1956).

twenty one

Role Model Influences on College Women's Career Aspirations

ELIZABETH M. ALMQUIST
AND SHIRLEY S. ANGRIST

If present trends continue, most educated women will work until marriage or the arrival of the first child, only to resume employment when their children are much older. In spite of the increasing participation of educated married women in the labor force (Ginzberg, 1968) the dedicated career woman is still rather rare, not much more prevalent than earlier (Oppenheimer, 1968). Participation in the labor force in adult life reflects many factors; at least one of these is career aspirations developed during the adolescent years. Research on career motivation has often attempted to characterize the *predominant* mode of college women's adult aspirations. Some researchers have argued that college women are likely to view their adult role as a dual one including both marriage and career (Shab, 1967), but others think that careers are a second choice and that planning is directed toward finding some occupation which would provide a career, *if* that became necessary (Empey, 1958). The strength of motivation for a career varies widely even among women at a professionally oriented and relatively homogeneous college (Almquist and Angrist, 1969). Most women plan to and will work at various times, but aspirations for work as a central feature of adult life, regardless of financial necessity and under conditions of free choice still do not characterize the majority.

What distinguishes the career salient women from their more conventional classmates? One explanation holds that career

From Merrill-Palmer Quarterly, Vol. 17, No. 3 (July, 1971). Reprinted by permission of Merrill-Palmer Quarterly and the author.

oriented women are deviant both in their early development and in their family relationships. In a previous paper we presented evidence and argument for the idea that such women may have had enriching family and childhood experiences which provide broader views of appropriate adult female roles. In this report, we expand on this notion that career women are products of broader sex role definitions by focusing on the various role models which may influence their career life style choices.

In studying differential role model influences on college women, we make two assumptions. (1) For women, career salience is a special type of achievement. Prevailing norms direct the female in our society to marry, rear children, and to provide support and assistance for the husband's career. Women who aspire to a career for themselves do not substitute the work role for the more traditional wife-mother-homemaker one, but are choosing an additional role (Turner, 1964). The majority of college women, even career oriented ones, expect to marry and rear children. A career aspiring college woman is still more ambitious; she wants to perform highly in activities besides those that accrue to the housewife. Hence our definition of career salience includes motivation to have both marriage and a career.

(2) The career aspirations of college women are explicable within a combined role-model-reference group framework. Following a recent statement by Theodore Kemper, a reference group is any

> group, collectivity, or person which the actor takes into account in some manner in the course of selecting a behavior from among a set of alternatives, or in making a judgment about a problematic issue. A reference group helps to orient the actor in a certain course, whether of action or attitude (Kemper, 1968, p. 32).

Kemper utilizes the reference group concept to explain achievement level striving and holds that his view is an improvement over McClelland's theory of need achievement.[1] Hence he identifies several functions or types of reference groups. *Normative* groups explicitly set norms and espouse values, and quite plainly expect the actor to comply with them, sanctioning the lack of compliance by punishment. Mere conformity with the demands of normative groups does not represent achievement but only minimal expected performance. It is for a second type of reference group, *the audience,* that the individual performs highly, attempting to assure recognition. The actor attributes certain values to the audience, attempting to behave in accordance with those values. He seeks the attention of the audience group actively, and it in turn bestows rewards for his performance. To this point Kemper and McClelland are apparently in agreement; McClelland holds that in order for achievement to be facilitated, high standards of excellence and at least feedback of information on the adequacy of performance are required. Kemper claims that the normative group provides the former and audience groups the latter. But Kemper insists that a third function must be served, that of the role model, of which McClelland makes no mention. The role model is one type of a comparison group:

> Usually an individual rather than a group . . . the role model demonstrates for the individual how something is done in the technical sense . . . (The role model) is concerned with the "how" question. The essential quality of the role model is that he possesses skills and displays techniques which the actor lacks (or thinks he lacks) and from whom, by observation and comparison with his own performance, the actor can learn (Kemper, 1968, p. 33).

Hence in order for achievement to occur, the actor also needs a role model to emulate. The role model does not motivate, influence, persuade or reward the actor; he (or she) merely provides a technical explication of how a role is to be performed.

It is difficult to separate empirically the analytically distinct functions of reference groups, e.g., is a specific referent serving a normative or an audience function? Kemper points out that the several functions of reference groups may be served by one group or person; such a fusion of effects may greatly facilitate achievement. However, it may be possible to characterize the predominant content of the influence of any particular referent. Furthermore some groups may be more potent for the career oriented women while others are more salient for the non-career oriented students.

Because our definition of career salience includes long term commitment to a career with the expectation that the career will be combined with marriage, women who aspire in this sense are choosing more than work or no work; they are making fairly explicit *life style* choices. Such a choice does not exist for men.

> That a man will spend at least one third of his adult life in gainful work is a premise on which the plans for his life are based. But for a woman, society creates not a decision but the necessity for a choice. She must decide whether to include work in her plans and if so how much of her life she should devote to it. If the answer is that she will include work is a serious way, she then arrives at the point at which the career thinking of men begins. (Bailyn, 1964, p. 702).

Reference groups function to mold life style aspirations, and role models specifically provide for the woman college student vivid demonstrations of how these life styles can be enacted. This is not to assert that the girl clearly perceives who influenced her or in exactly what way the influences occur. We assume in this research that influences on girls' life style choices operate both explicitly and covertly: of some influences, the recipient is aware, others may operate without explicit recognition by the persons involved. The task here is to obtain empirical evidence for underlying reference group processes.

Alice Rossi found that career salient college graduates had dated less frequently and were less likely to be married or have children than non-career salient women. Other differences[2] between the groups led her to believe that the career oriented women, home, family and motherhood had become negative reference groups (Rossi, 1967). An alternative interpretation of these findings is that career oriented women are less frequently associated with reference groups or involved in social activities which foster inculcation of the traditional feminine role. The following hypotheses reflect these assumptions.

1. Career oriented women are less often sorority members than are their non-career oriented classmates.
2. Career oriented women date less frequently in high school and college.
3. By senior year, career oriented women are less likely to be married, engaged, or going steady than are non-career oriented women.

By contrast, the next hypotheses illustrate the idea that career oriented women are differentially involved in a masculine world where career and work are paramount.

4. Career oriented women are more likely to prefer occupations similar to those chosen by their male peers.
5. Career oriented women will choose male-dominated oc-

cupations more frequently than their more conventional classmates.

6. Career oriented women will have had more jobs and more varied summer and part-time work experience.

Both career oriented and non-career oriented women have the family as a reference group, but we expect that the content of the influence differs. What will differ is the life style communicated by the family, and the key figures here are the parents. The amount of education they have, the type of work they do, whether the mother works at all or is active in leisure pursuits, should affect the girl's occupational inclinations. The existence of families of high socio-economic status connotes an emphasis on career for the father and the wife's role is more often one of being a help-mate to his career. Additionally the wife is expected to participate in community and self-enrichment activities. Higher socio-economic status students are less likely to be career oriented.

In order to realistically aspire to a career, young women require role models who illustrate how to combine marriage and career satisfactorily, and the most important model of this type are the students' mothers. Commitment to a career in teaching was related to the work histories of the mothers of in-service teachers (White, 1967). Among a small sample of college sophomores, the only familial background variable significantly related to the students' desire to work in the future was the mother's work orientation (Siegel and Curtis, 1963). Recent female doctorates were more likely to be currently in the labor force if their mother worked while they were growing up (Astin, 1968).

Finally the view of each parent as a sympathetic or helping person may mediate the girl's receptiveness to parental influence. Specific hypotheses then are:

7. Non-career salient women will have fathers with higher educational and occupational status than career salient women.

8. Career oriented women will more likely have working mothers and mothers with higher education, while non-career oriented women will have mothers who spend time on leisure activities.

9. The two groups of women will not differ in their negative or positive perceptions of parental personal characteristics.

One study of college women showed that the career oriented had been more influenced in their occupational choice by role models who embodied specifically occupation-related values and relatively less influenced by people (peers, family members) who embodied more generalized and less occupationally specific values. Career women also named more persons as influential than did non-career oriented women (Simpson and Simpson, 1963). From the present point of view, contact with role models is necessary in order to learn how to perform according to the requirements of the work role. Furthermore, students do not become committed to a career field without some positive relationships with role models who display the skills, meet the demands, and consciously enjoy the pleasures to be obtained from that pursuit. The most readily available models for students are first, their professors, and second, persons in a given occupation. Contact with more than one model will re-enforce the effects.

10. Career oriented women will have been more influenced by teachers and persons in a given occupation. Non-career women will have been influenced by family and peers in their occupational choice.

Procedures

The data derive from a longitudinal study of one class from the women's college of a small, private, co-educational and technologically oriented university. Questionnaires were administered every fall semester to the total class and tape-recorded interviews conducted among a sample of the class every spring semester over the four college years. The questionnaires dealt with adult role conceptions, occupational plans, work experience, classwork, grades, school activities, dating, social life and marriage plans. The interviews probed deeply into these same areas and occupational choice processes. In the senior year an attempt was made to interview the entire class. This report deals with 110 students for whom reasonably complete data were available. Ninety-five had been students at the university since freshmen year and fifteen transferred in as sophomores. Chi-square analysis is used to ascertain relationships between career salience and other variables. Except as indicated, data are taken from questionnaires.

Three items from the questionnaires form an index of career salience. Students who gave work-oriented responses on at least two of the questions were defined as career salient. Career oriented women indicated that fifteen years after college they would like to be married career women, with or without children; non-career oriented women wanted to be housewives.[3] In addition, career oriented women wanted to work after marriage even if their husbands earned an adequate salary. They definitely planned to work when their children were school age, but some were willing to work even with pre-schoolers in the household. Non-career salient women wanted to work only if their husband's salary were inadequate and generally would postpone a possible re-entry into the labor force until their children were much older.[4] The third question dealt with adult role alternatives. Here, given that they were trained for the occupation of their choice, married with children, and with no economic necessity for working, non-career oriented women preferred to spend leisure time participating in clubs, hobbies and volunteer activities. Career salient women preferred working either part or full time.[5] As a result of these procedures, fifty women, less than half the class, were termed career salient. Sixty students, about fifty-five percent of the sample, were designated as non-career oriented.

Several aspects of career planning substantiate the greater commitment of career oriented women, and generally support the operational definition of career salience. Career oriented women are somewhat more likely than their non-career oriented classmates to make a definite occupational choice during the first two years of college (Table 1). By senior year, nearly

Table 1 / Commitment Variables Associated with Career Salience

Variable	Career Salient (N=50)	Non-Career Salient (N=60)	Chi Square
Made definite occupational choice during first two years of college	32%	15%	$x^2=4.487$*
Very certain will pursue chosen occupation	46%	22%	$x^2=5.409$*
Plan to attend graduate or professional school	84%	52%	$x^2=11.957$***

*pL .05
***pL .001

one-half of the career oriented but only one-fifth of the non-career oriented felt very certain that they would actually pursue their chosen occupation. Some career salient students were deferring a definite choice until completion of post-graduate education. Fully four-fifths of these women, contrasted with half of the non-career oriented, indicated that they planned to attend graduate or professional school. These data tend to corroborate the differences between career and non-career oriented students.

Results

Social Life and Marriage Plans — In the class as a whole, two-thirds are sorority members, but over three-fourths of the non-career salient women are members and less than half of the career oriented are (Table 2). If we accept Scott's view that the

Table 2 / Social Life, Marriage Plans and Career Salience

Variable	Career Salient (N=50)	Non-Career Salient (N=60)	Chi Square Value
Sorority Membership (Yes)	47%	77%	$x^2=9.972$**
Dates in College Twice a week or more	45%	58%	$x^2=1.832$ N.S.
Marital Status, Seniors (Going steady, engaged or married)	37%	59%	$x^2=5-153$*

*pL .05
**pL .01

sorority functions largely as a family surrogate in maintaining social class and ethnic endogamy, and that its activities are organized around forming alliances with appropriate males (Scott, 1965), then it is not surprising that the marriage and family oriented women belong more frequently. The sorority serves to normatively sanction finding a marriage partner, provides role models to facilitate the learning of behavior patterns for attracting males, and as an audience group it rewards individuals successful in their quest. Because the several functions of reference groups are combined by the sorority, it serves as a unique framework for encouraging marriage. Since sorority largely ignores career planning, career oriented women can still be involved, although less frequently.

In spite of the possible implications of differential sorority membership, students did not differ significantly in frequency of dating. The results are in the direction predicted with more non-career oriented students having evening dates at least twice a week. By senior year, non-career oriented women were significantly more likely to be going steady, engaged, or married than the career oriented woman. On the face of it, it would seem logical to assume that women who date frequently and who are involved in specific marriage plans would be less oriented towards a career. Several students became career oriented during their senior year who had not been so previously, but they do not show a "flight toward career" resulting from panic over failing to attract a marriage partner. The interviews suggest some interdependence between career plans and relationship with a particular male. Some women stopped dating a male because he did not agree with their plans, some rather actively sought out males who did agree with them, and others had boy friends who encouraged their motivation for a career. Very few women reported that a male friend had influenced their occupational choice directly, and most women who were career oriented and planning to be married were able to make their plans for graduate school or work fit with their fiance's work plans as well. None indicated a cessation of their interest in a career as a result of their involvement in marriage plans.

Some excerpts from the interviews illustrate the ways in which marriage and career plans are made to mesh satisfactorily. One girl, when asked if she thought that getting married affected her plans for the future, replied:

> No. I probably wouldn't have kept going out with him if he didn't see things the way I did. A lot of people don't like women to work after they are married at all. It is just fine, he doesn't mind. He encouraged my interest in graduate school.

A non-career oriented girl seems to have resolved any possible conflict between career and marriage before it could become an issue:

> I have chosen to get married and I know that I can't have a career and raise a family. When my family get a little older I might go towards a career, but I don't think I can be successful with both.

There are jobs and there are careers. I had better take the job and make married life a career for a while.

Masculine and Work Reference Groups — Women who aspire to a career for themselves are more likely to have been involved with masculine reference groups. Indeed, many of the persons named by the students as important influences in choosing an occupation were males, and they were encountered within an explicit work context. The nature of this direct role model influence will be taken up below; for the moment some indirect measures of involvement in masculine reference groups will be discussed.

In this study students were asked to indicate occupations being chosen by their male and female friends. Responses were studied to determine if there were any similarity between occupations chosen by the subjects and their peers. Occupations were considered similar if they were alike either in subject matter or profession. Examples of similar fields are computer work and mathematics; similar professions are English teacher and history teacher. It is clear that non-career oriented women chose occupations similar to those reportedly chosen by girl friends. Career salient women more often chose an occupation similar to those chosen by both their male and female friends (Table 3). The fact that nearly two-thirds of the career salient women chose male dominated occupations for themselves may

Table 3 / Masculine and Work Reference Groups Associated with Career Salience

Variable	Career Salient (N=50)	Non-Career Salient (N=60)	Chi Square
Chose occupation similar to male friends	36%	13%	$x^2=7.201**$
Choose male-dominated occupation	66%	18%	$x^2=25.819***$
Held three or more jobs	66%	25%	$x^2=18.639***$
Held two or more different jobs	78%	25%	$x^2=30.656***$

**pL .01
***pL .001

explain the similarity to their male friends' choices. But it is also possible that career oriented women interact concerning occupational choice with both sexes rather than with women alone. This interpretation is congruent with the finding that career salient women named more and a broader array of persons as influential in their occupational choice.

Important involvement in masculine and work reference groups came through the students' own experience. A record of summer and part-time jobs held revealed that the study class had a large amount and variety of work experience. Although the school draws disproportionately from the upper socioeconomic levels, for the class as a whole, the average number of jobs held was about three, and the average number of different jobs was two. Only three girls report no work experience while twenty had held five or more jobs. Table 3 reveals that career oriented women have had more jobs and more different jobs than their non-career oriented classmates.

The relationship between work experience and career choices involves opportunities afforded for role learning. The neophyte has a chance to place herself in a particular role, with its attendant demands on performance, time, attention, and effort. She can decide whether she likes the role; this is dramatized by a few students who decided against a chosen occupation after some unhappy work experience in that field. Other girls reported an abrupt change in occupational choice because of a particularly unusual or interesting job. Work experience allows the student to test her own self conception against the work role requirements and to gain a clearer picture of her own ability through the expressed approval or disapproval of supervisory personnel. For students who were employed in their university departments, or in an occupational milieu related to their own vocational choice, the job may have provided contact with occupational role models who influenced their later career choices.

Familial Influence — A series of familial variables were examined to ascertain their possible significance in the development of career plans. As a first and primary group, the potential of the family is indeed very strong. However, with the exception of maternal employment and leisure activities, the data show little relation between parents as reference groups and outcomes on career salience. The mothers of career salient stu-

dents had slightly higher educational attainment, and the
fathers of non-career oriented students had higher educational
and occupational levels, but in no case do these trends reach
statistical significance (Table 4).

Table 4 / Family Life Style and Career Salience

Variable	Career Salient (N=50)	Non-Career Salient (N=60)	Chi Square
Father's occupation professional or managerial	45%	59%	$x^2=2.276$ N.S.
Father's education (At least some college)	55%	66%	$x^2=1.023$ N.S.
Mother's education (At least some college)	54%	45%	$x^2=.897$ N.S.
Proportion of positive characteristics attributed to parents	68%	79%	$x^2=6.736*$
Proportion of negative characteristics attributed to parents	37%	34%	$x^2=.254$ N.S.
Mother employed during student's college years	66%	22%	$x^2=22.031***$
Mother highly involved in leisure activities	25%	38%	$x^2=5.875*$

*pL .05
***pL .001

Students were asked to select from a list items which characterize their father, mother, or both parents. They could check
as many items as they wished. Negative items were "dismisses
my problems as unimportant," "hard to talk to," "often criticizes me unfairly," and "has little free time." The positive
items were "gives me advice," "offers sympathy and affection," "helps me with my problems," and "is a good listener."
Throughout the four years of college career salient and non-
career salient students did not differ in the number of positive
or negative characteristics attributed to mother, father, or both
parents. In senior year only, non-career oriented women check

slightly more positive statements, but the differences between the groups are small (Table 4).

Taken together this suggests that the emergence of career aspirations is not so closely related to family social class factors or to the girl's perception of her parents as individuals as it is to the general attitudes and aspirations developed in the family. Interview data show that students, regardless of their degree of career salience, perceive their parents as approving, supporting and encouraging their plans. An unhappy or tension-filled association between parents and child might serve to mediate the potential influence of the mother as a role model. With the absence of marked differences between career and non-career students either in socio-economic background or in relationships with parents, the positive impact of the mother as either a work or leisure role model operates rather freely.

The Mother as a Role Model — Detailed work histories for the students' mothers were constructed from student reports. Table 4 shows a strong association between maternal employment and daughters' work interest. Nearly two-thirds of the career salient but only about one-fifth of the non-career salient women have mothers currently employed. In the interviews students mentioned their mother's employment spontaneously and often discussed it at length. These girls learned a more favorable definition of the working mother role. They saw that combining marriage and career can be done, that it is enjoyable, and that their fathers do not object strenuously. One highly career oriented girl, who planned to marry and attend graduate school to prepare for a career in biological research was asked about her long range plans. Her reply:

> I know I am going to work; I enjoy it. I was probably influenced by my mother. She has worked the whole time, except when I was very small.

Another girl described the changes that occurred in her mother as a result of going back to work:

> My mother is working part time now and teaching two days a week. There are two little ones at home, aged seven and ten. She added a semester toward her master's degree, and all of a sudden she realized that she is very smart. She now does more things with my brother and sister. They have a happier home life, doing things now that before she would not have had time to do. She is going out

twice a week and having to look nice. I come home and she looks younger than she did before.

The results concerning maternal employment are strengthened if it is also pointed out that fully fifty percent of the non-career salient women do not recall that their mothers ever worked. Only twenty-two percent of the career salient women had mothers who were never employed in their knowledge. Moreover, among students whose mothers are currently working, the mothers of career oriented students are more often employed full time than are the mothers of non-career salient women who do work.

Career oriented women had a positive and favorable conception of their mothers, but sometimes show disdain for women who spend their time participating in clubs and volunteer activities. By contrast, non-career oriented women spoke favorably of spending time in these very activities. One girl said:

Why should I work when I can do so many other enjoyable things? I think that home and family is probably the most important thing a woman ever has to do. You must fulfill this requirement because a man just cannot. My life is probably not going to make that much difference on society, but maybe what my husband and children can do will. I would like to work, do volunteer work or spend time on my own hobbies, *if* I have the time left over.

Mothers of non-career salient girls participated more frequently in clubs, hobbies, community and volunteer work than did the mothers of career salient girls. The differences are moderate, but consistent and statistically significant (Table 4). Students occasionally pointed out that a woman could be interesting and well-informed without resorting to a job outside the home:

I would like to get married and have a family and I don't want to be a career woman. That is a very potent statement. I think my mother is a good example of what I would like to be and I have several girlfriends whose mothers are the same way. They are not career women yet they are very active in the community. I think you can keep up with what is going on in the world and you don't have to work all your life.

Non-career women tended to stress the need for a mother to care intensely and personally for her small children. Career

oriented women were also convinced of the necessity for taking personal care of their preschool children, but were adamant about returning to the labor force when their children entered school. They recognized that many household tasks could be delegated to others. One girl who plans to be a lawyer and hopes to marry one pointed out:

> We would both be capable of earning enough that I could hire a girl to do the work that you don't put your own personality in. Obviously things like decorating the house and doing your own cooking, raising the kids, you have to do it yourself. That is something you stamp your own individuality on, but if it is just a matter of making beds, sweeping the floors, or doing dishes, everybody does that more or less alike. For that you can get a hired girl. I don't think I would be hurting the kids any that way, not if I was home when they were.

Role Models and Occupational Choice

Both questionnaire and interview data confirm for this sample the finding of the Simpsons, that career salient women were more likely to indicate professors and persons in the occupation as the most important source of personal influence on their occupational choice. Non-career salient women were more likely to name family members or friends, but very often felt that no one had influenced their choice. Table 5 shows only the percentage who named at least one occupational role model and masks the fact that career oriented women often named several persons as influential in this process. This is well illustrated in

Table 5 / Role Model Influences on Career Salience

Variable	Career Salient (N=50)	Non-Career Salient (N=60)	Chi Square
Source of perceived influence on occupational choice (teachers and work role models)[1]	68%	23%	x^2=17.915***
Felt teachers consider her outstanding or bright	82%	54%	x^2=8.844**

[1] These data are from senior interviews. N for career salient = 38. N for non-career salient = 48.
**pL .01
***pL .001

the following exchange between the interviewer and a student who planned college teaching and research in chemistry:

Student: I guess my interest in chemistry originally stems from my father and my family. Our family is educationally oriented. My sister, my mother and my father are teachers. But I felt that teaching high school would not allow for the more intricate parts of chemistry, and I wanted to do research as well as teach. I decided to go more for college teaching.

Interviewer: Other than your family, do you know of other particular persons who might have influenced you?

Student: I would say my research advisor for the past two semesters. I consider him one of the few people who is really interested in other people. I guess in a way I am trying to copy him or something.

Interviewer: What would you want to copy about him?

Student: Just his interest in people. I feel that because of his vocation he can pursue both his interest in science and his interest in people, whereas if you are out in industry it is a great deal more difficult.

Contact with occupational role models came largely through work experience in an entry job, by assisting on faculty research, or through student originated independent study projects which involve the student directly and continuously with one or more faculty members. The pervasive influence of the college teacher-researcher work role model is further evident in the nine percent of the students who chose college teaching and another twelve percent who chose some aspect of research work. Contracts with persons in a given occupation were often made outside a work context but involved discussions in which the role model aided in clarifying and solving problems about future plans. One girl, when asked if any particular persons influenced her choice to do biological research in industry, replied:

Yes, a couple of my friends in biology that work in different companies. I just sit down and talk to them and become familiar with what people do. I learn about the attitudes of the companies, how they treat people. . . . One of my teachers had worked in industry before. He teaches you the very practical kind of stuff you will need to know, not just a classical education. When I get a job I won't have to say, "I never learned any of this and you are going to have to teach me from the beginning."

Non-career salient women seemed to make occupational decisions in more haphazard fashion. As one girl put it:

> I just kind of fell into teaching. My mother has always wanted me to take the teaching option for the security of it. I thought, well it is not going to take up too many electives, so I may as well go into education and I will have something behind me when I get married.

When these students did experience role model influence, they were frequently encouraged to choose occupations they could easily enter or leave in accordance with family needs, or occupations which would allow combining job with family responsibilities if it were necessary to work.

> Mrs. W. gave me the first organized impression I had of teaching, and she gave me more facts. She was very nice and a very good teacher. She would mention things like hours and the working conditions, and I guess it was just being part attitude and part facts that I got from her that made me decide to teach too.

Limited contact with career role models coupled with the more pervasive influence of family members led the non-career oriented women to stress the importance of family and motherhood, rather than career. When career salient women reported familial influence on their choice, the parents were referred to as strongly supportive of their daughter's intentions. Sometimes a member of the family served as a model for a specific occupation or as a connecting link to other models.

> My whole family are lawyers and I know many aspects of law from private practice to patent law to corporation law. My brother is a lawyer. I know a great many of his friends, most of whom are lawyers and I have spoken to them about it. I have some friends of the family who have daughters who are lawyers. I also know women in other professions (medicine) who think professions are great for women. Law is the type of work I would like to be doing.

Faculty and occupational role models were not exclusively men or women; students occasionally reported having contact with both. It is difficult to ascertain whether these influential persons were exemplars of the possible in combining marriage and career, and hence probably female, or if they present a technical explication of a particular occupational role, in which case the sex of the model is less relevant. Career salient women with working mothers already had the former, and for them faculty role models provide psychological incentives to select the particular occupation. These incentives include rewards for academic performance or work activity in which the model aids the neophyte in developing a self concept as a person capable of operating effectively in a given occupation.

Gold has pointed out that women in high level careers are potentially available as models, but students may "observe the rarity of the phenomena and infer the conditions which keep it so" (Gold, 1968:21).[6] In this sample, career oriented students were likely to have majored in departments which had a modest concentration of female faculty — the humanities and social sciences. In the natural sciences, departments which were almost exclusively male, less than half the students were strongly career oriented. But the major with the highest percentage of non-career oriented students was Home Economics, whose faculty is almost entirely female. Any attempt to explain this apparent curvilinear relationship[7] between the career salience of students and the sex composition of the faculty in major department should not generalize beyond the particulars of this university. Students are more likely to experience males as role models if only because of the predominance of males on college faculties. Male professionals give subtle emphasis to career but apparently it is necessary for students to perceive such careers as open to women as well.

Further research would be required to uncover the social psychological dynamics of the relationship between role model and neophyte, including the selection processes operating for both parties. Non-career women may not lack available role models so much as they are simply less interested or willing or able to enter into such a relationship. Non-career women were less likely to think that their teachers considered them to be bright or outstanding students (Table 5). Over eighty percent of the career oriented women felt that faculty members had a high opinion of them, but only half of the non-career oriented students perceived a favorable evaluation of this sort. These differentials reflected self-evaluations occur in spite of the fact that there are no marked differences in grades obtained by career and non-career oriented women. Because of their developing orientations, career women may be more amenable to potential influence, but the question of why some students are selected for special attention by faculty remains an open one.

Summary and Discussion

The findings are as follows:

1. Non-career salience is associated with sorority membership, being married, engaged, or going steady, but is not strongly related to amount of dating in college.
2. Career salience is related to choosing fields chosen by male peers.
3. Career salient students perceive their professors as having a more positive evaluation of their academic ability.
4. Career salience is related to having had more work experience in a greater variety of jobs.
5. Career salient students more frequently have working mothers while non-career salient students have mothers who tend to be more active in leisure pursuits.
6. Career salience is not significantly associated with the educational level of either parent, nor with the father's occupational level.
7. Non-career salience is slightly associated with positive perceptions of parental characteristics, but not with negative perceptions.

All of the above findings pertain largely to indirect sources of reference group influence. The other important finding involves more direct role model influence.

8. Non-career salient women felt that peers, family members, or no one had influenced their occupational choice. Career salient students had these same sources of influence but they were most strongly influenced by college professors and occupational role models.

From these findings, it should not be inferred that different reference groups alone account for differences in career orientations. It is also necessary to take into account the content of the influence of the specific referents which students have. With regard to peer groups, for example, non-career oriented students chose occupations similar to those chosen by their female peers, while career salient women picked fields chosen by both their male and female peers. Moreover, many of the career salient women were married or planning to be, but they had future mates who fostered their work plans, just as the non-career salient were attached to males who agreed with their lesser work orientation. Finally, knowing that the family serves as a reference group is not sufficient either, unless the nature of this influence is taken into account. The mother as a worker differs as a model from mother as a participant in leisure activities. We defined not only the types of reference groups which can influence the adult aspirations of college women, but also indicated the content of such potential influences.

For women, the importance of role models lies in their explication of a life style which incorporates work with family life. Occupational choice alone may be a temporary or changeable matter for a girl, but commitment to an adult life which includes work necessitates some notion of what such a life may be like. Adult career women, either as working mothers, female teachers or acquaintances in a given occupation, can serve as models of this life style.

We have not distinguished the sex of college professors or persons in an occupation who influenced the students' occupational choices. Little is known either about why or how some students come to be recipients of this type of influence or whether some students are more receptive to it. Generally career salient women perceived their faculty members as having a more positive evaluation of their studentship than did non-career women. Once the relationship is established it is clear that such role models not only provide a technical explication of how various jobs are performed, but they also present to the student an evaluation of her own abilities and prospects. Hence role models serve more than the limited function Kemper assigns. College professors and supervisory personnel on the job expect certain performance levels, thus serving as normative reference groups. Particularly when positive extra-work relationships develop between role model and neophyte, they can become a source of additional inter-personal rewards. As a result the student becomes further motivated; she has acquired an important audience. Thus role models act as more than technical explicators, they appear to combine the several functions of reference groups. These remarks should not be taken as derogatory of Kemper's reference group theory. Indeed, we are stressing the point that when the several functions are served by one group or person, this combination may be most facilitative of achievement.

NOTES

This is a revised version of a paper presented at the American Sociological Association Meetings, Washington, D.C., September, 1970. The research reported here was supported by the Scaife Fund of Margaret Morrison Carnegie College.

1. Kemper's discussion of McClelland's theory of n-achievement is based on David McClelland, *The Achieving Society*, Princeton: Van Nostrand, 1961, and David McClelland, John W. Atkinson, Russell A. Clark and Edgar L. Lowell, *The Achievement Motive*. New York: Appleton-Century-Crofts, 1953.

2. Career salient women were lower in family role salience; they reported lesser enjoyment of domestic activities, child care, contact with parents, homemaking tasks, and of planning and organizing things. They were consistently more interested in reading, study, and solo activities, exhibiting a pattern which differed from the model pattern of the majority in their age cohort (Rossi, 1967, pp. 4-5).

3. This item was termed adult role aspirations and read as follows:
Fifteen years from now would you like to be:
    (1) A housewife with no children
    (2) A housewife with one or more children
    (3) An unmarried career woman
    (4) A married career woman without children
    (5) A married career woman with children
The last three responses reflect a career orientation; only one person gave the third response.

4. Respondents rated themselves on whether they would want to work under each of the following conditions:
    (1) One child of school age, husband's salary adequate.
    (2) Two or more children of school age, husband's salary adequate.
Responses of "probably would" and "definitely would" were taken as high work orientation.

5. The specific question reads:
Assume that you are trained for the occupation of your choice, that you will marry and have children, and that your husband will earn enough so that you will never have to work unless you want to. Under these conditions which of the following would you prefer? (Circle one)
    (1) To participate in clubs or volunteer work
    (2) To spend time on hobbies, sports, or other activities

    (3) To work part-time in your chosen occupation
    (4) To work full-time in your chosen occupation
    (5) To concentrate on home and family
    (6) Other, explain briefly

On this question, "work part-time or full-time" were considered career oriented responses.

6. Gold notes that women faculty members may not serve as role models for several reasons. Students may associate such women with the negative aspects of the college experience, i.e., required courses, examinations and grading procedures. If faculty members are at the peak of their careers, modesty may prevent female students from assuming that they, too, can occupy such positions. In order to be "exemplars of the possible," role models at intermediary stages (as graduate students) are needed. Students may infer the prejudices operating against women in high level positions or discover some flaw in their appearance or personality. As a result, identification with these potential models may be impeded. Gold suggests that role models may have a more positive impact on women already committed to a career, and less on the undecided or family-oriented student.

7. The exact percentages of faculty who are female and student major who are career-oriented, respectively, were:

    Social Science — 27% and 65%
    Humanities — 23% and 58%
    Natural Sciences — 4% and 46%
    Home Economics — 87% and 27%

REFERENCES

Almquist, Elizabeth M. and Shirley S. Angrist, "Career Salience and Atypicality of Occupational Choice Among College Women," *Journal of Marriage and the Family*, 32 (May 1969): 242-249.

Astin, Helen S., "Factors Associated with the Participation of the Woman Doctorate in the Labor Force," *Personnel and Guidance Journal*, 45 (November 1967): 240-446.

Bailyn, Lotte, "Notes on the Role of Choice in the Psychology of Professional Women," *Daedalus*, 93 (Spring 1964): 700-710.

Empey, LaMar T., "Role Expectations of Young Women Regarding Marriage and a Career," *Marriage and Family Living*, 20 (May 1958): 152-155.

Ginzberg, Eli, *Life Styles of Educated Women*, (New York: Columbia University Press, 1966).

Ginzberg, Eli, "Paycheck and Apron-Revolution in Womanpower," *Industrial Relations*, 7 (May, 1968): 193-203.

Ginzberg, Eli, Sol W. Ginsburg, Sidney Axelrad and John L. Herna, *Occupational Choice: An Approach to a General Theory*, (New York: Columbia University Press, 1951).

Gold, Sonia, "Work and Leisure Models: Some Implications for Women's Higher Education," an unpublished paper (January, 1968).

Kemper, Theodore, "Reference Groups, Socialization and Achievement." *American Sociological Review,* 33 (February 1968): 31-45.

Masih, Lalit K., "Career Saliency and Its Relation to Certain Needs, Interests and Job Values." *Personnel and Guidance Journal,* 45 (March 1967): 653-658.

Oppenheimer, Valerie Kincaid, "The Sex-Labeling of Jobs," *Industrial Relations,* 7 (May 1968): 219-234.

Rossi, Alice S., "The Roots of Ambivalence in American Women." Paper presented at the Continuing Education Conference, Oakland University, Michigan, 1967.

Scott, John F., "The American College Sorority: Its Role in Class and Ethnic Endogamy." *American Sociological Review,* 30 (August 1965): 514-527.

Shab, Fred, "Southern College Women: A Comparison of Arts and Science Majors with Education Majors," *American Association of University Women Journal,* 60 (March 1967): 142-148.

Siegel, Alberta E. and Elizabeth A. Curtis, "Familial Correlates of Orientation Toward Future Employment Among College Women." *Journal of Educational Psychology,* 44 (January 1963): 33-37.

Simpson, Richard L. and Ida Simpson, "Occupational Choice Among Career-Oriented College Women." *Marriage and Family Living,* 33 (November 1963): 377-383.

Turner, Ralph H., "Role-Taking, Role Standpoint and Reference-Group Behavior." *American Journal of Sociology,* 61 (January 1956): 316-328.

Turner, Ralph, "Some Aspects of Women's Ambition." *American Journal of Sociology,* 70 (November 1964): 271-285.

White, Kinnard, "Social Background Variables Related to Career Commitment of Women Teachers." *Personnel and Guidance Journal,* 45 (March 1967): 48-52.

twenty-two

Interest of High School Girls in Dental Auxiliary Careers

LOIS K. COHEN, EDWARD M. KNOTT

The increasing demand for formally educated dental auxiliaries — assistants, hygienists, and technicians — indicates strongly that efforts should be expended to identify the potential sources of such manpower.[1] Once sufficient data are gathered to make it possible to determine the groups which are most interested in these auxiliary positions, the task for recruitment personnel can be facilitated as they can communicate information to these young persons in a far more efficient manner.

Some answers can be obtained from the results of a pilot study on high school students' interests in several health occupations, with particular emphasis on dental health. The study was financed by the United States Public Health Service, Division of Dental Health, and the data were gathered by the Department of Sociology of Rutgers University in 1961. A first report concerned the interest of high school boys in dentistry.[2] The present study is focused on the interest expressed by high school girls in dental auxiliary positions as well as on their general expectations for careers, because marriage and subsequent family obligations tend to encroach on this segment of the labor force supply.

Methodology

Through the cooperation of 7 New Jersey high schools, 756 junior and senior girls completed a self-administered questionnaire. Although college preparatory students were the primary focus of the study, 12 per cent of the respondents were enrolled

From JOURNAL OF DENTAL EDUCATION, Vol. 31, No. 1 (1967), pp. 20-27. Reprinted by permission.

in other programs, mostly commercial. The questionnaire included the following statements:

> Below is a list of jobs which many young persons are considering nowadays. Read the whole list carefully and "x" as many as *might possibly interest you* at all as jobs for yourself.

> Will you go over this list and "x" any that you probably *would not want to be*. ("x" as many as you definitely would *not* be interested in.)

Each of these statements was followed by a list of 31 occupations, including the dental auxiliary positions of assisting, hygiene, and laboratory technology. Nursing, an auxiliary occupation for the medical profession, was considered in this analysis as a useful comparison. On the basis of the answers, the students were divided into 3 categories of interest in each occupation:

1. *Positive.* These girls checked the given occupation as a job which might possibly interest them.
2. *Negative.* These girls checked the given occupation as a job in which they definitely were not interested.
3. *Neutral.* These girls did not indicate interest in or rejection of the given occupation.

Results

Of the 31 occupations, social work ranked first in positive choices, nursing sixth, dental assisting thirteenth, medicine sixteenth, nursing aide nineteenth, dental laboratory technology twenty-and-a-half, dental hygiene twenty-third, and dentistry twenty-eighth. The medical-related occupations ranked higher than the dental-related, and for the most part, the female-centered occupations ranked higher than the male-dominated ones. Within the dental area, greatest preference was expressed for dental assisting, and least for dental hygiene.

Students enrolled in the college preparatory classes represented nearly 90 per cent of the group. The number of girls in general, commercial, or "other" courses was small; thus an analysis as complete as for the college preparatory group was not possible. However, differences among the latter group in socio-economic background and in educational and occupational expectations seemed to distinguish types of girls who expressed interest in the auxiliary occupations.

Socio-economic Background

Regardless of social background characteristics, it is evident from Table 1 that more negative than positive interest was expressed for dental auxiliary occupations and nursing. The only times in which there was a greater amount of positive sentiment were among girls whose fathers were foremen and craftsmen, and among girls whose fathers had not graduated from high school. The positive interest was in nursing. However, these differences varied only by 2 and 4 per cent, respectively. What are more pertinent are the findings that much more positive interest was expressed for nursing than for the dental occupations, and, conversely, that less negativeness was shown toward nursing than toward the dental positions. Among the dental auxiliary occupations, dental assisting was the most popular choice and dental hygiene the least popular, when parental occupation and education were controlled.

Among these college preparatory students, it is apparent that the higher a student's social and economic status (determined by father's and mother's education, and father's occupation), the less likely she was to express positive interest in dental assisting and the more likely she was to state disinterest. Girls whose fathers had white-collar positions were less receptive to dental assisting than were girls whose fathers had blue-collar occupations. This relation between social background and interest in dental assisting is somewhat more pronounced when the education of parents is examined. For instance, 6 per cent of the students whose mothers had at least some college education stated a positive interest in the possibility of dental assisting as a future occupation compared with 16 per cent whose mothers had not graduated from high school.

Among college preparatory students expressing an interest in becoming a dental hygienist, the data are somewhat different. Although the number possibly interested in becoming a dental hygienist was small, as were the percentage differences, the data suggest that girls whose fathers are in the middle-range occupations (sales-clerical, foreman-craftsman) were slightly more prone to state an interest in dental hygiene than girls whose fathers are either top ranking or low ranking. Similarly, girls whose parents are high school graduates (6 per cent and 7 per cent, respectively, for father and mother), again in the middle educational range, stated more interest and less disinterest in dental hygiene.

It is true that there are more men than women actually engaged as dental technicians, but this occupation was included as a potential choice to complete the range of available major

Table 1 / Interest in Dental Auxiliary Occupations and Nursing among College Preparatory High School Girls (Percentages)*

	Positive				Negative				Number of Girls
	Assisting	Hygiene	Technology	Nursing	Assisting	Hygiene	Technology	Nursery	
Father's Occupation									
Professional-entrepreneurial	10	4	6	27	51	59	58	47	391
Sales-clerical	10	9	6	35	50	55	51	39	80
Foreman-craftsman	16	5	13	43	44	56	49	39	99
Other blue collar	13	4	2	33	35	52	52	46	52
Father's Education									
Some college or more	9	5	6	27	53	59	59	45	371
High school graduate	12	6	7	34	47	54	52	47	145
Not high school graduate	17	3	11	41	37	54	46	39	115
Mother's Education									
Some college or more	6	4	5	26	59	64	63	46	266
High school graduate	14	7	9	33	43	52	50	44	296
Not high school graduate	16	2	9	40	38	56	43	43	89

* Percentages do not add to 100, as neutral interest was eliminated.

dental auxiliary positions. It appears that girls whose fathers are foremen and craftsmen were more likely to prefer becoming a dental technician than girls whose fathers were engaged in any of the other occupations. Further, girls whose fathers and mothers did not complete high school were more likely to choose this occupation than girls whose parents had some higher education. Then, too, these girls were less likely to express disinterest.

Even though expressed interest for nursing was greater than that for the dental auxiliary occupations, this concern was somewhat dependent on social background characteristics. Forty-three per cent of the girls whose fathers were foremen and craftsmen stated a positive interest in nursing; whereas 27 per cent of those whose fathers were professionals, 35 per cent whose fathers were sales-clerical, and 33 per cent of those whose fathers were in other blue-collar jobs stated such positive interest. Conversely, less disinterest in nursing was apparent for girls from foreman-craftsmen backgrounds and sales-clerical parental backgrounds, the 2 middle-range categories. In general, the higher the parents' education, the less positive interest in nursing and the more the negative interest.

Future Plans

A second general pattern which emerged among college preparatory students was that the higher a student's own educational expectations for the future, the less likely she was to be interested in the health auxiliary occupations and the more likely she was to reject them. (Table 2) However, in the instances of positive interest in dental hygiene and laboratory technology, apparently there is the expectation of some college education.

The students were asked, "As far as you can tell now, how much more education will you *probably* get after you leave high school?" As their college preparatory enrollment would lead one to anticipate, some of the students planned to finish college (5 per cent) and a considerable number (22 per cent) were anticipating additional education above the high school level. However, this latter group rejected the dental auxiliary occupations to a greater extent than did those who expected less continued education. An interesting finding can be seen among girls who did not plan any college education and who did appear to be interested in nursing. Fifty-six per cent of these students were positively inclined toward nursing, whereas 34 per cent were negatively inclined.

The respondents were also asked, "As things stand now,

Table 2 / Interest in Dental Auxiliary Occupations and Nursing among College Preparatory High School Girls by Their Future Plans (Percentages)*

	Positive				Negative				Number of Girls
	Assisting	Hygiene	Technology	Nursing	Assisting	Hygiene	Technology	Nursing	
Probable Future Education									
No College	22	4	10	56	38	47	44	34	80
Some College	9	10	18	33	35	44	49	39	57
Finish College	12	6	8	29	45	56	54	46	374
College Plus	3	3	1	22	68	68	67	48	147
Probable Future Occupation									
Nonprofessional	21	1	6	32	38	58	56	49	99
Professional	9	6	7	31	51	57	55	44	540

* Percentages do not add to 100, as neutral interest was eliminated.

what do you think your future occupation probably *will* be (that is, other than being a wife and mother)?" A majority of the girls indicated that their future occupations would probably be professional in nature. Most of the others planned to enter the clerical field.

Interestingly enough, it was members of the latter group who were more likely to express positive interest in becoming a dental assistant, and it was those of the former group who tended to express a little more interest in dental hygiene. However, the expectation of being a professional or nonprofessional made no difference in choosing either dental technology or nursing. Perhaps the lines of demarcation distinguishing the professional nature of the occupations were unclear to the choosers.

The majority enrolled in a college preparatory program felt that their future plans included the possibility of combining a career with a home and family. (Table 3) It should be kept in mind that 30 per cent of those in college preparatory courses would rather not work. However, the fact that they were registered in programs geared toward higher education indicates that they may expect or be expected to work for a period of time, should the occasion arise.

Table 3 / Marriage and Career Plans of Students Enrolled in College Preparatory and Non-college Preparatory Courses (Percentages)

	Marriage Only	Rather Not Work	Like to Work but Don't Think Could Combine Career with Family
College Preparatory	1	30	20
Other Courses	2	47	19

	Like to Combine Career and Family	Career Even if It Postpones Marriage	Total
College Preparatory	36	13	100
Other Courses	22	10	100

Forty-seven per cent of those girls enrolled in general, commercial, or "other" courses preferred not to work after marriage. Thus, expectation for a career seems to be less of a consideration among those not in college preparatory classes.

Summary
1. The data from this study suggest that high school girls enrolled in college preparatory courses are more likely

a. to be negative than positive in attitude toward auxiliary occupations; and

b. to express positive interest first in nursing among the health occupations listed, next in dental assisting, next in dental technology, and last in hygiene.

2. The data show further that, on the basis of socio-economic factors concerned mainly with family background, the girls who expressed a positive interest in

a. *nursing* seemed to come from families where the father was a blue-collar (foreman-craftsman) worker, the parents had little education, and the girls tended to eliminate the possibility of a college education for themselves;

b. *dental assisting* tended to come from blue-collar families, where the parents were not high school graduates, and the girls did not expect to continue their education or pursue a professional occupation;

c. *laboratory technology* came from blue-collar families, where the parents had not completed high school, and the girls did not expect to finish college but did anticipate additional education; and

d. *dental hygiene* tended to come from a middle socio-economic background determined by the fathers' education (foreman-craftsman and sales-clerical) and by parents' education (high school graduates), and where there was a plan for some college education.

3. The data also show that, on the basis of marriage and family considerations, girls of the college preparatory group felt they could combine a career with family and home activities; whereas girls in non-college preparatory group felt they would rather not work after marriage.

Discussion

The choice of an occupation can be viewed as a decision-making process — whereby the person compares the image of the occupational role with his own evolving values, attitudes, goals, and capabilities, and thus chooses the best among the perceived alternatives. Further, a person's self-concept might be affected by socio-economic background, among other factors.[3]

Another component of the decision-making process is the amount of information on possible alternatives that is available to the chooser. Choices for women generally are limited to occupations which fit the concept of the wife-mother role (engrained in American girls during their childhood and adolescence), but they may also be influenced by the amount of accessible information. Among health auxiliary occupations, nursing may be the only one which simulates most closely the wife-mother model. Very likely, too, nursing is the role to which most publicity is given. Perhaps, the nature of the tasks and rewards — even the basic distinctions between dental hygienist, assistant, and technician — is less clear.

Even if information about all health auxiliaries were equally available, a recent study of nursing indicates that a motivating factor for recruiting women into that field was the extent to which self-identities are congruent with work roles.[4] Thus, it appears, from a practical point of application, that recruiters of dental auxiliaries must publicize the nature of the job alternatives through mass media and other educational facilities, as well as consider the possibility of stressing the traditional concept of the female role as it can be related to dental auxiliary work.

The Cornell nursing study suggested that nursing students in the State of New York tend to be recruited from a lower socioeconomic stratum than are students entering some of the other traditional women's occupations. Girls who had fathers who were blue-collar workers and earned low incomes, and who identified their origins as "lower middle class" or "working class" were more frequently found in the group of nursing students than were those from the comparison groups, for example, teachers and secretarial workers.[5]

Even though the present analysis does not concern students who are already committed to a health auxiliary field as was true in the above study, the current findings suggest a strong similarity. It was found that the college preparatory high school girls who expressed interest in nursing seemed to be drawn from lower-middle class families; i.e., the fathers are blue-collar workers, and the parents have had a little education, perhaps having completed high school. These findings are similar to the data on interest in the dental auxiliary occupations. In addition, the girls who were sampled expected to receive little education beyond high school.

These data imply that in order to meet the increasing demand for formally educated auxiliaries, the dental profession may find it fruitful to direct career information to these particular socio-economic and future interest" groupings in high school populations. The preparation of the materials might stress the differential tasks and rewards associated with the various types of occupations, thus relating the characteristics of the specific job requirements to the qualities of the potential recruits. Since the study population was not selected to be representative, generalizations about *all high school girls* must be strictly tentative. Thus, the inferences that have been drawn are suggestive, not definitive. In this respect, it is interesting to note that New Jersey, in actuality, makes less use of dental auxiliaries than other places in the United States. Future research might consider replicating this study in California, as that state accounted for almost 53 per cent of the total enrollment in dental assisting programs for 1963-1964.[6] There is the logical possibility that differential visibility of dental auxiliaries may be an influencing factor in attracting varying types of students. It is hoped that a future study of this kind will be conducted, if only to make more definitive the inferences that have been drawn from this New Jersey exploratory study.

NOTES

1. *Survey of Dentistry* — Final Report of the Commission on the Survey of Dentistry in the United States. Byron S. Hollinshead, Director. Washington, D.C.: American Council on Education, 1961. pp. 236-237.

2. Lefcowitz, Myron J., and Irelan, Lola M.: "Interest in Dentistry: A Pilot Study of High School Students: I. Effect of Social Status and Academic Ability." *J. Dent. Educ.*, 27, 48-54, 1963.

3. For a general statement and empirical study of the role of values and the congruence between self-image and occupational choices see Morris Rosenberg, *Occupations and Values*. Glencoe, Ill.: Free Press, 1957. 158 pp.

4. White, Rodney F.: *Female Identity and Work Roles: The Case of Nursing*. Ph.D. dissertation, Department of Sociology, University of Chicago, March 1964. 160 pp.

5. Williams, Robin M., and Goldsen, Rose K.: "Some Factors Relevant to Career Selection in Nursing: Progress Report." Report on study done under U.S.P.H.S. Grant G C 4465. Ithaca, New York: Cornell University, June 1964. Mimeographed.

6. From the files of the U.S. Public Health Service, Division of Dental Public Health and Resources, Manpower and Education Branch. Data were obtained from the Regional Dental Consultants.

twenty-three

Career Dreams of Teachers

BENJAMIN D. WRIGHT
SHIRLEY A. TUSKA

Message on the grade-school blackboard: Teacher loved Father. On the high-school blackboard the message is different: Teacher loved Teacher. Mother loved her well enough, but it was Teacher who inspired her and served as the model for her career. Message on the junior-high-school blackboard: Teacher neither liked nor disliked her parents to extremes, perhaps trying to hold on to both of them — and therefore fell between, into middle-school teaching.

These are the lessons we have learned from an intensive study of the childhood experiences and identifications of female prospective teachers at the different school levels.[1] Perhaps these lessons should also be learned by those who help prepare teachers, and children, for their future vocations.

That children will identify with adults important to them — especially their parents — and that these identifications will influence their choice of careers is, of course, a well-known fact. The psychological concept of "identification" is at least as old as Freud's *The Interpretation of Dreams*. But the systematic observation and explanation of identification, and how it works toward the choice of careers, have yet to be provided.

Our work started in 1960, out of discussions with Dr. Barbara Sherman, who had just embarked on a study of the identification of teachers with childhood authority figures. Later, after analyzing many personal anecdotes from female teachers at the different school levels (as well as those of women never inter-

From TRANS-action, Vol. 6, No. 1 (1968), pp. 43-47. Reprinted by permission of TRANS-action.

ested in becoming teachers), we began to wonder if the early lives of the women in these various groups had been different, presaging their different career choices. It seemed to us that teaching recreates a common and pervasive childhood environment (even if from a different viewpoint). Therefore it might offer a unique opportunity for a person to resolve childhood conflicts through identification with parents and teachers, or to even re-enact unresolved conflicts through identification with pupils.

Gradually we developed our theory. We believe that children live in a kind of family romance — a continuing drama in which different members of the family, and such influential outside adults as teachers, act out the pivotal roles of hero, rival, friend, and enemy of the child. The way the child perceives this romance and his role in it helps determine his personality, and therefore his inclinations toward a career.

Let us examine the different kinds of family romances, as described by our theory, and see if we can understand the connections between the childhood experience of the young women and their choice of careers.

In the "Father Romance" that we found to characterize the childhoods of female grade-school teachers, Father is the strong, influential person in the family — at least as far as the girl is concerned. The girl not only loves him and wants him as a friend, but considers him a hero and wants to be like him. Mother is either relatively colorless, or hostile. Of the pivotal roles — hero, friend, rival, or enemy — Mother can exert substantial influence only as enemy. In the romance between Father and daughter she remains passive. If she objected strongly, or tried to become a genuine rival, the competition would have to be resolved, bringing on that series of complications known as the Oedipus complex.

Mother may be passive for various reasons. She may have interests outside the family; she may be weak and childlike, willing to act out the role of another daughter; she may even identify with her daughter, having had as a child a similar romance with *her* father. Whatever the reason, in this case there is no significant Oedipal rivalry to be resolved.

In the "Mother Romance," the roles are reversed. Mother is strong and influential; the daughter loves and admires her, and wants her as friend and heroine. Father either appears seldom, or makes few waves. He is not a rival. If he exerts influence, it is as an enemy.

In this pattern, the reversed mirror image of the Father Romance, Father takes a back seat. As it happens, in our society this is a relatively common pattern, since there are few fathers who do not spend more time away from home than their wives do. In addition, like his female counterpart in the Father Romance, Father might be weak and withdrawn, have overriding, vital interests outside his family that keep him away, and so on. In any case, he does not compete. Mother has the field.

In the "Teacher Romance," the girl's relationship with her teacher, and its impact upon her, overshadow her relationship with her parents. We assume that either she did not get along with her parents, or her relations with Teacher were so good and satisfying that her parents faded into the background. In some cases, perhaps, her parents were so uneducated, or from such dull backgrounds (as with immigrants, or rural people moved to the city), that they were unable to compete. Generally, unsatisfying parental relations are most likely: Both parents were uninteresting or forbidding. Teacher therefore became the focus, the pathfinder to fulfillment and dreams — the one to be loved, possessed as a friend, admired as a heroine. If the parents do manage to step out of the background, they appear as enemies.

So far we have dealt with romances in which the child had, essentially, no rivals. In such romances it is not necessary for the child to resolve a conflict. But there are situations in which there is significant rivalry. Thus, when both Father and Mother play important roles in the child's life and have claims on the child's and each other's attention and affection, even though the child favors one, the other can be a serious rival.

How are such conflicts resolved? We must remember that having to compete for a favored parent is, for a child, no light thing. It entails conflict, guilt, and compromise.

In one of these Oedipal situations, the girl wants to possess Father as a friend — but unlike the Father Romance, this puts her into competition with Mother for his friendship. Or she desires Mother intensely, and enters into rivalry for her with Father. It is difficult for a child to win such a rivalry — unless, as with the earlier cases, the potential rivals are weak. In the Oedipal cases, the rival parent is strong and important, and thwarts the daughter's desire to be closer to the favored parent. Therefore the daughter must adjust. If she cannot win, she must modify her attachments. And it is this modification, this compromise, that leads to the resolution of the Oedipal rivalry.

This modification is achieved by intensive identifications with both parents. The expression, "If you can't lick them, join them," is apt. The child identifies with and becomes more and more like the rival parent. Affection from the favored parent is thus not endangered; and competition with the rival parent is diminished.

If the girl wants Father, she identifies with, and emulates, Mother. This brings her close to Father vicariously. This is the *feminine resolution* of the conflict. She becomes like Mother — including having an affectionate relationship with Father. Mother becomes heroine; Father becomes friend.

The *masculine resolution* turns the coin over. The girl identifies with and emulates Father in order to diminish rivalry and to be closer and more important to Mother. Father becomes hero, and she becomes like him. Mother is her friend.

The feminine resolution — a girl emulates Mother — brings out her feminine component. It leads to marriage and motherhood. The masculine resolution — a girl emulates Father — brings out the masculine component in the girl's character. It leads to professionalization.

This is what happens to the girls who have made successful Oedipal resolutions — resolutions of the rival situation. But what happens to the girls we discussed first — those who encountered no rivals in their family romances? What might we expect of *their* life careers?

These girls do not suffer the same conflicts. They do not need to placate one parent in order to retain favor with the other. The child can have, and be like, the desired parent at the same time.

The girl in this Father Romance therefore would incline toward a masculine professional life. But which profession would make it possible for her to both *be* and *have* Father at the same time? To *be* him, she must be a career professional; but to *have* him, she must be able to act like a good child with a good father herself, or be able to identify with well-fathered children. Perhaps the only profession that offers both opportunities in one job is teaching — especially with children.

As for the girl with a Mother Romance, how can she satisfy her emotional needs in her career? Naturally, she would be attracted to motherhood — but what kind? A girl with a mother-friend and a father-hero will look for a husband like Father; but the Mother Romance girl has Mother for both friend and heroine. The husband she would look for would not be like Father but like Mother. And she would be unlikely to try for a professional career.

What of the girl with a Teacher Romance? When she turned to Teacher, she turned away from a primary concern with her parents, away from her childhood — she found little joy in it. School was better than home. Being the student of a beloved teacher was better than being the child of her parents.

This type of girl has abandoned childhood; she has replaced dependency at home with self-assertion at school. We must expect that this will influence her self-concept, and her orientation toward career and life. The lack of satisfaction at home has promoted self-sufficiency — perhaps prematurely. Like the Father Romance girls, she too might well be a teacher; but a teacher driven by different motivations. The main interests of the Father Romance girl are childhood and family relations — she would gravitate toward that form of teaching that most satisfied those interests. The Teacher Romance girl wants to emulate her friend and heroine, Teacher. Her main interest will be in school and teaching itself, rather than in working with children.

This summary leads to certain hypotheses. If we examine the actual childhood memories of prospective teachers and non-teachers, we should discover these different patterns of childhood conditioning and family romances. Mother Romance girls, and those who achieved feminine resolutions to their Oedipal conflicts, should be rare among teachers, since they emulate or identify with Mother. Grade-school teachers should lean heavily toward the Father Romance pattern, since their working with very young children recreates the father-child relationship. High-school teachers should lean toward the Teacher Romance, since their main concern is not children but school and teaching.

To test these hypotheses, let us examine the childhood memories of young women who want to be each of the different kinds of prospective teachers — as well as the memories of those who do not intend to teach. In the charts that follow, the most important statistics are the percentages of each group recalling Mother, Father, or Teacher as most important.

Table 1 summarizes much of the data. The figures represent the percentage differences between the answers of prospective

Table 1 / The Influence of Teacher and Mother on Would-be-Teachers

| | Percentage differences in favor of girls who want to teach | | |
	Grade School	Middle School	High School
TEACHER			
Who most influenced me to become teacher	23	23	38
Whom I feared most	12	12	11
MOTHER			
Who most influenced me to become teacher	13	12	15
FATHER			
Who most influenced me to become teacher	9	6	0

teachers and of nonteachers — that is, for example, there were 23 percentage-points difference between the percentage of prospective grade-school teachers who were influenced by their teachers toward teaching and the percentage of nonteachers who were so influenced.

Generally, the prospective teacher — compared to the girl who does not intend to teach — more frequently, recalls that Teacher and Mother influenced her toward teaching. This "influence to become a teacher" is focused primarily on Teacher and then on Mother, but not — except among women planning to teach grade school — on Father.

The second point brought out by Table 1 is that the prospective teacher more often recalls Teacher as the person she feared most in childhood. What role does fear play in the professional motivation of teachers? Is this an instance of "identification with the aggressor" — when those who impress us, even through fear, influence us to be like them? If this is so, we might expect that one aspect of the influence of Teacher comes from her appearance as a threat. And — as we have described it in the Oedipal rivalry situations — how can a child deal with a person who seems a threat or interfering rival? By placating her through identification and imitation — by trying to be like her to minimize the conflict. Thus, even fear of Teacher can motivate a child toward becoming a teacher.

Of those who will become teachers, the woman planning to teach high school seems the most distinctive in her response.

Her salient recollections are in Table 2. In her childhood, Teacher was the most significant person. Not only does the

Table 2 / The Making of a High School Teacher

	Would-be high-school teachers compared to		
	Non-teachers	Grade School	Middle School
TEACHER			
ADMIRATION	17	16	10
Whom I most wanted to be like	24	20	16
Who was most successful in life	15	16	6
Whom I admired most	13	13	7
INFLUENCE	18	14	10
Who most influenced me to become a teacher	38	15	14
Who did the most with me	8	13	10
Who taught me the most	9	13	7
Whom I liked most	8	7	7
Whom I wanted to be with most	8	8	5
MOTHER			
Who liked me most	11	23	14
Who wanted to be with me most	13	16	10
ADMIRATION	—9	—8	—5
Whom I most wanted to be like	—19	—21	—17
FATHER			
Whom I was closest to	—9	—11	—8

prospective high-school teacher more frequently recall admiring Teacher and being influenced by Teacher than do the others, but she more frequently recalls Teacher as the one she liked the most and wanted to be with.

Mother also plays a special if one-sided part. In comparison with the others, the future high-school teacher more often recalls that Mother wanted to be with her most and liked her most. But she also less frequently recalls wanting to be like

Mother. It is as though Mother loved her well enough, but the daughter did not reciprocate. It was Teacher, not Mother, whom she loved and most wanted to be like.

Finally, the future high-school teacher less frequently recalls being close to Father than any of the others.

To sum up the prospective high-school teacher: She has the most possessive and emulative identifications with Teacher. Mother is a friend to her, but is not especially her friend. Father is away. Taking her as a type, if we sum up her childhood from her recollections, we can imagine her saying: "Teacher became the most important person in my life. I admired her, I loved her, I wanted to be like her — and so I, too, am going to be a teacher. She was friend, heroine, and inspiration to me. Mother loved me well enough, and was friendly, but I did not like her best, and I did not want to be like her. Father and I were not close."

The prospective grade-school teacher is the other type that stands out. Table 3 summarizes her most distinctive features.

Table 3 / The Making of Grade-School Teacher

	Would-be grade-school teachers compared to		
	Non-teacher	High School	Middle School
FATHER			
SYMPATHY	7	8	7
Who liked me most	11	13	12
Who wanted to be with me most	9	13	11
Who made feel best	9	5	5
INFLUENCE	7	7	4
Who most influenced me to become a teacher	9	9	3
Who taught me most	7	8	6
Who I disliked most	—9	—12	—3
INTERFERENCE	—8	—7	—4
Who frustrated me most	—14	—16	—6
MOTHER			
Who liked me most	—12	—23	—9
TEACHER INTERFERENCE			
Who frustrated me most	10	7	2

To her, Father is the significant figure. She recalls sympathy from and the influence of Father significantly more often than do the others; she recalls disliking him or being frustrated by him less often. In contrast to the prospective high-school teacher, she less often recalls that Mother liked her most, and more often recalls that Teacher frustrated her. Her statement would be something like: "Father is my best friend; he taught me most and frustrated me least. I would never reject him. But Teacher is my rival, and Mother is my enemy."

Generally, then, the data tend to reinforce our hypotheses. Teacher has most to do with making a high-school teacher, Father with making a grade-school teacher. The slightly negative part Teacher plays in the recollections of prospective grade-school teachers surprised us. We expected that the image of Teacher would be a beacon to all prospective teachers. But the data show that favorable recollections of Teacher are not more frequent among future grade-school teachers than among nonteaching women; and, significantly, that future grade-school women more frequently recall frustration with Teacher.

The characteristics of the prospective middle-school teacher are summarized in Table 4. By and large, she seems to fall be-

Table 4 / The Making of a Middle-School Teacher

	Would-be middle-school teachers compared to		
	Non-teachers	Grade School	High School
TEACHER			
ADMIRATION	7	7	—10
Who was most successful in life	9	10	—6
Whom I most wanted to please	8	6	2
MOTHER			
Whom I most feared	—9	—5	—10
Who understood me least	—9	—7	—2
FATHER			
Who frustrated me most	—8	—6	—10
Whom I disliked most	—7	—3	—9

tween the future grade-school and high-school teachers. She admires Teacher more than the grade-school woman, but less than the high-school woman. The grade-school woman had seemed estranged from Mother, and the high-school woman from Father — but the middle-school woman claims less distance from either. She is the golden mean. Less often than the would-be grade-school teacher, she recalls Mother as the one whom she most feared, who understood her least; less often than the would-be high-school teacher, she recalls Father as the one she disliked, who frustrated her more. She admires Teacher more than the woman who will teach grade school, but less than the woman who will teach high school.

The would-be grade-school teacher rejected Mother; the would-be high-school teacher got little from Father, but was, instead, strongly influenced by Teacher. Perhaps the would-be junior-high teacher is trying to hang on to both sides at once, to have both Mother *and* Father, to be a teacher *and still* be faithful to both parents. In effect, to teach both grade and high school at the same time — by teaching middle school.

To sum up: The actual childhood recollections of the prospective teachers indicate that:

(1) A high-school teacher has had a special admiring relationship with Teacher, built upon a loving but not longer stimulating relationship with Mother, and a poor or nonexistent relationship with Father.

(2) In contrast, a grade-school teacher has had a special sympathetic relationship with Father, facilitated by a poor relationship with Mother, sharpened by frustration with Teacher.

(3) The middle-school teacher is in-between on her admiration for Teacher, and, in effect, in her regard or dislike for her parents.

Comparing the findings with the family-romance theory, we find that, as predicted, the would-be high-school teacher is different from others in the direction of a Teacher Romance, while the would-be grade-school teacher is different in the direction of a Father Romance.

In the Teacher Romance, however, we predicted that Teacher would be friend and heroine, and parents would be the enemy. The actual observation shows that parents do *not* appear as enemy. Although Father is portrayed as relatively uninviting, the prospective high-school teacher recalls Mother as a friend who liked her — even if she did not influence her.

In the Father Romance, we predicted that Father would be the friend and hero, Mother the enemy. Here, the differences between hypothesis and findings are the ambiguity of Father in the hero role, and the possible presence of Teacher as a frustrating rival. The would-be grade-school teacher attributes great influence to Father — this distinguishes her from the others.

But as an explicit professional model to emulate, he is less directly useful to her than Teacher is to the prospective high-school teacher. Obviously, he is of the wrong sex and profession. Her admiration for and identification with him can therefore not express itself directly; she must use them to become her own heroine in the classroom.

Why was Teacher frustrating? Perhaps because when the would-be grade-school teacher went to school, this figure whom her loving father inspired her to be was not like him — and may even have reminded her of Mother.

Even when they become teachers, these women will still not be entirely free agents — their roles will still be affected by their childhood experiences. The grade-school teacher would like to recreate her own early family relationships. She would like to play the part of a loving and understanding father — what Father was to her. She would also like to continue to experience his love. By enjoying vicariously the attention she gives the children in her class, she can retain and relive the comfort and satisfaction of her Father Romance. Similarly, the high-school teacher, with her older students, can also retain and relive the Teacher Romance, as both Teacher and inspired student. Perhaps it is the family romance that makes the career worth pursuing.

NOTES

1. In this study we proceeded on the theory that how a young woman sees herself, what kind of teacher she becomes, and what people influence her are all important signs of what motivated her to become and remain a teacher in the first place. The past becomes incorporated into the present in the making of teachers; and we cannot understand present or future without it.

We designed a questionnaire that we believed, with proper analysis, could elicit this information. It was administered to 972 women enrolled in teacher-training programs in 12 institutions, about 40 percent coming from teachers colleges, and 30 percent each from teacher-preparation programs at universities and liberal-arts colleges. These young women were given the questionnaire first as students, second as practice teachers in their senior year (when experience begins to modify the dream, and, presumably, the answers on the questionnaire), and third as real teachers after graduation. The final sample of complete cases — those who answered all three times — was 508.

These young women were, on the average, 21 years old. They were of all classes, with a heavy concentration in the middle groups (21 percent upper-middle, 34 percent middle, 21 percent lower-middle); 38 percent of them were Protestant, 36 percent were Jewish, and 22 percent were Catholic. Eighty-five percent were single.

The answers from these 508 learning and beginning teachers were compared with those from a sample of experienced teachers (102 grade school, 94 junior high, 50 high) and with those from 153 non-teachers — young women, for the most part still in college, who had no plans to teach.

twenty-four

Academic Women

RUTH E. ECKERT and JOHN E. STECKLEIN

In a period when every source of high-level talent must be explored and utilized, special interest attaches to a study of women faculty members in American colleges. Although women account for only 22 per cent of all full-time academic staff members, both the numbers and the proportions of women college teachers must increase dramatically to meet soaring student enrolments. As several studies have shown,[1] the pool of underdeveloped talent is far larger for women than for men — making them the best single source for recruitment efforts.

A recent study of faculty members in one state — Minnesota[2] — including some representation of all 32 recognized higher institutions, throws interesting light on why women college teachers chose this field, how they view their jobs and what suggestions they have for recruiting and holding staff. Based on a 25 per cent stratified random sample of all full-time faculty members holding the rank of instructor or above and engaged in actual teaching, the Minnesota data were secured from 706 faculty members — or 94 per cent of all those whose cooperation had been invited. Of those who completed the four-page printed questionnaire, slightly more than a fourth (27.9 per cent or 197 respondents)[3] were women faculty members. About the same proportion of women (24 per cent) participated in the depth interviews conducted with almost a hundred of those who returned questionnaires.

The present article deals with an aspect not touched on in the general report, namely the similarities and differences in the responses given by men and women faculty members. It seemed

From LIBERAL EDUCATION, Vol. 45 (1959), pp. 390-397. Reprinted by permission.

desirable to find out whether these people selected college teaching for essentially the same reasons, whether they prepared similarly for their present jobs and whether they now appraised college teaching in much the same way. Implications of these findings for the recruiting and holding of women faculty members are suggested in a concluding section.

Background Information

To interpret properly the responses these women gave, both in the questionnaire and in interviews, it is important to know something of their personal and family backgrounds. More than two fifths (44 per cent) of them were born in Minnesota, as contrasted with only 25 per cent of the men, and likewise higher percentages of women came from other parts of the north-central area.[4] Like their male colleagues most of these women had grown up in middle- and lower-class homes, in which the fathers had been tradesmen, farmers, skilled or semi-skilled workers. Typically neither parent had gone beyond the tenth grade, although the fathers of one fourth and the mothers of one fifth of the women's sample had had some college training, pointed chiefly toward educational and religious vocations. About a fifth of the women faculty members came from homes where one or both parents had been teachers. But excepting the higher proportions of women faculty members who had grown up in the Minnesota area, home background factors did not appear to differentiate the women from their male associates.

As might be expected, a much higher percentage of the women were single (54 per cent as against 17 per cent of the men). And rather surprisingly, the typical woman was some six years older than her male counterpart (48 as against 42 years of age) — a difference that showed up consistently in all four types of colleges studied.[5] Whereas 46 per cent of the women had already reached their fiftieth birthday, only 26 per cent of the men were in this age group. The percentage of younger women attracted to college faculties has apparently been declining, despite the fact the college enrolments have more than doubled in the past twenty years.

Choice of College Teaching

Like their male colleagues few of these women had given any serious thought to college teaching during their undergraduate years, with only one in eight reporting this as a tentative choice of career at the time of graduation from college. As many of those interviewed noted, college teaching seemed to be a goal far removed from the aspirations of young women, although many planned to become elementary or secondary teachers (60 per cent of the women versus 35 per cent of the men reported this goal at the time of college graduation). There was also some indication that parents had encouraged this latter choice for their daughters but not for their sons.

Although few of these future college teachers had definitely made up their minds by the time of graduation from college to join a college or university faculty some day, a significantly higher percentage of the men who became college teachers reported that they had viewed this career favorably as a personal goal (66 per cent of the men versus 50 per cent of the women gave this response). This contrasts with the strikingly similar percentages (74 for men and 78 for women) who looked upon college teaching as a desirable career for other people.

The three reasons which women faculty members most often cited as influencing their final decision to become college teachers were the offer of a college teaching job, though they had not sought it (mentioned by 60 per cent of the women and only 32 per cent of the men), their interest in working with college-age students (mentioned by 49 and 44 per cent respectively) and their desire to continue study in their subject field (specified by 40 and 44 per cent respectively).

Women, to a significantly lesser degree than men, ascribed their final choice of this career to factors directly associated with the job itself, such as the possibility of carrying on research (18 versus 32 per cent for men), good working conditions (33 versus 46 per cent), and the academic and social advantages a college faculty member enjoys (18 versus 26 per cent). They appeared to have been more influenced by external circumstances, such as being counseled in this direction by a respected teacher or counselor (39 per cent reported this as a contributing factor as compared with only 19 per cent of the men) or by being offered a college-level job, as noted above.

These findings seem to reflect some reluctance on the part of young women to visualize themselves as college teachers and hence to seek such a post. This view is supported by their later specification of the single factor that had most influenced their decision, for equal numbers of women mentioned internal and situational factors, whereas men identified personal interests and motivations more than twice as frequently as external factors. For both men and women these final decisions were usually reached some years after college graduation.

Preparation for College Teaching

Almost half of the women (43 per cent) had received some type of academic recognition as undergraduates, such as election to Phi Beta Kappa or some other honor society, being granted a scholarship based on outstanding academic achievement or being graduated with honors. This was only slightly below the correlate figure (51 per cent) for men, suggesting that both groups had considerable potential for graduate work. Yet women students were much less likely to begin graduate work shortly after receiving their baccalaureate degrees. Although they had secured considerable parental help in financing their undergraduate work, they seemed to be on their own financially once they had their first degree. When asked how they managed to finance their advanced studies, significantly more women than men reported the use of personal savings, whereas men far exceeded women in the use of scholarships and fellowships, staff appointments as teaching and research assistants, GI aids and "earnings of a spouse" to finance extended periods of study.

This dearth of financial aids for women graduate students may partly explain why so few women continued to the doctorate, despite their excellent undergraduate records. Some earned only a single degree (13 per cent), supported in most instances by some advanced non-degree study, with the great majority reporting an M.A. or M.S. as their highest degree (49 per cent), again often buttressed by some study beyond this point. Only 26 per cent of the women, as contrasted with 51 per cent of the men, had earned their doctorates, even though the women had had six additional years' on the average in which to fulfill graduate requirements.

The great investment of time that many women faculty members had made in elementary and secondary teaching probably contributed to this differential in training. Three fifths of the women (61 per cent as contrasted with 36 per cent of the men) reported that their first full-time job after college graduation had been in this field. A significantly higher proportion of wom-

en had also come directly to their present college jobs from a
position in the lower schools (36 versus 17 per cent). Although
the typical woman faculty member was 48 years old, she had
been on a college or university faculty for only eight years,
which suggests how recently many women joined college staffs.

Current Positions

Several notable differences also emerged in an analysis of
these faculty members' current jobs. In indicating reasons for
joining their present staffs, women mentioned more often than
men that they liked the type of school, that they had been·
assigned to it (a response characteristic of members of religious
orders), or that the position had been "available." In contrast,
men tended to stress the reputation of the school, the research
opportunities it provided and the salary offered.

Only three fifths as many women as men had attained associate or full professorships (37 versus 56 per cent); they were
also seriously under-represented in certain types of institutions
(notably the university), and in certain subject fields, such as
mathematics, the biological and physical sciences and most
professional specialties. Two fields — the humanities and professional education — accounted for half of all the full-time
women teachers serving in these colleges. Some of those interviewed, including both men and women, felt that women were
discriminated against in many departments and that they could
not compete effectively with their male colleagues for promotions or salary increases.

The duties performed by men and women faculty members
in their present jobs also varied significantly, and in directions
suggested by the earlier findings. Women gave more of their
time to teaching and to services to student groups, whereas
men devoted relatively more time to research activities, committee work and off-campus projects. The largest single difference related to research, where 63 per cent of the women, as
compared with 36 per cent of the men, reported no time at all
spent on research and scholarly writing. Were the recommendations that these faculty members made for a redistribution
of their working time to be adopted, the above differences would
become even greater. Although both men and women agreed
that the greatest need for more time was in the area of research
and scholarly writing, a much higher percentage of men than

women (67 versus 47 per cent) stated this. On the other hand, a significantly higher percentage of women than men wanted to devote still more time to teaching and to student counseling, or said that they did not wish to see their present distribution of effort modified in any way.

Appraisals of College Teaching as a Career

When asked about the chief satisfactions they had experienced from faculty service, the vast majority of these faculty members agreed that they liked their present jobs and the status they enjoyed, professionally and socially, as college teachers. Women were more likely than men to mention "good students" and "desirable colleagues" as major sources of satisfaction, whereas male faculty members seemed to prize especially the opportunities that some college jobs provide for research and the freedom and independence enjoyed by college teachers. Both men and women indicated relatively few dissatisfactions, although men were more articulate than women about the limited time available for scholarly study and the low salaries received.

General evaluations that these faculty members made of their career showed that almost half of both groups were "very satisfied" and that most of the rest had experienced "moderate satisfaction" from their service as college teachers. But men seemed a little more reluctant than women to do it all over again, with 19 per cent of the men and 11 per cent of the women saying that they were either doubtful or would not again become college teachers if they were now faced with this decision.

Suggestions for Recruitment and Retention of Staff

Given an opportunity to comment on ways of attracting qualified people into college teaching, both men and women faculty members stressed the need to raise salaries, with men giving greater emphasis to this than women (66 versus 44 per cent). Men also attached somewhat greater weight to the need for providing faculty members with "reasonable" teaching assignments, adequate clerical help, assistance on research projects and greater job security. Women faculty members, on the other hand, more frequently stressed the importance of providing counseling and guidance regarding career opportunities in this field, making more scholarships and other financial aids available to qualified candidates and furnishing adequate pre-service education.

In commenting on ways in which colleges might successfully hold faculty members, once they had been recruited to college teaching, a larger percentage of men again emphasized higher salaries, reductions in teaching loads, better facilities for research and the provisions of leaves for study. Women significantly exceeded men on only a single item, namely that administrators should be more generous in their commendation of faculty achievements (mentioned by 11 per cent of the women and 3 per cent of the men).

Summary and Implications

The present study, based on almost 200 women faculty members in Minnesota's 32 public and private colleges, underscores the need to attract women to careers in college teaching. To an even greater degree than their male colleagues, the women presently teaching in Minnesota colleges appear to be there more by accident than by clear design. Despite excellent undergraduate records, they were handicapped financially in securing advanced training; this accounts partially for the long period many of them spent on elementary and secondary school staffs. In consequence, significantly fewer had earned a doctor's degree or had been promoted beyond an assistant professorship, despite the fact that the women were typically six years older than the male faculty members studied. Being burdened with the heavier teaching and service loads characteristic of junior-level positions, they also had little opportunity to do the research and scholarly writing on which professional advancement so often depends.

Despite such handicaps, these women faculty members appeared to be as satisfied with their choice of career as their male colleagues were and even more ready to reaffirm it, given the opportunity to re-make the decision. But the pattern of their reported satisfactions differed somewhat, with a greater emphasis placed on good human relations as contrasted with the emphasis that men gave to material rewards, opportunities to do creative work in their subject fields and the freedom and independence associated with faculty service. Recommendations given for recruiting and retaining qualified faculty members revealed similar differences, with the women apparently more sensitive to the human factors, such as providing counseling for prospective faculty members and developing harmonious administrative-faculty relationships, and the men more concerned about program adjustments, research facilities and the rewards given for effective service.

At least three major implications can be drawn from these findings for the future staffing of college and university programs. In the first place, a more determined effort must be made to acquaint women undergraduates with the opportunities and satisfactions of careers in this field. If this is done effectively, many of those who had planned to teach in the lower schools may view such service as a possible stepping-stone to a college position, and others, whose primary commitment is to a subject field rather than to the teaching function, will glimpse the rich possibilitites of developing their scholarly interests through membership in a college faculty. Several faculty members suggested in their interviews that the college teaching profession should be talked about and made more attractive to grade school and high school students; other urged that promising undergraduate students be used as assistants and student teachers in order to get them actively involved in the field.

Secondly, financial support for graduate studies must be made more widely available to qualified women students. To defer such study until a young teacher can finance the program for herself often results in the long postponement or abandonment of such plans. Studies are urgently needed to find out what financial aids in the way of graduate scholarships, fellowships and assistantships are now open to qualified women students and what the major blocks may be to making full use of these opportunities.

The in-service education of women faculty members likewise demands attention. Since most women teachers have not completed a doctoral program, they stand in special need of leaves for advanced study and of adjustments in their loads that will encourage completion of a thesis and other types of scholarly endeavor. Encouragement in this direction given by perceptive administrators and colleagues will reinforce these efforts, since women faculty members appear to be strongly influenced by such recognition. In institutions where faculty members, without regard to sex, are helped to reach their full professional stature and to know the abiding satisfactions of college teaching, both men and women students will be attracted to careers in this field. Women faculty members who are geinuinely respected and honored on the local campus may be particularly effective in this respect, since their presence will help gifted women students to identify themselves with the role of the college teacher and to prepare themselves for this service.

NOTES

1. Dael, Wolfle, *America's Resources of Specialized Talent,* Harper & Brothers, New York, 1954, and the Educational Policies Commission, *Manpower and Education,* National Education Association, Washington, D.C., 1957.

2. John E. Stecklein and Ruth E. Eckert, *An Exploratory Study of Factors Influencing the Choice of College Teaching as a Career,* conducted under a grant from the Cooperative Research Program, U.S. Office of Education, 1958.

3. These 197 women included 158 in four-year colleges (86 in priivate liberal arts colleges, 29 in state colleges, and 43 at the University of Minnesota) and 39 teaching in junior colleges. The statistics used in the present report are based on those teaching baccalaureate and advanced programs.

4. Where differences are mentioned in the text, they satisfy at least the .05 level of confidence (indicating that chance alone would account for these differences only once in twenty instances). Those characterized as "significant" meet th .01 confidence level, which provides a more rigorous test of their importance.

5. See Stecklein and Eckert, *op. cit.,* for separate analyses of the junior college, private liberal arts college, state college and university samples, on this and other points touched on in the present article.

twenty-five

Differential Recruitment of Female Professionals: A Case Study of Clergywomen

ARTHUR R. JONES, JR. AND LEE TAYLOR

The process of recruitment into professional work is part of the social structure of occupations which defines who is acceptable for a particular work position and the manner by which one achieves acceptability. Major elements of occupational recruitment include the sociopsychological process of career choice, the occupational socialization process, and the structural aspects of occupational organization which function to select qualified individuals who aspire to work positions in the occupation.[1]

The pattern of occupational recruitment into the professions in this country is typically male biased due primarily to the historic segregation of professional activity by sex. In recent years, however, boundary maintenance around professional work based on sex segregation has weakened. An examination of Census data (Table 1) indicates the extent of participation of women in traditionally male dominated professions. Understanding the recruitment situation for female aspirants to professional activities which historically have been defined by society as unappropriate for women is important in light of new norms which allow for their choice to enter the professions as a career experience.

The purpose of this paper is to present research findings that focus upon an occupational situation for females which on the one hand provides the institutionalized space required to make a career choice for a profession but which, on the other hand,

Paper presented at the annual meeting of the Southern Sociological Society, Atlanta, Georgia, April, 1964. Printed by permission.

Table 1 / Females Employed in the Labor Force and in
Selected Professions, 1940-1960.

Employment and Occupation	Percent Employed in			Percent Increase in Number Employed	
	1960	1950	1940	1940-50	1950-60
Total employed	32.7	27.9	24.7	41.6	34.2
Professions	38.1	43.6	45.8	40.0	41.1
Clergy	2.3	4.1	2.3	116.8	−31.2
Technical Engineer	0.8	1.2	..	..	11.0
Lawyer, Judge	3.5	3.4	2.3	55.2	18.5
Physician, Surgeon	6.8	6.1	4.6	54.5	32.0

Source: U.S. Bureau of the Census. *Sixteenth Census of the United States: 1940. Population.* Vol. III, *Labor Force.* U. S. Government Printing Office, Washington, 1943. Table 58; and *U. S. Census of the Population: 1960. Detailed Characteristics.* Final Report PC (1)-1D. U. S. Government Printing Office, Washington, 1963. Table 202.

lacks normative patterns that would facilitate their normal entry into a traditionally male profession, the clergy.

Source of Data and Methodology

The data are from questionnaires completed by members of a national association of clergywomen. Although 60 per cent (146) of the schedules were returned 18 per cent were excluded primarily because the respondents were religious practitioners other than clergywomen. It was impossible to predetermine this factor prior to the mailing of the questionnaires. Thus this report is based on an analysis of 42 per cent of the schedules returned.

The instrument consisted of both structure-response and open-end questions which were derived from theoretical assumptions about recruitment, namely, that it is processual[2] and is largely determined by occupational structure.[3]

The Nature of Recruitment

Only two kinds of recruitment are emphasized in this paper, the occupational organization which structures entry into the occupation according to formally prescribed criteria as well as informal criteria and the choice process.

Occupational choices, as one comes closer in time to the point of actual entry into the labor force, are brought into further correspondence with reality factors constituted by the requirements of the occupational structure. In occupations which provide social space for the female sex, given this perception, a certain number of women will qualify and be selected to fill appropriate positions. In occupations not defined as appropriate for women, real choices toward such occupations do not typically prevail, if the woman is intent upon entering the labor force.

Concerning the occupational structure, entry may be controlled by the profession itself, as in the case of independent professions like law and medicine. Even when certification and licensing is provided for by state examining boards, such action is normally congruent with the judgments of the profession which otherwise sets and maintains standards of professional acceptability. In the case of salaried professionals, and many newer professions, control over recruitment is moderated and distributed between the profession and other social structures. In both types of organizations indicated recruitment specifically involves the articulation of normative patterns which function to systematically and selectively encourage, or discourage, individuals from entering a particular profession.

Recruitment and entry into the clergy[4] may be controlled by professionals only, by professionals and a non-occupational organization, or by a non-occupational organization alone. (By reference to a non-occupational organization we mean the congregation or parish which, in some religious situations, alone has power to authorize the ministry of an aspirant. In addition it should be noted that although the congregation is not an occupational organization, it frequently functions as part of the occupational recruitment structure for the clergy.) The latter particularly occurs when the polity of a religious body is congregational. This should not be taken to mean that informally clergymen themselves do not play an important role in the recruitment process by recommending and sponsoring new ministers to positions in the profession.

These dimensions of recruitment as related to the clergy have generally functioned to exclude or discourage women from seeking admission to the profession. Social space to articulate a career choice is provided females in 77 religious bodies, 6 or 30 per cent of all religious bodies (1952). The latest major religious bodies to grant ordination and full clergy rights to women were the Presbyterian Church, U.S.A., and the Methodist

Church in 1956. The following analysis provides insight into the recruitment process for women where no institutionalized social space provides them with a normal career entry experience.

The Recruitment Environment of Clergywomen

The general early-life environment of clergywomen is highly religious. To this extent they are provided with a favorable orientation to the occupation which they later enter. This early experience is taken to be a basic socializing influence upon their development of a level of occupational aspiration which directs them toward the clergy.[5]

The religious histories of the clergywomen's parents indicated both membership and generally intensive participation in religious groups.[6] Eighty-two per cent held membership in a religious body, and 69 per cent attended religious services regularly. This background is consistent with Ginsberg's pilot study where ". . . almost without exception, future ministers were exposed from earliest childhood to religious experiences and institutions, (which) were reinforced in puberty and early adolescence."[7] Moreover, Ginsberg reported "that without the opportunity to live in — and respond to — a strongly religious environment . . . few would think seriously of the ministry as a life work."[8] It would be incorrect to reason that given the characteristic of a strongly religious background an individual will become a religious practitioner. Research evidence, however, does indicate that very few people select the ministry as a career without a certain kind of previous socialization to religious systems.

Thus in the early environment of the clergywomen studied the unusual situation existed in which the values and orientation of the religious group (the key position in the group being that of clergyman) also constituted part of the belief and value orientation of the parishioner's home life. Not only was it possible for the child to perceive at a relatively early age the social existence of the profession of the clergy, but more important, the values which justified the existence of the profession were reinforced in the child through home and family experiences constituted in part by a significantly religious environment.

Early association and participation in a religious system continued throughout puberty and adolescence. By age 17 over four-fifths of the respondents had become members of their respective religious bodies. Although structures controlling membership status in religious bodies varies, it is noted that during these phases of their lives they exhibited behavior that was appropriate according to the norms of their religious reference groups. That is, they fulfilled the expectation that one should acquire membership status, and by observing this act they were further linked ideologically with the values of a religious reference group.

Occupational choices occurred in context of the early recruitment environment discussed above. The content of the choices of the respondents to enter the clergy is revealing. Only one-fifth explicitly articulated their choosing the ministry as a profession as a result of a "call of God." The remaining four-fifths articulated their choice as due to influences deriving from their social backgrounds. They most often viewed their entry as a developmental experience rather than as a unique experience.

The final decision of selecting the ministry as their profession occurred during the period from late adolescence to the middle adult years. Some scheduled their education and training upon this decision when it occurred early enough; others indicated that they had shifted areas of study while in a religious seminary from other programs of training to the clergy. Three clergywomen stated that later in their lives they were invited to assume the position of minister in churches formerly served by their pastor-husbands who were deceased at the time of the study.

These findings reflect the manifest social space available for women in certain religious bodies to articulate a choice for the clergy as a profession.

Only one-third of the clergywomen were able to move into ministerial positions immediately upon the completion of their educational careers or other certification by their respective religious bodies. For the remaining two-thirds entry into their chosen professions was interrupted due to a lack of structures to facilitate their selection into positions. It was therefore necessary for them to enter alternative careers until positions in the clergy became available to them. Fifty-eight per cent of these entered the labor force at the level of professions, primarily in the field of teaching. Five per cent entered managerial or other business enterprises, and 14 per cent entered clerical-sales work. Twenty-one per cent entered church-related work other than the clergy. Two per cent worked as laborers before they were able to move to a church.

The lack of an occupational structure to systematically move female aspirants into the clergy is reflected in their comments. One respondent stated

> I was going to finish two years of college, teach, earn money, and finish in religious college and the seminary. Doors closed and because of finances, I finished four years of college before going to the seminary. Superintendents were reluctant to give me a student church, so I taught and paid back my debt.

Another indicated her perception of the dialogue between the persons responsible for her placement in the ministry. One of the boys needs the job. We've got to stick together.

These comments may be interpreted in contrast with the recruitment of males into the ministry, and of females into occupational categories readily defined as appropriate for them by society.

According to Blau, after appraisal of the occupational marketplace the individual's first preference, if unattainable, is modified to fit other occupational alternatives which would be more realistic to achieve.[10] On one level, this thesis is apparently borne out by the subsequent occupational behavior of the respondents who could not achieve their original career preference. However, there is no formulation in this thesis to account for the strength or saliency of the original preference as a force to motivate the individual to continue to seek a position as minister until an opening presented itself.

In order to account for this occurrence in the occupational behavior of the respondents the findings indicate that a continual association with religious reference groups played an important role in their career determination. Although the majority did not move into the ministry systematically following their real choice and/or training, continued association with religious reference groups reinforced their original decision to enter the ministry. Thus while not serving in a position as minister it was possible to otherwise continue to associate with a religious system. This was accomplished by first of all maintaining active membership status with religious groups, second, by substituting for ministers whose pulpits were temporarily vacant, and third, by teaching in religious education programs in their churches. This type of behavioral and ideological association with religious practices and values thus provided a realistic basis for their continuing to maintain an original career choice to pursue a desired professional experience.

Conclusion

This paper presents the problem of recruitment for women who aspire to enter the clergy. The findings revealed an occupational situation in change. From a historical period of strict sex segregation in this country, it is now possible to identify a limited social space which facilitates the choosing of the clergy as a profession by women. Structural norms, however, which control the actual procedure for entry into the profession for women have not sufficiently developed. Consequently, clergywomen do not typically find a systematic movement into this field of work. Rather they most often have to accept nonclerical positions until they are able to move into a ministerial position that subsequently opens for them. Ideological association with religious groups functions to preserve the saliency of their original career choice to become ministers when opportunity arises. On the basis of these findings it is reasonable to suggest inquiry into the recruitment structure facing women who aspire to other traditional male-dominated professions.

NOTES

1. Theodore Caplow, *The Sociology of Work* (Minneapolis: University of Minnesota Press, 1954), pp. 102-106; Margaret Cussler, *The Woman Executive* (New York: Harcourt, Brace and Co., 1958), pp. 3-26; Eli Ginsberg, *et al.*, *Occupational Choice: An Approach to a General Theory* (New York: Columbia University Press, 1951), pp. 185-198. See also Ginsberg's ch. 12 which deals with applying the theory of occupational choice to the career experience of women. William J. McGlothlin, *Patterns of Professional Education* (New York: G. P. Putnam's Sons, 1960, Ch. 5, "Recruitment and Selection of Students;" "Special Recruitment Issue," *Social Work Education*, 5 April, 1957); Ernest F. White, "Recruitment and Training of Professional Personnel," *Journal of Jewish Communal Service*, 33 (Fall, 1956), 97.

2. Ginzberg, *Loc cit.*

3. Peter M. Blau, *et al.*, "Occupational Choice: A Conceptual Framework," *Industrial and Labor Relations Review*, 9 (July, 1956), 531-543.

4. See especially Joseph Fichter, *Religion as an Occupation* (South Bend, Ind.: University of Notre Dame Press, 1961), for sources of recruits for the Catholic clergy. For Protestants see James M. Gustafson, "The Clergy in the United States," *Daedalus* 92 (Fall, 1963), especially pp. 741-3 concerning recruitment.

5. Archibald O. Haller and Irwin W. Miller, *The Occupational Aspiration Scale: Theory, Structure, and Correlates* (Michigan Agricultural Experiment Station Technical Bulletin 288, 1963), pp. 9-17.

6. See "Women in the Ministry," in Benson Y. Landis, (ed.), *The Yearbook of American Churches: 1964* (New York: National Council of Churches, 1964), p. 283.

7. Ginzberg, *op. cit.*, p. 14F.

8. *Ibid.*

9. Compare James Otis Smith and Gideon Sjoberg, "Origins and Career Patterns of Leading Protestant Clergymen," *Social Forces*, 34 (May, 1961), 294.

10. Blau, *op. cit.*, p. 533.

V

Adult Socialization and
Career Commitment

Self-Concept, Occupational Role Expectations, and Occupational Choice in Nursing and Social Work

ANNE J. DAVIS

Social work and nursing resemble one another in being considered traditional women's occupations, in recruiting predominately middle-class women, and in being oriented to service. In view of these similarities, the question arises as to what factors influence the occupational choice of these students.

The Problem

This study explored the differences in the self-concept and occupational role expectations of women students in nursing and social work. The following hypotheses were tested.

Hypotheses 1: There will be a significant difference in family background between women students who have chosen nursing as an occupation and women students who have chosen social work as an occupation.

Hypotheses 2: There will be a significant difference in the self-concept between women students who have chosen nursing as an occupation and women students who have chosen social work as an occupation.

Hypotheses 3: There will be a significant difference in the occupational role expectations of nursing between women students who have chosen nursing as an occupation and women students who have chosen social work as an occupation.

Hypotheses 4: There will be a significant difference in the occupational role expectations of social work between women stu-

From NURSING RESEARCH, Vol. 18, No. 1 (1969), pp. 55-59. Copyright 1969, The American Journal of Nursing Company. Reproduced by permission.

dents who have chosen nursing as an occupation and women students who have chosen social work as an occupation.

Hypotheses 5: There will be a significant positive relationship between the nursing students' self-concept and their role expectations of nursing.

Hypotheses 6: There will be a significant positive relationship between the social work students' self-concept and their role expectations of social work.

Theoretical Framework

Sarbin's role theory, that of self and role in interaction, served as the theoretical framework (1). Sarbin defined *self* as those ideas the individual has of himself which he has learned in relationship with others, and *role* as organized actions of a person coordinated with a given position or status. Self and role interact since the self strives for consistency and selects those roles compatible with the self-concept, and these role experiences, in turn, either do or do not reinforce the concept of the self. When the self-concept and the role are incompatible, conflict arises. The self-concept is not only, in part, a product of social roles, but also seems to be a major determinant of occupational role-taking, that is, of occupational choice. People tend to view a vocation as favorable or unfavorable for them because their ideas of that occupation either do or do not fit into their concept of themselves (2).

Sample and Methodology

In fall 1967, 100 juniors entering social work (N = 50) and nursing (N = 50) at the University of California participated in the study. A total of 74 nursing students responded to the Adjective Check List and the questionnaire but since there were only 50 female social work students available to participate in the study, the 74 nursing students were random sampled to produce an equal number of 50 in both groups to permit efficient statistical manipulation. They responded to the Gough Adjective Check List (ACL) which described 1) the self, 2) personality characteristics needed to function effectively in the nursing role, and 3) personality characteristics needed to function effectively in the social work role (3). A questionnaire provided demographic and supplementary occupational role expectation data.

Statistical Treatment of the Data

Analysis of the data from the Adjective Check List was accomplished in two complementary phases. In order to control the total experimental Type I error, and to avoid the additive effects of this kind of error, it was required to reduce the total of 57 variables to a more manageable number of composite variables which would adequately represent the entire matrix of measures. The technique of cluster analysis, as outlined by Tryon, which selects groups of highly collinear variables which can be shown to reproduce the total correlation in a matrix, was used (4). It seemed necessary to execute a cluster analysis on the pooled sample in order to determine the most general salient dimensions common to the entire subject group and to submit the resulting set of simultaneous composite variables to a discriminant analysis to determine if these composite key cluster variables could, when properly weighted, distinguish between the social worker group and the nurse group. The discriminant analysis as performed did reveal that the two groups were discriminated even on the basis of the general dimensions derived from the combined matrices.

In cluster analysis, as in factor analysis, the order in which the composite clusters of collinear variables is derived is important to an understanding of the dimensional structure of the total set of variables.

The initial cluster derived from the analysis usually accounts for a greater proportion of the common variance; subsequent clusters, derived from the residual matrix, account for a lesser, but statistically independent, proportion of the variance. The meaning assigned to each of the clusters is the province of the analyst. Although the total procedure of the analyses has been programmed for performance by computer, the completion of the analysis is not automatic. All decisions upon which the finally accepted solution is based are made by the analyst on the basis of unique knowledge of the subjects and the measurement devices being used.

To establish that these variables differentiated between social work and nursing students, the following statistical procedure was undertaken. The answers to items which preliminarily indicated differences rather than similarities between the groups were rescaled in order to approximate the assumed underlying continuous variables. In order to perform a discriminant function analysis with the associated Hotelling's T^2 and the F-ratio on these recorded scores, it was necessary to calculate the differences between the means of each group, and the discriminant function coefficients for each of the variables. With this data, it was then possible to determine the squared distance (Mahalanobis's D^2) between the two groups, the generalized (Hotelling's) T^2, and the variance ratio (F). In this instance, $F_{8,91df} = 2.10343$. The interpolated value of $F_{8,91df}$ at the .95 level is 2.06; therefore, the difference between the groups on these clusters is statistically significant.

It is often the case that one or more measures will not be effectively predictive or discriminative when used simultaneously. Still it is more important to the understanding of the structure of such a relationship that some hierarchy be established to show which of the simultaneous measures are more effective and which are less effective as discriminators. Probably the most feasible method for obtaining relative effectiveness may be contribution of the variables to the numerical values of Delta (Δ), which corresponds to the sum of squares for regression in an analysis dealing with a numerical criterion. This procedure was undertaken for both the ACL cluster and the questionnaire variables.

An identical statistical procedure was done on the demographic and supplementary occupational role expectations data obtained from the questionnaire. In this instance $F_{21,75df} = 3.82069$. The interpolated value of $F_{21,75df}$ at the .95 level is 1.66; therefore, the differences between the two groups on these 21 variables are statistically significant.

Demographic Data

Data obtained from the questionnaire indicated that the nursing students and the social work students shared certain characteristics which lent themselves to a descriptive presentation, since no statistically significant differences occurred between the two groups. The following discussion provides a composite picture based on the combined frequencies of nursing and social work students' responses on the variables which demonstrate similarities rather than differences between the two groups.

Students in this study were in their early twenties, single, and expected to work during their adult lives. Parents were living, married to one another, and the father assumed the role of breadwinner. Students took a college preparatory program in high school and generally received a Grade Point Average of B during the first two years of college. More than one-half of the fathers and one-third of the mothers graduated from college and many of these completed graduate study. About one-half of the fathers were professionals or semi-professional while almost one-fourth of the mothers fell into the professional category.

During the occupational choice process, both groups discussed the matter most with their girlfriend, next most with mother, and third most with father. Also, the girlfriend provided the most help during this time and supported the occupational choice as the right one for the student. Medicine and other health sciences and teaching constituted the two most considered occupational alternatives. Twenty per cent of their mothers and 40 per cent of their girlfriends worked in the occupation of choice or a closely allied one but the extent to which these people served as occupational role models did not differentiate between the student groups.

Table 1 shows the questionnaire variables ranked in order of relative effectiveness from most effective to least effective in differentiating between the social work students and the nursing students.

The one variable which most effectively differentiated between the two groups was the period when they decided on their occupation. Most nursing students made this decision during grade or high school while social work students generally waited until after they entered college, usually during the sophomore year. Social work students also experienced more difficulty in choosing an occupation.

On both religious and ethnic background factors, social work students were characterized by more diversity than nursing students. There were more Jewish students and students who had no particular religious affiliation in the social work group than in the nursing group. Among the nursing students, there were fewer Oriental students and no Negroes or Spanish Americans whereas these groups were represented in the social work student group.

More nursing students than social work students discussed occupational choice with high school counselors and college

Table 1 / Questionnaire Variables in Order of Relative Effectiveness from Most Effective to Least Effective in Differentiating Students — Significant at .05 Level

Variables	$a_1 d_1$*	Proportion
When Chose Occupation	0.0090860	0.17686
Mother's View of Choice	0.0074088	0.14421
Freedom in Nursing Role	0.0046680	0.09086
Boyfriend's View of Choice	0.0036062	0.07019
Occupational Role Model — Father	0.0030368	0.05911
Talked with College Teacher	0.0026464	0.05151
Helpful — Mother	0.0023800	0.04632
Religion**	0.0023594	0.04592
Creativity in Nursing Role	0.0022200	0.04321
Ethnic Background	0.0022200	0.03384
Talked with High School Counselor	0.0017388	0.03170
Helpful — High School Counselor	0.0016260	0.03165
Father's View of Choice	0.0016104	0.03133
Occupational Role Model — Relative	0.0011340	0.02207
Choice Difficulty	0.0011184	0.02177
Creativity in Social Worker Role	0.0006070	0.01182
Helpful — College Teacher	0.0002698	0.00525
High School Counselor's View of Choice	0.0002640	0.00513
Family Annual Income	0.0002508	0.00488
College Major***	0.0003020	0.00058

* Difference between the group means x discriminant function coefficients.
** Large Religious categories were utilized — Buddhist, Catholic, Jewish, Protestant.
*** Categories — Biological/Physical Science, Social Science, Pre-professional, Other, None.

teachers and found them more helpful. Both student groups discussed career plans with their mothers; however, nursing students received greater benefit from these discussions.

The majority of nursing students' parents viewed nursing as the right occupation for their daughters, whereas the parents of social work students expressed mixed reactions including the opinion that social work was not good enough as an occupation. A somewhat similar pattern emerged in the boyfriends' attitudes toward the occupational choices. More nursing students had fathers and a relative other than parents who could serve as an occupational role model.

Nursing and social work students differed on their major during the first two years of college. Most nursing students enrolled in the pre-professional program, but most social work students majored in a social science-humanities program.

Both groups came from homes with incomes above the national average, but nursing students reported a higher annual family income than did social work students.

Self-concept and Occupational Role Expectations

From the data presented in Tables 2 and 3, it is possible to state that a correlation existed between the students' self-concept and the role expectations of their respective chosen occupation.

Table 2 indicates that social work students described their self-concept predominately as independent, spontaneous, and assertative. They rarely included the adjectives: industrious, methodical, and dependable, but these best described the qualities required in the nursing role as viewed by social work students. These same students characterized the social worker as capable, forceful, and strong-willed although, and to a lesser extent, they also included in this role-description such words as self-denying, adaptable, and co-operative.

The nursing students' self-concept was best described as dependable, methodical, capable, and conscientious with some tendency to be submissive and sustain subordinate roles (Table 3). Their major expectations of the nursing role called for an industrious, methodical, and dependable individual with an ability to submit and sustain subordinate roles while being co-operative, considerate, conventional, and adaptable. Their expectations of the social worker role could best be realized by a cooperative, considerate, adaptable, and curious person although nursing students also expected social workers to be aggressive, forceful, and strong-willed in their role.

The students differed in their expectations of nursing as to the freedom and opportunity for creativity in the role. The major difference occurred on the question of freedom in planning and carrying out patient care. The majority of social work students disagreed with this expectation. The nursing students were more equally divided between agreement and disagreement with somewhat more agreeing on this occupational expectation. Not as sharp a difference appeared on the question of nurses having an opportunity to be creative in their work. Both groups agreed more than they disagreed but the nursing students agreed significantly more with this occupational role expectation. The majority in both groups agreed that nurses were

Table 2 / ACL Key Clusters* and Their Definers —
Social Work Students

Cluster 1: Self: Tendency to be Independent, Spontaneous and
Assertative
    Definers
    Self — Autonomy
    Self — Change
    Self — Deference
    Self — Liability

Cluster 2: Nurse: Tendency to be Self-Controlled, Methodical, and
Dependable
    Definers
    Nurse — Order
    Nurse — Endurance
    Nurse — Self-Control
    Nurse — Autonomy
    Nurse — Aggressive

Cluster 3: Standard Total Number of Adjectives Checked: Tendency
to Reflect Surgency and Drive and a Relative Absence of Repressive
Tendencies
    Definers
    Social Worker — Standard Total Number
    Nurse — Standard Total Number
    Self — Standard Total Number

Cluster 4: Social Worker: Tendency to be Aggressive, Forceful,
and Strong-Willed
    Definers
    Social Worker — Dominance
    Social Worker — Achievement
    Social Worker — Self-confidence
    Social Worker — Abasement

Cluster 5: Social Worker: Tendency to be Self-Denying,
Adaptable, and Co-operative
    Definers
    Social Worker — Aggressive
    Social Worker — Nurturance
    Social Worker — Affiliation
    Social Worker — Deference

Cluster 6: Self: Tendency to be Industrious, Methodical
and Dependable
    Definers
    Self — Achievement
    Self — Endurance
    Self — Order
    Self — Dominance

---

* In Tables 2 and 3 the order of the clusters is important since the initial cluster
accounts for a greater proportion of the common variance.

Table 3 / Eight ACL Key Clusters and Their Definers —
Nursing Students

___

Cluster 1: Nurse: Tendency to be Industrious, Methodical and
Dependable
    Nurse — Achievement
    Nurse — Endurance
    Nurse — Dominance
    Nurse — Order
Cluster 2: Self: Tendency to be Dependable, Methodical, Capable,
and Conscientious
    Self — Endurance
    Self — Intraception
    Self — Order
    Self — Self-Control
Cluster 3: Social Worker: Tendency to be Considerate, Cooperative,
Curious, and Adaptable
    Social Worker — Personal Adjustment
    Social Worker — Intraception
    Social Worker — Nurturance
    Social Worker — Affiliation
Cluster 4: Standard Total Number: Tendency to Reflect Surgency
and Drive and a Relative Absence of Repression Tendencies
    Nurse — Standard Total Number of Adjectives Checked
    Social Worker — Standard Total Number of Adjectives Checked
    Self — Standard Total Number of Adjectives Checked
Cluster 5: Social Worker: Tendency to be Aggressive, Forceful, and
Strong-Willed
    Social Worker — Dominance
    Social Worker — Self-confidence
    Social Worker — Achievement
    Social Worker — Abasement
Cluster 6: Self: Tendency to be Submissive and
Sustain Subordinate Roles
    Self — Deference
    Self — Autonomy
    Self — Abasement
    Self — Aggression
Cluster 7: Nurse: Tendency to be Submissive and
Sustain Subordinate Roles
    Nurse — Abasement
    Nurse — Deference
    Nurse — Dominance
    Nurse — Autonomy
Cluster 8: Nurse: Tendency to be Co-operative, Considerate,
Conventional, and Adaptable
    Nurse — Personal Adjustment
    Nurse — Self-control
    Nurse — Affiliation
    Nurse — Nurturance

highly regarded by colleagues such as physicians and psychologists so no difference occurred in this occupational expectation. As to freedom in the social work role, nursing students agreed more often to this as a possibility than the social work students, although the social work students believed freedom was more possible in this role than in the nursing role. Both student groups very much agreed that social workers could be creative in their role but nursing students agreed somewhat more with this expectation.

Implications

This study provides additional supportive data for the theory that people tend to view an occupational role as favorable or unfavorable for them because their ideas of that occupation either do or do not fit into their self-concept.

One interpretation of the findings is that, although these social work and nursing students' expectations of the nursing role derived from different perspectives, they both perceived it as reflecting a more traditional definition of the role of women who choose to prepare for a career in the women's occupations.

To function in the nursing role requires self-controlled, methodical, and dependable behavior and the ability to be submissive and to maintain subordinate roles, which although it limits occupational freedom, does perhaps gain regard from male colleagues such as physicians and psychologists.

The social work role presents less stringent role boundaries and this may account for the students' difficulty in making their choice in this field. It seems to reflect a role in the process of moving away from this traditional definition to include more aggressive and autonomous behavior in the role expectations. This makes for occupational freedom but perhaps at the price of strained collegial relationships.

Social work students' responses to the ACL showed that their first cluster defined the self. This would seem to indicate that while these social work students tend to think of themselves primarily as individuals and only secondarily as social workers, the reverse is true for the nursing students. In this instance, nursing appears to be a more encompassing occupational role than social work.

One factor concerning the nurse's role, which cannot be overlooked, is the tendency for the lay public to connect this role almost exclusively with the hospital. In this work situation, the outsider may view the nurse as dominant, self-assured, and strong-willed vis-a-vis the patient so that she can obtain his cooperation in treatment; however, the role also may be viewed as subordinate to the physician who makes the decisions concerning overall care of the patient. Although these two aspects of the nursing role may exist in the outsider's view, their confinement to the inner world of one institution, the hospital, aids in producing a clearer occupational image for acceptance or rejection as a career choice. No such institutionally encased role comes to mind when considering the social worker.

Summary

This study undertook an exploration of the differences in the self-concept and occupational role expectations of women students who had chosen nursing and social work as their occupations. One hundred social work and nursing students in their junior year at the University of California completed the Gough Adjective Check List which described 1) the self, 2) the social worker, and 3) the nurse. In addition, a questionnaire provided demographic and supplementary data on occupational role expectations. Five hypotheses relative to the differences were tested and all were supported. The one variable from the questionnaire which most effectively differentiated the two groups was the period when they decided on their occupation with most nursing students making this decision while in grade school or high school, while social work students generally waited until after they entered college, and then, often until the sophomore year.

On the Gough Adjective Check List social work students described themselves predominately as independent, spontaneous, and assertative. Their self-concept rarely included the adjectives: industrious, methodical, and dependable, but these best described their view of the qualities required in the nursing role. These same students characterized the social worker as capable, forceful, and strong-willed. The nursing students' self-concept was best described as dependable, methodical, capable, and conscientious with some tendency to be submissive and to sustain subordinate roles. Their major expectations of the nursing role called for an industrious, methodical, and dependable individual with an ability to submit and sustain subordinate roles while being cooperative, considerate, conventional, and adaptable. Their expectations of the social worker role could best be realized by a co-operative, considerate, adaptable, and curious person although nursing students also expected social workers to be aggressive, forceful, and strong-willed in their role.

REFERENCES

1. Sarbin, T. R., Role theory, in *Handbook of Social Psychology,* ed. by Gardner Lindzey. Cambridge, Mass., Addison-Wesley Publishing Co., 1954, Vol. 1, pp. 223-258.
2. Super, D. E., and others. *Vocational Development; a Framework for Research.* New York, Bureau of Publications, Teachers College, Columbia University, 1957.
3. Gough, H. G., and Heilburn, A. B., Jr., *The Adjective Check List Manual.* Palo Alto, Calif., Consulting Psychologists Press, 1965.
4. Tryon, R. C., *Cluster and Factor Structure.* Tolman Hall Library, University of California, Berkeley. (Unpublished)

twenty-seven

Women Preparing to Teach

FRED SCHAB

The continuing public interest in the problems of the schools, as evidenced by the writings of Conant, Rickover, and, more indirectly, Mrs. Friedan, prompted me to investigate the values which women preparing for teaching place upon this career. The subjects of this investigation included almost all of the junior and senior women enrolled in the College of Education at the University of Georgia. Of this total of 226, 119 were elementary education majors and 107 secondary education majors.

The following table presents the similarities and differences in some aspects of their personal backgrounds:

	Elementary	Secondary
Single	84.0%	93.5%
Married	15.9%	6.5%
Engaged	21.0%	10.2%
Parents Graduated From College	43.6%	34.5%

An immediate difference of potential effect upon the teaching profession appears in the figures shown in the married and engaged categories. Twice as many elementary majors were already committed to domesticity as their main career. The fact that more secondary majors came from noncollege parental backgrounds may only partially explain the lesser interest in rapid domestication.

Very little difference was found between the two groups of

From AAUW JOURNAL, Vol. 61, No. 2 (1968), pp. 60-61.
Reprinted by permission.

teacher-trainees in their responses to the question "What are you most interested in?"

Marriage alone is preferred by 20.9 percent of the elementary group and 20.5 percent of the secondary group. None of the elementary group opted for a career alone, but 2.7 percent of the secondary subjects would prefer only a career. A combination of career and marriage appealed to 79.1 percent of the elementary group and 76.8 percent of the secondary teacher-trainees.

The subjects were then asked what they would be adequately prepared for, having attained a college education. Of the elementary subjects, 10.9 percent replied "Career," .8 percent "Marriage," and 88.3 percent "Both Career and Marriage." Corresponding percentages of the secondary group were 14.9 percent and 84.2 percent.

College as Preparation for Marriage?

Extreme pessimism about college as a preparation for marriage alone is to be noted. More secondary majors, again, felt confident of preparation for a career, but both groups were quite convinced they will be adequately prepared for the combined endeavors of career and marriage. When asked about the compatibility between career and marriage, the elementary majors were more positively (95.8%) convinced of this than the others (89.7%).

Again elementary majors responded predictably when the question, "How important is marriage to you?", was asked. Elementary trainees were 73.3 percent sure it was very important compared with 56.3 percent of the others. The secondary group also indicated more caution in the selection of a mate. Thirty-four and five-tenths stated they would marry *"only if the right man appears."*

When asked about the preferred time for marriage, the responses given were as follows: "before graduation" was the choice of 17.9 percent of the elementary trainees and 10.2 percent of the secondary; answers scaled down in considerable detail to "uncertain," with .7 percent of the elementary group so responding and none of the others.

The choice of "before graduation" corresponded with the figures already obtained from the married and engaged students. The elementary majors, again, appear more domestically inclined. The secondary women appear more career-minded and, although only a few would put off marriage until after age twenty-five, this was five times as many as in the elementary group.

Children Temporary Setback

There can be no doubt about the effect of childbearing upon the progress of the teaching career of either group of women. Another set of responses indicated the permanency of the effect of the arrival of children. Twenty-two and four-tenths percent of the future elementary teachers felt a child will end their careers, and 17.5 percent of the secondary trainees believed they will be more loyal to their careers than the elementary group. Both groups were quite sure they will resume their career efforts after their children no longer require their full attention. An interruption, therefore, of fifteen to twenty years may be anticipated in the careers of both sets of prospective teachers.

The next question asked for methods by which these women hoped to prevent a loss of career skills envisaged by this long interval in their careers.

Of the elementary group, 21.5 percent, and 32 percent of the secondary, would keep up by reading in their major interest. Wide general reading was the envisioned course in the case of 53.7 percent of the elementary, 48.4 percent of the secondary. Thirteen and two-tenths of the elementary trainees would take up adult education studies, 9.8 percent of the secondary. But the majority felt that their skill will deteriorate during the child-bearing years.

It is evident that more than seventy percent of both groups believed reading of some kind will help them retain their professional skills while housekeeping. Only about ten percent would consider adult education, or extension, courses. The almost complete absence of refresher courses for ex-teachers accounts for the small percentage of those choosing this method of skill retention.

Conclusions

The tentative conclusions to be drawn from the beliefs recorded by the two groups of future teachers can be stated as follows:

First, elementary majors are twice as interested in immediate domestication as are secondary majors. Therefore the present shortage and dropout of elementary teachers is certain to be continued.

Second, woman secondary majors cannot be depended upon to stay on the job either, since two-thirds of them plan to stop teaching when children arrive.

Third, about three-fourths of both groups plan to resume teaching after an interval of fifteen to twenty years. There is good reason to doubt their readiness to resume teaching at the previous level of efficiency. One example of what can occur stems from the coming of educational television. Women trained twenty years ago would be gravely handicapped if ignorant of the uses of this learning tool.

Organized systems of retraining are necessary. Because of the shortage, these exteachers will find employment easily without much concern for their "antique" skills. Teachers' colleges will need to offer more flexible programs of courses to fit the housekeeping schedules of these future returnees. This, added to the valuable experiences gained from child-rearing and community activities, may bring more mature teachers back into the profession and benefit our schools more, perhaps, than the raw recruits who left teaching after only a few years' experience several decades ago.

twenty-eight

The Perspective of College Women

WALTER L. WALLACE

Whenever we have presented separate data for male and female students in the preceding chapters, differences between these status categories have been evident. Sometimes these have been differences in the strength of a particular association, and sometimes they have been differences in the direction of an association. But throughout, with almost unbroken regularity, we have found lower levels of grades orientation and lower levels of graduate school aspiration among women than among men. Moreover, consistent with this, female freshmen generally lost their grades orientation faster and adopted graduate school aspirations slower than did male freshmen.

These and other specific sex differences shown by our data so far do not seem to be discrete or unconnected. Rather, their very regularity intimates that they may be shadows of more far-reaching differences in the content of socialization for college men and women.

As previously stated, we view socialization as involving progressive differentiation within each of the norms and norm constituents relevant to the organization in question. It is clear, however, that not all statuses, occasions, responses, and consequences which are relevant to a given organization are peculiar to it alone. In fact, one of the meanings of the statement that certain organizations "belong" to a certain society is that the former adopt or import (or have thrust upon them) some of the statuses, occasions, responses, and consequences which are general in the society at large. Thus, although a given organization may have a large number of statuses (and other norm constituents) which are peculiar to itself (e.g., freshman, foreman, quarterback, archbishop), the organization simply adopts some statuses (and other norm constituents) which are common in the larger society and by this adoption becomes part of that society.

Obviously, sex status was such an adopted distinction at Midwest College, and along with that distinction many interrelated occasions, responses, and consequences were imported into the college which modified its operation in important ways. Our purpose in this chapter is to explore the manner in which student socialization was complicated by the fact that an adopted status distinction cut across the more indigenous freshman-nonfreshman distinction which has occupied us so far.

Two Dimensions of Sex-related Attitude Differences

An integral part of women's adolescence in the society at large is the realization that their adult social status generally depends on that of the men they marry, rather than on their own performances.[1] Thus the search for satisfactory marriage partners takes on, for women, not only the problems of individual personality gratification which it carries for men, it also becomes one of women's prime arenas of social competition for adult status validation. Because of this, the American cultural specification that personal "success" consists in upward generational mobility (i.e., achieving higher social status than one's parents) can apply to women as well as to men, although the means which are appropriate to the pursuit of such mobility differ between the sexes. However, matters are different with respect to the specification that success also consists in upward career mobility (i.e., a lifetime of movement to ever higher statuses) (Lipset, 1953; Bettelheim, 1962). For men (particularly those of the middle class), whose personal success is worked out chiefly in their occupations and jobs, careers tend as a matter of course to become a succession of departures and arrivals in which each achievement or failure is followed by a new competition in a new arena (Warner and Abbeglin, 1955, pp. 80-82). But because a woman's socially defined success is typically dependent not on her own occupational and job mobility but on her husband's, and because she is culturally enjoined against the corollary of job mobility, namely marital mobility,[2] there is only one comparable departure and arrival in her life cycle: her exchange of a father-determined social status for a husband-determined one. Career mobility and its marital equivalents are therefore both relatively closed to women and social judgment of the latter's personal success must hinge more exclusively on generational mobility via marriage.[3]

A woman's selection of a husband can thus be a more significant, because more singular, rite of passage to adult status than is a man's selection of an occupation. There are, however, at least two major differences (beyond the most obvious ones) between the processes, as distinct from the consequences, of the respective choices. First, in order to succeed maritally a woman must persuade her chosen to choose her ("he chased her until she caught him"). That is, the process of striving for success in the romantic and marital arena consists chiefly in manipulating people and in eliciting their personal affect, and the relevant skills are therefore "personal appeal" and "attractiveness." In varying degrees of contrast with this, striving for success in the occupational arena more often consists in the manipulation of "things" — whether sledgehammers, scalpels, or symbols — and the important skills are less likely to be related to sociability.[4]

The second difference has two aspects: For one thing, selection of a desired mate and successful competition for his or her attentions are apt to occur much closer together in time (for the middle class) than are choice of occupation and occupational success. Secondarily, the individual man's equipment for achieving success in most semiprofessional and professional occupations increases in effectiveness over the post-college years toward a high point during middle age or later. The individual woman's equipment for romantic and marital (as distinct from family) success, however, is culturally declared to be at a maximum very early in life — during the years covered by college careers, to be exact. From these observations it seems fair to conclude that a second sex-related difference in modes of seeking access to adult social positions is that husband choice tends to be consummatory of past and present competitions, while occupational choice is more often preparatory for future competitions.

Now we need only combine these differences with our basic view of college as an organizational experience which social- izes and selectively recruits adolescents for adult social posi- tions to arrive at the speculation that men and women are likely to differ in their outlooks on college in ways which correspond to the people-thing and consummatory-preparatory dimensions we have just outlined. This speculation may be diagrammed by cross-classifying the latter two dimensions (Fig. 1).[5] The or-

	Thing Manupulation	People Manupulation
Preparatory	High School College Graduate School	Coeducational High School
Consummatory	Job	Coeducational College
	(Masculine) Occupational Mode of Success-Striving	(Feminine) Marital Mode of Success-Striving

Figure 1. Preparatory and Consummatory Organizational Setting of Two Modes of Success Striving

ganizational settings in which the indicated process typically takes place for youths who attend college are entered into each cell.[6]

Our data support these notions about sex-differentiated sig- nificances of college experience in several ways. For example, the "people" emphasis of women was already reflected on en- tering college in September: freshman women were nearly five times as likely to be oriented toward falling in love and getting married as a goal of their college careers; more apt to empha- size having a good time socially; and more apt to stress being accepted and liked by their fellow-students, than were fresh- man men. The "consummatory" dimension of women's atti- tudes toward college is implied by the fact that they were only half as likely to want to attend graduate or professional school after college as were freshman men. Moreover, on entering col- lege, the women were much less apt to make the "preparatory" instrumental connection between getting good grades in college and the goal of going to graduate school. This is shown by the fact that the association between these attitudes among freshmen in September was .43 (N = 147) for men, but .05 (N = 175) for women. On the other hand, women were more likely to make the "consummatory" instrumental connection between seeking to be accepted and liked by one's fellow-students and the goal of falling in love and getting married: the associations were .18 among men, but .48 among women.

Strong precollege influence toward sex-differentiation of attitudes relating to college life can, of course, be attributed to parents. For example, the association between freshmen's desire to please their parents and their desire to attend graduate or professional school was +.47 for men, but −.37 for women, in September. On the other hand, as noted in Chapter 2, the associations between the freshmen's desire to please their parents and (a) their desire to fall in love and marry while in college and (b) their desire to be accepted and liked by fellow-students were about twice as high for men as for women.

It would therefore appear that freshman men and women arrived at the gates of Midwest College from quite different attitudinal approaches, and began their college careers with orientations which generally conformed to Figure 1. But our primary concern in this study is not so much with what students brought to college as with what happened to them in college. Let us pursue this question by first examining data on non-freshmen, who may be presumed to have survived the shocks of socialization to which freshmen were still subject.[7]

The logic underlying the presentation of Table 1 is as follows: If the hypotheses which Figure 1 suggests about sex-related differences in the meaning of college are true, then the strictly academic side of college life (i.e., grades, principally) is likely to be viewed by women as a set of bothersome regulations which has to be put up with while one gets on with the real purpose of college. To men, however, the academic side of college will tend to appear more directly related to the purpose they had in coming to college. It seems to follow from this that among college women, a close approach to marital success (without actually getting married) will be accompanied by overt expression of disinterest in academics, while among men an equally close approach to marriage will have no relation (or even positive relation) to orientation to academic matters. It

Table 1 / Per Cent Expressing Indicated Attitudes and Behavior,
Holding Constant Marital-Romantic Status (Nonfreshmen)

Attitudes and Behavior	Marital-Romantic Status		
	Married	Engaged or Going Steady	Neither
Men			
High grades orientation	50 (10)	39 (100)	43 (182)
Graduate school aspiration	100 (13)	80 (117)	79 (216)
Graduate school expectation	54 (13)	64 (114)	60 (211)
Women			
High grades orientation	50 (6)	17 (76)	30 (156)
Graduate school aspiration	33 (6)	49 (88)	50 (184)
Graduate school expectation	(6)	19 (87)	34 (181)

should be noted that we are not here hypothesizing a necessary causal sequence between these two variables (although a sequence will be shown in the freshman data). It may be that approach to marital success causes women's hypothesized lack of interest in academics: i.e., they may "drop the mask" of organizational compliance when they become confident that their nonacademic, marital, purpose is about to be accomplished; or they may feel compelled to devote as much attention and energy as possible to accomplishing the marital purpose which is now so near at hand. On the other hand, it may be that lack of interest in academics is a causal factor in women's approach to marriage: "Men seldom make passes at girls who wear glasses." It may also be that both lack of interest in academics and coming close to marrying are caused by some other factor, say, sex-role socialization in the family and through the mass media. Our guess is that all three causal sequences are true, but regardless of whether all or any are true, the essential point for our present purpose is that college men will not have the same experience as women in this regard. We hypothesize that college men will experience approach to marriage and their academic orientations as unrelated, or positively related. In this case, as for women, a positive relationship could prevail as a result of at least three causal sequences, and none is more necessary to our hypothesis than another. Table 1 is therefore an attempt to examine the hypothesis of sex difference in the meaning of college from a correlational, rather than causal, point of view, and in general the data confirm the hypothesis.

We find that among the men, being engaged or going steady (as opposed to being neither engaged nor going steady) had no relation to grades orientation, to graduate school aspiration, or to graduate school expectation. The relation of romantic status to grades orientation and to graduate school expectation among the women, however, was distinctly negative, as predicted. We show data on married students chiefly for completeness, since it seems likely that marriage can bear on women's attitudes toward college in ways which radically differ from the effects of close approach to marriage. Nevertheless, it can be noted that all the married men wanted to go on to graduate or professional school after college and that they manifested a rather high level of grades orientation.

In general, therefore, the data on nonfreshmen conform well to predictions based on Figure 1. But when we examine data on changes among freshman newcomers, we are confronted by findings which contradict our predictions (and our data on non-freshmen) in almost every detail. Thus Table 2 indicates that freshman women who entered college already engaged or going steady sustained their grades orientation level better than did

Table 2 / Per Cent with High Grades Orientation, Holding Constant Romantic Status° in September (Freshmen)

Date of Observation	Men		Women	
	Romantic Status			
	Engaged or Going Steady	Neither	Engaged or Going Steady	Neither
September	100	71	64	75
November	43	50	43	34
	(21)	(104)	(14)	(132)
September–November change	—57	—30	—33	—55

° One male married freshman was excluded from this table.

other freshman women, while the reverse was the case among the men. Notice that when the freshmen entered college, in September, the relations between romantic status and grades orientation were as our hypothesis would predict, but attitude changes in college took these relations in the contrary direction. The same sort of observations can also be made of Tables 3 and 4: freshman women who were engaged or going steady either

Table 3 / Per Cent with Graduate School Aspirations, Holding Constant Romantic Status ' in September (Freshmen)

Date of Observation	Men		Women	
	Romantic Status			
	Engaged or Going Steady	Neither	Engaged or Going Steady	Neither
September	58	47	12	28
November	58	73	41	36
	(24)	(118)	(17)	(151)
September-November change	0	+49	+33	+11

' One male married freshman was excluded from this table.

Table 4 / Per Cent with Graduate School Expectations, Holding Constant Romantic Status' in September (Freshmen)

Date of Observation	Men		Women	
	Romantic Status			
	Engaged or Going Steady	Neither	Engaged or Going Steady	Neither
September	76	51	8	27
November	59	56	25	25
	(17)	(101)	(12)	(120)
September-November change	—22	+10	+18	—3

' One male married freshman was excluded from this table.

maintained or increased their graduate school aspiration and expectation, while other freshman women lost such interest; freshman men who were engaged or going steady lost interest in graduate school, while other freshmen sustained or gained interest.

The key to comprehending this many-sided nonfreshman versus freshman reversal seems to lie in the probability that several related situations (which we will document as well as our data allow) were true. First, it seems most probable that freshmen who, on their second day on campus, said they were engaged or going steady were referring to persons "back home." That is, such freshmen were unlikely to be engaged or going steady with Midwest College students so early in their college careers. Second, the romantic attachments which freshmen did then have in mind provided the women involved in them with strong extracollege "anchorages" for their affections and fidelities, thereby removing such women from the mainstream of their peers' social system and locating them in unusual social environments which brought about unusual patterns of attitude change. Third, freshman men who said they were engaged or going steady in September were considerably more cavalier about these attachments and appear to have galloped off in pursuit of replacements for their now absent fiancées and steadies almost as soon as they arrived at college. Finally, it would appear that eventually both freshman women and freshman men tended to transfer their affections to fellow Midwest College students. It was only then that the patterns predicted by Figure 1 and confirmed by Table 1 emerged. Let us now review the evidence for these conclusions and discuss the conclusions themselves in somewhat greater detail.

First and most important, it is apparent from Table 5 that freshman women who said they were engaged or going steady in September were much more likely to continue their engagements or steady dating in the following November than were freshman men. Thus 95 per cent of freshman women who were engaged or going steady in September were still so attached seven weeks later, as compared with an unseemly 54 per cent among freshman men. That most of the engagements and steady dating relationships to which the freshman women, at least, referred in September involved off-campus, "back home," young men is suggested by the finding that although the engaged or going-steady women dated more in high school than did other women (as one would expect), they dated much less than did other freshman women after they reached college. The obvious implication is that the young men who were the objects of the engaged or steady dating freshman women's affections

Table 5 / Per Cent Reporting Dating-Related Attitudes and Behavior, Holding Constant Romantic Status

| Attitudes and Behavior | Men | | Women | |
| | September Romantic Status[a] | | | |
	Engaged or Going Steady	Neither	Engaged or Going Steady	Neither
	Freshmen			
Engaged or going steady in November	54 (24)	13 (119)	95 (19)	9 (151)
September desire for love and marriage	32 (25)	25 (121)	53 (19)	66 (153)
November high dating orientation	50 (20)	21 (104)	57 (14)	49 (128)
April high dating orientation	38 (13)	30 (77)	64 (11)	48 (103)
Dating more than once a week in high school	62 (24	34 (121)	79 (19)	40 (153)
Dating more than 8 hours per week in November	42 (24)	24 (119)	21 (19)	38 (151)
Dating more than 8 hours per week in April	50 (20)	29 (108)	38 (13)	48 (141)
	Nonfreshmen			
	November Romantic Status[a]			
November high dating orientation	60 (96)	30 (176)	71 (70)	49 (147)
Dating more than 8 hours per week in November	68 (118)	32 (215)	68 (88)	33 (184)

[a] One male married freshman and thirteen male and six female married nonfreshmen were excluded from this table.

had been present in high school, but were no longer present in college. Our guess is that most engaged or going-steady freshman men were also attached in September to girls whom they had left behind in coming to Midwest College, but Table 5 offers no empirical support for this guess, probably because of the very rapid breakup of freshman men's original romantic attachments.

In this latter connection, it is interesting to contrast the fact that freshman women who entered college engaged or going steady tended to date *less* in college, and were initially *less* oriented toward falling in love and getting married in college than were other, unattached women with the findings among men: engaged or going-steady men were likely to date *more* in college, and be *more* desirous of finding love and marriage in college, than were unattached men. It would seem that fidelity can account for the findings among the women; apparently, they were being faithful to the "boys back home." The reversed situation among the men, however, can be explained in at least two ways: either the freshman men who said they were engaged or going steady in September meant that they were attached at that time to women who were already on the Midwest College campus, or they (the freshman men) were simply less monogamous with respect to the girls whom they left back home. If the former alternative were true, it would imply that these freshman men were already engaged or going steady with sophomore, junior, or senior women at the time the former arrived on campus — since Table 5 has already indicated that few freshman women could have been attached to them. This does not seem likely, since the relatively high turnover in engagements and steady dating relationships which Table 5 shows among the men during just seven weeks seems to suggest that the female partners to the initial relationships were not present, while new potential partners were. It would appear, therefore, that as far as romantic attachments back home were concerned, it was a man's privilege to change his mind and he exercised it, quickly. One might guess that going steady or becoming engaged while in high school tended to whet a young man's appetite, not so much for the favors of his particular fiancée or steady, but for those of girls in general. In other words, first romantic success seems typically to have made young women act like Juliet, but made young men act like Don

Juan. When placed in the context of propositions represented by Figure 1, of course, these findings and conclusions lead us to speculate that the normative conditions which are most conducive to a given partner's romantic fidelity are those in which marriage is the prime adult status-conferring achievement.[8] Since these conditions presently hold more for women than for men, they may account for our evidence of freshman women's greater reluctance to change romantic partners.

But these general conditions are confounded for the individual woman when she enters an organizational setting different from that of her fiancé or steady, where members tend to pursue marriage with other members of the same organization, where her newness makes her especially attractive to eligible men (until she learns their reputations, how the date-rating system works, what the standard "lines" are, and how to handle all three in appropriate ways), and where the eligible men probably show greater promise of occupational success than did the "boy back home." Under these conditions, our data suggest that women are likely, in time, to transfer their affections from outside to inside the organization. Thus Table 5 indicates that by November, freshman women who had come to college in September engaged or going steady valued dating (presumably with on-campus men) slightly more than did women who had arrived on campus unattached, and by April the former were considerably more oriented to dating than were the latter. Although actual dating frequency seems to have lagged behind the change in dating orientation, it is clear that between November and April attached women were catching up with unattached women in terms of dating frequency. It does not seem unreasonable to suggest, therefore, that the nonfreshman data (also shown in Table 5) present a picture of the presumably stable states of romantic matters toward which freshman women as well as men were moving, albeit at different rates. One should note the general symmetry of data between nonfreshman men and women, except that more men than women were engaged or going steady — which suggests the possibility that in the end women had the stronger endogamous tendency (organizationally speaking), while more men may have found fiancées and steadies outside the Midwest College student body.[9]

All the evidence therefore points to initially wide and systematic differences in the dating patterns of those freshman men and women who came to college romantically attached. These differences were almost bound to reflect themselves in IE differences, and we can now show that the latter enable us to account exactly for the unexpected directions of grades orientation and graduate school aspiration-expectation change which we encountered in Tables 2, 3, and 4.

Thus Table 6 makes it clear that being engaged or going steady implied that a freshman man would build a relatively wide acquaintanceship with nonfreshman women,[10] but a severely limited acquaintanceship with his fellow freshman males. Earlier we found that among freshman men, the nonfreshman female IE proportion was positively associated with grades-orientation decline, while freshman male IE proportion was negatively associated with it. These are exactly the observations needed to explain the freshman male changes shown in Table 2. Also earlier we found little or no association between freshman male IE proportion and graduate school aspiration change, but the negative association with nonfreshman female IE proportion needed to explain the findings of Table 3 is present.

Table 6 / Associations (Yule's Q) between Romantic Status[a] in September and November IE Proportions (P) (Freshmen)

Sex and Class	Men	Women
(P) Opposite-sex freshmen	.00	−.28
(P) Opposite-sex nonfreshmen	+.37	−.18
(P) Own-sex freshmen	−.47	+.16
(P) Own-sex nonfreshmen	+.06	−.06
	(142)[b]	(168)[b]

Note: A positive Q means that being engaged or going steady was associated with a high proportion.

[a] "Engaged or going steady" versus "neither." One male married freshman was excluded from this table.

[b] Number of cases in the fourfold table from which Q's were computed.

Returning to Table 6 and examining the data on freshman women we find that, for all the reasons discussed above, being engaged or going steady was correlated with women avoiding members of the opposite sex (whether freshman or nonfreshman) and with wide acquaintanceship among members of their own sex and college class. The same earlier findings tell us that such distributions of IE proportions can account for the otherwise anomalous grades orientation and graduate school aspiration changes shown in Tables 2, 3, and, by implication, **4.**

Thus what began as an apparent contradiction of the hypothesis of sex-differentiated meanings of college experience ends as a complex and strong confirmation of it, once we take into account the fact that attitudes can play a part in selecting a certain kind of social environment and that the selected environment can then influence other attitudes of little relevance to the original selecting attitude.

NOTES

The data for this study derived from questionnaires administered in 1959 and 1960 to the student body and faculty of a small coeducational midwestern liberal arts college of high academic reputation. The various methods which were combined in the analysis consisted of survey and sociometric, cross-sectional and longitudinal. For details of the purpose, methods and techniques used see the author's introduction to *Student Culture.*

1. For a discussion which develops different implications of this point from those which we emphasize here, see Parsons (1954, pp. 299-322).

2. Despite the prevalence of divorces, it seems reasonable to guess that women generally enter (or are culturally enjoined to enter) each marriage with the expectation that it will be permanent. Men, however, most often take a particular job with the expectation and hope that it will *not* be permanent, and that they will soon be moving on to a higher-placed job.

3. In emphasizing that social approval is given for one or the other of two modes (occupational and marital) of reaching a single success goal (generational mobility), depending on the sex of the actor, we are simply applying the principle (set forth in the discussion of norm constituent in Chap. 1) that the predictable social consequences of a given response are always status specific.

4. The steady increase in people-manipulating occupations which are filled by men would seem to carry some interesting implications for our present cultural definition of masculinity.

5. The relations of this schema to Parsons', Bales', and Shils' (1953) and Parsons' and Smelser's (1956) paradigms of phases and functional imperatives in social action are more complex than space and present focus permit us to discuss fully. Still, it may briefly be pointed out that our cell *a* (Thing-Preparatory) seems to correspond best to the Latency phase; cell *b* to the Integrative phase; cell *c* to the Goal Attainment phase; and cell *d* to the Adaptive phase of a system of

social action which might be termed the Generational Replacement System: Insofar as the social system of present interest, the college, appears twice in Fig. 1 (in what would be the L and G phases), it reflects the observation that a system may function in one way or another, depending upon the kind of participants supplied to it. Insofar as Fig. 1 differentiates kinds of participants by status (in this case, sex), it reflects the observation that the personal significance of social status is precisely its implication of different experiences of the same system. Our schema therefore implies testable hypotheses addressed to the twofold problem of (1) the operation of a social system given different kinds of participants, and (2) the experience of different kinds of participants, given the same social system.

6. We specify coeducational high school and college for women's marital success strivings for obvious reasons. But an investigation of the role of women's colleges in these strivings should be of interest. There are intimations that Vassar, for example, plays such a role (Bushnell, 1962, pp. 500, 509).

7. In the next chapter we discuss faculty attitudes toward female students and the former's probable influence on the latter.

8. Ultimately, this is simply the hypothesis that the person who has the greater social stake in something will value it more, identify with it more, and remain faithful to it longer.

9. One characteristic of Midwest College (and perhaps of many other small coeducational colleges) was its high rate of female transfers, at the end of the sophomore year, to large state universities. Female student informants freely attributed this to the lack of unattached, eligible, interested males at Midwest College, and said that women transferred to state universities mainly in search of men and marriage. This also testifies to the power of college women's marital success motivation to subordinate academic success motivations.

10. Table 5 suggests that this freshman acquaintance with nonfreshman women was probably the result of dating. This may seem unusual in view of the recognized tendency of women to date up in age and seniority. However, two observations may clarify the apparent peculiarity: (1) A college student body has an artificially truncated age and seniority hierarchy, so that freshman women have the greatest possibility of dating up inside the college, and senior women have no such possibility with respect to seniority and a severely limited one with respect to age. (2) Freshman women were probably especially attractive to nonfreshman men because, being new to the college culture, the former were innocent of whatever romantic "styles" the latter had developed and were therefore easily impressed by them. Freshman women were also probably especially attracted to nonfreshman men because such men occupied an appropriately superior age and seniority status category, and because they

were obviously bound for high statuses in the adult world. As a result of these two considerations, it is highly likely that some non-freshman women not only dated down, but dated entering freshman men, partly because so many freshman women were dating up. Thus in November forty (27 per cent) freshman men said they spent more than eight hours per week on dates, and sixty-one (35 per cent) freshman women said they did likewise. But among seniors, sixty-nine (50 per cent) men and only twenty-six (37 per cent) women reported more than eight hours of dates per week. (As validation of these data it may be noted that the total number of male respondents who said in November that they dated more than eight hours per week was 191. This figure closely matches the 183 female respondents who gave a similar report.) Moreover, among freshman women, the association between hours spent dating and IE proportion opposite-sex nonfreshmen was .51, while the association with IE proportion opposite-sex freshmen dropped to .34. The corresponding associations among freshman men were .34 and .32.

REFERENCES

Bettelheim, B. *The Problem of Generations, Daedalus,* 1962, 92, 68-96.

Bushnell, J. H. *Student Culture at Vassar,* in N. Sanford, ed., *The American College.* New York: John Wiley and Sons, 1962.

Lipset, S. M. *Social Mobility and Occupational Career Patterns,* II: Social Mobility. In R. Bendix and S. M. Lipset, eds., *Class, Status, and Power.* Glencoe, Ill.: The Free Press, 1953.

Parsons, T. *Essays in Sociological Theory.* Glencoe, Ill.: The Free Press, 1954.

Parsons, T., Bales, R. F., and Shils, E. A. *Working Papers in the Theory of Action.* Glencoe, Ill.: The Free Press, 1953.

Parsons, T., and Smelser, N. J. *Economy and Society.* New York: Free Press of Glencoe, 1956.

Warner, W. L., and Abbeglin, J. C. *Big Business Leaders in America.* New York: Harper and Bros., 1955.

twenty-nine

The Female in Engineering

STANLEY S. ROBIN

Four distinctly separate lines of thought converge in the concern about and analysis of the female engineer. First, while predated by the attention of elites, mass concern for the profession of engineering, its quality, adequacy, and performance probably began with the start of active space exploration. For Americans the initial Soviet successes and American failures in 1957 and 1958 dramatically emphasized the state of American engineering (Furness, 1957; *Life*, 1957; O'Neil, 1957; Price, 1957; *Time*, 1957; Wallace, 1957). In the wake of outraged national pride, shaken self-image, and cold war considerations, remonstrations aimed in various directions about the declining number of American engineers being produced and the increasing number of Soviet engineers being turned out, were common.[1] In this light the utilization of the female as engineering "man power" is relevant. Females are seen as an untapped and major source of engineers in a perceived shortage of engineers — an undeveloped national resource.

The second thread of analysis impinging on the issue of female engineers is the sociological concern for occupational recruitment and socialization. Common to industrial sociology and the sociology of education, research and theory in this area focuses upon the nature of differential recruitment among variously defined social categories and the subsequent results of occupational socialization (Davis, 1961). Here the proclivity of

From Stanley S. Robin, "The Female in Engineering," in Robert Perrucci and Joel E. Gerstl, *The Engineers and the Social System*, 1969, pp. 203-218. Reprinted by permission of John Wiley & Sons, Inc.

females to enter engineering and their acceptance into the occupation is at issue.

A third approach to the understanding of females in engineering deals with the etiology and characteristics of the ongoing changes in the status of females in American society. Increased independence of the female, loss of the double standard, increased participation in sectors of the society once considered exclusively reserved for males, and the altered occupational expectations of females, mark this line of inquiry (Hunt, 1965). The entrance of the female into engineering, and her functioning, in comparison to her entrance into other fields, and female participation in engineering in other societies, provide clues to the social factors influencing the "assimilation" of females into engineering (Evan, 1957).

Fourth, a modern feminism is noted in discussions of the female engineer. This approach, a frankly value position and ideological commitment, stresses the "rightful," "equal," and "proper" place of the female in society. Concepts of social justice abound in the writings, along with the expressed fear that the initial impetus of feminism is waning. Here the matter of the female engineer is cause for unabashed lament (Rossi, 1964a).

The need for more than one perspective in the understanding of the position of the female engineer is clearly seen through a comparison of the trends in general female participation in the labor force and their participation in engineering.

Examination of Table 1 shows in detail the basis for the general statement that women are comprising an increasing segment of the labor force. In the span of two and one-half decades, the labor force has changed in composition from one-fourth female to more than one-third female. In the same time period, the proportion of females who are in the labor force has increased from 28% to 36%. With the exception of the World War II period, the increase in female participation has been linear and steady. By 1962, both the percentage of the labor force composed of females and the percentage of all females in the labor force approximated the levels found under conditions of war-time production necessities and the acute manpower shortage of the 1940-1945 period.

The data for these twenty-five years can be seen as an extension of long-term trends in the employment of women in the

Table 1 / Women in the Labor Force[a]

Year	Number	Percent of All Workers	Percent of All Women
	Women Workers (14 Years and Over) Recent Highlights[b]		
April 1962	24,052,000	34	36
Start of sixties (April, 1960)	23,239,000	33	36
Mid-fifties (April, 1955)	20,154,000	31	34
Korean War (April, 1953)	19,296,000	31	33
Pre-Korean War (April, 1950)	18,063,000	29	32
Post World War II (April, 1947)	16,320,000	28	30
World War II (April, 1945)	19,570,000	36	37
Pre-World War II (March, 1940)	13,840,000	25	28
	Long Term Trends[c]		
1930 (April)	10,396,000		24
1920 (June)	8,229,000		23
1900 (June)	4,999,000		20
1890 (June)	3,704,000		18

[a] Adapted from "Working Women," Esther Peterson, *Daedalus*, Spring 1964, p. 672.
[b] "Current Population Reports," for civilian labor force.
[c] Decennial census for total labor force, excluding armed forces, U.S. Department of Labor, Bureau of Labor Statistics, and U.S. Department of Commerce, Bureau of Census.

United States. The percentage of all females employed rose steadily by one third, from 18 to 24% during the 1890-1930 period.

To conclude from these data that female participation in all segments of the labor force in general and in engineering in particular has followed this pattern is specious. There has been an apparent selectivity in the sort of positions females have occupied in the labor force.

The occupations calling for education beyond the college undergraduate level have disproportionately small representation of females. In the National Opinion Research Center study, *Great Aspirations*, James Davis (1961, p. 18) concludes, ". . . women are less likely to plan further study even when matched (with males) on ability and specific career." He points to the data that indicate that in a matched sample of males and females 38.8% of the males in the upper fifth of their graduating class planned to go immediately to graduate school, while only 23.6% of the females so planned. In general, we can conclude that the increase in female participation in the labor force has primarily occurred in the lower paying, lower prestige, nonprofessional occupations.

Of equal importance, for our treatment of the female in engineering, is the fact that there is a nonrandom selection by females among occupations requiring postgraduate or professional level education. In 1940, for example, 1.2% of the physicians were female, 6.1% of the lawyers were female, and 3.5% of the clergy were female. During the same period, 23.2% of college teachers were female (Rossi, 1964b).

In this overview of female participation in the professions, women in engineering occupy a special position — that of the least participation in a major professional category (Torpy, 1964). While women in professional employment generally increased in the 1950-1960 decade, the percentage of women in engineering has decreased during the same period. While a decline in percentage is not confined to women engineers, comparisons with other professional categories show that in 1960 in the United States, 7% of physicians and surgeons employed were women, 9% of the natural scientists, 2% of the earth scientists, 4% of the physicists, 26% of the mathematicians, 27% of the biological scientists, and less than 1% of the engineers (Rossi, 1964b; Torpy, 1964). Comparisons with other professional, occupational categories show that 32% employed in journalism and 4% in the ministry were females[2] (Rossi, 1964b). These figures become even more arresting when compared to the large proportions of women in many of these occupations in other societies (16 and 75% of physicians in England and the Soviet Union, respectively, are female)[3] (Degler, 1964).

The future participation of women in engineering may be extrapolated from some preliminary data gathered from universities with engineering curricula. It can be seen that the percentage of females enrolled in university engineering programs, as shown in Table 2, agrees with data presented about the proportion of females in engineering. In all cases, women represent less than 1% of the total students enrolled in engineering. Moreover, during the decade covered by these data there is no systematic change in the participation of females in university engineering programs. In this period, females also represented a smaller proportion of engineers graduated than they do engineering students enrolled. Females average .86 of a percent of

Table 2 / Comparison of Males and Females Enrolled and Granted Degrees in Engineering Programs in a Sample of Ten United States Universities[a]

Year	Number of Males Enrolled	Percent of Males Enrolled	Number of Females Enrolled	Percent of Females Enrolled	Number of Males Graduated	Percent of Males Graduated	Number of Females Graduated	Percent of Females Graduated	Ratio of Males Graduated to Enrolled	Ratio of Females Graduated to Enrolled
1955-56	23,030	99.32	169	.68	2,625	99.44	15	.56	.114	.089
1956-57	25,915	99.22	204	.78	3,586	99.59	15	.41	.138	.074
1957-58	26,047	99.05	252	.95	4,108	99.62	16	.38	.158	.063
1958-59	24,840	99.15	214	.85	3,459	99.29	25	.71	.139	.116
1959-60	23,031	99.07	218	.93	4,237	99.70	13	.30	.184	.060
1960-61	23,474	99.12	209	.88	4,118	99.45	23	.55	.175	.110
1961-62	23,562	99.13	208	.87	3,742	99.63	14	.37	.159	.067
1962-63	22,861	99.05	220	.95	2,855	99.31	20	.69	.125	.091
1963-64[b]	19,774	99.13	175	.87	3,370	99.56	15	.44	.170	.086

[a] These data were compiled from ten randomly chosen universities: University of California, Los Angeles, University of Colorado, Georgia Institute of Technology, Louisiana State University, University of New Hampshire, Ohio State University, Purdue University, University of Tennessee, University of Washington, University of Wisconsin.
[b] Only nine universities are included in this year.

the students enrolled and .49 of a percent of students graduated. There is no increase, during this decade of the proportions of females graduating with engineering degrees.

From these data and from the examination of the ratio of males graduated to enrolled and ratio of females graduated to enrolled, the conclusion is reasonable that, in addition to selecting engineering as an occupation in such relatively small proportions, females are considerably less likely to emerge with engineering degrees than their male counterparts. This generalization stands in the face of other data that indicate that females are, by standard academic measures, as intellectually capable or more so than their male counterparts (Davis, 1961, Section VII, Table 6; Robin, 1962). These findings will prove valuable to subsequent analysis.

The female in engineering can be seen as an extreme example of the general case of the females in the professions. The question that remains is why the female should be found in such minute proportions in a field which has been, is, and will be suffering from a shortage of qualified persons?

The major pattern of analysis involves social psychological study of females in American society. Typically the question is asked: what is happening to the American female personality structure and/or role assumption and definition and/or subculture in the face of rapid cultural change? Such analysis centers about (1) changes in occupational demands and opportunities due to increasing industrialization (Cavan, 1963); (2) changes in value and normative structures about the worth, dignity, and personal development of individuals; and (3) the changing place of the females, with social-psychological repercussions, due to the factors above[4] (Gruerbert and Krech, 1952; Komarovsky, 1950; Komarovsky, 1952; Rose, 1951; Rossi, 1964b; Seward, 1945; Wallin, 1950; Zopoleon, 1950).

Females have been categorized and studied in light of their responses to these factors. For the most part, these categories represent various degrees of female socialization into the changing norms about appropriate female behavior, occupational and other. The "most emancipated" of these females, sometimes designated as "pioneers" (Rossi, 1964b), "liberals" (Seward, 1945), or the "career woman" (Parsons, 1947) are found to want to achieve and function in all areas of the society. Other research focuses on the difficulties females have meeting changed expectations and explores ambivalence arising in females (Komarovsky, 1950; Rose, 1951; Wallin, 1950). Still other research attempts to specify the social conditions antecedent to the development of these female types and their participation in the labor force (Hunt, 1965; Masuka, Matsuoka, and Kawamura, 1962; Smith, Ramsey, and Gastillo, 1963).

If there is sufficient evidence to note the entrance of some types of females in the hitherto male occupations (Degler, 1964; Hunt, 1965; Torpy, 1964), why is engineering so little manned by females? For the specific case of engineering, some illumination may arise from a look at engineering and engineers.

From his research concerning students who have graduated from engineering programs and intend to pursue engineering further, Davis (1961, p. 64) notes, "In general we can say that individuals going into the sciences and engineering tend to be low on extroversion and sophistication. . . ." Additionally, "Engineering, accounting and agriculture attract a rather stolid type who is low in emotionality, sophistication, extroversion and intellectual urbanism" (Davis, 1961, p. 65).

What about engineers actively pursuing their profession? In a series of articles, Harrison, Hunt, and Jackson (1954) found mechanical engineers tend to do less nontechnical reading than other college graduates. They are also characterized as "anti-intellectual," having few "cultural interests" and intellectual concerns external to their fields.

Supporting these data is the research of Harold L. Wilensky who indicates that engineers, as compared with lawyers and professors, read fewer "quality" newspapers, rate as less important "serious" content of newspapers, read fewer "quality" magazines, and watch fewer "educational" and "special" programs. Indiscriminate TV viewing (allowing whatever comes on the channel to stay, from one show to another) is higher among engineers than lawyers and professors. In fact, the media-consuming patterns of engineers approaches the patterns of the "middle class" (nonprofessional white-collar and blue-collar workers) in several of the above categories (Wilensky, 1964).

Augmenting these data and moving back to the educational setting, a sample of engineering professors indicated that they expect their students seldom to do original work, agree only moderately on the value of a liberal arts background, mostly agree that knowledge is unambiguous, arrive at no consensus that "reading good literature will make better engineers," mostly disagree that introspection is not good for engineers and mostly disagree that the "unusual person (oddball)" has no place in engineering (Robin, 1962). It must be remembered that this last research cited deals with an atypical sample of engineers: professors. Accordingly, the narrowness of interest and outlook in extraprofessional matters seen in other research is significantly moderated.

The sociological and psychological research available concerning engineers specifically lead us to the conclusion that engineers, while professionally dedicated, are narrow of interest, stolid, relatively uninterested in "cultural" things and not inclined to general intellectual pursuits.

"Sophistication appears to be correlated with sex, as the careers which attract people who rate themselves as sophisticated are mainly those with a high proportion of women . . ." (Davis, 1961, p. 64). This generalization agrees with and is reflective of older studies of value and personality characteristics of females in American society (Allport, Vernon and Lindzey, 1951; Gough, 1952; Strong, 1945; Termin and Miles, 1936). Intellectual sophistication, defined as broad interests, emotional sensitiveness, a "liberal arts" approach to learning, responsiveness to art and literature, and relative tolerance of intellectual creativity and deviation, seems to be a salient characteristic of academically oriented females.

From the preceding discussion it seems useful to distinguish two types of factors inhibiting the entrance of females into engineering. First, there are the variables which act in general to exclude females from proportional participation in professional and high status career activities and second, there are the particular characteristics of engineering and role of the engineer.

Many females do not select engineering as an occupation because their socialization has produced "traditional" or "domestic" females for whom an occupational career is not a viable alternative. Others decline engineering because the traditional image of the profession as a masculine pursuit is strong. Still others fear a discrimination in engineering occupations. Some "emancipated" females find themselves prevented by social circumstances such as marriage, children, and other traditional obligations. Finally, even "emancipated" females are subject to the ambivalence of a socialization in a society where a rapidly changing normative system fails to provide clear sanctions for wholehearted participation in fields like engineering (Rose, 1951; Rossi, 1964b; Seward, 1945).

These factors, however, are of the first type; they provide a framework for explanation of the general tendency for women to be underrepresented in the other professions as well as engineering. They do not address themselves specifically to the dramatically low frequency of females in engineering. The differences in female participation in engineering, compared to other professional fields, must be found in other factors. Why do *so few* intellectually capable, professionally oriented, socially emancipated females enter engineering? The answer here offered lies in the comparison of the characteristics of such females and the characteristics, as discussed above, of engineers. The outlook of engineers, the sorts of persons self-selected and, presumably, the socialization compatible with and reinforcing of the characteristics of engineers are fundamentally incompatible with the interests, aspirations, and personal characteristics of females who would otherwise select the field for an occupational career. These females select other professions and careers — as the data clearly indicate.

If the offered explanation is valid, evidence of this incompatibility should be found in the behavior and experiences of the small proportion of females who do attempt to become engineers. For this purpose, we turn to a research done with the cooperation of the Society of Women Engineers (Robin, 1962).

This analysis was designed to specify sources and types of role conflict that might make it more difficult for females to assume and function in the role of engineer. The major focus was to determine the degree to which female engineering students, as opposed to male engineering students, could agree to and accept the specific norms that comprise the role of engineering student and engineer. To the extent that an individual or category of individuals cannot recognize or accept the norms within a role, to that extent those individuals are able to assume the role with less effectiveness and/or are unlikely to assume the role at all.[5]

The research was conducted with samples of (1) engineering faculty at Purdue University, (2) male engineering students at Purdue University, (3) female engineering students at Purdue

University, and (4) a national sample of female engineering students. All student samples were comprised of juniors and seniors.

Set in the context of role theory the research was designed to explore the possibility that female engineering students conceive of the role of engineering student and the role of engineer differently than do male engineering students. If this proved to be the case, in what fashion is the female role different? The final question was what difference, if any, did an altered female role make in the pursuit of an engineering program?

Remembering that we are dealing with a selected group of females, those few choosing to enter engineering, we first wish to notice whether there are significant differences in attitudes and expectations about engineering between males and females in engineering programs. There is a difference between males and females in the branches of engineering selected, with males selecting electrical and mechanical engineering with greatest frequency and females selecting chemical engineering. There was no significant difference, however, between the males and females in violation of prior expectations about the engineering program (two thirds of each sample reported expectations fulfilled) and professional plans (almost all expected to graduate and over two thirds wanted to be hired by large firms). Each sample expected to function as professional engineers (71% for males, 72% for females). Clearly, both males and females had, to a large extent, equivalent professional expectations.

Nevertheless, role differences between the male and female engineering students did exist. They can be summarized as follows: the female sample expected, significantly more often, to receive technical information from fellow students. They were significantly less strong in their expectations that one cannot complete an engineering program without being "deadly serious" about it. They agreed more that engineering students are expected to extend course materials by seeking extra work. The female sample agreed more strongly than the male sample that a liberal arts background is essential training for student engineers. The males, unlike the females, were more prone to agree that intellectual interests and pursuits are damaging to their training and performance.

The females agreed that there is a need for engineering students to learn draftsmanship — there is no consensus[6] on this point within the male sample. There is consensus among the females that basic design is not more important than testing or development; the males are split on this point. The females agreed that the "right" answer is not characteristic of engineering, and the problematical does exist; the males achieved no consensus on this point. High-level nontechnical reading was agreed upon as beneficial to those in engineering by the female sample — the male sample here achieved no consensus. The females stated that there is room for the unusual, less-conforming person in engineering, while males are divided on that point.

The males expect that knowledge in engineering is definite and unambiguous, while females do not have consensus on that expectation. The male sample states that they expect good work to result in good professional relationships, but females are divided and achieve no consensus on that point.

From these differences in norms, we can see a pattern of role differences. It appears that the females' student engineering role, in addition to being demonstrably different from the male role, involves more tolerance of ambiguity both in professional and relational spheres. There is a discernible emphasis on liberal arts and "intellectual" expectations in the female role that is largely excluded from the male role. The females tend more to accept "paper work" in their role (and projected professional role), than do the males. Finally, the females see their social relationships in the area of engineering as having more autonomy from their technical performance.

The nature of these differences makes feasible the tentative conclusion that the females who do elect engineering as an occupation include general feminine norms into the student role and expect to function with them in the role of engineer. What are the repercussions for females and for engineering of these role changes?

The females who enrolled in the Purdue engineering programs were, agreeing with data previously mentioned, intellectually outstanding. The entrance examination scores of the female sample were uniformly high. Their ranks in high school graduating classes were significantly higher than the average of engineering students. There were no significant role differences between the males (Purdue sample) and females (national sample) and the number of hours of study expected, perceived relationships with instructors, desired characteristics of engineers, categories of difficult courses, and definition of engineering.

Examination of the engineering faculty description of the student engineer's role shows that it is substantively closer to the male students than the female. It is the female's role picture of the student in engineering that deviates, using the audience of engineering professors as a standard. In spite of the common expectations of males and females about the norms of the student *qua* student (expected number of hours of study, relationships with instructors, etc.), the mean grade index for females at Purdue was 2.09 in engineering courses ($F = 0$, $A = 4$) or just above a "C." A matched sample of males had a mean-grade index of 2.95 or just under a "B." (These differences are significant at the .001 level.) Thus the performance of females in academic engineering programs is substantially inferior to that of the males.

If the intrusion of feminine norms into the student engineer role does reduce the ability of the female to function — if it is this factor rather than others — an additional test is necessary. All female engineering students were given a masculinity-femininity test. (Incidentally, female engineering students were not significantly more masculine than a general sample of college co-eds.) Separating the more masculine females from the rest of the sample, a role picture of the student engineer role was obtained that lay in content intermediate between the male and female student roles. The masculine females made significantly higher grades than their more feminine counterparts, and the correlation, in the female sample, between grades in engineering courses and masculinity was .52. Thus it seems that the introduction of feminine norms into the role reduces performance; the reduction of feminine norms yields an increase in performance.

Even among the few who enter engineering, the tendency is to counter the definition and characteristics of the engineer by the introduction of feminine interests and behavior. This results in lower grades, less faculty approval, and helps explain the data (Table 2) indicating that fewer females than males who enter engineering programs finish with an engineering degree. One might hypothesize that those who finish are the more masculine females — but they represent few of those starting.

The analysis presented here can be seen in two parts: (1) the factors, beyond those found for other professional occupations, that make engineering unattractive for the female; and (2) what happens to females, in the educational setting, who attempt to become engineers. The elements of analysis are distinct but not separate. The proclivity of females to import feminine norms into the student role supports the initial analysis of the incompatibility of feminine characteristics and engineering. The dysfunction of the female student role helps explain the paucity of female engineers. Finally, and most important, the difficulties of the female student engineer may yield insight into problems of the female engineer functioning in her role as professional engineer.

In the opening sections of this chapter, emphasis was put upon the perceived need for engineers. Mention was also made of the feminist position, which states that women ought to be engineers (or doctors or bank presidents) because they too are people. How shall we answer these concerns?

The general factors inhibiting the entrance of females in general into occupations of high skill, professional standing, and high status may be declining (Torpy, 1964). If this is so, it is occurring slowly. The additional particular factors affecting engineering are not likely to change rapidly. The structure of female socialization and, through it, personality characteristics seem to lead away from rather than toward engineering, specifically among the career oriented. The nature of engineering and the characteristics of those in it seem unlikely to change. This is especially true if the tendency toward the increasing division of labor continues to separate engineers from scientists. If the above is maintained, then educational experiences of females in engineering programs are not likely to change, and the pattern of female nonparticipation in engineering will be reinforced.

In sum, the preceding discussion has different implications for the four approaches to females in engineering, outlined initially. There is no indication that females in significant numbers will become a source of engineering manpower. Both the data reviewed and the reasoning pursued lead to the conclusion that, in our society, females will compose a minute and marginal segment of engineers. Sources of engineering manpower will have to be found in the male population.

From the perspective of the analysis of occupational recruitment and socialization, this treatment of females and engineering stands as an example of the sorts of variables and considerations utilized to provide generalizations. These data about the nature of engineers and their role may, however, be used to address the question: from what social categories might we expect additional engineers to be recruited successfully?

The third approach, focusing on the change of status of females in American society, illuminates the issue of the type of female likely to encounter these societal changes in such a fashion that they "live" them. If we assume that there is a vanguard of females both productive of and responding to changes in female behavior, the characteristics of these females indicate their lack of fit into roles like engineering. Speculation might be advanced that if, over time, increasing proportions of females respond to those emancipating social changes, perhaps additional more appropriate social psychological types will become available to engineering. Information presented over the 1950-1960 period do not indicate this occurrence, but a single decade remains a poor test of this proposition.

The modern feminist should be alerted to the logic of selectivity. As feminism views the traditional role of the female as "bondage," the workings of a relative, as opposed to an absolute deprivation, may yield frustration. Participation of females in *all* segments of professional occupational and intellectual life is not only sought but impatiently expected. Quite aside from conscious volitional opposition, the social and psychological reasons for limited and selected participation in some societal roles must be appreciated. It seems quite likely that the able, far ranging, and intellectually broad spirits championing feminism would be among the first to avoid encapsulation in the role of engineer.

Words of comfort for those concerned do not come easily. Unless there is a conscious manipulation of the social structure and attendant norms probably within universities — though with limited effect if confined there — the involvement of females in engineering will remain low by any standard of comparison.

NOTES

1. Evidence exists that elites are still concerned, a decade later, American space successes notwithstanding (*Science*, 1967).

2. In contrast to Rossi, Bock (1967) presents data indicating that females in the ministry have declined from 3% in 1900 to 2.3% in 1960 in spite of a numerical increase. While problems of definition are apparent for this occupation, even the conservative estimate shows the females to be better represented in the clergy than in engineering.

3. These figures are for 1950. Evan also cites the figure of 50% for women engineers in the U.S.S.R.

4. This value is interestingly reflected in an implicitly culture-bound personality theory (Maslow, 1943).

5. There are several distinct sorts of role conflict, as explored along with antecedent conditions, by Gross, Mason, and McEachern (1958), Biddle and Thomas (1966), and Ivey and Robin (1966).

6. "No consensus," here, means that the sample in question did not achieve 50% or above agreement to the norms as the lower limit of a confidence interval with .05 as the level of confidence.

REFERENCES

Allport, G. W., P. E. Vernon, and G. Lindzey, *Study of Values,* Houghton Mifflin, 1951.

Biddle, Bruce J. and Edwin, J. Thomas, *Role Theory,* Wiley, New York, 1966, pp. 3-62.

Bock, Wilbur E., "The Female Clergy: A Case of Professional Marginality," *American Journal of Sociology,* 72 (1967), pp. 521-539.

Cavan, Ruth Shonle, *The American Family,* Thomas Y. Crowell, New York, 1963, pp. 40-76, 511-534.

"Crisis in Education," *Life,* 44 (12), March 24, 1958, pp. 25-37.

Davis, James A., *Great Aspirations,* National Opinion Research Center, University of Chicago, 1961.

Degler, Carl N., "The Changing Place of Women in America," *Daedalus,* 93 (1964), pp. 653-670.

Evan, William M., "Recruitment of Women in the Engineering Profession," *Science,* March 1957, pp. 387-389.

Furness, C. C., "Why Did U.S. Lose the Race? Critics Speak Up," *Life,* 43 (17), October 21, 1957, pp. 22-30.

Gough, H. G., "Identifying Psychological Femininity," *Educational Psychological Monographs,* 12 (1952), pp. 427-439.

Gross, Neal, Ward S. Mason, and Alexander W. McEachern, *Explorations in Role Analysis: Studies of the School Superintendency Role,* Wiley, New York, 1958, pp. 3-70, 244-251.

Gruerbert, Sidonia and Hilda Krech, *The Many Lives of a Modern Woman: A Guide to Happiness in Her Complex Role,* Doubleday, New York, 1952.

Harrison, R., W. Hunt, and T. Jackson, "Profile of the Mechanical Engineer I.: Ability," *Personnel Psychology,* 8 (1955), pp. 219-234.

_____, "Profile of the Mechanical Engineer II: Interests," *Personnel Psychology*, 8 (1955), pp. 315-333.

_____, "Profile of the Mechanical Engineer III: Personality," *Personnel Psychology*, 8 (1955), pp. 469-490.

Hunt, Chester L., "Female Occupational Roles and Urban Sex Ratios in the U.S., Japan and Philippines," *Social Forces*, 43 (3), 1965, pp. 407-417.

Ivey, Allen and Stanley S. Robin, "Role Theory, Role Conflict and Counseling: A Conceptual Framework," *Journal of Counseling Psychology*, 13 (1), 1966.

Komarovsky, Mirra, "Cultural Contradictions and Sex Roles," *American Journal of Sociology*, 52 (1946), pp. 148-189.

_____, "Functional Analysis of Sex Roles," *American Sociological Review*, 15 (1950), pp. 508-516.

Maslow, A. H., "A Theory of Human Motivation," *Psychological Review*, 50 (1943), pp. 370-396.

Masuka, Edna C., Jitsuichi Matsuoka, and Nozumu Kawamura, "Role Conflicts in the Family," *Social Forces*, 41 (1962), p. 5.

O'Neil, Paul, "U.S. Change of Mind," *Life*, 44 (9), March 3, 1958, pp. 91-100.

Parsons, Talcott, "Age and Sex in the Social Structure of the United States," *American Sociological Review*, 7 (1947), pp. 608-612.

Price, George R., "Arguing the Case for Being Panicky," *Life*, 43 (20), November 11, 1957, pp. 125-132.

Robin, Stanley S., *A Comparison of Male-Female Roles in Engineering*, unpublished dissertation, Purdue University, 1962.

Rose, Arnold M., "The Adequacy of Women's Expectations for Adult Roles," *Social Forces*, 30 (1951), pp. 69-77.

Rossi, Alice S., "Equality Between the Sexes: An Immodest Proposal," *Daedalus*, 93 (2), 1964a, pp. 607-652.

_____, *Why So Few Women Become Engineers, Doctors and Scientists*, unpublished paper given for Symposium on American Women in Science and Engineering, Massachusetts Institute of Technology, Cambridge, Massachusetts, October, 1964b.

Science, 156 (3772), 1967, p. 227, *Demand for Engineers and Technicians, 1966*, Engineers Joint Council.

Seward, Georgina, "Cultural Conflict and the Feminine Role," *Journal of Social Psychology*, 22 (1945), pp. 177-194.

Smith, Robert J., Charles E. Ramsey, and Gelia Gastillo, "Parental Authority and Job Choice: Sex Differences in Three Cultures," *American Journal of Sociology*, 49 (1963), pp. 143-150.

Strong, E. K., Jr., *Vocational Interests of Men and Women*, Stanford University Press, Stanford, California, 1945.

Termin, Lewis M. and Catherine C. Miles, *Sex and Personality*, McGraw Hill, 1936.

Time, 70 (21), November 18, 1957, pp. 20-25.

Time, 70 (23), December 3, 1957, pp. 13-14.

Torpy, W. G., "A More Significant Role for Women Engineers," *American Association of University Women Journal,* 57 (1964), pp. 59-71.

Vincent, Melvin J. and Jackson Mayers, *New Foundations in Industrial Sociology,* D. Van Nostrand, Princeton, 1959, pp. 149-159.

Wallace, Robert, "First Hard Facts on All Russian Sciences," *Life,* 43 (25), December 16, 1957, pp. 109-122.

Wallin, Paul, "Cultural Contradictions and Sex Roles: A Repeat Study," *American Sociological Review,* 15 (1950), pp. 288-293.

Wilensky, Harold, "Mass Society and Mass Culture," *American Sociological Review,* 29 (1964), pp. 173-197.

Zopoleon, Marguerite, "Women in the Professions," *Journal of Social Issues,* 6 (1950), pp. 13-24.

thirty

The University of Michigan:
Graduate Limbo for Women

DAVID BOROFF

A D. H. Lawrence scholar at the University of Michigan mused about how that writer, so passionately absorbed in the role of woman, would react to women graduate students. "I think Lawrence would see a certain smallness and dispiritedness about them," he said. "Yet many of these women students are attracted to Lawrence. I think it's partly their desire to be genuine women since they [women graduate students] are outside the pale. In _The Rainbow,_ Lawrence deals with a high school teacher and the exhaustion that comes from controlling kids. I guess he would feel the same about graduate students."

People talk this way about the woman graduate student. The stereotype is grim and forbidding. In her manless state, the legend goes, she prowls the alley-ways of academia out of sheer desperation. She is alleged to be formidably plain, a girl who does little to improve her natural disadvantages. Most cruel of all is the charge that she is aggressively intelligent, maimed by a fatal confusion about what should be her authentic feminine role.

"They're just out of it," a flip woman undergraduate said dismissively. "They don't have any pizazz; they're kind of unloved and unhappy. And eh, how they dress! Full cotton skirts and sturdy brown oxfords with ripple soles!"

Why is there such an incredible disparity between the official portrait of the American coed — all winsome bust and rump and lively chatter — and that of the woman graduate student whose crabbed lineaments are reminiscent of nothing so much as the Museum of Modern Art's haunting show of neurotica titled "New Images of Man?" The coed and the woman graduate student are so little separated by time, why is it they are so far apart in spirit? Graduate study is becoming popular these days, and women, though laggards, are flocking to graduate schools all over the country. (The figures for 1957-1958 show that roughly 198,000 men and 80,000 women were enrolled as resident, degree-hunting graduate students — an all-time high.)

Why do women go to graduate school? What sort of lives do they lead there? Are they academic stalwarts, or, as some assert, displaced persons lost in dusty library stacks?

I took these questions with me on a visit to the graduate school at the University of Michigan — one of the great centers for advanced study in this country. Located in Ann Arbor, forty miles from Detroit, the University of Michigan dominates the town. It *is* the town. In fact, it has spilled out of the narrow confines of the community and has a new North Campus — largely devoted to scientific research — just outside of Ann Arbor. The statistics of the university are awesome. The land, buildings, and equipment are capitalized at over $205 million. The school comprises 19,946 acres of very expensive real estate, 141 major buildings, and accommodates 24,000 students. The campus is a crowded one, with buildings reflecting the hundred-year growth of the university. There are grimy old Victorian piles with the legend "Chemistry" or "Classics" over the entrance, quaint mementos of the days when a little building could house an entire department. And there are gleaming new structures, all glass and red brick, which have sprung up in profusion during the current educational push. The university is not distinguished for the beauty of its campus — it is far too congested for that. But it turns out an impressive product; in recent decades, *Who's Who in America* has listed more graduates of the University of Michigan than of any other college — and that includes Yale and Harvard.

The country over, graduate schools size each other up remorselessly; even obscure little undergraduate colleges are kept busy grading the giants. Although there is no official ranking of graduate schools, there is a kind of crystallized quasi-official gossip about which schools, and which departments are up and which are down. (Undergraduates, in fact, learn about where to go for graduate study from their professors whose eyes are cocked on the national scene. Each academic area or discipline has national, even international boundaries, and what happens at Berkeley or Harvard or Michigan is of intense interest everywhere.) According to a recent poll of heads of graduate departments in leading universities, the University of Michigan's Horace H. Rackham School of Graduate Studies ranks fifth nationally, surpassed only by the graduate schools at Harvard, California (Berkeley), Columbia, and Yale. Following Michigan, according to the poll, are such distinguished graduate schools as those at Chicago, Princeton, Wisconsin, Cornell, Illinois, Pennsylvania, Minnesota, Stanford, UCLA, Indiana, Johns Hopkins, Northwestern, Ohio State, NYU, and Washington, in that order. The unwary are reminded that these are approximate ratings and have no relevance to particular departments, which may be rated higher or lower than a school's over-all ranking would suggest. Michigan's graduate departments seem to hover around the level of the school's rating — a meritorious fifth. There are exceptions: Michigan runs second only to Harvard in psychology, third in philosophy, while its chemistry and economics departments rank fairly low among the academic behemoths.

The University of Michigan, in short, has a lead role in that efflorescence of higher education which is a feature of our time. It has its share of academic luminaries (anthropologist Leslie A. White, for example, well known for his cultural theory of evolution, and man of science George E. Uhlenbeck, codiscoverer of the "electron spin"). And it attracts first-rate graduate students. They come from all over the country, and from dozens of foreign lands as well, turning Ann Arbor into kind of a small, tree-shaded New York — impersonal, feverish, full of busy and pre-occupied people. In a week at the university, only one student I passed said "Hello." There is little Midwestern bonhomie.

There are over five thousand graduate students at Michigan, of whom about 1,500 were women. There are, in addition, about 236 women among the roughly 2,700 students engaged in graduate-professional studies such as dentistry and medicine. During my visit, I made the rounds with women graduate students. I attended classes in which they are students (notebooks open, pens nervously busy), and where they teach (they merely switch from flats to heels). I surveyed their surprisingly decorous drinking places (beer only), looked in at their apartments (as neat and austere as monkish cells), and talked endlessly with them.

First, we should dismiss the nasty canard about their looks. If they are less than glamorous collectively, they are a cross-section of the young women of America, ranging from the breathtaking — a small minority — to the plain. What they have in common is an indifference to dress. Never were so many skirts and blouses slopped into service.

Why do they come? The stereotype of the unloved and lonely has only slender truth. At Michigan about 40 per cent of the women graduate students are married. Most elected to go on with their education for correct and wholesome motives. Single or married, they find that the B.A., except for elementary or secondary school teaching, is preparation all too often for only routine jobs. Professional requirements are scaled up these days, and increasingly graduate training, even the Ph.D., is essential for *interesting* work.

There are those for whom academic values have always been paramount. An anthropology student, with a blazing interest in American Indians, recalled, "My mother tells me that when I was born, I didn't let out a birth cry but a war whoop." Proudly this student showed me two photographs of herself — one as a pig-tailed five-year-old brandishing a toy tomahawk, and another as a graduate student, wearing authentic Indian costume acquired on a field trip.

Usually, the women who make it into graduate school were strong students all through college, and somewhere in their history there was a fructifying relationship with a professor, who helped them gradually to incorporate the values of academic life: the sheer pleasure of learning, the heady joys of discussion, the athletic exhilaration of tracking down a research problem.

There are those, of course, who merely drift into graduate work. "If a girl graduates from college and isn't engaged, what should she do?" a pretty girl asked. "She can go to New York for a career, but I like academic life, so this is what I did."

An M.A. candidate in mathematics, who had majored in education, said she simply didn't feel ready to teach. Her year at Michigan was a buffer between college and the cloistered elementary school classroom — a kind of final sowing of academic wild oats.

Scholastic joys can be intense. Women graduate students at Michigan never worked harder, they say, never had a more grinding sense of how little they knew and of how much they have yet to learn. I watched a classics student hover with exquisite pleasure over a photograph of a Roman tombstone. She was attempting to restore the inscription — part of her work for a course in epigraphy. For another course, one in papyrology, she had just deciphered an original second-century papyrus from Egypt. (It turned out to be a prosaic receipt for wheat given to a landowner by a farmer as rent for his farm.)

Most graduate students find considerable nervous excitement in the search for, and discovery of the academic father, a distinguished professor who initiates the young person into the Sacred Mysteries of the Discipline. But at best, graduate study is a tough grind. Even professors comfortably ensconced in cushy academic posts rarely get sentimental about the grubby days of their apprenticeship. "The system beats you down," a male historian commented. Some graduate students tell you that academic life in a graduate school is less fun intellectually than undergraduate days. What they are complaining about more than anything else is the changeover from the role of cultural consumer — an agreeable role — to that of cultural producer. Not all Ph.D. candidates have an affinity for research (for instance, about half do none to speak of once the degree is safely in hand).

In graduate study there are massive, omnipresent pressures. First, there are the courses (thirty credits for the M.A., sixty for the Ph.D.) At the University of Michigan a grade under C does not count as graduate credit, and the required average is a robust B. Looming menacingly are foreign language exams and prelims, which are comprehensive exams frankly designed to liquidate the academically infirm. And after these fierce bouts there is the herculean struggle of the dissertation.

Each university has its own *modus operandi*. At some schools one merely registers for classes, attendance is optional, but Judgment Day overtakes the self-indulgent at the prelims or orals, and students pay then for every delicious Monday morning they slept late and missed class. Elsewhere, the courses are demanding, while the prelims and dissertation are almost a formality. At some places, students are looked after solicitously and shoved through the rat race by faculty sponsors; at others, they are desolately on their own — academic orphans, unloved and unwanted until they are close to the Ph.D. and show real promise. But graduate schools have one thing in common: one way or another, they are all rough.

Unlike the B.A., which is now almost as common as a driver's license, the Ph.D. — or even its poor, despised cousin, the Ed.D. — cannot be claimed as a democratic right. Candidates sweat and strain after the doctorate for five, ten, and even fifteen years — dazed inmates of a book-lined limbo — and the mortality rate is high. Almost any sophisticated cocktail party in a large city is likely these days to have a few aborted Ph.D.'s, many of whom, by the way, go on to distinguished nonacademic careers.

Often it is the dissertation that sends the scholars scuttling off into business. The squeeze is merciless. On the one hand, students are expected to work meticulously on their dissertations, to follow truth wherever it leads. On the other hand, they had better snap to it, for there is a rigid timetable for academic achievement. At Michigan, the doctorate must be attained within seven years, or there are penalties like taking courses and exams over — a demoralizing business!

After the massive effort of the dissertation, there is the wan ceremony of depositing three copies of the manuscript in the graduate school office. A 600-word abstract is prepared for *Dissertation Abstracts*. Then, in a symbolically revealing act, the dissertation is reduced to microfilm. And that is more or less the end of it, unless the brand-new Ph.D. starts to send it out to university presses for possible publication.

Graduate students lead a curiously straitened life, physically and intellectually. "You're isolated in little cells," a graduate student at Michigan said. "There are lots of buildings I've never been in and never shall. Occasionally, very occasionally, I'm aware that I'm on a college campus."

"You could die here," a girl said, "and the only way they would know is when the cadaver began to stink."

Another graduate student was acrimonious about graduate study as an *obstacle* to liberal education. "For people who just want to learn," she said, "I don't know if it's any good. You have to sort of sneak learning in between all those required books. There really ought to be institutions for intellectual people who don't plan to become professors." (A recent publication, *The Graduate School and the Decline of Liberal Education*, by Earl J. McGrath, makes much the same proposal; McGrath comes out boldly for reconstituting graduate schools as centers of liberal arts instead of specialized academic shops.)

The girls are prone to talk of their unheroic martyrdom

with infinite relish. In an affluent society, they are a stubborn pocket of poverty, a slum in the nouveau riche suburb of academia. The financial take for professors in good universities is handsome, but for the female graduate student, life is skimpy. Chaucer's clerk of Oxford, with his lean horse and threadbare garb, has as his spiritual descendent the female academic. The men do nicely these days, thank you, between their grants and their spouses. (As a current gag has it, the graduate student lives by the sweat of his *Frau.*) But women keep alive the old tautology — the poor student. There are, to be sure, hundreds of teaching fellowships and grants; but men do better in this department than women, and even these rarely exceed $2,000 a year. The unmarried girls, therefore, are in a very low income group. Luxury items that enhance morale are usually excised — perfume, good cosmetics, decent clothes. The woman graduate student becomes that most sexless of creatures: an academic drone, indifferently dressed.

Worst of all, she often cannot make up her mind about the future. If she is merely an M.A. candidate, the internal pressures are comparatively mild. The end is in sight. But the Ph.D. seems like an interminable grind, a vast expense of spirit. *And then what?* The truth is that many women are academically motivated but professionally confused. Men rush headlong through the degree if they can muster the psychic and intellectual resources. But women tend to delay — and there is objective evidence of this. A recent study at Harvard and Radcliffe, revealed that while 26 per cent of the men took from four to ten years to complete their Ph.D. — an excessive period — the percentage of dawdlers among Radcliffe women was even higher: 44 per cent. And the women delay for what seems to be a good reason. If they are single, getting the degree means an end to the interregnum between college and marriage: It means facing up to the next, even more terrifying, phase of their life. What next?

Next is likely to be a small, obscure college somewhere in the hinterland, for the juicy academic plums usually go to male Ph.D.'s. Ever more terrible, the next step may be that final entombment in a small *women's* college — no fate more harrowing than that. So the female graduate student bogs down in her dissertation. What's the rush?

As a result, the bitterness, the anxieties, the nervous fretting about is-it-worth-it are as real as the academic ardors. The girls love academic life, and they hate it. They hang on gamely in a giddy cycle of elation and depression.

"It's common to call up a friend here and say, 'What's new?' " a Michigan graduate student explains. "And someone will answer, 'Marian's cracking up today.' "

"We sometimes feel it's a kind of doom," a history student said dolefully, and then recited a bleak catalogue of the evils of graduate study: "Always having to prove yourself, not being able to read the novel you want to read, the tensions of prelims, being grown up and yet being told what to do, not being able to travel — you just get fed up with this sordid life."

Nor is there relief when they get home. A young woman from Milwaukee remarked, "You don't feel like an eccentric until you go home. In my city there's a fine German word they use for us — *überstudiert* (overstudied)."

A pretty Brooklyn College graduate reported that her classmates back in Flatbush describe her half-admiringly, half-scornfully as "idealistic." They add complacently, "We just went after that diamond ring and got it."

Small towns are even worse. A girl from a hamlet in back-country Missouri runs the gauntlet of three questions every vacation: Are you still in school? When are you getting married? When are you coming back to Missouri to live?

Certainly, there is little in the social life of graduate school that would make an impressive tale to throw up to probing friends back home. On the face of things, graduate school is an unmarried girl's dream country — virtually a male harem. There are almost four men in the Michigan graduate school for every woman. But the resounding if extravagant lament about graduate men is: "They're either married — or impossible!"

The melancholy reality is that a girl can be a stunner and yet get lost socially: there are departments with a scarcity of marriageable men. The school of social work, for example, is heavy in women; classics has lots of priests. And there is little mobility. Unlike undergraduates who roam at will — meeting people of many kinds and in many fields through "activities" and their sororities and fraternities — graduate students do not often cross departmental lines. Girls date the men in the department. And the further they go in a field, the harder they find it to establish rapport with someone outside it. (I'll have to marry in the profession," a philosophy student said. "Engineers bore me.")

Generally, there is little split between work and play. There is a good deal of relaxing during the day in departmental hangouts. Philosophy people, for example, foregather in the Commons Room, where they habitually have their lunch (a sandwich prepared at home, coffee from the hot plate). Other departments use snack-bars scattered through the buildings. (There are, of course, well-appointed dining rooms in the two student unions, but graduate students eat there only on state occasions.) At ten or eleven in the evening, after a long session of solitary labor, the hardier graduate students meet for a beer or a cup of coffee.

The social pattern is informal — sometimes bleakly so. (Nothing is so oppressive as mandatory informality.) There is no place to go — only student beer joints. Detroit is near enough but few graduate students have cars. And if they do (usually decrepit relics), it seems a senseless frivolity to go barreling around night clubs after a hard day of somber academic work. (One couple, appalled by the invincible squalor of their lives, got dressed one evening in all their finery and walked grandly to The Michigan, the local movie house.)

The evenings, in graduate school, are likely to be merely extensions of the days: academic discussion ("A cat is never a cat, it's always a symbol," an English major complained), gossip, love, if luck is there. Sometimes graduate students go to the Pretzel Bell, famed U. of Michigan drinking place, and wistfully look on at the standard ritual. (When a student reaches twenty-one, the legal beer-drinking age in Michigan, a huge bell peals in celebration, while the boy or girl stands triumphantly on a table downing schooner after schooner of beer handed up by jubilant friends.) But the graduate students are really out of it, estranged from these innocent pleasures as they are from the banks of the Huron River or the leafy bowers of Nichal's Arboretum, where, in the spring, undergraduates go to make love. That whole delightful if censurable side of American higher education in the college as playground for adolescents is firmly sealed off from graduate students. They live in an ambiance of undergraduate fun, but they may not reach out for it. Theirs is a new-found and chafing academic dignity.

"We're mostly friends," a girl said of the men in her life. It sounds Jamesian, I know, but that's the way it is." However, relationships grow in depth, and, according to many girls, have "more substance than the fluffy undergraduate stuff." To be sure, dating the boy in the next seat has its asperities. "It's just too bad if he gets a B, and you get an A minus," a girl said. "But we don't want the weaklings anyway."

Another graduate student sketched a hideous portrait of the "hungry female": around thirty, with a Ph.D. or close to it, and no husband. She throws parties to which she invites young men in the hope they will come alone. (She hates and fears the pretty young things who turn up on these occasions.) The hapless hostess, according to this informant, almost invariably "ends up on the floor quite tight, snuggled up to one of these young men." Only slightly less disagreeable are the parties given by groups of such women relentlessly "trying to find someone" — a pursuit which effectively excludes fun.

Among the most abrasive features of this graduate-school life, women say, are the rebuffs they must endure from the masculine world. Given their own self-doubts, they find these assaults that come from smug masculine purlieus particularly punishing.

It may be disguised antifeminism, or it may issue from a realistic appraisal of their performance, but the conviction exists that women graduate students are not really in earnest and are less likely than ever to do distinguished work. "When it comes to night assignments on a research project," a psychology professor said peevishly, "they'll ditch me if they have a date."

Some professors feel cheated of the possibility of academic immortality when they have too many female students. The chance to transmit a body of ideas — canonization through disciples — is lessened by women, whose academic career is likely to be ephemeral.

A psychology professor, now an administrator, spoke of the antifeminist bias of his colleagues with startling candor: "I was struck by the geeing and hawing of the liberals in the department when they were faced with lots of good women applicants. The argument advanced was that we had limited resources and were faced with a dire need for teachers. And we had to consider the length of service candidates might offer. Some good women lost out as a result." He wishes society — and women — were more flexible. He would like to see part-time teaching jobs made available to married women, and some sort of retraining period arranged for female Ph.D.'s who absent themselves from the profession while their children are young.

One of Michigan's departmental chairmen thinks women ought to complete their Ph.D.'s not at twenty-eight but at forty-eight, when their child-raising chores are done, so that there would be no lag between their studies and their teaching. (Because she interrupts her career, the woman Ph.D. often teaches with a set of skills and a body of information ten or fifteen years out of date.)

Even praise of women graduate students is tinged with a certain condescension. "They have the right virtues," a dean observed. "They're neat and punctual." An English professor said: "They're more patient and systematic than men. They're likely to do very well with bibliographic problems [just about the dreariest area of literary scholarship]. Relatively few have shown marked originality. Very often they make good teachers of Freshman Composition because they're patient and diligent." (In most English departments, teaching Freshman Composition is viewed as a humiliating serfdom.)

These views, though not untypical, are nonsense. Given the right incitements, women could achieve as much in scholarship as men. They fail precisely in the measure they are made to fail. This is an example of what sociologists call "the self-fulfilling prophecy." Made woozy by propaganda, the girls in time see themselves as a minority group immured in a cheerless academic ghetto. (A shapely ex-model from Miami Beach, now implausibly installed as a teaching fellow in philosophy, tells with wry amusement that her dates ask her quite seriously, "Do you know how to dance?" The young men in that other, and now distant phase of her life, used to ask very different questions.)

A young woman, a Ph.D. in psychology, who often counsels graduate students sees them as a "special, self-selected group." She doubts that many girls go to graduate school merely because they have nothing better to do. "I wonder," she speculated aloud, "whether they would drop graduate work if they got married. They tend to idealize marriage. They overlook the tedium. If it comes down to it, I'm not sure they would give up their studies."

Certainly, there *are* many girls who have tried to make the best of both marriage and graduate study. For the most part, they manage very well. A political science major, whose sultry, theatrically sexy appearance belies a discerning mind, had a problem. She was getting married in June, and her fiance — also a graduate student — was scheduled to go into the army. However, graduate work had just opened up for her in that first, exhilarating breakthrough when academic life begins to seem more like an adventure than a disease. She had received a grant for the next year, and was slated to some exciting research connected with the behavior of voters in the Presidential election. She finally decided to return to Michigan in the fall (instead of following her husband from army pillar to post), even though it meant forging ahead of him. Meanwhile, she has drafted the blueprint of their future career. Their academic areas overlap — she is in political science, while he is in sociology. "He's very creative and imaginative," she said, "but I am logical and systematic. He'll have the ideas, and I'll operationalize them."

A girl pushing steadily toward a Ph.D. in physics is married to a physicist with a mere B.A. "But he's brilliant," she expostulated. "Each of us has his own area of superiority." And physics dovetails neatly with the requirements of domestic life, for she is in the theoretical branch — "pencil and paper stuff."

Another young woman is studying art history; her husband is a Ph.D. candidate in anthropology. At exam time, there is a double strand of distress. "We beat the kids at the same time," she said. Money is tight, and so two nights a week she works as a waitress in a local espresso shop. "Sometimes at the end of a day," she mused, "I think of the things I've done and I'm entertained by the incongruities — looking after the kids, attending class, and then dressing as exotically as possible for the espresso place."

The life of the woman graduate student is full of such incongruities and ambivalences. "The further a young woman goes in the academic world," Michigan's dean of women observes, "the further she removes herself from the normal complex of wife and mother. This is the unseen drama."

But a few things are clear. Women are academically gifted, even if they are constantly being tripped up or tripping themselves up. As matters now stand, their resources are mostly going to waste — either rusting unused or dissipated in suburban boondoggling. And when they persist in using their skills, they are confronted with the unnerving question, "But don't you want to fulfill yourself as a woman?"

The problem will no doubt answer itself soon. The demand for college teachers during the next decade will be so intense that the barriers will topple. As more women join the ranks of graduate students, it will no longer seem a heresy when they devote themselves to the intellectual life. The gates of the ghetto will swing open.

thirty-one

Career Expectations of
Negro Women Graduates

JOSEPH H. FICHTER

Sociological generalizations about Negro women have become commonplace and seem to derive mainly from historical reconstructions and from data on the masses of relatively poorly educated Negroes. There are generalizations about the cultural subsystem in which the female family role is dominant and in which the woman's occupational status is emphasized. Even among the Negro college graduates . . . a Negro woman is more likely to be the head of a household than is a white. More Negro women than men get the bachelor's degree, while the opposite is true for whites.[1] Like whites, however, a higher proportion of Negro men than women take postgraduate and professional training.

Throughout this report,[2] we are making racial comparisons between Negro and white college graduates and also regional comparisons between southern and nonsouthern graduates. In many instances, the sexual comparison also seems significant, since women have different expectations of a life career, they enter different fields of graduate study, they get better grades in high school and college, and their social attitudes are often different from those of men. In contrast to other college graduates responding to this survey, there is a much higher proportion of women than of men from the predominantly Negro colleges. This is almost exactly the same as the distribution of Negro women (62 percent) and men (38 percent) age 25 to 34 who are college graduates, as reported in the U.S. Census of 1960 for

From MONTHLY LABOR REVIEW, Vol. 90, No. 11 (1967), pp. 36-42. Reprinted by permission.

the southern region. The median years of schooling among Negroes in this age bracket are 9.8 years for women and 8.7 years for men.

Although the differences between the men and women among the graduates of predominantly Negro colleges tend to reflect also the status of the male American Negro, we are [here] mainly focusing on the female Negro graduate, as compared with the female southern white graduate and the "other" female nonsouthern graduate. Negro women who have finished college constitute only 5.2 percent of southern Negro women age 25 to 34 and can hardly be called a representative reflection of American Negro womanhood.

What kind of person, then, is the typical American Negro woman? If she is defined by the modal category, that is, by the largest number having similar characteristics, she would be a southern woman who did not go to college. Consequently, our study gives no information about her. We might consider the Negro woman who is a college graduate an "ideal type" in the sense that her educational achievement is remarkably higher than the average for her race.

Marriage Plans

Since marriage and child rearing are significant aspects of the female role and must be considered in relation to both occupational careers and postgraduate study, it seems important to look at the racial contrasts in this regard.[3] At the point of college commencement, the female graduate of a predominantly Negro college is somewhat more likely than the southern white woman or other American female graduates to be single and have no definite marriage plans. Yet those who are married are significantly less likely than the two other categories to be childless. The average number of children is 1.20 for female graduates of predominantly Negro colleges, 0.71 for southern whites, and 0.86 for other female graduates.

We asked our respondents to tell us in what ways they thought marriage would affect their plans both for postgraduate study and for their future occupational career. The most important finding here is that the woman graduate of a predominantly Negro college is about one-half as likely as the southern white woman and the other female graduates to say that marriage would make it difficult for her ever to go to graduate or professional school.

This is a clear indication of a fact for which we have further overwhelming evidence: That the educated Negro woman either does not want, cannot afford, or is culturally conditioned against the notion of marriage and family to the exclusion of other roles. Only 4 percent of the Negro women estimate that marriage would make it difficult for them to have any kind of a career at all. Furthermore, only one-tenth of the Negro women, as compared with about one-fourth of the other female graduates, say that marriage "would enable me to be the homemaker I really want to be instead of working."

What these female graduates prefer and what they really expect in the relationship between family and occupation are seen in Table 1. Practically no one of either race wants a career to the exclusion of marriage, and hardly any of these women

Table 1 / Female Graduates' First Preference for Life Career, and Realistic Expectation, by Race[1]

Life career	First preference			Realistic expectation		
	PNI	PSW	All other wo- men	PNI	PSW	All other wo- men
	Per- cent	Per- cent	Per- cent	Per- cent	Per- cent	Per- cent
Housewife only	8	14	8	5	8	5
Work only before children are born	16	19	20	11	27	24
Work after children are grown	13	31	35	8	22	34
Occasional work throughout	11	10	12	19	18	17
Combine family and career	40	23	20	37	16	12
Combine family and steady job	7	1	1	3	3	2
Marriage and career; no children	3	1	2	3	1	1
No marriage; career only	2	1	2	3	5	5
Number	1,928	1,877	10,031	1,762	1,864	9,835
No response	337	202	937	503	215	1,133

[1] See text footnote 2.

would prefer to have a marriage which excludes children completely. The significant differences in preference occur in the two responses on combining marriage and child rearing with either a professional career or steady employment. Here we find that almost one-half (47 percent) of the Negro women, compared with one-fourth (24 percent) of the southern white women and even fewer (21 percent) of the others, would really prefer to combine the familiar role with the occupational role. The response that is most popular with the white women of both categories is to be employed before children are born and only after children are grown.

When we compare [the data in this table], we see an increase in the minority who expect to have a career without marriage and a decrease in the minority who expect to be housewives only, without outside employment. The large differences again in the work orientation of the Negro college woman, who is more than twice as likely (40 percent) as the southern white woman (19 percent) and the others (14 percent) to say that she realistically expects to combine marriage, child rearing, and gainful employment. In contrast to their preference to work only until children are born, the percentage of Negro women decreases and that of white women increases in their expectation of realizing this end. But there is both a large racial and regional difference in the women expecting to work only before having children and then only after the children are grown.

It is clearly demonstrated that the great majority of American women college graduates of both races expect, and would prefer, to have some gainful employment after marriage, at least at certain times and under certain conditions. . . . The general impression is that these female respondents tend to state a preference for that which they realistically expect to experience, and this seems to be the case more with the Negro women than with the white women. Statistics of the Department of Labor reveal that a larger proportion of Negro married women than of white married women are actually in the labor force. Our data reveal that three-fifths (59 percent) of the Negro female graduates expect to work occasionally or regularly throughout their married life, and the same proportion (58 percent) say that this is what they want. Only about one-third of the white female graduates have this expectation and preference.

The Man's Point of View

Table 2 provides the opportunity for an interesting three-way comparison, showing what these women think their husband or fiance prefers for them, compared with what we have seen

Table 2 / Men's Preference for Wife's Role, as Seen by Male and Female Graduates, by Race[1]

Life career	Female graduates' belief of role their own husband or fiance prefers for them			Male graduates' preference of life career for their own wife[2]		
	PNI	PSW	All other women	PNI	PSW	All other men
	Per-cent	Per-cent	Per-cent	Per-cent	Per-cent	Per-cent
Housewife only	22	31	18	24	34	25
Work only before children are born	25	26	34	26	35	34
Work after children are grown	10	19	29	10	16	25
Occasional work throughout	14	9	8	12	6	6
Combine family and career	22	12	9	22	7	8
Combine family and steady job	6	2	1	5	1	1
Marriage and career; no children	1	1	1	1	1	1
Number	1,365	1,206	5,646	1,032	2,840	11,607
No response	900	873	5,322	246	363	1,345

[1] See text footnote 2.
[2] Questionnaire item was answered regardless of marital status.

they prefer for themselves, then showing what the male respondents to this survey would prefer for their wives. In the first place, all three categories of female graduates believe that their men prefer less employment for them than they prefer for themselves. But there is still a significant racial difference, in that many more of the Negro women (42 percent) than of the southern whites (23 percent) or of the other female graduates (18 percent) say that their men prefer them to work regularly or occasionally throughout their married life.

The fact is that the male graduates have an even greater preference that their wives have a minimum of outside employment than the female graduates realize. In this matter, the racial contrast also persists, with a much larger proportion of male Negroes (39 percent) than of male southern whites (14 percent) or other male graduates (15 percent) saying they prefer that their wives work regularly or occasionally throughout their married lives. Furthermore, there is a remarkable similarity between the distribution of responses of Negro men and women in this regard. These data show that the attitudes on marriage, child rearing, and wife's occasional role are most dissimilar between male and female whites and most similar between male and female Negroes. Here again, the male Negro's preferences may well be much closer to the realities of the female Negro's role than are those of the male white to those of the female white.

These cross-sex comparisons of opinions provide one of the clearest indications of the familial and occupational status of Negro women. We have seen in other items of the survey that the fundamental differences among these college graduates are racial. Southern white college graduates are much more similar to other American whites than they are to Negroes. . . . Women are more likely to think that men want their wives to be housewives only, while men are less likely to think women themselves want to be housewives only.

Chances of Finding a Husband

Prodding further into the racial differences in opinion and attitude, we asked a series of questions about women in relation to dating, marriage, and children. The educational discrepancy between the races seems to be reflected in the fact that more Negroes than whites agree with the statement that a single woman who gets an advanced degree will have a hard time finding a husband. Negro women have more years of schooling than Negro men, and more of them go to college and obtain the bachelor's degree. At this point, fewer of them (21 percent) are married than are the female southern white graduates (27 percent), but more of them are married than are the other female graduates (17 percent), so that the fact of having had a college education does not seem a significant deterrent to marriage.

The statement in question, however, concerns advanced or postgraduate degrees. More Negroes of both sexes than whites feel that the advanced degree does lessen a woman's chances of finding a husband. Since marriage is a principal goal of practically all these women, of both races, we would suspect that they would want to avoid experiences — like going to graduate school — that might make it difficult to get married. The reverse of this question, whether marriage hinders graduate study, we have already discussed. On that matter, we found a significant racial difference in opinion: The Negro woman was much more confident than the white woman that she could go on, even though married, to postgraduate study and professional training. We also saw that the female Negro college graduate was much less interested than the white college graduate in being "merely" a homemaker.

We can draw from these various data the generalization that men want their women to stay home and out of the labor market more than the women want to do so. This seems to be reflected in the fact that more men than women, of both races and both regions, want the woman to avoid an occupation that would be difficult to combine with child rearing. The racial difference, however, seems more significant than the sex difference in this regard. A larger proportion of Negro men (66 percent) and women (60 percent) than of whites of either sex want to be sure that they have children. They say this in spite of the fact that the Negro woman is more likely than the white woman to combine child rearing and gainful employment.

Working Mothers

These responses revolve around an important sociological hypothesis that is pertinent to our investigation. When women of ability, talent, and interest get into gainful employment, do they have smaller families? If so, do they want this? Compared with white women, a larger percentage of Negro women of all levels of educational background, both single and married, have been gainfully employed. In spite of Negro women's greater participation in the labor force, the Negro birth rate has been higher than the white. We have seen here that the married female Negro graduate is more likely than the female white graduate to have children and to have a larger family.

It appears, then, that neither the amount of schooling nor the extent of employment has the negative effect on childbearing for

Negro women that it has for white women. Putting this in another way, we may suggest that trained and talented Negro women, even though married, are more likely than their white counterparts to make a contribution to society through the professions and occupations. Considering that the neglect of male Negro talent and the lower status and role of the Negro husband are a continuing problem, we have no way of estimating if the pattern of female Negro employment will change so that it resembles that of female white employment.

Certain other questions we asked about women and careers elicited responses with an expected difference in opinion by sex, the largest of which concerns the statement that a woman should not seek advanced degrees unless she expects to work in her field almost all her adult life. Men favor this statement more than women, but the difference in opinion between white men and women is much greater than that between Negro men and women. The statement that a man can make long-range plans for his life but a woman has to take things as they come gets agreement from one-fifth of the men of both races. In the light of other findings, it seems appropriate that a smaller percentage of Negro women than of white women agree with this statement, the implication being that Negro women have been less likely than white women simply to "take things as they come."

"Feminine" Careers

Whether or not the majority of our respondents see certain career fields and occupations as "masculine" and others as "feminine," the fact is that there is a sharp sex differential both in the major areas of college study these graduates choose and in the occupational fields they enter. For example, women are more likely to go into social work and into grade school and high school teaching, while men are more likely to go into business fields, the physical sciences, medicine, and law. What is of immediate interest at this point, however, is the racial comparison of female graduates in these areas. [There is] a remarkable similarity in the general fields of major academic preparation among female respondents. The Negro women are somewhat more likely to go in for teacher preparation than are the white women, but the difference is not as great as we might have expected. On the other hand, white women seem to have majored more in the humanities in college than did the Negro women.

When we look at Table 3, which reports the career and occupational fields these college graduates are actually entering, we find an even greater similarity across racial lines. For example, the same proportion (55 percent) of Negro and southern white female graduates, and only a slightly higher proportion (59 percent) of the other female graduates, will be in the teaching field.[4] Since job opportunities in the business world are notoriously poor for Negroes, we would expect a smaller proportion of Negro women than of white women to take up a career in business. This is not the case, however; we find that most of these Negro women have prepared themselves for secretarial services or for other clerical and office work. They do not expect to be in jobs like advertising, accounting, sales, marketing, and finance. There is a racial difference in the proportions of women entering the field of social work; Negro women find more job opportunities there than exist in certain other occupational areas. They are twice as likely as the white women to become social workers.

Table 3 / Career Fields Entered by Female Graduates, by Race[1]

Career field	PNI	PSW	All other women
	Percent	Percent	Percent
Social work	10	5	4
Physical sciences	3	4	3
Health and medical fields	8	7	9
Biological sciences	4	2	2
Business fields	6	6	5
Elementary and secondary education	23	24	28
Other educational fields	32	31	31
Social sciences	6	5	6
Humanities	8	15	11
Number	2,051	1,873	10,127
No response	214	206	841

[1] See text footnote 2.

There are certain activities that cut across a number of specific jobs, and we asked our respondents which of these they thought would be the most important activity in their own occupation. Again we find a remarkable similarity across racial lines: two-thirds of all the female graduates say they would be more occupied with teaching than anything else. The next most frequently mentioned activity is professional service to patients or clients, and the statistical difference in response between the races is insignificant. In the most general terms, what we are finding here is that, regardless of the occupational field they enter, women around the country and across racial lines tend to have the same distribution of work activities on the job itself.

The Most Interesting Jobs

In an attempt to learn more about the interests and abilities of these graduating women, we presented a series of eight occupations or professions and asked them to check off their agreement with a list of statements about each occupation. One of these statements was: "This sort of work would be very interesting." Regardless of sex differences, which are of course very significant in occupational preferences, we found some similarities among the women across racial lines. For example, teaching at the college and high school level was "very interesting" to more than two-thirds of the respondents in all categories.

The smallest proportion of both Negro and white female graduates consider engineering an interesting occupation. This is also an occupation for which women college graduates did not prepare and which they do not intend to enter. On the other hand, although these women did not emphasize the sciences in their college majors, and although relatively few of them are going to make a career in scientific fields, one-half of them think they would find the work of a research scientist very interesting. Here again, there is close agreement across racial lines.

If we look at these comparative responses as a kind of "job rating," we find that the female graduates agree on the rank order of the most interesting jobs: College professor, high school teacher, and research scientist. We find they also agree that the least interesting job is that of engineer. A considerable racial difference shows up in the rating of three jobs: Proportionately more Negro women than white women find the business executive's job interesting, but proportionately more white women than Negro women find a lawyer's or physician's work more interesting. There are fewer female Negro lawyers and physicians in the United States than female white, even allowing for the racial and educational composition of the female population. Even fewer Negro women than white women become business executives, so that if we correlated job potential with the interest one has in a job, we would expect even fewer Negro women than whites to find the job of business executive interesting.

Yes I Can

One of the more significant findings of our study, however, is ... that the female Negro with a college education has a great deal more confidence in her own abilities than does the female white graduate. Using the same list of eight selected occupations, we asked them to weigh the statement: "I don't have the ability to do this kind of work." On every one of these occupations the proportions of Negro women who say that they do not have the necessary ability are lower than those of white women. Practically all these graduates of both races consider high school teaching within their competence, but only 8 percent of the Negro women, compared with 22 percent of the female nonsouthern graduates, feel that they lack the ability to be a college professor.

The smallest proportions of female Negro graduates had said they would find the work of physicians and engineers interesting. The largest proportions of women of both races admit they lack the ability to do the work required by these two professions. The ranking of these eight occupations, from that requiring the least ability to that requiring the most, is the same for both races, except that the white women think the research scientist's job takes more ability than the lawyer's while the Negro women do not.

We asked further whether the respondent felt she had an unsuitable personality for work in each of the eight occupations. In most instances, the female white graduates are about twice as likely as the Negroes to think they do not have a suitable personality for the occupation. Three-tenths of the white women say this about the jobs of physician and musician, two-fifths about the research scientist, engineer, and lawyer, and one-half about the business executive. The ranking of the eight occupations, from those for which most have a suitable personality to those for which least have it, is roughly the same across racial lines. The large difference is still in the percentage of Negro women compared with the whites who feel they have a suitable personality for these jobs. . . .

In making comparisons with southern and nonsouthern female whites, we found that there were always smaller proportions of female Negroes who were ready to admit that they did not have the ability to do the work. This seems to imply great self-confidence in their own abilities in spite of the demonstrably poorer schooling of Negroes and in spite of a lack of broad experience in many of these occupations. We had thought this phenomenon would carry over into the class distinctions within the Negro group, but it does not. In other words, the women from the least educated families are not significantly less willing than the others to admit they do not have ability for these various occupations. In the occupations of law, music, and medicine, more of the lower class women than of the others admit a lack of ability to do the job.

An even more telling difference in occupational self-appraisal between Negro and white female college graduates had shown up in the question whether they felt they had an unsuitable personality for the selected occupations. In every instance, a significantly higher proportion of female whites than of Negroes admitted they had an unsuitable personality for the work. In every instance except law, a higher proportion of Negro women from the better educated families admit they do not have a suitable personality for the particular occupation. The percentage differences are not large (except for the job of high school teacher), but they tend to support the hypothesis that lower class Negroes — even those with a college education — express an unusual amount of confidence in themselves.

Aspirations and Expectations

In recapitulating these findings, we note that the sex differences in Negro respondents coincide with differences between white and Negro college graduates in general. One of the most significant differences between the Negro and white female college graduates lies in their life expectations concerning the combination of marriage, family, and occupation. Negro women have a stronger work orientation than white women. Even though they want marriage and a family, they are not as ready as white women to say it would interfere either with postgraduate study or with their occupational career.

These findings provide a broad insight into the peculiar position of the educated Negro woman in the American society. Probably because of various occupational pressures, Negro women are more educated than Negro men and are more likely than white women to be gainfully employed. From the point of view of both family and career, they come to prefer that which they have learned to expect, that is, to combine marriage, child rearing, and gainful employment. Having children seems to be a more important value for Negroes of both sexes than it is for whites.

Like the female white graduates, the Negro women expect that their main occupational function will be teaching, but a higher proportion of female Negroes than of whites will go into social work. They are as interested as the whites in teaching at both the college and the high school level, but they are much less likely than the whites to say they do not have the talent, or that they have an unsuitable personality, for any of the occupations about which we asked them. Although their ultimate aspirations for graduate degrees are much higher than those of whites, the year after commencement will find fewer female Negroes than whites either working for a postgraduate degree or taking nondegree courses. A smaller proportion of female Negroes than of whites had a definite job commitment after graduation.

The class comparisons among women within the Negro group do not show much difference in orientation toward marriage and career. It appears that the employment preferences and expectations of Negro women emerge from traditional patterns which are not greatly altered by class position. The significant class difference lies in the type of occupational field these Negro women enter. Teaching at the elementary and secondary levels is more attractive to the women from the least educated families, and it will absorb proportionately more of them than of the upper class women. The latter tend to have somewhat less confidence in the suitability of their personality for the various job requirements.

NOTES

This article is taken from Father Joseph H. Fichter's report on his study of 1964 graduates of predominately Negro colleges, prepared for the National Institutes of Health and with the joint sponsorship of the

U. S. Department of Labor and the National Science Foundation. Sub-heads have been added, and tabular material combined to make up the tables printed in this excerpt.

1. Hurley H. Doddy, "The Progress of the Negro in Higher Education," *Journal of Negro Education,* Fall 1963, pp. 485-492, calls this one of the "deviations" in Negro higher education, and finds that the sex disproportion is increasing. Between 1950 and 1960, the relative increase in college enrollment was larger for Negro women (6.3 percent) than for Negro men (1.8 percent).

2. Three distinct student populations were utilized in the study. The principal population, that of the Negro, is derived from a study of 50 predominantly Negro institutions (PNI), nearly all of them in the South. The second and third populations, "Predominantly Southern White" (PSW) and "All Other," are derived from the National Opinion Research Center's companion study of the national 1964 senior class, but excludes respondents from the two predominantly Negro schools which fell into the sample of that study. A discussion of the sample design and execution is presented in the appendix to Fr. Fichter's report, *Graduates of Predominantly Negro Colleges — Class of 1964* (U.S. Department of Health, Education, and Welfare, Public Health Service, 1967), PHS Publication 1571.

3. It is an interesting fact that a larger proportion of white women (66.7 percent) than of Negro women (60.5 percent) are married. Perhaps it is even more interesting that a larger proportion of Negro women (21.3 percent) than of white women (16 percent) had *not* given birth to a child, according to the 1960 U.S. census.

4. Doddy's complaint that the large proportion of Negroes going into the "traditionally safe" field of teaching is a "deviation" of Negro higher education seems to overlook the fact that this is a female phenomenon and that white women also go in disproportionately for teaching. See Doddy, op. cit. If there is a disproportionate entrance of Negro women into some field compared with that of white women, the field seems to be social work rather than teaching.

thirty-two

Factors Associated with the Participation of Women Doctorates in the Labor Force

HELEN S. ASTIN

Participation of women in the labor force has been increasing steadily. While women in 1920 constituted 20 per cent of the working force, today they make up more than 32 per cent of it. The percentage of married women among those who work has also shown a steady increase. In 1962, 60 per cent of the women in the labor force were married, as compared to only 23 per cent in 1920 (*American Women,* 1963). Since the rate of participation by women in the labor force is in direct proportion to their educational level (1960 Census), motivation and ability would appear to be at least equal in importance to economic necessity in the women's decision to work. However, the fact that the proportion of unemployed women in the labor force decreases with increasing education suggests that the educated woman's participation in the labor force is determined not only by her own needs and career interests, but also by the availability of job opportunities.

In spite of these trends of increasing participation of women in the labor force, women workers in general are found primarily in clerical occupations and household work. Among the professions, they are found principally in nursing and elementary school teaching. The representation of women in fields requiring advanced training is unimpressive, particularly in scientific fields. Less than one per cent of engineers are women (Rossi, 1965) and less than three per cent of the doctorates in physical sciences are awarded to women (Harmon & Soldz, 1963).

From PERSONNEL AND GUIDANCE JOURNAL, Vol. 46, No. 3 (1967), 240-246. Reprinted by permission.

The present study was designed to investigate the employment status and career commitment of women doctorates. The primary interest was to identify the personal and environmental factors that are associated with the labor force participation of women doctorates.

The population for this study included all women who received earned doctorates in the years 1957 and 1958. These two years were selected because they provided a post-doctoral period of seven to eight years for the study of factors influencing career development.

Sample and Procedures

The doctorate files of the National Academy of Sciences-Office of Scientific Personnel list a total of 1,979 women as doctorate recipients in 1957 and 1958. Their current addresses were obtained through university alumni files and professional directories. These subjects were mailed a 41-item structured questionnaire dealing with work experience, marital status, awards and achievements, publications, domestic and community activities, problems encountered in career development, and other personal data.

Excluding the ineligible cases (i.e., 21 deaths, 6 males, and graduate students without doctorates who were misplaced in the doctorate files of the Academy, and 21 cases who never received questionnaires due to a clerical error) the 1,547 completed questionnaires constitute 80.1 per cent of the sample. However, further excluding 69 undelivered questionnaires, we obtained an 83.1 per cent rate of return of completed questionnaires. A short version of the questionnaire was mailed on a postcard to those who had not responded and was completed by an additional 106 women (5.7 per cent).

In all, 209 subjects (10.7 per cent) did not respond to either questionnaire or postcard inquiries. From these cases a random subsample of 69 subjects, who had United States addresses, was selected for a telephone follow-up. Thirty-six per cent of this subsample was reached and information secured on their employment and marital status. The rate of unemployment among these 69 subjects was higher than among respondents (18.2 and 8.6 per cent, respectively). Marital status was identical in both groups. Further, the non-respondent group contained a greater proportion of foreign-born women and foreign residents than the sample of respondents. Lost or undelivered mail sent overseas may have accounted for part of the non-response rate in this group.

Twenty-eight measures of the subject's personal and family background characteristics were selected as pre-doctoral or "control" variables: year of birth, citizenship status at the time of the doctorate, grades, and scores on intelligence tests[1] obtained in high school; parents' level of education, occupation, and birthplace; major field of doctorate study (scored as six separate dichotomies: Physical Sciences, Biological Sciences, Social Sciences, Psychology, Arts and Humanities, and Education), whether or not stipend support was received during graduate training, and the quality of the doctorate institution;[2] and four additional dichotomies: whether or not she was a nun, whether or not she was married at the time of the doctorate, whether or not she is currently married, and whether or not she is currently retired. Although the latter two variables are not "pre-doctoral," it was considered necessary to control their contribution to the criterion before the effects of some of the environmental variables could be assessed.

Nineteen variables describing the subject's environmental experiences since obtaining the doctorate were selected as additional predictors of full-time employment. They were: residence in the United States (versus foreign residence); size of current home town; number of children (including four dichotomous variables indicating whether the subject has any pre-school, elementary school, high school, or college age (and older children); husband's educational attainment (college graduate, Ph.D. degree, or professional degree); husband's occupation based on a five-group classification (Natural Science, Social Science, Medicine, Business and Law, College or University Professor); and husband's annual gross income. Also included were three variables describing the subject's post-doctoral career experiences; whether she has been a post-doctorate fellow; whether her first job was in an academic setting; and whether or not her first job after receiving the doctorate was full-time. The criterion or dependent variable for the analysis was whether or not the subject was employed full-time at the present time (that is, as of December, 1965).

The statistical method used to analyze the effects of the different variables on employment status was step-wise multiple regression.[3] Performing the regression analysis in step-wise fashion permits one to control the effects of each independent variable in a pre-determined sequence. Thus, the investigator seeks to enter into regression first those variables that could bias the relationship between the dependent variable and subsequent independent variables. For instance, in this study we were interested in examining the effects of certain environmental experiences, such as having children, upon the criterion of full-time employment. However, since having children is obviously dependent on certain antecedent conditions (e.g., being married), it is important first to control the effects of these antecedent variables. Otherwise, the apparent "effect" of the environmental variable (having children) on employment status may simply be an artifact of our failure to control the relevant antecedent variables (e.g., being married). One can never be sure that all relevant biasing variables have been adequately controlled, but it is important to control as many as possible.

Variables were entered into the regression generally in chronological sequence. Thus, the last "control" variables entered into the equation were the dichotomies, "retired" and "currently married." Following the regression of the criterion on all control variables, the environmental variables were entered into the equation in a "free" step-wise fashion until no additional variable could significantly reduce the residual sum of squares in the criterion.

Results and Discussion

Ninety-one per cent of the women doctorates of 1957 and 1958 are in the labor force. Of these, 81 per cent work full-time (see Table 1).

The employment status of these women varies with their marital status, i.e., married women do not participate in the labor force as fully as the single women. The greatest loss of talent among married women doctorates occurs in the Natural Sciences.[4] Eighteen per cent of those in the Natural Sciences are not in the labor force, as compared to 10 per cent in the Humanities and 11 per cent in Education. The Humanities and Education have also the highest rate of full-time employment among the married doctorate holders.

Whether or not a woman who has earned a doctorate in one of the specialized fields participates fully in the labor force is

Table 1 / Present Employment Status of Women Doctorates (N=1,547)

	Full Time			Part Time			Not in Labor Force		
	Total %	Married %	Single %	Total %	Married %	Single %	Total %	Married %	Single %
Psychology	70.9	65.5	89.7	19.3	23.4	5.1	9.7	11.1	5.1
Social Sciences	80.7	70.9	89.7	12.1	17.2	7.3	7.2	11.8	2.9
Natural Sciences	75.7	61.7	96.7	12.3	20.3	0.0	12.0	18.1	3.3
Humanities	83.6	73.2	93.3	8.9	16.6	1.7	7.4	10.2	5.0
Education	90.7	83.2	97.1	3.0	5.4	1.4	6.3	11.4	1.4
Total	81.3	70.2	94.8	10.1	16.8	2.1	8.6	13.0	3.0

dependent on a number of personal and environmental factors. We have already observed that those women doctorates who marry are less likely to be fully employed seven to eight years after receiving their degree than are those who remain single. Women of different field specialties also demonstrate different degrees of participation in the labor force. The regression analyses enabled us to investigate more fully the effect of these factors upon full-time employment.

Table 2 presents the effects of selected personal characteristics and predoctoral experiences on full-time employment of women doctorates. It appears that the older the woman doctorate is, the more likely she is to be employed on a full-time basis. This relationship appears to be due to the fact that the younger woman doctorate is more likely to have children at home (see Table 3).

Although the field of the doctorate, by itself, is related to full-time employment status, the fields did not contribute to the final prediction of full-time employment after other personal variables and pre-doctoral experiences entered the equation. Psychology as a field carried a negative predictive weight until marital status entered the equation. It would appear, then, that psychologists tend not to work on a full-time basis as often as do other women doctorates, primarily because a greater proportion of psychologists get married.

When "being married at the time of the doctorate" was forced

Table 2 / Full-Time Employment of Women Doctorates as a
Function of Personal Characteristics and
Pre-Doctoral Experience (N=1,547)

Variables	Multiple r	Partial r with Residual Criterion	p Associated with Reduction in Sum of Squares
Birth date	.200	−.200	p < .001
Intelligence score	.226	−.108	p < .01
Mother worked while subject was growing up[a]	.260	+.028	p > .05
Early marriage	.288	−.124	p < .001
Is currently married	.410	−.300	p < .001
Retired	.454	−.213	p < .001
Assistantship as a graduate stipend source[a]	.457	+.038	p > .05

[a] Although the variables "mother worked" and "Assistantship" did not appear to reduce the sum of squares significantly when they entered the equation, their predictive value increased significantly at the last solution of the analysis after all the personal and pre-doctoral experience variables had entered.

Table 3 / Full-Time Employment of Women Doctorates as a Function
of Post-Doctoral Experiences and Present Environmental
Predictor Variables after Control of Personal
and Pre-Doctoral Experience Variables (N=1,547)

Predictor Variables	Multiple r	Partial r of Entering Variable with Residual Criterion	p Associated with Reduction of Sum of Squares
Pre-school children (some vs. none)	.511	−.254	p < .001
First job after the doctorate was full-time	.551	+.238	p < .001
Husband's income	.562	−.135	p < .001
Post-doctorate fellowship	.570	+.078	p < .01
Husband's occupation in Law or Business Administration	.572	+.059	p < .05
College or older age children (some vs. none)	.574	+.058	p < .05
Husband's occupation in the Social Sciences	.576	+.055	p < .05
Size of town	.578	+.057	p < .05
Number of children	.582	−.051	p < .05

into the equation, it carried a negative predictive value for full-time employment. However, when "currently married" entered the equation, the weight for "early marriage"[5] became *positive*. It appears that among women doctorates who get married, those who marry after the doctorate are less likely to be working full-time seven to eight years later than are those who married during or before graduate school.

If the subject's mother worked while she was growing up, she is more likely to be employed full-time today. Although it is difficult to account for such a finding without much more evidence, it is interesting to speculate about possible psychodynamic processes that may be operating in the career development of the woman doctorate. For example, the woman whose mother was employed while she was growing up may be better able to

Table 4 / Full-Time Employment of Women Doctorates as a Function of Personal and Environmental Variables (N=1,547)

Variables	Beta Coefficients	p Associated with Reduction in Sum of Squares
Is currently married	−.266	p < .001
Pre-school children (some vs. none)	−.255	p < .001
Retired	−.192	p < .001
First job after the doctorate was full-time	+.187	p < .001
Husband's income	−.135	p < .01
Early marriage	+.128	p < .01
Has been married	−.084	p < .01
Elementary school children	−.076	p < .01
Post doctorate fellowship	+.062	p < .01
Husband's occupation in Law or Business Administration	+.058	p < .01
Mother worked when subject was growing up	+.058	p < .01
College or older age children	+.057	p < .05
Assistantship as graduate stipend source	+.057	p < .05
Husband's occupation in the Social Sciences	+.050	p < .05
Size of town	+.046	p < .05
Intelligence score	−.041	p < .05

resolve the conflicting feminine roles of housewife and career woman. That is, seeing her own mother handling the double role while she was a child better enables her to accept and manage these dual roles herself today.

Women who hold assistantships during their graduate years are more likely to be working full-time today than are women who did not have assistantships. The fact that a person is able to complete graduate studies while working as a graduate assistant may be indicative of certain energy levels or motivational characteristics that enable this same person to work full-time in addition to being married.

The results of the analyses of the environmental variables that followed the control of the 28 personal variables are shown in Table 3. Nine of the 19 environmental variables contributed significantly to the prediction of full-time employment.

If a woman doctorate has pre-school children she is much less likely to be employed on a full-time basis at the present time than the woman doctorate who has no pre-school children. Also, her husband's present income is a factor in her decision to work full-time. More specifically, it seems that if a woman doctorate is married to a man with an adequate income, she is less likely to work, or if she does indeed work, she is more likely to hold a part-time job.

The woman doctorate's career behavior immediately after receiving the Ph.D. is positively related to her present career commitment, independent of pre-school children or other environmental factors. That is, if she participated fully in the labor force during her first job after earning the doctorate, or if she has been a post-doctorate fellow, she is a likely candidate for full-time employment seven or eight years later. Although women who are able to go through graduate training and receive a doctorate degree are — almost by definition — highly motivated, this finding indicates that there are still important variations in their degree of career commitment. These variations, which can be observed almost as soon as graduate training is completed, tend to persist for some years.

The husband's occupation is also related to the employment status of the woman doctorate, independent of his education and income. Women who marry lawyers, businessmen, or social scientists are much more likely to be working than are women who marry men in other fields. It may be that women with a greater commitment to their careers tend to marry men

in these fields, or that men in these occupations are more accepting and encouraging of their wife's work and career activities. Another possible explanation is based on the finding that
the size of the town in which the woman doctorate lives is positively related to her participation in the labor force. Perhaps
those women who marry men employed in law, business, or
social science are more likely to live in larger towns.

Although the variables employed in this study yielded a multiple correlation of .58 with the criterion of full-time employment, the differential contribution of the personal and environmental variables are of interest and contribute further to our
understanding of the factors that affect a woman doctorate's
decision to participate fully in the labor force today.

It is evident that if she is married and has children of pre-
school age she is not as likely to work full-time. In terms of the
magnitude of their relationships to full-time employment, these
two variables are by far the most important of the environmental factors that contribute to non-participation in the labor
force among women doctorates. Nevertheless, there are still
other characteristics and environmental conditions that contribute independently to the decision to work on a full-time
basis. These include several behaviors exhibited earlier, such
as early full-time participation in the labor force, being a post-
doctoral fellow, and being a graduate assistant while in training, all of which indicate strong motivation, high energy level,
and full commitment to a career.

Certain characteristics of the woman doctorate's husband
also appear to be important factors in her decision to work full-
time. In addition, early marriage and growing up in a home
where the mother works appear to be indicative of less conflict
with problems of combining a career with family responsibilities.

The fact that intelligence test score contributes negatively to
the prediction of full-time employment is difficult to explain.
Perhaps the women in Psychology, who do not participate in
the labor force as fully as do women in other fields, also tend
to attain higher scores on measured intelligence. We have already seen that the psychologists tend to work on a part-time
basis rather than withdraw completely from the labor force
(see Table 1). It may be that if a woman doctorate is faced with
the decision of working part-time or not working at all, she may
choose the part-time job; but if such jobs are not readily avail-

able, she will be forced not to work at all. If our assumptions about women psychologists are correct, then the negative weight for the intelligence test score is a reflection of the fact that these women may be more likely to engage in part-time jobs. This line of reasoning was further supported when we examined the differential contribution of these variables in the prediction of the dichotomous criterion: employment full-time plus part-time versus no employment. In this analysis the intelligence score did not contribute significantly to the prediction, indicating that those doctorates who work part-time have slightly higher scores on measured intelligence than do those who work full-time.

The partial correlations reported in Table 5 demonstrate some of the relationships that exist between full-time employ-

Table 5 / Partial Correlations between the Criterion of Full-Time Employment and Certain Job Characteristics and Other Variables, after Control of Personal Variables and Environmental Variables (N=1,547)

Variables	Partial r
Attending professional meetings	+.25**
Hours per week spent on domestic activities	−.24**
Annual professional income	+.22**
Employing a housekeeper	+.18**
Membership in professional organizations	+.15**
Papers presented at professional meetings	+.11**
Health	+.09**
Employer: a higher education institution	−.09**
Employer: government	+.08**
Teaching position	−.08**
Husband's negative attitudes toward wife's working	−.08**
Administrative work	+.08**
Books published	+.07*
Honors received	+.07*
Articles published	+.07*
Amount of professional reading	+.07*
Experiences in salary discrimination	+.07*
Administrative position	+.06*
Research position	+.06*
Use of day care centers for pre-school children	−.06*
Employer discrimination regarding delegation of authority to women	+.06*

* $p < .05$
** $p < .01$

ment and other variables such as job characteristics, professional activities, etc., after control of the personal and environmental variables.

The woman doctorate who works full-time, compared to the woman doctorate who does not, tends to participate more frequently in professional meetings and to be an active member of a number of professional organizations. The employment of a full-time housekeeper enables her to spend less time in domestic activities, which undoubtedly allows her to be more efficient in her professional work. She appears to be more productive in scholarly endeavors, as measured by the number of articles and books published in her field of specialization. She also earns a good deal more income, but more often claims that her employer discriminates against professional women employees.

Finally, women doctorates who work full-time, compared to those who either do not work or work only part-time, are more likely to be engaged in research or administrative activities and to be employed by governmental agencies.

NOTES

1. The measured intelligence scores referred to in this study were the scores that these subjcts attained when they were in high school. The scores have been converted to AGCT equivalent scores, and have been normalized with a mean of 50 and a standard deviation of 10.

2. The subject's score on the quality of her doctoral institution was based on a six-point scale that was developed utilizing Cartter's data (1966). A score of one represents the highest overall institutional quality that resulted from averaging the scores that the different departments received. A score of six indicates that the school was not rated.

3. The step-wise multiple regression analysis computer program was a BIMD computer program with further elaborations and refinements added to it by R. J. Panos of the American Council on Education.

4. Natural Sciences include the Physical Sciences and the Biological Sciences; Social Sciences include all Social Sciences except Psychology. The Humanities include the English specialties and the Arts; Education includes all sub-specialties within Education; Psychology, all the sub-specialties within Psychology.

5. The variable "early marriage" indicates that the subject was married at the time of the doctorate.

REFERENCES

Cartter, A. M., *An Assessment of Quality in Graduate Education.* Washington, D.C.: American Council on Education, 1966.

Harmon, L. R. & Soldz, H., *Doctorate Production in United States Universities, 1920-1962,* Washington, D.C.: National Academy of Sciences-National Research Council, 1963.

1960 Census of Population, Educational Attainment. Washington, D.C.: U.S. Government Printing Office, 1963.

American Women. Report of the President's Commission on the Status of Women. Washington, D.C.: U.S. Government Printing Office, 1963.

Rossi, A. S., "Women in Science: Why so few?" *Science,* 1965, *148,* No. 3674.

thirty-three

An Analysis of the Factors Influencing Married Women's Actual or Planned Work Participation

Much has been written by both laymen and social scientists about a conflict of women's roles in American culture. It is here proposed that a more fruitful avenue of analysis is one that considers the factors which permit a satisfactory arrangement in relationship to a woman's performance in more than one role.

The purpose of this research was to attempt to discover the factors that are related to actual or planned participation of married women with children in the labor force. All hypotheses tested were within the framework of the study's orientation of a workable arrangement being established between performance in the labor force and performance as a housewife and mother.

Certain factors seemed to be either favorable or unfavorable, that is, seemed to either inhibit or encourage women to enter the occupational sphere. The following specific factors included in the study were mentioned by the respondents during the pretest:

1. Educational background of the wife
2. Specialized training received by the wife[1]
3. Attitudes of the husband toward the wife's actual or potential participation in the labor force
4. Husband's help with child care
5. Husband's help with household chores
6. Ages of the children
7. Wife's work experience before marriage
8. Wife's previous occupation

From AMERICAN SOCIOLOGICAL REVIEW, Vol. 26, No. 1 (1961), pp. 91-96. Reprinted by permission.

9. Availability of employment

[10. Debts of the family unit

/ 11. The family's planning to purchase big items

In addition other variables such as socio-economic status and the traditional or companionship[2] attitude the women had toward marriage were considered.

Hypotheses

The principal hypotheses examined were:

1. A woman will perform or plan to perform in both the traditional and career, or in the companionship and career roles, when her husband's attitude toward outside employment supports this decision.

2. The performance of married women with children in the labor force or the planning to perform in the labor force will occur when employment for which the woman is qualified is available.

3. The higher the socio-economic background of the family, the more likely the married woman with children is to "choose" to perform in the labor force.

4. A woman will perform or plan to perform the career role as well as the traditional (housewife and mother) role or companionship role when she has achieved a "high" educational level,[3] or has had "specialized" training.

5. The performance of married women with children in the labor force or the planning to perform in the labor force will occur when women have husbands who accept an obligation for helping with the care of children and with household chores.

6. The performance of married women with children in the labor force or the planning to perform in the labor force will occur if these women performed in an occupation before marriage that required "high" educational achievement or specialized training.

7. Married women with children will perform in the labor force or plan to participate in the labor force if they had continued to work after marriage.

8. Women with children will participate in the labor force or will plan to participate in the labor force when the family unit has debts.

9. Women with children will participate or plan to partici-

pate in the labor force when the family unit plans to purchase big items.

A description of the actual study is presented in the following discussion.

Description of the Sample

Two hundred married women with children, living in housing developments in a suburban town, Livingston, New Jersey, comprised the sample. Sampling of this kind was considered advantageous as:

1. Families with children concentrate in developments.

2. Using a lower priced development (W) and a development of middle-priced homes (C), (as compared to other areas in town), permitted a comparison of data in relationship to the economic factors.

3. The income distribution was high enough to permit the observation of factors other than financial need in relationship to participation in the occupational sphere.

As the study developed, it became apparent that both samples could be combined for analysis because of the small differences in relationship to all characteristics.

All the respondents, with the exception of one, were homeowners. They were white, and, 50.2 per cent were Protestant, 31.0 per cent were Catholic, 16.5 per cent Jewish and one half of one per cent Greek Orthodox. The median income of husbands was $7900 per year. The median age of the women was thirty-six years. 59.3 per cent of the working women and 62 per cent of the husbands were classified as professional, technical, and managerial.[4] One half of the respondents were either working or planning to work. Because of the income distribution of the particular sample utilized, it was possible to look at factors other than the financial that were related to the woman's participation in the labor force.

When comparing the selected sample with national statistics, it was found that the median income of the husbands of the respondents was much higher. Also, a higher proportion of both husbands and working wives were classified as professional, technical, and kindred workers, according to Census Bureau definitions of such occupational categories. It is also apparent that although the religious distribution came close to the reli-

gious distribution of the nation, there was a slightly higher proportion of Jewish and Catholic respondents. The proportion of
married women working approximated within five per cent the
figures given in the national statistics. The average age of the
working women in this sample was 38.4 years which is about
the same as the figure of 39 years given in the national statistics.

General Procedure

Each house in each of the developments was visited, and
those family units not meeting the standards set for sample selection were eliminated.[5]

Both an interview schedule consisting of 64 items and the
Motz Role Inventory[6] which contained items that classified the
women in either the traditional or companionship role, were
administered. Anonymity of responses was assured by the investigator.

The sample interviewed consisted of twenty-three women
who were employed full time, twenty-six who were employed
part time, sixty-two who were planning to work, and eighty-
nine who did not plan to enter the labor force. Thus, the variables were analyzed in relationship to these work status categories.

Findings

With the variables in mind, a series of tetrachoric correlations were undertaken with participation or planned participation in the labor force as the dependent variable. This method
was used as it facilitated a dichotomous analysis and is a direct
estimate of correlation.

Tetrachoric correlation coefficient were computed with the
cosine pi formula.

When comparing both working women and women planning
to enter the labor force with those women not planning to enter
the labor force, the factors affecting the women's participation
in the occupational sphere are: the positive attitude of the husband toward the wife's decision to participate in the labor
force, the wife's occupation before marriage being classified
as professional, technical or managerial, the wife's participation in the labor force after marriage, the high educational level
of the wife, and the woman having received specialized training. In addition, the husband's help with both household chores

and the care of children affected only the working woman's participation. Table 1 presents these factors, when comparing

Table 1 / Tetrachoric Coefficients of Correlation of Factors Related to Participation and Planned Participation in the Work Force as Compared to Not Planning to Work (Variables Grouped)

Variables	$r$tet. Working Category	$r$tet. Planning to Work Category
Husband's attitude		
Positive attitude of husband	.92	.88
Husband helps with chores	.55	.21
Husband helps with care of children	.41	.26
Career orientation		
Occupation before marriage being professional, technical or managerial	.72	.74
Worked after marriage	.60	.55
High educational level (B.S., B.A. or beyond)	.56	.47
Specialized training beyond high school	.43	.44
Husband's occupation being professional, technical or managerial	.16	.18
Others		
Children of school age	.27	—.14
Family debts	.17	.04
Planning the purchase of big items	.04	.08
Availability of work	.14	—.06

the categories of planned and actual work participation with the category of women not working.

The scores obtained for the responses to the Motz Role Inventory were also analyzed in relationship to the work status categories. The scores which are presented in Table 2 indicated that there was not only a relationship between working outside of the home and being classified in the companionship role, but also between the amount of time the woman was employed outside of the home, and the companionship role. Thus, observing the four work status categories in the following order: (1)

Table 2 / Distribution of Female Respondents in Motz Role
Inventory Classifications, by Work Status
Categories — Sample C

	Full Time N=12	Part Time N=12	Planning to Work N=33	Not Planning to Work N=45	Totals N=102
Traditional	25.0%	41.7%	69.7%	84.4%	69
Companionship	75.0	58.3	30.3	15.6	33

Distribution of Female Respondents in Motz Role Inventory
Classifications, by Work Status Categories — Sample W

	Full Time N=11	Part Time N=14	Planning to Work N=29	Not Planning to Work N=44	Totals N=98
Traditional	27.3%	57.2%	55.2%	86.3%	65
Companionship	72.7	42.8	44.8	13.7	33

Distribution of Female Respondents in Motz Role Inventory
Classifications, by Work Status Categories — Total Sample

	Full Time N=23	Part Time N=26	Planning to Work N=62	Not Planning to Work N=89	Totals N=200
Traditional	26.0%	50.0%	63.0%	85.4%	134
Companionship	74.0	50.0	37.0	14.6	66

women working full time, (2) women working part-time, (3)
women planning to work, and (4) those not planning to work,
there was a steady and marked decline of those women who
could be classified in a companionship role. These findings differ significantly from those reported by Motz.[7] Motz reported
that women who worked full time tended toward conventional
(traditional) conceptions as compared to those who were employed part time and tended toward companionship conceptions.

The correlation (^{r}tet) between the companionship attitude
and work participation was .71. Considering the relationship
between the husband's positive attitude and the wife working,
the correlation was .92, as shown in Table 1. The correlation

between the companionship attitude and the woman planning to work was .47. And the correlation between the husband's attitude and planning to work was .88. Thus, it is the husband's attitude which is the most important factor when considering companionship and traditional attitudes in relationship to actual or planned work participation by married women. Table 3 shows this distribution of husband's attitude toward outside employment.

It is interesting to note that a high percentage of the women in the labor force, especially those employed full time, were employed in occupations classified as professional, technical, or managerial. All the women employed described their occupations as pleasant or very pleasant, except for three respondents. These three respondents were the same respondents who stated that they were working for financial reasons. They were also performing in occupations which were not professional.

The findings of this study tend to confirm certain hypotheses which are presented in rank order according to the importance of the factor:

A woman will perform or plan to perform in both the traditional and career roles or the companionship and career roles:

1. When her husband's attitude toward her outside employment is positive.

2. When she performed in an occupation before marriage which required high educational achievement or specialized training.

3. When the woman continued to work after marriage.

4. When the woman has achieved a high professional level or has had specialized training.

5. When her husband accepts an obligation for child care and household chores.

6. When her children are of school age.

Differential availability of employment, the high socio-economic background of the family, the wife's work experience before marriage,[8] debts of the family unit, and plans to purchase big items, showed little or no relationship to planned or actual work participation.

In relationship to family debts and plans to purchase big items, the chain of causation and the sequence of events are important for consideration. Thus, it is suggested that debts and plans to purchase big items were effects, not causes, of partici-

Table 3 / Distribution of Husband's Attitude Toward Outside
Employment, by Work Status Categories — Sample C

	Part Time N=12	Full Time N=12	Planning to Work N=33	Not Planning to Work N=45	Totals N=102
Objects only to full time employment	75.0%	0.0%	48.5%	17.8%	33
Objects to both full and part time	0.0	8.3	3.0	71.1	34
No objections	25.0	91.7	48.5	8.9	34
Never discussed	0.0	0.0	0.0	2.2	1

Distribution of Husband's Attitude Toward Outside Employment,
by Work Status Categories — Sample W

	Part Time N=14	Full Time N=11	Planning to Work N=29	Not Planning to Work N=44	Totals N=98
Objects only to full time employment	69.3%	0.0%	44.9%	18.2%	30
Objects to both full and part time	7.1	9.1	13.8	70.5	37
No objections	28.6	90.9	41.3	11.3	31

Distribution of Husband's Attitude Toward Outside Employment,
by Work Status Categories — Total Sample

	Part Time N=26	Full Time N=23	Planning to Work N=62	Not Planning to Work N=89	Totals N=200
Objects only to full time employment	69.3%	0.0%	46.8%	17.9%	63
Objects to both full and part time	3.3	8.7	8.1	70.9	71
No objections	26.9	91.3	45.1	10.1	65
Never discussed	0.0	0.0	0.0	1.1	1

pation in the labor force. It is after the woman enters the occupational sphere that the family is able to pay debts and to purchase new items.

Some Theoretical Considerations

Robin Williams[9] stated that there are important pressures to preserve the traditional role of women, and that some social arrangements are necessary to insure that the necessary functions will be performed. He listed the following as such social arrangements: (1) extra family service, (2) low birth rates, (3) the nuclear family. In this study the husband's assistance with child care and household chores facilitated the wife's performance in the labor force.

Nelson Foote's[10] discussion of the change in marriage patterns and the role of women used the term "professionalization" to summarize the interrelationship of variables and trends which appeared most influential in redefining a woman's role in marriage. Some of the variables were: (1) the use and stabilization of real income, (2) freer access to higher education, (3) lowered number of hours of the work day and work week, (4) less time in conducting a household . . . receiving the husband's assistance, and (5) attitude change toward working women. The women comprising the sample in this research were members of family units that had an income which could be described as high when compared to the national statistics on family income. Also, in reference to the variables listed by Foote, a large proportion of these respondents had achieved a "high" educational level. And, while not a discriminating factor, employment for which these women were qualified was available.

Considering the factors of "lowered number of hours of the work day and work week," and "less time in conducting a household . . . receiving the husband's assistance," listed by Foote, the women who worked part time in this present study indicated that they experienced a minimum amount of difficulty as a result of entering the labor force, and the women planning to work received assistance from their husbands in household chores and child care.

Dr. Foote, in summarizing the interrelationship of variables which appeared most influential in redefining women's roles, also listed the broadening application of the career concept, and a self-conscious emphasis on basic or continuous personal development. It is interesting to note that many of the reasons given for employment or planned employment by the respondents in this study can be described as part of the process of "continuous personal development." When asked why they were working or planning to work outside the home, some of the reasons given by the respondents, as noted in Table 4, were:

Table 4 / Reasons Given for Present Employment Given by Respondents, by Work Status Categories

	Part Time N=26	Full Time N=23	Total N=49
Outside stimulation	23.2%	21.8%	11
Additional income	30.7	30.4	15
Job offered	11.5	0.0	3
Additional income and outside stimulation	7.7	21.8	7
Enjoy occupation	11.5	4.3	4
Husband disabled	0.0	4.3	1
Utilize education and training	15.4	17.4	8

(1) outside stimulation, (2) additional income, (3) job offered, (4) additional income and outside stimulation, (5) enjoyed work, and (6) to utilize education.

Both Foote and Kirkpatrick[11] stressed the role of upper-middle class women who become the leaders in adopting a new role. Foote also mentioned the changing attitude toward working women as influencing the new role. The women in this study perceived the community attitude on the part of their neighbors toward work participation as favorable if adequate provisions were made for the care of the children. Clearly, this is related to La Piere's[12] emphasis on the status group as an important key to social organization. Specifically, control is exercised by the group through interdependent action, especially in reference to the actor's need for prestige and esteem.

Summary

To summarize, career orientation[13] of the wife and the favorable attitude of the husband were the determining factors in influencing actual or planned participation. The discussions of familial roles on a more popular level have emphasized the change of the division of labor within the home in terms of the husband's assistance with chores. However, this analysis suggested the factor of the husband's help with child care especially as it affects the wife's participation in the labor force.

In addition, children being of school age was a variable which affected participation in the labor force. The children being of pre-school age was considered as a temporary inhibiting factor in relationship to those women who planned to work outside of the home, as seen in Table 5.

Table 5 / Distribution of Ages of Children of Female Respondents, by Work Status Categories

	Working N=49	Planning to Work N=62	Not Planning to Work N=89	Totals N=200
Under school age	49.1%	74.2%	66.3%	129
School age	50.1	25.8	33.7	71

Because of the selective nature of this sample, the generalizability of the analysis is limited. However, the analysis does suggest areas for additional research such as: (1) reasons other than financial which motivate a woman's participation in the labor force, (2) the changing attitude of the community toward working women and how this affects the attitude of the husband, (3) part time employment as facilitating performance in the dual role, and (4) the differential significance of the husband's assistance with household chores and child care in the family unit.

The analysis also illustrates that role and role expectations can be utilized as conceptual tools in empirical research. The roles of women are viewed in their manifold relationship to the social system.

NOTES

I gratefully acknowledge the considerable help and guidance of Dr. Nelson N. Foote.

1. "Specialized Training" refers to educational training beyond high school and other than college training, such as secretarial school, etc.

2. *Companionship role* is not limited to activities associated with

domesticity. These activities may take a variety of forms. An important aspect of the "companionship" patterns for women is the sharing of decisions and responsibilities associated with all phases of married life. The Motz Role Inventory utilized in this research classified the women in either the *traditional* or *companionship* role.

3. "High educational level" in this study refers to four years or more of college training.

4. This classification is a combination of two categories given by the United States Bureau of the Census in *Census of Population, Classified Index of Occupations and Industries,* Washington: Government Printing Office, 1950, pp. IX-X.

5. The homes eliminated for interviewing purposes were those inhabited by widows, widowers, divorced persons, families without children, unmarried individuals, and those where the youngest child was over eighteen years of age. Of the 248 homes visited in both developments, thirty did not meet the criteria set up for sample selection, eighteen refused to be interviewed, leaving a total sample of 200 married women with children.

6. The role inventory developed by Annabelle Motz not only classified the responses of the subjects, but also revealed the consistency of responses to the various roles. The role inventory also provided a reliability check on many of the items included in the interview schedule. For a complete description of the role inventory, see Annabelle Motz, "A Role Conception Inventory: A Tool for Research," *American Sociological Review,* 17 (August, 1952), pp. 465-471.

7. See A. Motz, "Conception of Marital Roles by Status Group," *Marriage and Family Living,* 12 (December, 1950), p. 136.

8. Work experience refers to whether the woman was employed in the labor force before she was married.

9. Robin Williams, Jr., *American Society,* New York: Alfred A. Knopf, 1952, p. 59.

10. Nelson Foote, "Change in American Marriage Patterns and the Role of Women," *Eugenics Quarterly,* 1 (December, 1954), pp. 254-260.

11. Clifford Kirkpatrick, *The Family,* New York: The Ronald Press Co., 1935, p. 137.

12. Richard T. La Piere, *A Theory of Social Control,* New York: McGraw-Hill Book Co., Inc., 1954.

13. Career orientation is a phrase which summarizes the interrelationship of such variables as: (1) wife's performance in an occupation before marriage, classified as professional, technical and managerial, (2) high educational achievement, (3) the specialized training of the wife, (4) work experience after marriage, and (5) the husband's professional or managerial status.

VI

Career Patterns and Marriage

College Women Seven Years After Graduation: Resurvey of Women Graduates, Class of 1957

Introduction

A longitudinal survey of women at important stages of their lifespan is one tool for gaining greater insight into their needs and interests under changing personal and economic circumstances. Conducted in the sixties, such a survey reflects growing interest in women's response to the new and challenging opportunities facing them and in the extent and variety of their participation in today's world. The urgency for obtaining factual knowledge is heightened by the marked rise over the past quarter century in the number and percentage of married women[1] who combine home responsibilities and paid employment.

In 1940 the number of married women workers was just over 4 million. By 1965 it had reached 14.7 million and was approaching the 18 million level estimated for 1970. Over this 25-year period the percentage of wives who work jumped from 15 to 35 percent. A further increase is anticipated in the future.

Questions arise about women's growing desire to utilize their abilities and education in the workplace as well as in the home. When and why are more and more married women deciding they want a paid job? What obstacles or problems interfere with their efforts or desires to work? Are they able to obtain the jobs they want and are qualified for? How firm is the attachment of college-educated women to the labor force, and how significant is their availability as a skilled labor reserve? Are adult women seriously interested in obtaining more education or training?

Bulletin 292, United States Department of Labor, Women's Bureau, Washington, D.C., 1966.

467

How important are volunteer activities in the lives of married women?

Answers to some of these questions are available from a group of women college graduates surveyed in 1964. They are largely the same group of June 1957 graduates who participated in a survey made in the winter of 1957-58.[2] That survey was conducted jointly by the Women's Bureau and the National Vocational Guidance Association. It involved participation of a scientifically selected sample of 153 women's colleges and co-educational universities and of almost 6,000 women graduates.

Primary focus of the earlier survey was on the relationship between undergraduate education and subsequent employment of recent women graduates. Attention was given particularly to the influence of the graduates' marital status, the extent of their advanced education and additional job training, and their attitudes toward future employment. The widespread interest stimulated by the survey findings indicated a need for additional information covering later periods of a woman's life.

The audience for such information is considerable. Both the population and the work force of college women are expanding in the United States. By 1965 more than 4 million women aged 18 years and over in the population had obtained a college degree. About 2.5 million, or 58 percent of the total, had a paid job. When women 18 to 64 years of age were counted in the 1940 census, there were only slightly more than three-quarters of a million college women workers — about 52 percent of the 1.5 million college woman population.

Traditionally, college women have engaged in paid employment to a greater extent than women with lesser amounts of formal education. The increase in the labor force participation of college women during the 25-year period has not been as sharp as that of all women 18 years of age and over. For the latter group the participation rate rose from 30 percent in 1940 to 40 percent in 1965.

In the 1964 resurvey, questionnaires were mailed to 5,846 graduates after their names and addresses had been updated from the records of alumnae associations or college and university offices. The sample group represented almost 88,000 women who were graduated in June 1957 from colleges and universities granting bachelor's degrees and classified as coeducational or women's colleges. The second survey centered on the interrelated influences on college women of their under-graduate education, postgraduate specializations, family and community activities, and work careers.

The women college graduates resurveyed in 1964 were at an age when most were married and mothers of young children. Many had left the work force because of household and child care responsibilities. The high rate of survey response in 1964 is a testimonial to the graduates' interest in the survey purpose and findings. Fully 84 percent of the graduates to whom questionnaires were mailed participated in the survey. On the basis of telephone calls made to a few nonrespondents, there is reason to believe that many who failed to return the questionnaire never received it.

Graduates expressed appreciation to the Women's Bureau for making the survey and inviting their participation, as the following comments indicate:

"It is gratifying to know that an attempt is being made to solve the problems of women in our society."

"This inquiry stimulated me to think about my future responsibilities to myself and others — something often obscured in day-to-day living."

"I appreciate the opportunity to be part of this study, since I read your former report and am always interested in this type of information."

Even more important than the complimentary references to the survey are the comments which confirm that its substance touched on vital aspects of the graduates' lives. Illustrative remarks were:

"Dissatisfaction with previous work experience I blame largely on lack of proper guidance and counseling. My plans for future employment and education hinge just now on obtaining counseling assistance. I would be interested in the results of this survey and in knowing whether my problem is unusual."

"It is a source of great frustration to be unable to use one's education or training during this period."

"It is important for a woman to belong to the mainstream of life just as her husband and children do, so that she does not try to see the world and live only through their experiences."

"The most difficult problem for me has been working out a pattern of family living that permitted definitions of mother-child and wife-husband roles acceptable to everyone and compatible with professional commitments."

"Despite obviously negative financial reward, I suddenly felt desire to use dormant, stagnating mental abilities, and to have an identification other than as someone's wife or mother. Rebuilding my professional self has been rewarding to my family and myself. I have more self-respect and the 'other me' is fascinating to my children."

"I think we make a great mistake in American culture by promoting the idea that the man's job should be superior to that of his wife. We promote guilt in women regarding success and allow waste in regard to what women can contribute to our country. We associate job and contribution with the roles of masculinity and femininity in an unrealistic way. Why deny that a woman can be very feminine while using all her potential as a woman, whether working and/or keeping house?"

Survey Highlights

Rising interest of college women in paid employment and continuing education was confirmed by this second followup survey of June 1957 women college graduates. When questioned 7 years after graduation, more than one-fourth of the survey women said they wanted a career and almost one-half had some other type of future work plan. Less than one-fifth indicated no interest in paid employment.

In response to inquiries about their educational plans, almost three-fourths of the graduates recorded affirmative interest in further training or education — principally university courses. Slightly over half of those desiring more education were motivated by job-connected reasons; the remainder by cultural or personal interests.

A majority of the June 1957 women graduates (51 percent) were part of the work force 7 years after graduation. Thirty-nine percent had full time jobs, 10 percent had part time jobs, and 2 percent were seeking work. The size of the work group had declined considerably since the earlier survey in the winter of 1957-58, when it constituted 85 percent of the recent graduates. Most of the survey women employed in 1964 had worked continuously since graduation, but a few had stopped work for a while — primarily to attend school or have children. At the time of the survey, over three-fifths of the graduates were married women with young children, and slightly over one-fourth of them were employed.

The college women surveyed had averaged 5.5 years of employment since graduation. A measure of their attachment to the labor force is revealed in the fact that as many as 43 percent of the total group had worked at least 6 years during the 7-year period. It is significant also that 32 percent had had only one employer since graduation.

The graduates' jobs, in terms of broad occupational groups, were generally similar in the two survey periods. Teachers (60 percent) continued to be predominant in the 1964 occupational distribution, followed by nurses (6 percent) and secretaries (4 percent). But 89 percent of the employed graduates held professional jobs in 1964, as compared with just 83 percent in 1957-58. The proportion performing clerical work dropped to 8 percent in 1964 from 14 percent in 1957-58.

Salaries of the June 1957 women graduates were on the average almost 60 percent higher in 1964 than in 1957-58. Average annual salary[3] of the graduates was $5,947 in 1964. An average of $3,739 had been reported by the members of the class employed in 1957-58.

Almost half the June 1957 women graduates had taken at least one graduate course since leaving college, but only 15 percent had earned a master's degree by 1964 and less than 1 percent had their doctorate. The largest group of graduates with an advanced degree had specialized in education. However, the undergraduate fields in which the highest proportions of graduates obtained an advanced degree were sociology or social work, foreign languages, history, chemistry and other physical sciences, music, psychology, and social sciences.

Characteristics of Graduates

At the time of the second survey, the June 1957 women graduates were at an age when their childrearing and other family responsibilities were near the maximum. As many as 70 percent were 28 or 29 years of age, and 91 percent were between 27 and 34 years.

By 1964, 81 percent of the survey graduates were married — in marked contrast to the 38 percent who were married when surveyed 6 months after graduation. An additional 4 percent of the graduates were widowed, separated, or divorced. Over three-fourths of the graduates who had ever been married had children; virtually all in this group had children of preschool age. As few as 3 percent of the graduates had only older children (6 years and over). The percentage of graduates who had never married dropped to 16 percent in 1964 from 60 percent in 1957-58.

The predominant family groups for whom the graduates and/ or their husbands had major financial responsibility in 1964 consisted of two adults and two children (28 percent), two adults and one child (20 percent), two adults and three children or more (16 percent), and two adults and no children (16 percent). The fact that few of today's young marrieds support another adult was reflected in the survey statistic that just 2 percent of the families dependent on the graduate or her husband consisted of three or more adults.

In terms of the total survey group, the regions in which the June 1957 women graduates resided were relatively similar in 1964 and the winter of 1957-58. Nevertheless, in 1964 slightly more of the graduates were living in the West; slightly fewer in the North Central States and the Northeast.

An examination of the State addresses of individual graduates in the two survey periods revealed their relatively high mobility. In 1964 as many as 20 percent of the graduates were in a region different from 6½ years earlier, and an additional 16 percent were in a different State in the same region. About 61 percent of the graduates lived in the same State both periods. Of course, many of these had changed residences within their State.

The concentration of today's population in urban areas also was characteristic of the survey group. About 54 percent of the graduates dwelt in a metropolitan area in 1964; another 39 percent in a small town or city. Only 6 percent resided on a farm or in open country.

Continuing Education of Graduates

During the 7-year period since graduation, 15 percent of the women had earned a master's degree, but less than 1 percent had earned a doctor's degree. The women with graduate degrees tended to cluster in a few subject areas. Fully 2 out of 3 of the women with a doctorate had specialized in the health fields (largely medicine); most of the others in chemistry or physical sciences, journalism, or social sciences. Of those with a master's degree, 43 percent did graduate work in education; 9 percent in English; and 8 percent in sociology or social work.

In terms of undergraduate field of study, the highest proportions of women with an advanced degree were those whose major had been sociology or social work (27 percent); foreign languages (24 percent); history (23 percent); chemistry and physical sciences (23 percent); or music (23 percent). Those with relatively few advanced degrees had had undergraduate majors in home economics (8 percent), religion (8 percent), or the health fields (3 percent). (The principle undergraduate major of the doctors of medicine was biological science; few of them had majored in a health field.)

In most of the graduate fields reported, the majority of women with advanced degrees were continuing to specialize in the field of their undergraduate major. For example, 95 percent of those with advanced degrees in nursing had undergraduate majors in nursing. Likewise, there was a close similarity in subject matter for 90 percent of those with advanced degrees in foreign languages; 79 percent, in English and journalism; and 57 percent, in education and physical education. The major exceptions were the graduate fields of library science, social sciences, and health. In none of these exceptions did a majority of the graduates with advanced degrees have undergraduate majors in the same field of study.

Reflecting the widespread interest of college women in continuing education, fully 46 percent of the survey women had taken at least one graduate or professional course since college graduation. Many had taken non-professional courses — mostly cultural or recreational in nature. Relatively few had taken business, vocational, or technical courses following graduation.

When surveyed in 1964, 17 percent of the June 1957 class were enrolled in graduate or professional schools, and an additional 29 percent reported having taken previous postgraduate courses. About three-fourths of the current enrollees were candidates for a degree (usually a master's degree) or a certificate (usually a teaching certificate).

Education was the predominant field of study of the women in the June 1957 class during their postgraduate years as well as during their undergraduate years. For almost half the women with postgraduate courses, education was the major graduate subject. Other numerically important graduate fields among the survey women were English (6 percent), nursing (5 percent), and sociology or social work (4 percent).

Financial aid was received by more than one-fourth of the women who had done some graduate work. Of this group, more than three-fifths were awarded a fellowship, a scholarship, or a grant; one-fourth, an assistantship or traineeship.

Fields in which the highest percentages of graduates obtained financial assistance were sociology or social work (67 percent); biological sciences (63 percent); mathematics (61 percent) social sciences (51 percent); foreign languages (49 percent); and nursing (47 percent). However, only low percentages of graduate students received financial aid among those specializing in education (14 percent); business and commerce (22 percent); home economics (25 percent); and library science (25 percent). In general, these figures reflect the relative availability of aid among the various fields of graduate study.

Graduates who were continuing their education were frequently motivated by their desire to advance professionally, as noted in the following remarks:

"I decided to return to school to continue my education and get a Ph.D. in biochemistry. The primary reason was 3 years of very frustrating work experiences. . . . The feeling seemed to be that it was not worthwhile to train women for more than the most menial laboratory jobs, since they do not stay at one job very long. They get married. . . . The only way to move upward is with more education."

"I have experienced some prejudice on the part of employers to hire women in a traditionally man's job [pharmacist]. Even under the merit system of Civil Service, there is some prejudice against women, and promotions are not on the same basis as for men. An additional degree might help, so I'm getting it."

In their efforts to engage in graduate study, some women encountered such obstacles as age requirements, restrictions on financial aid, and limited course offerings. Illustrative comments follow:

"Although I am interested in earning a Ph.D. degree in psychology, I feel that this will be almost impossible. In the area of psychology, most major universities require full-time enrollment in a Ph.D. program. Also there is a trend toward placing a ceiling on the age at which one can enroll in a Ph.D. program. Even if it were possible to be accepted as a part-time student, nearly all financial aid in the form of scholarships and fellowships is available only to full-time students."

"Grants and loans often do not permit the student to work full-time and go to school part time. I had to pay for all my education because financial responsibilities would not allow me to attend school full time."

"I wish that more postgraduate courses were available closer to home and at more convenient locations."

However, one graduate who was attending school reported favorable circumstances both in her community and at home.

"I am especially fortunate because five universities and colleges are within commuting range. I am further blessed by having a husband and parents who encourage women to greater educational achievement and, in fact, are pushing me to complete a master's."

Employment Status in 1964

Slightly over half (51 percent) of the women graduates were in the labor force when surveyed in 1964, 7 years after their college graduation[4]. Forty-nine percent were employed: 39 percent, full time and 10 percent, part time. The fact that very few (only 2 percent) were looking for a job reflected the brisk demand for trained workers in 1964.

The percentage of workers in the survey group had dropped considerably from the 85 percent level recorded in the winter of 1957-58, just about 6 months after graduation. The proportion of women attending school only was also down — from 8 percent in 1957-58 to 4 percent in 1964. Similarly, those combining school attendance with employment declined from 13 to 9 percent. As might be expected, the group of women neither working nor attending school grew from 7 to 45 percent over the 6½-year span.

The degree level of the women graduates had a marked influence on the extent of their employment. The percentages employed in 1964 ranged from 91 percent of those with a doctorate to 71 percent of those with a master's degree, and 45 percent of those with a baccalaureate. On the other hand, the proportions not in the labor force were 4, 21, and 50 percent, respectively. The remaining proportions of the group were attending school or seeking work.

The employment status of the graduates varied by under-graduate major also. That the music majors included the highest proportion (65 percent) of employed graduates may be related to the fact that music teachers can adapt their work to family life more easily than many other kinds of workers can. The relatively high amount of employment among women who had majored in health fields (61 percent) may be explained by the rising job demand and fairly high salaries in the health services. On the other hand, fairly low salary rates may have influenced the relatively small extent of labor force participation among women who majored in religion (33 percent), home economics (39 percent), art (45 percent), and English (45 percent).

Only minor differences in the graduates' extent of employment appeared to stem from the region or the type of area where they were living in 1964. By region the percentage who were working ranged from 47 percent in the Northeast to 51 percent in the South and also in the West. As for residential areas, jobs were held by 50 percent of the women in large metropolitan cities, where employment opportunities are relatively abundant. But this proportion of employed was only slightly above the 48 percent for graduates living in small cities or towns and the 45 percent for those on farms or in open country.

The majority (67 percent) of the graduates working in 1964 were employed by governmental organizations, chiefly local boards of education. About 29 percent were employed by private organizations, and only 4 percent were self-employed. The predominant industry of the graduates' employers was educational service (68 percent), followed by medical service (12 percent), and social or religious service (4 percent).

When asked why they were working in 1964, more than two-thirds of the graduates gave a financial reason; one-fifth, a work-oriented reason. More than three-fourths of the single graduates and nine-tenths of the widowed, separated, and divorced graduates needed to support themselves or others, and almost half of the married graduates wanted to increase family income. Interest in having a career stimulated employment among relatively large proportions of single women and of married women with only older children (6 years of age or over) or with no children.

The graduates noted numerous hindrances to satisfactory

work experiences, particularly in regard to hiring, pay, and advancement opportunities. A few of their comments were:

"I now live in a small town where job opportunities for college women are not readily available. Teaching is almost all there is."

"I'm unhappy and disturbed to hear reports that many school systems, especially in larger cities, do not like or refuse to hire female teachers over 40 years of age."

"Past experience in an executive training program in the merchandising field shows tremendous barriers still exist against women. Lower pay and lack of advancement are common."

"Promotions are not easily obtained by women. My rank [assistant professor of English] bothers some of my colleagues. Not until this year was my pay on a comparable level with men in our department."

"In this area of the country, jobs in my field [chemistry] are very limited; and where available, there is much prejudice against women. However, I work for my husband and enjoy doing it."

"I cannot resist the opportunity to express continued distress that in so many areas of business women are denied advancement and salary commensurate with their education, experience, and proved ability because of their sex. It is most difficult to see so many men hired at immediately higher salaries in better jobs, to help train them, and yet sincerely to feel — even after many years — that they never prove themselves to be even equal in performance — much less superior."

Family Status and Employment

Family responsibilities were a paramount concern in the lives of most of the college women 7 years after graduation, since 85 percent of the women were or had been married and 66 percent were mothers of children under 18 years of age. Whether or not the graduates were employed was strongly affected by their family status.

Mothers of young children (under 6 years old) were the only group of survey graduates in which a majority were not in the labor force in 1964. Only 26 percent of this group had paying jobs and about half of these women worked part time. In addition, 2 percent were seeking work. By contrast, 93 percent of both the single graduates and the widowed, separated, or divorced graduates were employed, and 1 percent in each of these groups were looking for a job. Among married women with only older children (6 years of age or over) and those with no children, the proportions in the labor force were 90 percent and 80 percent respectively.

In addition to their family status, various other factors were important to the married graduates when they decided whether or not to work outside the home. A principal consideration was the attitude of the husbands toward their wives' employment. When the married graduates were questioned about the husbands' attitudes, more than half described the attitudes as favorable, and more than one-fourth as neutral. Less than one-fifth thought their husbands were opposed to their participation in the work force.

The highest proportion of favorable replies (82 percent) was reported by wives who were already working, and the fewest favorable replies (37 percent) by wives not in the work force. The percentages of husbands in the two groups described as opposed to their wives employment were 4 percent and 28 percent respectively. In each of these employment status groups there was relatively little difference in the response of those with or without children.

Some of the women not working in 1964 volunteered the view that their husbands would no longer oppose their working outside the home when their children become older. On the other hand, some of those working thought their husbands would disapprove if the employment were full time rather than part time. But despite the few qualified answers given to this question, the overall response reflects the changing attitude of society in favor of the employment of married women.

A few comments of the wives reveal the high value they place on their husband's attitudes, as follows:

"I would love to work, but my husband feels that my place is in the home caring for my family. Counseling and opportunities are needed for a woman who can't or won't devote full time to a job but needs to be doing something of importance other than just being chief cook and bottle washer. Clubs aren't important enough."

"A favorable attitude of the husband is vital to the working wife, in my opinion."

"I am extremely active in many extracurricular areas of my field [teaching chemistry]. This is possible only because I'm married to an extraordinary man who is more interested in me as a professional colleague and partner than in the accumulation of dirt in our house."

The employment status of the husband and the kind of occupation he holds are other factors which may exert strong influence on a wife's employment status. Among the large group of survey women whose husbands were employed in 1964, 38 percent of the wives had paid jobs. However, in the smaller groups in which the husbands were attending school or were neither working nor attending school, as many as 62 percent and 68 percent, respectively, of the wives were employed.

In terms of the husband's occupation, the highest proportions of wives who were working were among those whose husbands were employed as laborers (88 percent), service workers (69 percent), operatives (60 percent), or clerical workers (56 percent). Conversely, relatively small percentages of wives were employed when their husbands were farm workers (32 percent), professional workers (35 percent), or managers, officials, or proprietors (36 percent).

The ability of a mother to make satisfactory arrangements for the care of her children is also an important determinant in her decision regarding paid employment. Approximately three-tenths of the mothers in the class of June 1957 were employed in 1964. During their working hours, two-thirds[5] of the group had child care arrangements for their children in their own home; about one-sixth outside their home. Most of the other working mothers, primarily those with older children (6 to 17 years of age) only, had adjusted their work so that their children were not alone or considered that their children were old enough to care for themselves.

Among both the mothers who were working and those not working there was considerable feeling that insufficient attention was being given to their needs and problems. The following comments shed light on their situations and views:

"Our society has made virtually no provision for a woman with young children who wants or needs to work. Many young talented women I know are frustrated in their attempt to escape the boredom they feel at home by engaging in activities even on a part time basis. It is simply too expensive to hire a full time nursemaid for care of young children. It's a horrible and discouraging struggle for those brave enough to make the attempt to work."

"I would consider taking a job now if excellent inexpensive day care centers were available for children."

"I have contemplated private duty nursing, but felt the financial gain at this time would be hardly worthwhile since I would have to hire a babysitter. I think the establishment of really good inexpensive day nurseries — maybe government-run — would get many young mothers back to nursing and teaching."

"To make it possible to unleash more female brainpower, there should be a healthy, realistic federal income tax deduction for all gainfully employed women who must pay baby sitters in order to work."

"I recently was interviewed for a good job for which I was well qualified, but the employer would not hire a woman with little children. As long as employers refuse to take chances, people like myself must either be underemployed or unemployed. . . . It is stupid to ask women to keep out of things until their children are grown."

"I find substitute teaching the perfect answer for a wife and mother. It keeps my credential active and enables me to stay current in the teaching profession. Beside the good pay, the hours are convenient for my children. It also gets me away from everyday chores, and I feel like a person in my own right again."

Another concern that influenced the graduates' interest in paid employment was their ability to obtain satisfactory employees to assist with housework. Slightly more than one-fifth of the June 1957 women graduates engaged a household worker in 1964. The extent of employing household workers ranged from 28 percent among the employed married graduates to 14 percent among the single graduates. Only among the employed married graduates was there a significant proportion (7 percent) who had at least 40 hours of paid housework a week. Most of the graduates with household assistance had 8 hours a week or less.

A short workweek was considered by some of the graduates as a satisfactory solution to handling dual responsibilities at home and in the workplace. About one-third of the employed married graduates had a part time job (less than 35 hours a week); the majority of this group worked no more than 16 hours a week. Of the employed married women with young children (under 6 years), about half were working on a part time basis.

Remarks such as the following indicate growing interest in the promotion of part time employment opportunities, particularly for educated women who wish to keep in touch with their profession while their children are young:

"Satisfying professional opportunities for young mothers on a part time basis would help so much in providing that thread of continuity between college, graduate school, early employment, and later years of education and employment. Whatever can be done to advance these opportunities and gain acceptance, by employers particularly, of the part time employment of professional workers, will be widely welcomed by many of us."

"There seems to be a tremendous lack of information available concerning part time work for married women with children, who cannot spend a full week away from home, but who have a college degree and adequate work experience to qualify them for interesting jobs. Do these jobs exist? If so, it seems impossible to find out about them."

For some women, a partial answer to their wish to combine home and work activities is found by performing paid work in their own home. Of the survey women who were married, 5 percent were doing paid work at home. More than two-fifths of these women were teaching or tutoring; other significant proportions were engaged in writing, typing, secretarial work, research, bookkeeping, child care, or telephone selling. A few specific jobs included a free-lance artist working on greeting cards, a music teacher, a reader of high school papers, an abstractor of chemistry reports, a sales counselor, a thesis editor and typist, and a translator.

Occupational Patterns

More than four-fifths of the employed women graduates considered their 1964 job the kind they wished to hold. Most of those with another preference named teaching; some were already teaching but were interested in another job in the field. Significant numbers of other dissatisfied graduates wanted a job in nursing or other health work, entertainment or the arts, or social work.

Consistent with this general indication of satisfaction with job choice was the report by a majority (53 percent) of the graduates that the chief reason for taking their present job was that it was "interesting work." Other major reasons named were good hours and working conditions (17 percent) and good pay (13 percent). Relatively small proportions said they accepted their present job because of a promotion (3 percent), advancement opportunities (4 percent), or chance to be creative (5 percent).

Teaching, the occupation of 59.9 percent of the employed graduates in 1964, continued to be of their favorite. As in the winter of 1957-58, the next largest occupational groups were those of nurses (6.4 percent) and secretaries and stenographers (4.4 percent). Despite this concentration, the graduates' occupations covered a broad gamut of fields and levels of responsibility. Among the rather unusual positions held in 1964 were those of security analysis investment officer, highway engineer technician, college mathematics professor, clinical psychologist, Peace Corps volunteer, assistant hospital administrator, professional cellist, film actress, senior programmer, assistant theater designer, radio performer, geography editor, and company staff physician.

About 9 of every 10 survey graduates employed in 1964 had a professional job. The increase in the proportion of graduates in professional occupations since the winter of 1957-58, when only 83 percent were professional workers, is probably due to the improved job status of some of the graduates, including those who had been graduate students, and to the relatively greater tendency of those with nonprofessional jobs to leave the labor force. Although the increase in professional representation was distributed among numerous professions, it was most noticeable for three. The percentage of employed graduates with jobs as teachers rose from 58.8 to 59.9 percent; as editors, copywriters, and reporters, from 0.8 to 1.7 percent; and as social, welfare, and recreation workers, from 2.8 to 3.2 percent. In addition, 1.6 percent of the women employed in 1964 were librarians, a group with insufficient numbers to warrant reporting in 1957-58. Professional groups with a relatively significant decrease in representation over the 6½-year period were home economists, down from 1.2 to 0.5 percent, and dietitians, down from 1.4 to 0.9 percent.

Graduates holding clerical jobs decreased from 14 percent of the total employed in 1957-58 to 8 percent in 1964. Those clerical groups with significantly decreased representation were secretaries and stenographers, down from 6.7 to 4.4 percent, and miscellaneous clerical workers, down from 6.2 to 2.4 percent.

Comparison of the employment status in 1964 for each of the

various occupational groups in 1957-58 provides some indication of the relative extent of withdrawal from the labor force. Occupations with the highest percentages of women who were out of the labor force in 1964 were home economists (63 percent), secretaries and stenographers (56 percent), dietitians (54 percent), religious workers (53 percent), buyers and sales workers (52 percent), and social and welfare workers (51 percent). Occupations with the lowest percentages out of the labor force in 1964 were artists, musicians, and actresses (34 percent), therapists (35 percent), recreation workers (36 percent), and bookkeeping and accounting clerks (37 percent). Teachers also had a relatively low withdrawal rate; 43 percent of their group were out of the labor force in 1964.

The graduates had a generally high opinion of the relevancy of their formal education to their 1964 employment. However, fewer reported a direct relationship in 1964 than in 1957-58. Sixty-eight percent of the June 1957 graduates employed in 1964 — as compared with 86 percent employed 6½ years earlier — considered that there was a direct relationship between their undergraduate major and their current job. In regard to the relationship between their 1964 job and their graduate education, three-fourths said it was direct; an additional one-seventh, indirect.

The undergraduate subjects that generally had the closest relationship with the jobs held in 1964 were education and other job-oriented majors. For example, of the graduates employed in 1964, 93 percent of those who had majored in nursing in college were working as nurses, and 87 percent of those with an education major were teaching. Also, half or more of the employed graduates who had majored in physical education, English, foreign languages, music, home economics, history, and mathematics were teachers. Among other employed graduates, 43 percent of those with majors in the health fields (excluding nursing) were working as biological technicians and 20 percent as therapists; 37 percent with sociology or social work majors as social, welfare, or recreation workers; and 31 percent with biological science majors as biological technicians. Of the chemistry majors, 25 percent were working as chemists and 19 percent as biological technicians.

Many graduates volunteered statements about the rewarding aspects of their particular profession, usually because of its opportunities for social service, stimulating challenges, or easy accommodation of home and work schedules. Occupations receiving special praise included teacher, children's librarian, medical technologist, recreation worker, computer programmer, and physicist.

A few of the graduates, however, were disillusioned by their employment experiences, particularly in fields where men still predominate, as illustrated in the following remarks:

"Although I have a B.S. in chemical engineering and spent 6 months looking for a job, I ended up working as a reports librarian because it was the only offer I got. Thus, the end of chemical engineering for me."

"I tried for over 2 years to get a job as a mathematician and found private industry very prejudiced against hiring women as mathematicians — especially in research and related fields."

"From my own experience and that of others I have known, I believe it is sound advice for students majoring in one of the arts fields to get an education degree first and then pursue the arts degree. In seeking employment or earning dollars for further study, this would be more beneficial."

"Analytical chemists — especially women analysts — are second class citizens of the chemical world. If I ever work again I might teach but would more likely do stenographic work. This is women's work, traditional and respectable."

"I have found a significant degree of discrimination against women in fields of mathematics and higher education. Also there seems to be a consistently small proportion of fellowship and assistantships awarded to female applicants."

"I feel the position of women in the business world is difficult because of male competition. The teaching profession is more comfortable for a woman because here she is accepted. . . . Much as I would like to see women get ahead in business, I feel they don't generally, because things are made difficult for them."

"It is unfortunate that school systems have a hiring preference for men over women in administrative and/or supervisory jobs, and that individuals from outside the system are hired for these positions."

"As often as we move, it would be nice if nationwide requirements for teacher certification were standard. I have a currently valid credential to teach in one State, but another State won't renew my certification because the required undergraduate credits which I have received since college graduation were earned in the night program of a junior college instead of a 4-year college."

Graduates' Salaries in 1964

An average of $5,947 was earned in 1964 by women out of college 7 years and employed full time in the United States. The salary was more than half again as large as their $3,739 average in the winter of 1957-58, about 6 months after their graduation.

The highest average salaries earned by the June 1957 women graduates were received by those employed as chemists, mathematicians, or statisticians ($8,039), followed by managers or officials ($7,466), and professional workers in schools, excluding teachers, ($6,744). The teachers, with an average salary of $5,890, earned slightly less than the average for the total group of survey graduates. Lowest average earnings were reported by the secretaries and stenographers ($4,527), miscellaneous clerical workers ($4,813), and librarians ($5,658).

Fully 20 percent of the employed graduates earned $7,000 or over in 1964; only 5 percent less than $4,000. The graduates' earnings were generally highest in the West ($6,358) and Northeast ($6,266), and lowest in the South ($5,215).

The positive influence of advanced education on salary levels was corroborated by the $6,409 average salary of graduates with a master's degree and the $5,800 average of those with a baccalaureate only. The earnings of the few survey graduates with a doctorate degree are not reported because most were resident physicians in hospitals and had typically low earnings.

In terms of their undergraduate major, graduates with the highest average salaries in 1964 were those who had majored in mathematics ($7,517), chemistry ($6,535), or psychology ($6,393). The large group of graduates with an education major averaged $5,877 — slightly below the average for the total group. Lowest average salaries were received by graduates with a major in music ($5,566) or business and commerce ($5,568).

Complaints of low pay or salary discrimination were voiced by some of the graduates, as illustrated by the following:

"Women are still discriminated against in business. . . . As a commercial artist, I am paid considerably less than a 24-year old man who has a fifth of my education and background — and much less talent. I also find it ironic that a 19-year-old secretary with one previous job makes only $5 a week less than I."

"I am still appalled at the low scale of women's wages and that the old battle of the sexes still prevails in hiring women executives in this day and age.

"I do feel that wages are drastically low for this profession [nursing] and must be remedied before the shortage becomes greater."

Work Histories of Graduates

The women had an average of 5.5 years' paid employment between their graduation from college in June 1957 and the 1964 survey. The fact that as many as 27 percent had worked throughout the 7-year interval, and an additional 16 percent for at least 6 years, supports the view that college women are making significant economic use of their college education. Only 3 percent of the survey graduates had not had any paid employment since graduation. Nine out of ten of those with some employment history had worked primarily on a full time basis.

There were several indications that the women in the June 1957 class had considerable job stability. In the positions held in 1964, they had spent an average of 3.9 years. As many as 32 percent had worked for only one employer between graduation and 1964. The average number of jobs the group had held was 2.6 — which was also the average number of employers for whom they had worked. Factors tending to increase job changes were that some graduates had quit to accompany their husbands to new locations and some teachers had taken temporary jobs during the summer.

Principal reasons given by the June 1957 women graduates for leaving the work force were the birth and care of their children (72 percent), marriage (12 percent), and moves to a new location (7 percent). The majority of the single graduates who left work, however, left to attend school. About three-fifths of the married women without children who left did so because of marriage, location moves, or household responsibilities; some left because they were expecting a child in the near future. Of the total group of graduates not in the labor force in 1964, almost half were last employed in 1961-63.

Future Employment Plans

Four of every 5 graduates, when asked about their anticipated activities, included paid employment in their plans. As many as 27 percent of the total group said they wanted to have a career. These included almost two-thirds of the single women, almost three-fourths of the married women with older children

(6 to 17 years of age) only, and fully three-fourths of the widowed, separated, or divorced women. Almost two-fifths of the total group planned to resume work when family responsibilities were less demanding.

The employment plans of the graduates bore a strong relationship to their employment status in 1964. Those who wanted a career included over half the employed graduates but less than 1 percent of those not in the work force. On the other hand, more than one-third of those not working did not plan to work in the future.

The extent of the graduates' interest in employment increased during the 6½ years' survey interval, as revealed by comparison of the graduates' employment plans in 1964 and in the winter of 1957-58. Of those who had said in 1957-58 that they did not plan to work in the future, only two-fifths gave the same response in 1964. One-tenth of the group wanted a career and the remainder had some work plan. Of those planning in 1957-58 to pursue a career, about three-fifths felt the same way in 1964 and only 5 percent had no future work plan.

One-tenth of the graduates not employed in 1964 reported immediate plans to seek work. The majority of these women wanted a part time job. Teaching or related work was preferred by almost two-thirds of the "near-future" job seekers; nursing by one-tenth. When questioned about the main reason for preferring a certain type of work, almost one-half said it was work for which they had been trained, and one-third work that was interesting.

About one-eighth of all the survey graduates indicated they would like to receive counseling assistance regarding employment. One graduate, 28 years of age, who was not interested in counseling, added, "No, too late now." The percentage of those wanting counseling was slightly higher among the employed than among those not employed.

Remarks of the graduates regarding counseling assistance related not only to their present needs but also to their conviction that more employment information should be given young women in high school and college. Typical remarks follow:

"Greatly interested in counseling assistance. Feel this is the answer to many a graduate's problem after trying first job — then being so disappointed in outcome."

"At this point, I feel that I would have prepared myself more carefully for a profession had I taken the time to find out where my real interest and ability to perform should be directed."

"There is a tremendous need for occupational guidance on the college level. Most college students have no idea of the wide range of occupations that might be available and do not consider the practical consequences of taking subjects just because they're interested in them."

"I have a desire to return to work when my children are in school full time. I feel the greatest need for women in my present position is guidance. There should be more information about the availability of jobs."

"I feel that employment opportunities for women college graduates are grossly lacking or underpublished. Women graduates in liberal arts are often aware of no other type of employment than teaching."

"I think a State job placement and counseling service for college graduates would be very valuable."

Numerous graduates revealed serious intentions of returning to the work force when childrearing demands diminished, as noted below:

"I plan to return to work when my oldest child is in high school for two reasons: (1) to pay for a college education for each child; and (2) to regain contact with and make contribution to the community outside the home and family unit."

"If I go back to work after my children are in school, it would be a teaching job. My reasons would be the enjoyment I get from teaching, plus my feeling that those who are capable and qualified owe it to the community to contribute to the care and education of all children, not just their own. I would plan to spend a good share of my wages to employ household help."

"I want to go back to work in the near future but, as I see it now, on a part time basis. I am hoping to find something to do that I will enjoy without taking too much away from my home and family. As do many of my friends, I regret the lack of contact with people and using my mind and education."

"I do not believe that my previous educational training has been wasted just because I am not now working in the field for which I was trained. I was not sorry to give up teaching for my family, and I feel my children need me to be with them in their early years. My time is coming again when I can do more for myself."

"Although I enjoyed teaching and felt successful in it, I would like to start anew in another entirely unrelated field and return to school to train for it. Perhaps nursing or secretarial work or optometry would be satisfactory."

Future Educational Plans

Almost as many graduates included further education in their future plans as mentioned paid employment. Over three-fourths of the employed and over two-thirds of those not employed said they were planning to continue their education. The majority were considering a variety of university courses, but significant proportions named refresher courses in their professional field or enrollment in a teacher certification program.

A job-oriented reason for seeking additional education was given by slightly over half the graduates with an education plan or interest. In this group about three-fifths wanted further education for job advancement purposes; the remainder wished to obtain preparation or a teaching certificate. Graduates who did not relate their desire for more education to employment said they had a general educational or cultural reason or were working toward a degree.

About two-thirds of the survey graduates felt they were keeping up to date in their professional field. This favorable view was reported by twice as many of those employed (88 percent) as of those not employed (44 percent). Most of the employed were keeping up to date by working in their professional field. In addition, many were doing outside reading, attending conferences, and taking courses. More than four-fifths of those not employed who reported they were keeping up to date were reading journals, magazines, or books in their field. Other significant methods used by this group to update their knowledge and skills were by maintaining contacts with others in their profession (24 percent), taking courses (17 percent), and attending meetings, conferences, or workshops (14 percent).

Graduates' statements about their educational plans and needs ranged from firm declarations of intent to return to school to earnest appeals for more assistance in bridging the homemaking period between jobs.

"Fully intend and look forward to becoming an accredited children's librarian and will return to graduate school once my husband has completed medical training and is in practice."

"I plan to go back to college on a regular basis to get a master's degree after my husband acquires his degree. He then would be available to babysit with our son."

"I think now that our oldest child has started the first grade, my interest in education and teaching is higher then it has ever been since graduation. I find myself wishing I were back in the classroom. When all my children are in school, I hope to start teaching after completing some refresher courses."

"My degree in liberal arts prepared me for absolutely nothing. I would like to go back and get some kind of training that would prepare me for some field of work — not necessarily to use in the immediate future but as security if the need should ever arise for me to work."

"In a profession such as nursing, I find that reading professional publications is not enough to keep one up to date. Unused skills are readily lost. The only alternative seems to be part time work, which is frequently undesirable to the mother of preschool children. Surely some program could be developed which would help nurses maintain skills and interests through this period."

"Teacher certification courses are too time consuming. There should be intensive home-study courses or night courses for qualified students. Most courses drag too slowly and waste time. They are also very costly."

"I feel that educational institutions should make more effort to enable college-trained women to come back to school for graduate work and refresher-type courses."

Volunteer Activities

In 1964 over three-fourths of the women out of college 7 years were active members of one or more voluntary organizations. The majority were affiliated with a religious institution. Significant proportions also belonged to a social or recreational club (40 percent), a community, welfare, or social service organization (38 percent), a professional society (34 percent), or a school or educational group (33 percent).

When asked whether they were volunteer workers for community or national organizations, more than two-thirds of the graduates answered affirmatively. A few worked as many as 40 hours a month in a voluntary capacity. Most spent from 9 to 16 hours (29 percent), 5 to 8 hours (25 percent), or 4 hours or less (23 percent) a month in volunteer service.

Some of the women noted that they would like to do more volunteer work but were deterred by childrearing demands or by frequent moves of the husband to new communities. One revealed that when she engaged in extensive volunteer work she was encouraged by her husband to get a paid job and bring home a paycheck. Another speculated that the reason her husband preferred her to be a volunteer rather than a paid worker was that her volunteer status affected his ego less. Despite these conflicting influences, however, many of the women wanted to and did engage in some volunteer work — often along with homemaking and/or employment activities — because they wanted to perform some social service or to keep in touch with their community.

Conclusions

In this period of rising interest in women's employment status, the views, accomplishments, and needs of the women who were surveyed 7 years after college reflected the changing social and economic climate of the Nation. By their questionnaire answers and observations, many of the women revealed that they were paying increased attention to fashioning a dynamic life pattern, thinking ahead to the time when their current responsibilities would lessen and they would be seeking a new assortment of meaningful activities.

The widespread desire of college women to participate in economic and/or community activities outside the home was substantiated by the high rate of response to the survey, as well as by their thoughtful statements. A significant number of the survey women, some of whom were wives and mothers, had found jobs that utilized their capabilities and education to advantage. But social attitudes or economic forces restricted fulfillment of the personal goals of others.

Some of those who encountered difficulties reported job barriers or rebuffs, particularly when they tried to follow earlier pioneers in occupational fields with relatively few women. Others found limited willingness on the part of employers to hire them for jobs commensurate with their abilities or to provide equitable pay and suitable work arrangements. A few were affected adversely by prejudices against working mothers. For some, there was an insufficient number of schools and colleges with convenient and suitable courses for housewives. And still others were frustrated in their efforts to reconcile work or school activities with homemaking schedules.

Nevertheless, the most influential factor affecting the economic status of these women was the Nation's generally high level of economic activity in 1964. With rising demand for trained and skilled workers in virtually every profession, college women were in a relatively advantageous employment position. Employers, some of whom might have been reluctant to hire women if skilled men had been available, were more willing than usual to give women a chance to show their worth in new fields of employment. If recent legislative and related developments improve women's employment opportunities as expected, these college women — like other women — can look forward to further success in toppling traditional barriers to better economic status.

In their search for a useful and satisfying life, the survey women generally had a positive outlook. Few revealed negative or defeatist thinking that might limit their ability to find appropriate solutions to their employment problems. Instead, they questioned social or economic prejudices in a forthright manner and analyzed their difficulties objectively.

Questions arise about subsequent actions of this group of women. Will they retain their self-confidence and determination to reenter the work force as the years following graduation increase? Will the interruption in job career be shorter for them than it was for older alumnae? Will they follow through on their stated plans for additional education?

The search for answers to questions such as these could stimulate subsequent study at the next important stage in their lives — when their youngest child is in school. Then the latent desire to return to work may reach the decisionmaking stage. Continuing concern by society about the activities and needs of educated women is essential — not only to enable them to make their maximum contribution to society but, even more importantly, to help them satisfy their individual aspirations and lead rewarding lives.

NOTES

The 30 tables of this study have been omitted here but may be referred to in Bulletin 292, United States Department of Labor, Women's Bureau, Washington, D.C. 1966.

1. In this report the terms "married women" and "working wives" refer to women with husband present.

2. First Jobs of College Women — Report on Women Graduates, Class of 1957. Women's Bureau Bull. 268.

3. In this report "average" refers to arithmetic mean.

4. This percentage is the same as that reported by the Bureau of Labor Statistics in its Special Labor Force Report No. 53, "Educational Attainment of Workers, March 1964." Among women who were 25 to 34 years of age and had 4 years or more of college, 51 percent were in the labor force in March 1964.

5. For comparison with information for all working mothers, see "Child Care Arrangements of the Nation's Working Mothers, 1965," a preliminary report of the Children's Bureau, U.S. Department of Health, Education, and Welfare, and the Women's Bureau, U.S. Department of Labor.

thirty-five

Marriage and Medicine

CAROL LOPATE

A woman's goal, like that of men, is to develop a life style that uses her energies and capabilities in such a way that she functions in her various roles efficiently and productively, with sufficient integration among these roles to give her at least some personal satisfaction in each.[1]

Considered from this standpoint, women physicians more than other professional women achieve a healthy balance between fulfillment of their professional and sexual goals. In contrast to the old attitude that women doctors could only be spinsters and "hen medics," over three-fourths of all women physicians are married (over half, to other physicians), and the majority of them have children.[2] In fact, those physicians who do marry have averaged three children, or slightly more children than reported by other married women in their socio-economic class.[3] According to actual statistics, women entering medicine also have statistically a far greater probability of combining marriage and a career than women beginning graduate work in the physical or social sciences.

Sociologists and psychologists, as well as popular writers, have explored the conflicts or assets (depending on their point of view) which arise when a woman takes on the responsibilities of a career in addition to her family. The arguments against — neglect of spouse and children, aggressive competition between marital partners, undermining the "bread-winning status" of the man, etc. — have been offset by glowing reports of

From *Women in Medicine* by Carol Lopate, 1968, pp. 145-168. Reprinted with permission of the publisher, The Johns Hopkins Press, for the JOSIAH MACY, JR. FOUNDATION.

494

the positive results: increased stimulation in the home, greater compatibility between husband and wife, and above all, fulfillment of the woman's potential. The most reasonable viewpoint on the subject is probably the one given by Elizabeth Herzog of the Children's Bureau, who states:

> Consensus of the research to date is that gainful employment of the wife is not a significant factor in either marriage success or failure. It is a peg on which conflict can be hung, a socially approved area in which to disagree.[4]

For the woman and those dependent on her love and services, being a physician may imply more than the ordinary amount of energy taken away from the family. While women generally avoid professions such as engineering because of their "masculine" image, Alice Rossi reports that in her sample of college-educated women this was not the problem; rather, "four out of five say that women do not go into medicine because 'it is too demanding to combine with family responsibilities.' "[5] According to Rossi:

> This seems to flow from an image of the doctor modelled on the general practitioner of horse-and-buggy days, on call night and day, seven days a week. There is no room in this image for the contemporary partnerships, group practices, increased specialization, staff appointments, restricted house calls, etc., which are increasingly characteristic of the medical profession. Training to become a doctor may be hard for a woman unless she postpones marriage or at least child-bearing, but once she has a medical degree, a pediatric partnership or appointments as a staff pathologist or anesthetist might actually provide more flexibility of routine and shorter hours of work than a job as a laboratory technician.[6]

Rossi's evaluation of the possibilities for relaxed scheduling in the life of a woman physician may be overly optimistic. Most women do not practice part-time, and many give 60 to 70 hours a week to their profession. In a recent survey, 54.5 per cent of the women physicians reported having worked over 2,000 hours in 1964 (full-time), 30.5 per cent less than 2,000 hours (part-time); another 6.1 per cent reported activity but did not specify hours, and only 8.9 per cent said they were not working at all.[7] The percentage of women reporting relatively full-time activity ranged from 86.4 per cent of the single women to 72.6 per cent of the married women with no children to 55.3 per cent of those with one or two children, to 39.3 per cent of those with three or more children.[8]

Two reasons may be given for the fact that such a high percentage of women doctors work full-time, as opposed to women in other fields. In the first place, because of the shortage of physicians and their vital importance to the community, women physicians may have more of a sense of responsibility to fulfill the demands made on their professional services. Particularly for those in private or group practice, it is nearly impossible to keep down the size of the practice as it tends to grow year by year: when a patient is referred to a doctor, it is hard to say no, even if her 40 hours have already been scheduled. The alternative of a salaried position may provide more clear-cut and regular schedules, but even here part-time often implies taking home papers and records or seeing patients "after hours."

In the second place, without resorting to undue generalization, it is clear that the type of woman who enters medicine is usually endowed with more than average energy and motivation and a desire to work to her full capacity. The obstacles of the pre-medical and medical training years discussed in earlier chapters weed out most of those girls with less willfulness and ambition, and those who survive feel strong enough to want both a career and a family.

Most amazing is the fact that such a large proportion of women in medicine do, to a large degree, follow through with their career plans. Whatever the girl's hopes may be, however, it is her husband, if she marries, who ultimately determines the possibility of continuing in her profession while being a wife and mother. Edna Rostow, in an article on "Conflict and Accommodation" in the lives of American women, states:

> For a woman to perform in two worlds, as men do, her marriage must countenance her dual goals and support her in seeking them. The marriage relation is seen more and more consciously as a process in which husband and wife co-operate on many levels in order to permit each separately and both together to achieve a number of goals and satisfy a number of needs — not the least of them the need to control or eliminate destructive elements between them. . . . For a woman to accept from her husband the kind of help that man has traditionally taken as his due from his wife, however, can be an emotionally complicated experience for both.[9]

"The right husband" is one of the most common requirements set up by women physicians themselves for combining a
medical career with marriage. Without a husband who actively
supports his wife's career, most women physicians maintain
that there can be only two solutions: divorce, or sacrifice of the
medical career. The self-conscious gratitude of these women
toward their husbands for helping them maintain their professional lives is impressive. Even those who acknowledge that
their husbands give little practical assistance to ease their work
burden — "He usually reads the paper or looks over his journal
while I do the dishes" — emphasize the importance of their
husbands' emotional support. "He tells me I'm so much more
stimulating to be with, now that I've returned to work," said
one woman who had retired to become a full-time housewife
while her children were young. "My husband has always been
very willing to overlook short-order meals or a rug that needed
vacuuming so that I could continue my job at the hospital," another remarked.

Since many women physicians still feel the responsibility to
fulfill their traditional duties as housewife and mother, there
may be a confusion at times as to how much one should ask of
one's husband, or allow him to do when he does offer. In many
cases, the lack of time may bring about a simple solution: the
wife cannot do everything, and someone else must give a hand
somewhere. Feeling themselves to be capable and strong, many
women physicians, however, do not like to ask. "I try to get
home in time to straighten up the house and make a full course
dinner," said a resident who had been married less than a year.
"I don't think it's right for him to have to put on a kitchen
apron."

Another woman, who had just finished a strenuous year of
internship, described how her husband had rushed home from
the hospital (he was already a licensed pathologist) to relieve
the babysitter and change a diaper, and how he had often spent
long evenings alone with their two babies while she had to remain at the hospital. "I used to feel sorry for him!" she recalled.
Her experiences during this period had convinced her to take a
residency program which would allow her to be home regularly
and for long enough periods to hold up her end of the familial
responsibilities. Although she made no mention of her husband's having complained, it was obvious that she — and prob-

ably both of them — could not adapt to such a reversal of roles for long.

Because many of the responsibilities and roles are not the traditional ones which husband and wife expect when they first marry, compromise and adaptation become a very conscious part of the lives of women physicians and their husbands. Dr. Rosa Lee Nemir, former President of the American Medical Women's Association, described the process of adaptation in her own marriage in the following way:

> There are periods when one or the other ascends, but you have to cherish both lives. It's like putting bulbs in the ground at the right time. You always have to keep your interests and wits alive. When it's a crucial period in my medical life my husband has to become a partner and give me emotional support. Then the next year I may say, I'll pay more attention to you than I ever did before.

When the marriage occurs after the couple's ways of living and working are rather set, the adjustment may take a somewhat different course than when the two are starting out. If both members are far along in their careers when the marriage occurs, they may give each other greater leeway and be less inclined to mold the other in his or her image, since their ways of living and working have already settled into a somewhat rigid form. One woman, who put off marriage until she had completed her residency and passed her specialty boards, reported her anxiety as the wedding approached that her career, which meant so much to her, would be disturbed by her new life. She was used to getting up at five in the morning, for instance, to write reports and work on articles; these were her most creative hours of the day. "I asked my fiancé if we might have separate bedrooms when we were married," she smiled, "so that I wouldn't disturb him when I did my work. He thought I was crazy, but agreed — if I felt I needed it. Well, the situation never arose. Once I was married, I found that I didn't want to get up in the morning as I had done before. I still did my writing, but I found other, more convenient times to do it."

Marriages among medical students, interns, and residents, while increasing the possibility of financial and other difficulties, bring the partners together at an age when adaptation is usually easier for both. The relatively new concept of a "partnership" marriage is reflected in the burgeoning number of couples who join their private and professional lives in a more co-operative manner than was the norm several decades ago. One young Harvard graduate expressed this attitude jokingly: "All couples should be incorporated, so that whoever hires one of them has to hire the other."

Over half of all husbands of women physicians are themselves doctors. Women physicians, in fact, appear to gravitate towards mates in their own profession more than do women in other fields. In a study of women professionals in New York State, 58 per cent of the women physicians, in contrast to 50 per cent of the women lawyers, 50 per cent of the women dentists, 17 per cent of the women educational administrators, and none of the women in nursing administration were married to men in their own professions.[10] Unfortunately, no data have been gathered on the number of physician-couples who actually practice together or who do co-operative research. A guess is that an increasing number are doing so, although married medical teams are by no means a new phenomenon. At Stanford, Dr. Emile Holman, the distinguished cardiovascular surgeon, and Dr. Ann Purdy, who established the first cardiac clinic for children in San Francisco, were an outstanding example a generation ago.

Even when the husband is in a different profession, there can be an enormous degree of sharing and co-operation. An illustration of the eager involvement of a lawyer in his physician-wife's career is given by Morton Hunt in *Her Infinite Variety*. The lawyer recalls the early years of his marriage when his wife was still a medical student:

> My practice was growing fast and I could have afforded a nice place, but in order to save her travel time I moved in with her into her little dormitory room. For a year and a half, I'd come back to that little place after a long day in court, take her out for a quick dinner, and then help her study until late at night, or help her relax sometimes by telling her stories about my cases, or hobnobbing with the other med students. I got to be the best midnight scrambled-egg cook on an illegal electric burner that you ever heard of. It was a grind, but I really loved the whole atmosphere — it was almost like being on some kind of wartime mission.

And looking back on his life with his wife-physician, he explains:

There *are* times when I think how much simpler it all was for my father — he would just come home and take his ease, and let everybody fuss over him. He was the one who counted, and everything was arranged to suit him. Sometimes I wish it were that way with me. But then Rosalie and I go out to dinner and I see people our own age sitting opposite each other but staring around sideways or looking at their food, and not having anything at all to say to each other. We're still like each other's dates — after eighteen years. We always find each other interesting, and its amazing to see how she really looks especially pretty and full of bounce after she's just pulled off a tricky operation and is still all excited and pleased by it, even though she's really dead-tired. I can't be sure how all this would have worked out if I weren't pretty successful in my own field, but I am. She has great respect for what I do, and she has even come to court a few times to hear me. She's very much a women with me, but once in a while, if she tries to take over a little too much, I call her "Doctor" very respectfully, and she gets nettled for a minute, and then laughs and turns it off.[11]

The threat of competition between two professionals married to each other may, in many cases, be something which is more feared than actually experienced. "Competition" — a word which to many women still has such negative connotations that it can barely be discussed for longer than it takes to make a complete denial of its existence in their lives — is often a positive glue and source of stimulation to professional as well as non-professional couples. In casual discussion, the word may call up visions of the wife increasing her salary to match her husband's, or refusing to carry out those wifely duties which might make her subservient in her own and her husband's eyes. As a constructive force, however, competition may prompt both parties to read outside their fields, to "keep up with" their mates, or to work hard for a position that the mate will be proud of. Not only do more men appear to be able today to take independently successful wives than ever before, but women professionals still have a long way to go before they become as openly aggressive and competitive as some people fear they are. Most women doctors, because of children or their own lesser aspirations, limit their professional careers and do not succeed to as high a level as their husbands. In the few cases where they have married below their own professional prestige level,[12] there has been an attempt to preserve the traditional ranking. "At work I head a program and manage my duties the way I think best, but at home my husband is the boss, and I like it that way," stated one physician. Another woman who had married a man with no college degree refused a position as chief of a government service because she would outrank her husband socially and economically. Whether or not she unconsciously married someone with less education than she because it would limit her own achievement is difficult to say. In general, women physicians stress the importance of having a husband who is successful in his own world, whatever he does. If the woman feels that his self-confidence is secure and not at stake in her success, she will have the freedom to go as far as she herself wants.

A common notion is that the competition implicit when both mates have professional status will lead more easily to divorce; this attitude is defended by citing the fact that there is a somewhat higher divorce rate among women physicians than among the general female population.[13] However, the higher rate of divorce is probably due much less to competition than to a laissez-faire attitude which can arise when both partners have busy schedules. Because people have such fear of open aggression in interpersonal relations, they assume that the tragedy of divorce can only stem from the bloody battles which must surely occur when two people are strong. What is more common is the situation in which the physician, extending her highly-controlled manner into her home, allows both of them to drift further and further away until either a divorce occurs or the marriage continues only in name. In interviews with women doctors, one gains the impression that they are sometimes able to shed their husbands in much the same way that a general loses a horse shot from under him — without forfeiting momentum in their careers. A woman doctor who married in the first year of medical school and divorced several years later, admitted that she had felt nothing throughout the whole divorce proceedings — no one around her had guessed that anything was amiss — and she had not even cried during it. One day about a year later, during her internship, an elder physician scolded her in front of a patient for making a sloppy presentation. At this moment, through the tears of professional humiliation, she was able to feel all the accumulated pain of the other experience.

It would be unfair to leave out the positive side of the higher divorce rate among women physicians and other professional women. Having an economically rewarding as well as emotionally fulfilling career, they need marriage neither as the sole financial nor emotional center for their lives. In many cases, where an untrained woman might feel forced to hang on to a bad situation, a self-sufficient doctor would be free to work out a better life.

Physician-Mothers and Conflicting Commitments

In her own way, the modern professional woman may come closer to the Renaissance ideal of self-fulfillment along many lines than her male contemporaries. Although women doctors do not achieve as many "firsts" in their fields as do the men, they usually express themselves in a wider range of abilities and interests over their lives. For this reason, it is often difficult for themselves and others to evaluate their success. According to the psychologist, David McClelland:

> The phrase "part time" catches a lot of the essence of the feminine style of life in a very practical sense. Women will be part time daughters, part time mothers, part time wives, part time cooks, part time intellectuals, part time workers. They may spend part of their lives being wholly wives and mothers and another part being wholly intellectuals. But their psychology permits this degree of alternation more easily than for a man who will often blindly follow a single course. A woman's success is less easily visible by the same token, because it consists of the sum of all these activities rather than the result of a single-minded pursuit of one.[14]

The ranks of women physicians, probably more than any other professional women's group, have furnished models to prove that the effective balance of many different activities is one of the more common miracles to be encountered in the world. They have larger families than do women lawyers or academic women and, at the same time, their record for the amount of time given to their profession is better than that of either of the other groups.[15] In a way which is admirable and sometimes frightening, they show a great capacity to have their cake and eat it too.

Needless to say, combining medicine with raising a family is not an easy task: it requires much energy and planning to do well by husband, children, and profession, and, what is equally important, to see that she herself does not suffer. The paradox is that what may appear in one light as perhaps being a little self-indulgent (i.e., having your cake, etc.) yields the practical result of being placed in a position in which the woman's own subsequent demands cannot be listened to, least of all by herself. She has to operate with a great degree of responsibility, and with the ever-present reminder that she has no right to neglect any of her jobs for relief — because she herself has taken them on. In effect, she is submerging herself in a tunnel of obligations for ten or twenty years, with little time to come up for air, but with the conviction that this is the most satisfying kind of life that can be had.

The dangers to this course are strain and a loss of touch with herself. One psychiatrist said:

> The demands of psychiatric patients on the one hand and of young children on the other are very exhausting, and I am often fatigued. Though I get through at my office each day at 2:00 p.m., I find there is little time to do anything for *myself.*

Some women physicians report that they simply relinquish any thoughts of taking care of themselves while their children are young. For those who continue working throughout this period, it may seem like an extended internship with two centers of crises: the hospital and the home.

Although women doctors have great resources and energy, their assumption of more and more responsibilities may bring them to a limit where one activity must be sacrificed or curtailed for another. The most usual circumstance effecting this occurs when they have children. The appearance of children may solidify a marriage and may help the woman to maintain her feminine identity while working in a man's world, but her capacity for involvement in her career and husband is more likely to undergo reduction. One important medical staff member was asked which of the three — career, husband, or children — was more likely to be put off a little by a woman doctor when the going got rough. Her answer was brief and decisive: "Well, the children certainly don't suffer." When pressed for the next in line, she was a little more evasive and finally said: "I believe, and I think most women physicians believe, that they have a very real duty to use their medical education and serve the community's health problems." The question was dropped at that, but the intimation of who the third place candidate might be was clear.

With their wives bustling between patients and children (and often having little time for personal adornment or special attentiveness), it· is not surprising that husbands often take a more "conservative" line about having the woman return home during the child-rearing years than the women themselves. In a study of college graduates:

> . . . although one-half of the women thought it appropriate for a woman to take a part time job if a child is a pre-schooler, only one-third of the men approved. One-fourth of the men and only 14 per cent of the women thought a full time job should not be taken until the children were "all grown up."[16]

While the man says that having his wife stay home is for the children's sake, this attitude may actually be triggered by his own sense of being the neglected and forgotten party. Such feelings often depart when the woman learns how to juggle her roles and loses some of her time-consuming anxiety; although with all of these responsibilities, the amount of time that the couple has alone together cannot help but decrease. A woman dermatologist, who lived in the suburbs but practiced in the city, told me that she commuted with her husband each morning and evening: their forty-five minutes together on the train was the only guaranteed time during the day which they had alone, and they put it to good use.

When the doctor leaves her position or practice to give birth to her child, an important question for her to settle is: When should she go back? Some stay at home little more than the time needed for the delivery and are back at work a week later. Others try to spend the first six months with the child. Still others feel that they are needed at home during the child's formative years, until he goes off to pre-school or kindergarten. Women physicians interviewed often reported that they had spent much longer at home with one child than with another; their decision to remain at home or return to work was usually determined either by the feasibility of taking maternity leave or by their own energy. (Many hospitals, for instance, still do not guarantee a job to a physician-mother who leaves for six months to have her child, even though men are given two year's military leave.) Of course, personal convictions about child-rearing also play a significant role.

There is confusion among women doctors — probably as great as among the population as a whole in this epoch — about what the needs of a young child are for his mother and what the responsibilities of a mother are to her child. Living in a sea of half-facts and hypotheses and waiting for the "final" research reports to come in (if they ever do), the woman physician goes ahead and does what she feels she has to do. Comparing afterwards her own children and those of her friends and neighbors, she justifies her decision by her children's successes and blames herself for their failures. "If I had stayed home when he was little, he might not have that allergy," said one. Another who did remain at home for the first few years wondered whether her return to work could have been accomplished with less heartache if she had never tried to become a full-time mother.

Betty Friedan tells of the response of an orthodox Jewish woman, a doctor's wife and herself a physician, to returning to work after devoting years to her husband and four children.

> An unassertive, quiet woman, she exerted almost unbelievable effort to obtain her license after fifteen years of inactivity. She told me apologetically: "You just can't stop being interested. I tried to make myself, but I couldn't." And she confessed that when she gets a night call, she sneaks out guiltily as if she were meeting a lover.[17]

Women who continue working, or who return to work while their children are still in school, often show great determination to see that each child gets sufficient care and stimulation. Although the mothers' days are spent away from home, they emphasize the quality of the interaction with their children rather than mere quantity. Some mother-physicians have said they feel that they are able to give their children more when they are working, because they actively enjoy the time spent with them and are not as distracted as they would be were they home all day long. One mother, and her husband, had bought a house in the country to which the whole family retired every Friday afternoon for a concentrated weekend. As her children grew older and the stimulation of the city outshone the pleasures of the cottage and family life, she devised alternative activities which would continue to bring the family together regularly. Another said that she carefully scanned the newspaper during her coffee breaks at the hospital to plan a weekly excursion with her children. When the day came, she often found herself with several additional children from the neighborhood, which pleased her, since most of their mothers did not work.

Women physicians, even when relatively satisfied with the job they are doing both at home and at work, confess to having the feeling of being torn between their responsibilities in the two areas. As one woman expressed it, "I can't help resenting a lot of the time I spend away from home. I'd like to be able to share more with my children. But it's probably my loss more than theirs. . ." Another put it this way: "I feel as if I'm always apologizing, either to my profession when I have to go home, or to other women who say, 'Oh, I couldn't leave my child.' "

Morton Hunt has observed that, "The woman who works although she does not need the money is a thorn in the flesh of her friends."[18] Women doctors are acutely aware of the hostile reactions which their professional commitment arouses in nonworking mothers; they may try to keep it a secret at casual social gatherings in order to prevent the "deep freeze" which sometimes ensues when it becomes known. One woman said that she rarely heard direct remarks against her. "More often I hear of them via the grapevine: 'You must be making a pile of money.' "

Early one morning, as a physician and mother of three children was hurrying off to work after having solved a crisis with the housekeeper and gotten her oldest off to school, she was stopped by a woman pushing a stroller. "How do you do," said the other woman. "You're Dr. X, aren't you? I'm Dr. So-and-so from down the street. But I gave up medicine to be a mother to my childen." The doctor who told me this story added that during the next years she had become a much better friend of her neighbor than their first meeting might have forecasted. Behind the woman's aggressive introduction lay an unhappiness at having given up her profession. (She had dropped out before receiving her license and could find nothing on a part time basis which she felt would justify the sacrifice of time spent with her children.) After many long talks with the practicing physician, she began studying to pass her boards and eventually found a job which required her services only part of the day, a few days a week; in this manner she slowly returned to medicine. The assistance and encouragement given by the practicing doctor was not merely altruistic, however; as she herself intimated, women who "sacrifice" themselves to family life and raising children always make a professional woman feel a little guilty about maintaining her independent identity.

The Practical Problems of Child Care

One variable in a woman's decision either to continue working or to give up her profession while her children are small is the actual physical help available to her. In much of the writing about women in medicine and how they do or do not fulfill their responsibilities to the profession, the emphasis is placed on inherent motivation — their ability to stick it out no matter what the obstacles — and little attention is given to the very real difficulties they face and what might be done to make it easier for the professional woman with children.

The business of employing a woman to take care of one's children involves many potential obstacles. One of the first considerations is the character of the baby sitter. Many women physicians, probably because of their original concern for health and their desire to ensure adequate protection in this area, hire retired nurses or nurses' aides to take care of their children. In several instances, the physicians said they had paid a nurse the equivalent of her hospital salary so that she would give up her job to take care of the children. On the other hand, some women felt that in choosing a mother-substitute for the baby, "anyone who is warm and kind" would be satisfactory. One doctor said that she wanted "someone who will tell me when she is disgusted with my children as well as when she thinks they are adorable and has had a good day with them."

The difficulties inherent in even the best mother-substitutes are well known. No other person can feel exactly the same as the mother does about all aspects of child-rearing, and not the worst of eventualities is the mother's suspicion that her child is giving a little too much affection to his baby sitter. One physician was resentful that her housekeeper had won her little daughter over by a lack of discipline. The woman fed the little girl, instead of forcing her to feed herself — it was less work and quicker, since the housekeeper avoided having to clean up the mess — and then when the mother came home and tried to get the girl to eat her evening meal, the child became quite passive, waiting for her mother to help her the way the other woman did. Another physician commented a little wistfully that her two children ran into the arms of the babysitter when the woman arrived each morning, and were often busy with their play when she herself came home.

A physician practicing in the suburbs believed that not enough consideration is given to the "social situation currently facing women who plan to enter careers." Elaborating on her feelings in this respect, she said:

> It is now no longer possible for a woman who has normal desires for a family to combine motherhood and a career, largely due to the increasing impossibility of securing adequate domestic help. I was able to do it, with some difficulty, when my children were small and can continue now only because they are old enough to manage and help out. I would not encourage my own daughter to hope for a career involving commitments outside the home and then face the frustration of being unable to use her skills and potential. As a psychiatrist, I am frequently called on to treat the consequences of this frustration.
>
> I believe that unless the government takes steps to remedy the present situation, and to free the manpower inherent in married women, it will only worsen. A career and children today demand superhuman motivation from a mother which can only include neglect of children.

Since 1940, resources for child care and household help have shrunk from 18 per cent of the employed women to 8 per cent; at the same time, more and more mothers have entered the labor market.[19] Nothing has been done to raise the status of housekeepers in the United States, and as a result, fewer and fewer women are willing to offer this service. The decrease is also not surprising when one considers that the job has few of the protections and benefits other workers take for granted, and no future or possibility for advancement. It is at present nearly impossible to find child care facilities of sufficient quality to give a working mother the tranquility needed to do her job well. A general practitioner, who had obviously had a series of bad experiences, expressed her feelings on the situation rather bluntly:

> No one but derelicts, failures, drifters and convicts even applies. To stay with one family more than a month is unusual, and if the lady of the house isn't there to supervise, the idea is to steal as much as possible either directly or indirectly. No one ever heard of training

for such a job and the employment agencies are interested only in their percentages.

While it is still possible to find good help, it is generally recognized that provisions are inadequate. One resident, at the end of her wits, told me that she had had six housekeepers in the past year, all of whom had left unexpectedly, and that she was going to relinquish her position at the end of the month to give her children a more settled life. Another physician said that after many unsuccessful trials, she had finally come upon a way of handling her child care problems: she hired several women on a part time basis, often mothers who had themselves children to care for and could thus appreciate the difficulties of a mother with more than one responsibility. With the resources of two or three women at hand, she could nearly always find one of them to cover for her — one of the greatest difficulties of the woman physician who is subject to emergency calls.

Two proposals have recently been made to raise the status of women offering housekeeping and child care services, thus ensuring a higher quality and greater number of women taking on these jobs. The President's Commission on the Status of Women suggested in its 1963 report that household workers should be unionized, and that facilities should be established to train women in child care.[20]

The women physicians who are at present most contented with their arrangements are probably those with relatives or friends nearby upon whom they can depend. Even the mother-in-law whose child-rearing philosophy seems "outdated," or who is more permissive than one would like her to be, is more apt to be a loving and dependable baby-sitter than a stranger. In addition, it is a rare relative who demands the same salary as a woman hired on the outside, and the saving of this expense can be a great boon to the mother who wants to work, but who, under normal conditions, would not have been able to finance it.

Three alternatives are open to the physician-mother determined to work but unable to secure adequate housekeeping or child care in her own locality. The first, the importing of domestic help from Europe, has become more widespread in recent years. The young women secured in this way provide the family with the stimulation of a foreign language and tradition. They also bring their problems of adjusting to a new, bewildering society, which gives the employer an added responsibility that may be enriching or troublesome, depending on the situation. The total cost of hiring a foreign girl is usually no more than domestic help.

The second alternative is the day-care center. Although such institutions are still rare, government-run centers have been established in most of the metropolitan areas of the United States, and many large hospitals now have crèches and nurseries for their personnel. The reluctance of women physicians to use these centers is based perhaps on an emotional connection with the Brave New World picture of depersonalized child care. And there is an association with the lower-classes, since many centers are presently in lower-class housing projects and/or connected to welfare centers. A resident at a city hospital observed that while there was a crèche in the hospital for the children of employees, it had become exclusively the place for the children of janitorial help, aides, and perhaps a minority of nurses. Few of the physicians in the hospital had heard of its existence, and still fewer would consider leaving their children there, even though doing so would give them the opportunity to drop in and see the child during the day. A hospital administrator said that when a crèche in his hospital had first opened, he had encouraged women doctors and other higher status personnel to use it, but they had taken the conservative position of waiting to see how it would turn out first. In the interim the crèche had become utilized by unskilled and semi-skilled personnel. "They should have come in right at the beginning, to set the pace!" he said.

Interestingly, even in the U.S.S.R. and other Eastern European socialist countries where women are actively encouraged to work, the official attitudes toward child-care facilities have not been completely ironed out. The majority of working women in Russia have no choice but to use domestic help or to raise the children themselves, and, as a result, they end up bearing a disproportionate share of the work load. Government policy itself has appeared to favor this solution.

Although the government has allocated substantial investment funds over the years to the expansion of child care facilities, it has been unwilling to assign this program sufficient resources to satisfy demand. On the contrary, it has chosen to compel most working women to make their own arrangements — with members of their families or outside help — for the care of their young children. This policy can hardly be considered beneficial to the working mothers. From the standpoint of the regime's overriding goal of economic growth, however, the imposition of hardship on the working mother and a slightly lower rate of participation of women in the labor force have apparently been considered preferable to the diversion of investment funds and other resources to additional child care facilities.[21]

At a panel discussion in Prague on love, sex, and the family in January, 1967, Milan Novak, a repairman and poet, spoke against women who turn their children over to "cold and uninterested institutions." Mr. Novak demanded that the state pay mothers a living wage for the job of raising children. "Raising children is a form of production, too," he said, "and a Socialist state owes wages according to productivity."[22]

While this idea may sound far-fetched, the President's Commission on the Status of Women argued for something quite similar, realizing that it could not be an immediate solution. The report stated, "The idea of treating homemaking as having a real monetary value, and so a kind of dignity, has important repercussions for women's choices of where and how they'll work, for it could do much to change the present status of the woman domestic worker."[23]

A third solution — along with foreign maids and day-care centers — is for the doctor to practice in an office in her own home. While some assistance with cleaning and even child care may still be needed, she is nearby to supervise and to help in case an emergency should arise. By staying at home, she can cut down on the extra costs of working outside: transportation, lunches, etc. Practicing at home also provides a kind of relaxation which is impossible with any outside job. Those who have adopted it to their satisfaction are often the most zealous partisans for this approach. Dr. Joanne Denko, a psychiatrist, reports in the *Journal of the American Medical Women's Association* that, having set up an office on an enclosed porch of her home, she is free to treat child patients on this porch or in her back yard at the sandbox. She can schedule her patients to coincide with her young son's nap-time, or in the evening when his father is home to take care of him. By making use of this flexible scheduling, she is able to control her own son's upbringing far more than she could if she were away at the office during the daytime. "In these years before he goes to school I try to teach him things he won't learn there. I make a conscious effort to impress on him values I consider important, rudiments of scientific method, and sensitivity to beauty."[24] She lists a series of such educational experiences: introducing him to forms, colors, smells, and textures in nature, encouraging him to have scientific observation but "not to discourage in him the imaginative, metaphoric, almost poetic way children think until adults stifle it," and going for long walks in the country.

> All these pursuits are inordinately time-consuming and would not be possible if I were either a full time physician or a standard harassed wife-housekeeper-cook-nurse-mother. Admittedly, the investment by society in my education is not now bringing maximal returns. But this is my compromise with the investment I make in my child.[25]

This points up one of the problematic characteristics of working at home: that it is more suitable to part-time than full-time work, and those who begin it with plans for the latter schedule usually switch to the former. Even doctors who continue full-time work feel a loss of the demarcation between their family and professional lives. A pediatrician who had maintained an office in her house for a time while her children were young observed that, in retrospect, she thought the quality of her work had not been as good as it would have been had she found someone to assume entire responsibility for the children while she went to an office. An additional problem (although one which can be overcome) is that contacts with other doctors — and thus referrals — decrease: for the woman who goes immediately from training into such a practice, it can take some time to build up a remunerative clientele.

*   *   *   *   *

A universal complaint among women physicians, whether they employ full-time housekeepers or share the job with part-time workers, is the cost of help to substitute for them at home. Many pay up to $100 a week for full-time help, and the fees may actually be higher when the household helper lives in. During the internship and residency, if the doctor has children, her salary may easily be less than what she pays her housekeeper or baby sitter. If she is in a part-time program, she may spend double her salary from the hospital for someone to take care of her children. The Radcliffe Institute is the only organization until now to realize the importance of this cost in discouraging the mother from continuing her career: Radcliffe physicians-in-training receive the difference between salary and child-care expenses, so that they will not sustain a heavy financial loss through training.

Even with a full salary, many women physicians do not add substantially to their family's total income while the children are young. Some resign themselves to not earning this additional income, but their husbands may be less reconciled, particularly if they are concerned about the welfare of the children with a working mother and wonder what is gained by the wife's job. According to a *New York Times* article on the subject:

> The $15,000-a-year wife married to a husband who earns $20,000 adds about $3,300 to the family's net income, after taxes and her expenses of $5,000 for a housekeeper or nurse for her two children and $1,500 for her own lunches, extra clothes, carfare, and the like. The family has about $3,300 a year more because she works than if they depended on the husband's income alone. In the case of lower salary levels the advantage is much less.[26]

Two solutions might be offered to this problem: government subsidy for child care expense, or tax deductions for the cost of housekeeping and baby sitting to the working mother. The latter approach is more widely known and espoused by women doctors. It has a plausible justification: a man can deduct his business expenses, while a woman cannot take off the child care salary she pays, although it is an expense necessary for her work. A baby sitter is considered a cost which must be borne by the woman alone; the government wants women to work, but thus far has provided no encouragement.

> How my blood used to boil as I would drive to the hospital in my business-expense-deducted automobile after paying $10.00 in cash for the middle-of-the-night babysitter without whom I could not practice medicine. No deduction. But as for the car, well I could always walk . . .

Such problems are not unique to women physicians. At the Governor's Conference on Women in New York in the fall of 1966, working women of all professions reported that their salaries could barely meet the costs of their going to work, and the request was made that child care expenses be tax deductible. At present, deductions for child care extend only to those women whose incomes are necessary for the support of the family: in other words, those who are divorced, widowed, or for some other reason the sole support, or those whose income combined with their husband's does not exceed the minimum level of $6,000. While it is true that mother-physicians may have to make more concessions than they are presently willing to make — accepting crèches and day-care centers, for example — the government also has a responsibility to ease the burden of these women if their skills and knowledge are to be fully utilized.

NOTES

This study is based on questionnaires and interviews of male and female physicians, medical school deans, educators, and students.

1. Lotte Bailyn, "Notes on the Role of Choice in the Psychology of Professional Women," in Robert J. Lifton (ed.), *The Woman in America* (Boston: Houghton Mifflin, 1965), p. 237.

2. Lee Powers, Harry Wiesenfelder, and Rexford C. Parmelee, "Practice Patterns of Women and Men Physicians," Preliminary Report (October, 1966), Tables 4-B and 7.

3. "The Case against the Female M.D." *Medical Economics* (December, 1961).

4. Elizabeth Herzog, *Children of Working Mothers* (Washington: U.S. Department of Health, Education, and Welfare, Children's Bureau, 1960).

5. Alice S. Rossi, "Why So Few Women Become Engineers, Doctors, and Scientists." In Jacquelyn A. Mattfield and Carol G. Van Aken (eds.), *Women and the Scientific Professions* (Cambridge: The M.I.T. Press, 1965), p. 97.

6. *Ibid.*

7. Powers, Wiesenfelder, and Parmelee, "Practice Patterns," Table 10.

8. *Ibid.,* Table 15.

9. Edna G. Rostow, "Conflict and Accommodation," in Robert J. Lifton (ed.), *The Woman in America,* p. 224.

10. Rita L. Stafford, "An Analysis of Consciously Recalled Motivating Factors and Subsequent Professional Involvement for American Women in New York State" (unpublished Ph.D. dissertation, School of Education, New York University, 1967), p. 317.

11. Morton M. Hunt, *Her Infinite Variety* (New York: Harper and Row, 1962), pp. 281-82.

12. Although no statistics are available on the number of women physicians married to nonprofessionals, my impression from interviews with women doctors, corroborated by data on women in other professions, suggests that the nonprofessional husband is a rarity. In Ginzberg's study of women receiving graduate training at Columbia University, for instance, only one-fourth had husbands who did not have at least one graduate degree. See Eli Ginzberg and associates, *Life Styles of Educated Women* (New York: Columbia University Press, 1966), p. 25.

13. Data on physicians from Powers, Wiesenfelder, and Parmelee, "Practice Patterns," Table 3. Data on general population from Paul H. Jacobson, *American Marriage and Divorce* (New York: Rhinehart, 1959), p. 159.

14. David C. McClelland, "Wanted: A New Self-image for Woman," in Robert J. Liifton (ed.), *The Woman in America*, pp. 187-88.

15. Stafford, "An Analysis of Consciously Recalled Motivating Factors and Subsequent Professional Involvement" (pp. 346 and 348) compares women physicians and lawyers by the number of hours per week and per year given to the profession. Jessie Bernard, *Academic Women* (Cleveland: Meridian, 1966), pp. 85-95 gives statistics on career patterns among academic women.

16. Rossi, "Why So Few Women Become Engineers, Doctors, and Scientists," p. 87.

17. Betty Friedan, *The Feminine Mystique* (New York: Dell, 1963), p. 340.

18. Hunt, *Her Infinite Variety*, p. 271.

19. Margaret Mead and Frances Balgley Kaplan (eds.), *American Women: Report of the President's Commission on the Status of Women*, and other publications of the Commission (New York: Charles Scribner's Sons, 1965), p. 41.

20. *Ibid.*, pp. 40 and 224.

21. Norton Dodge, *Women in the Soviet Economy* (Baltimore: The Johns Hopkins Press, 1966), p. 241.

22. "Sex Advice Given by Czech Panel," *New York Times* (January 19, 1967).

23. Mead and Kaplan, *American Women*, p. 187.

24. Joanne D. Denko, "Managing a practice and a home simultaneously; one woman's solution," *J. Amer. Med. Wom. Ass.* 20, no. 8 (1965): 765.

25. *Ibid.*

26. Elizabeth Fowler, "Personal Finance; Working Wife Finds that her Pay Doesn't Double the Family's Income," *New York Times* (December 29, 1966).

thirty-six

Career Patterns of Married Couples

LYNDA LYTLE HOLMSTROM

Careers, as Everett Hughes has emphasized, are played out within some kind of organized system. Thus to understand them, one must look at both the person and the institution. One must ask both questions about the individual and about the work system.[1]

The present study sought, using this framework, to understand the career patterns and contingencies which occur when both a husband and a wife have highly demanding careers. Specifically, the study focused on twenty couples in which both the husband and the wife were professionals. In each couple the wife had a doctorate — either in the physical sciences, social sciences, or the humanities. And she had an independent professional career of her own. Thus, these were deviant couples. They were challenging the system as it now exists in the United States. They had to face a whole series of barriers. These barriers are based on the assumption that only one spouse will work. And furthermore, these barriers assume that it is the husband who will work.

Both the husbands and wives in these twenty couples were interviewed. The couple was taken as the unit of analysis. This is different from many studies. Investigators interested in women's careers have typically taken the woman as the focus of the study, and have talked of how her career is influenced by her husband. This is, of course, important. But it seemed important to also investigate whether the opposite was true. And indeed the results of the study show that the husband's career is influ-

Revised version of a paper read at the Seventh World Congress of Sociology, Varna, Bulgaria, September 14-19, 1970, at the Round Table in Honor of Everett C. Hughes. Printed by permission of the author.

enced by that of his wife a lot more than most studies have previously indicated.

In the brief space allotted here, the focus will be on four career contingencies that these couples faced. The first three are due to the current structure of the professions in the United States. They are 1) the pressures for geographic mobility, 2) status inconsistencies of professional women because the professions are dominated by men, and 3) the pressure for full-time and uninterrupted careers. The fourth contingency has to do with the current structure of the family in the United States. It is the difficulty of raising children in the isolated nuclear family when both spouses work.

The first problem concerns the pressures for geographic mobility. It is advantageous, from the viewpoint of career advancement, if a person can determine his geographic residence independently of the interests of other members of the family. Most often it is a question of mobility. It is an advantage to be able to move about. There are more employment opportunities if a person is not restricted to one locale. People are given incentives to move in what Everett Hughes calls the itinerant job market.[2] In other words, there are incentives to move from employer to employer rather than going up the ladder in a single institution. And of course frequently a change of employer means a change of city too. The converse of this mobility is that a person needs to be able to remain in one locale long enough to finish school or to fulfill a job commitment. He cannot be taken away to some other geographic area because of the interests of other members of the family.

The typical "solution" in the United States has been to discourage women from the pursuit of a serious career at all. This is particularly true of married women. However, since most women expect to marry, the practical effect of discouraging married women is to discourage almost all women. By not permitting the wife to have competing career interests, she is left free to follow her husband on his itinerant circuit of jobs.

But in the two-career family, which was under study, the situation is more complex. It would be to each spouse's advantage to choose a geographic residence independently of the other's interests. Career opportunities may beckon the husband and wife in opposite directions. And yet presumably they wish to remain together as a family.

The couples in the study were asked how they had dealt with the issue of moving in the itinerant job market. In fifteen of the twenty couples this was an issue which had arisen since they had married.

In every one of these fifteen cases, the wife's decision about where to live had been significantly influenced by the career of her husband at least once. In most of these cases a move had occurred. The couple either negotiated simultaneously for a set of positions, moved taking account of the careers of both people, or the wife had followed the husband. This is not a surprising finding. It is very much in keeping with the social expectation that the husband's career is the important determinant of geographic residence, and the wife should follow her husband.

Turning the question around, however, there is a much more interesting finding. In most of these same couples, the husband's decision about where to live was significantly influenced by the career of his wife at least once. In most of these cases, a move occurred. The couple negotiated simultaneously for a set of positions, they moved taking account of the careers of both people, or the husband actually followed the wife. In a few cases, the decision was to not move or to postpone a move; for example, the husband remained somewhere an additional length of time while the wife finished up some research work that she was doing. This finding that the husband's geographic residence is influenced by the wife's career is of much greater surprise and interest. Previous studies have not paid much attention to this aspect; it is usually the opposite finding which is emphasized.

These couples deviated a great deal from the traditional middle-class pattern of the wife following the husband. But even so, they were still a long way from equality of the sexes. Although both spouses' careers were seen as very important, the husband's was still seen as more important than the wife's when deciding where to live. If ambition and plans were altered, it was the wife who typically made the bigger sacrifice. The women accommodated to their husbands' careers more than vice versa. It was among the wives, not the husbands, that instances occurred of giving up a tenured position with no new position yet in sight, accepting employment at a strictly undergraduate institution despite an interest in teaching graduate students, or interrupting a dissertation in order to move for the other person's job.

A second set of career contingencies is associated with the male dominance of the professions in the United States. Everett Hughes long ago called attention to how certain combinations of status-determining characteristics may make for contradictions of status.[3] A certain set of auxiilary characteristics comes to be associated with a status, and then these auxiliary characteristics are expected of its incumbents. It seems, for example, entirely natural that all Catholic priests should be men, although women are often more religious. And Hughes called attention to the fact that for many favored statuses and positions in the United States, the expected characterisics have traditionally been white, Anglo-Saxon, male and Protestant.

Even today the combined characteristics of female and professional can produce contradictions and dilemmas of status in a multitude of settings. Very often the rules of the game — the etiquette and so on — simply assume that the professional will be a man. If the professional is a woman, then there will be many occasions on which other people will not know whether to respond to her primarily as a professional or as a woman. A dilemma of this kind recently occurred in England when a woman judge was appointed to the High Court of Justice. A protocol crisis occurred over what the lawyers should call her. "My Lord" seemed confusing. But "Mrs. Justice" somehow did not sound right. Eventually it was decreed that for reasons of protocol the lady should be referred to as a man.[4]

The women in the study also reported a great variety of such contradictions. In one couple, a woman reported that she was very good at climbing towers and walking out on beams like a steeple jack; but, she said, sometimes there were "stuffy old men" who did not like to see a woman doing such a thing on the job. In another couple, the wife was an accomplished scientist with an international reputation. But when this couple moved to a new university, other people suddenly perceived her more as a woman than as a scientist. The method of dealing with the status dilemma was to maintain the fiction that she assisted her husband in his work. For example, the wife's work depended on access to very expensive equipment to gather data. Everybody knew that she did the empirical work and that he was the theoretician. Yet everybody maintained the fiction that he was the one who used the equipment and that she just went along to help him. When the work schedule came out saying who could use the equipment when, his name — not hers — appeared on the list. Eventually the husband got together with a friend of his and raised a big fuss, saying that they would "no longer tolerate such antiquated rules." A big battle raged through the university on her behalf. As a last ditch stand, the director was reduced to saying, "Well it's not easy to have her there regularly because there's no ladies' room." Fortunately, the couple finally won the battle. It was formally acknowledged that the wife used, and was entitled to use, the scientific equipment.

These status inconsistencies directly affect the women. But they sometimes also indirectly affect the husband. For example, in the couple just mentioned there was one time when the husband's career was affected by the kind of discriminatory treatment which his wife received. In one decision about where to accept employment, they turned down job offers at an institution where previously the wife had been made to feel uncomfortable. Thus the fact that "women were not welcome" influenced not only the wife's career, but also the husband's.

In the same way, more blatant forms of discrimination against women can also indirectly affect the men to whom they are married. Any factor which makes it harder for the wife to find employment also makes it harder for a couple to find career opportunities together. For example, one woman described her experience of applying to graduate school. One place where she and her husband applied said they did not grant Ph.D.'s to women. So the couple went elsewhere. Discrimination against this woman also affected her husband's career. It influenced where he went to graduate school.

A third set of career contingencies is associated with the pressure for full-time work and for uninterrupted careers. In the United States, preference is given to the individual who works or studies full-time and who does not have an interrupted career. Anything less than full-time employment may be difficult to obtain. Or, even if obtained, it may mean that one will be treated like a second-class citizen. For example, in many universities voting privileges are extended only to full-time members of the faculty; part-time people — no matter how well known or how committed they are to their work — are not allowed to vote in university affairs. Likewise, interruptions in employment may be looked on with disdain; "gaps in the vita" are hard to explain away.

To some degree, part-time status and career interruptions are matters of perception.[5] In actual fact, employers and educational institutions do make many special arrangements for part-time work and leaves of absence. The catch is that they only do it for individuals with socially acceptable reasons. And domestic responsibilities have not been one of these reasons. A man, if he divides his time between two part-time professional jobs, may be perceived as working full time. A woman, if she divides her time between work and family, may be perceived as working only part-time. Likewise, there is a difference between how different career interruptions are defined. Men often interrupt their careers for military service. Women often interrupt their careers for child rearing. For example, in the present study, half the women had interrupted careers — usually because of child rearing. And half the men had interrupted careers — typically for military duty. Thus half the women and half the men spent time away from their professions — but for different reasons. And these interruptions have, at least up to now, been perceived very differently by employers and school officials. In a curious paradox of human values men have been criticized only slightly for career interruptions in which their task was to kill off other members of the human race; but women have been severely criticized for taking time away from their profession in order to raise the next generation.

This pressure for continual full-time devotion to one's career has at least two effects. One is that any person who wishes to pursue a career less than full time, has to make special arrangements to do so. It is not an institutionalized pattern. Each person who wishes to do this must make some kind of *ad hoc* arrangement. For example, in the sample studied at least two women had to wage major battles with a university in order to be allowed to attend graduate school on a part-time basis. There just was no precedent for this sort of thing.

The second effect is that pressure for full-time commitment to one's career creates a very hectic time schedule. Time becomes a precious commodity — limited in supply and greatly in demand. A serious career requires an expenditure of a great deal of time. A family makes many demands on a person's time too; it is hard to develop a meaningful relationship with another person unless one has time in one's life for them.

Most of the women who were interviewed felt pressed for time. This is not surprising considering that there were many activities competing for their attention. Most of the men also felt pressed for time. These men said they felt this pressure either because of their own work responsibilities, the time they felt their family demanded, or complications from the fact that the wife also had a career. These husbands and wives made comments like "When the alarm goes off in the morning it's like the horses off at the races," and "In terms of time, our lives have been pretty much like a countdown for a rocket."

The women, in particular, responded to these pressures of time by organizing their use of this scarce resource. They budgeted time almost like one might budget money. They were very conscious — to use Everett Hughes' term — of their economy of time and effort.[6] The general tendency of the women was to follow a very complicated routine; different activities were allotted to a certain regular time in the weekly schedule.

Not only did most of the women have an organized routine, but a few went so far as to suggest that if a woman was not capable of being organized then it probably would not be possible to pursue a career. The pressures of time are also seen in that several couples reported that the husband and wife had competed with each other for time. For example, one woman reported that she and her husband had fought consistently about time commitments. She said they had not competed with each other professionally, but they had competed over whose schedule would have first priority.

A fourth set of career contingencies is associated with the family — especially child rearing. One striking feature of the family in the United States is the peculiar isolation of the middle-class nuclear family. The husband and wife are the only two adults around. They are literally responsible for all the tasks involved in earning a living and running a home. In the absence of other adult relatives, servants, and child-care centers, the wife in most middle-class couples is literally forced to remain at home to care for children when they are young. So the question is, what happens when the wife has an independent career of her own.

In the couples studied, most women received help in caring

for their children from their husbands and/or from hired help. In most couples with children, the husband gave his wife considerable assistance on a regular basis with the routine aspects of child care. Most couples had also employed help to assist them in caring for their children when they were young. The arrangements varied from full-time live-in help to day-time baby sitters who came to their home a certain number of hours.

The presence of children increased the complexities of scheduling. It affected the economy of time and effort of both the husband and the wife. Most of the husbands with children — even those on rather rigid work schedules — had had to take over at home for their wives at least occasionally; for example, they had done things like stay home half the day when the couple was unexpectedly without a baby sitter. A few husbands who had flexible work schedules, had been willing to do a lot of their work at home and do a large share of the baby-sitting; these couples had been able and willing to arrange their schedules so that the husband and wife took turns being at home. This shows, once again, the usefulness of taking the couple as the unit of analysis. The career contingencies associated with two careers in a family affected not only the women, but also the men.

In conclusion, perhaps some comments on change would be appropriate. At present the occupational system and family system in the United States create many career contingencies which make it very difficult for both spouses to follow careers. Many of these contingencies have to do with the inflexibility of occupations and the isolation of the nuclear family. Thus two changes would be particularly helpful.

The first suggestion is to promote more flexible work schedules for both men and women. A flexible schedule means having some choice over which particular hours one will work, even though the total number of hours may remain constant. The present study showed, that for women who had combined career with major responsibilities for child rearing, flexibility of hours was often more important than the absolute number of hours involved. For example, one woman found it easier to work nine to six rather than eight to five, because the former made it easier to get the children off to school. Also, flexibility of work involves the idea that a person, especially when his or her children are young, should be able to work "less than full time" without being unduly penalized for this. The idea that men as well as women might work less when their children are young has already come up for discussion in other countries such as Sweden.

The second suggestion is that day-time child-care centers be established in the United States. The present study showed that it is difficult in the United States for a parent in a two-career family to combine professional and child-rearing responsibilities because there are no collective solutions to these problems. Most of the men and women who were interviewed expressed positive attitudes toward the idea of child-care centers. Such centers, of course, have already been built in a number of other countries — the Soviet Union, Sweden, and Denmark, to name just a few. Hopefully, in the future, the United States will follow their lead in this matter.

NOTES

The research reported in this paper was done under Grant No. 91-23-68-45 from the Manpower Administration, U. S. Department of Labor, under the Manpower Administration, U. S. Department of Labor, under the authority of Title I of the Manpower Development and Training Act of 1962, as amended. Reseachers undertaking such projects under Government sponsorship are encouraged to express freely their professional judgment. Therefore, points of view or opinions stated in this document do not necessarily represent the official position or policy of the Department of Labor. Reproduction in whole or part is permitted for any purpose of the United States Government.

1. Everett Cherrington Hughes, *Men and Their Work* (Glencoe, Ill.: Free Press, 1958), p. 8.

2. *Ibid.,* p. 136.

3. Everett Cherrington Hughes, "Dilemmas and Contradictions of Status," *American Journal of Sociology,* 50 (March, 1945), pp. 353-59.

4. Cynthia Fuchs Epstein, *Woman's Place* (Berkeley: Univ. of California Press, 1970), pp. 88-89.

5. Hughes has written on the variability of what is defined as full-time work. Everett C. Hughes, "Neo-Feminism: An Essay on Woman's Work," (Mimeographed).

6. The concept level and direction of effort has been important in Hughes' work on student culture. See Howard S. Becker *et al., Boys in White: Student Culture in Medical School* (Chicago: Univ. of Chicago Press, 1961) and Howard S. Becker, Blanche Geer, and Everett C. Hughes, *Making the Grade: The Academic Side of College Life* (New York: Wiley, 1968).

thirty-seven

The Married Professional Social Worker

JOHN E. TROPMAN

The need for manpower in the social work profession has never
been greater. Private and public agencies are short of staff at the
same time that new ventures to help those in need are opening
up even greater opportunities for the social work profession.
Indeed, so great is the demand for people in the helping professions, that social work is in danger of "competition" for many
positions from people with all manner of training in personal
and social helping. The law of supply and demand could produce
a plethora of "professions" and "training schools" of dubious
quality. To meet manpower needs, and to prevent an unwise
"mushrooming" of various mental health professionals, the
social work profession must be able to staff many positions now
unfilled.

One factor which is contributing to the manpower shortage is
the number of trained professionals who are not working at professional tasks. Professional women social workers with a husband and family typically spend important portions of their time
carrying out familial duties — time which is thus lost to the profession. The kind of employment picture which these women
present has important implications for training policy. It can be
argued that if such women, once trained, become substantially
lost to the profession, then a case can be made for not training
them at all. On the other hand, it may be that women at certain

From JOURNAL OF MARRIAGE AND THE FAMILY, Vol. 30, No. 4 (1968),
pp. 661-665. Reprinted by permission of the author and the National Council on Family Relations.

points in the life cycle are exceptionally good professional investments. Exactly what, in fact, is the employment pattern of professionally trained women social workers is a topic which generates considerable affect, a fact which in itself indicates a lack of empirical evidence. This research note is a beginning step toward developing some of those facts.

Specifically, in this research the investigators were interested in the actual amount of attrition in a sample of professionally trained women social workers. Secondly, previous research had suggested that there is a relationship between employment and the timing of marriage, and the investigators wished to reinvestigate this finding.[1] Thirdly, they were interested in the relationship of employment patterns to the age of children in the professional woman's family. It seems "obvious" that the professional woman's employment picture would be related to the age of her children, but such "obvious" relationships are often the ones which need to be investigated the most. Finally, the investigators were interested in the problem of "role conflict" among professionally trained women. There is much discussion and little evidence in this area, and even a small amount of data would be useful.

The Sample

The sample was composed of married women social workers who had received the master's degree from the School of Social Service Administration, The University of Chicago, between 1938 and 1958. They had to be currently married, have children, and reside in Cook County, Illinois. The lists of the School were inspected, and the names of the 130 women who met these criteria were selected. Of the 130, it was possible to interview 117, or about 90 percent. Of the 117, seven had left the field of social work, leaving an effective sample size of 110. It should be noted that most of the interviewing was done by women who were themselves in the second year of the professional social work program. The effect which this status might have had on the information elicited is impossible to assess. The interviews averaged about one and one-half hours in length, using a combination of closed and open-ended questions on the schedule. The interviewers reported that, generally speaking, the interviewers were very willing to answer the questions and often engaged in some considerable additional discussion on the general topic.

It should be underscored, however, that there are definite limitations to a sample such as this one. There is no way of telling whether certain types of women were likely to leave the city. While the investigators "assume" that there is no significant difference between the women who stayed and those who left, this assumption arises more from necessity than certainty. Additionally, the Chicago employment picture, though internally varied, may differ in significant respects from the employment picture in other communities. For a variety of reasons, more (or fewer) women might be working in other communities. The reader is cautioned that the Chicago situation thus may be a rather specialized one and not a good basis for generalization.

Recognizing limitations does not mean the cessation of research. But it does devolve upon the writer to draw generalizations only to the extent the sample will permit, and it devolves upon the reader not to assign to the writer findings of a generality greater than he can legitimately claim.

Characteristics of the Sample

The respondents married men of good education and relatively high socioeconomic status. The majority fell into Classes I and II on a modified Hollingshead- and Redlich-type scale.[2] The median income of the husbands in the group was $13,000 per year. The respondents were primarily Jewish (63/110) and Protestant (42/110).* There were only five Catholics. The median age of the respondents was approximately 40 years.

(1)   The Work Experience of the Women

That there is indeed some considerable attrition can be seen from Table 1. Of the 110 women, 20 were employed full time, and an additional 25 were employed part time. The remaining

Table 1 / The Employment of Professional Women Social Workers in Social Work

Total	Current Employment Status		
	Full Time	Part Time	Un-employed
110 (100%)	20 (18%)	25 (23%)	65 (59%)

* Because the sample size of 110 is so close to 100, it seems unnecessary to compute percentages continually since they will be only slightly smaller than the actual frequencies. Hence, throughout this report the frequencies will be reported over the relevant base as shown.

group, 65/110, were not employed at all. The rate of attrition is thus over 50%. Such a rate is high by any standards.

This percentage is, of course, a figure for one moment in time only. One can raise a question about the total work experience for each woman. Perhaps over time the picture is less bleak.

On the basis of detailed work histories, the total time each woman had actually worked was ascertained. This figure was divided by the total amount of time she had available for work. The resulting figure, multiplied by 100, gave a score for each woman called the Employment Quotient, or E.Q. The E.Q. is thus a simple statement of the work experience of each woman. Considering the entire sample, one finds that the average E.Q. is 43.9 percent. Had every woman worked for all of the time she had available to her, the E.Q. would have been 100 percent. Thus, on the average, the women in the sample have worked a little over 40 percent of the time available to them to work. Put another way, the women have, on the average, been unemployed about 57 percent of the time. Thus the current proportion of unemployment (60/110) is only slightly higher than the work experience seen historically. The findings are thus only slightly less dismal.

In this sample, at least, there can be no question that there is a high attrition rate of professionally trained women. Should these figures be applicable on a national scale, there would be every cause for concern. While there is no way to assess the degree to which this sample is representative of the national scene, the author might note that it is perhaps most easy to get work in a large metropolis. The cities of Chicago, New York, and San Francisco provide a heavy complement of social work opportunity. Thus it should be understood that this paper is discussing employment patterns under conditions of reasonable opportunity. What might happen as the opportunity, and especially the opportunity for part-time work, becomes constricted, is cause for additional concern.

(2) Employment Patterns and Timing of Marriage

It has been hypothesized in the literature that women who enter professional training already married are more likely to work than those who receive the degree before they are married.[3] This understanding is based upon the assumption that, if a woman decides to go to school and is married, she has somehow weighed the duties of marriage as part of her overall calculus in the decision to go to school. If she can be married and go to school, it is also likely that she can be married and work. The unmarried professional woman is expected to cease working upon marriage, her new duties being perhaps more pressing.

It is true that women who were married before admission to professional school work more than women who were married afterwards. This finding can be seen in Table 2A.

Table 2A / Professional Women Social Workers by Current Employment Status and Marital Status at Admission to Professional School

Marital Status	Current Employment Status		
	Total	Employed	Unemployed
Total	110	45	65
	(100%)	(41%)	(59%)
Married Before Admission	29	19	10
	(100%)	(66%)	(34%)
Married After Admission	81	26	55
	(100%)	(32%)	(68%)

However, if one inspects the data more closely and controls for the age of the children, this difference evaporates. This finding is presented in Table 2B.

Table 2B / Professional Women Social Workers by Current Employment Status, Marital Status at Admission to Professional School, and Age of Youngest Child

Age of Youngest Child and Marital Status at Admission	Current Employment Status		
	Total	Employed	Unemployed
Total	110	45	65
	(100%)	(41%)	(59%)
Age Less Than Six			
Married Before	12	5	7
	(100%)	(42%)	(50%)
Married After	50	9	41
	(100%)	(18%)	(82%)
Age More Than Six			
Married Before	17	14	3
	(100%)	(83%)	(17%)
Married After	31	17	14
	(100%)	(55%)	(45%)

The more significant variable seemed to be the presence or absence of young children, rather than the timing of marriage in relationship to admission. This finding suggested that the relationship of children to the timing of admission would be a salient feature. To explore this idea, the investigator looked at the subset of women who were admitted after the birth of the first child. It can be seen from Table 3 that the presence of

Table 3 / Professional Women Social Workers by Parity Status at Admission to Professional School and Current Employment Status

Parity Status	Current Employment Status			
	Total	Full Time	Part Time	Unem- ployed
Total	110 (100%)	20 (18%)	25 (23%)	65 (59%)
Admitted After the Birth of First Child	22 (100%)	13 (59%)	6 (27%)	3 (14%)
Admitted Before the Birth of First Child	88 (100%)	7 (08%)	19 (22%)	62 (70%)

children before a woman is admitted is a favorable sign in terms of her future employment. Of the 22 respondents who received the degree after the birth of the first child, 19 are working and 13/19 are working full time. On the other hand, of the 88 women who received their degree before the birth of the first child, only 26 are working, and 7/26 are working full time. It seems, then, that the child-care calculus is one which enters most strongly here. If a woman who has children decided to go back to school and get her degree, then it is most likely that she will work also upon completion of her degree and even quite likely that she will work full time, something which is not at all true of the childless graduate.

This finding should give admissions officers pause. Although the findings are something less than definitive, they do suggest that each school should look into its own experience in this regard. It may be that schools are admitting those women who are unlikely to work and not admitting those who are a very good employment risk.

(3) Employment and Child Care

The special importance of children in relationship to professional women's work experience, which has just been noted, deserves some special attention. Of primary interest is the factor of child care. Usually, it is thought, the woman will remain home to care for the child until the child begins school, at about the age of six. Thus, the presence of a child or children under six becomes an important variable.

Women whose youngest child is under six do work less than women whose youngest child is over six. These results can be seen in Table 4. Of the 62 women whose youngest child is under

Table 4 / Professional Women Social Workers by Age of Youngest Child and Current Employment Status

Age of Youngest Child	Current Employment Status			
	Total	Full Time	Part Time	Unemployed
Total	110 (100%)	20 (18%)	25 (23%)	65 (59%)
Less Than Six Years	62 (100%)	1 (02%)	13 (21%)	48 (77%)
More Than Six Years	48 (100%)	19 (40%)	12 (25%)	17 (35%)

six, 14 (23.0 percent) are working; of the 48 women whose youngest child is over six, 31 (65.0 percent) are working.

Not only is the decision to work or not affected, but of those working, the presence of younger children affects the decision to work or not to work full time. Of the 14 women who have children under six and are working, only 1/14 is working full time, whereas 19/31 working mothers who have children over six are working full time. Thus a woman with a child under six is less likely to work, and, if she does work, she is less likely to work full time.

(4) Role Conflict

It is "obvious" to many people that the professional woman has a conflict between the role of wife and mother and her role as a professional person. Since this was a study of professional women, it provided a perfect opportunity to consider some aspects of the "role conflict" problem, even though it was marginal to the overall focus of the study. The respondents were asked the following question:

> It has been said that the married professional woman in our society has a built in conflict between her investment in her family and her desire for a career. Could you tell me to what extent you feel affected by this kind of conflict? (Use non-directive probes, i.e., "What do you mean?" "In what way?" to clarify the answer.)

The responses were inspected to see whether there was any mention of conflict at all. If there was some mentioned, the response was coded "some"; if there was no mention of conflict, the response was coded "none." The distribution of the full 117 respondents, including those who had left the field of social work, can be seen in Table 5. In terms of the total sample, a

Table 5 / Professional Women Social Workers Reporting Role Conflict

	Role Conflict	
Total	Some	None
117	41	76
(100%)	(35%)	(65%)

majority (76/117) reported no conflict. This result was a surprise and certainly at variance with the hypothesis that such conflict is a ubiquitous feature of the professional woman's landscape.

The absence of conflict in a majority of cases, however, leaves one with the interesting minority to consider. Even with these, many expected relationships did not "pan out." With one exception, conflict might have been randomly distributed among the professional women. The exception developed out of an idea found useful in a study of the nursing profession.[4] In that study a distinction between an "intellectual" and a "service" approach was suggested.

It seemed that a similar distinction might obtain here. The investigators defined those women with academic majors in college (mostly in the social sciences) as having an "intellectual" orientation and those women with a pre-professional social work major as having a "service" orientation. The cross-tabulation with conflict can be seen in Table 6, a result which holds even when one controls for employment. The academic majors

Table 6 / Professional Women Social Workers, by Reported
Conflict and Undergraduate Major

Undergraduate Major	Conflict		
	Total	Some	None
Total	117	41	76
Pre-professional	26	3	23
	(100%)	(11%)	(89%)
Academic	91	38	53
	(100%)	(42%)	(58%)

reported far greater conflict. Of that group, 38/91 reported
some conflict; of the pre-professional major group, only 3/26 reported some conflict. How can this relationship be interpreted?

The difference, it appears, may lie in what a woman wants
from work, and in this case, from social work. The service-
oriented person may simply wish to offer help and may see her
job as an extension and possible substitute for tasks typically
performed in the home. Kadushin has capsulized this idea when
he commented that:

> The professional role of the social worker is, in a large measure,
> an extension of the traditional female functions of nurturing and
> support, of the traditional female concern with children and the
> family.[5]

Kadushin's description may apply to some, but not all, social
workers.

On the contrary, the intellectually oriented person may be
more interested in the ideas involved in the work, rather than
in the work itself. It might be said that such a person has an
intellectual, but not an affectual, grasp of social work process.

What appears possible, then, is that there are two rather
different orientations toward the social work experience, which
indeed may be indicative of larger orientations to life experience. If this is so, then the differences one sees here are between
the major orientations, rather than their manifestations. The explanation goes somewhat as follows. The investigator suggests
that, for the service-oriented women, there may be a greater
degree of "role substitutability" between the wife and mother
role and the work role than is the case for the intellectually
orientated women. In other words, for the service-orientated

group, there is a similarity of demands and satisfactions in both role sets. If this is the case, there would be little or no "built in conflict between . . . family . . . and . . . career." One can be substituted for the other with a minimum of conflict.

If, however, the role sets of workplace and home are seen as fundamentally different, then the choice between them is in effect a choice between two styles of life, a choice which would certainly produce some conflict. The intellectually orientated woman may seek from work a different set of satisfactions from those which she receives from home. The boundaries between them may be less permeable. Reported conflict is the result.

However, one must add to this interpretation the fact that these role orientations do not carry equal social legitimacy. For the woman with a service orientation, both work and home roles may be a vehicle for carrying out traditionally assigned responsibilities. For the intellectually orientated woman, the satisfactions of home and work are different. By choosing work, she may, in her own mind, be abandoning the traditional role; if she does not work, she may feel less than fully satisfied. Both situations are productive of conflict.

This explanation is a hypothetical one, which needs to be tested with further research. Its intent, however, is to make an interpretation of conflict which is definitional, in the sense that it looks to a particular woman's definition of the situation as a means to understanding conflict. It has the additional value of explaining why many women do not report conflict when they exist in a structural situation which should be most productive of conflict. In short, they do not see the roles as incompatible, and thus they have little or no conflict.

Finally, this extensive discussion of conflict should be seen against the background of the general absence of conflict in the study sample. This finding in itself deserves further investigation into other samples of professional women social workers and other professional women.

Summary

This study has investigated the employment patterns of trained women social workers. A substantial attrition rate was found to exist, with over half of the women being unemployed. For the majority of women, the demands of child care seemed to be a dominant factor in keeping women out of the labor market. It might well be that, were social work employers to be more flexible in hours of work and in arranging part-time work, a number of women could be attracted back into the labor market. Were employers willing to provide child-care service, additional gains might be made. While such suggestions might seem radical to social work employers, the shortage of trained workers necessitates something being done, and these steps are relatively uncomplicated and within the easy reach of most employing agencies.

NOTES

An earlier version of this paper was given at a meeting of the Society for Social Research in Chicago. The author would like to acknowledge the help of Dr. William Reid, Director of Social Casework Research, Community Service Society of New York, and Professors Henry J. Meyer and Rosemary Sarri, of the University of Michigan School of Social Work, for providing helpful comments and encouragement. I should also like to thank the School of Social Service Administration of The University of Chicago, where this research was carried out. Data for the research were collected September, 1962 — June, 1963.

1. T. Lewin, *Employment Patterns of Married Women Social Workers: A Study of One Hundred Graduates of the New York School of Social Work,* unpublished Ph.D. dissertation, The University of Chicago.

2. A. Hollingshead and F. Redlich, *Social Class and Mental Illness,* New York: Wiley, 1958.

3. Lewin, *op. cit.*

4. J. Shuval, "Perceived Role Components of Nursing in Israel," *American Sociological Review,* 28:1 (February, 1963).

5. A. Kadushin, "The Prestige of Social Work — Facts and Factors," *Social Work,* 3:2 (April, 1958), p. 40.

thirty-eight

The Inactive Nurse

DOROTHY E. REESE
STANLEY E. SIEGEL
ARTHUR TESTOFF

The nurse-population ratio in the United States increased from 249 per 100,000 in 1950 to 297 per 100,000 in 1962, even though the rate of graduation from basic schools remained almost constant at 30,000 a year. The increase was largely due to the return of inactive nurses, many of whom work part time.

Obviously, then, one way to meet the country's ever-increasing need for nursing service is to bring nurses back to active practice in greater numbers. We need to know why these women are inactive and what their plans for returning to active nursing employment might be.

To find answers to these questions, the Division of Nursing, U.S. Public Health Service, began studies in 1961 in 12 states. Objectives of the studies were: to estimate the proportion of inactive registered nurses likely to return to nursing; to determine the reasons for the inactive status of the study population; to determine the characteristics of inactive nurses; and to help states determine the extent to which this group represents a potential resource for expanding medical care programs by their return to full- or part-time work.

The 12 participating states were Montana, Kansas, Vermont, Alabama, North Carolina, Georgia, New Mexico, South Dakota, Rhode Island, Mississippi, Oregon, and Wisconsin. All inactive, currently registered nurses living in these states were sent questionnaires. Nurses who did not maintain current registration were not included in the 12-state study.

From AMERICAN JOURNAL OF NURSING, Vol. 64, No. 11 (1964), pp. 124-127. Reprinted by permission of the authors and The American Journal of Nursing Company.

The rate of response to the questionnaire was 78 percent, ranging from 91 percent in South Dakota to 61 percent in Georgia.

Potential Reservoir

Of the 10,141 inactive nurses responding in 12 states, 44 percent (4,503) planned to return to active practice; 55 percent did not plan to return; and 1 percent did not answer this question (see the pie graph on page 540). Wisconsin had the highest proportion of respondents intending to return, 57 percent; North Carolina the lowest, 32 percent. At the time of the study there were approximately 230,000 professional registered nurses in the U.S. who were not employed in nursing. If the nurses in the 12 study states are representative of the nation as a whole, from 74,000 to 131,000 might be expected to return over a period of years.

Reasons for Inactive Status

A list of 14 reasons for being inactive was included in the questionnaire. Respondents were asked to indicate the most important reason for not being currently employed as a nurse for pay. For both inactive nurses who plan to work and those who do not plan to return, the reason "I believe a mother should be in the home while her children are young" ranked highest. This reason was given as the most important by 49 percent (2,197) of the 4,503 nurses who planned to return to active practice and by 31 percent (1,708) of the 5,516 nurses who did not plan to return. The table on page 538 shows the other most important reasons for being inactive.

The Nurses' Characteristics

As might be expected, a large percentage (90 percent) of the inactive nurses are married, as compared with 61 percent of active nurses in the 12 states. More than two thirds of the inactive nurses are 39 years of age or younger, as compared with 56 percent of the active nurses.

Of the nurses planning to return to work, 90 percent of them (4,042) have children, 83 percent (3,335) have two or more children. More than 72 percent (2,926) of these children are four years old or under.

Why Aren't They Practicing?

Reason for being inactive	Number planning to return	Number not planning to return
I believe a mother should be in the home while her children are young.	2,197	1,708
I cannot make suitable arrangement for the care of my child or children.	481	159
My husband prefers that I do not work.	292	644
The salary I would get would not make it worthwhile.	264	237
Other.	250	352
I am reluctant to return because I have not engaged in nursing practice for a while.	192	255
Employers cannot utilize the working hours I could be available.	188	53
I prefer to be a homemaker.	151	750
I am not able to engage in active nursing practice because of my health.	150	889
Employment opportunities in my field of practice are not available.	98	68
No reason.	77	134
The lack of domestic help for household tasks prevents me from being active in nursing.	56	46
I am enrolled as a full-time student obtaining further preparation in nursing.	48	6
I have transportation difficulties.	46	44
I prefer to give my available time as a volunteer worker in community activities.	10	71
I am not at present interested in nursing as an occupation	3	100

As the age level of the nurses increases, the proportion who intend to return to active practice decreases. Although nurses 39 years of age or younger constituted 69 percent of the study population they represent 85 percent of those planning to return to work.

Intention To Return

The longer a nurse is inactive the less likely she is to return to active status (see Fig. 1). After being inactive only one year, the intention to return drops markedly, and each two-year interval

PLANNING TO COME BACK?

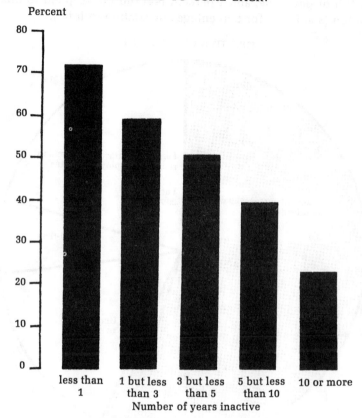

Percent

Number of years inactive

THE LONGER A NURSE is out of active nursing practice, the less likely she is to return.

reveals a substantial decrease in the proportion intending to return.

Of the 4,503 nurses who do plan to return, 901 intend to do so in less than 2 years. As many as 1,558 nurses were undecided about when they will return. This indecision may reflect the uncertainty of the nurse about her family responsibilities and the availability of satisfying employment which can be fitted into those responsibilities.

Of the 4,503 nurses who plan to return, 47 percent (2,122) plan to return part time and 15 percent (689) full time. Thirty-seven percent (1,658) were uncertain whether they would return full or part time, and 1 percent (44) did not respond to this question (see Fig. 2 for percentages in relation to total).

FULL TIME OR PART TIME?

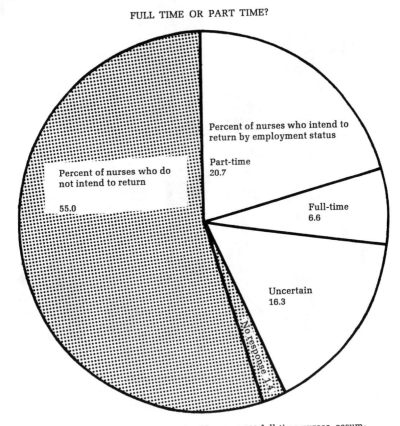

Percent of nurses who intend to return by employment status

Part-time
20.7

Percent of nurses who do not intend to return

55.0

Full-time
6.6

Uncertain
16.3

No response 1.4

THOSE PLANNING TO RETURN add up to 1,700 full-time nurses, assuming that part time means half time.

THOSE PLANNING TO RETURN add up to 1,700 full-time nurses, assuming that part time means half time.

Of a total of 679 nurses who would work full time, 224 plan to return to active nursing practice within two years. Among the 2,122 nurses who intend to return part time, a group of 527 expects to return within 2 years and an even larger group of 766 plans to return in 3 to 10 years.

The expectation to return to full time employment ranged from 7 percent in Rhode Island to 29 percent in Mississippi. The percent of those who expect to return to work on a part-time basis ranged from 31 in Alabama to 59 in Wisconsin.

Desire for Refresher Work

Of the 4,503 nurses who plan to return to active nursing practice, 65 percent would like a refresher course within the next 12 months, while 28 percent do not; 7 percent did not respond to this question.

Interest in such a course was high among the groups planning to return to work within 3 years, more than 70 percent, as well as those who planned to return within 3 to 10 years, more than 57 percent.

More than 60 percent of the nurses who have been inactive less than 10 years want a refresher course. This strong interest was expressed by those who have been inactive for a very short time, less than 1 year, as well as by those who have been inactive from 5 to 10 years.

Position and Field

Participants were asked to indicate the position and the field of employment to which they were most likely to return. In responding, the nurses were probably influenced by their previous experience, their knowledge of available positions in their geographic areas, and their fields of interest. For example, many nurses with public health experience noted that they would like to work in the health department, but that there were no vacancies.

More than half of the nurses indicated that they would be likely to return to the hospital field. About a fourth were undecided about the field to which they might return. Others indicated an interest in employment in a doctor's office, in private duty, public health, and nursing education — fields in which working hours might be more suitably arranged to coincide with family schedules. Almost two thirds of the respondents said they would be most likely to return to staff nursing positions. Again, about one-fifth of the nurses were undecided.

Interest in Home Care

In all the states except Montana the nurses were asked: "Communities are developing or extending public health programs to give bedside nursing care to patients at home. Would you accept employment in this field if you could have preparation for this field of nursing?"

Of the 4,503 nurses who plan to return, 34 percent (1,529) were willing to give bedside nursing care to patients at home: 434 on a regular basis, 877 on occasion as needed, and 218 were uncertain about the type of schedule they could assume.

Of the 434 nurses who were willing to work regularly, 61 percent were willing to work 20 hours or more per week; and 30 percent were willing to work 40 hours or more.

Local Possibilities

Of the 14 reasons given for inactive status, about half were amenable to possible solution by local action. For example, where a sizeable number of nurses said "Employers cannot utilize the working hours I could be available," changes in work schedules might be arranged to capitalize on the availability of these nurses. If many indicated "I cannot make suitable arrangements for the care of my child or children," a day care center might be set up in or near the health agency to provide for adequate child care for preschool and school age children.

As to child care services, many working mothers other than nurses have children who require care during the hours in which the mother is employed. The report of the President's Commission on the Status of Women states that child care services should be available for children of families at all economic levels (1). It says further that costs should be met by fees scaled to parent's ability to pay, by contributions from voluntary agencies, and by public appropriations. Public recognition of the need for community child care centers is growing. Moreover, some hospitals have initiated day care programs for children which have been successful in helping to attract and retain staff (2).

There are regional differences in the responses about salary. Most of those who mentioned salary lived in the southern and southeastern parts of the country. However, even here the reasons for not working were largely related to family responsibilities and particularly to the care of children.

Part-time Employment

Forty-seven percent of the nurses who plan to return expressed an interest in working part time. The increasing use of part-time nurses has been documented by a study of general hospitals (3). Another study showed that 23 percent of the nurses who began to work on a part-time basis following a refresher course later converted to full-time employment (4). Thus the return part time may be the first step in returning to full-time employment.

Maintaining Skills

Inactive nurses' interest in refresher courses may indicate an awareness of and a concern with the rapidity with which medical and scientific progress alters nursing care of patients. Courses in medical-surgical nursing, therefore, are essential in the use of the inactive nurse resource. The returning nurse, of course, needs orientation to the agency and unit in which she is to work. She also needs time for adjustments to the work situation. The returning nurse quickly becomes discouraged by being asked to carry unreasonably large and unfamiliar assignments.

To utilize fully the potential of the inactive nurse reservoir, local groups must plan for the re-education or retraining of nurses to function effectively in the modern, changing, nursing setting. Opal David speaks of this: "In professional groups such as nursing there might be increased attention to the development of imaginative ways to update and employ colleagues who have been occupied with babies and other home responsibilities." (5)

There is much emphasis these days on continuing education for practitioners and on the use of more modern teaching methods such as closed circuit television and programmed learning. Surely there are possibilities here for developing educational opportunities for inactive nurses who wish to keep up to date. What kinds of continuing education programs are needed for those who are not practicing? Research is needed to determine the special requirements of the inactive nurses and to determine how their needs might best be met.

Home Care

There is increasing emphasis on meeting the medical and nursing needs of the chronically ill and aged in the home rather than in institutions. It is noteworthy that more than one third of the nurses planning to return expressed an interest in giving bedside nursing care to patients at home. Edna Brandt and her associates described the use of nurses for home nursing service in a rural setting (6). In this project "resident nurses" in a rural community were trained to give part-time professional nursing service to chronically ill patients at home. This is one example of how the inactive nurse might be brought back and illustrates a way in which her available time can be matched with patient care needs.

NOTES

1. U.S. President's Commission on the Status of Women, *American Women*. Report of . . . Washington, D.C., U.S. Government Printing Office, 1963; p. 20.

2. Adler, Patricia, and others. "Day Care Services Help Recruit Nurses," *Amer. J. Nurs. 63:97-100,* Sept. 1963.

3. Testoff, Arthur, and others. "Analysis of Part-Time Nursing in General Hospitals," *Hospitals* 37:54, 56, 58-60, Sept. 1, 1963.

4. Reese, Dorothy E., and others. "How Many Caps Went on Again," Nurs. *Outlook* 10:517-519, Aug. 1962.

5. David, Opal D. "Anticipating the Future for Students and Teachers in Nursing: Concepts about Women Are Changing," *Amer. J. Nurs.* 62:82-84, Dec. 1962.

6. Brandt, Edna J., and others. "A Home Nursing Service in a Rural County, *Amer. J. Public Health*, 51:1294-1305, Sept. 1961.

thirty-nine

Career and Family Orientations of Husbands and Wives in Relation to Marital Happiness[1]

LOTTE BAILYN

The role of the educated married woman has been the subject of much debate in the past few decades. People concerned with the economy and the professions have urged trained women with families to enter the labor market — and women have responded, though their participation in the highest job levels is still limited (Fogarty, Rapopart, & Rapoport, 1967; Rendel, 1968). Some family experts, on the other hand, have warned about the possible disintegration of the family that would result if women forsook their traditional roles, though research findings, on the whole, have not supported this fear (Goode, 1963; Nye & Hoffman, 1963).

Both research and ideological pronouncements, however, have dealt almost exclusively with the life situation of the woman: with the complications and rewards she faces in trying to combine family and work. And though the importance of the husband is always assumed, little systematic attention has been given to the interplay between the chosen life style of an educated woman and that of her husband. Only recently have some writers begun to analyze the process by which men achieve an integration of family and their own work, and there has virtually been no study relating to married women's work patterns that deals simultaneously with husbands and wives.[2]

The hypothesis under investigation in this paper is that an educated, married woman's resolution of the 'career-family' dilemma cannot be adequately evaluated without knowledge of her husband's resolution — of the way he fits his work and

From HUMAN RELATIONS, Vol. 23, No. 2 (1970), pp. 97-113. Reprinted by permission.

his family into his life. In particular, it deals with the patterns that result when husbands with varying orientations to their families and their careers are combined with wives who also differ on this dimension, and it evaluates the different combinations by the degree of marital happiness associated with each.[3] The investigation is based on data from some two hundred British women, all university graduates of the year 1960, and from their husbands.[4]

Husband's Orientation

It is assumed in our society that every man will spend a major portion of his time and energy on his work; and, indeed, every husband in the sample does so.[5] Yet the degree of men's involvement with their occupation varies greatly. Moore (1969) distinguishes between two approaches to work: '*conditioning* (implying a reluctant adjustment to a harsh reality) or *commitment* (enthusiastic acceptance of pleasurable duties' p. 868). Masih (1967) identifies career-saliency as a dimension along which people vary and define it as consisting of three elements: 'a) the degree to which a person is career motivated, b) the degree to which an occupation is important as a source of satisfaction, and c) the degree of priority ascribed to occupation among other sources of satisfaction' (pp. 653-4). Similar distinctions exist in the extent to which a married man's satisfactions are determined by his family, and it is the relative weight of these two potential sources of satisfaction — career and family — that is used to differentiate the husbands in the sample.

The specific measure is based on the following questions:

(a) Which of the following gives you the most satisfaction in your life?

(b) Which gives you the next greatest satisfaction?

Your career or occupation
Family relationships
Leisure time recreational activities
Religious beliefs or activities
Participation as a citizen in affairs of your community
Participation in activities directed towards
    national or international betterment
Running a home
Other

Over half of the husbands (58 percent) indicated that they derived most satisfaction from their families; a little over one fourth (27 percent) said their careers were most satisfying; only 14 men, a mere 6 percent of the sample, checked the third most frequent choice — leisure time recreational activities. Further, over two thirds (69 percent) of those whose greatest satisfaction comes from their families gave career as the source of their next greatest satisfaction, and over four fifths (82 percent) of those listing career first chose family as second. All in all, as may be seen in Table 1, only seven men did not mention either career or family as a source of great satisfaction for them.[6]

Table 1 / Husband's Sources of Satisfaction

Mentioned as source of satisfaction:		No.	%	
Only Family		51	23	
1st choice		40	18	Family-oriented
2nd choice		11	5	
	140			
Both Family and Career Family first		89	41	
Career first		50	23	
Only Career	70	20	9	Career-oriented
1st choice		11	5	
2nd choice		9	4	
Neither Career nor Family		7	3	
TOTAL		217[a]	99	

[a] 6 men who did not answer this question at all were eliminated from the analysis.

The 210 men who did mention career or family or both as sources of satisfaction in their lives, may be divided according to their primary emphasis, as indicated in *Table 1*. The 140 whose family relationships are their sole or greatest source of satisfaction comprise the group that is family-oriented; the 70 whose satisfactions stem more from their careers are considered career-oriented, a ratio of 2:1 in favor of the family.

The group of husbands as a whole, then, has a strong family

emphasis. All are married and 88 percent either had children or were expecting their first child at the time they filled in their questionnaire, and both marriage and children increase the likelihood of men listing family relationships as their main source of satisfaction in life (Fogarty, Rapoport, & Rapoport, 1970 [in press], ch. V). Further, this group of men all became part of the sample by being willing to answer a 'spouse questionnaire' for a study in which their wives, as 1960 university graduates, were the primary targets. This means that their family relations were close enough for them to cooperate with their wives in a joint venture, which, in itself, probably preselects those who are more oriented to their families. Also, not all of these men are university graduates themselves; on the contrary, almost one fourth of these husbands of university graduates had themselves not graduated from university and these tend to emphasize family more than do their counterparts who did graduate from university and who show a greater commitment to occupation.[7]

Still, both orientations are present in the sample: there are those whose primary emphasis is on their careers and those who emphasize their families more. The distinction is embedded in many aspects of a man's life; it cannot be isolated from his other attitudes or life experiences. Masih (1967) found that one of the main differences between male students whose careers were very salient for them and those for whom this was not the case, was the former group's lesser interest in interaction with the opposite sex and greater desire for 'enduring' long periods of work. In relation to a job, the 'high-saliency' group showed less concern about the security of steady work than did the group whose careers were less salient. In the present sample, too, such distinctions exist. The man whose primary emphasis is on his family is more concerned with human contact in the realm of work; the career-oriented men, in contrast, emphasized intellectual fulfillment more.[8] The latter group is more ambitious: 63 percent of the men whose primary emphasis is on their careers, as opposed to 49 percent of those more oriented to their families, fall into the ambitious category.[9]

These, then, are some of the characteristics that differentiate career-oriented from family-oriented men. They are obviously relevant to what happens when these men marry wives who differ in the degree to which they incorporate work into their lives.

Wife's Orientation

The diversity of educated women's lives makes it particularly difficult to find a meaningful way of describing their career orientation at an early stage in their family life.[10] For the men in the sample, all of whom are married and working and, presumably, expecting to continue this double pattern, the relative contribution of these two realms to their satisfactions in life is a meaningful way of assessing career-family orientation. But these conditions do not hold for the women.[11] As has already been indicated, 88 percent of the wives in the sample either had children or were expecting their first child. And, only eight years after their graduation, the children were young: 83 percent of the families with children had at least one child under three. Thus, the pull of the traditional expectation that mothers of small children stay home must have been quite strong for these women.

Nonetheless, at the time of filling in the questionnaire, 46 percent of the wives were engaged in work for which they were paid, though only 15 percent were working more than 30 hours per week, and most of these (73 percent) were recruited from the small group without children. But, by itself, the fact of working is not a good indicator of career orientation. At any given moment in their lives, some wives who are working are doing so only out of necessity, waiting perhaps for circumstances to arise that would allow them to stop, and, conversely, some who are not working wish they could. In our sample, 45 percent of the non-working wives are not satisfied with their 'unemployed' state; and among the sub-sample who are engaged in gainful work, fully 40 percent say specifically that are *not* in favor of married women engaging in a career — of having any long-range occupational commitments.[12]

And even anticipated future work patterns — though not subject to these forces of the immediate situation — are not as good a measure of career commitment as one might wish. In the present state of flux in women's roles, the difficulties involved in any chosen style — and all paths have their difficulties — may lead one to view an opposing style as unrealistically attractive.[13] There is evidence, for instance, for the existence of what might be called the 'traditional dream' — an expectation on the part of married women that having children will make family life all-fulfilling for them. That this anticipation is not always met in reality is attested to by the fact that over one third (36 percent) of the wives with children expect to be working more or less continuously, even when their youngest child is under three, as contrasted with only 19 percent of the married women who have not yet had their first child.

If, then, one is interested in a woman's career commitment at an early stage in her family life, it is necessary to find a way of gauging it; that is, as little contaminated as possible by the specific circumstances she finds herself in at that time, or by unrealistic expectations of the future — whether these take the form of a traditional or of a 'pioneering' dream.

The measure chosen, which seems to meet these requirements, is based on two elements: whether or not a woman is generally — abstractly — in favor of married women having a career, and whether or not she gets personal satisfaction from her career or occupation. The first element is measured by a question that asked everyone in the sample to give his attitude 'to married women engaging in a career (i.e. in which there is a long-term occupational commitment).' Forty-five percent (N = 101) of the wives indicated they were 'in favor'; 29 percent (N = 64) were 'mixed or neutral'; and 26 percent (N = 58) were 'against' married women engaging in a career. The second element — the satisfaction a woman derives from pursuing such an activity — is based on the same question that was used to determine the men's career orientation. But because of the preponderance of family and other home-oriented responses among the women, the answers were categorized differently. All the women who mentioned career as either their first (only 15 did so) or next greatest source of satisfaction in life were considered career-satisfied: 30 percent of the sample (67 people) fell into this group.

The measure of career orientation among the wives is derived from the relation between these two elements, as indicated in Table 2. Those 45 women, (20 percent of the sample), who are in favor of married women pursuing careers and who themselves get satisfaction from their own career activities, we have called *integrated,* to indicate a predisposition to integrate a career with their family life. Those 99 women, on the other hand — almost half of the sample — who are not in favor of married women engaging in occupations requiring a long-term commitment and whose satisfactions do not depend on work outside the family, comprise the *traditional* group, the group subscribing to the conventional pattern for women. In between is a mixed group con-

Table 2 / Wives' Career Orientations

Sources of Major Satisfaction:[b]	Attitude to Married Women Having a Career.[a]	
	In Favor	*Not in Favor*
Career Mentioned	Integrated N = 45	Mixed (work-oriented) N = 22
Career Not Mentioned	Mixed (ideaologically committed) N = 56	Traditional N = 99

	N	%
Integrated	45	20
Mixed	78	35
Traditional	99	45
TOTAL	222	100

[a] 3 wives who did not answer this question are classified as 'not in favor.'
[b] 1 woman who did not answer this question is eliminated from the table.

sisting mainly of wives who favor women having careers but for whom a career or occupation is not personally a major source of satisfaction, as well as a small group (10 percent of the sample) who do get satisfaction from work, even though ideologically they are not in favor of married women pursuing careers.

Thus there is a similar tendency among the women to that of the men: the ratio of traditional to career-integrated wives is just about the same (2:1) as the ratio of family-oriented men to career-oriented men. It is important, however, not to equate traditional wives with family-oriented men. Rather, by the definition of our measures as well as by the forces working in society today, it is the wives who integrate a career with their family responsibilities, whose style of life is more analogous to that of family-oriented men, i.e., those men who add to their traditional concerns with a career, a primary emphasis on their families. Both career-integrated wives and family-oriented husbands have foresaken the expected concentration of their sex on only one of these two realms; both have added to their traditional concerns an emphasis on the realm most commonly associated with the other sex.

These analogies are based, of course, on the presumption that a woman's career orientation will bear some relation to the actual career pattern she will follow in her life. There is evidence that indicates this to be likely: nearly all (88 percent) of the wives in the career-integrated group were working at the time of the questionnaire; and, over three fifths (61 percent) were planning to work more or less continuously, even when their youngest child was under three (a plan held by only a quarter of the other wives in the sample). The career-integrated wives, thus, are recruited primarily from those who are now working and are satisfied with this work, who feel it is proper for married women to have a career, and who themselves plan to continue to include work as part of their life styles. And this work is an addition to, not a substitute for, a family. These wives are already married and only two do not plan to have any children (out of a total of five in the whole sample). But they do seem more likely to limit the size of their families: only 32 percent plan to have more than two children; more than half of the other wives have this plan (61 percent of the traditionally-oriented wives hope for three or more children).

Couples' Patterns

When, now, the orientations of husbands are combined with those of their wives, 209 couples emerge whose distribution among the various patterns is given in Table 3. As the table

Table 3 / Distribution of Couple Patterns
(Number of People in Each Combination)

	Husband's Career-Family Orientation	
Wife's Career Orientation:	Emphasis on Family	Emphasis on Career
Traditional	60 [64]ᵃ (29%)	35 [31] (17%)
Mixed	53 [48] (25%)	19 [24] (9%)
Integrated	27 [28] (13%)	15 [14] (7%)
	N = 209ᵇ (100%)	

ᵃ Numbers in brackets indicate the frequencies expected in each cell if the two orientations are independent of each other: $\chi = 2.75$, P = .25.
ᵇ This number represents the number of men who could be classified by their career family orientation (210, see Table 1) minus the one wife whose orientation to her career is unknown.

shows, there is hardly any relation between husbands' and wives' orientations: career-oriented men are no more likely to marry traditional wives than are those whose emphasis is more on their families; nor do women who hope to integrate a career with their family lives show any preference for either family or career orientation in the men they marry. Clearly, career-family orientation is not a salient dimension when marriage decisions are made. Though such a state of affairs may not be optimal from the point of view of the individual marriage (and it sometimes is not, as will be seen), from the point of view of this study it is very useful since it permits one to investigate the different combinations of career orientations without too much concern for the possible effect of other related factors.

As was mentioned at the start, this paper is concerned with the extent of marital happiness associated with these different patterns. The following question, which was asked of every person in the sample, is used as the basis for classifying couples according to marital happiness.[14]

Taking things together, how do you really feel about your marriage?

Very happy
Pretty happy
Sometimes happy, sometimes unhappy
Not very happy
Unhappy

Sixty-one percent of the wives and 61 percent of the husbands stated that they were 'very happy' with their marriages; 25 percent and 28 percent, respectively, indicated that their marriages were 'pretty happy'; no wife said that her marriage was less than 'sometimes happy, sometimes unhappy,' though four husbands did. Not all couples agreed on the degree of their marital satisfaction: 13 percent of the husbands indicated a greater degree of happiness than did their wives; 12 percent of the wives rated themselves happier. Since consensus is a better way of characterizing a couple than is one partner's perception alone, only marriages in which *both* partners said that they were 'very happy' are classified as happy.[15] Fifty-five percent of the couples fall into this category.

It is obvious from Table 4 — which indicates the marital happiness associated with each of the various combinations of career orientation — that one pattern stands out from all the others: marriages of men whose exclusive or primary emphasis is on their careers to women who themselves place store on integrating a career with their family lives are not very happy.

Table 4 / Couple Patterns and Marital Happiness
(% of Couples with Very Happy Marriages)

	Husband's Career-Family Orientation	
	Emphasis on Family	Emphasis on Career
Wife's Orientation:		
		Conventional Pattern
Traditional	62% (N = 60)	54% (N = 35)
Mixed	62% (N = 53)	53% (N = 19)
Integrated	56% (N = 27)	13% (N = 15)
	Co-ordinate Patterns	

As a matter of fact, the number of couples in this group who describe their marriages as 'very happy' is so low that it is not possible, with the present sample, to investigate the conditions that contribute to or might ease the strains of this pattern. It should be mentioned, however, that neither of the two couples of this pattern whose marriages are very happy has children; it should also be said that both husbands are in favor of married women having a career,[16] and both are very satisfied with their own work. It seems, then, that under special conditions this pattern can be accompanied by a happy marriage, but the conditions are rare in this sample.

All the other combinations in Table 4 seem to be associated with about the same degree of marital happiness: between one half and two thirds of the marriages in each group are very satisfactory to both partners. In discussing the conditions that facilitate these successes, we shall emphasize two patterns: the conventional pattern (upper right cell of Table 4) and the co-ordinate pattern (lower left). Traditional wives married to career-oriented husbands represent the pattern, here called conventional, in which family roles are probably most differentiated by sex, with the man primarily oriented to his career and his wife primarily to the home. In contrast, it seems likely that the least differentiation of roles along traditionally accepted sex-linked lines occurs in the marriages of career-integrated wives to men who, though involved in a career, place primary emphasis on their families — the couples of the co-ordinate pattern.[17]

Table 5, which gives the basic data for this discussion, also includes information on the upper left cell of Table 4, in which traditional wives are paired with family-oriented husbands. This combination has the wife's orientation in common with the conventional pattern and the husband's orientation in common with the co-ordinate one. It thus allows one to make inferences as to the relative influence of each partner's orientation on the success of the contrasting family styles.

Conventional Pattern

According to prevailing social expectations, the conventional pattern would not seem to require any particular justification. But when one considers the separation of interests it implies, with the husband primarily concerned with his work and the wife with house and family, it becomes less obvious why such a pattern is assumed to be such a satisfactory one. It is not altogether surprising, therefore, that marital happiness is increased under conditions that minimize the built-in separation of interests of this pattern. A look at the first column of Table 5[18] shows that the more children conventional couples have, the less likely they are to have very happy marriages (item 1). More children, by increasing the care and time necessary to meet the needs of the family, would seem to exaggerate the differentiation of roles in a pattern in which the family is the more or less exclusive concern of one partner. Moreover, item 2 shows that the proportion of happy marriages declines the more satisfied the husband in this pattern is with his present work situation. Such an increase in satisfaction, by adding strong motivational support to the husband's primary concern with his work, would also seem to exaggerate the differentiation of roles implicit in the pattern. Finally, the conventional pattern is the only one in which marital satisfaction is greater when the fields of husband and wife overlap (item 3). Such a common interest seems particularly important for the success of a pattern based on rather strict differentiation of roles.

Table 5 also shows that the conventional pattern is the only one in which marital happiness is negatively associated with in-

Table 5 / Factors Associated with Marital Happiness for
Different Couple Patterns
(% of Couples with Very Happy Marriages)

| | COUPLE PATTERNS | | |
| | Conventional | | Co-ordinate |
	career traditional (N=35)	family traditional (N=60)	family integrated (N=27)
Husband's Primary Emphasis: Wife's Career Orientation:			
1. Number of Children:	%	%	%
none (N=33)[a]	67 (N=9)	[100 (N=3)][b]	50 (N=6)
one (N=41)	63 (N=8)	64 (N=14)	[75 (N=4)]
two (N=101)	47 (N=15)	52 (N=29)	53 (N=15)
three or more (N=34)	[33 (N=3)]	71 (N=14)	[50 (N=2)]
2. Husband's Feelings About his Present Work Situation:[c]			
extremely satisfied (N=51)	43 (N=7)	78 (N=18)	[100 (N=4)]
somewhat satisfied (N=115)	55 (N=22)	65 (N=31)	53 (N=15)
neutral or dissatisfied (N=39)	67 (N=6)	22 (N=9)	29 (N=7)
3. Relation of Own and Spouse's Field of Work:[d]			
overlapping (N=97)	67 (N=18)	53 (N=30)	57 (N=14)
distinct (N=100)	41 (N=17)	69 (N=29)	58 (N=12)
4. Husband's Income:			
high (>£2000/year) (N=75)	36 (N=14)	77 (N=22)	70 (N=10)
low (≤£2000/year) (N=128)	67 (N=21)	57 (N=35)	44 (N=16)
Mothers' Work Status While Growing Up:			
5. wife's mother did not work (N=93)	62 (N=16)	71 (N=31)	62 (N=8)
wife's mother did work (N=114)	47 (N=19)	56 (N=27)	53 (N=19)
6. husband's mother did not work (N=85)	33 (N=12)	62 (N=32)	83 (N=6)
husband's mother did work (N=124)	65 (N=23)	61 (N=28)	48 (N=21)
7. Dominant Values of Social Circle:[e]			
intellectual, academic (N=95)	71 (N=14)	67 (N=21)	58 (N=19)
suburban (N=110)	46 (N=24)	65 (N=40)	62 (N=8)

8. Attitude of Social Circle to Women Working:[f]
   same opportunities as
   men (N=46)   [25 (N=4)]   58 (N=12)   56 (N=9)
   women's work
   secondary to home
   and family
   obligations (N=111) 50 (N=24)   70 (N=30)   58 (N=12)
   very mixed feelings
   (N=44)   83 (N=6)   53 (N=15)   50 (N=6)

9. Division of Labor in Household (supervision
   and care of children; shopping for food):[g]
   only wife usually
   does it (N=102)   61 (N=18)   55 (N=29)   43 (N=14)
   wife has some help
   (N=104)   44 (N=16)   67 (N=30)   69 (N=13)

[a] Numbers in parentheses indicate the number in the given category in the sample. They do not always add up to 209 because No Answers have been eliminated.

[b] Percentages in brackets are based on very small N's.

[c] In general, how do you feel about your present work situation? (If you are not working, indicate your feelings about being unemployed).
   Extremely satisfied
   Somewhat satisfied
   Neutral
   Somewhat dissatisfied
   Extremely dissatisfied
The last 3 categories are combined.

[d] Do you consider that your own field of work and your spouse's field of work outside the home are:
   Very close and similar to one another
   Overlapping to some extent, but with major areas of difference
   Quite distinct from one another
The first 2 categories are combined. Couples are classified on the basis of information from the wife.

[e] Looking at your social circle as a whole, how would you characterize their main values or interests?
   a. Suburban (emphasis on home, garden, kids, community etc.)
   b. Intellectual, academic
   A dominant value or characteristic
   A secondary characteristic
   Not a characteristic
N's represent the number of people who said the given factor was 'a dominant value or characteristic.' Some may have given this response to both of the listed factors. Couples are classified on the basis of information from the wife.

[f] Looking at your social circle as a whole, how would you describe their attitude to women working?
   i. Most people feel that women ought to have same opportunity to pursue an important career as men
   ii. Most feel that women ought to be able to work a bit but not so as to allow it to interfere with home and family obligations
   iii. Women ought not to work outside the home
   Very mixed feelings (some feel like i, some feel like ii, some like iii)
Categories ii and iii have been combined. Couples are classified on the basis of information from the wife.

[g] Who usually does each of these things in your household?
   a. Supervision and care of children
   b. Shopping for food
   Husband
   Wife
   Both
   Domestic help
   No one in household
Those who responded 'wife' to both of these areas are compared to all the rest. Couples are classified on the basis of information from the wife.

come — in which there is a larger percentage of happy marriages when income is low than when it is high (item 4). Further analysis shows this to be particularly true when the husband's ambition is low. Under this condition, only 17 percent of those with high incomes have very happy marriages, as compared with 71 percent of those whose incomes are low. In other words, marital happiness is very low indeed if the husband in a conventional couple combines low ambition with high income. In this situation he has, perhaps, the least justification for his primary emphasis on career, since it is based neither on his ambition nor on the need to make money.[19] Both of these — career ambition and need for family income — are traditionally accepted reasons for a husband's one-sided emphasis on his work; when neither is in force, the conventional pattern is not very successful.

That the conventional pattern is not automatically satisfactory but needs some justification is shown also by one other item in Table 5. Item 6 shows that a greater proportion of conventional marriages are happy if the husband's mother worked while he was growing up than if she did not work. That is, the pattern seems to be *less* satisfactory if it is 'conventional' as far as the husband's personal experience is concerned — if, that is, it is merely a continuation in his adult life of the traditional pattern in which he grew up; it is *more* satisfactory if it represents a new family style in the husband's experience and is not merely fulfilling a social and personal expectation.

Thus it seems that the conventional pattern, if it is to be associated with marital hapiness, requires support from a number of directions: some common focus or justification seems to be necessary. Items 7 and 8 of Table 5 show, further, that its success is also dependent on suppport from the social circle in which it functions. The proportion of happy, conventional marriages decreases when a dominant value of the couple's social circle is the suburban one with emphasis on home, garden, kids, community, etc. (item 7) — a value more in line with a family-centered pattern — and when 'most people [in the couple's social circle) feel that women ought to have the same opportunity to pursue an important career as men' (item 8) — an attitude more consistent with a less differentiated pattern of family life.

Co-ordinate Pattern

The kind of support necessary for the success of the co-ordinate pattern is quite different from that required by the conventional one. As items 7 and 8 of the last column in Table 5 indicate, the attitudes and values of the couple's social circle are not associated with marital happiness in this case (though it is of interest that, compared to the sample as a whole, a large proportion of couples in this group describe their social circles as predominantly intellectual and as having an equalitarian attitude to women's careers). Nor does the community of interest represented by overlapping fields (item 3) relate to marital happiness of co-ordinate couples. Rather, the factors associated with happy co-ordinate marriages are more managerial ones, those that ease the physical burdens of integrating the realms of family and work. The proportion of happy marriages in this pattern is greater when the wife is not alone responsible for the care of the house and the children (item 9) and, perhaps not unrelated, when income is high (item 4).

It has previously been hypothesized that family-oriented men, like career-integrated women, are oriented to both work and family and seek satisfaction in both spheres, a similarity that should make the differentiation of roles in the co-ordinate pattern more dependent on the particular personal characteristics of the partners than on those prescribed by social expectations. It was suggested, in other words, that the co-ordinate pattern represents a true integration of the realms of family and work for both husband and wife and is in no way a mere reversal of traditional family roles. Evidence from Table 5 supports this line of reasoning. In contrast to the conventional pattern, happiness of co-ordinate marriages increases as the husband's work satisfaction increases (item 2). Also, further analysis shows that the proportion of happy co-ordinate marriages is particularly great when high income is combined with high ambition of the husband: 83 percent of these couples have very happy marriages. Thus, the family-orientation of the husband whose co-ordinate marriage is successful is not a substitute for work; on the contrary, work is both important and satisfactory to such a man and his family emphasis is based on choice, not on default.[20]

In one respect, the conditions associated with marital happiness of the co-ordinate pattern are similar to those of the conventional one: in both cases, marital happiness is greater if the style of the family is different from the one in which the husband grew up. Item 6 of Table 5 shows that co-ordinate marriages are happier if the husband's mother did not work while he was growing up than if she did. Couple patterns that represent a personally new style for the husband are thus more likely to be happy, no matter what that style may be.

The fact that the wife's mother plays no such differentiating role[21] is a first indication, perhaps, of the relative importance of the husband's orientation as compared to that of his wife in determining the personal satisfaction associated with a particular family pattern. Further corroboration comes from a look at the second column of Table 5. Couples in this column, as was previously stated, share the wife's traditional orientation with conventional couples and the husband's family emphasis with co-ordinate ones. For almost every item in Table 5, the distribution of happy marriages in this middle column matches that of the third column — the co-ordinate pattern — more closely than it does the first one — the conventional pattern. It is the husband's orientation, therefore — which the middle and co-ordinate columns have in common — more than that of the wife, that is crucial for the effects we have discussed.

The data of this study thus corroborate the hypothesis, stated at the start, that husband's mode of integrating family and work in his own life is crucial for the success — at least in terms of marital satisfaction — of any attempt of his wife to include a career in her life. There is evidence, as a matter of fact, that identifying the conditions under which men find it possible to give primary emphasis to their families while at the same time functioning satisfactorily in their own careers may be even more relevant to the problem of careers for married women than the continued emphasis on the difficulties women face in integrating family and work.

NOTES

1. This paper is part of a larger study of highly qualified women and their careers sponsored by The Leverhulme Trust in a grant to Political and Economic Planning (P.E.P.) under the direction of Michael Fogarty and Rhona Rapoport (P.E.P.) and Robert Rapoport (Tavistock Institute) London. The author worked with the Rapoports on their 'couples' data in 1969. The report on the overall study will

appear in Fogarty, Rapoport & Rapoport (1970, in press). The data on which the present paper on couples is based come from a sample of British university graduates questioned in 1968, eight years after finishing university. The sampling frame was provided by Professor R. Kelsall from a National Survey of 1960 Graduates directed by R. K. Kelsall, A. Poole and A. Moore. The data were collected by Research Services Ltd., and some of the analysis was done with the assistance of L. Hawkins of Survey Analysis Ltd., London, using his newly developed Conversational Mode Survey Analysis Program. Some of the items in the survey, upon which this paper is based, are drawn from a questionnaire designed by Alice Rossi in her study of university graduates (which was associated with James Davis' survey of graduates) conducted by The National Opinion Research Center, Chicago, Illinois. Thanks are due to all of the above mentioned, but the author is particularly grateful to the Rapoports for their help at all stages of the work for this paper.

2. For an analysis of the problems confronting the professional woman who tries to combine career and family see Bailyn (1965). Writers who have concerned themselves with the relation of family and work in men as well as women include Brim (1968), who feels that one focus in the study of adult socialization should be on 'the two-way process of influence between the world of work and the world of the family in their varying demands upon the adult' (p. 203); Alice Rossi (1965a), whose emphasis on 'the development of a more androgynous conception of sex role' (p. 130) underlies all her work in this field; and Rapoport & Rapoport (1965), who emphasize the integration of the two realms at various periods of transition in the life cycle, an emphasis that has guided much of their research, including the study on which this paper is based. Their investigation of the 'dual-career family' (Rapoport & Rapoport, 1969) — an arrangement 'in which both husband and wife pursue careers (i.e. jobs which are highly salient personally, have a developmental sequence and require a high degree of commitment) and at the same time establish a family life with at least one child' (p. 3) — is one of the few that analyzes the work and family roles of husbands and wives simultaneously. See also Blood & Wolfe (1960) for a discussion of the effects of the comparative work participation of husband and wife on various aspects of the husband-wife relationship, though, not untypically, this information comes from interviews with wives only.

3. Other terms of evaluation are also possible: in particular, one would want to know about the consequences of the various combinations for the character of work produced by the couple, whether by one or both partners. It is entirely possible that a combination that is fully satisfactory to the individual couple may not be the most creative in its contribution to society. An evaluation in terms of work

would be related to such questions as the distribution of talent and the special needs of the most creative minds. In this paper, we limit the context of our evaluation to the family.

4. Full details of the total sample (which includes men and women graduates, both married and single) are available in Fogarty, Rapoport & Rapoport (1970, in press). Here it is only necessary to say that each of 449 married women in the sample who had agreed to cooperate with the survey received two lengthy identical questionnaires through the mail: one for themselves and one for their husbands. Of these 348 (78 percent) returned their own questionnaires; 223 (64 percent) of the husbands of this group of respondents also returned questionnaires. These 446 questionnaires (223 filled in by the women; 223 by their husbands) comprise the data on which this paper is based. The 223 married women whose husbands also responded, were compared on a number of items to those who only returned their own questionnaires. The only differences found were in the small group without children. In that group, the wives in the 'couples' sample show somewhat greater marital happiness, are somewhat more likely to be working at the present time, and also hope for somewhat fewer children. Thus the 'couples' wives — as compared to the total sample of married women — slightly overrepresent the group of childless, working, happily married wives, who are not planning on large families. By far the larger proportion of the couples, however, already had children; and in this group the relevant distributions are very similar to the sample of married women as a whole. More differences, as will be seen below, exist between the spouses of these wives and the sample of married men university graduates.

5. The few characteristics of husbands that have been studied in relation to married women's careers include occupation and income, attitude to women's work, willingness to help with household tasks (e.g. Mulvey, 1963; Weil, 1961). But there has been no effort to explore the relevance of men's attitudes to their own work and the part played in their lives by career and family.

6. This response may reflect a transient family-work situation: four of these seven have no children, the husbands in these couples are generally not very satisfied with their present work situation, and a disproportionate number of wives in this group did not answer questions relating to their anticipated future work patterns.

7. 74 percent of the husbands who did not graduate from university are family-oriented as opposed to 64 percent of the university graduates. When compared to the married men in the target sample of university graduates, husbands in the 'couples' group are also somewhat more likely to have working wives and to approve of this arrangement.

8. Each person was asked to indicate which of a number of

'factors which contribute to their personal ideals for a career' he personally considered most important. Two of these related to people:

Responses	% giving each response:	
	career-oriented (N = 70)	family-oriented (N = 140)
an opportunity to work with people rather than exclusively with things and ideas	13%	19%
an opportunity to be helpful to other people	4%	8%
Total People Responses	17%	27%
Three concerned intellectual fulfillment: a chance to use intellectual problem solving abilities	24%	19%
an opportunity to show what I can accomplish	17%	7%
an opportunity to be creative	11%	8%
Total Intellectual Responses	52%	34%

9. Included in the ambitious category are those men who, when asked to 'characterize your level of ambition' at the present time, said they wanted 'to get to the top'; as well as those who wanted only 'to hold a high position' but who, on another question, rated themselves as 'very' or 'somewhat ambitious'; and, finally, five who did not answer the main question but who rated themselves as 'very ambitious.' It should be noted that this difference in ambition is limited to husbands whose incomes are rated low ($\leqslant$£2000/year). The group that combines low income with low ambition — of which 74 percent are family-oriented — stands out in a number of ways: it contains more non-graduates than any other, and the men in this group who did graduate from university received less good degrees; they rated themselves as less assertive (based on self-ratings on three interrelated characteristics: 'competitive occupationally,' 'competitive socially,' and 'dominant'), and were less satisfied with their intellectual abilities; they gave the fewest work-oriented responses when considering their ideal jobs and were least satisfied with their present work situations. Their family orientation is a part of this syndrome.

10. Obviously this is not true if one can study women at a stage of their lives late enough to allow classification according to the actual work patterns they have followed. The problem here is to get a measure that can be presumed to be a fairly good predictor of these patterns.

11. Masih (1967), for instance, found that judges had much more

trouble classifying female students according to the degree of their career-saliency than they had with men.

12. Not all of these 40 percent, of course, actually dislike working. We shall see later that some wives are ideologically against married women having long-range career plans but actually get a great deal of satisfaction from their own work. Orden & Bradburn (1969), who asked their married women respondents whether they would work if they didn't need the money, found that only 23 percent of their college graduates answered negatively (*Table 3,* p. 398).

13. Alice Rossi (1965b) indicates the way experience tempers the expectations of the women college graduates she studied:

> . . . the pioneers [women whose long-range goals are in heavily masculine fields such as natural sciences, medicine, economics] had romantic notions concerning careers and work which the reality of advanced study and employment temper, and the homemakers (women with no career goal other than being 'housewives') had romantic notions concerning marriage and family roles which the reality of marriage and motherhood tempers (p. 81).

14. Obviously we are not suggesting that all the meaningful aspects of a marriage can be represented by a global question on professed marital happiness. Yet, there is evidence that such a question correlates sufficiently well with more refined ways of measuring success in marriage to make it a useful indicator for our purposes. In the present questionnaire the global question followed two others concerning the marital relationship: how well the respondent felt he was doing as a husband or wife and whether he ever felt he had married the wrong kind of person. Andrew Bebbington developed an index of marital satisfaction based on all three questions as well as on a measure of conflict based on the number of disagreements the couples had on a variety of subjects. Of all the items involved, the question used here had the highest correlation with the resulting index. Similarly, in a study of married women, Nye & MacDougall (1959, as presented in Nye & Hoffman, 1963, pp. 270-1) found that a global question on marital happiness along with questions on arguments and quarrels and on actual or contemplated separation met the Guttman criteria of scalability, hence, presumably, they all reflect a single dimension of marital success. In a more refined analysis of marriage happiness, based on data from married men and women (though not on couples), Orden & Bradburn (1968) develop a two-dimensional model of marriage adjustment: one dimension is positive, relating to the satisfactions — both the sociability and the companionship that husbands and wives share — of marriage; the other is negative, and concerns the tensions in marriage. The two aspects are independent of each other, yet they relate in the expected direction to a person's self-

ratings of marital happiness. In comparing their Marriage Adjustment Balance Scale, which is based on the difference of the scores on the two dimensions, to self-ratings of marital happiness, they conclude that there is little to choose between the two approaches if one's interest is in a summary measure of marital happiness, though the MABS has the advantage of allowing one to consider its components separately.

15. These distributions are very close to those of a number of other surveys which have asked for self-ratings on marital happiness, ratings which have been found to be very stable over time; further, other studies have found that the validity of self-ratings is increased when they are checked by those of the spouse (Orden & Bradburn, 1968).

16. It is of interest that this is the *only* pattern whose success is at all dependent on the husband's attitude toward careers for married women. Most of the studies that have shown this factor to be important were based on a woman's assessment of her husband's attitude (e.g. Weil, 1961). In our sample, where we know the wife's perception of her husband's attitude as well as his actual views, we find that 69 percent of the wives gauge their husbands accurately — match, on a three-point scale, his stated view. With a 30 percent error of assessment, it is possible that the correlations found in previous studies reflect a woman's rationalization and justification of her behavior as much as they do the actual influence of her husband's attitude.

17. Rapoport & Rapoport (1969) in their investigation of the 'dual-career family' chose couples in which both partners had a career — couples who, in our terms, could fit into either of the bottom two cells of Table 4. Yet 'with the exception of one of the couples studied, family life in general and children in particular were highly salient' (p. 9). Thus, their couples seem to represent the pattern we have called co-ordinate. Other people have also investigated the marital adjustment of employed married women (see e.g. Orden & Bradburn, 1969). But the large difference between the degree of marital happiness associated with the bottom two cells of Table 4 makes it difficult to compare their results with ours.

18. In this discussion, we shall only refer to factors that make at least a 25 percent difference in marital happiness. The proportion of happy marriages is about .5 in the groups under consideration. Under this condition, the probability of getting as large a difference as .25 or more is approximately .05 for equal samples of n = 30.

19. The direction of causality here is by no means clear. It is entirely possible that such a person emphasizes his career as a response to an unhappy marriage. In general, we view the association between

a person's career-family orientation and his marital happiness as the result of a process of reciprocal influence — a process that can, however, be affected by other aspects of the person's temperament or experience at any point. We do not view marital happiness, therefore, as a direct consequence of a given pattern of career-family orientations, but see it, rather, as one of a number of factors that seem to go together under certain conditions.

20. It should be noted, however, that such an integration can result in a serious problem of physical and psychological overload (Rapoport & Rapoport, 1969) and is probably not compatible with the superinvolvement with career that has been expected in some professions.

21. We are talking here about a differentiating role in relation to marital happiness. There is a slight tendency (as shown by the N's in parentheses) for wives whose mothers worked to be somewhat more frequently in the integrated group than there is for those whose mothers did not work.

REFERENCES

Bailyn, L. (1965). "Notes on the Role of Choice in the Psychology of Professional Women," in R. J. Lifton, ed., *The Woman in America*. Boston: Houghton Mifflin.

Blood, R. O., Jr. & Wolfe, D. M. (1960). *Husbands and Wives: the Dynamics of Married Living*. Glencoe, Ill.: Free Press.

Brim, O. (1968). "Adult Socialization," in J. Clausen, ed., *Socialization and Society*. Boston: Little, Brown.

Fogarty, M., Rapoport, R. & Rapoport, R. N., (1967). *Women and Top Jobs*. London: Political and Economic Planning (P.E.P.)

Fogarty, M., Rapoport, R. & Rapoport, R. N. (1970, in press). *Careers and Families: Sex Roles and Achievements*. London: Allen & Unwin.

Goode, W. J. (1963). *World Revolution and Family Patterns*. Glencoe, Free Press; London: Collier-Macmillan.

Masih, L. K. (1967). "Career Saliency and its Relation to Certain Needs, Interests, and Job Values," *Personnel & Guidance J.* 45, 653-8.

Moore, W. E. (1969). "Occupational Socialization," in D. A. Goslin, ed., *Handbook of Socialization Theory and Research*. Chicago: Rand McNally.

Mulvey, M. C. (1963). "Psychological and Sociological Factors in Prediction of Career Patterns of Women," *Genetic Psych. Mon.* 68, 309-86.

Nye, F. I. & Hoffman, L. W. (1963). *The Employed Mother in America*. Chicago: Rand McNally.

Nye, F. I. & MacDougall, E. (1959). "The Dependent Variable in Marital Research," *Pacific Sociol. Rev.* 2, 67-70.

Orden, S. R. & Bradburn, N. M. (1968). "Dimensions of Marriage Happiness," *Am. J. Sociol.* 73, 715-31.

Orden, S. R. & Bradburn, N. M. (1969). "Working Wives and Marriage Happiness," *Am. J. Sociol.* 74, 392-407.

Rapoport, R. N. & Rapoport, R. (1965). "Work and Family in Contemporary Society," *Am. Sociol. Rev.* 30, 381-394.

Rapoport, R. & Rapoport, R. N. (1969). "The Dual-career Family: A Variant Pattern and Social Change," *Hum. Relat.* 22, 3-30.

Rendel, M. *et al.* (1968). *Equality for Women*. London: Fabian Society.

Rossi, A. S. (1965a). "Equality between the Sexes: An Immodest Proposal," in R. J. Lifton, ed., *The Woman in America*. Boston: Houghton Mifflin.

Rossi, A. S. (1965b). "Barriers to the Career Choice of Engineering, Medicine, or Science among American Women, in J. A. Mattfield & C. G. Van Aken, eds., *Women and the Scientific Professions: The M.I.T. Symposium on American Women in Science and Engineering*. Cambridge, Mass.: M.I.T. Press.

Weil, M. W. (1961). "An Analysis of the Factors Influencing Married Women's Actual or Planned Work Participation," *Am. Sociol. Rev.* 26, 91-6.

forty

Professional and Non-professional Women as Mothers

FAYE HIGIER VON MERING

Patterns of maternal behavior have been explained in terms of differences in biological drives, early personality predispositions, and general socio-cultural experience. Viewing maternal conduct from a different perspective, the present study focuses on the influence of role-identification. Comparing professional and non-professional women as mothers, the study anticipated differences, which, if demonstrable, could be related to differences in the aims and organization of the American maternal role on one hand and the professional role on the other.

Briefly, the theoretical position adopted here is that conformity with the expectations of the maternal rôle depends immediately on identification with its basic aims and not wholly upon generalized drives, needs, or canons of value derived from other orders of experience. The study proceeds on two assumptions. The first is that the basic aims of the American maternal role are child-centered, with the accent on serving the interests of the child. The second assumption is that both groups of mothers studied, the professional and the non-professional, will pursue this purpose but will differ in the ways they go about it. Such anticipated variations in selection, assumed to be equally compatible with serving the child's interests, will be interpreted in the light of differences in role activity and hence of the socially adaptive needs of the mother.

Guided by considerations of variations in role activity, the controlling hypothesis of the study can be stated as follows:

From THE JOURNAL OF SOCIAL PSYCHOLOGY, Vol. 42 (1955), pp. 21-34. Reprinted by permission of Otto von Mering and The Journal Press.

The professionally-active mother by virtue of her dual social roles is expected to regard the child as a potential adult. She defines childhood as a period when adult standards should be learned, and hence, emphasizes the disciplinary and independence training functions of the parent. In contrast, the mother identified exclusively with the maternal role is expected to regard the child as a unique person with special personality and dependency needs appropriate to his level of development. She considers childhood to be a period when these needs should be understood and gratified. Hence, this mother, relative to the professionally-active mother, minimizes the disciplinary and independence training functions and maximizes the empathetic, understanding, and protective functions of the parent.

The hypothesis expresses implicitly the bearing that differences in role experiences are anticipated to have on child-training. Thus the role experience of the non-professional mother can be shown to be basically *person-oriented*, and hence, this mother is expected to deal with the child primarily as a personality, to recognize and gratify his needs and wishes. On the other hand, the professionally-active mother, with her partial identification with the world of performance and achievement, is expected to be more *standard-oriented*, and hence, to stress the importance of the child's achievement of adult norms. Therefore, this mother is expected to minimize understanding and protection and to emphasize early discipline. Again, one could reasonably anticipate that mothers exclusively identified with the maternal role would reflect a role-type orientation of *collective service* in the sense that they would be more likely to accommodate the child's frame of reference and set aside the claims of their own. On the other hand, the professionally-active women could be expected to reveal a role-type orientation of *creative autonomy*, which would be expressed in promoting self-sufficiency in the child and early mastery of social, intellectual, and ethical norms.

The vehicle for illustration of the hypothesis is an interview-type investigation of a sample of 25 college graduates. A reasonable homogeneity of socio-cultural interests was largely assured by the fact that all of the subjects possessed a B.A. or an advanced degree from the same college and that all lived in the residential sections of the city where the college is located. Selection of the subjects was also governed by the necessity of limiting the age range of their children to the years of 4 to 12.[1]

Conforming to the terms of the hypothesis, the sample ultimately chosen consisted of three groups of mothers: 8 are professionally-active (Group I); 8 have had more previous professional or semi-professional experience (Group II); and 8 have had no experience of this type at all (Group III). One woman was later added to the sample and left unclassified.

a. *Basic categories of analysis.* A wide range of behavioral and psychological indices were used so that the results of each could be cross-checked with the others. Outlined below are some of the most important items:

(1) *Scale of Expectations,* or the balance of rules and preferences vs. choices and suggestions expressed by the subjects for 13 areas of child-training. (These areas include food, sex, and toilet habits; acquisition of cognitive values; relations with parents, siblings, and peers; manners, property, hygiene, and household responsibility.)

The scale of expectations was used to determine the degree of emphasis on discipline-authority functions.

(2) *Reasons for expectations,* i.e., on grounds of (a) *parental prerogative,* (b) *the personality needs of the parent,* (c) *objective standards,* (d) *discipline.* Only the standard of discipline requires explanation. It occurs when the mother justifies a rule on the grounds that it will teach the child adult responsibility, renunciation, and regularity. Studying the mother's reasons for rules helps to discriminate between authoritarian or self-centered motives vs. a genuine desire to create an effective and autonomous adult.

(3) *Understanding,* or any attempted diagnosis by the mother of the child's motives or needs underlying his conformity or resistance to rules. The incidence of understanding expressed in an interview is a basic index of the degree of the subject's awareness of the child's personality needs.

(4) *Empathy,* or awareness of the child's needs for gratification. Such awareness is expressed when the mother states the child's likes and dislikes. Empathy is considered as a non-analytical dimension of awareness of the child's personality needs.

(5) *Independence Training vs. Protectiveness.* The degree of protectiveness vs. emphasis on independence training is defined in terms of the degree of (a) control over the child's

physical movements, (b) emphasis on his assumption of household duties, (c) encouragement of social contacts.

(6) *Techniques of communication*, e.g., "reasoning," "ordering," etc.

b. *General interview plan and techniques of summary*. The
interview schedule opened with a series of questions on the
mother's background, training, working history, community
work, her assessment of her husband as a father, and also on the
division of labor between husband and wife. The bulk of the interview was occupied by questions relevant to the above six
topics of child-rearing.

The discussion on each topic was opened by such a general
question as, "Do you have rules about manners and observing
decorum?" Such a general question, specified when needed,
stimulated the subject to discuss her point of view *in extenso*,
to explain what she does and does not expect, the reasons for
her expectations, her concern for the child's wishes and needs,
and her manner of communication with him.

By recording all interview responses to these issues for each
of the 13 areas of child-training, the investigator was able to
obtain a total frequency for rules, preferences, suggestions, and
choices; for each type of justification of rules; for each instance
in which empathy and understanding are expressed; and finally,
for several types of communication practices.

The frequency of each item were expressed in terms of its
proportion to the total number of expectations mentioned by
each subject and each test group. Group differences were expressed in terms of the median distribution and for important
measures, in terms of chi square values.

Results and Conclusions

Representing an ascending scale of relative permissiveness
and prescriptiveness, the scale of expectations is at once the
most richly detailed and the most sensitive measure of the degree of emphasis on discipline-authority functions. The terms of
the scale are (a) *choices*, or the absence of conformity expectations, (b) *suggestions*, or mild recommendations of desirable
action, (c) *preferences*, or strongly recommended action and (d)
rules, or unqualified expectations that a particular response will
be forthcoming.[2]

One set of examples taken on the issue of verbal aggression

towards the parent will illustrate the extremes of variation found within the interviews:

> *Mrs. Faris:* Allows *choice* to a 7-year-old boy.
> (Group II) "I am addressed as a 'stinker.' My husband hasn't accepted it. They'll change. Basically Robert has respect for us. These things are very superficial."
> *Mrs. Bailey:* Expresses a long-standing *rule* for her children.
> (Group I) "— and, of course, the children have never been permitted to speak disrespectfully."

The range of variation illustrated on the issue of verbal abuse to parents reflects in a specific situation what proved to be true generally. On the whole, the professionally-active mothers of Group I expressed more rules and preferences and in this sense expected more from their children than did the mothers of Group II and III. This was by no means true for all issues, but in 7 out of 13 areas of child-training, including manners, household responsibilities, and acquisition of cognitive values, Group I women proved the most prescriptive. . . . Only in the case of household responsibility are group differences actually significant.

However, the final statistical summary did yield significant findings. A comparison of the total proportion of choices and suggestions to the total number of expectations revealed group differences significant below the .05 level. Confirming these findings is the comparison of simply the proportion of choices to rules. In this comparison, of the 7 women with the lowest proportion of choices, 6 belonged to Group I.

Analysis of the modes of justification of rules shed further light on group differences and, at the same time, indicated certain similarities that marked the sample as a relatively homogeneous population. The similarities consisted in the fact that all three groups preferred to justify their rules in terms of some objective standard and, conversely, were less inclined to claim justification on grounds of their personal needs or their prerogatives as parents.

The material on modes of justification suggested certain basic similarities within the sample. All three test groups leaned strongly in the direction of the objective standard type of justification involving either ethical or rationalistic reasons for rules. Among the total number of relevant responses, 151 involved "non-empirical" standards, and 242 involved rationalistic or pragmatic standards. Only 181 responses could be classified as personalistic, and only 30 belonged to the parental prerogative category. The preponderance of the objective standard response virtually obliterated significant group differences. Only tendencies were observed. For example, Group III mothers tended to invoke personalistic appeals more frequently than did the others while Group I mothers showed a greater tendency to invoke the non-empirical type of objective standard.

There was one variety of objective standard, however, which proved to be such a highly significant focus of group differences that it was dealt with separately. This is the standard of discipline.

With marked frequency the professionally-active mothers tended to justify their rules on the specific grounds that the child should have experience with responsible, renunciatory, and routinized behavior. Underlying this disciplinary orientation is the premise that frustration is a basic part of life and that the child must learn how to cope with it so that he will be prepared for the adult life to come. On the other hand, it is precisely this frustration which the mothers of Groups II and III feel should be avoided. From their point of view, the child should be allowed to enjoy himself now because "he will probably be kicked around later."

The difference between a disciplinary and a non-disciplinary orientation is illustrated in the following paired example:

I) *Mrs. Brown:* (Group I) Emphasizes "self-sufficiency" as the standard for household duties, a typical disciplinary approach.

"I have a housekeeper all the time, but I think also that children should be given things to do. They're now at the ages of 7 and 8 and they have certain obligations to perform. — I try to make them self-sufficient. There are just too many parasites in our society."

Mrs. Hill: (Group III) In contrast, Mrs. Hill expresses the practical standard that help is needed when the maid is off and also the personalistic orientation that she doesn't want to be a slave.

"When we are here without a waitress, they will be perfectly helpful and do things for me. — It isn't too definite, however. Once in a while I'll blow off steam. — I don't want them to get the idea that their mother is a slave. . . ."

The distinctively disciplinary orientation of Group I mothers, which is illustrated in the above example, can be attested statistically. In the distribution of the incidence of invocation of the standard of discipline the average incidence for Group I was 2.39 as compared with 1.56 for Group II and .65 for Group III. Differences were found significant at the .001 level.[3]

Relevant to the issues of authority and discipline were the data on techniques of communication. Classifying these techniques into *informative* types, such as "reasoning" or "cautioning" as opposed to *non-informative* types, such as "ordering" or "yelling," the investigation found that in all three test groups the former greatly outnumbered the latter. For the sample as a whole, the median frequency of the informative types was 5.88 as opposed to a median 1.55 for the non-informative types. Group differences proved negligible.

In the assessment of relative emphasis on understanding functions, the study explored a wide variety of data, but particular stress was laid on the actual evidence of the mother's understanding as expressed in her report of how she handled the child. The difference in levels of understanding proved to be a difference in the number of times during the course of an interview that a subject diagnosed the child's needs underlying his resistance or conformity to rules. Naturally, the quality of diagnosis differed enormously, but, unfortunately, it is possible here only to illustrate the quantitative expression of understanding.

Two examples, taken on the issue of sibling relations, will illustrate the difference between high and low levels of understanding:

Mrs. Holmes: (Group II) Mrs. Holmes expresses what is typical for her group. She is sensitive to the psycho-dynamics of sibling rivalry, which can be seen from her analysis of the child's drawing. Also, she shows some knowledge of technical psychology despite the fact that her training was far removed from child-care. Finally, she is convinced that the child is passing through a "normal" stage, a type of diagnosis typical for Groups II and III.

"Well, I have been kicked particularly by Barbara, and, of course, their aggression towards one another is inevitable. — I don't interfere very much unless Peggy becomes terribly outmaneuvered. Sometimes Jean will take advantage of Peggy. It's funny. Peggy did a free drawing of a fight with Jean. She drew a child with an enormous head. It looked like a monster, and it was very big. Then, in the other portions of the drawing, there was a little monster, and these two monsters were fighting madly with each other. The amusing thing was that Peggy decided that the larger one was herself. Isn't it wonderful? It was a perfect fantasy of a wish-fulfillment. I think this is normal though. When I was a child, I wasn't allowed to express my aggression, and I find the fact that the children do very reassuring."

Mrs. Bailey: (Group I) In this question-answer sequence, emphasis is placed on the expectation without any analysis of the problematic nature of sibling relations.

"Q. Has there ever been a period when Joan and Richard quarreled with one another?"

"A. That is relatively rare. Quarreling is not part of the family pattern. They seem, as a matter of fact, to be relatively indifferent to one another."

The two examples relevant to the issue of understanding reflect a marked pattern of differentiation within the sample as a whole. Group II mothers, as compared with the others, exhibited a significantly higher level of analytical understanding as measured by the sheer incidence of effort to diagnose the child's problems. The average incidence for Group II is 7.15 as compared with 4.68 for Group I and 5.00 for Group III. Differences were found significant at the .001 level.

Awareness of the child's gratification needs constitutes another function of the parent examined by the study. This awareness, basically empathetic rather than analytical, was considered present when the subject conveyed the child's experience of contentment or frustration by the use of such terms as, "he likes," "he hates," "he wants," or "he enjoys." One paired example showing the presence and the absence of empathy will suffice as illustration.

Example: A comparison of Mrs. Farley and Mrs. Hunt on the issue of playing in the front room. Both have rules on the subject, but Mrs. Farley pauses to recognize that the children *enjoy* jumping and to express her wish that they be *happy,* while Mrs. Hunt, though emphasizing the child's rights, ignores the question of the child's subjective feeling,

Mrs. Farley: (Group III) "We have to draw the line somewhere, of course. — They are not to touch the things in this room. In the sun parlor they can do anything they like. . . ." "I wonder whether I am keeping them happy. I feel they should be made happy now because they'll be kicked around later. You simply have to let them do it and enjoy themselves. They bang around in the sun parlor. That's designed for them. They like to jump up and down on the studio couch in the sun parlor but what kid doesn't?"

Mrs. Hunt: (Group II) "Yes, we feel very strongly. When they were small, they couldn't be free in this room and tear everything up. They had their own things and we had ours. They could play roughly but they did that in their rooms."

The above examples illustrate a recognizable, though not a statistically significant, trend within the sample. Mothers of Groups II and III tend to express the child's wishes and experience of frustration or contentment more frequently than do the mothers of Group I. Differences were significant only at the .10 level. The above examples also suggest that Group II mothers have a tendency to be more analytical than empathetic, emphasizing psychological concepts rather than the child's direct emotional experience.

In the assessment of relative emphasis on protection vs. independence training functions, a variety of data proves relevant, some indicating similarities within the sample and others indicating suggestive or significant group differences.

Similarities within the sample were clearly indicated on certain critical issues. Thus 23 of the 25 mothers encourage a measure of self-help, and only two mothers indicated that performing some kind of household task was completely a matter of choice. The sample as a whole proved relatively prescriptive on the issues of household duties, prescriptive in the sense that rules and preference preponderated over choices and suggestions. In contrast to its behavior on the issue of household duties, the sample as a whole was relatively permissive on the issue of the child's physical movements. In this area, choices and suggestions predominate over rules and preferences, which means that most subjects try to give the child as large a scope of choice as possible in his place of play, participation in sports, use of his bicycle, etc.

Other basic uniformities were observable. Fundamentally, the subjects foster rather than limit the child's social contacts. This can be seen in the fact that all three test groups treat the area of "play with friends" permissively. How the child plays and with whom he plays are much more frequently issues of choices and suggestions rather than of rules or preferences. Again, the general pattern of fostering the child's social contacts can be seen in the fact that all but four of them have sent their children to nursery school.

Within the context of similarities, certain differences in group behavior become distinctly visible. The most striking difference revolved about the issue of household duties. On this issue Group I mothers expressed the largest proportion of rules and preferences and Group III mothers reversed the pattern for the sample by expressing more choices and suggestions. Group differences were significant below the .02 level.

Though there were no other variations relevant to the question of fostering independence that proved as significant, still what variations that did occur formed a relatively consistent pattern. Thus, for example, the only area of child-training for which Group I mothers expressed more choices and suggestions than the other groups was the area of "physical safety." In all other areas, Group I mothers revealed a medium or maximum prescriptiveness. The pattern of significant prescriptiveness on issues of household duties plus a rare permissiveness on issues of physical safety seems to mesh with the striking tendency of Group I mothers to conceptualize the importance of "self-sufficiency."

Summary and Conclusions

The study emerged with two sets of results, those suggesting similarities between the three test groups and those indicating significant lines of cleavage.

The similarities indicate that the study was dealing with a relatively homogeneous group in certain fundamental respects. For example, it was true for all three test groups that democratic techniques of communications and objective modes of justification far exceeded the frequencies of alternative types. Here group differences were comparatively insignificant. The majority of each group are more likely to "explain" or "reason" than "order" or "yell." When they justify rules, they are more likely to invoke an objective standard than retire into the absolutism of parental authority or invoke their personal needs.

It is also true that the majority of subjects of each group tend to eschew patterns of extreme overprotection. This is clearly suggested by the fact that all but two mothers exert some pressure on the child to perform household duties. On the other hand, in areas where protectiveness could be theoretically anticipated, such as in matters of physical safety, conditions of play, and range of social contacts, most of the mothers allow their children a considerable range of choice.

Using the balance of choices and suggestions vs. preferences and rules as a guide-post, the investigator found certain similarities between the three test groups in patterns of normative emphasis. For example, a pattern of permissiveness tended to predominate on issues of the physical disciplines and also on

Table 1 / Summary of Basic Group Differences

Data	Group Proportions			X^2	D.F.	Significance
	I	II	III			
Ch. + Sug.	176	197	211*	5.050	1	.02 > P < .05
Total Ex.	384	372	400			
Choices	112	135	137*	6.191	1	.01 > P < .02
Rule + Ch.	233	234	235			
Discipline	46	29	13	21.257	2	P < .001
Total Ex.	384	372	400			
Understand.	90	133	100	17.118	2	P < .001
Total Ex.	384	372	400			
Empathy	78	102	101	5.473	2	.05 > P < .10
Total Ex.	384	372	400			

Abbreviations: Ch. Choices; Sug. Suggestions; Ex. Expectations.

 * In these two comparisons, the proportions for Groups II and III were so close that they were combined.

issues relevant to the acquisition of cognitive values. On the other hand, rules and preferences tended to predominate on issues pertaining to relations with siblings and peers, manners, hygiene, and property-honesty. The similarities between the three test groups in patterns of normative emphasis forms an important background for the conclusion that the professionally-active mothers differ from the others more in the *level* of expectation than in the *kind* of expectation.

Out of the similarities marking the sample as a homogenous population several visible lines of cleavage emerge which lend support to the hypothesis of the study. The most important findings were these:

1. The professionally-active mothers exhibited a significantly higher scale of expectation than did the mothers of the other two

groups. With few exceptions, group differences followed the normative pattern of the sample as a whole. Consequently, the mothers of Group I differed in the level rather than in the kind of expectations they have of their children.

2. Group II mothers exhibit a significantly higher level of analytical understanding while Group I mothers score the lowest.

3. In the distribution on awareness of gratification needs, there is a marked though not statistically significant trend suggesting that the mothers of Group II and Group III recognize their children's wishes more frequently than do the professionally-active women.

4. The professionally-active mothers place a significantly greater emphasis on discipline as a justification for their rules.

5. The professionally-active mothers place significantly greater emphasis on encouraging their children to perform household tasks.

Discussion

The weight of the most important evidence suggests strongly that the professionally-active mothers emphasize the discipline and independence training functions of the parent, and that the mothers currently identified with the maternal role exclusively emphasize the protective, empathetic, and understanding functions.

One further conclusion deserves mention. The extraordinary high rating of Group II mothers in understanding, together with a variety of other evidence, suggest that they tend to adopt the role of clinician toward their children and in this sense, tend to "professionalize" the maternal role.

If the results of this study can be reproduced in a large-scale investigation, the immediate implication would be that maternal behavior is at once selective and adaptive, varying sensitively with role-specific aims and hence not necessarily determined either by biological structure, the experience of preadolescence, or even by the claims of the "total culture." Naturally, this implication is more of a promise than an established fact, but the empirical results at least lend support to this possible conclusion.

The results of the study allow for the interpretation (a) that all three groups of mothers observed are motivated by an ultimately similar definition of prescribed role purpose and (b) that the variations stem from a selection among acceptable alternatives as a result of different adaptive needs. The interpretation of similarity of motivation, posited to result from common identification with the maternal role, is suggested by the fact that the varying functions performed by the professional and non-professional groups are both compatible with the central purpose of serving the child's interests. Except in isolated instances of neglect, overprotectiveness, or authoritarianism, relative emphasis on independence training vs. protectiveness or on discipline and teaching vs. empathy and understanding could be understood in terms of serving the child's interests. The emphasis of the professional mother's child-training is on equipping the child to cope effectively with the rules and techniques of his culture. The accent of the non-professional mothers is to insure the child's emotional security. Both orientations, within definable limits, involve care and concern for the child and have functional value for his development.

The observable differences in accent can be interpreted in the light of the concepts of selection and adaptation. It is clear from the above discussion and the empirical results that the American maternal rôle allows for a range of choice in defining the characteristics of the child and consequently the range of function a mother can perform. The material presented here suggests that the professional mothers define the child as a potential adult who must learn to deal effectively with the adult world. Hence, these women tend to emphasize the discipline and independence training functions of the parent. On the other hand, the non-professional mothers appear to view the child not as a potential adult but as a unique social personality whose needs should be allowed spontaneous expression and at the very least understood. Hence, discipline is minimized and empathy accented.

The reasons for the observed differences, while undoubtedly related to personality, can at least be shown to vary with differences in role experience and hence with adaptive needs. Thus, the specific behavior of mothers indentified exclusively with the maternal role appears to reflect the role characteristics of person-orientation, collective service, diffuseness in purpose and spontaneous, non-intellectual relations. On the other hand, the mothers also identified with the professional role, with its accent on standards, individual achievement, and deliberate action, could be understood as accepting the basic norm of the maternal role and at the same time, placing a different though appropriate construction on the nature of the obligations they are to perform.

The material and interpretations presented here have simply illustrated the role perspective on maternal conduct without disproving the relevance of other points of view. The purpose is not to insist that this perspective is the only correct one, but rather, that it promises to explain important facets of the data. Perhaps the most basic contribution of the study is that it underscores the importance of measuring variations in maternal behavior in terms of an action frame of reference and consequently avoids the difficulties created sometimes by purely psychobiological interpretations. Often in theoretical discussions of the biological and personality components of maternity, a standard of measurement will be employed without reference to the action context. For example, variations in maternal behavior will be described in terms of such alternatives as masculine vs. feminine tendencies, or nurturant and protective vs. cognitive and intellectual orientations to the child. As a result of this type of analysis, populations of women come to be divided into "maternal" vs. "non-maternal" types. Thus, the sentiment is often expressed in psychoanalytic and even anthropological quarters that women who are "sober" and "intellectual" with their children will never know what "true motherliness" is, implying that "true" maternity is basically "emotional," basically a unitary quality which some women possess and others don't. If this or other similar standards were employed, the professional women and even the analytical women of Group II would appear suspect as mothers. In short, the theory of this study, with its emphasis on the concept of role standards and selective adaptation, would make it at least theoretically possible to account for widespead variability without introducing the assumption that numbers of women who are clearly identified with specified social roles are biologically or psychologically non-maternal types.

NOTES

Summary of a thesis presented in partial fulfillment of the requirements for the degree of Doctor of Philosophy in the Department of Social Relations, Harvard University, 1952.

1. Due to the unavoidably wide age range among the profession-

ally-active mothers, which was duplicated within the other test groups, it was necessary to deal with a wide range for the children. The attendant difficulties were largely offset by adjustments of interview questions and by the adoption of conventions in rating the interview material.

2. In scoring each type of expectation, a much more precise set of definitions was employed than is indicated in the text. . . . In view of the difficulties of content analysis the reliability level of the scoring techniques proved fairly satisfactory. Correlating its own list of choices, suggestions, etc., with those of an independent judge, this investigation found the following *rho* values: choices, .89; suggestions, .35; preferences, .69; and rules, .78.

3. The frequency of any item like the standard of discipline was determined in terms of the proportion of the incidence of the item to the total number of expectations. (See Table 1 for raw proportions). For convenience in discussion, the resultant percentages were divided by .05.

REFERENCES

Abraham, K., "Manifestations of the Female Castration Complex," *Inter. J. Psychoanal.*, 1922, 3, 1-29.

Baldwin, A., *et al.*, "Patterns of Parent Behavior, "*Psychol. Monog.*, 1945, No. 3, 108.

Deutsch, H. *Psychology of Women.* New York: Grune & Stratton, 1945.

Dollard, J., & Davis, A. *Children of Bondage.* Washington: Amer. Council Educ., 1940.

Foley, P., "Early Responsibility and Affect Hunger as Selective Criteria in Maternal Overprotection," *Smith Coll. Stud. Soc. Work*, 1932, 3, 209-233.

Freud, S., *The Psychology of Women. New Introductory Lectures on Psychoanalysis.* New York: Norton, 1933, 153-185.

―――. "Infantile Genital Organization of the Libido," *Inter. J. Psychoanal.*, 1924, 125-129.

Levy, D., *Maternal Overprotection.* New York: Columbia Univ. Press, 1943.

Mead, M., *From the South Seas.* New York: Morrow, 1939.

―――. *Male and Female.* New York: Morrow, 1949.

Newell, N. W., "Dynamics of Maternal Rejection," *Amer. J. Orthopsychiat.*, 1934, 387-401.

Parsons, T., *Essays in Sociological Theory, Pure and Applied.* Glencoe, Ill.: Free Press, 1949.

―――. *The Social System.* Glencoe, Ill.: Free Press, 1951.

Radke, M. J., *The Relation of Parental Authority to Children's Be-*

havior and Attitudes. Minneapolis: Univ. Minnesota Press, 1946.

Wiesner, B., *et al*. *Maternal Behavior in the Rat*. Edinburgh: Oliver & Boyd, 1933.

Zilboorg, G., "Side-lights on Parent-child Antagonism, *Amer. J. Orthopsychiat.*, 1932, 2, 35-43.

————. "Masculine and Feminine," *Psychiatry,* 1944, 7, 257-396.

VII

The Marginal Professional

forty-one

Women as a Minority Group in Higher Academics

ANN E. DAVIS

The purpose of this paper is to explore the role of women in our culture, in academia, in a few professions, and in the field of sociology. Some of the issues examined are the problems encountered by women as members of an academic minority group, the relative success women have in academic careers, and the manner in which women's educational and social capacities are used. This investigation ranges beyond the stated limits, giving rise to more questions than it answers, and concludes with suggestions regarding areas in need of further clarification by the professional community.

A Look at the Role of Women in the United States

Our concern lies in discovering some clues as to why women drop out of academic endeavor at a higher rate than men; why they are not considered good risks for academic jobs (at least in status universities); why such a large proportion of women with advanced degrees withdraw from active participation in their field; and, lastly, whether discrimination is practiced against women.

Surveying the literature on the role of women in general was at first considered too large a task for a paper of this length, but a preliminary search of the literature yielded the interesting fact that in comprehensive texts no more than a page is usually devoted to the subject. In the indexes of many sociological volumes there is no mention of "women," "role feminine," or even the category "family." This is in contrast to lengthy dis-

From THE AMERICAN SOCIOLOGIST, Vol. 4, No. 2 (1969), pp. 95-99. Reprinted by permission.

cussions of delinquency, socio-economic status, race, labor, and numerous other well-known sociological areas.

When one of our foremost sociological therorists, Talcott Parsons, in his volume on social structure and personality (1964: 242), refers to the woman's role, he says, "If child-rearing has been the primary center of the feminine role, occupational achievement has been that of the masculine." Interestingly, Parsons relates loss of status to job loss in men's roles only:

> There are very important reasons why the "job" should have come to be such an important focus in the role organization of our type of society, and within this more general category, why the career and its peak should be so important. . . . If, given the overwhelming importance of this category of contribution, the individual is no longer wanted or needed, or if his capacity declines, the obvious conclusion seems to be that he should be placed in a lower category of social worth . . . (1964: 242).

Parsons discusses the woman's role in another context:

> Given the independence of the nuclear family, given its spatial separation from work and its personal diffuse character as opposed to the business world, the division of sex role by which the husband alone enters the occupational sphere is a mechanism that minimizes rivalry within marriage and promotes family solidarity (1964: 242).

There are suggestions in some of the sociological literature that women are in a difficult and sometimes unspecified role. Parsons (1942), in his essay, "Age and Sex in the Social Structure of the United States," analyzes the various avenues of expression available to women: domesticity; glamour; and good companion, as expressed in such pursuits as humanitarianism and club activities. He suggests that careers for women are destructive to marriage owing to competitiveness with the male. He does not elaborate on the academic career woman but mentions that it takes an unusual type of woman, and marriage, to make the adjustment.

Much literature, academic and otherwise, has been devoted to a survey of the opportunities and joys of the domestic role. Inherent is the assumption that the woman will pattern her choices around those of the husband, upon whom depends the status of the family unit. Educators troubled by the question of educating women have spoken about the education of women for marriage, philosophizing that better education ensures a better wife, one able to give more to her husband and children. In the large study, *The American College* (Sanford, ed., 1962), the writers state that the woman's career aspirations are subordinated to the man's and that higher education may create adjustment problems in the marital role, but that the woman should take heart in that she can claim a place in the occupations at a later date. The assumption is that she can enter the occupational structure after the children are raised.

In a best seller, *The Feminine Mystique*, Betty Friedan (1963), a Ph.D. in psychology, emotionally presents the case of what she terms "the woman without an identity," tied to her husband's image and dependent upon him for stimulation. She feels that women are denied the opportunity to grow as individuals, to seek goals, and to feel pride in their accomplishments. She cites as a consequence that women entirely dependent upon their families for gratification raise children who are not self-reliant and who become dependent adults. Housework, she feels, is a dull, unrewarding, and shallow concern that leaves socially isolated and frustrated wives who are unable to be mature, warm, or responsive wives and mothers.

Mrs. Friedan explores at great length the evolution of the woman's role and asks what has happened to the independent women in the women's civil rights movements and those who were originators of the free-thinking women's colleges. She places blame for the retreat into childbearing and into the isolation of the modern home on the women, and on the anthropologists and sociologists.

Margaret Mead receives considerable attention, and blame, for fostering the domestic womanly image of woman, whose rightful place by nature is in breast-feeding children and becoming fulfilled in the bearing of these children and, in general, keeping the home fires well tended. Mrs. Friedan accuses the sociologist of authoritatively imbedding (as fact) the image of the woman's role as in the home and subordinated to the male's role. She states that, in describing what "is," the structural functionalist sociologists have given rise to a dogma asserting what "must" be. Lastly, she criticizes the educators for educating women to the home and for replacing mental stimulation with courses on marital adjustment and home economics. Mrs. Friedan's cry regarding the unhappy woman, admittedly emotional, and frequently unscientific, is nevertheless thought-provoking.

Kingsley Davis and other sociologists of equal repute have become conecerned with women's roles from the point of view of the waste of talent by American society. Davis states:

> We make less use of talented women in the labor force than do some rival nations (notably Russia). In fact, although the greatest disregard of talent is assumed to arise from class and racial inequality, this source of loss is probably less than that involving women. When we consider that female participation in the labor force is a public issue from a purely quantitative point of view as well, we can see the practical importance of research on womanpower (1965: 328-329).

There has been national concern about school drop-outs and the problem of encouraging some of the brighter youths to seek college educations. A survey of the literature leads a reader to the discovery that frequently the largest proportion of school drop-outs are girls, girls who have married or for whom college is not held as functional.

In general, then, we are left with the picture of the woman's role in America as properly being that of domesticity and child rearing, all of which is accompanied by insinuations that careers are difficult, if not ill-advised, as female pursuits. We feel that there is also confusion about the role, perhaps unhappiness in it for some women, and there is a probable loss of national talent involved in the manner in which the role is traditionally performed.

The Academic Woman

An outstanding book about the academic woman has been written by Jessie Bernard (1964), a sociologist and the wife of the late Dr. Bernard, also a sociologist. She writes about educated women, their characteristics, and the problems they encounter. The result of independent research supported by a National Institute of Mental Health Grant, her volume also includes materials from other studies. Mrs. Bernard is associated with Pennsylvania State University and is a past vice president of the American Sociological Society.

Ben Euwema (1964), the author's dean, writes in the foreword that the author should be commended for a very honest attempt to avoid a platform for women's rights and perhaps also for underplaying what she believes is discrimination against the academic woman. In his experience, he has found, "certain departments will hire no women at all; others will not promote women to higher academic posts; and most departments have a strong prejudice against female administrators . . ." (1964: xi). He feels that married career women have a whole set of disadvantages for which the university makes no provision. He states that we cannot afford to shut out one-half of our population from the academic work force (1964: xi-xii).

In his introduction to the book, David Riesman is perhaps even more lucid in his commentary. He speaks of the noncompetitiveness of women and the manner in which they remain outside the informal communications system that is deemed such an essential aid in getting important job positions (1964: xvi). He feels that, as a minority group, women do not band together and therefore exert no pressures to gain advancement, as might the Negro. Women, he speculates, may be their own worst enemies. "The evidence lies in the tacit league of educated housewives accusing working mothers of neglecting their families, or the preference of women college students for men teachers, or the dislike of women to be 'bossed' by other women . . ." (1964:15). He further says, "Since married women can become 'men of knowledge' only with the support or at least non-reluctance of their husbands, much depends on the latter's security and this in turn depends on the cultural and subcultural definitions as to the proper division of labor among husband and wife . . ." (1964:21). He reflects on what other discoveries might be made, other laws emphasized, or altered patterns of scientific and academic organization preferred or discovered, if women had a larger influence on scientific work (1964:19). Such discrimination as there may be, he states, occurs earlier in the life cycle and reflects mammoth cultural attitudes as to proper sex roles rather than specific academic hostility (1964:23).

In her book, Jessie Bernard utilizes all available information to survey the issues. Of a total labor force of 72,706,000 in July of 1960, only 382,644, or one-half of 1 per cent, were in the academic profession. Of those in academic work, women constituted 19.5 per cent of all faculty members and 11.4 per cent of the professional staff for organized research (1964:30). She states that women are represented in the teaching profession roughly in the same proportions as they are in the general labor force; therefore, if the percentage of women in academics is small, it is partly due to the fact that the number of women in the labor force is small (1964:52).

Of the graduating high school population in 1959, 39 per cent of the women were enrolled in college. Of the total U.S. population in 1958, 22.7 per cent of the women were married by age eighteen as opposed to 3.4 per cent of the men (Bernard, 1964: 58). A Woodrow Wilson Foundation report on women entering doctoral programs at Columbia showed that 2 to 3 per cent of the women who became doctoral candidates in the period 1945 to 1951 earned their degrees by 1956, as compared to 5 to 13 per cent of the men (Bernard, 1964: 57). Mrs. Bernard gives evidence that financial grants are as available to women as to men; therefore she concludes, the answer to the lack of women in academic life and in the labor force lies in their lack of motivation to enter these fields.

She examines a fact noted by others, that there has been a drop of 5.1 per cent of women on faculties between 1930 and 1962 (Bernard, 1964: 39). Since this decline cannot be attributed to a lack of demand for teachers or to a lack of growth in educational institutions, Mrs. Bernard believes an explanation may lie in the shift in philosophy and function of the women's colleges. Schools such as Vassar, Wellesley, and Smith have been hiring men as teachers and administrators in an effort to upgrade their academic image. Also, there may be a complementary factor in the inability of universities to locate interested and qualified women to fill the posts.

Examining the question of lack of motivation, Mrs. Bernard explores the psychological and social nature of women and discrimination against them in the academic professions, as well as the liability of marriage insofar as a career is concerned. She presents material indicating that the careers of women are hindered to a great extent by marriage and children. Academic women are about 15 per cent less likely to be married than average, or non-academic women and they have half as many children. As many as 25 per cent of the women, after receiving their doctorates, drop out of the field to marry and raise families (1964: Chaps. 14 and 15).

The liability of marriage and childbearing is frequently cited by administrators as a reason for not hiring women. There is the fear that the woman will not complete her work, will marry, will give primary concern to the home, and will be a professional only to a limited degree. Because of the greater risk involved in the training of women, Milton Eisenhower has been quoted as saying, it costs $200,000 to train each woman.

In view of these facts, often given as reasons for the differential treatment of women, it is difficult to discern the real areas of prejudice. Prejudice remains a subtle interplay of half-truths, used in some cases when not necessary. Discrimination, when and if it exists, appears to operate against the best women because only the best succeed; the best women may be hampered by the lesser.

"In a study of 706 college teachers in Minnesota, 27 per cent of whom were women, it was found that the women were much more tentative, much more modest, and much more influenced by others in their career choices than men . . ." (Bernard, 1964: 65). Mrs. Bernard feels that the quest in academia is highly competitive — almost an initiation by endurance into a fraternity. The bywords, such as "defense of thesis," emphasize the aggressive ability of the intellectual to defend himself, perhaps, more than his product. Women are not generally socialized into such a role and do not compete in the same manner; in fact, outward aggressiveness on the part of the woman is labeled as masculine and is not considered flattering to her.

Women, on the whole, hold lower-status jobs in academic work. Thirty-eight per cent of academic males are located in schools of high academic rank, as opposed to 22 per cent of women. In the lower-ranked institutions, academic women constitute 16 per cent of the teacher group as opposed to 8 per cent of the men (Bernard, 1964: 93). Universities are characterized as looking predominantly for men of knowledge and not for teachers per se. Women are shown to be more interested in teaching and less interested, as well as less productive, in writing. A reverse argument can be stated, that the demands of the university operate to stimulate publication, and thus those employed in status universities are more likely to publish.

"The professor or man of knowledge deals with controversial hence usually with advanced aspects of his discipline. He stands for a point of view in the field" (Bernard, 1964: 117). He makes use of and systematizes, even if he does not produce, the research. These men are generalizers, dealers in the abstract, not always teachers. The individual, frequently the woman, who devotes most of her time to teaching is confined to the required courses and is not expected to be a social critic or to promote the promising disciples in the field. The man of knowledge must be an innovator and a person who often rejects the *status quo*. This type of person, it stands to reason, is seen as aggressive. As noted before, women do not use aggression in the same way as men. Research cited in the book (Bernard, 1964: 130) provides an interesting commentary on this situation: students do not consider women teachers to be as convincing as men teachers in the same field.

The Woman as a Professional Sociologist

To be more specific regarding the academic field, sociology was chosen for a detailed examination of the general problems that have thus far been discussed. Owing to the lack of printed material on this subject, interviews with five professors (four in sociology and one in anthropology) were conducted as a means of gathering insights.[1] These were informal discussions geared toward the professor's subjective appraisal of the woman's role in sociology. It should be mentioned that of the 148 students in the graduate department of sociology at U.C.L.A. in 1966, 48 were women, accounting for 32 per cent of the total graduate population.

The professors felt that women hold a lesser or minority position in the field, that they are probably not as productive in terms of publications contributing to academic knowledge, and that they are less likely to be hired as professors in status universities. They held that women were employed in research organizations proportionately more frequently than men. This situation, with two exceptions, was attributed to the woman's role, which appears to prevent the pursuit of an uninterrupted career because of a prodominant affiliation as a wife or mother who patterns her life around that of her husband. Two professors, while granting the fact that there are role pressures upon women, felt that a problem of equal importance is discrimination in the sense that men are preferentially hired over women; further, they felt that the lesser ability of women may be a myth perpetuated by men for their self-protection, or at least ease.

A topic raised by most, and of subsidiary interest, was that of married academic couples. Anti-nepotism regulations at some institutions preclude the hiring of husband-and-wife teams. It was suggested that a sizable number of academic women publish and work jointly with their husbands, and that usually the husband remains the professionally known or dominant member of the team. Briefly discussed in relation to this was the element of competitiveness in academic marriage, or competitiveness in male-female relations in general, and the unfavorable effect that it may have on the heterosexual or marital relationship.

Men and Women Sociologists: A Job Comparison

To evaluate adequately the question of what women as sociologists do, some original research was necessary. From the University of California's sociology department, these statistics were obtained (for the time period 1948 to 1964): Of 500 candidates for the Ph.D. degree, 27 succeeded. Five of the doctorates granted were to women, a total of 18.5 per cent of the group. This is higher than the proportion of women in professional sociology, for which the figure in 1963 was 12.5 per cent (as cited below). The above figures nonetheless show what appears to be a greater mortality rate among women Ph.D. aspirants than among men.

A brief attempt at a comparison with the field of anthropology was made by means of an interview held with the chairman of that department (also at the University of California). The consensus among sociology professors was that anthropology, as a field, was more favorable to women, and the chairman agreed. He attributed the more favorable climate and philosophy of anthropology in part to the fact that women can be used as field observers in primitive cultures, where they have easier access to information from primitive women. Famous women anthropologists such as Ruth Benedict and Margaret Mead were cited as examples of, as well as reasons for, this more favorable climate. The chairman also tendered his personal philosophy that women by their nature belong in the domestic role. This position, as we previously noted, is emphasized in the works of Margaret Mead, who uses primitive cultures to explore and document woman's basic nature.

Of the 151 students enrolled in graduate study in the department of anthropology, 56 were women, or 37 per cent of the total. Of 49 Ph.D.'s awarded since 1930, 8 went to women, or approximately 16 per cent. This is proportionately 2.5 per cent less than in the field of sociology. There is, in fact, the possibility of a slightly higher mortality rate among women in that profession than in sociology, contrary to expectation.

The Directory of the American Sociological Association (1963) was consulted to arrive at a factual analysis of the number of women in the field and their employment. The only members included in the analysis were fellows, life members, active members, and emeritus or honorary members. To achieve these titles a member must be a Ph.D. or have equivalent professional training in sociology, substantial professional achievement in sociology, or substantial professional achievement in a closely related field, provided that the applicant's interests and activities have a sociological emphasis (American Sociological Association, 1963: 174). As it happened, the sample consisted primarily of Ph.D's. The analysis, which involved manual counting, yielded the following results.

In 1963, the Association had 3,080 such members, of whom 385 were women, or exactly 12.5 per cent.[2] The total population of 385 women was used in determining where the women were employed or, more simply, what they were doing. Mutually exclusive employment categories were developed, and each woman was assigned to only one. This analysis is presented in the following table along with comparable figures for a sample of 670 men. The sample of men was chosen by counting every fourth man (the membership listing was in alphabetical order)

Occupations of Professional Sociologists

Type of Employment	Women		Men	
	Per Cent	(N)	Per Cent	(N)
College professor	51	(200)	71	(480)
Employee in private industry	1	(7)	2	(16)
Employee in research organization	9	(37)	4	(28)
Local, state, and private welfare employee	8	(32)	6	(44)
Federal welfare employee	3	(14)	4	(28)
Secondary, private, and public school employee	.9	(3)	.4	(3)
Religious vocation	.2	(1)	.4	(3)
Writer	.9	(3)		
Retired	1	(5)	.9	(6)
No occupation listed	21	(83)	9	(62)

and assigning him to an exclusive category.[3] The categories are by employer. For instance, assignments to the research category were made when it was apparent that the individual was employed by a research concern or where research was designated as the individual's first function. Assignments to the teacher category were made when the primary listing was given as professor at a specific college. All other assignments were made on the same basis, that of the individual's primary employment function.

The table illustrates some interesting facts. Men are 20 per cent more likely to be college teachers, and women are found twice as often in research, though the figure is small for both. A notable fact is that 21 per cent of all women (recall that most have Ph.D.'s) are listed without a work affiliation, in contrast to only 9 per cent of the men. Of additional interest, a separate count revealed that approximately 6 per cent of all women sociologists are nuns.

In Summary

The foregoing material can serve both as an indictment of, and a cause for, restricting the role of academic women, as well as an accounting of the reasons why women withdraw from the professions. To label the interplay of variables as discrimination is not wholly accurate, but neither can the material be taken as cause for maintaining the *status quo*. We continue to be faced with the facts that good intellectual ability among women is being wasted as a social and national resource and that lack of clarity about the female role may be productive of personal unhappiness. Ultimately, there is the question of whether, because of the acquiescence of women, we are culturally perpetuating for the benefit of men a model of women that is not inherent in womanhood.

NOTES

1. Interviews were held at the University of California at Los Angeles in the spring of 1966.

2. The possibility of error is acknowledged, owing not only to human error in manual counting, but also to the difficulty of establishing sex by name alone.

3. Some error is acknowledged because of the difficulty of precise assignments of categories to some people, e.g., the coexistence of the research and teaching functions.

REFERENCES

American Sociological Association Directory. Washington, D.C.: American Sociological Association, 1963.

Bernard, Jessie, *Academic Women*. University Park: Pennsylvania State Press, 1964.

Davis, K., "The Sociology of Demographic Behavior." Pp. 309-333 in Robert K. Merton, Leonard Broom, Leonard Cottrell, eds., *Sociology Today*. New York: Harper and Row, 1959.

Euwema, B., Foreword in Bernard, 1964.

Friedan, Betty, *The Feminine Mystique*. New York. Dell, 1963.

Parsons, Talcott, *Social Structure and Personality*. New York: Free Press of Glencoe, 1964.

Parsons, Talcott, "Age and Sex in the Social Structure of the United States," *American Sociological Review* 7 (October): 604-616, 1942.

Riesman, D., Introduction in Bernard, 1964.

Sanford, N., ed., *The American College*. New York: Wiley, 1962.

forty-two

The Female Clergy: A Case of
Professional Marginality

E. WILBUR BOCK

Most professions have been traditionally defined as open only to males and have been male dominated and male controlled. The boundaries of these occupations have been tightly maintained by the occupants and by the public at large. Recently, however, the barriers have been lowered, and women have entered many of these occupations in increasing numbers. The opening of professional roles to women has probably been greater for the whites than for the Negroes, and the number of professional alternatives remains relatively greater for white females.[1]

Practical considerations may help open professional avenues for women. The lack of males to fill the increasing number of professional positions may necessitate greater reliance on female occupants to perform these roles. Norms have been developed and structures have been created for the recruitment, training, and placement of women in these "male" professions. Although females are increasingly being encouraged to enter these occupations, they frequently find themselves on the fringe of their profession. They are not completely accepted by the public or by their male colleague in their professional roles. Their experience in the labor force is likely to be that of professional marginality.

However, the degree of marginality of women varies among the different professions. One profession that apparently is

From AMERICAN JOURNAL OF SOCIOLOGY, Vol. 72, No. 5 (1967), pp. 531-539. Reprinted by permission of the author and The University of Chicago Press.

quite, if not the most, resistant to change is the clergy,[2] which has not only been defined as masculine but as "sacredly" masculine. The father figure, a prominent feature of Christianity, is also a predominant ingredient in the image of the clergy. Sacred tradition has therefore helped maintain the boundaries of the clerical profession.

There has been much publicity regarding the increasing number of churches without religious leadership. This perceived threat of the decline in the provision of ministers could possibly help remove some of the barriers to the admission of women to the clergy. Although there has been no publicity regarding the state of religious leadership among Negroes, a recent study indicated that the lack of Negro clergy may be far more acute than that of the white clergy.[3] Negro females may, thus, have relatively greater opportunities to occupy ministerial positions than their white colleagues.

Although there have been some changes to permit women to become clergy,[4] these changes have met opposition both within and without the professional bodies of clergy.[5] After much deliberation, some major denominations have finally allowed women the full rights or ordination.[6] Females, however, do not necessarily serve in the ministerial role after they have been ordained.[7] One recent outcome of the debate over the ordination of women was the apparent creation of a "fourth order" of clergy in the Episcopal hierarchy so that a woman could be included in the clerical role. This clergywoman, however, will not perform marriages or administer communion.[8]

Opposition to women as clergy has varied not only among the large church bodies but has also varied among types of church organizations. Sect-type groups appear to approve of female clergy to a greater extent than do church-type groups; at least a much larger percentage of clergywomen are affiliated with sect-type than with church-type groups.[9] Even here, however, Negro females probably have a greater opportunity to serve as clergywomen than do white females, since Negroes are more likely than whites to be affiliated with sect-type groups or congregationally based churches. The greater approval of clergywomen by sects than by denominations reflects differences regarding definitions of the clergy.[10] The association of female clergy with sect-type organizations should be reflected in the characteristics of most clergywomen, since their characteristics are related to the social use of sect membership from which they are recruited and which they, in turn, serve.

The characteristics of clergywomen are affected, however, not only by the varying amounts of opposition to them but also by the conflict between roles expected of clergy and other roles expected of females. The roles required of the clergy often conflict with those traditionally required of women. The expected greater orientation toward marriage and the family on the part of the female often precludes her consideration of the clergy as an occupation. If she enters such an occupation, conflict between roles of clergy and roles of marriage and family may result either in leaving the ministry and "disappearing into marriage" or foregoing marriage and family for the sake of a career.[11] This role conflict can, of course, occur between any career and marriage and family expectations. The conflict may be more acute, however, in the case of the ministry because this occupation is defined as a leadership position which tends to make exclusive and extensive demands on the role player. The husband may resent his wife's being a clergywoman, unless perhaps he also occupies a position of leadership (e.g., if he also is clergy). This conflict in role systems can be expected to be reflected in the characteristics of female clergy who probably must decide which system of action is to be most important in their lives: career or family. In the case of the clergy, the acuteness of the conflict may be too great to permit females to operate effectively or satisfactorily in both action systems.

Propositions

The above considerations led to the formulation of the following general propositions which guided the present investigation.

Proposition I. — There has been an increase in the number of clergywomen since the beginning of the present century. This increase has not been great, however, due to the lingering opposition to clergywomen, and the proportion of clergy who are female has remained small.

Proposition II. — A larger percentage of female than of male clergy is Negro. This is expected because the white female has more professional alternatives than the Negro female, and because of the greater association of the Negro than of the white with sect-type organizations.

Proposition III. — The female clergy is older, on the average, than the male clergy. This is expected because the lack of commitment to this occupation and the strong attractiveness of the alternatives are more likely to be experienced by the younger than by the older females.

Proposition IV. — The female clergy has obtained a lower level of education than the male clergy. The general opposition to clergywomen would lead the more highly educated women to enter other professions. At the same time, the sects continue to recruit from a less educated social base and accept a less educated clergy, including women.

Proposition V. — The clergywoman is less likely than the clergyman to be married and to be living with spouse. This is expected because of the conflicts between clergy and marriage roles.

Data and Method

Data for the present report were drawn from tabulations published by the U.S. Bureau of the Census. Information regarding a number of significant variables allowed comparisons of male[12] and female clergy, comparisons of white and Negro clergy, as well as the determination of changes occurring in each of these racial and sex categories. The factors on which information was available are racial composition, age, educational attainment, and marital status. Some information was available for each of the decades from 1900 to 1960. Certain comparisons, however, could be made only for shorter periods of time due to the nature of the census reports. Whenever possible, the analysis was limited to employed clergy, although the information on certain variables was available only for experienced clergy.

Findings

Census data support the proposition that the number of clergywomen has increased between 1900 and 1960. There were 4,695 clergywomen in the United States in 1960, an increase of about 38 per cent since the turn of the century, at which time there were 3,405 clergywomen (see Table 1). However, the male clergy increased approximately 81 per cent during this period, so that the percentages of females in the total clergy decreased somewhat from 3.0 per cent in 1900 to 2.3 per cent in 1960.

Moreover, the number of clergywomen displayed great fluctuations between 1900 and 1960, with increases between 1910 and 1950, but decreases between 1900 and 1910 and between 1950 and 1960. The percentages of females in the total clergy de-

Table 1 / Percentages of Employed Female Clergy in Specified Racial Categories, 1900-1960

Year	N	Total	White	Negro	Other Non-white
			Race		
1900	3,405	100.0	95.05	4.9	0.05
1910	685	100.0	89.6	10.0	0.4
1920	1,787	100.5*	87.2	12.8	0.05
1930	3,276	100.0	84.6	15.1	0.3
1940	3,148	†	†	†	†
1950	6,777	100.0	89.6	10.4	0 0
1960	4,695	100.0	87.5	11.5	1.0

* Because of rounding, the percentages do not add to 100.00.
† Racial composition of clergywomen was not available for 1940.
Source: U.S. Bureau of the Census, *Twelfth Census of the United States: 1900, Statistics of Occupations* (Washington, D.C.; Government Printing Office, 1904), Table 36, p. cxiii, and Table 37, p. cxiv; U.S. Bureau of the Census, *Thirteenth Census of the United States: 1910,* Vol. IV: *Population — Occupational Statistics* (Washington, D.C.: Government Printing Office, 1914), Table 6. p. 428; U.S. Bureau of the Census, *Fourteenth Census of the United States: 1920,* Vol. IV: *Population — Occupations* (Washington, D.C.: Government Printing Office, 1923), chap. iii, Table 5, p. 342; U.S. Bureau of the Census, *Fifteenth Census of the United States: 1930,* Vol. V: *Population — General Reports on Occupations* (Washington, D.C.: Government Printing Office, 1933), chap. iii, Table 3, pp. 83-84; U.S. Bureau of the Census, *U.S. Census of Population: 1950,* Vol. IV: *Special Reports,* Part 1, chap. B, "Occupational Characteristics" (Washington, D.C.: Government Printing Office, 1956), Table 3, p. 29; U.S. Bureau of the Census, *U.S. Census of Population: 1960, Subject Reports, Occupational Characteristics,* Final Report PC(2)-7A (Washington, D.C.: Government Printing Office, 1963), Table 3, p. 21.

creased from 3.0 in 1900 to 0.6 in 1910, increased steadily to 4 0 in 1950 and decreased to 2.3 in 1960.

The remarkable fluctuations by decades in the number of clergywomen are difficult to interpret. They may result from opposition experienced in the ministry, conflict between marital and clerical roles, the lack of strong commitment to the clergy as a career, and the existence of professional alternatives. However, the fact that the fluctuations by decade are quite uneven would necessitate the assumption that these explanatory factors are also unevenly experienced from decade to decade. Since there is no known evidence to support this assumption, the explanation of the fluctuations in the number of clergywomen remains conjecture.

Even if these "explanations" were valid, they would, of course, have a differential effect on the various categories of women. The discussion of each of the subsequent propositions notes which of the categories have fluctuated the most, and which of the factors mentioned above might help to explain these differentials.

The second proposition, that a larger percentage of female than of male clergy is Negro, is not supported by census data in any decade until 1960.

One method of ascertaining the degree to which Negro and white females contribute their proportionate shares to the clergywomen is to compare the percentages of the male clergy that is Negro with the corresponding percentages of the female clergy. Such comparisons show that the male had higher percentages of Negroes than the female clergy between 1900 and 1950. During this period, however, the percentage of clergymen that was Negro decreased,[13] while the percentage of clergywomen that was Negro increased (see Table 1). Thus, relative to the male clergy, Negroes did not contribute disproportionately to clergywomen until 1960, at which time the female clergy had a higher percentage of Negroes than the male clergy (11.5 per cent versus 6.7 per cent).

However, it has long been noted that, relative to the total male population, Negro males have made up a disproportionately large percentage of male clergy. This same "predisposition" to become clergy may or may not be true for Negro females. One way of answering this question is to compare the percentage of the white clergy that is female with a corresponding percentage of the Negro clergy (see Table 2). Such comparisons show higher

Table 2 / Percentages of the Total Employed Clergy that is Female, According to Specified Racial Categories, 1900-1960

Year	Race			
	White		Negro	
	N	Per Cent	N	Per Cent
1900	3,207	3.3	164	1.1
1910	614	0.6	68	0.4
1920		1.4	228	1.2
1930	2,772	2.3	494	2.0
1940	*	*	*	*
1950	6,450	4.5	750	4.0
1960	3,859	2.1	508	3.7

* Racial composition of clergywomen was not available for 1940.
Source: See Table 1.

percentages in the white clergy than in the Negro clergy between 1900 and 1960, during which time these differences diminished. In 1960, the percentage of females in the Negro clergy was higher than that in the white. Thus, relative to the Negro males, the Negro females did not contribute disproportionately to the clergy until 1960.

The increasing visibility of Negroes among female clergy is probably related to the decreasing number of Negro clergymen. The steady loss of Negro clergymen since 1930 may have provided more opportunities for Negro women to serve as clergy. The increasing number of white clergymen during that period has probably limited the number of opportunities for white clergywomen.

The third proposition, that female clergy are relatively older than male clergy, is not supported by census data in any decade of the present century until 1960. (The changes that have occurred in the age composition of the female clergy are indicated in Table 3 for those years in which census data were tabulated in comparable age categories according to race or color.)

Table 3 / Percentages of the Employed Clergywomen Who Were in Specified Age Classes, by Color, United States, 1900, 1930, 1950 and 1960

Color and Year	N	Age Levels					
		Total	Under 35	35-44	45-54	55-64	65 and over
White:							
1900	3,207	100.0	53.0	21.6	12.9	9.5	3.0
1930	2,772	100.0	25.0	25.5	24.2	17.2	8.1
1950	6,450	100.0	31.1	25.6	20.5	15.8	7.0
1960	3,859	100.0	19.6	21.8	28.3	14.2	16.1
Non-white:*							
1900	164	100.0	32.6	32.5	20.2	9.2	5.5
1930	494	100.0	20.3	33.5	30.0	12.2	4.0
1950	750	100.0	16.0	16.0	28.0	24.0	16.0
1960	550	100.0	14.9	10.9	29.6	19.0	25.6

* The figures for 1900 and 1930 are for Negroes only; those for 1950 and 1960 are for all non-whites.

Source: U.S. Bureau of the Census, *Twelfth Census of the United States: 1900, Statistics of Occupations* (Washington, D.C.: Government Printing Office, 1904), Table 5, pp. 20-21, Table 6, pp. 24-25, Table 7, pp. 28-29, and Table 9, pp. 36-37; U.S. Bureau of the Census, *Fifteenth Census of the United States: 1930,* Vol. V: *Population — General Reports on Occupations* (Washington, D.C.: Government Printing Office, 1933), chap. iv, Table 7, pp. 154-55, Table 8, pp. 174-75, and Table 9, pp. 192-93; U.S. Bureau of the Census, *U.S. Census of Population: 1950,* Vol. IV: *Special Reports,* Part 1, chap. B, "Occupational Characteristics" (Washington, D.C.: Government Printing Office, 1956), Table 6, p. 75, and Table 7, p. 87; U.S. Bureau of the Census, *U.S. Census of Population 1960, Subject Reports, Occupational Characteristics,* Final Report PC(2)-7A (Washington, D.C.: Government Printing Office, 1963), Table 6, p. 81, and Table 7, p. 101.

Regardless of race, today there is a tendency for clergywomen generally to be older than male clergy. The median age for clergymen in 1960, for example, was 43.2, while that of clergywomen was 48.7.[14] Whereas in earlier decades of the present century there were higher percentages of female clergy under thirty-five years of age than was true of the male clergy, there has been an apparent tendency for clergywomen to experience a greater "aging process" than clergymen from 1900 to 1960. Both white and Negro female clergy have displayed greater fluctuations in number at the younger than at the older ages (over forty-five) than was true for male clergy. Thus, it may be more difficult to recruit and keep relatively young clergywomen than young clergymen.

Census data support the proposition that clergywomen have attained a relatively lower level of education than clergymen. (The information in Table 4 is based on census reports for the

Table 4 / Percentages of the Experienced Clergywomen who Completed Specified Numbers of Years in School, by Color, United States, 1950-60

Color and Year	N	Level of Education Attained					
		Total	Elementary School or Less	High School		College	
				1-3 Years	4 Years	1-3 Years	4 Years or More
White:							
1950	6,540	97.7*	18.8	10.1	22.0	22.9	22.9
1960	3,859	100.0	14.6	16.6	23.3	22.9	22.6
Non-white:							
1950	780	96.1*	34.6	23.1	15.4	11.5	11.5
1960	550	100.0	32.7	11.1	18.0	12.0	26.2

* Because of rounding and the omission from census reports of persons not reporting their educational status, percentages do not total 100.0.
Source: U.S. Bureau of the Census, *U.S. Census of Population: 1950*, Vol. IV: *Special Reports*, Part 1, chap. B, "Occupational Characteristics" (Washington, D.C.: Government Printing Office, 1956), Table 10, p. 107, and Table 11, p. 115; U.S. Bureau of the Census, *U.S. Census of Population: 1960*, *Subject Reports, Occupational Characteristics*, Final Report PC(2)-7A (Washington, D.C.: Government Printing Office, 1963), Table 9, p. 123, and Table 10, p. 137.

two decades for which data were available. It was assumed that treating non-whites as Negroes would not bias the interpretation unduly.)

White and Negro female clergy tend to be of lower educational status than their male colleagues. The median number of completed years of school in 1950 was 16.0 plus for clergymen and 12.8 for clergywomen; comparable figures for 1960 were 17.1 and 12.8. Differences between the sexes in educational attainment were more marked among white than among Negro clergy.

Given the age and racial composition of the clergywomen, however, the low level of attained education is perhaps to be expected. Since no direct comparisons regarding attained education could be made between clergywomen and clergymen, or between clergywomen and females in the total labor force (with age and color controlled), indirect standardization was used.[15] This method indicated that the educational attainment of clergywomen, given their age and racial composition, was no less than that of the female labor force. In fact, clergywomen had attained a level of education greater than the female labor force would lead one to expect. In comparison with other working females, then, clergywomen appear in a favorable light. In comparison with other female professionals, however, and in comparison with clergymen, the lower educational attainment of clergywomen (regardless of age and racial composition) remains conspicuous.

The median educational attainment of clergywomen apparently did not increase to any great extent between 1950 and 1960. Census data disclosed further that, with increasing education, females were more likely to enter professional occupations but less likely to use the ministry as a professional outlet. These highly educated women were more likely to enter other professions in which they were accepted by the public.

Census data support the proposition that clergywomen are less likely than clergymen to be married and to be living with spouse. (Although data were available from previous census reports, only those for 1960 are presented in this paper for the sake of brevity.)

The census report for 1960 indicates that clergywomen are more likely than clergymen to be single, widowed, or divorced (see Table 5).[16] These differences in marital status were apparent in every census report since 1900. Additional information provided by the 1960 census report indicates that, among the married, the spouses of clergywomen are more likely to be absent than those of clergymen (7.1 per cent versus 1.7 per cent).

The marital status of clergywomen, however, may be due to

Table 5 / Percentages of the Experienced Clergy Who Were in Specified Marital Categories, by Sex, United States, 1960

Sex	N	Marital Categories				
		Total	Single	Married	Widowed	Divorced
Male	196,367	100.0	22.2	76.5	0.9	0.4
Female	4,409	100.0	23.4	57.8	15.2	3.6

Source: U.S. Bureau of the Census U.S. Census of Population: 1960, Subject Reports,
Occupational Characteristics, Final Report PC(2)-7A (Washington, D.C.: Government
Printing Office, 1963), Table 12, p. 174.

·their age and racial composition. Indirect standardization indicated the marital status of clergywomen, given their age and
racial composition, was the same as that of the female labor
force. Although clergywomen do not differ maritally from other
females of the same age and racial composition, they do differ
from clergymen in this respect. Census data allowed the marital
status of clergymen and clergywomen to be compared directly
within each age category. Such comparisons established the
fact that, age for age, female clergy are less likely to be married
than are male clergy.

It has been suggested above that this marital deviance reflects
various solutions to the conflict between marital and occupational roles. The fact that clergywomen are more likely than
clergymen to work part-time suggests one solution to the conflict between requirements of family and career. The fact that
clergywomen have a relatively high percentage of absent
spouses may have resulted from another type of solution. The
relatively high percentage of divorced clergywomen hints at still
another possibility. And widowhood, perhaps, frees the female
from both marital and family responsibilities, forces her to
work, and affords her the opportunity to assume the ministerial
role previously occupied by her husband. These solutions could,
of course, hold true for many other occupations that women perform. That they might hold true for the clergywomen suggests,
at least, that ministerial roles for females are different or differentially experienced from those same roles for males.

The author proposes, however, that the most significant evidence for the conflict between career and marital orientations is
the large amount of fluctuation in number of young (25-44
years of age) single clergywomen. As young single females enter
the ministry, they face opposition, experience role conflict, and
do not perform the roles for which they thought they were pre-

pared. Consequently, they leave the ministry for a more satis-factory alternative. Whether these clergywomen are "disappear-ing into marriage" or choosing another career awaits field re-search.[17]

Conclusions

Census data provide little evidence for the increased pro-fessionalization of clergywomen, greater acceptance of women as clergy, more use of the clergy by women as an occupational outlet, or improvement of the composite "woman preacher."[18] In fact, the data may be interpreted to question attributing the very label of "profession" to these females. In some characteris-tics (e.g., educational attainment), they are more like the general labor force than like other professionals. The differences be-tween male and female clergy in age, educational attainment, and marital status are quite conspicuous, and these distinctions suggest that clergy roles are different for females than for males or are differentially experienced by the two sexes. The opportu-nities for females to act as clergy are more limited than for males, and these limitations have produced a composite picture of the female clergy that *at least suggests* professional margin-ality.

NOTES

1. Census data for 1960 indicated that, in comparison with their white colleagues, Negro female professionals were concentrated in a smaller number of professional occupations.

2. The American Association of Women Ministers was founded in 1919 with the stated purpose "To promote equal ecclesiastical rights for women and to encourage young women to take up the work of the ministry." The organization claims a membership of 250 women who are licensed, ordained, or authorized to preach. It holds annual meetings and publishes a quarterly, *Woman's Pulpit* (reported in *Encyclopedia of Associations*, Vol I: *National Organizations of the United States* [Detroit: Book Tower, 1964], p. 758.

3. E. Wilbur Bock, "The Decline of the Negro Clergy: Changes in Formal Religious Leadership in the United States in the Twentieth Century" (paper presented at the annual meeting of the Southern Sociological Society, New Orleans, Louisiana, April, 1966 [mimeo-graphed]).

4. Recent books on the sociology of religion suggest that the ad-mission of women to the clergy may be one of the most significant

changes taking place in church organizations (see David O. Moberg, *The Church as a Social Institution* [Englewood Cliffs, N.J.: Prentice-Hall Inc., 1962], pp. 508-9; Glenn M. Vernon, *Sociology of Religion* [New York: McGraw-Hill Book Co., 1962], pp. 198-99; and especially W. Seward Salisbury, *Religion in American Culture* [Homewood, Ill.: Dorsey Press, 1964], pp. 284-88.

5. Compare, e.g., a Gallup poll, which reported in 1947 that 47 per cent of the respondents were unconvinced that women should be clergy, with a Minnesota poll, which reported in 1956 that 59 per cent of the respondents were willing for women to be clergy (see "Public Still Reluctant To Accept Women Clergy," *Christian Century*, LXIV [July 16, 1947], 869; and Moberg, *op. cit.*).

6. Salisbury, *op cit.*, pp. 285-86.

7. "Women in the Churches," *Christian Century*, LXIX (May 21, 1952), 606-7; and "Breakthrough for the Woman Minister," *Christian Century*, LXXIV (January 23, 1957), 100. Jones and Taylor report that only one-third of their sample of clergywomen was able to move directly into ministerial positions upon completion of education and certification. Two-thirds of these women found it necessary to enter other occupations until ministerial positions were available to them (see Arthur R. Jones, Jr., and Lee Taylor, "Differential Recruitment of Female Professionals: A Case Study of Clergywomen" (paper presented at the annual meeting of the Southern Sociological Society, Atlanta, Georgia, April 1965 (mimeographed), p. 5]).

8. "California Woman 'Recognized' as Episcopal Clergy Member," *Lutheran*, III (October 13, 1965), 31.

9. George F. Ketcham (ed.), *Yearbook of American Churches* (New York: National Council of Churches of Christ in the U.S.A., 1951), pp. 239-43; Benson Y. Landis (ed.), *Yearbook of American Churches* (New York: National Council of Churches of Christ in the U.S.A., 1952), pp. 264-65; and Benson Y. Landis (ed.), *Yearbook of American Churches* (New York: National Council of Churches of Christ in the U.S.A., 1964), p. 283.

10. The sect emphasizes the saliency of clerical roles compared with other social roles, priority of the preaching role compared with other clerical roles, the "call" as compared with formal education, and lay leadership (see, e.g., John Scanzoni, "Resolution of Occupational-Conjugal Role Conflict in Clergy Marriages," *Journal of Marriage and the Family*, XXVII [August, 1965], 396-402).

11. Cf. Jessie Bernard, *Academic Women* (University Park: Pennsylvania State University Press, 1964), in which the author argues that the decline since 1930 in the proportion of academic personnel who are women is due partially to the "flight into maternity" as well as to the increasing attraction of other professional careers.

12. For the sake of brevity, only a limited amount of census data

on male clergy is reported here. A more complete presentation of these data is to be made in a separate article (see also Bock, *op. cit.*).

13. *Ibid.*

14. This difference in age is greater than would have been expected from comparisons of male and female professionals and of males and females in the general labor force.

15. The following steps were involved in indirect standardization: (1) determining what proportions of persons in the labor force at each age level had attained given levels of education, (2) distributing the number of clergy of each age level across levels of education in the same proportions as the labor force, (3) summing across age levels within educational levels, and (4) using these summary figures on each educational level as standards for comparisons with the actual number of clergy at each educational level. This procedure was performed for each color and sex category separately. The method, of course, involved the assumption that at each age level the distribution of educational attainment (or any other variable under consideration) was similar to that of the labor force. The validity of this assumption remains an unknown (see George W. Barclay, *Techniques of Population Analysis* [New York: John Wiley & Sons, 1958], pp. 174-77, for a discussion of indirect standardization).

16. The percentages of unmarried male and female clergy appear to be approximately the same in Table 5. However, when the presence of Catholic priests among male clergy is taken into account, the differences in percentages between unmarried clergywomen and clergymen became even more noticeable.

17. Data from earlier census reports (1900, 1920, and 1930) indicated that the large percentage of single clergywomen is probably due more to white females while the large percentage of widowed clergywomen is probably due to Negro females. If "flight into marriage" is occurring, it may more likely be experienced by white than by Negro clergywomen. On the other hand, the assumption of the ministerial role of the deceased husband may be experienced by a greater percentage of Negro than of white clergywomen.

18. See, e.g., "Breakthrough for the Woman Minister," *op. cit.*, p. 100, where the anticipation was that "A significant result of the Methodist and Presbyterian, USA, actions in 1956 is likely to be enhancement of the quality of the composite 'woman preacher.' "

forty-three

Women in Science: Why So Few?

ALICE S. ROSSI

Where women are concerned, the late 1940's and the 1950's were marked by a national mood of domesticity demonstrated by the rapid rise in the birth rate and the flight of families to the suburbs. It was a period of high praise for woman's domestic role. That mood has shifted in the 1960's. Educators, employers, government officials, and manpower specialists are urging women to enter more fully into the occupational life of the nation. A President's Commission on the Status of Women has recently issued a set of wide-ranging recommendations to this end (1). Particular stress has been put on the need for women in fields in which there is a critical shortage of manpower — teaching, science, and engineering — and conferences on women in science have been held under federal auspices, at Marymount College in 1963 and at the Massachusetts Institute of Technology in 1964.

What can we expect as a result of this campaign? Working women in the industrial, service, and clerical occupations will probably experience an improvement in status. The implementation of the Equal Pay Act and the retraining possible under the Manpower Development and Training Act will be of help to such women, as will all attempts to improve community child-care and housekeeping facilities, increased tax deductions for families including a working mother, and the like. A steady supply of older, married women secretaries, clerks, machine tenders, and technicians seems assured.

From SCIENCE, Vol. 148, No. 3674 (1965), pp. 1196-1202. Reprinted by permission of the author and SCIENCE. Copyright 1965 by the American Association for the Advancement of Science.

A second group directly benefiting from the campaign consists of women residents of the national and state capitals. There is a renewal of optimism among women in government employment, and some indications that in Washington itself their opportunities for advancement may be increasing. But a very large proportion of women in all grades of the Civil Service are unmarried, and a very large proportion of those who are married have no children (2).

Most college-educated women in this country are married and living with their husbands and children. Whether we are interested in the status of women or in the needs of science or both, I do not think we can expect any appreciable increase in the representation of women in the top professions unless that fact is taken into account. As long as it is mostly spinsters or widows who are appointed or elected or promoted to a college presidency, a national commission, a senatorship, or a high post in a government agency or scientific institute, we cannot consider that a solution has been found to the problem of women's status in American society. Marriage, parenthood, and meaningful work are major experiences in the adventure of life. No society can consider that the disadvantages of women have been overcome so long as the pursuit of a career exacts a personal deprivation of marriage and parenthood, or the pursuit of happiness in marriage and family life robs a woman of fulfillment in meaningful work.

The Present Situation

How many women are there in the fields of science and engineering in the United States, and what are their characteristics? The latest figures available are from the 1960 Census. In 1960 (3), only 9 percent of the employed natural scientists and less than 1 percent of the engineers were women (See Table 1). Within these broad fields, there was considerable variation: from 2 percent in the earth sciences and 4 percent in physics to 26 percent in mathematics and 27 percent in the biological sciences (4). Women lost rather than gained ground in the sciences between 1950 and 1960, for although they appeared in greater absolute numbers in 1960, the rate of increase was much lower than that of men. Thus while there was a 209 percent increase in the number of women mathematicians, the number of male mathematicians increased 428 percent, so that the propor-

Table 1 / Employment of Women in Sciences and Engineering, 1950 and 1960, as Percentage of Total Personnel, and Rate of Increase of Each Sex (3).

Occupation	Female (%)		Increase (%)	
	1950	1960	Female	Male
Biologists	28	27	38.2	56.2
Chemists	10	9	—3.6	13.5
Geologists, geophysicists	6	2	—27.3	81.1
Mathematicians	38	26	209.8	428.1
Physicists	6	4	20.2	92.5
All natural scientists	11	9	10.4	30.0
All engineers	1.2	0.8	11.0	64.3

tion of women actually declined from 38 percent to 26 percent in that decade. Hiestand (5) has shown that this is a characteristic of all occupations undergoing an accelerated rate of growth. The majority group in the labor force is white men, and it is their growth pattern which defines the rapidly growing fields. Since women constitute a far smaller proportion of the total labor force, they can usually provide only a small proportion of the added manpower in rapidly growing fields. That this is not the whole story, however, is suggested by the fact that in fields like medicine and law, which have not had the same accelerated rates of growth, women were no better represented in 1960 than in 1950.

Women employed in the scientific and engineering fields in 1960 were less likely than men to have advanced degrees, particularly the Ph.D., less likely to be employed in industry, considerably less likely to be married; they earned less money and worked fewer hours per week. At each level of educational attainment the median salary of men was markedly higher than that of women. Half the women scientists but only one-fourth of the men worked in educational institutions, and men were four times as likely as women to be in industrial management (6). Among those who were teaching science, women were more likely than men to work less than 35 hours a week; significantly larger proportions of men reported work weeks in excess of 40 hours. As of 1960, the chances were rather slim that a woman in engineering or science would find part-time employment other than in teaching. For example, the proportion reporting fewer than 35 hours a week was 41 percent among women teaching chemistry above the secondary school level, but only 9 percent among women identifying themselves as "chemists" (7, table 4).

Four out of five men scientists but only two out of five women scientists were married and living with their spouses (7, table 3). Since these figures represent employed women only, they exaggerate the proportion of unmarried women among those trained as scientists. Significant numbers of women have been trained in the professions but withdraw for varying periods of time to home and child-rearing. Table 2 shows what proportions

Table 2 / Voluntary Withdrawal from Labor Force* in Selected Professions, by Age and Sex (7); Expressed in Percentages.

Profession and sex	Age		
	25 to 44	45 to 64	65 or older
Natural scientists			
Women	51	13	61
Men	2	1	57
Engineers			
Women	31	13	42
Men	1	4	58
Secondary school teachers			
Women	34	13	65
Men	2	2	54
Physicians-surgeons			
Women	19	10	31
Men	2	2	25

* The labor force is defined as all persons, whether currently employed or not, who have worked in the stated capacity during the last 10 years. The figures are as of 1960.

of experienced professional men and women in 1960 were in the labor reserve (defined as those not employed and not seeking employment but who worked in a given field within the previous 10 years) (8). Among men, there is little withdrawal from the active labor force before age 65; among young men the proportion is typically under 5 percent. Among women, sizable proportions withdraw, particularly in the 24 to 44 age group, when family responsibilities are at their peak.

There are considerable differences among the professions, however, in this regard. Women doctors have very low withdrawal rates, whereas the rates for women secondary school teachers and engineers are moderately high. It is rather surprising to find that women scientists have an even higher rate of voluntary withdrawal than the teachers — 51 percent as against 34 percent. One might expect that having undertaken careers in science, still a pioneer field for women, these women would have motivation high enough to offset the easier accommodation of work and family responsibilities to school teaching. Apparently this is not so.

What about the future supply of women in science? An examination of the career plans of younger women, in a study of college seniors of the class of 1961 by the National Opinion Research Center (9), indicates no new trend toward more women physicists and engineers, although there is an increase of women headed for the biological sciences. Among college seniors planning graduate work in physics 8 percent were female, in engineering 1 percent, in chemistry 20 percent, in mathematics 28 percent, in all biological sciences 43 percent. Furthermore, some of these women will become secondary school science teachers rather than practicing scientists. A follow-up study one year after graduation showed that among those actually enrolled in graduate school, the percent female in the physical sciences was 16, in the biological sciences 34 (10). If the pattern shown in Table 2 holds for this younger group of women, by 1965 about half of them will have voluntarily withdrawn at least temporarily from advanced training or jobs in science.

Several questions emerge from the foregoing review. Why are there so few women in science? Why are they less apt to get advanced degrees than men? Why are they less apt to marry? Why do they withdraw from their fields?

The Priority of Marriage

What a man "does" defines his status, but whom she marries defines a woman's. In meeting strangers, one can "place" a man socially by asking what he does, a woman by asking what her husband does. This is particularly true for the top professional and technical strata of American society. Only small proportions of the wives of doctors, scientists, engineers, and lawyers are employed, ranging (in 1960) from a low of 16 percent of doctors' wives to a high of 25 percent of scientists' wives (7, table 12). In contrast, 44 to 47 percent of the wives of librarians, social workers, and school teachers are employed.

This has decided implications for the paths young women see

as open to them for success in American life. A man must express his intelligence and ambition in the occupational sphere. A woman's ambition can find an outlet in marriage or in work, seldom in both. If a woman has a successful husband, there are no cultural pressures upon her to use her intelligence or training in the work of the world. In fact her husband may resist a desire on her part for such a separate career, for a wife with leisure is one symbol of his success, and a wife's career might require him to carry some of the parental responsibilities his wife has carried for him.

I think it is the awareness that marriage and careers are not now compatible for women in the upper middle class (despite protestations to the contrary in recent years) that lies behind the often pathetic vacillations of high school and college girls between the pursuit of social popularity (a route to successful marriage) and excellence in scholarship (a route to successful careers). Surely it plays a role in the different concerns parents have for their adolescent boys and girls — the educational goals of their sons and the dating patterns of their daughters.

A sample of women college graduates 3 years beyond graduation were asked the following question (11): "An American woman can be very successful in a variety of ways. Which of the following would you most like to be yourself?" The most frequent answers were: to be the mother of several accomplished children and to be the wife of a prominent man. Yet some echoes of earlier aspirations and the imprint of their college education are found in their responses to the further question, "Which of the following do you personally admire very much?" Four out of five chose winners of scientific, scholarly, or artistic awards. They admire the minority within their sex who have careers, but choose themselves to live in the shadows of their husbands' and children's accomplishments.

Unless there are changes in the organization of professional and technical work or in the attitudes of men towards women's roles, it seems likely that fewer rather than more college-trained women will pursue serious careers in the future, for there has been a steady increase in the proportion of the male labor force found in the top occupations. This is not to say that wives of such men will not work. They will, particularly early in the marriage when their earnings supplement university stipends to support the graduate training of their husbands. And we shall hear from these women again when they reach their forties. As long as their husbands are not "too" successful, they may become social workers, teachers, computer programmers, professional or technical aides in laboratories or offices. Only rarely will they become doctors, lawyers, scientists, or engineers. Harriet Martineau's observation in 1834 that the "prosperity of America is a circumstance unfavorable to its women," meaning women are not "put to the proof as to what they are capable of thinking and doing" (12), is as true for the upper middle class in 1964 as it was when she compared America with England on her first visit to the young nation.

It is ironic that with a life span now long enough to experience many and varied adventures of the mind, the spirit, and the senses, the major life experiences of marriage and parenthood and the intellectual excitement of advanced study are compressed into the same narrow few years of early adulthood. Instead of savoring each to the full and in their turn, we feast upon all three simultaneously as on a triple-decker sandwich. This quickened pace of life and the earlier age at which marriage, parenthood, and occupational success take place play an important role in lowering the career aspirations of women and in deflecting them from the pursuit of such goals as they have. There is not enough time in late adolescence for young women to evolve a value system of their own and a sense of direction toward an individual goal, for they are committing themselves prematurely to marriage and adapting to the goals of their husbands at the expense of their own emotional and intellectual growth.

Men are more conservative than women concerning the role of careers in the lives of women. Much larger proportions of college-trained men than women in the NORC career development study (11) believed women should not choose a career difficult to combine with child-rearing, and disapproved of women's working when they have preschool children. The same men were between two and three times more likely than the women to say there was "no need at all" for the major recommendations made by the President's Commission on the Status of Women — increased child-care facilities, equal opportunity in hiring and promotion, and encouraging more women to enter the professions and national political office.

Women see the sharp differences between their own views

and those of "most men." Women in the NORC sample were given a brief account of a hypothetical family conflict and asked how they themselves would resolve it and how they thought "most wives" and "most husbands" would resolve it. In the story, a woman graduated from college with honors in biology, married, and held a teaching job while her husband completed law school. Now he has a degree and a good job. Both wish to have children, but she would like to take an advanced degree in biology and eventually pursue a career in biological research. The respondents were asked what decision the couple should make: to start a family and have the wife get the degree later; to start a family and give up the wife's career goal; to postpone child-bearing and let the wife get the degree now; or carry out both wishes simultaneously. Only one-fourth of the women thought the couple should start the family now, with the wife either giving up or postponing her training and career plans; but half of them believed these two decisions would be favored by "most wives," and three-fourths that it would be favored by "most husbands."

In actual fact, most women do as they say most husbands would prefer: they are less apt to complete any advanced training, highly likely to work after marriage and then withdraw for the child-bearing and -rearing years. The typical pattern of work for American women shows two peaks of employment, the first in their early twenties, the second in the 40 to 55 age group. As seen in Table 2, this withdrawal in the 24 to 44 age group is particularly high for women in the sciences. Thus in their expressed attitudes, women are less conservative than men, but their actual behavior reflects an adaptation to the views of men.

Effect of Interruption of Career

During the last 5 years there has been a mushrooming of centers for counseling and retraining older women who wish to return to professional employment. I think there is a danger that by thus institutionalizing the withdrawal-and-return pattern of college-educated women, we may reduce even further the likelihood that women will enter the top professions. Older women who have not worked for many years may be retrained and contribute significantly to personnel shortages at the lower professional levels as laboratory assistants, technical writers, nurses, and school teachers, but only rarely as doctors, full-fledged scientists, and engineers. Not only is training for such fields a long and difficult process, but the pace of technological and scientific knowledge has been so rapid that even those who remain in these fields have difficulty keeping up, let alone those who return to advanced training after a 10-year break.

Even more fundamental, however, is the effect on potential creativity of withdrawal precisely during early adulthood. Lehman's researches into the relation between age and achievement (13) have shown that the quality of intellectual output is strongly related to age, and that in the sciences the peak of creative work is reached in the late twenties and early thirties. The small number of women included in his samples showed their most creative years to be no different from those of the men. They were making their major contributions during the very years when most American women withdraw and devote a decade or more to home and family.

If more women are to choose science and remain active in science, it must be possible for them to do so without lengthy interruption of their careers during their potentially most creative years. There has to be a better balance between marital, parental, and career obligations and pleasures for both sexes: work must be *less* dominant than it is in the lives of men in order for it to be *more* dominant in the lives of women.

New View of the Maternal Role

Women will not be strongly motivated to remain active professionally during the early years of child-rearing simply out of concern for the effect of withdrawal upon their intellectual creativity. The development of their children is a concern equal to if not greater than their own work. Until very recently, there was a widely held belief than any separation of the mother and the child would have dire consequences for the emotional development of the child, and many women who worked throughout their children's early years did so with considerable anxiety about the effect of their daily absence upon their children. It is only very recently that this myth has been laid to rest. A current volume of some 22 empirical studies on the employed mother (14) has shown that maternal employment has no unfavorable effects upon children. Of much greater importance than employment per se are the mother's reasons for working, the quality of the care the child receives in her absence, and the attitudes of her husband. In the last few years, social scientists have begun to stress the desirable rather than the unfavorable consequences of maternal employment (15, p. 615).

There is a second body of research on child development that reflects a further shift in the concept of the maternal role. For years psychologists focused rather exclusively on the mother's feelings toward and physical care and training of the child. Now there is increasing emphasis on the role of mothers in their children's cognitive development. It has been found that how well the child takes to his early school experiences is strongly related to whether he has had stimulating experience with language and ideas during his preschool years. The better educated the mother, the greater will this stimulation of the child tend to be. There is research currently under way testing the hypothesis that it is the lack of cognitive stimulation that contributes most heavily to poor school performance among lower-working-class children (16).

The implications for social action in behalf of children in culturally deprived homes are clear: enrich the environment of the very young child by means of child-care facilities designed to provide such cognitive stimulation (17). The implications as regards children of college-educated parents are less clear-cut. Some child specialists may say that the mother is more necessary at home than ever, not only to love and care for the child but to stimulate the growing mind of the child. This is to stress the role of the mother as a *teacher*. She may be even more effective, however, as an *example* to the child. If she is utilizing her education in a professional job which keeps her alert and involved with things of the mind, she may transmit far more zest for learning than the educated mother who shelves her books along with her diploma. With the view that maternal employment will harm the child now shown to be unfounded, younger women are potentially free of one source of anxiety if they choose to pursue a profession.

Women and Science: Incompatible?

What is there about women on the one hand, and science on the other, that leads to such a very low affinity between them in American society? What are the major characteristics of the scientist, and why are women in our society less apt to have these characteristics than men?

The following thumbnail sketch of the scientist is based largely on the intensive research of Roe *(18)* on eminent physicists and biologists. Two caveats must be noted. First, there have been no detailed psychological studies of women scientists in any way comparable to those of men scientists. Some studies suggest that differences in students' interests and values are more closely related to their fields of study than to sex differences, but in drawing a portrait of the characteristics of the scientist it is an assumption rather than an empirically established fact that women scientists do not differ from men scientists in the major characteristics relevant to their occupational role. Secondly, Roe's studies of scientists were conducted in the 1940's with men largely in their fifties at that time. Whether younger men entering the considerably changed world of science in the 1960's and 1970's will differ we do not know, though a comparison of physics students with the physics faculty at a major university in the 1950's shows such striking similarity in personality and social traits as to suggest little change from generation to generation *(19)*.

The four characteristics Roe found most typical of outstanding natural scientists are the following:

1) *High intellectual ability,* particularly spatial and mathematical.

2) *Persistence in work;* intense channeling of energy in work such that the greatest personal satisfaction was experienced when working.

3) *Extreme independence,* showing itself in childhood as a preference for a few close friends rather than extensive or organized social groups, and preference for working alone; in adulthood as a marked independence of intense relations with others and a preference for being free of all supervision.

4) *Apartness from others;* low interest in social activities, with neither preference for an active social life nor guilt concerning such tendencies toward social withdrawal.

All four characteristics manifest themselves early in life; hence a predisposition toward science as a career goal is established long before the college student makes a formal commitment to a "major." Furthermore, these are all characteristics girls in American society are considerably less apt to have than boys. Both at home and at school, girls are socialized in directions least likely to predispose them toward science as a career. What are these sex differences during the formative years?

Intellectual Ability

For many years it was assumed that there were practically no sex differences in intelligence, for studies relying on the Stanford-Binet intelligence test showed almost no differences between boys and girls. It had somehow been forgotten that, in standardizing this test, items which revealed consistent sex differences were discarded so that the scores of boys and girls could be evaluated against the same norms. During more recent years, as specific tests were constructed to measure different dimensions of intellectual and creative ability, consistent sex differences began to emerge.

These differences may be summarized as follows (20): Girls talk at younger ages, put words together into sentences somewhat sooner, and learn to read more easily than boys. After the fifth or sixth grade, however, boys do as well as girls in reading comprehension, though girls show somewhat greater verbal fluency. In mathematical skills there are no sex differences during the early school years, but during high school boys begin to excel, and by the time they take the Scholastic Aptitude Tests the boys score an average of 50 points higher on the mathematical portion, while girls score only 8 or 10 points higher on the verbal portion. Throughout school boys do better on spatial tests (for example, detecting a simple figure embedded in a more complex one), which suggests that "boys perceive more analytically, while the girls are more global, more influenced by all the elements of the field together" (20, p. 29).

Thus girls develop cognitive abilities along somewhat different lines than boys, and enter adolescence with a style of thinking less appropriate to scientific work. Any final interpretation of this sex difference awaits further research, but what is known to date is that one key lies in the kind and degree of training in independence the child receives. Bing (21) found that high verbal ability is fostered by a close relationship with a demanding and somewhat intrusive mother, while high mathematical abilities were enhanced by allowing a child a considerable degree of freedom to experiment on his own. Children whose scores on standard intelligence tests rise between their 6th and 10th years are highly likely to have been six-year-olds who were "competitive, self-assertive, independent and dominant in interaction with other children," while those who showed declining scores were "passive, shy and dependent" youngsters at six (20, p. 33).

Early Family Influences

If we look more closely at the family environment of the young child, we can guess at some of the sources of this difference in cognitive style between boys and girls. The scientist's characteristics of independence, persistence in work, and social isolation are mirrored in significant differences between the father and the mother as seen through the eyes of the child. No matter what the father works at, the child sees him leave the family to pursue it; it is a normal part of every day's expectation that father will not be present. Mother, in contrast, is usually at home and instantly available, someone who takes care of the thousand details of home and family life, none of them so important that she cannot be easily interrupted. Even when he is at home, father may be far less "available" than mother.

It is easy for the child to conclude from daily observation that men work for long stretches of time at something important, and that men are less involved with people than women are. There is a consistency between these observations of the parents and the characteristics of young children. Very young girls have a greater interest in other people than boys have and are influenced to a greater extent by what other people think of them. Coleman (22) has found that in adolescence, girls are far more often involved in same-sex cliques than boys, who are more often independent loners. Girls comply with the demands of social situations more than boys do, whether at home in doing what parents ask of them or at school in doing what teachers ask. In short, by the example of their parents boys receive encouragement to stand on their own, to be alone, to aim high, and girls are encouraged to be cooperative and responsive to people and to minister to their needs.

The result of these early influences is a marked contrast between men and women in the values that underlie their career choices. Rosenberg (23) and more recently Davis (24) have indicated that the occupational value which most sharply differentiates the career choices of women from those of men has to do with the orientation toward people. Women strongly prefer fields in which they work with people rather than things, and hence we find college-trained women most heavily represented in the humanities, the applied aspects of the social sciences, education, and the health professions. Some of these differences persist even among men and women who have chosen the same occupational field. Women are more often found teaching science than doing science. Women college teachers mention as most satisfying about their campus jobs "good students" and "desirable colleagues," whereas men teachers stress "opportunity to do research" and "freedom and independence" (25).

For most American women, growing up has meant shifting from being taken care of in a well-peopled social environment to taking care of others. If we want more women to enter science, not only as teachers of science but as scientists, some quite basic changes must take place in the ways girls are reared. If girls are to develop the analytic and mathematical abilities science requires, parents and teachers must encourage them in independence and self-reliance instead of pleasing feminine submission; stimulate and reward girls' efforts to satisfy their curiosity about the world as they do those of boys; encourage in girls not unthinking conformity but alert intelligence that asks why and rejects the easy answers. A childhood model of the quiet, good, sweet girl will not produce many women scientists or scholars, doctors or engineers. It will produce the competent, loyal laboratory assistant "who will not operate so readily on her own," as Pollard wrote recently in describing his preference for a female rather than a male laboratory assistant (26).

Summary and Conclusions

American society has prided itself on its concern for the fullest development of each individual's creative potential. As a nation, we have become sensitive to the social handicaps of race and class but have remained quite insensitive to those imposed because of sex. Those women who have entered the top professional fields have had to have extraordinary motivation, thick skins, exceptional ability, and some unusual pattern of socialization in order to reach their occupational destinations. In their backgrounds one is likely to find a professional mother, an unusually supportive father, or dedicated and stimulating teachers.

If we want more women scientists, there are several big tasks ahead:

1) We must educate boys and girls for all their major adult roles — as parents, spouses, workers, and creatures of leisure. This means giving more stress in education, at home and at school, to the future family roles of boys and the future occupational roles of girls. Women will not stop viewing work as a stopgap until meaningful work is taken for granted in the lives of women as it is in the lives of men.

2) We must stop restricting and lowering the occupational goals of girls on the pretext of counseling them to be "realistic." If women have difficulty handling the triple roles of member of a profession, wife, and mother, their difficulties should be recognized as a social problem to be dealt with by social engineering rather than be left to each individual woman to solve as best she can. Conflicts and difficulties are not necessarily a social evil to be avoided; they can be a spur to creative social change.

3) We must apply our technological skill to a rationalization of home maintenance (15). The domestic responsibilities of employed women and their husbands would be considerably lightened if there were house-care service firms, for example, with teams of trained male and female workers making the rounds of client households, accomplishing in a few hours per home and with more thoroughness what the single domestic servant does poorly in two days of work at a barely living wage.

4) We must encourage men to be more articulate about themselves as males and about women. Three out of five married women doctors and engineers have husbands in their own or related fields. The views of young and able women concerning marriage and careers could be changed far more effectively by the men who have found marriage to professional women a satisfying experience than by exhortations of professional women, or of manpower specialists and family-living instructors whose own wives are homemakers.

The physiological differences between male and female are sufficiently clear and so fundamental to self-definition that no change in the direction of greater similarity between male and female social roles is going to disturb the sex identity of children or adults. No one would be confused if men were more tender and expressive and women more aggressive and intellectual. If anything, greater similarity in family and occupational roles would add zest and vitality to the relations between men and women and minimize the social segregation of the sexes. An increase in the number of women scientists would be only one of many desirable outcomes to the social changes that I have here urged.

NOTES

1. *American Women: Report of the President's Commission on the Status of Women, 1963* (Government Printing Office, Washington, D.C., 1963).

2. *Report of the Committee on Federal Employment to the President's Commission on the Status of Women* (Government Printing Office, Washington, D.C., 1963), pp. 104-105.

3. *1960 Census of Population* (Government Printing Office, Washington, D.C.), vol. 1, pt. 1, Table 202.

4. Scientific personnel in government employment do not show so high a proportion of women in the biological sciences: the proportion female by major scientific field among those federally employed is 8 percent for physical sciences, 4 percent for biological sciences, 1 percent for engineering (2, Appendix D).

5. D. Hiestand. *Economic Growth and Employment Opportunities for Minorities* (Columbia Univ. Press, New York, 1964).

6. 1962 National Register data, reported in *Physics: Education, Employment, Financial Support, A Statistical Handbook* (American Institute of Physics, New York, 1964).

7. *1960 Census of Population: Characteristics of Professional Workers* (Government Printing Office, Washington, D.C.).

8. *Ibid.*, rates calculated from data in Tables 3 and 6.

9. J. Davis, *Great Aspirations: The Graduate School Plans of America's College Seniors* (Aldine, Chicago, 1964), pp. 154-155.

10. N. Miller, "One year after commencement," *National Opinion Research Center, Chicago, Report No. 92* (1963), pp. 125-126.

11. Preliminary results of a recent questionnaire sent to the same sample as in Davis (9).

12. H. Martineau, *Society in America*, S. M. Lipset, Ed. (Doubleday, New York, abridged ed., 1962), p. 295.

13. H. Lehman, *Age and Achievement* (Princeton University Press, Princeton, N. J., 1953).

14. A. Rossi, *Daedalus* 93, 615 (1964).

15. F. I. Nye and L. W. Hoffman, *The Employed Mother in America* (Rand McNally, Chicago, 1963).

16. R. Hess, *J. Marriage and the Family* 26, 422 (1964).

17. One experimental day-care center in Syracuse, New York, will test the effect of an optimal environment for 6-month-to-3-year-old children on learning readiness at school age. B. M. Caldwell and J. B. Richmond, *ibid.*, p. 481.

18. A. Roe. "A psychological study of eminent biologists," *Psychol. Monograph No. 65* (1951), p. 331; "A psychological study of physical scientists," *Genet. Psychol. Monograph No. 43* (1951); "Psychological study of research scientists," *Psychol. Monograph No. 67* (1953), p. 2; "Crucial life experiences in the development of scientists," in *Talent and Education,* E. Torrance, Ed. (Univ. of Minnesota Press. Minneapolis, 1960); *The Making of a Scientist* (Dodd, Mead, New York, 1963).

19. G. Stern, M. Stein, B. Bloom, *Methods in Personality Assessment* (Free Press, Glencoe, Ill., 1956).

20. E. Maccoby, "Woman's intellect," in *The Potential of Women,* S. Farber and R. Wilson, Eds. (McGraw-Hill, New York, 1963), gives a more detailed summary of sex differences in intellectual ability.

21. E. Bing, *Child Development* 34, 631 (1963).

22. J. Coleman, *The Adolescent Society* (Free Press, Glencoe, Ill., 1961).

23. M. Rosenberg, *Occupations and Values* (Free Press, Glencoe, Ill., 1957).

24. J. Davis, *Undergraduate Career Decisions,* in press.

25. R. Eckert and J. Stecklein, "Job motivations and satisfactions of college teachers," *U. S. Office of Education Coop. Res. Monograph No. 7* (1961).

26. E. Pollard, *Science* 145, 1018 (1964).

forty-four

Women in Architecture

BEATRICE DINERMAN

Women constitute less than one per cent of the total number of registered architects in the United States — under 100 out of a total of some 20,000. Only one architect in 200 is a woman and women represent less than 5 per cent of all architectural students.

Why do so few women choose to join the profession? Is there something inherently masculine about the field of architecture, requiring certain traits and capabilities not generally associated with feminine attributes? Why does the architectural profession appear to welcome women into its ranks and, at the same time, continue to erect subtle discriminatory barriers against them? And, most important of all, what can be done to stimulate more women to enter the profession and assure them a gracious reception from both clients and colleagues?

Architecture, much like law, engineering, and business, has always been thought of as a man's field. This distinction, an outgrowth of a cultural heritage that assigns quite different, mutually exclusive roles to men and women, has had an unquestionable impact on the architectural profession, diverting the energies of girls who might otherwise be attracted to architecture into more acceptable "feminine" careers.

The image of the architect as a masculine figure is a holdover from an earlier era when architects were closely related to unprofessional, skilled craftsmen, and much of their work involved considerable physical strength and direct contact with construction crews, often in a supervisory capacity. Today, architecture requires more intelligence than manual expertise; the average architect spends far more time at his desk than straddling the steel framework of some building under construction.

Ignoring this shift in emphasis, the lay public has continued to view the architect as a relatively tough, masculine figure. Girls planning a career and firms employing architects are influenced by this stereotype.

This traditional, sex-linked division of labor has produced a number of potent myths concerning a woman's ability to function effectively in a field such as architecture. Doubts range from her very intelligence and competence, to her loyalty to the profession in terms of the pull toward home and family, to an excessive emotional involvement which could prevent an objective approach toward her professional responsibilities.

Architectural school deans across the country report no appreciable distinctions between their male and female students, clearly refuting the myth of inherent, sex-linked capabilities. On the contrary, it would appear that women tend to outperform men scholastically, exhibiting far greater motivation and far greater drive and accounting for a far greater proportion of top students.

"Although only 2 per cent of our students are women, they usually rank in the upper 5 per cent of their class," reports Dean Emil Fischer of the College of Architecture and Design at Kansas State University. "In general" he continues, "women seem to be more definitely motivated and try to excel. Once they choose the profession of architecture, they apply their total energy toward becoming as proficient as possible." Women students who succeed in completing their program have tremendous drive, motivation and superior performance.

Not only are women architects as competent as men, they share an equal dedication to their work, successfully overcoming the temptation to leave school, marry and raise a family. Architectural school deans report that the percentage of female dropouts is generally no higher than for men. While marriage and motherhood are dropout factors in some cases, more often those women who do discontinue their studies leave for much the same reasons as men — financial problems, or a change in career focus, or some personal setback.

"Marriage does not seem to be a factor," says Dean Robert Dietz of the College of Architecture and Urban Planning at the

University of Washington. "Like the men, they simply keep on going to school, even during periods of obvious expectancy." In observing that most women students continue their studies and graduate, Joseph Sabatella, assistant dean in the department of architecture at the University of Florida, attributes this tenacity to the fact that "women who enter the program have generally made an extensive study of their relationship to the profession prior to beginning. Consequently, they posses higher interest and motivation."

Such observations could well represent a significant step forward in encouraging women to enter the architectural profession in greater numbers. Yet, the imperative of changing social tradition so that girls are no longer conditioned to see certain occupations as being masculine by nature remains a tremendous challenge. This exceedingly difficult task will, above all, place an ever increasing burden on educational counseling.

Unfortunately, high school and college counselors, far from encouraging more women to enter architecture, have had a negative influence. In raising the question with a representative sampling of female architects, close to two-thirds reported receiving no encouragement whatsoever from either professional counselors or university faculty members. In fact, over half of this group was actively *discouraged* from choosing architecture as a career, with sex representing the determining factor in virtually every case.

In tackling the problem of attracting more women into architecture, several constructive steps have been suggested: a greater emphasis on positive educational counseling; a central employment registry for women seeking architectural positions; the greater availability of part-time work; development of refresher courses for women architects who, having dropped out of the field to raise a family, now choose to return to their profession; research into sources of domestic help for professional mothers and tax relief for women so employed; an educational campaign designed to change the image of achitecture by, for example, depicting women architects at work in career brochures; and a more active involvement by architectural associations and by the women architects themselves.

But, the success of even a most rigorous program of this nature hinges on another question: Does the architectural profession truly *want* women as colleagues?

Most women architects feel they have been subjected to some degree of bias because of their sex, noting a wide variety of discriminatory practices.

Female architects agree that their most serious setback occurs in getting their *first* architectural position. "There is no doubt that discrimination exists" is the unequivocal conclusion of one self-employed West Coast female architect. "Some employers hire a woman so they can feel heroic, but most firms are more conservative, using a variety of excuses and rationalizations for not hiring a woman." Given the choice between an equally qualified male and female job applicant, the architectural firm will invariably select the male.

Other barriers mentioned most frequently include income disparities for comparable work, the need to specialize in residential architecture in order to win even a minimum of acceptance, and an intense degree of prejudice from contractors which forces architectural firms to limit their female professionals to office work, making advancement to managerial levels and to field supervisory positions so difficult as to be virtually impossible.

Women are often not even interviewed by certain firms for jobs such as project coordinator or field supervisor. One female architect engaged in a successful practice with her architect husband is more intense in her reaction, claiming that "a so-called preference for female architects in residential design is little more than a placebo, diverting attention from severe restrictions against women in other architectural specialties and transforming the female architect into little more than a glorified interior decorator." An ability to devote careful attention to small details is an essential characteristic of the competent architect, yet a woman's special faculty for such attention, used extensively as an excuse for limiting her to tedious, routine responsibilities, is totally ignored when her architectural potential is being considered.

Women architects are especially resentful of the fact that more is expected of them in terms of competence, personal standards, and working relations with others, viewing such expectations as discrimination via the "double standard." "In order to be equal," comments one experienced, middle-aged female architect in private practice, "a woman must be *more* than equal. Men anticipate her failure and so she must prove herself again and again." And, in fact, female architects are unified in their observation that women architects, to be accepted, must be exceptionally competent, possess an extreme degree of perseverance and stamina, work twice as hard, be gifted with both a thick skin and a sense of humor, and exhibit a consistently excellent disposition in their working relations with others.

Women architects are not alone in their recognition of sex discrimination. The existence of prejudice in the field, and the degree to which such restrictions might well underly a reluctance of women to enter the profession, have been noted by quite a number of unbiased and objective sources.

Robert J. Piper, in his educational brochure *Opportunities In An Architectural Career,* comments that while there are many openings for women in the field, the opportunities for men are considerably greater, noting that "women are usually subject to lower salary schedules than are men — even for comparable work."

The Bureau of Labor Statistics made a similar observation in its 1967 *Occupational Opportunities Handbook,* terming the employment outlook for women architects "less favorable" than for men. While predicting ready employment for capable female draftsmen, the Bureau concluded that few women are able to establish themselves in private practice where earnings are much greater than those received by even a highly paid salaried employee of an established architectural firm.

Many architectural schools exhibit strong concern over the limited opportunities available for even their finest female graduates, noting a reluctance by numerous firms to even consider employing a female architect as a matter of company policy. Other barriers mentioned include restricted opportunities for advancement, the virtual exclusion of women from managerial positions and/or field responsibilities, lower pay scales, prejudicial attitudes by contractors and construction crew members who resent taking orders from a woman, and a myriad of intangible, psychological obstacles stemming from a general reluctance to consider the female architect as being the equal of her male counterpart.

Some female architects attribute sex prejudice to an economic rationale — a belief that male architects don't want their field invaded by outside competition. Most women reject this explanation, placing greater emphasis on the fact that the successful female architect is viewed as a threat to the very masculinity and ego strength of her male colleagues.

This conviction is reflected in the type of advice offered by women architects to their sisters in the field. "The successful woman architect must take advantage of all opportunities to allow her male colleagues to express their ego," advises a female project architect for a leading university. "Men will only favor the female architect if they feel she needs their support. As she becomes strong, self-sufficient and comes to occupy a leading role, these same men will turn bitter and resentful."

As Ethel Charles so cogently stated in an address before the Royal Association of British Architects, "This should not be a case of men versus women, but a case of individual capability and aptitude. I suppose the reason why women should not practice architecture is because they have not practiced it before, and this is no reason at all."

forty-five

What You Should Know About Women Engineers

HERBERT POPPER

If you have been looking forward to getting a bright, pert, girl chemical engineer for your department one of these days, take heart — your chances are improving. The latest survey of the Society of Women Engineers showed 243 girls enrolled in chemical engineering, compared with 199 in 1963, and 169 in 1961. In fact, more girls were enrolled in chemical engineering than in any other engineering discipline (electrical, civil and mechanical engineering were next, in that order).[1]

Encouraging as these statistics are to those who would like more women engineers — or engineers of both sexes — to enter the profession, it might well be asked why the numbers aren't even higher. Considering the present and projected shortages of young chemical engineers, remembering that there are 27 million U.S. working women who make up about 36% of the nation's "manpower" force, and keeping in mind that almost as many girls show basic mathematical and technical aptitudes as do their male counterparts, why isn't the enrollment figure, say, 2,430 instead of 243? Would 2,430 girls really be too much of a good thing?

To help answer this question, let us quickly examine the validity of some of the reservations a male engineer or manager may have about giving women engineers a much bigger role; we will then take up various suggestions for positive action.

Engineering and the Feminine Mystique

Some of us feel instinctively that engineering is a male field, and that any females who enter its domain are either unfeminine to begin with or will become defeminized before they are through. According to this line of reasoning, the fact that more than a third of the engineers in Russia are female merely proves that their women are less feminine than ours — after all, they also have more female shot-putting champions than we do, but would you want your little daughter or kid sister to try out for the shot-putting team in school?

This line of reasoning is certainly open to attack. Now that more and more chemical engineering is being done in air-conditioned offices or in landscaped technical centers, and less and less of it involves exchanging invectives with burly chemical operators on the rickety operating platforms of distillation towers during howling gales on the night shift, there appears little justification for maintaining that all engineering is inherently defeminizing. Indeed, the female engineers that I interviewed when researching this article in New York were charmingly feminine. And the 320 delegates whom I had a chance to observe this July at the Second International Conference of Women Engineers and Scientists in Cambridge, England, certainly represented a perfectly normal cross section of femininity. (In fact, a civil engineer from Poland with whom I chatted at Cambridge reminded me somewhat more of Sophia Loren than of any female shot-putter.) Therefore, I think we should bury the stereotyped image of the woman engineer as a cold, hard, overintelligent female who trudges through life in her flat-heeled shoes and tailored suit;[2] a few women engineers may be like that, just as a few nurses or schoolteachers may be, but most are not. And today, there is no reason why they should be.

Women engineers have even been able to do field work in engineering without becoming defeminized. I spoke with one who used to service gas wells out in the oil country; another one who does cost engineering requiring occasional field trips. The latter, a pretty young professional engineer, reports that she heard less profanity on the construction site than she hears in the home office, and that she was treated with great chivalry by the construction workers.

Of course, there are certain types of field work that still are not suitable for most women — at isolated sites, for instance. Also, some states have "protective" laws (many of them now under attack by women's groups) that limit the numbers of hours or the night-shift work that women may put in. Incidentally, a protective Texas law bars women employees in places where unspecified "immoral conditions" exist,[3] but I am sure this law does not represent any sort of barrier to women engineers who want to work in Texas chemical plants.

All in all, it has been proved that there are many types of field-work, as well as most types of home-office or technical-center work, that women can perform with distinction, and without sacrificing an ounce of their feminine charm.

Do Women Have Staying Power?

A serious question is raised by many employers as to whether it pays to give young women engineers extended training, since they may wander off to raise a family.

This question is a complex one. Time has been on the side of women. At one time, the new male chemical engineer was likely to spend at least a good part of his career with the company that gave him his first job. Now, job mobility has increased to the point where the average tenure on the first job is less than three years. Therefore, women can and do point out that there is a certain degree of risk in training anybody — male or female — and that this risk may sometimes be less with females.

Here is the way one staff engineer puts it. She is Christine Konecny, presently employed as a plastics engineer at Magna-flux Corp. in Los Angeles. She worked for eight years before taking a five-year leave of absence to raise a family; since then she has worked for over 12 years without missing a day:

> "When I have hired technical personnel, I have found that it is the sincerity, character and background of a person, rather than the person's sex, that provides the clue as to whether he or she will continue with an engineering career and contribute to the company.
>
> "Consider the effort a girl had to expend to get an engineering degree, and the expense involved. Because of her minority status, she faced more obstacles than did the average male student. She probably had to work just a little harder, and she had to overcome not only the prejudices of others, but her own inner qualms and inhibitions. After four or five years of hard work, that degree means more that just a piece of paper. The pursuit of a career is something real and, with few exceptions, is undertaken with great sincerity.
>
> "If she eventually leaves to raise a family, the chances are she

will try to keep up with what is going on in her field, and return one day. (During my own semi-retirement, I kept very active in professional organizations.) Prior to returning, she may take a refresher course of some kind to upgrade her knowledge; the fact that more and more of such courses are being offered to working engineers is in her favor.

"I believe our nation's greatest natural resource is brain power, and that women are part of this natural resource — a part that has been overlooked for a long time. Given an opportunity, women will prove their value. Most women engineers are so intent on proving themselves that I think you will find they will work with more zeal and professional dedication thaan the run-of-the-mill male engineer."

Mrs. Konecny touched on an important and somewhat controversial point in discussing the problem of "keeping up" during the semi-retirement period. Technology is changing so fast that a woman who stays out a dozen years, say, instead of five or six, may have great difficulty picking up the pieces unless she has spent considerable effort keeping herself up to date. Understandably, not all women are motivated to expend this effort while they are raising a family and completely away from the job. Some part-time work or consulting assignments can be a big help in bridging the gap, and in supplying the motivation to keep up to date via a self-study and participation in the activities of professional societies.

Many women engineers are doing just that, in Europe as well as in the United States. For instance, Dr. Nicole Bécarud, a charming chemical engineer from France whom I encountered at the Cambridge Conference, is a part-time technical advisor on food industry problems; she works for Fédération des Industries de l'Alimentation, in Paris. She expects to return to full-time chemical engineering when her sons are a little older, feeling that the satisfaction of a professional technical career can be perfectly combined with the satisfaction of raising a family.

Of course, one must beware of sweeping generalizations here; some highly intelligent and dynamic women can apparently find permanent and complete fulfillment in their family, household, social and cultural activities. But others cannot — and they would seem to be much better off pursuing rewarding careers of their own instead of trying to find an outlet for self-expression by over-managing the children, joining every club in sight, second-guessing their husband's career decisions, or even "helping their husbands get ahead." Along these lines, a recent survey by the *Wall Street Journal* suggests that the imbalance between a mentally active husband with a challenging career, and a mentally active wife with an unchallenging household, can be a bigger threat to the tranquillity of some marriages than any strains that might come about from dual careers.[4]

The next decade or two will undoubtedly see great strides in educational methods and information technology; this will greatly facilitate the job of the woman engineer who is trying to keep up to date while raising a family. John B. Parrish, professor of economics at the University of Illinois and a member of various federal manpower committees, offers this prediction:[5]

"The woman engineer of the future will marry a professional man before or shortly after getting her first degree. She will earn a second-level and perhaps a third-level degree. She may have children before leaving the university campus; or she may obtain the degrees, work for three to five years and then drop out for child raising. In either case, she will acquire or maintain professional competence by means of an automatic study carrel (electronic information booth). Through telecommunication she will attend engineering classes, observe research projects, discuss problems with teachers and engineers on the job. The turn of a dial on a console will give access to all engineering literature, including search, retrieval and display of any desired volume, article, report or blueprint. If convenience requires, she can retransmit the display to panels in other rooms — to the kitchen while making coffee, to the nursery while tending the children. Another console dial will give access to a computer network for analytical tasks.

"If enrolled in formal course work, examinations will be written in her study carrel, transmitted to a mechanical grader, the grade transmitted back to the carrel, to faculty and to academic administrative personnel. This air-conditioned automatic information carrel will be made available at low subsidized cost through a federal government scientific manpower agency. She will insist it be in colors, so that it harmonizes with the decor of the other rooms in the house or apartment.

"If she takes time out from professional practice while children are small, she will return to part-time or full-time practice fully updated; in fact, probably more so than her male colleagues undergoing professional obsolescence through narrow specialization. Her husband will need to have frequent recourse to this information carrel to keep up professionally with his wife."

Female Charm: Asset or Handicap?

In the preceding sections, I have used such terms as pretty and charming to describe some of the female engineers I have met. This, of course, raises a question that is in the back of the minds of some managers. Will the assignment of a pretty girl engineer to an all-male department cause major distraction and disrupt efficiency?

In general, the answer would seem to be no. If the men do spend some time in nonbusiness conversations with her at the beginning, this time is largely taken away from nonbusiness conversations the men would have had among themselves anyway. In other words, she may change the pattern of nonbusiness conversation, but probably not the extent of it, particularly if she wants to get her own work done.

After a while, the novelty wears off, she becomes accepted, and her distraction-potential goes down. As one pretty girl engineer put it, "The only time the men in my department get distracted now is when a new secretary walks through. I guess I've become assimilated."

There are times when feminine charm can be a real asset. For instance, an executive for a British instrumentation firm told me that he sometimes uses one of his capable and comely girl electrical engineers to explain portions of contract proposals to customers as a "change of pace" during long negotiating sessions. At first, the customer's reaction is usually polite, tolerant amusement. But after he asks a few searching questions and finds out that the girl really knows what she is talking about, she can often get her explanation across better or faster than a man could.

Thus, charm — when used as a supplement to brain power and perseverance — can be a very legitimate asset. When used as a *substitute*, it can represent a danger, but no girl has been able to get through an engineering curriculum on charm alone. After she graduates, in the unlikely event she relies on charm to get her out of tight spots or to give her an unfair advantage, it is up to us men to display our maturity and set her straight — and to judge her by her performance on the same basis as that of her male counterpart.

This brings us to the question of promoting the woman engineer. Some companies do this very gingerly, on the theory that most men do not like to be supervised or "managed" by a woman. This is a complex sociological question, and one I do not want to get into in detail; several good articles have appeared on the subject.[6] Let me just cite three comments from lady engineers:

1. "Some managers feel that a young woman engineer is just killing time, waiting to go off and start raising a family, and they tend to assign her to a routine or blind-alley job where she is most likely to be expendable. How far or fast she advances thus depends on her dynamic personality, to a greater extent than is the case for a man."

2. "Advancement was slow until they realized I intended to make a career of engineering; thereafter, I had equal treatment."

3. "I have some supervisory responsibility over seven male engineers and ten technicians. They respect me because I know my field and how to handle people. I can talk their language on the job; I make sure to recognize their good work and fight for them when it comes time for raises. Yes, some men are sensitive to criticism, particularly when it comes from a woman, but good judgment can go a long way here. I don't refrain from criticism, but I do try to put it on the basis of 'we goofed' rather than 'you goofed.' "[7]

Let me just add that several of these supervisory engineers quite impressed me with their appreciation of human relations; I can certainly think of far worse fates for a young male engineer than to work for one of these ladies.

The Case for Women Engineers

Returning to the scarcity question for a minute, I realize that the extent of the present or future engineering shortage is subject to controversy.

On the one hand, the Engineering Manpower Commission predicts that demand for engineering graduates will average 69,000 per year during the next decade, in contrast to an estimated average supply of only 41,000 per year. (The present yield is about 36,000 new B.S.-level engineers per year.) The report envisions a steady decline in engineering enrollments as a percentage of the entering freshman class. Despite the great increase in the number of students entering college, engineering enrollments and degrees are growing much more slowly. Thus, according to the commission, the engineering shortage is likely to get much worse.

On the other hand, some engineers maintain that there is no critical engineering shortage now, nor is there likely to be one. They say that they will start believing "all this shortage talk" when new engineering graduates start making more money than union plumbers, or when the salaries of veteran engineers start to zoom just like mercury prices zoomed during the recent mercury shortage, or when engineers are forced to delegate all noncreative work to technicians.

Let's take an in-between viewpoint. While the scarcity of engineers in the chemical process industries is not equally manifest in all fields and at all level of experience, and probably will never reach a uniform stage of criticality, it is nevertheless true that shortage of help has already forced many engineers to take their vacations at inconvenient times, to put in unpaid overtime instead of taking continuing education courses, and to pass up opportunities for professional recognition via prepared papers or published articles because "our department is one man short." College recruiters have had several very rough years in a row, and while this has given engineering seniors a unique chance to see the length and breadth of this country at company expense, there is much to be said for a saner atmosphere.

And this is where women engineers come in. If we are going to increase engineering enrollment, we can:

1. Make the engineering curriculum easier so that young men of marginal aptitude and ability will not only be attracted to it for financial reasons, but will be able to survive it despite their shortcomings, or

2. Encourage young women of high aptitude and ability to take up engineering, without lowering educational standards.

Because of current trends in engineering education (e.g., the necessity of including more and more courses in the curriculum), the second alternative would seem to make more sense than the first.

But are there enough young women with a high degree of technical aptitude? Most women come close to panic when they have to change a tire, don't they?

Here we must not confuse mechanical aptitude with technical aptitude. Women do indeed lag behind men in mechanical aptitude; this is inherent in our culture, the rules being that little girls play with dolls while little boys play with trucks and tinker with other mechanical toys. But *technical* aptitude involves something else again — to a greater and greater extent, it involves mathematical and analytical ability, with a dash of chemistry and the natural sciences. Here the gap between boys and girls is much smaller; indeed, some people maintain that there would be no gap at all if only true aptitude (rather than aptitude plus some acquired knowledge) could be measured. To be conservative, let us accept a gap; let us accept one test-survey of high school students that showed 6.3% of the boys and 4.2% of the girls to have aptitude for engineering.[2] This suggests that up to 40% of all engineers could very well be women — a far cry from the 0.7% of today,* and probably enough to solve the engineering shortage of the next decade.

What Can We Do About All This?

Becoming convinced that women chemical engineers can represent good business as well as a worthy sociological cause is the first step. The next step is to take positive action either to increase the supply of these engineers, or to use the existing supply most effectively. In the latter regard, we can:

1. Maintain an open rather than tradition-bound mind on what jobs can or cannot be handle by women. Note this comment from one engineering executive: "If we think a woman applicant or recruit can do the job, we now let the personnel department hire her and then assign her to the supervisor. We've found that if we let the supervisor of an all-male department make this hiring decision, he'll find some reason for insisting that only a man would be suitable."

2. Treat the person as a professional. Any professional likes to think that his or her success will depend on individual performance and contributions, and will not be affected by "stereotype" attributes. This applies to good as well as bad attributes — most of the girl engineers I have met struck me as alert, direct, purposeful, very alive and well-adjusted, but I don't

* According to a just-released survey by Josephine Webb of the Society of Women Engineers, there are 5,200 women engineers in the U. S., compared with 750,000 males. Taking chemical engineering alone, there are 1,180 women vs. 123,750 males. (There are more women in chemical engineering than in any other single engineering discipline, but the percentage is still only about 1%.)

want to imply that all girl engineers are necessarily this way or that way — they have to be evaluated as individuals, just like anybody else.

But what can be done to increase the supply of women engineers? The importance of this question is evident from these figures: The girl engineers who graduated in 1966 from 26 leading universities got an average of five job offers each, some getting as many as eight or ten. About two-thirds of the women graduates accepted jobs from campus recruiters, and didn't have to knock on any doors. Salary offers averaged $7,570 at the B.S. level, $9,900 for an M.S., and $11,800 for a Ph.D; this is only about 5% lower than starting salaries offered to male graduates. Thus, it would seem that women engineers, unlike their predecessors who sometimes had to resort to suffragette tactics to see the personnel manager, are beginning to enjoy a seller's market, and one that will become even tighter unless the supply of graduates is increased rather significantly. And here we all have a part to play.

For one thing, we can use our influence in our community and among our circle of friends to dispel the notion that engineering, like lumberjacking, is strictly for men. Unfortunately, the reaction of many parents to a daughter who wants to become an engineer is, "Good grief, where did we go wrong?" We can do a lot to counter this attitude — after all, there are about 120,000 of us chemical engineers alone, and each of us has several non-engineering families in our circle of friends. Let's put in a good word for engineering where we can, with girls as well as boys. There are a lot of good personal reasons why a girl who shows some aptitude should at least consider engineering — it pays better than teaching, for instance, and may well be less strenuous. The curriculum is tough, but you can often go further with a bachelor's degree in engineering than you can with a master's degree in mathematics or chemistry. And I have met several girls with degrees in liberal arts, economics, statistics or library science who were doing rather routine work and who wished they had obtained a technical degree — but not one who wanted to trade in her technical degree for one of the nontechnical ones.

Let us try to get our message across to junior and senior high schools, as well as to colleges and to individuals. The Society of Women Engineers (SWE) is trying to do this via speaking engagements; perhaps we should help. It might make a big impression on girls if we men told them that we really wanted them in engineering. Perhaps they need to feel needed. As Evelyn Harrison of the SWE recently put it, "Many girls are indoctrinated against a career in engineering by their mothers, teachers and school counselors even if they display high aptitude. By the time a girl is entering college, her mind has often become patterned in such a way that she would be unable to survive an engineering course even if she wanted to. That is why it is so important to reach the 14- and 15-year olds who have not yet been totally conditioned against becoming engineers."

Janet Hershkowitz, the lone girl to obtain a B.S. in chemical engineering from Polytechnic Institute of Brooklyn this year, confirms the importance of reaching girls in high school:

"A lot of my old girl friends were good in science and math, but they never considered going into engineering because they felt it was a rugged occupation with a 'For Men Only' label. No one ever told them that most engineering jobs were no more unladylike than jobs in chemistry, for instance. Actually, I didn't know very much about engineering either, but I thought I liked applied science even better than pure science, and I refused to believe that engineering could be as rugged and exclusively masculine as all that. So I started out in college as a chemical engineering major, and never found any reason for changing. Although the curriculum was rough, the work was rewarding and sometimes even fun. And you don't have to sacrifice your social activities altogether. A lot of the problems that I was solemnly warned about — for instance, the alleged difficulty of lugging heavy equipment around in engineering laboratory courses — just never materialized. And now that I have worked as a process engineer for an oil company this summer, I feel even more strongly that there are a lot of information voids and downright misconceptions about engineering careers — particularly where girls are concerned — that should be corrected at the high school level."

Curriculums are also a factor. If you are active on school boards, or know someone who is, make sure the curriculums don't shunt girls out of engineering careers before they even understand what they are shunted out of.

An action of a different kind that would also have mutual benefits is to provide part-time assignments for lady engineers who are raising a family and are not yet ready to return on a full-time basis. Such an assignment would provide a base for keeping up to date via self-study, while helping solve many a department's short-handedness. This is being done at the Wright-Patterson Air Force Base, where an engineering job is sometimes split down the middle between two women: They share the salary, sick-leave and vacation benefits; one works in the morning, the other in the afternoon. When the woman is ready to return full-time, she does not have the handicap of a ten- or twelve-year gap in her working knowledge. From the employer's viewpoint, he benefits because the women work at peak efficiency during their half-day stints, and will need less retraining later on.

The girl engineers who have entered industry have certainly proved to be not only an adornment, but a lucrative source of technical talent. This source can be developed much further. If we want to help develop it, let's see what we can do to persuade students, parents and counsellors that a technical career can be compatible with a happy marriage and that, in some cases, an engineering slide-rule can be a girl's best friend.

NOTES

1. Biennial Survey of Undergraduate Women Engineering Day Students, Winter 1966, conducted by the Student Activities Committee of the Society of Women Engineers.

2. Peden I. C., Women in Engineering Careers, Ch. 10 in "The World of Engineering," Whinnery, J. R., ed., McGraw-Hill, 1965.

3. Staff article, "Sex and Civil Rights: Women's Groups Fight Last Vestiges of Bias on Job, Before the Law," *Wall St. J.*, May 22, 1967.

4. Staff article, "Price of Success? Growing Job Demands Shatter the Marriages of More Executives," *Wall St. J.*, May 10, 1967.

5. Parrish, J. B., "Future Role of Women in U. S. Science and Engineering," presented at Second Intl. Conf. of Women Engineers and Scientists, Cambridge, England, July 7, 1967.

6. For a good discussion, including a review of the Civil Rights Act of 1964 and other federal legislation, see Famularo, J. J., "Woman Power," *J. of College Placement*, Apr.-May 1967, p. 32.

7. Dunleavy, Ann D., private communication.

forty-six

Women in the Law

JAMES J. WHITE

Evidence of Discrimination

As it is used in this article, "discrimination" includes every differentiation, whether or not it is rational or functional. It includes both the racist's selection of one of his own race in preference to a more able member of another race and an ill person's selection of the best neurosurgeon in preference to the next best one. Initial support for the conclusion that the male-female income differential is caused principally by discrimination against women comes from the fact that our statistics rule out or render unlikely the other most plausible explanations. On the basis of the available figures and analysis one can conclude with near certainty that the income differential between the men and women was not caused by any of the following factors: (1) the fact that women were employed only part time; (2) a lack of experience on the part of the women lawyers; (3) lower class rank and less law review participation by the women; (4) a difference in schools attended; or (5) different types of employers. In addition, the statistics and analysis indicate, although with less certainty, that the income difference was not caused by (1) response bias among the members of the sample; (2) differences between the general type of work performed by the men and women; or (3) differences in the type of jobs sought. If one rejects forgetfulness and lying as plausible explanations for the large income differential which was observed, he is left with only one plausible hypothesis[1] to explain

From MICHIGAN LAW REVIEW, Vol. 65, No. 6 (1967), pp. 1084-1095. Reprinted by permission.

the income differential, namely discrimination on the basis of sex against women lawyers by employers and clients.

A second and more direct piece of evidence of this discrimination is the response of the 63 placement directors and deans who answered our placement questionnaire: 6 stated that any discrimination against female law graduates is "insignificant"; 43 believed that such discrimination is "significant"; and 14 stated that it is "extensive." These observers speak with authority and from long and extensive experience with the interviewing and hiring processes at a number of our busiest law school placement offices.[2]

Further evidence of discrimination is provided by the response of women to the question: "Do you believe that you have been the object of discrimination because of your sex by your present, former, or by any potential employer from whom you sought a job?" The following exhibit shows that more than half believe they probably have been the object of such discrimination and that more than a third are "certain" that they have been discriminated against.

Exhibit 1 / Beliefs of Females Concerning Discrimination

Degree	Per Cent of Females (N = 1148)
Certainly discriminated against	38.2%
Almost certainly	9.6%
Probably	17.6%
Probably not	15.8%
Certainly not	18.8%

Doubtless many disappointed female lawyers blame their lack of success upon discrimination and, for that reason, the figures on the above table should probably be discounted by a certain percentage. The question gave the respondent an opportunity to say that she was only "almost" certain or that it was only "probable" that she had been discriminated against, yet 38% of the women chose to state that they were "certain" that they had been the victims of discrimination. In view of lawyers' notorious propensity to qualify and equivocate, the absolute quality of these answers, made exclusively by lawyers who had the opportunity to select several degrees of equivocation, suggests that one should not discount the answers too greatly.[3]

Finally, discrimination against women lawyers is suggested by the female response to the question, "How many of each of the following types of employers stated a policy to you against the hiring of women as lawyers?" On 1,963 separate occasions, potential employers are reported to have actually stated to a female respondent a policy against the hiring of women lawyers. Even if we discount this number by a considerable margin, it still constitutes persuasive evidence of employer discrimination on the basis of sex.

Exhibit 2 / Employers Who Stated a Policy Against the Hiring of Women Lawyers

Type of Employer	Number of Statements of Discrimination Policies	Number of Women to Whom at Least One Statement Was Made
Law firm — 30 and over	474	218
16 to 30	322	141
5 to 15	325	149
4 or under	271	125
Federal government	88	79
State and local government	95	63
Judges	78	52
Corporations	125	66
Banks & trust companies	111	56
Unions	22	5
Non-law jobs	52	28
Totals:	1963	982

It does not necessarily follow that one who states he has a policy against the hiring of women in fact has and carries out such a policy. However, one can imagine few circumstances under which it would be beneficial for the employer to state a policy of discrimination which he did not practice. In some southern societies, the pressure to discriminate against Negroes might be so great that even one who did not oppose Negroes would feel compelled to express opposition, but surely the pressure to discriminate against women has not reached such a pitch.

The combination of this evidence — the apparent failure of other hypotheses to explain the income differential, the statements of the placement officers and deans, the opinions of the female respondents, and finally the reported statements of the employers themselves — convinces me that discrimination against women lawyers by their potential employers is at least a substantial cause, and probably the principal cause, for the income differential which we have observed between men and women.

Is the Discrimination Functional?

For present purposes, discrimination by any private employer may be considered functional to the extent that it is likely to produce a greater economic gain for him than he would have received had he not so discriminated. For example, the failure of the Green Bay Packers to select women as defensive linemen is discrimination, yet it is entirely functional and appropriate; women do not exhibit the massive size, strong backs, and powerful limbs which are the requisites of the position. Similarly, women may have psychological or intellectual limitations which make them less effective lawyers than are men. If this is true, some or all of the discrimination against women lawyers is functional and, perhaps, defensible.

Because the qualifications of a defensive lineman are relatively simple and obvious, it is easy to tell which discriminations in selections for that position are dictated by its function and which are not. However, there is no such agreement about the necessary, or even the desirable, attributes of an "effective lawyer." Indeed, such attributes are kaleidoscopic, elusive, and difficult to generalize. At one end of the legal spectrum is the lawyer who does nothing but appear before juries; at the other end is the man employed by a governmental agency or a very large firm who is an expert on some obsure and complex statute or body of law. The latter in his relish for and mastery of the statutory intricacies resembles the scholar; the former in his enjoyment of the pomp and show of the courtroom resembles the actor. The same personal characteristics which are vital to the success of one of these men would spell the doom of the other. And between these two extremes lie 300,000 American lawyers who exhibit infinitely varied mixtures of a number of roles, including actor, scholar, and counselor.

Nonetheless, it probably is possible to identify a few characteristics which are desirable for the performance of every lawyer function (for example, intelligence), and others which would be helpful to sizeable slices of the legal profession (for example, ability to inspire confidence in clients). The data produced by this study are not extensive, but they do provide a basis for comparing men and women as to certain of these functional attributes — intelligence, emotional suitability, probable length of service, and ability to inspire confidence in clients.

Both class standing and law review participation probably bear a direct relation to intelligence.[5] These are two common indicators of intellectual ability used by employers, who often specify that only persons on law review or with certain grades or class standing may apply for jobs with them. The data provide no basis for discrimination against women on either of these grounds. There was no statistically significant difference between the men and women in either class standing or law review participation.

I know of no data which give a suitable inventory of an emotional makeup of women lawyers, nor do I know of any which compare female lawyers either with other women or with male lawyers.[6] Absent a systematic psychological inventory, one should take care to avoid two inviting errors in analyzing the emotional composition of women lawyers. The first is to attribute the common characteristics of all women to that tiny percentage of women who happen to be lawyers. One random selection of 15,663 female college graduates netted only 44 who were going to become lawyers.[7] Whatever the process which culled out these 44, it is a hasty judgment which says that they exhibit all of the attributes of the remaining 15,619. On the contrary, it is entirely possible that "women" exhibit certain attributes and that "women lawyers" exhibit substantially different ones. The second error is to color all 7,000 females lawyers with the attributes of one or two of them. Since women make up no more than 3% of the bar, it is possible to engage actively in practice and yet not have extensive contact with women lawyers. Nevertheless, I have quizzed few lawyers or law teachers who did not have definite, and often outspoken, views about the emotional composition of that group, although often these generalizations are based on only a handful of experiences with one or two women lawyers. Since this study is limited to women who are lawyers and includes approximately 1,300 of them, it suffers from neither of these errors.

Two areas of our study — one dealing with trial practice and the other with motives for attending law school — yielded information which is relevant to the question of emotional suitability. First, the idea that women shrink from the combat of litigation is not supported by the data, which show that the women appeared in court with nearly the same frequency as did the men.[8] Seven per cent of the full-time employed women listed "litigation" as the type of work (singular) they performed; 7.2% of the men listed litigation. Moreover, 45.6% of all the females in full-time private practice stated that they engaged in litigation and 27.7% stated that they did criminal work. The study did not compare male and female success in litigation, but it showed at a minimum that a sizeable body of the women were actively engaged in trial practice.

It is sometimes suggested that women are less able at certain kinds of practice because, unlike men, they are not motivated by a wholesome ambition to earn money and get ahead. However, the thought that women are exclusively or even principally motivated to enter law by "bleeding heart" motives or that they are untouched by crasser motives is contradicted by the data discussed above.

We know far too little about the psychological composition of the female lawyer to state with certainty how she differs from other females or from male lawyers. Clearly some current ideas about the female lawyer's psychological composition cannot be empirically supported. Such incidental data as the study produced on motives for attending law school and frequency of court appearance should inspire a vigorous skepticism about other notions concerning a woman's emotional suitability for various kinds of practice.

It is often stated that a woman is a less desirable employee-lawyer than is a male because she will quit working to get married, to have a child, or to devote more time to her family just when she is gaining sufficient experience to be a valuable employee. The data show that many women had changed jobs several times at the time they answered the questionnaire and that a larger share of the women than men had ceased practice entirely. However, they do not support the common expectation that there is a vast difference between male and female performance on this point. Rather, the striking thing about the data is that both men and women changed jobs quite frequently.

At the end of three years, only 30% of the males in the class of 1962 and 29% of the females in that class were still at their first jobs. At the end of seven years, the corresponding percentages fall to 14.5% and 11.1% respectively. Except for the class of 1959, the percentage of women in each class who were still at their first jobs at the time they answered the questionnaire did not differ from the corresponding percentage of the males by a statistically significant margin. However, if the men from all classes are compared with all of the women, the difference is statistically significant. (Exhibit 3)

Exhibit 3 / Job Movement
(Still at First Job in 1965 — No Job Changes)

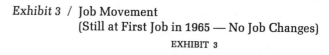

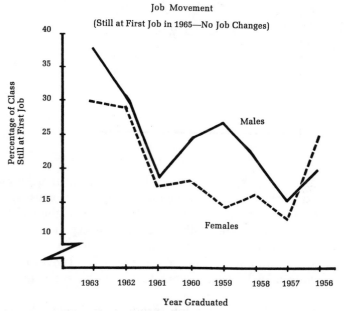

As is indicated in Exhibit 4, a significantly larger percentage of women than men had left their *second* jobs, in four of eight classes. The fact that the male turnover with respect to the second job is lower by a significant margin in the three oldest classes might suggest that this job turnover differential grows wider with the passage of time, as more women leave practice because of growing family commitments. Yet the first job data show no such trend, and the number of women permanently re-entering practice after a spell of child-rearing and house-keeping may actually cause a reduction in turnover among fe-male lawyers who have been out of law school for more than ten years. The data give us no reliable answers to these questions.

Exhibit 4 / Job Movement
   (Still at Second Job in 1965 — 1 Job Change)

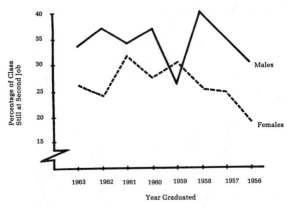

EXHIBIT 4

Job Movement

(Still at Second Job in 1965—1 Job Change)

In summary, our gross data show a slightly greater female job turnover in the first job after law school;[9] they also suggest that job turnover of women is higher than that for men thereafter. Moreover, if a large share of the female non-respondents are housewives,[10] and if no corresponding percentage of the male non-respondents are not working, the actual job turnover of all female lawyers may be even higher than that reflected in our data.

But, even if the total female job turnover is higher than our data suggest, that fact alone does not prove that a woman is a less desirable employee than is a man, for high turnover can re-sult from many causes. It can be caused by employee fickleness, but it can also be caused by poor pay or other inadequacies of the job. If women are as effective lawyers as are men but are nevertheless paid less money than are comparably employed men, one might expect women to seek new jobs more frequently.

On the other hand, some of the standard female motivations for job change — the urge to motherhood, the need to devote time to one's family or to move with one's husband to a new location — are all peculiar to women and may be less subject to control by employer offers of more money and greater status than are the typical male motivations for job change. Without information indicating which changes are caused by employer discrimination and which are caused by the demands of a husband or a family, high job turnover neither proves nor disproves that discrimination against women is functional. The naked statistic of frequent job change is equally consistent with either hypothesis.

The data do explode the myth that few married women and no mothers practice law. Few women ceased work because of marriage alone, and more than 25% of the full-time employed women were mothers of small children. One can only guess how many more might work full time if more employers tailored positions so that the hours and responsibilities were compatible with a mother's other responsibilities.

Every law firm, except one with a shrinking practice, has the problem of transferring a client's sometimes fragile allegiance from senior men to competent younger men without losing the client's patronage. If the young lawyer is a Jew, a Negro, or a woman, this problem may be aggravated by the clients' own prejudices.[11] One of the most frequently stated fears about women lawyers is that clients will not place their confidence in them. Our data did indicate that women see fewer clients than do men by a statistically significant margin. This difference was particularly great among those who were employed by large firms and who had been out of law school for four or more years.

Despite this statistically significant difference in the frequency of client contact, the data do not really support the conclusion that clients will not place their confidence in women lawyers. First, it is not possible to tell from our data whether the lower frequency of female client contact was due to clients' resistance or to mistaken beliefs of women lawyers and their employers about client resistance. Second, the data show a very substantial amount of client contact on the part of women employed by corporations and by firms of 15 or under. If the hypothesis about client resistance were correct, one would expect women to be concentrated in jobs which required little or no client contact. Yet in the smaller firms and corporations, women saw approximately seven clients for every ten seen by men.

Of course these data do not prove that all clients will place their confidence in a woman lawyer as readily as in a male lawyer. The figures tell nothing about the kind of clients which the women saw. Perhaps they were spread across the spectrum of legal practice, but they may have been concentrated in the probate and domestic relations field.[12] Furthermore, the figures do not indicate whether the clients were satisfied with the service, nor do they indicate whether the employers had to undertake a more extensive and careful introduction than would have been required with a male. They do show, however, that any vision of the woman as exclusively a back-room and library worker is badly distorted.

The survey did not solicit conclusive or comprehensive data on the question whether discrimination against women lawyers is functional. It tells us nothing about the relative ability of men and women to acquire clients or about the importance of that function to employers. Moreover, the information on court appearances and frequency of client contact fall far short of the systematic psychological inventory which we need in order even to begin evaluating the contention that discrimination against women lawyers is functional. Nonetheless, the information which the survey did gather makes some of the stoutest citadels in the rational discrimination fortress look vulnerable. "Women can't stand the rigors of trial practice" — but the full-time employed women appeared in court nearly as often as did the men. "Clients won't put up with a woman" — but, except in one kind of practice, the women saw seven clients for every ten that men saw. "Women quit work to marry and have children" — but 27% of the full-time employed women were married *and* had children. "Women lawyers are just bleeding hearts who do not understand the usual business motives" — but equally as many men admitted the importance of the "bleeding heart" motive and a large share of the women rated monetary motives very important in their choice of law as a career. These data have convinced me that much of the enormous income differential between the males and females is attributable to nonfunctional discrimination.

Exhibit 5 / Average Number of Clients Seen per Week

EXHIBIT 5

Average Number of Clients Seen per Week

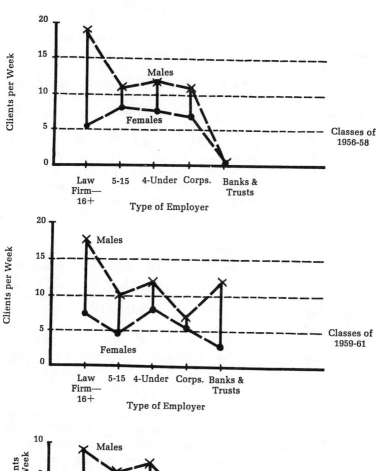

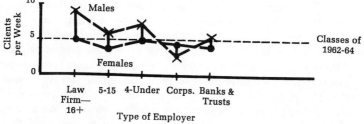

NOTES

1. If a disproportionate share of the females are Jewish, some of the income differential may be explained by discrimination against them because they are Jewish. Since the questionnaire did not collect any information on race, religion or ethnic background, we could not calculate the effect, if any, of such discrimination, and, absent data showing a disproportionate percentage of Jews among the females and lacking evidence about the extent and effect of anti-Semitic discrimination against lawyers, I have chosen to classify this hypothesis as "not plausible."

2. Among those indicating a belief that discrimination against women in hiring is significant or extensive are representatives of the placement offices at six out of the nine schools which we classified as prestige institutions.

3. The women who were most certain they had been discriminated against also earned the least money. Perhaps this fact proves the accuracy of their opinion. On the other hand, it may only indicate that their belief is a rationalization for low income. The average present income of full-time employed women in relation to their responses to the discrimination question is as follows:

Discrimination	1964 Income		
	Classes of 1956-58	Classes of 1959-61	Classes of 1962-65
"certain"	$8,700	$7,000	$6,400
balance of responses	$9,100	$8,100	$6,600

4. The large ratio of reported statements of a discrimination policy to the total number of interviews is consistent with our data in some cases but inconsistent with other data which we have collected. The percentage of female lawyers finding an initial job with a law firm of 30 or more is not statistically different from the percentage of males finding jobs with that employer. If these firms in fact discriminate as extensively as the reported policies would indicate, it is difficult to understand how such a large percentage of females could find employment with them. The explanation may lie in the fact that some other firms of 30 or more in fact hire more than their proportionate share of females. Since females make up less than 3% of the lawyer population, anyone who has 30 to 50 employees and who hires two women will have employed a higher percentage of the female lawyer population than of the male lawyer population, and thus will have offset somewhat the aggregate discrimination. Another explanation may be found by an examination of the positions which women hold with

those firms. Some women may have responded that law firms who in fact hire women for second-class positions nevertheless have a "policy against hiring women."

5. Since law review participation is usually determined in part by class standing, the former may be only an additional indication of the latter's effect.

6. Alice S. Rossi, who is with the National Opinion Research Center at the University of Chicago, is conducting a study of a large sample of female college graduates. This study should ultimately produce information about the characteristics of women who undertake practice in the traditional male professions, but it probably will not give specific information about female lawyers.

7. This sample is random in the sense that it was chosen from colleges which were randomly selected.

8. The difference between the average number of court appearances made by the males and the females is statistically significant.

Average Number of Court Appearances Per Year		
Year Graduated	Females	Males
1964	2.4	4.1
1963	4.0	7.7
1962	5.8	7.9
1961	9.2	10.0
1960	7.4	9.2
1959	9.6	10.2
1958	7.3	9.1
1957	7.8	10.5
1956	8.2	10.3

9. Because the sample was not large enough, we could not make a meaningful comparison of female turnover by type of job. Such data might reveal quite different patterns among jobs and between male and female employees depending upon the type of job.

10. We have no reason to believe either that they are or are not.

11. Despite the fact that employer discrimination based on clients' prejudices is functional, it has been prohibited by the Civil Rights Act of 1964.

12. Some members of the bar assume that probate and domestic relations clients find female counsel more acceptable than other clients do. One can question why these clients should react differently to female lawyers than do others.

forty-seven

Prejudice Against Female Artists

BERNARD ROSENBERG and NORRIS FLIEGEL

When the woman artist complains that it is difficult for her to gain a foothold in the art world, she's not simply being paranoid. For all her achievements, she must be prepared to deal with bias, prejudice, or outright hostility — and it emanates from many sources. At least one well-known and successful modern female painter felt compelled for some time to exhibit under an assumed male name. She thought, probably with justification, that as a woman she would not receive anything like the same treatment, the same objective reception automatically accorded to men. Shades of Currer Bell, George Sand, and George Eliot! Some women deny being sensitive to all of this, but they recognize that it exists; many are extremely thin-skinned about it:

> I've never had any self-consciousness about being a woman artist, but many men have. Certain dealers, for example, A. Z., have said that they would never take a woman artist, and women artists are considered by museum directors as a separate deal. But I know that some women painters can be easily insulted, especially if anyone should say, "As a woman artist, what do you think?" They'll even walk out of a party or some such thing.

That certain gallery owners still openly refuse to show or represent the female painter is a well-known "trade secret." This action is rationalized in a variety of ways, all easily refuted. Some of our respondents interpret it at the level of artistic evaluation: "I think many gallery owners wouldn't take women at all. I think they've decided that it's impossible for a woman to be a great artist." Some put it on a purely economic basis: "If I were a gallery owner or dealer, I wouldn't feel necessarily that a woman artist would be harder to handle. But she would be harder to sell; she would be harder to promote." This argument might carry some weight if it were not well understood that the "tastes" of most collectors are molded by others, including art dealers and gallery owners. Many collectors reveal anti-female biases in their buying patterns, which include the price they are willing to pay for a woman's work, but this too is a posture they have learned to assume.

One artist, whose observations may strike closer to home, guesses that "some dealers just don't like women." Since they do not find it politic to express that feeling openly, many dealers rationalize their prejudice by seeing women as "difficult to deal with." One put it this way: "The women I have known have been difficult in dealer relationships. Whether they are more difficult than men, I don't know. I've known some pretty difficult men in gallery relationships too. But I know there are a lot of dealers who do not like women painters and give that as a reason. How valid it is, I don't know." Museum directors are apparently guilty of the same reactions as gallery owners, although it is not as easy, from our data, to establish this feeling as fact.

Under these conditions we hear one famous woman artist say diffidently: "Women artists have a difficult time getting accepted. They don't get the same prices or get shown or get bought. But that's just in the world of making a living and that's not why anyone becomes a painter." Her point is valid, yet one could hardly expect the same kind of indifference from those women who are still struggling for recognition. Still, most of them do manage to maintain a professional perspective:

> I think that if you get hung up on how we're treated in the market-place, you lose sight of our whole purpose and involvement. I mean at times everybody has a gripe about everything. Lots of things are unfair, depending on what is important to people at the time. I'm not unrealistic, but you're not an artist to make money and be treated nice, although it's helpful in the long run.

But since artists themselves are the most influential "taste-makers," it is the reaction of her peers which, at least initially, has the greatest impact on the female painter. Since men still effectively dominate the art world, their reactions become most important. And here a woman has special problems. The feelings of older artists toward her are predominantly negative; younger men may profess greater tolerance and acceptance, but there are still no "male artists in shining armor" to grant her or her ventures unqualified support or passionate endorsement.

Under these circumstances it is not surprising that she finds it difficult to survive as an artist. If she wishes to exist in the art world as it is presently constituted, she must make one of two choices: she can passively accept the treatment accorded her, or she can aggressively resist and struggle with and against it. But to dramatize the perverseness of her situation, one male painter complains:

> Let's just say that I can't think of any woman artist that I would be interested in, either as a person or as a woman. I think they're all too cranky and unreasonable. Or if they're reasonable, they are so damn reasonable that I can't stand them. Why are they that way? They're that way because they are that way. They just can't be different, I guess.

Thus she is damned if she does and damned if she doesn't, and it is the rare male who can see the irrationality of it all. Oldsters are quick to condemn her for always imitating men, but they do not see how little latitude they give her to develop naturally. They may suggest that "real" women have their own art styles, and that if they only stuck to them everything would be fine, but they also make it clear that they view "feminine" styles as inferior to their own.

Criticisms of the female for being excessively "reasonable and compliant" remain rare; accusations of masculinity and aggressiveness are the norm. Men frequently characterize their female counterparts, with varying degrees of resentment and understanding, as hostile, competitive, and overly assertive:

> They have to pay a price in femininity. They become more agressive. Successful women artists tend to be castrators. I would say so, definitely.
>
> Some of them are very masculine, practically a masculine protest, especially some of the people who are abstract expressionists.
>
> I think most women seem to think in terms of being a man. And therefore they think that in order to be a painter, they have to do

it bigger and better and more. That doesn't necessarily make better art.

The fact that most artists are males affects the women. One of the dangers they run then is wearing their balls around their necks in order to prove they aren't women. You know, overpainting and being too masculine in their painting just to prove they're not women. This affects their painting at times because they seem to be leaning over backward to be unfeminine.

You see, most women try to imitate the characteristics of a man, and I think that's very bad. They're trying to be something that they're not. There's a difference of temperament involved. It's a question of competition, which is a pity, because a number of them are very talented painters, women painters, and you can't even tell. It seems as if they refuse to be themselves.

It's hard to think that women artists are women and that they really aren't men. If you see them, they're terribly aggressive and not female; they try to act tough and it's hard for them to be tender. I wouldn't be certain that this is completely fair, but there's an awful lot of evidence to go on.

And on they go. They may qualify and hedge, and sometimes they are quite as critical of themselves, but their attempts to soften harsh judgments are rather halfhearted:

There can be a great deal of self-centeredness. There can be a certain fantasy about their importance, or they can put on masks and mannerisms of very great efficiency and direct action. I think that's enough for you to get the idea.

I would say that most of them are very aggressive. I would say so about most of them, but certainly not all of them. Most of them are really pushers though, you just can't get away from it. They're really pushers. They have themselves a wheelbarrow and they're pushing it in front of them all the time. Pushing through, breaking through, going right on through. I don't know whether it is because this is the way they are or what the world has done to them. Some of them have never been out in the world and I don't really know if they've ever been invited. They take their work with them everywhere, and at any time they will say, "Here it is and let's have a show." But I suppose many men do the same thing.

It is beyond our competence and our data to judge the accuracy or objectivity of these pronouncements. Our own observations would lead us to be much more generous in characterizing the female artist as a person, but only an occasional comment from male respondents is less severe than those quoted above. Truly favorable remarks could be numbered on one hand. An eminent artist, considered something of a maverick in the art world, tried to be moderate as he reflected on women artists. However, since he began by admitting his pre-conception that *all* women are highly competitive, and there-fore aggressive, his contribution did little to alter an essentially negative image; his sympathy with women's difficulties was less than overwhelming, although he did try to be disinterested:

> I think it is probably true to a great degree because, you know, they fight terrific pressures from other women who say, "Oh really, you want to be a big mother?" So it's like the same when they do work. They work with great vengeance, like "I am a female." But they all seem like females. They're like women. I mean, they're not like a man to me, even if I'm not attracted to them physically. So what? They've had affairs and they want to get married. They are just like any other women.

At the same time, however, he stands out among our male artists because he strives to maintain some measure of reason. He experiences women artists as human beings, normally per-plexed by having more than their share of difficulties.

One thoughtful male artist, while concurring in the judgment that female artists are excessively assertive, showed equal in-terest (no one else did) in colleagues who are so easily put on the defensive by them. He conceded that the world of art has always been a "male stronghold," but his subsequent attempts to ex-plain male reluctance to admit the female as only a matter of habit and custom rang a little hollow. Although we may not be inclined to accept his analysis of a very complex situation, he at least makes no plea for innate male superiority. He even ac-cepts the idea that women will eventually win through to serious artistic expression, against all odds and in the face of all interested parties:

> As for women, they are aggressive. But it's hard for the male world to accept the infringement of the female world. It has gone on for ages and suddenly there is this phenomenon of the woman sticking her head in. In spite of it, there is no reason why there shouldn't be a female Rembrandt or Leonardo.

The unequivocal assertion that women not only have talent but their potential for realizing it is as great as a man's, is in this context both bold and rare. Only one other interviewee was willing to take so strong a stand. One of our soberest and most guarded male respondents bewilderedly and fatalistically conceded that: "Some women are very good. What can you do? They're fantastically good artists." This concession to the female was unique. The man who made it was also willing to interpret feminine behavior at a much less malevolent level; here again he stood alone. His perceptions were exactly those of his confrères, but he drew opposite inference from them:

> Well, I think there have always been women painters, but I think today there are probably many more serious ones, because they seem to have incomes. If they didn't have an income, I don't think they could be too serious. That's because I think it's much harder for a woman to have people pay attention to her. If she makes it, she's either very rich or she's dynamic. The ones I meet are unusual, as women go. They are more alive or something; they're more intense, more dynamic. Even more than the men are. Women artists either have money or they can get their hands on it. A man can be a slob or something; he doesn't have to be anything special. The women seem to be. The ones that are just coming around are more alert, are more intense, and are even more determined.

NOTE

The data for this study derive from unstructured, informal or focused interviews of 29 artists, all of whom were considered to be "successful" painters and sculptors. Seven of the respondents were women. The study was conducted in 1961-62 in New York City.

VIII

Female Professionalism and Social Change

Women Lawyers and Their Profession: Inconsistency of Social Controls and Their Consequences for Professional Performance

CYNTHIA F. EPSTEIN

Women who have professional careers are subjected to a different and often inconsistent social control system than are men. They often get different messages regarding what is expected of them and what will happen to them if they do or do not meet these expectations. The controls which motivate and punish the male professional and insure normative conformity[1] are differentially applied to the female.

These ambiguous, inconsistent and often contradictory controls deprive women of a meaningful pattern of motivation, makes difficult their conformity to professional norms and ensures that most women will not perform at the peak of their potential or rise to the peak of their profession.

The consequences of this reward-punishment system operate contrary to the professed values of the educational system and the society, and the stated goals of the professions, although they tend to shield the existing structure of the professions from change. For the professional woman, the reward system generates ambivalence and failure.

Interviews with more than 50 women attorneys practicing in New York City and its suburbs[2] showed clearly that these women were exposed to different expectations than male colleagues regarding standards of behavior and professional com-

Paper presented at the 64th annual meeting of the American Sociological Association, San Francisco, California, September, 1969. Printed by permission.

petence. In addition, expectations regarding appropriate female sex-role behavior often were in conflict with norms governing occupational-role behavior. Other lawyers did not judge women lawyers' conformity to professional norms without at the same time evaluating their fulfillment of female-associated roles. Even the profession's elite — its normkeepers — were likely to believe that different professional criteria apply to men and women.

Thus, the women lawyers studied experienced simultaneously the expectations linked to the status of the lawyer, those linked to the hybrid status of woman lawyer, and those associated with their status as women.[3] Since these expectations were apt to be contradictory, considerable ambivalence occurred. These women lawyers not only had trouble meeting certain professional norms because of the inconsistency with which they were expected to adhere to them,[4] but also because the punishments and rewards attached to these expectations were inconsistently applied.

Similar professional performances were differentially rewarded and, to compound the ambiguity, substantial variations in performance often received the same reward. As a result, many women experienced confusion or hostility, and some deviated from professional norms or withdrew entirely from the discomfort which the ambiguity created. It was not that these women could not perform their professional tasks, but that for lawyers of their age, experience and ability as demonstrated by law school performance and record, they chose low-level jobs and part-time work. They demonstrably lacked the career aspirations common to the legal profession. At the same time, however, they breached professional etiquette by inappropriately over-producing or overreacting in an effort to "prove" themselves.[5]

By some standards, the women lawyers in this sample might be considered "successes"; the paradox lies in the fact that their measure of ability and success did not reinforce their commitment to the profession or fire their ambitions; they did not expect, or hope to reach the top or even the lesser professional peaks.

Social scientists from Plato to Parsons have assumed that people are socialized through rewards — honor, money and love — and through punishments — fear, degradation, and discomfort. This applies as well to adult socialization processes — for example, socialization in occupational roles. The allocation of rewards and punishments experienced by the novice professional continues beyond the learning stage and ideally becomes a kind of maintenance system by which the person is motivated to adhere to the occupational norms he has learned.

The control system works because it is more clear and logical than not and because it is usually universalistically applied and communicated to all who play a part in it.

Although suspicions may be voiced that loopholes exist, that the undeserving do succeed, most people assume that this is not typical. These are considered breakdowns in the system. "Mainstream" society believes it *is* possible to make correct judgments about performance, and it further assumes that correct judgments will be made and should be made to keep the record clear and the system on its tracks.

Because the professions' centers of control have remained in the hands of homogeneous elites there has been little challenge of the legitimacy of their control systems. In one such high-level profession, the law, most practitioners do believe that excellence is rewarded and those lawyers who are widely believed to be excellent receive high rewards. Attorneys often fight for large stakes in terms of lives and money, and, to a considerable extent, competence or skill will determine *who* wins; it thus would seem to be to the law firm's advantage to choose the most capable people and to promote them rapidly to positions of responsibility.

We are interested here in how the legal profession's system of rewards and punishments work with reference to a sub-group within the profession — women lawyers — to see how the rewards are allocated and what are their consequences.

All norms permit a range of acceptable performance of the tasks linked to the status. Thus the lawyer is permitted latitude in his performance as a professional. He may work short or long hours; he may read widely in legal literature or only barely keep up with pertinent statutes. But short of violating ethics to a point where he is disbarred or rejected by colleagues, he is still a lawyer and considered so by his role network. Yet some lawyers are considered to be *more professional* than others.

The work of Smigel, O'Gorman and Carlin[6] suggests that in law there is a relationship between quality of reward and quality of adherence to professional norms. It is indisputable that high prestige and income are considered the due of a lawyer who fulfills professional norms by working at one of the "most professional" specialties; for example, corporate work, the judiciary, or litigation at the appeal level. Wall Street attorneys are "lawyer's lawyers" and are paid better on the average than lone practitioners who perform real estate closings and handle divorce proceedings. Matrimonial specialists are considered to be less professional because they deal with matters that are considered to be paralegal by members of the profession. Women lawyers have something in common with lawyers at the lower end of the prestige scale. They are not asked or expected to conform to the highest standards in the range of professional norms, yet they are different in the sense that they are not told that they have "failed" when performing the low-level tasks of law. "Justice" seems violated in the payoff system for women lawyers both from their profession and from the society.

The achievement of success in a profession probably is a guarantee of recognition as a "success" by the wider society. Professions are the elites of the occupational world and their practitioners are not only more highly regarded by society[7] but they attain higher incomes on the average than those in other occupations.[8] It is probably safe to say that a man who stands at the top of his profession will receive acclaim beyond the profession, even from those who do not have competence to evaluate his performance. A man *expects* to be rated and rewarded by the bestowal of money and acclaim if he has talent and works hard. The relationship between work and rewards is construed as "justice"; lack of reward for excellence is seen as "injustice."[9]

It is interesting to note that the "halo effect" of professional success on the man's reputation outside his profession may not occur for women. That is, prestige in the professional sphere may not bring the woman prestige in her family or among her friends, and may even bring her condemnation. Furthermore, this lack may not generate a culturally normative protest against "injustice." The woman herself may view the situation as unjust, but she may also feel that it is inappropriate to protest it. Yet the definition of what constitutes "justice" for women professionals varies substantially from the definition applied to men.[10]

The range of relationships between the performance of the women lawyers studied and the rewards granted them is set out schematically in the following typology:

A TYPOLOGY OF REWARDS AND SANCTIONS* AS RELATED TO FULFILLMENT OF PROFESSIONAL NORMS

	Rewards	Sanctions
Fulfillment of Norms	(1) $+ +$	(2) $+ -$
Failure to Fulfill Norms	(3) $- +$	(4) $- -$

The tables may be read as follows:

Type 1 — the individual has fulfilled the norms and is rewarded.

Type 2 — the individual has fulfilled the norms and is sanctioned.

Type 3 — the individual has *not* fulfilled the norms and is rewarded.

Type 4 — the individual has not fulfilled the norms and is sanctioned.

* "Sanctions" is used in this paper only in its negative sense, implying penalties, punishment or other forms of disapproval.

Types (1) and (4) are the expected examples of "justice": rewards for successful performance, sanctions for failure. They are mechanisms of the control system which insure commitment and conformity to professional norms. Types (2) and (3) are examples of "injustice,"[11] and creates conditions which disrupt commitment to the profession's norms.

We are not concerned here with the random injustices that men as well as women must face in professional life, but with situations in which type 2 or type 3 consequences are not publicly defined as unjust. The two are examples of the patterned ambivalence resulting from the association of sex-status with professional status.

Type 1: the individual has fulfilled
the norms and is rewarded

The "just" reward pattern of Type 1 undoubtedly matches the reward system applied to most male lawyers. In my study, the question arose: are women lawyers subject to the same pattern and to what extent? The women I interviewed seemed highly qualified, using as an indicator, performance at law school — more than a third were editors of their law reviews and 70% had done very well![12] Of course it is impossible to know how far these women might have gone if they were not women, but measuring them according to standards of income and attainment of partnership in a firm seemed good general indicators. We would have liked to measure them on a prestige scale but we had insufficient information about their professional reputations to do this.

Income is one indicator of success that can be measured with accuracy. The women lawyers in the sample reported fairly high earnings — a median of $13,500 per year — and 40 per cent of the respondents reported earning $16,000 or more per year. The incomes reported by respondents who worked full time — two thirds of the full sample — averaged nearly $20,000 per year.

Precise information is unavailable on the incomes of male New York attorneys, but it is clear that the incomes reported by these women lawyers, though lower than their male colleagues' incomes, are reasonably close to what the males' earnings would be if they were in the same types of practices — the "female specializations" of matrimonial and real estate law and probate work. But although justice prevailed for some within the profession, cultural complications outside undermine the payoff of income.

These women rarely seemed to view their incomes as a desired symbol of success or as an unmitigated reward. There was even evidence that some respondents would view a sharp gain in income as an intolerable burden on their relationships with their husbands. Few men view a rise in their incomes as a burden.

These professional women's sense of reward was related primarily to their husbands' incomes. They reported feeling a sense of accomplishment from their earnings, but it was true that those reporting the highest incomes generally were married to wealthy men and expressed the feeling that their personal earnings had ceased to matter. Only a handful of these women reported that they now worked for money, although many had been quite poor when they entered practice. Significantly, as many high-income respondents dropped out of practice as stayed in.

Partnership is another indicator of reward, but it is more difficult to appraise because the *prestige* conferred by "partnership" is measured by the size of the firm, the specialty to which the partnership is attached, and how many years it has taken the lawyer to become a partner. "Justice" prevailed for a number of women in the sample. Nine were partners but with varying qualities of prestige. (Of the nine women in the sample who were partners, one was a partner-semi-retired in a large firm, and four were partners in medium-sized firms — all of good reputation.) Four others were partners of another type — they were in smaller firms, three of them in partnerships with husbands. By the standard of the profession these women must be considered successes even if they had not attained the pinnacle of the profession. Griffen[13] has cited some statistics on a national scale, a bit old now, unfortunately, which indicate that on average when women attain partnerships it does not tend to be partnership of the *highest* quality.

Besides the few women in the sample who had attained high prestige through partnerships in "good" firms, some others achieved jobs of high rank — one as a judge, several as private practitioners with large practices, one as an important city commissioner. But although these women were successful, they were not *as* successful as the men who constituted their reference group or as measured by their own standards of achievement. The judge, for example, felt that she could have gotten a *better* judgeship (i.e. to a higher court) had she been a man.

*Type 4: the individual has not fulfilled
the norms and is sanctioned*

This too is another instance of logic in the system. The case of the professional who fails and is sanctioned by loss of reputation or job is as clear-cut for the woman professional as it is for the male.

There is justice here too. Women are in fact punished for violating professional norms. The women who worked part-time and had more discontinuous career lines made less money on average than male colleagues and were not awarded high-ranking jobs. Since they did not aim high and exhibited little assertiveness, they were not given career-line jobs or assigned clients who could assure them positions of power. In short, there are certain "absolute" professional standards which, if not met, can be expected to result in relatively negative consequences for career aspirants. These, by and large, are the uninteresting cases.

The next two types are those which create the most ambiguity:

*Type 2: the individual has fulfilled
the norms and is sanctioned*

Two major patterns fall in this classification: the woman who is *not rewarded* for good professional performance, and the career woman who becomes a professional success but is punished for it. The first is a case of unequal and "unjust" reward. The second is the result of role-conflict which stems from expectations that fulfillment of role obligations attached to one status — the professional one — will entail violation of role obligations attached to another or other statuses — the female sex and family statuses.[14]

Many women lawyers felt that they were notoriously under-rewarded for good professional performance. Many had the experience of seeing the men in their firms rising to partnership while they were frozen at the associate rank despite demonstrably equivalent competence. Even women who could be considered successful by male career standards often feel relatively deprived; that is, they believe they should be regarded as *great!*

One lawyer in the study who was a partner in a "distinguished old firm," and whose income was substantial, felt that her progression to the top had taken too long. Although she had risen to partnership in this firm from a job as legal stenographer, the status-sequence had spanned a 20-year period. Other lawyers in the firm, however, who had joined the legal staff when she did, had become partners far sooner.[15] Her account indicated that she may accurately be described as a Type 2 case:

> I struggled on and saw everyone getting ahead of me becoming partner; I couldn't because I was a woman. No one ever thought of it. And I didn't have the nerve to approach the subject. I just assumed that virtue would be rewarded even if you kept your mouth shut, which it isn't. Until one day I couldn't stand it any longer . . . and I decided to try.

Part of the problem stems from women's lack of power in the bargaining process. Power is itself a reward, but some power must somehow be attained to bargain successfully for more. No powerful client will permit an important case to be handled by an associate, but women do not often have powerful clients who will press the firm to make them partners. They are also not well situated in the informal social network in which business contacts are made, and they thus bring fewer clients into the firm than a male lawyer might. The lawyer who had waited so long for partnership pointed out that if she had brought a substantial number of clients to the firm, she could not have been refused partnership, because she could have threatened to leave and take them with her.

One of the respondents was asked if she would have left her firm if she had not been made a partner. Her response shows the extent to which improper rewards affect motivation:

I: What would you have done if you had been refused partnership?

R: I would have left. I felt that my dignity was being impaired.

I: Do you think you would have gone to another firm?

R: No. I wouldn't have. I would have left because I have my family.

I: You would have given up law entirely?

R: I think I would have.

The case of the woman who succeeds in her profession but is punished for the supposed violation of her female role obligations — a violation which is assumed to be true by virtue of her success — is equally destructive. Here the woman is the object of sanctions, both from alters in the professional sphere who believe that success detracts from a woman's femininity and from alters in her family who feel that her success makes their relationships with her uncomfortable.

Although men acquire added ranking in *all* spheres when they are rated a success in their work, the woman seems to be subject to a zero-sum evaluation in which the greater her occupational accomplishment, the more likely she is to be rated lower in her performance of female roles. This evaluation usually is not the result of direct observation of whether she can take care of both her clients and family, but is due to cultural *assumptions* that she is neglecting her family. A few lawyers in the study felt sufficiently aware of the potential loss of ranking in their family roles to over-compensate for it. The extreme of this behavior is typified by one lawyer who grossed $100,000 a year, who insisted on getting up at 6:00 in the morning to clean house before the children's nurse arrived. Most, however, had learned to delegate such chores.

The successful woman lawyer continually meets expressions

of ambivalence in the evaluation of her role performance. Respondents reported being told that they were taking work away from less successful male lawyers. One was told she "thought like a man" by her colleagues, who offered it as a compliment but implied that she was less of a woman for it. Two successful women who did trial work claimed that opposing attorneys complained they often won by female "wiles"; but other respondents were told by male lawyers that women attorneys who do not use wiles are "masculine."

To some extent women have the same experiences as men who are being "cooled out"[16] of the running for important jobs. The messages, for example, are disguised as protective *"concerns."* One respondent reported that an employer denied her promotion because "it would be too demanding of her energy"; another, because "her husband would be angry"; another, because she would be hurt by hostility in a truly male domain. Some women saw through such explanations and experienced them as sanctions, but many accepted them at face value. This was especially so when it was a husband/partner who was doing the "cooling out."

In wife-husband partnerships especially, the wife may be prevented by the husband-partner from attaining too much success, or, too much *visible* success. This may be the unintended consequence of the division of labor in which the wife takes over the "invisible" tasks of the practice — office and research work — or the husband assumes responsibility for a case at the point at which it is to be completed, making the "victory" his.

Type 3: the individual has not fulfilled the norms and is rewarded

The case of the woman who does not comply with professional norms but who is rewarded anyway is sociologically interesting because it runs counter to common sense, and arouses the cultural distaste for those who "get something for nothing." Type 3 incorporates two sets of phenomena. In the first, the woman is given too much acclaim for only routine performance. In the second, the woman violates professional norms by her *lack* of commitment, expressed by working only occasionally or dropping out altogether at the peak of her career, yet continues to be the recipient of prestige awards from family and community, although probably not from professional colleagues. She gets honor for *having been* a lawyer, although her male counterpart would be sanctioned as a "has-been" and a failure.

The "rewards" the woman may attain in these cases must be considered *secondary gains* — and as such, are *substitute* rewards that persons with "inappropriate" statuses may enjoy instead of the rewards usually given for conformity to professional role expectations. Both cases are based on normative expectations of the woman's *inability* to perform the occupational role *continuously* and with full commitment.[17]

When the expectation of failure is sufficiently institutionalized, everyone is pleasantly surprised if the woman manages all the same to meet professional norms. Although few women admit it, comments of male lawyers indicate that women often receive more praise and notice at a lower rank in the professional hierarchy than a man would, and for a lower level of performance as well.[18] This "gain" has a clear drawback. The woman gets more for doing less, but is more satisfied with less[19] and has less incentive to aim higher.

Women, especially married women, settle for lower incomes, because having any *at all* gives them a feeling of accomplishment and making *too much* might cause trouble. Even single women in the sample who were concerned about providing for themselves did not have high economic aspirations.

For women lawyers especially, membership in a high-ranking male occupation is itself an indicator of great success in the world outside the profession. The women in the study who had a network of friends who were not lawyers felt little impulse to rise within the profession; they had attained sufficient rank by just entering law. The woman's network, whether or not her friends were working women, was always important in evaluating her career.

One-third of the lawyers worked at law part-time and unlike men did so with full approval and esteem. None felt they should do more work than they did. Of course, part-time activity is considered appropriate for women, and they actively seek it. Even the full-time lawyers who were single or married without children said they could leave full-time employment without any qualms if family demands were greater.

Women in the sample stated that they could maintain their lawyer-status even if they did not practice. One who had not practiced in twenty years was still referred to as a "lawyer" by her friends. Women who had given up practice were pleased to be considered lawyers, and still felt they were.

And women don't *have to* give up the status of lawyer. Once having *achieved* their occupational status they can keep it without fulfilling the obligations attached to it. Since it is unusual for a woman to attain the status of lawyer, it is a distinguishing characteristic which becomes affixed to those who achieve it. Countless names of so-called women "lawyers" who no longer were in practice were given to me by men and women both in and out of the legal profession when it was known I was doing a study of women lawyers.

The professionally trained woman who does not practice at all, or whose practice is minimal — a person who is a *failure* in terms of professional norms — will still be given deference and prestige in her community. She is sought for community leadership posts, while the male lawyer who retires to a lower-status job before retirement is probably ignored.

To sum up: The ambivalence of expectations and rewards faced by women professionals arises from the following conflict: they face (1) Normative prescriptions for attainment of occupational success which demand that the professional demonstrate commitment, talent and hard work. (2) But normative prescriptions weigh against women's occupational success because the female role requires a lack of assertiveness and a non-competitive work role vis-à-vis men and is assumed to require a fundamental commitment to home and family. (3) There are also normative prescriptions that women cannot conform to professional norms, with the consequence that different standards are applied to their performance. (4) Women professionals are subject to a contradictory reward structure which may confer rewards not commensurate with the levels of their performance or contributions to the profession. Furthermore, success in a profession may brand women as failures in the larger society, or, concomitantly, failure in a profession may result in rewards from the larger society. My conclusion is that although the control systems with respect to women seems to be an institutionalized evasion of professional norms in that they often run counter to the official professional norm of achievement, it is not a failure, but a relatively successful control process. By undercutting the motivation of women lawyers to engage their talents at the highest levels, it maintains the cohesion of the collegial group; makes for ease of social intercourse in the *male* legal community; and reduces competition by closing higher level opportunities to women.

It is not the aim of the system, but it is its consequence. Whether or not recent changes in law — those having to do with widening its client-structure and extending practice into the areas of social welfare and civil rights will affect the aspects of its control system relating to women — as it has for blacks — is unknown. The percentage of women in law has remained constant at about three percent. A decade ago, the 20 top Wall Street firms had 435 partners, one of them a woman. Today these same firms, which have grown substantially, include three women partners, hardly a revolutionary change. The "positive" consequence for the profession of women's limited participation is mirrored in the greater society the way it is now structured. Should women generally have intensive commitment to career and profession, the potential for strains in the family are certainly increased, and problems created in time, effort and emotional priorities. These are now fairly well fixed by a ranking system which generally places the male and his work as pivotal and the woman and children's activities contingent. This means that in a society where women do not really have an obligation not to work outside the home (we would lose one third of our labor force, if this were true), they are, nevertheless, directed not to try very hard in the outside world. So it is in the professions, and in the larger society as well.

NOTES

Note: The research reported in this paper was supported by a pre-doctoral fellowship of National Institutes of Health and by a grant from the Manpower Administration, U. S. Department of Labor. The author is indebted to Howard Epstein and William J. Goode for their comments and suggestions.

1. Although Goode defines "statuses as the class of roles which is institutionalized," women professionals are assumed to possess a status (noninstitutionalized) different from the usual by reason of their sex. Thus, "woman lawyer" is assumed to be a different status than "lawyer." Moreover, there is no institutionalized set of expectations linked to the role relationship between the status of "woman lawyer" and role partners such as clients and colleagues. This case is

similar to those Goode points to when elements in role relationships are becoming institutionalized or noninstitutionalized (both of which might apply in the case of the woman lawyer), such as the changing status obligations of parents-children, husbands-wives. William J. Goode, "Norm Commitment and Conformity to Role-Status Obligations," *American Journal of Sociology*, 66 (1960), 249-50.

2. Interviewing for the study was conducted during 1965-1966. A full report appears in my Ph.D. dissertation, "Women and Professional Careers: The Case of the Woman Lawyer," New York, Columbia University, 1968.

3. School superintendents in Gross's study suffered from differential expectations attached to one role. Neal Gross, Ward S. Mason and Alexander W. McEachern, *Explorations in Role Analysis,* (New York: John Wiley and Sons, 1958). Women lawyers suffer from differential expectations of one role-set (i.e., the professional) about their *two* statuses (as woman and as lawyer).

4. Harriet Zuckerman has brought to my attention one example of the different and lower standards used in evaluating eminence of women as compared with men in American society. Because Americans of achievement listed in *Who's Who*, a directory of prominent people in the United States, tend to be almost entirely men, a separate volume, *Who's Who of American Women* was introduced in 1958. In establishing criteria for inclusion the editors noted in their preface to that first edition that they were "scaling down" the *Who's Who* standards because (as a letter to potential listees stated) for women, "national or international prominence . . . is not a requisite." (See Preface to *Who's Who of American Women*, First Edition, 1958-1959, [Chicago: A. N. Marquis Company], and most recent form letter dated 1968.)

5. See my dissertation, *op. cit.,* pp. 240-243.

6. Erwin O. Smigel, *Wall Street Lawyer* (New York: Free Press of Glencoe, 1964); Hubert J. O'Gorman, *Lawyers and Matrimonial Cases* (New York: Free Press of Glencoe, 1963); Jerome Carlin, *Lawyers' Ethics: A Survey of the New York City Bar* (New York: Russell Sage Foundation, 1966).

7. For evidence for the U. S. and other societies see National Opinion Research Center, "Jobs and Occupations: A Popular Evaluation," in Reinhart Bendix and S. M. Lipset, eds., *Class, Status and Power* (Glencoe, The Free Press, 1953), pp. 412-14; Alex Inkeles and Peter Rossi, "National Comparisons of Occupational Prestige," *The American Journal of Sociology*, LXI (1966), 329-39.

8. U. S. Bureau of the Census, Statistical Abstract of the United States: 1960 (Washington, D. C.: Government Printing Office), p. 325. Only groups such as the owners and managers of large businesses consistently attain higher incomes than successful professionals.

9. Homans poses this "role" of distributive justice as: "a man's rewards in exchange with others should be proportional to his investments." George Casper Homans, *Social Behavior: Its Elementary Forms* (N.Y.: Harcourt, Brace and World, 1961), p. 325.

10. If, according to Homans, justice is an equation between investment and reward, and women are believed to make less of an investment (background characteristics such as sex, race and ethnicity are included with hard work as "investments"), then, he asserts, they should not expect as much reward as a man who has "put in" a *higher* investment (i.e., by being male). Homans further suggests that being Negro or a woman is an *unchanging* value, unlike "experience" (another investment), which increases with time. *Ibid.*, pp. 236-37. If one takes the legal profession as the context in which the appraisal of justice is being made, the woman is not unfairly treated, since it is true that, on balance, women are believed to have a lesser investment in the structure than do men. If "society" is taken as the structure, the balance scale is not as clearly weighted. If women in law (as a group) is taken as structure, then a different system of weights and values surely emerges. We do not agree with Homans that we are using an "olympian" view of justice when we appraise as "injustice" the situation in which women get a lesser reward for hard work than men. Goffman's perception of the situation seems to hold more truth: that "in America at present, *separate* systems of honor seem to be on the decline," and that even those with so-called "abnormal" characteristics have come to believe *they* "deserve a fair chance and a fair break." Erving Goffman, *Stigma: Notes on the Management of Spoiled Identity* (Prentice-Hall, Inc., 1963), p. 7.

11. See George C. Homan's discussion of the "principle of distributive justice" and its application for behavior, *op. cit.*, pp. 232-64.

12. Epstein, dissertation, *op. cit.*, p. 147.

13. Verna Elizabeth Griffen, *Employment Possibilities for Women in Legal Work*, U.S. Department of Labor, U.S. Government Printing Office, Washington, D.C., 1958. Her information is from *The Bar Register: 1957*, which rates 3,000 firms as preeminent in the profession on the basis of investigations and recommendations from local bar members and groups. Thirty-two of the 3,000 firms listed women as partners. The 32 firms reported 35 women among their 262 partners.

14. This has as source and consequence two types of sociological ambivalence. The first, specified by Robert K. Merton and Elinor Barber, "Sociological Ambivalence," Ed. Tiryakian, (Ed.), *Sociological Theory, Values and Sociocultural Change,* (New York: Free Press of Glencoe, 1963), pp. 91-120, comes from conflicting demands of different statuses ordinarily involving different people (e.g., demands of the senior partner *vs.* demands of the woman attorney's husband). The second is a type in which ambivalence arises from conflicting ex-

pectations of role partners in a role-set attached to one status because of visibility of the role incumbent's other statuses.

15. Smigel reports that nine to eleven years is considered an "appropriate" amount of time for becoming a partner in a Wall Street firm (*Wall Street Lawyer, op. cit.*, p. 92), and the time span has decreased recently to an average of seven. Erwin O. Smigel, "Wall Street Lawyers Reconsidered," *New York*, August 18, 1969, p. 4.

16. I am grateful to William J. Goode for pointing out the application of the "cooling out" process for woman lawyers.

17. It is assumed that a woman cannot meet the demands of both work and home and that she will or should limit the professional role *first*. One must at least mention that assumptions are still with us concerning women's biologically imposed limitations — their underendowment of intellect and overendowment of "emotion."

18. Cf. the *Time* magazine comment on women in law, that "many Portias admit with a touch of asperity that they are often overpraised by men for a performance that would be regarded as merely competent in another male." (March 6, 1964, p. 48)

19. George Homans frames this as "occupational justice," since "by the standards current in American industry, the female sex is considered to have made a lower investment than the male, and so by distributive justice, to deserve a less good job than the male. This kind of discrimination may well vex a woman, but it has its compensations. It means that she expects less than a man does, and so is more satisfied if she gets anything like as much. . . . There is much evidence that on the average the women in American industry are more satisfied than the men. . . . The high investments of . . . men tended to make them less satisfied, and the low investments of . . . women tend(ed) to make them more satisfied with pay and promotion than was justified by the sheer quantity of pay and promotion either . . . received(d)." *Op. cit.*, p. 274.

forty-nine

Do "Bad Girls" Become Good Nurses?

CYNTHIA KRUEGER

"I solemnly pledge myself before God and in the presence of this assembly to pass my life in purity and to practice my profession faithfully. . . ." The student nurse is then capped, and her purity becomes a purely personal matter.

Before the capping ceremony, however, the student nurse's virtue is a very public concern. In fact, the nursing school may consider it the measure of her "suitability" for the profession. As the Florence Nightingale pledge above implies, traditional nursing is based on two standards: The good nurse must be medically expert, and morally fit as well.

"What we do in our private lives is our own business," some student nurses complain. "It has nothing to do with whether or not we're good nurses." And, in fact, a study I recently completed on the leisure behavior of student nurses confirms this view: Their off-duty behavior should not be used as a measure of their nursing ability. When it is, the effect on the nursing profession is an unhealthy one. For it is precisely the moralistic Florence Nightingales, the favorites of the nursing-school administration, who after graduation turn out to be those least likely to answer the profession's real need — the critical need for nurses who can meet the rigorous medical standards and the grueling workloads of the nation's hospitals.

The study of student nurses spanned a four-year period and was conducted at a small, Midwestern diploma school of nursing that I will call General Hospital School of Nursing. Members of the class of '65, from the day they entered until the date they

From TRANS-action, Vol. 5, No. 8 (1968), pp. 31-36. Reprinted by permission of TRANS-action.

graduated, were tested and retested by St. Louis's Medical Care Research Center project on the professionalization of nurses. By the end of their second year of training, the students had been given a wide range of tests on personality attributes, self-conception, and perception of the hospital nurses' role. Then, to gain a first-hand look at the informal side of their lives, I took a room in the nurses' dormitory and began my study of their off-duty behavior and its relationship, if any, to their professional training.

Medicine and Men

In the dormitory and off-duty, the 52 students in the class of '65 behaved like most other women students. They studied, gossiped, and dated. Their two major interests were medicine and men. For example, most of the girls viewed nursing as a useful addition to marriage and motherhood rather than as an alternative to it. And nurse's training itself was seen as a time for hunting a suitable marriage partner, as well as a period of professional preparation.

The girls' relationship to medicine was a personalized one. Their discussions of medicine centered not on abstract disease categories, but on the problems of individual patients. And even then, the girls were usually much more interested in the personal and social likes of the patients than in their medical difficulties. For the students, the patients and their family visitors were simply people — which made them suitable objects for anecdotes, crushes, and flattering or unflattering personal evaluations.

Similarly, the hospital physicians and other medical personnel were evaluated in personal terms. A doctor might be described as crabby, good-looking, or a flirt – but his medical skill was rarely mentioned. The hospital nurses were generally not discussed unless one of them had caused a student some trouble, or had been especially helpful.

This personal approach to the medical setting served, I think, to cast the students' medical experiences — some of them definitely painful or shocking to girls just out of high school — into more familiar and more manageable terms. By viewing the players in these often dramatic medical scenes as ordinary people, the students were better able to view the scenes themselves as ordinary, everyday events. The students' informal way of seeing and talking about both patients and hospital personnel, then, rather effectively eliminated more harsh medical content from topics based in that setting.

The other major topic of conversation — and the one that aroused most enthusiasm and stimulated most activity — was men. Getting a date and then getting ready for it were subjects of conversation throughout the entire dormitory. "Getting involved" and becoming "uninvolved" were major and recurrent events in the girls' lives. Thus the degree of intimacy one was enjoying, the concomitant danger of pregnancy, and plans of what to do about it were frequent topics of more private conversations. Although some girls did not date, or rarely dated, they never advertised a lack of interest in men. For at General Hospital School of Nursing, being popular with men generally raised one's standing in the eyes of the other students.

If a girl became engaged, for example, it was cause for general rejoicing. Even members of rival or antagonistic cliques would congratulate her, particularly if she had received a diamond that was unusually large. In part, this rejoicing seemed to be because the competition for dates had been decreased, if only by one. And for the girl who had become engaged, the event removed her from an area of cryptic evaluation by her fellow students — whether or not she could swing dates.

The importance of having dates was increased by the fact that they were rather hard to obtain. Romantic involvements with patients seldom arose. When they did, they were met with administrative veto. Attempts to arrange interschool affairs with students at a nearby school of pharmacy were also quashed by the administration, which, the girls felt, wanted them to "keep their noses in the books all the time."

Naturally, despite the rule barring dates with hospital personnel, the girls carefully scrutinized each new crop of medical interns. Intricate plots to "catch" them were concocted, and each unmarried intern must have felt like Mr. America — until most of the girls became disenchanted or concluded that the situation was hopeless. After this, the girls would ignore or merely tolerate the interns, or treat them with measured antagonism.

Another element that appeared to increase the girls' preoccupation with dating was the low allowances that they received from their parents. On the average, the girls' allowances for personal expenses were only about $5 per week. This made dating a form of financial relief, and many dates were evaluated in terms of how much money the boy spent.

Enforcing the Rules

These broad aspects of student-nursing life are similar to the pursuits of women students elsewhere. But the parallels should not be ovedrawn: At General Hospital School of Nursing, intellectual interests were minimal and discussions of class work infrequent. A concern with medicine was there, of course, but as noted, it was transformed from a scientific interest into more understandable, personal terms.

The nursing school itself had problems similar to those of girls' schools and women's colleges everywhere. A school of this sort, finding itself acting *in loco parentis* (in place of the parent), must continually reassure parents that their girls are being properly taken care of — protected against the dangers of the world and shielded from its temptations. In addition, the school must not only produce competent graduates, but in the process protect its own good name. Toward this end, it often set up an elaborate system of rules to govern the students' leisure-time conduct — rules that can become very difficult to enforce gracefully when the students regard them as stupid and unfair. In these circumstances, the school may become the enemy, to be circumvented or defeated.

At the General Hospital School of Nursing, enforcing the rules was particularly hard. On duty, students were exhorted to "be mature." Off duty, students were governed by regulations that denied them the same maturity their professional role required. Contradictory demands were evident even in the students' work. While they were enjoined, for example, to show *responsibility* on the wards, they also had to follow ward procedures that they regarded as impractical and that were *not* followed by practicing nurses. In short, the student nurses had to contend with the strain of being accorded a limited and inconsistent adult status.

This conflict was magnified by the dual nature of the nursing profession itself. The legendary view of Florence Nightingale as the personification of traditional Christian female morality prompts the nursing school to stand as the guardian of the girls' virtue. But while virtue may be important, technical advances in medicine demand increasing emphasis on medical expertise. At General Hospital School of Nursing — as at most other three-year diploma schools — tradition prevailed. The administration wished to increase the medical expertise of its graduates, but at minimal sacrifice of personal characteristics that have traditionally defined the "good" nurse.

The tension between these two separate and partially divergent ideologies is probably greatest at church-related schools of nursing. When I was double-checking my findings at one church-related school, one student there told me, "Between God and Florence Nightingale, we can't do anything right." Besides, another volunteered, "It's all a sham; Florence Nightingale died of syphilis — we *all* know *that*." (Miss Nightingale reportedly acquired syphilis from the wounds of men she nursed.)

The ultimate sanction available to a school is its power to expel students. At General Hospital, a student could be asked to leave "at any time if the student's personality, conduct, health, or level of achievement makes it seem inadvisable that she should continue. . . . Students are forbidden to bring full, partially full, or empty liquor bottles into the Nurses' Residence. Any student found possessing the above materials will be brought before the Advisory Board of the Student Council and will be subject to expulsion from the School."

Besides these basic caveats, both academic and ward evaluations — necessary for remaining in school — seemed to be influenced by a student's personal qualities. The student handbook itself stated that each case should be evaluated individually, and the girls' reports indicated that this was most assuredly the way evaluations were handled. This was the way, they said, that the administration and faculty encouraged some students to withdraw, or assisted others to remain in school. Even where the crucial issue of expulsion was concerned, cases were decided not by any objective, universal standard, but by a blanket judgment on the part of the authorities as to whether a girl was "suited for nursing."

The Company She Keeps

Success as a student at the training hospital centered on the individual's reputation. And reputation itself was not an individual characteristic; it was identified through a group. A girl, it seemed, was known to the administration by the company she kept.

Off duty, the girls I studied usually separated into nine informal groups. While each group had its own distinctive features, there were two that seemed to define the extremes of student behavior. The students consistently named one group — which included the two class officers — as being the one the administration most approved of. The "wild" ones, by contrast, received every possible vote — including their own — as being the group whom the administration most disliked. The wild ones were those who broke the rules and didn't exhibit the "right kind of attitudes toward the school." Members of the student-officer group, on the other hand, were described as "ideal."

Unlike the other eight groups, the student officers, for the most part, pursued individual pastimes. Four of the eight were engaged to be married and two more soon would be, which undoubtedly prompted them to go off on their own. But even after work, while others busily visited each other, the girls in the student-officer group would each separate to their own rooms, nap, and read before going to dinner.

This group was a quiet one, seldom laughing or talking loudly. None of the members smoked, three drank (which came as a surprise to some in the group), and all but one went to church regularly. Though some topics, like drinking, were not widely discussed among group members, the clique was nevertheless close-knit. About once every two weeks the eight of them would cook a communal dinner. During weekends, they frequently visited one another's homes.

The two class officers in this group spent considerable time mediating between the students and the administration, in the process often assuming the attitudes and postures of the administration.

The wild students, on the other hand, considered themselves nonconformists. This group had six members, one of whom was a freshman. (This in itself was deviant, since all other groups were segregated along class lines.) The wild ones traveled together as a single unit once the separation dictated by the workday was over. After work, they would regularly meet in one of the dorm rooms — they all lived on the same floor — to plan the rest of the evening. At that time, they would recall funny or irritating experiences of the day and reminisce about recent parties that they had enjoyed or trouble they had suffered.

The wild ones were loud, and they laughed a lot. Jokes and gossip in this group were always heavily accented by swearing and by the customary reference — "the bitch" — extended generously to non-group members.

During the summer of 1964 none of these girls were engaged, and a great part of their time was spent getting dates and planning parties. Although the girls actually didn't drink much, they took pride in their reputations as heavy drinkers. Another badge of honor they wore was frequenting bars that were, if not actually considered "off limits," frowned upon by the school administration.

Almost every evening, those who did not have dates — generally four of them — would go to their favorite hangout. There they were often given free drinks and money for the jukebox by the owner, who felt the girls were "good for business." Since the girls usually danced with each other, offering suggestive modifications on the twist, dog, swim, and so on, they were good for business. The other patrons — mostly men — would watch their performance with appreciation, then buy the girls more drinks. The girls wanted to have fun, but they would grow abrupt with any man who was overly aggressive or vulgar. And a man would also get the impression it was time for him to leave their table if he stayed longer than the drinks he had bought for them lasted.

Even though the girls were always the bar's center of attraction, they felt that their past experiences there were far more enjoyable than the present ones. They reported that they had slowed down quite a bit — because they were afraid of the school administration. "If we were really doing something wrong, it would be different," one complained. "Hell, anything we do is wrong. If you listen to the rumors, there's nothing we haven't done. . . . We were even prostitues at the Bat [a motel in the area]." The administration, one girl contended, actually "had people spying on us. Of course, most of those brownnoses were only too happy to do it."

The girls would save their allowances, or baby-sit, to rent a motel room for one or both nights of party weekends. Very often, their liquor — as well as some of the money required for the room — would be furnished by one of the girls' mothers.

The wild ones spent very little time alone. Group membership seemed to carry with it the obligation, perhaps as well as the desire, to be with the other members of the group. They did not want visitors, for the group thrived on secrets. An outsider posed the threat of carrying tales and getting them into trouble.

Rule-Making and Apathy

While the student-officer group and the wild ones were near opposites in their behavior and attitudes toward such things as swearing and drinking, the most noticeable differences between them centered on their reaction to the school rules.

Though the wild ones relished attacking the school's rules, they would sometimes admit that the rules didn't really bother them much. "Hell, I'm glad we have to get in at a decent hour," confessed one student. "Otherwise I'd *never* get any sleep." But when a rule did happen to interfere with what the girls wanted to do, it would be bitterly condemned. And then it was not merely the content of the rule that the group attacked, but the "nerviness" or presumptuousness of the rule.

None of the student-officer group ever criticized the rules. They regarded the rules as facts of life, to be accepted without question. On one occasion, these girls indicated that I could not eat in the hospital cafeteria because I was not wearing a skirt. (I was wearing shorts.) They followed this statement with no explanation and no criticism. They were simply stating a fact.

In some instances, the student officers wanted *more* rules governing off-duty behavior. During the month of July, for instance, they first obtained administration approval and then met with the student body to vote on a dress restriction. The student leaders favored a rule calling for rather formal attire when girls went down to the dormitory basement to use the candy machine. This rule, they felt, would make it easier for them, and the others who dated, to use the nearby basement recreation room for entertainment.

During the meeting called for a vote on this rule, the wild ones worked hard to convey the impression that they were totally uninterested in the proceedings. They set one another's hair, pretended to doze, and yawned loudly whenever someone made a point either for or against the proposed rule. When a vote was finally taken, the girls made a production of raising their arms halfway for each side. After all, they said, student government was just a "figurehead deal." Besides, they thought it was terribly funny that the question of dressing to go down to the basement candy machine could become a big issue.

The student-leader group, on the other hand, viewed its position as the rule-making group with a good deal of seriousness. And even when these girls had no hand in framing a rule, they would support it. One rule handed down from the administration that summer — a rule originated by the administration and presented to the students as an accomplished fact — limited the amount of food each girl could take from the cafeteria. The student-officer group did not oppose the rule at all. As one member explained it, "Some girls really overdo it, and take much more than they actually want." Another added, "There's really an awful lot of waste."

As expected, the wild ones attacked the rule with gusto. They considered it an affront. "What business do *they* have," one demanded; "telling us how much we can eat?" "I'd like to see [the head administrator] live on that amount of food," volunteered another girl. "She probably eats that much for breakfast." The wild ones were most concerned about what the rule's effect upon the dining-room activities represented — another encroachment by the administration into their private lives. They were not interested — as were the student leaders — in evaluating the rule in terms of the possible underlying factors that led to its promulgation.

In short, the student officers were apologists for the school administration. During their term of office, the amount of student-initiated change in the school was minimal. The officers themselves spoke of "student apathy." But, of course, the real question is whether student apathy was the cause of the administration's domination of student government, or whether — more likely — the traditionally heavy hand of the administration was the cause of student apathy.

"Damn Good Nurses"

The wild ones, because they took pride in their capabilities as nurses, were never worried about their class or ward performance. "We're damn good nurses" was their typical evaluation of themselves, and this evaluation was confirmed by other members of the class.

The administration took a different view of the wild group.

The head administrator regarded them as deviant, but felt that they were controllable. "Oh, we know how to handle girls like them," she said without alarm. "There's a group of rebels in almost every class." However, one member of their group had been asked to withdraw during her first year; thus, the wild ones never seemed comforted by the administrator's rather relaxed attitude. And if this administrator treated them with some measure of equanimity, other officials were clearly not so charitable.

The final student report — which remained in a girl's permanent dossier — was filled out by the assistant head of the school, and her profiles of the wild students regularly pointed out some unflattering characteristic: They were "insensitive to patients," "bossy," "had problems with authority," or were summed up by the cursory and subtly censorious evaluation of "average student, average nurse." On the other hand, the members of the student-officer group were almost without exception described as "excellent nurses" — "understanding, sincere, and considerate." The wild ones seemed faintly obsessed with the ironies of their situation: "Wouldn't that be a bitch . . . to come this far and then get kicked out for something that isn't even any of their business?" They expressed various opinions as to why they had *not* been expelled: "If they didn't need their slave labor so much in that damned hospital, we'd all be out on our asses." Other tentative explanations of administrative tolerance for them included the possibility that Miss X (the head administrator) was aware of the fact that they were good nurses, and for that reason allowed them to remain in school. More frequently, however, the explanations were that "maybe she [Miss X] was wild when she was young," or "maybe she doesn't know." "Yes, she knows," observed others, "but she doesn't give a damn. She's letting us get through anyway."

Regardless of why the wild ones were not expelled, the fact remains that they did serve as negative role models for the other student nurses. As sociologist Kai T. Erikson has noted, behavior labeled as deviant defines the boundaries for the social system in which the deviance occurs. In any social system, deviance throws into sharp relief the modes of behavior that are accepted — and the individuals who are acceptable. The deviant wild ones apparently constituted the outside limits of what, in terms of personal behavior, the nursing-school system would tolerate.

Since the nursing school used students as comparisons for one another, the members of the student-officer group were, in a way, deviants too. In any system and under any label, those people who are perceived as the embodiment of the ideal often put the teeth into the treatment given to those who violate that ideal. Conversely, those who violate the ideal serve to highlight those who fly high within the organizational framework. At General Hospital School of Nursing, the student-officer group set the upper limit of the system, while the wild group set the lower one.

But the example of the wild ones also adds a human dimension to Erikson's theory. Their deviance seems to have resulted from disagreement over where limits of the system lay. The wild ones disagreed that the school's territory extended into their private lives. They felt that the authority of the school, rather than extending to questions of morality and personal habits, should be confined to areas of nursing expertise. In this sense, the wild ones were engaged in a struggle to establish or maintain a realm of personal autonomy.

Who Are the Nurses Now?

Upon graduation, the formal evaluations made of the class of '65 suddenly ended. No longer was a girl's private life construed as having an important bearing on her expertise as a nurse. In fact, out of school and on the job, all except one of the wild students continued working at the school-affiliated hospital. Their dissatisfaction with the school, apparently, had not spread to dissatisfaction with nursing itself. By their junior year they had already established close working relationships with several doctors in the hospital, and evidently loyalty to the hospital gradually supplanted the antagonism the girls felt for the school. The rules, the right attitude, and the right moral reputation, it turns out, might have something to do with being a good *student* nurse, but very little to do with being a good *working* nurse.

In contrast to the wild ones, only one of the student-officer group went into hospital nursing. Most of them chose work that didn't require the level of professional expertise demanded by the hospital. Instead, they chose clinic or private-office work — or fulltime marriage positions.

The nursing school's preferential treatment of the student-officer group and condemnatory attitude toward the wild students raises some important questions. Foremost is the question of whether the nursing schools are geared to producing what we really need — not paragons of womanly virtue, but thoroughly trained, medically expert nurses. At a time when the United States faces a need of 300,000 trained nurses, and when the nurses themselves are prepared to strike to lighten their workloads by relief from traditional chores such as serving meals, the traditional emphasis on virtue seems at best irrelevant.

If the General Hospital School of Nursing is typical, then perhaps the nation's nursing schools need to revise their attitudes — as well as their courses — to meet the new demands now being placed on the nursing profession.

fifty

Employer Acceptance of the
Mature Home Economist

LOUISE A. STEDMAN and
PAUL S. ANDERSON

Is business interested in the mature home economist on a full-
or part-time basis? Does business know how a home economist
can improve business services and production? Is the mature
home economist whose family is approaching maturity destined
to a marginal career? Does she have professional career possibilities at all? Is the home economist who has been a full-time
homemaker for a decade or even longer prepared to return to a
career, and are employers prepared to hire her?

These are questions which provide the focus of a recent
study[1] of employment possibilities for mature home economists
conducted by the School of Home Economics at the University
of Minnesota in co-operation with the placement service of the
College of Agriculture, Forestry, and Home Economics. In brief,
this study sought to discover what the employment prospects
would be for mature home economics graduates who might seek
employment in the Twin Cities (Minneapolis-St. Paul metropolitan region) area.

In this study, the term "mature home economist" referred to
a person with a bachelor's or higher degree in home economics
who had been a full-time homemaker for several years and who
might be a candidate for part-time or full-time employment at a
professional level. Normally, a person of this type would have
a family of several children. These children in most circumstances would be of school age. In some cases, the home econ-

From JOURNAL OF HOME ECONOMICS, Vol. 57, No. 10 (1965), pp. 767-
772. Reprinted by permission of authors and JOURNAL OF HOME
ECONOMICS.

omist might have been continuously or intermittently employed both after marriage and the arrival of children.

There were several important reasons for conducting this study. The most immediate were personal experiences of the staff in the School of Home Economics which suggested that many alumnae and other home economics graduates might be served by employment information for mature home economists. In addition, an investigation conducted by the Twin Cities home economists in homemaking in connection with the School of Home Economics had revealed that there was significant interest in employment opportunities and in refresher training in home economics. The Minnesota Plan for Continuing Education had also stimulated interest in employment and careers for mature women.[2]

In a broader sense, of course, these findings were indications of the national trend toward increased employment of women in many areas. This arises from several circumstances. Increasingly, women are marrying earlier, thus having children at earlier ages; and usually last children are born at relatively young ages of the mother. Consequently, as child-rearing responsibilities decline, women are available for employment at an age when a long-term career is still a serious possibility.[3]

The reasons for entering a career are many. Probably the most common is that the additional income provides savings for college education of the children in the family. There are other compelling reasons, not the least of which is that of personal self-fulfillment.[4]

Method

Though the focus of the study ultimately centered on the problems of the mature home economist, the methodological design was developed from the theory that the role of the mature home economist could not be understood without a knowledge as well of the over-all setting of employment within a particular organization. Thus, the basic questionnaire (see pages 702-4) contained 37 items related to both the role of the home economist and the nature of the employer's organization. The information gathered has, of course, utility for curriculum policy and placement of recently graduated home economists as well as immediate significance for the study of mature home economists.

The questionnaire was developed in consultation with staff members of the School of Home Economics in various professional areas. It was then pretested with six employers. (The data from these interviews were retained in the final sample.)

Pretesting revealed that the questionnaire could best be administered nondirectively in a conversational technique rather than in a categorical question-answer interview. This approach, aside from providing the basic information, improved rapport and provided much additional information because the interviewee was able to lead the conversation into areas of particular interest to him. Normally, two staff persons were available for each interview. One staff person took detailed notes. The other checked items on the questionnaire check list as they were discussed.

At the same time that the questionnaire was in preparation, a careful investigation was being made to determine the sample of employers to be interviewed. Since for practical reasons the study was limited to the Twin Cities area, a comprehensive analysis of all potential Twin Cities employers of home economists was conducted. Basically, the yellow sections of the telephone directories were reviewed in detail to discover both employers and specific categories of employers. From the approximately 23,572 businesses in the Twin Cities area, about 2,000 were identified as possible (potential, actual, or remotely potential) employers of home economists. These 2,000 employers were finally classified into 25 basic categories. (See page 706.)

On the basis of these 25 categories, a sample of employers was selected on a subjective and judgmental basis, rather than on a random basis. Employers were chosen on the basis of known interest and employment of home economists (current employers) or on the basis of an estimated potential employment possibility for a home economist (potential employers). No specific universal criteria were applied, but rather an attempt was made to get information from a great range of potential and current employers of home economists. Thus, for example, some of the largest merchandisers and food manufacturers in the metropolitan area were contacted as well as some of the smallest specialty businesses, such as kitchen designers and loft-type clothing manufacturers.

An indicator of the employment prospects for home economists in major employment categories was derived by analyzing placement of University of Minnesota School of Home Economics graduates with Bachelor of Science degrees during the period 1957 to 1962. This analysis is shown on page 706. A better indicator would have been employment of home economists of greater maturity, but data on these home economists were not readily available. On the basis of this analysis, employers were classified into two groups: actual or current employers of home economists and potential employers.

This classification of employers proved to be relatively reliable. In only one case did subsequent investigation reveal employment of a home economist in a potential category (mass media). However, some home economists were being employed as occasional consultants by firms in so-called "potential categories."

Upon completion of this analysis, a preliminary sample of approximately 200 potential and existing employers was isolated from the 2,000 employers listed in the basic 25 categories. Interviews were held with 46 of this group — 22 current employers and 24 potential employers. The screening of employers was done on subjective criteria, taking into account geographical location, significance of firm or agency, and special knowledge available about particular organizations. Employers in all major employment categories were interviewed to make the sample at least geographically representative of the metropolitan area.

Interviews were conducted at the highest possible level of management or ownership. Usually the vice-president of personnel or his equivalent was the employer representative interviewed.

Hypothesis and Findings

It was expected that employment prospects for mature home economists would be found to be comparatively poor. This hypothesis was posited because placement experience had led the investigators to the conclusion that employers hold a generally negative view regarding the placement of professional women and lack an understanding of the basic qualifications of a professional home economist.

Given this hypothesis it was not possible to logically derive subhypotheses regarding employer views on retraining home economists, the significance of part-time employment, and other issues. It was expected that answers to these questions could be obtained only after either persuading the employer to consider home economists as employees or after asking him to consider these other questions as if he were seriously interested in employing home economists. The general findings of this study, noted in detail below, indicated that the major hypothesis and subhypotheses were phrased too negatively or pessimistically and that, in fact, issues such as retraining were relevant in the employer's mind. Consequently, there was no need for either persuasion or "as if" staging of the interview.

An analysis of the data from the 46 interviews reveals differential support for these hypotheses. *First of all, there was no extensive indication of specific negative feelings with regard to the employment of the mature home economist.* Seventeen (77 per cent) of the 22 current employers of home economists indicated an interest in employing mature home economists either full time or part time.

Further, 21 (90 per cent) of the 24 potential employers of home economists indicated a serious interest in considering home economists for full-time or part-time employment. Thus, in the complete sample, 83 per cent of the 46 firms indicated a positive acceptance of the mature home economist.

The prevalence of acceptance of mature home economists was supported by various arguments. The position of many employers is reflected by this comment of one personnel director: "I don't care how old they are as long as they can perform the duties adequately." About 34 of the employers interviewed indicated they would consider employing either young or mature home economists.

However, some employers (4) who reacted positively to the employment of mature home economists voluntarily *indicated a preference for this type of employee.* They argued that the mature home economist is less likely to leave employment and often has more mature judgment than the recent graduate.

All employers responding positively on the questionnaire nonetheless indicated that a mature home economist must give assurance to her employer that family responsibilities would not seriously interfere with work responsibilities and that, in any employment interview, this dimension of personal situation would be probed in depth. Specifically, the personal representative seeks absolute assurance that children of the mature home economist's household will be well cared for by another responsible person, relative, or housekeeper, in the event of illness, major or minor.

The few employers indicating a negative view regarding employment of mature home economists all give special reasons related to the nature of their business or activity. One firm required extensive travel which, in the view of the personnel representative, could be performed only by a single person. Another felt that in view of the rate of change of techniques and knowledge, a person without continuous work experience would lack adequate "know-how." Two organizations indicated that mature home economists had not been successful in their operations and were reluctant to hire mature home economists, though the personnel representative reflected no personal bias.

View of Qualifications of the Home Economist

All of the employers were asked several questions regarding their view of the educational background and professional capacity of a home economist. These questions (see page 703) were:

18. What do you think home economists do and can do?
19. What kind of training do you think the home economists receive?
20. What kind of training do you think the home economists should receive?
21. What are the kinds and types of positions you have in your firm for which home economists qualify?

Despite the almost overwhelming acceptance of the home economist in the employment setting, as noted above, most employers reflected a diffuse and imprecise view of the qualifications of a professional home economist. Of the total sample, only six of the 46 employers were able to answer questions 18 and 19 with any degree of accuracy. These employers all have home economists on their staffs. The other employers, both potential and actual, reflected confusion regarding specific qualifications and, in a majority of cases, viewed the home economist as a skills-oriented person.

EMPLOYER QUESTIONNAIRE
I. BASIC INFORMATION REGARDING FIRM OR AGENCY:
— 1. Name of firm or agency
—   Address
—   Home office
—   Personnel officer
—   Date of interview
—   Ownership of company
—   Principal home economist

—   Major stockholder
—   Chairman of board
—   2. What are the major activities of your firm?
II. GROWTH OF FIRM OR AGENCY:
—   3. Changes in sales from 1953 to 1963
—   4. Established any new divisions? Yes.... No....
—   5. If so, what are they?
—   6. Any areas of research? Yes.... No....
III. EMPLOYMENT ORGANIZATION OF FIRM OR AGENCY:
    Do you think of your firm as having any particular image?
—   7. Kinds of positions available for college graduates
— ·8. Summarize the major criteria which you apply in hiring professional employees.
—   9. Formal training program? Yes.... No....
—10. Describe the training program for college graduates.
—11. Firm's policy on encouraging further education or study.
—12. Pay range of nonprofessional union help.
—13. Salary range for new professional employees
—14. Salary levels for home economists hired now
—15. Difference between salary offerings to professional men and women in organization? Yes.... No....
—16. If so, what is the approximate difference?
—17. Any new positions created in the last 10 years
IV. HOME ECONOMIST IN FIRM OR AGENCY:
—18. What do you think home economists do and can do?
—19. What kind of training do you think home economists receive?
—20. What kind of training do you think home economists should receive?
—21. What are the kinds and types of positions you have in your firm for which home economists qualify?
—22. How many home economists do you have currently employed?
—23. Does your firm have need for MS or PhD level personnel? Yes.... No....
—24. What does this advanced personnel do?
—25. Would home economists fit into any of these positions?
—26. Is there particular graduate training that would be suitable?
—26a. What is the turnover of home economists?
—27. Does this raise any alternatives for considering home economists as employees for your business that you may have overlooked? Yes.... No....
—28. Can you visualize any opportunities in your firm to combine existing duties of professional or nonprofessional employees into new positions for which home economists would uniquely qualify?
—29. Are there any qualities you look for in hiring home economists

that are essentially different from those of other professional employees?

—30. If you had available home economists whose families are now in school, would you consider these home economists for permanent employment? Yes.... No....

—31. If you had available home economists whose families are grown and they wish to return to work would you consider them for permanent employment? Yes.... No....

—32. Do you feel refresher courses would be helpful or essential?

V. PART-TIME EMPLOYMENT:

—33. Can you tell us of opportunities for home economists in your organization that are part-time, summer, or seasonal?

May be home economists with families in school —
Mature home economists —
Must be graduate home economists —
Can be undergraduates who are enrolled in home economics —
No preference —

—34. Could two part-time people fill a full-time position?

—35. Are there categories of employment in your organization in which you have difficulty in finding suitable people?

—36. What are the big problems in your business?

—37. Do you have specific positions for home economists which we could assist in filling now?

The data on these items may be summarized as follows: The six employers able to provide answers on questions 18 and 19 viewed the home economist's role as professional and had a general idea both of the range of major areas and a knowledge of curricula, so that, for example, they knew that home economists must carry a basic sequence in the liberal arts and the sciences in addition to specialization within home economics. Two employers (one current employer and one potential) categorically defined home economics training as professional. The remaining 38 employers' uninformed views reflected different patterns at different levels of analysis. First, most of these employers viewed a home economist as a person with basic homemaking skills. One employer, who since has become interested in employing home economists in a professional and creative role, said: "Well, what can home economists do? I've always thought they would make wonderful wives. But how can they fit into our business?"

Second, employers in this group tended to view home economists as filling highly traditional employment roles but were unable to conceive of alternative employment opportunities. One current employer, in serious need of research laboratory workers, had not thought of employing home economists in food laboratory research even though some high school graduates without suitable training had been trained by the company for this type of work at considerable expense. In another case, an executive who uses consulting home economists expressed the view that home economists were too skills-oriented for mass-media work. Thus, probably intimately related to the problems of lack of professional image is the rigidity employers show with regard to the variety of employment for which home economists are qualified.

Third, employers tend to have an understanding of specialized aspects of home economics training related to their particular activity, but they do not have a clear knowledge of other aspects of home economics training. Thus, officials of organizations which hire home economists as interior decorators and dietitians, for example, are aware of the specialized course work requirements but largely uninformed with regard to other dimensions of curricula.

In sum, current employers of home economists, as might be expected, had a clearer view of the basic education of the home economist. At the same time, it must be noted that only 7 of the 22 current employers reflected a clear professional view of the home economist; the remaining 15 showed various degrees of knowledge depending upon the specialization of the home economists they employed but lacked a general knowledge of the profession. Finally, of the 24 potential employers, only one reflected a professional view of home economists.

Employers Support Retraining

A basic concern of this study was the relevance of retraining of mature home economists to employability either in part-time or full-time employment. Given the prevailing ethos in support of education, it might be expected that employers would support this type of program. In fact, 60 per cent of the employers indicated that they felt a mature home economist with refresher training would definitely be a more attractive employee. The balance of the firms showing a positive interest in employment of home economists indicated definite interest in retrained personnel but with some qualifications. The firms which did not reflect a positive interest in the home economist did not, of course, reflect an opinion on this item. The qualifications voiced by some firms arose out of special circumstances which might be applied with regard to a particular potential employee. Thus, a merchandiser said that a person previously in merchandising would probably not need refresher training. Another expressed the view that if persons were up to date on current concepts and knowledge, refresher training would be unnecessary. Another employer indicated that the company training program was sufficient for their own needs.

HOME ECONOMICS EMPLOYMENT CATEGORIES

Major Employment Categories in Twin Cities Business and Industry Related to Home Economics, Based on Placement 1957 through 1962

Employment Categories	Current Employers	Potential Employers
1. Appliances, equipment, and utensils		0
2. Associations, organizations	X	
3. Buildings — residential and commercial; architects		0
4. Interior decorating	X	
5. Business management		0
6. Churches and church organizations		0
7. Cleaning and laundry		0
8. Clothing — manufacturing and wholesale	X	
9. Florists		0
10. Food manufacturing	X	
11. Food service management, food merchandising, retail and wholesale	X	
12. Government offices	X	
13. Hospitals	X	
14. Household furnishings		0
15. Manufacturers, miscellaneous	X	
16. Mass media, publishers		0
17. Merchandising — retail and wholesale		
18. Miscellaneous (itemize)		0
19. Nursing homes, retirement homes		0
20. Public Relations and advertising		0
21. Research	X	
22. Restaurants and hotels		0
23. Schools	X	
24. Social service agencies		0
25. Utilities	X	

Contrasted with these specialized views was the more general view that retraining was essential. One employer indicated that such a program would be supportive of company policy of providing professional retraining every ten years. Most employers voiced support in more general terms without being able to speak definitively of suitable curricula or necessary general preparation.

Conclusions

In summary, the evidence of this study does not support the hypothesis that employers have a negative view with regard to employment of mature home economists, but it does support the view that the perception of the home economist is confused. *Thus, with the provision that adequate care will be provided for minor children, most employers reflected a serious interest in employing mature home economists.* Employers generally supported the notion of refresher training and indicated that such refresher training would make the mature home economist a more attractive employee.

Consequences and Continuation

This study has been a brief and partial investigation of employer attitudes regarding mature home economists. The findings from the standpoint of an action program in the development of professional home economists have been encouraging. The broad verbal acceptance of the mature home economist suggests that the employment opportunities are extensive, particularly if retraining can be initiated and employers can be educated to a more comprehensive understanding of the education and varied capabilities of home economists.

NOTES

1. The College of Agriculture, Forestry, and Home Economics of the University of Minnesota received a grant from the Sears-Roebuck Foundation for the purpose of surveying and studying the business firms in the Twin Cities relative to opportunities for the mature home economist on a part-time or full-time basis.

2. The Minnesota Plan for Continuing Education is a Carnegie-Foundation-supported program at the University of Minnesota which assists women, particularly mature women, in obtaining undergradu-

ate, refresher, and graduate collegiate education. It is directed by Dr. Vera Schletzer.

3. Esther Peterson, "Working Women," *Daedalus.* 93 (Spring 1964), p. 676; National Manpower Council, *Womanpower.* New York: Columbia University Press, 1957, p. 19.

4. Peterson, *op. cit.*, pp. 313-315.

fifty-one

Women and Medicine in a Changing World

JOHN KOSA

It is an interesting experience for the sociologist to re-examine an old research topic: while doing so, the passage of time will teach him something new about his old topic and, in addition, teach him something about social change which by necessity affects every sociological problem. A case in point is the problem of women physicians about which the present writer did research some years ago.[1] At that time the small number of female physicians (less than 6 percent of all physicians in the country) was regarded as a traditional feature of medicine, and their presence and role represented relatively unimportant issues among the many other concerns of medical manpower policy. Since then, however, the new social trends have removed this issue from its previous place of unimportance and placed it among the conspicuous and perhaps even popular issues of our present-day social consciousness. In view of this it might be rewarding to re-examine how much the social change of the last few years has affected the basic relationship of female role and medical career and how much progress women have made in gaining their proper places in medicine.

An additional personal note will illuminate the issue. In 1967 the present writer began another research with the aim of exploring the motivation of women entering medicine. He interviewed with the aid of semi-structured schedules 20 female residents working in the hospitals of two large metropolitan centers of the country; after that the project was discontinued because it was felt that, in view of the great social change just

Written especially for this book.

taking place in society at large and in health services as a particular field, it would be hardly worth while to complete a motivational study of this kind. The 20 lengthy interviews obtained, although fragmentary parts of an unfinished study, revealed some aspects of the motivation of women in medicine; their results are partly corroborated by other research[2] and their brief summary presented below might be generally useful.

1. Twelve of the 20 female physicians interviewed were children of physicians and the rest came from the background of professional-managerial families. Although physicians generally tend to be recruited from high socio-economic strata, our impression was that medicine as a family occupation and high socio-economic status were even more pronounced among female than among male physicians.

2. Money, or rather, lack of money, never seemed to have presented a problem in the lives of the respondents. As for the future, the women clearly stated that they were not interested in making money and competing with men for well-paying medical positions. Without exception they planned to avoid the most entrepreneurial form of medical practice, private solo practice with its usually high financial reward and equally heavy work load, as well as those specialties (e.g., surgery) which are known to secure above-the-average incomes.

3. The respondents agreed that medicine as an occupation suits only a few exceptional women who are not interested in the social amenities of college life, but are greatly committed to having a career of their own, who have great self-confidence and much energy (both physical and mental) and are not loath to face some embarrassing situations in life.

4. They agreed that marriage and medical career are compatible for women provided reasonable family planning is observed. But medicine is definitely not for girls who are of the "housefrau" type, who wish to get married early or have many children.

5. They seemed to agree (although with some exceptions and with some qualifications) that there were no formal restrictions upon female medical students or women in medicine, but at the same time certain informal restrictions existed both on the part of the public (such as an unwillingness of men to accept women as their doctors) and medical institutions as well (such as the hiring practices of certain hospitals and the admission policy of certain special boards).

6. They agreed that the female role does restrict medical careers and makes it difficult, or perhaps impossible, for women to give the same undivided attention and time to their work as their male colleagues do. They thought that shorter working hours, shorter careers in terms of years, and greater reliance on part-time positions were particularly for women.

There cannot be much doubt that these comments characterized rather well the problems of medical women in the 1960's; yet, by the time the respondents articulated them, they had to recognize signs of a changing world also. The country as a whole was in the midst of a major social transformation which in its accomplishments promised to amount to a more or less peaceful revolution. Its most conspicuous and closely interrelated manifestations were the civil rights movement, the war on poverty, and the women's liberation movement which in their present state appear to change the entire social texture of America. Their effect in the field of medicine can be briefly assessed.

The civil rights movement, among other achievements, opened the doors of the medical schools before the children of minority groups.[3] Their entry represented the admission of a new type of student, hardly seen before in most of our medical colleges. At the same time it gave a new impetus to the demand that women, too, should be admitted in greater numbers to the schools of medicine.

The war on poverty carried broader medical implications. It demanded better health care for the poverty population (and, in fact, for the nation as a whole) and, in defiance of the traditions of entrepreneurial medicine, made many innovative efforts to achieve that aim. It established federally financed health programs, neighborhood health centers and other facilities for providing the needed care and it popularized new models of medical care such as comprehensive and community care systems.[4] With such an expansion of the field, at a time when the shortage of trained medical manpower was acutely felt, it required the services of more doctors, and particularly of female doctors. It created many new salaried positions in the fields of family medicine and maternal and child health; the positions were eminently suited to women but there were not enough women to fill them. Perhaps for the first time in history, medical journals carried vacancy announcements which expressed a preference for women. The conservative medical groups did not hesitate to propose solutions (such as the employment of females in auxiliary capacities as mere helpers of busy doctors) which were designed to keep medicine an exclusively male profession, but their attempts could not offset what seemed to be the requirement of the time. The war on poverty convincingly proved before the whole nation that more women doctors were needed.

Women's liberation movement, as the third major force on the social scene, is as complex in its aim and mass appeal as the civil rights movement or the war on poverty.[5] Its main aim can be properly described as essentially social-psychological: the liberation of women from the antiquated interpretation of the female role which has restricted them to the often glorified duties of serving children and spouses and renouncing their personal self-development in fields of their own choice. A logical consequence of this aim is the growing interest among women in finding appropriate places within the context of professional work, places which do not relegate them to auxiliary roles in serving men bosses (as nurses serve physicians), yet, do not necessarily put them into direct competition with men.

Thus, the major social movements of the last decade have built up a strong pressure toward establishing an equality of the sexes and, within this broad scope, toward admitting more women into medicine, admitting them without those mainly informal restrictions that operated before. In view of this, one has to ask the question: What were the results and achievements of those social movements as far as women's place in medicine is concerned?

As the first and undoubtedly most important result one has to point to the increasing admission of women to the country's medical schools. In 1960 exactly 600 women applicants were accepted by the medical schools of the United States who made up 7.0 percent of all applicants admitted, while in 1968 (the last year for which data are available) 976 women applicants were accepted, making up 9.7 percent of all applicants admitted.[6] The percentage increase from 7.0 to 9.7 is by no means spectacular, but the later figure is almost double of the average admission rate of women in the 1950's. Moreover, some further figures should also be considered for a better understanding of the general trend.

Between 1960 and 1968 the total number of applicants to medical schools greatly increased, but the percentage of women among the total applicants remained the same, about 8 to 9 percent. Thus, the percentage of admitted applicants was pretty much the same for both sexes and female applicants had the same chances as male applicants to gain admission to medical schools. In particular, there was no discriminatory difference between the Medical College Admission Test scores of men and women applicants.[7] In view of such facts one is willing to share the opinion of a female physician, herself a member of an admission committee, that in the mid-sixties medical schools on the whole admitted students "on the basis of the quality of the applicants" and without any discrimination for sex.[8] One may, of course, inquire into the reasons why so few women decide to go into medicine and apply to medical colleges; some answers to these will be presented below.

Another encouraging sign should also be noted. Up to the mid-sixties a small number of medical schools produced an unduly large proportion of women physicians, while other medical schools practically excluded women from among their students. The Women's Medical College of Pennsylvania (Philadelphia) was historically the leading institution for the production of women physicians; about 1965, one out of every 15 women physicians in the United States was the alumna of Woman's Medical College. In addition, four more medical schools made noteworthy contributions to the training of female physicians: the University of Puerto Rico (with 16.2 percent of its total medical graduates being women), University of California, San Francisco (11.1 percent of all graduates being women), Johns Hopkins University (10.7 percent) and Boston University (10.1 percent). On the other hand, in three medical schools less than one percent of the graduates were women: St. Louis University had a rate of 0.9 percent of women among its graduates, Jefferson Medical College only 0.3 percent, while Dartmouth none.[9] There can be no doubt that such variations in the percentages reflect the policy of the institutions involved, and institutional policies can seldom remain insensitive, at any rate not for any length of time, to general social trends. As the available fragmentary data indicate, the present-day social pressure has made its impact felt, and some medical schools, instead of waiting for applicants to come at their own choosing, have taken steps to recruit women or, at any rate, call the attention of college girls to the opportunities in medicine. One may question how general and how well planned this recruitment activity is, but, in any case, it represents a significant departure from previous practices.

The acceptance of women by the medical profession and the

public at large also seems to change, although the results still appear to be somewhat vague, showing promises for the future rather than actual achievements. The limited acceptance of women by the medical system is well reflected by the fact that the sexes are unequally distributed among the various specialties and types of practice. For example, women are overrepresented in pediatrics, psychiatry, anesthesiology and pathology, but grossly underrepresented in general surgery and all surgical specialties. Similarly, women are more likely than men to work in salaried positions, but less likely than men to be in private practice and, particularly, in private solo practice.[10]

It can be hardly expected that the recent social trends would affect women's preference for pediatrics or their conspicuous absence from surgery. But a new and rapidly growing field of medical specialization has been initiated, that of family medicine, which seems to hold a great appeal to women and, when fully established, may help towards a more equal distribution of women in medical fields. At the same time, we are witnessing a general restructuring of medical practice arrangements whereby the old forms of entrepreneurial practice decline in importance and an increasing number of physicians come to depend in an increasing degree on salaried incomes. Thus, the general trend is toward an equalization between the sexes in types of practice and perhaps even in the arrangements for holding part-time positions.

It has been repeatedly observed that certain segments of the public prefer the man to the woman physician and the latter experience a reluctant acceptance in some situations of the doctor-patient relationships. Thus, one study asked 1500 low-income mothers in the Boston area what kind of doctor they like most. Thirteen percent of the respondents checked "man," while only 2 percent of them checked "woman." Such answers indicate a slight preference for men doctors but, at the same time, suggest that the overwhelming majority of mothers do not consider sex as a factor that would determine their liking or disliking doctors. It is not known what answers men would have given to the same question, but it is generally assumed that men prefer male physicians, with the lower-class masculine males and adolescent boys being most reluctant toward getting in bodily contact with women physicians during physical examinations.

Another study of interest asked housewives in a middle class and a working-class suburb about their possible acceptance of, not female doctors, but auxiliary medical personnel and concluded that middle-class housewives were much more likely than working-class ones to accept female auxiliary workers.[11] A combination of the data suggests that, among women, the reluctance in accepting women physicians is the function of lower educational attainments, underprivileged status, and a certain feeling of alienation — and such facts and attitudes, although they represent real problematic factors in present-day medical care, can be changed by social movements and educational efforts. Perhaps the women's liberation movement is in itself a force that will make women professionals more acceptable to the public.

These are the achievements of the last few years and they appear to be rather modest. Perhaps they can be better evaluated if we compare them to the situation in some other countries. Among all the countries known, the Soviet Union has the greatest number of women physicians: in 1963, 75 percent of all doctors were women and, although this proportion might have somewhat declined since then, medicine is there for all practical purposes a female profession much the same way as school teaching is in this country.[12] It should be added, however, that in the Soviet Union practically all doctors are employees of the state health system, they work shorter hours, have considerably less relative income and less prestige than doctors in the United States.[13] No other country comes near to the preponderance of women found in the Soviet Union. In the Philippines, Finland and Israel one out of every four doctors is a woman, in Germany and Italy one out of every five, in England and Sweden one out of every six, while in the United States one out of every fourteen.[14]

In view of this world situation, why has our progress been so slow and what further achievements can we expect in the near future? Any answer to these questions must consider those many social factors that affect the entry of women into medicine. The antiquated definitions of the female role are rapidly changing and a momentous social movement demands a greater representation of women in medicine; but such pressures are counterbalanced by many forces that militate against the increase in the number of professional women. Paradoxically enough, the foremost of the opposing forces is our general affluence.

In those countries where the proportion óf women doctors is the highest, the level of income and the standard of living is considerably lower than in the United States. In the Soviet Union and the Philippines a family needs two independent incomes to sustain itself on a level comparable to that of the American middle class and even in England the average income of a general practitioner imposes a certain modesty upon his standard of living. Under these circumstances many young women plan to, and later have to, spend the major part of their productive years in the labor force. Hence, the financial rewards that medicine holds out have a great appeal to women and motivate many women to invest in their future careers the education and work that the practice of medicine requires. In the United States, however, the same financial reward has little appeal to women. The young middle-class girl who has to make a decision about entering medical school, is likely to visualize her future as marriage with a middle-class boy who after his graduation will be able to maintain his family on the customary standard of living. Hence, few young girls are willing to take the rigors of professional education and career. Characteristically enough, the years of American affluence witness a proportional but general decline of women among the students of graduate schools.[15]

In addition we have to consider the fact that in present-day American medicine entrepreneurship and charisma are the two hallmarks of successful doctors.[16] The former affects professional income directly because it enables the physician to increase his income through greater work load, longer work hours, managerial skill or capital investment; while charisma, which specifies the physician as leader in times of distress, greatly contributes to personal prestige and status. But both of them are male characteristics, contrary to the female role; their psychological bases are less likely to be present in the female personality and, under any circumstances and for many reasons, females usually do not display them in their work career. Thus, it is small wonder that one factor that restricts the acceptance of female physicians is the preference of the public for a male on occasions of dramatic illnesses and related emergency situations when the charismatic leadership of the doctor is most needed. Although the present trend is quite clearly towards a bureaucratic medical care (exemplified by governmentally sponsored health facilities and group practices) where the individual performance of the single practitioner has a reduced importance, both entrepreneurship and charisma are likely to stay with American medicine and affect the future status of women physicians.

To sum it up, there is a strong social trend toward increasing the role of women in medicine and, at the same time, there are strong counterbalancing forces which tend to keep down the number entering medicine as well as the number of women achieving positions of medical leadership. The outcome of such opposing trends is characteristic of our changing world in general: some progress but rather small and slow. The number of women students has increased in medical schools but, in view of the present rate, it cannot be expected that women physicians will make up any time in the near future more than 10 percent of the country's practicing physicians, nor can it be expected that the number and power of women in positions of medical leadership will change in any noticeable degree.

Provided the present social forces continue to operate, what can be done to increase the progress of women in medicine? One recommendation presents itself and it should be considered: a more meaningful recruitment of women on the part of medical schools. So far medical students, and women in particular, have tended to come from the upper crust of our society, this small group which can furnish but few exceptional young women who are willing to select medicine as their career. Now it is reasonable to ask that the base from which future physicians are recruited should be radically expanded. This requires major changes in the admission policy of the schools and the life style of the student, and such a profound change is without precedent in the history of our medical education. Yet, it is a task that can, and must, be accomplished; medical schools must direct their recruitment activities to young women of the hitherto neglected social clases. So far many young girls from the less fortunate classes have given up their plans for a medical career because they knew that such plans were impractical. In the future a new and imaginative recruitment policy might be able to change this long-standing attitude and find untapped woman power. But at present, as far as women and medicine are concerned, our changing world has presented us with many new problems without bringing any of those problems to their final solution.

NOTES

1. John Kosa and Robert E. Coker, "The Female Physician in Public Health: Conflict and Reconciliation of the Sex and Professional Roles," *Sociology and Social Research* 49 (April 1965), 294-305.

2. The literature on women physicians is not extensive and of uneven quality. The thorough studies by Carol Lopate (*Women in Medicine.* Baltimore, Md.: The Johns Hopkins Press, 1968) and Susan Chapin Holton ("The Woman Physician: A Study of Role Conflict," *Journal of Medical Women's Association,* 24 (August 1969), 638-645 offer the essential picture. They are supplemented by May E. Roman, "Women and Psychiatry," *Journal of the American Medical Women's Association* 24 (August 1969), 629-636. Many official pamphlets give statistical background data: *Special Report on Women and Graduate Study* (Resources for Medical Research, Report No. 13, June 1968), US Dept. of HEW — National Institute of Health; see further the Special Statistical Series of the American Medical Association (*Selected Characteristics of the Physician Population* by C. N. Theodore and J. N. Haug, Chicago: AMA, 1968; and *Medical School Alumni* by C. N. Theodore, G. E. Sutter and J. N. Haug, Chicago: AMA, 1968) which omit any textual interpretation of the printed tabular material, making the published data almost impossible to handle. *The Fuller Utilization of the Woman Physician* (Washington, D.C.: Women's Bureau, U.S. Dept. of Labor, January 1968) presents essentially promotional material. Two excellent studies describe the situation in England: Margot Jefferys and Patricia M. Elliott, *Women in Medicine.* London: Office of Health Economics, 1966; and Margot Jefferys, Suzette Gauvain and Ozdemir Gulesen, "Comparison of Men and Women in Medical Training," *Lancet,* No. 7400, June 26, 1965, 1381-1383.

3. M. S. Melton, "Health Manpower and Negro Health: The Negro Physician," *Journal of Medical Education,* 43 (July 1968); Herbert M. Morais, *The History of the Negro in Medicine.* Washington, D.C.: Publishers Company, 1968; Dennis B. Dove, "Minority Enrollment in U.S. Medical Schools," *Journal of Medical Education,* 45 (March 1970), 179-181.

4. John Kosa, Aaron Antonovsky and Irving K. Zola (eds.), *Poverty and Health.* Cambridge, Mass.: Harvard University Press, 1969.

5. As for the background see the series of reprints of older books collected in the *Source Library of the Women's Movement* (Source Book Press, so far 40 titles.) As for the present time see *American Women. The Report of the President's Commission on the Status of Women.* New York: Scribner's, 1965; Jacquelyn A. Mattfeld and Carol G. Van Aken (eds.), *Women and the Scientific Professions.* Cambridge, Mass.: M.I.T. Press, 1965. Of the voluminous popular literature just a few items should be mentioned: Betty Friedan, *The*

Feminine Mystique. New York: W. W. Norton, 1963; Kate Millett, *Sexual Politics.* New York: Doubleday, 1970; Robin Morgan (ed.), *Sisterhood Is Powerful.* New York: Random House, 1970.

6. Frank T. Stritter, Jack G. Hutton and W. F. Dube, "Study of U.S. Medical School Applicants," *Journal of Medical Education,* 45 (April 1970), 195-205.

7. Lopate, *Women in Medicine,* p. 72.

8. Helen S. Pitman, "Admission of Women to HMS," *Harvard Medical Alumni Bulletin,* 43 (Spring, 1969), p. 3.

9. *Medical School Alumni,* p. 8.

10. Holton, "The Woman Physician," p. 639; *Selected Characteristics of the Physician Population,* pp. 33-38; *The Fuller Utilization of the Woman Physician,* p. 73.

11. Unpublished data from the study of "Health Care Among Low-income Families," that the author carried out together with Joel J. Alpert, Robert J. Haggerty, Leon Robertson and Margaret C. Heagarty (Harvard Medical School).

12. Mark G. Field, *Soviet Socialized Medicine.* New York: Free Press, 1967, pp. 118-120.

13. Alexander Solzhenitsyn's famous novel (*Cancer Ward.* New York: Farrar, Straus, 1969) gives an interesting description of the social status and life style of Soviet doctors.

14. *The Fuller Utilization of the Woman Physician,* p. 9.

15. Eli Ginzberg, "The Woman Physician," in his *Men, Money and Medicine.* New York: Columbia University Press, 1969, 135-147.

16. John Kosa, "Entrepreneurship and Charisma in the Medical Profession," *Social Science and Medicine,* 4 (July 1970), 25-40.

fifty-two

Women in Academe

PATRICIA ALBJERG GRAHAM

American colleges and universities, struggling to accustom themselves to the state of siege mentality in which, it seems, their present and future work must be carried out, are in for another round of crisis — this one dealing with the "woman question." In colleges and universities throughout the country, high pressure has been applied by women intent on securing rights equal to those of men in academic position and preferment. In this atmosphere, many academic administrators must look wistfully back to the first two centuries of higher education in the United States, when women were simply excluded from collegiate precincts. From the founding of Harvard in 1636 to the opening of Oberlin in 1837, it was not possible for a young woman to attend college in this country. By the mid-19th century, some American colleges had begun to admit women to their classes, in response to pressures similar in some respects to those affecting higher education in the United States today. One source of the pressure was ideological — the conviction that women were entitled to the same educational opportunities as men. From this stimulus, which, significantly, was contemporaneous with the abolition movement, came the establishment of certain colleges designed specifically for women, and of others which admitted both men and women. But the major impetus for women's higher education came in the second half of the 19th century, a time of dire economic need for many colleges, caused chiefly by shrinking masculine enrollments. The sag in college attendance was attributed to the Civil War, to economic

From SCIENCE, Vol. 169, No. 3952 (1970), pp. 1284-1290. Reprinted by permission.

depressions, and to dissatisfaction with the college curriculum. College trustees and presidents saw women as potential sources of tuition revenues that would permit the colleges to remain open. The principal reason, then, for the 19th-century breakthrough in admitting women to colleges with men was economic rather than ideological, and these circumstances were not highly conducive to developing plans that would take particular account of the educational needs of women. Even such state institutions as the University of Wisconsin first admitted women during the Civil War when many men students had joined the army.

After the Civil War very few colleges were established solely for men, the major exception being Roman Catholic institutions. The most important women's colleges were still in the East, where traditional institutions of the Ivy League — as it would later be called — dominated the educational scene; these, on the whole, saw no need to include women. In the West, where endowments were small or nonexistent and the financial pressures were greater, resistance to the admission of women was much less. There the critical institutions were state universities, and by the turn of the century most were coeducational. There, too, the denominational colleges, limited as they were in endowments and dependent upon tuition, and now in competition with the less expensive public institutions, frequently became coeducational. The argument is sometimes made that the important role the women on the frontier played is substantially responsible for the greater degree of coeducation in the West. Although this may have been a factor, it seems not to have been as determining a one as the economic considerations, or as the nascent women's rights movement, which was heavily centered in the East. Well into the 20th century the single-sex colleges in the East remained the prestigious places for young women to be educated.

By 1920 women constituted 47 percent of the undergraduates in the country and were receiving roughly 15 percent of the Ph.D.'s. In 1930 the proportion remained about the same. Today women constitute only 40 percent of the undergraduate student body and receive about 10 percent of the doctorates. The total number of students, of course, has increased enormously during these years. Although the percentage of women receiving doctorates is rising gradually from a low in the late 1950's and early 1960's, it still has not reached the high attained in the late 1920's. Various studies have also shown that between 75 and 90 percent of the "well-qualified" students who do not go on to college are women.

In the present movement toward coeducation at some of the well-known single-sex colleges, particularly Princeton, Yale, Vassar, and Sarah Lawrence, economic considerations are again an important basis for the decision to admit members of the opposite sex. The current financial dilemmas of many colleges and universities are well known, but the cure is no longer simply a matter of enlarging the student body. Although these institutions are not short of applicants, some of them at least believe that the most outstanding high school graduates are choosing other, coeducational colleges because of a desire not to be isolated from young persons of the opposite sex. This is an economic argument of a rather more sophisticated type, based on considerations of human capital. In some cases the admission of women follows by several decades the abolition of quotas for Jews and, more recently, the initiation of efforts to admit blacks. Again, the parallel with the mid-19th century is striking: the women's rights advocates rode the coattails of the abolitionists much as the current feminists are trailing the black power movement.

The Current Situation

What, then, is the current situation for women in academe? Women constitute about 18 percent of the staffs of institutions of higher education, being distributed principally at small colleges and universities and in the lower ranks of other institutions. They tend to be concentrated in such fields as education, social service, home economics, and nursing. For example, 6 of the 11 women who were full professors at the University of Chicago in 1968-69 (there are 464 men full professors) were in social work. At present 2 percent of the full professors at the University of Chicago are women, in contrast to 8 percent at the turn of the century, when Chicago was (as it still is) one of the top half dozen universities in the nation. Alice Rossi reports (1) that 30 percent of the Ph.D.'s awarded in sociology go to women but that only 1 percent of the full professors in sociology in top graduate schools are women, 5 percent are associate professors, and 39 percent are subprofessorial appointees, such as "research associates."

The 2 percent figure for the proportion of full professors who are women also applies at Stanford University, where 15 percent of the graduate students are women. At Columbia University, which has probably granted more doctorates to women than any other institution and has for years enrolled a high proportion of women in its graduate departments (about 20 percent), just over 2 percent of the full professors are women. Barnard College, the women's undergraduate division of Columbia, which has its own faculty, for many years in the first third of the 20th century hired women primarily, as did most of the other women's colleges. Since World War II the proportion of men professors has risen steadily. Barnard still has a higher proportion of women on its faculty than any other of the "Seven Sister" colleges (only six of which have separate faculties), probably because there are more highly educated women in New York City than in South Hadley or Poughkeepsie. The representation of women at Barnard in 1968-69 in the professorial ranks is still weighted heavily at the bottom, with women constituting 82 percent of the non-professorial teaching staff, 64 percent of the assistant professors, 54 percent of the associate professors, and a mere 22 percent of the full professors. Nonetheless, Barnard still has a woman president, whereas only one of the other five faculties (Wellesley) is presided over by a woman. Mary I. Bunting heads Radcliffe, but it does not have a separate faculty. In the last 5 years men have replaced women presidents at Vassar, Bryn Mawr, and Sarah Lawrence. Both Smith and Mount Holyoke have men presidents. Kirkland, the newest bidder for prestige as a women's coordinate college, has a man president.

Recent studies, such as Helen S. Astin's (2), indicate that, contrary to the dire pronouncements of some graduate school officers, women who receive Ph.D.'s are likely to use them in a professional capacity. Ninety-one percent of the women who received doctorates in 1957-58 were employed in 1964, and 79 percent of them had not interrupted their careers during that time (2, p. 57). Even more startling to those of both sexes who assume that the reason women are not in better positions is that they do not publish enough is the research of Rita Simon, Shirley Merritt Clark, and Kathleen Galway (3), which showed that married women Ph.D.'s who were employed full time published slightly more than either men Ph.D.'s or unmarried women Ph.D.'s.

Other studies, such as one made by Lindsey R. Harmon and

another by the National Academy of Sciences (NAS), report, on the basis of various measures, that women doctorate holders have somewhat greater academic ability than their male counterparts (4). Further, women who were married at the time of receiving the Ph.D. were more capable academically than their unmarried female contemporaries. Nonetheless, the fate of married women Ph.D.'s is somewhat discouraging. The NAS report states:

> In general, the rate at which women achieve the status of full professor is slower than for men, the average lag varying from two to five years in the bio-sciences and up to as much as a decade in the social sciences. There is a marital status difference also. Considering data on women for all fields combined, the single women lead the married ones by five to ten years. At any given time, 10 to 20 per cent more of the single than married women have achieved full professor status.

Not surprisingly, the NAS also found that the salaries received by married women in general were 70 to 75 percent of those received by men at the same interval after receipt of the doctorate. Salaries of single women were more variable, but on the average they were somewhat higher than those of the married women, though still markedly lower than men's salaries.

Possible Explanations

Discrimination. One can think of various explanations for the considerable discrepancy between the ability and the professional position of women Ph.D.'s. One possibility is overt discrimination, but obvious disregard of women scholars is not as common today as it was in earlier years. The confident announcement of a senior professor in a leading history department less than 10 years ago that, as long as he was a member of the department, there would never be a woman professor in it was at the time accepted without a murmur. His view held sway until his retirement. Now, in that department of nearly 50 full-time members, one full professor and one assistant professor, both in esoteric specialties, are women. Explanations given by the department for the absence of women from the populous fields of European and American history are vague. For many years about 15 percent of the graduate students in that department have been women. The discrimination is now much more subtle and less easily countered.

Internal ambivalences. Preeminent among the reasons for the poor representation of women in the higher echelons of the professional world is a psychological-cultural one. Ellen and Kenneth Keniston of Yale University have written perceptively about the "internal ambivalences" that most American women feel about combining career and family (5). These ambivalences are especially acute in the years between 18 and 25, years which, in this society, men generally devote to intense preparation for a career. For women these years are likely to be a time in which they seek affirmation of their femininity, an activity likely to be at variance with serious vocational commitment. These activities are certainly not the only ones young people engage in, but they are likely to be the ones invested with the greatest psychic energy.

Some young women are able to do graduate work and to do it well in these years, but few pass through this period without severe qualms about the desirability of planning for a demanding professional life. Men, too, are beset by a variety of doubts during these years, but for the majority of them, at least, academic success does not bring substantial psychic problems as it does for women. Matina Horner has recently given unfinished stories, identical except for the name of the protagonist, to groups of young men and women for comment (6).In one set "Bill" is at the top of his medical school class; in the other set "Anne" is at the top. Both the young men and the young women believed that Bill was headed for a bright and happy future whereas many believed that Anne would face many problems as a result of her academic achievement. Matina Horner concludes,

> For women, then, the desire to achieve is often contaminated by what I call the *motive to avoid success.* I define it as the fear that success in competitive achievement situations will lead to negative consequences, such as unpopularity and loss of femininity.

To expect young women to buck the cultural standards for females is to demand of them much more than is expected of any man attempting to succeed in his field, since men are supposed to be successful. The problem for young women is not eased by the fact that they see few women occupying positions of importance in the academic, professional, and business worlds. Some of those who are there are unmarried, and few young women deliberately choose the single life. Others are the rare individuals who manage to marry a brilliant and successful husband, have five children, write intelligently on a variety of topics, assume a major administrative position, and at the age of 40, be featured on the beauty pages of a woman's magazine. Most young women rightly recognize such an achievement as truly exceptional, and girls in this society do not think of themselves as conquerors of the world. "Models" of this sort sometimes lack effectiveness because undergraduates simply refuse to aspire to such heights.

Aspiration and expectation. The problem of aspiration is closely tied to the internal ambivalences. If one is uncertain about whether one should have a career, one cannot aspire, either publicly or privately, to be an art historian, a plasma physicist, or a professor of philosophy. Women's low expectations for themselves so infect the society that both men and women refuse to think of women as generally likely to occupy important posts. A riddle currently popular in the cocktail party circuit concerns a father and son driving down a highway. There is a terrible accident in which the father is killed, and the son, critically injured, is rushed to a hospital. There the surgeon approaches the patient and suddenly cries, "My God, that's my son!" The group is then asked how this story can be true. All sorts of replies requiring immense ingenuity are forthcoming: complicated stepfather relationships are suggested, sometimes even artifical insemination. Almost invariably the storyteller must supply the answer: "The surgeon is his mother."

The problem, then, of aspiration and of expectation is acute. The Kenistons have pointed to the absence of an aristocratic tradition in American as one factor depressing the level of women's aims. They point out that in Europe "women of the upper classes have had enough leisure and freedom from family needs to permit them, if they choose, to 'work' outside their homes." Except in the South and possibly in the Boston area — both places which have nurtured a number of unusual and talented women — the United States has lacked, not to say discouraged the growth of, such a leisured class. The South, which in this respect as in so many others does not fit the usual generalizations, has produced some of the best-known contemporary writers in America, such as Flannery O'Connor, Katherine Anne Porter, Eudora Welty, and Carson McCullers.

But Boston and the South cannot change the nation, much as

both have sometimes wished to try. There are few hard data on the question, but the number of women Ph.D.'s in the United States today who have close ties to another cultural heritage is probably substantial. For example, both the first woman full professor at Princeton (who was apointed to the professorship in 1968) and the recently named special assistant to the president for coeducation, at Yale, the former a Ph.D. in sociology and the latter a Ph.D. in chemistry, came to the United States as young girls, one from Austria and the other from Germany. The author of the most recent major work on women Ph.D.'s herself grew up in Greece. A leader of the Columbia Women's Liberation Movement is English. All these women have direct experience with another culture and presumably recognize a greater variety of options for women than the stereotype of middle America currently exemplified by Mrs. Nixon and Mrs. Agnew.

Another substantial category of women Ph.D.'s is comprised of the daughters of professional women. Learned pediatricians and psychiatrists to the contrary, the daughters of working mothers seem more inclined to pursue definite career patterns than other women are. My own mother received her Ph.D. in 1925 and taught in Alabama State College for Women until her marriage and then only sporadically (she was a victim of the nepotism rule). When Princeton hired its first female assistant dean this year,the university selected a woman whose mother is director of the New Jersey State Council on Aging. Mary Bunting's mother was a leader in public education in New York City.

No doubt Princeton and other universities are completely unaware of the way in which their women fit into these three major categories, but the fit is striking. Incidentally, Princeton's second woman full professor, who will join the faculty in the fall of 1970, is a Virginian by birth.

The "internal ambivalences" remain for the girl of more or less ordinary ability. If she wants to marry, bear children, and also have a serious and responsible position, whom can she find to exemplify such a pattern? Unless she has gone to one of the women's colleges, which still have larger proportions of women faculty than coeducational institutions have, she is not likely to find many models, although probably more now than she would have found 5 or 10 years ago. If she is impolitic enough to suggest that something is wrong with a society in which it appears so difficult for a woman to achieve these kinds of goals, she is likely to be subjected to the harshest kind of argument — not anger but ridicule, as evidenced by the recent article in *Harper's* by a young Harvard graduate who had returned to the United States after several years in Europe and found to his consternation that a feminist movement was under way. In her formative state she may well opt out of a Ph.D. program or accept a "research associate" position instead of holding out for the degree or the assistant or associate professorship she deserves.

Publication. Another major reason usually given for the low proportion of women in top positions in universities is that they do not publish. This may well be true, despite the Simon-Clark-Galway study, which indicated that married women Ph.D.'s publish slightly more than men Ph.D.'s do. Simple numbers of items on bibliographies are not a guide to quality. Probably one of the most important reasons why most women Ph.D.'s do not publish as widely as men Ph.D's do, if this is indeed true, is that they are not put into positions in which they must. Research and writing for publication are not easy, and a great many people would not publish unless it was necessary. For example, if a young man is appointed an assistant professor at a major university shortly after receiving his Ph.D., the chances are better than nine out of ten that he is married. Presumably he is supporting his wife and his growing family. He knows that if he expects to remain at the university beyond his 6 or so allotted years as an assistant professor, he must publish. Furthermore, as his family grows he needs more money, and his wife, whose status in a community is largely a reflection of her husband's position, is usually eager for him to be promoted and may even be willing to help him with his research. Most important, a man expects to be a success, at least in a modest way, and most men are willing to exert some effort to achieve this.

A woman's situation is very different. One of the cardinal social rules is that she should not be more successful than her husband, especially in his line of work. Nearly half of the recent women Ph.D.'s who are married have husbands who also have professional degrees. For example, all but one of the husbands of the married women Ph.D.'s holding professional appointments at Princeton in 1970 have doctorates. The remaining one expects to receive his Ph.D. at Harvard soon. But people in some circles question whether a woman with an advanced degree should succeed at all. The chances are that, if she is married, her place of residence has been selected because it offers the best position for her husband, not for her. Often, if she is teaching, it is in an institution less prestigious than her husband's, and there she is under less pressure to publish. Sometimes she rationalizes her nonresearch on the basis that research would not be helpful to her professionally anyway, so why should she bother. Her chances of having secretarial help and graduate-student assistance are probably less than those of men professors. In short, incentives for her to do research are generally missing.

Single women, who theoretically have much greater geographic mobility than married women, can seek a position in an institution in which extensive publication is not expected. In fact, until very recently that was about the only place in which they were likely to be hired, since the faculties of the most prestigious institutions were almost entirely male. Unless she published, she would probably not be hired away from the small institution at a higher academic rank. Often she need not publish because departments frequently assign onerous committee duties to women, who accept them too willingly and then use them as excuses for not doing research.

The problem of time. Another serious obstacle to women's (particularly married women's) professional advancement is the simple one of time. There are just not enough hours in the day to do all she must. A recent UNESCO study (7) revealed that the average working mother had 2.8 hours of free time on a typical weekday, as compared with 4.1 for a working man.

Another way of viewing this question is to note that women Ph.D.'s in the United States spend about 28 hours per week, on the average, on household tasks (2, p. 95). Although we are fond of talking of the great advances made by technology in freeing women from domestic tasks, the working mother's concern for her children is not eased by possession of an automatic washer-dryer or dishwasher. What she needs, and what she finds increasingly difficult to find, is household help — persons who are competent and reliable and will assist her in caring for her children and running her house. Day care centers are certainly needed, but even they do not solve the problem of having to vacuum the living room and change the beds.

The suburban syndrome. Related to the problem of time and of inadequate household help is the suburban syndrome, in which both of these problems are accentuated. More and more

Americans live in outlying urban areas, and it becomes harder and harder for wives to find jobs that do not take them away from their homes for long periods of the day. If one must spend 3 hours each day commuting and then come home to perform the customary domestic chores, the amount of energy left at the end of the day is small indeed. In suburban communities domestic help is notoriously difficult to find. Complicating the picture even further is the usual social custom of such towns, in which people generally entertain at dinner parties in their own homes. In a city it is still possible to entertain one's friends by taking them to restaurants or concerts, but in many suburban communities there are no public facilities where one can spend a pleasant evening. The home and the overtired woman are expected to provide the serene environment in which friends can enjoy themselves. An obvious solution is simply to reduce one's social life to the barest minimum, but this exceedingly common way of dealing with the problem works hardships on the professional woman's family and on the woman herself.

The nepotism rule. A final obstacle that a woman Ph.D. (or sometimes her husband) faces is the nepotism rule, written or unwritten, that still prevails on many campuses. Although more and more institutions are now willing to have two members of the same family teaching in one institution, few regard with enthusiasm the prospect of having a husband and wife in the same department, particularly if both are at the professorial level. Since many professional women met their husbands in graduate school (the proportion of women Ph.D.'s married to Ph.D.'s in the same field is very high in all fields except that of education, where women are less likely to be married), the question of husbands and wives being employed in the same department is very likely to occur. Rarely is the wife given the superior appointment. Typically she takes a job in another institution or works part-time as a "research associate" at her husband's institution.

Corrective Measures

If these are the problems that affect professional women on academic faculties, what are some of the steps institutions might take to alleviate them? Until very recently universities were, on the whole, not conscious of discrimination against women. Administrators were — and many still are — fond of making pious statements to the effect that all persons were treated equally, that none was discriminated against. To say this is to raise the question of what "equality" really is. Is it simply applying the same rule in all situations, or is it rather recognizing that the rules themselves may favor one group over another? For many years we gave standardized I.Q. and achievement tests to youngsters and assumed that we were treating them equally because we were giving all students identical tests. In recent years we have come to see the fallacy of this policy, and we recognize that these tests have a "cultural bias." Although they met the standard of abstract equality, they failed to meet the comparably important one of actual equality. So it is with many of the policies in the university, which apply primarily to men. Women who wish to teach must meet these similarly "culturally biased" standards, and what is called equality in academe is only abstract equality and not actual equality.

Appointment to senior faculty and administrative posts. In order to achieve genuine or actual equality for women, colleges and universities need to make some adaptations. Preeminent among these is the need to recognize women's situations in their own academic communities and then to support them adequately. Probably the most important single factor in creating an environment that is as hospitable to the aspirations of women as to men is to appoint women in significant numbers to senior faculty and administrative posts in the university. Just as "tokenism" has been rejected for the blacks, so it must be rejected for the less militant feminine majority. The appointment of women to faculty posts will provide evidence for both male and female students, and for faculty colleagues, that teaching and scholarship of the highest standards can be attained by women as well as by men. The presence of women in senior administrative positions will also encourage the able young undergraduate and graduate women at the university to believe that a secretarial career, even a glorified one, need not be their vocational ambition, and it will remind the young men who will later be employers of women that women too can be expert executives. Male professors should see successful women of their own age among their colleagues, in order that the entire faculty can justifiably encourage women students to pursue additional studies or accept demanding positions that are in line with their talents.

No doubt it is also necessary, on most campuses, to increase the number of young women in the junior faculty and administrative positions at the university, but this is generally neither as crucial nor as difficult as the senior appointments. Many mature male professors find it much easier to appoint young women to junior and subordinate positions (where they have little power) than to appoint women of their own age to positions truly equivalent to their own. Sometimes it is possible to appoint women of mature years to junior administrative positions which might otherwise be filled by bright young men but this kind of appointment may be more damaging than no female appointment at all. Few intelligent, alert coeds look forward to being rewarded in their middle years by promotion from departmental secretary to administrative associate when other administrative associates are 25-year-old men. At one leading university three assistant deans were men in their twenties or thirties; the fourth was a woman in her fifties. Many traditionally coeducational colleges are now replacing the separate dean of women and dean of men by a dean of students. Generally this reorganization, which is thought to be "progressive," means that a man is appointed. At one Midwestern state university where this was done the Dean of Women was nationally known and widely respected. The Dean of Students, who became her immediate superior, had no standing outside the community and not much locally, but he was of the same sex as the all-male administration of the university, which had been coeducational since its founding in 1869.

Ideally the women at the university should represent a variety of life styles, just as the male faculty members do. Some should be dedicated, and probably single, scholar-teachers, and others should be women who manage successfully to cope with the demands of academic life and of home and family. Some may be concerned with the particular educational needs of women students, but others may not. In appointing women professors the institution will look first for scholarliness and teaching ability, not militant feminism. As the number of women on the faculty grows, the responsibility of individual women for exemplifying female academic accomplishment will decline, and this is as it should be. When there are but a few women on a faculty, excessive demands are made upon them; not only must each fulfill the usual academic requirements but she must serve as the token woman on all kinds of committees.

Part-time professorial appointments. If the academic institutions do move vigorously to appoint more women to their faculties, they might well consider expanding the number of part-time professorial appointments with full perquisites. "Part-time" has a poor reputation among academic administrators, largely because it is assumed that the part-time person is one who is in effect "moonlighting" from a full-time job. With women scholars this is not quite the case. They have no prior institutional loyalty or obligation. Women scholars, particularly those who are married, might welcome the opportunity to teach on a part-time basis with full professional recognition. The demands on their time and energies at home are often considerable, as noted above, but at present, if they wish to be taken seriously in their fields, they must accept full-time positions. To do so frequently requires an unusual endowment of energy. If they do not wish to teach full-time, they are generally consigned to the ranks of lecturers and instructors, where they are not eligible for sabbatical leaves and other academic perquisites. Such circumstances tend to depress the status of women in the university and do not foster conditions in which they are likely to do research, which is the major means of getting out of the lower-ranking positions.

If universities permitted and even encouraged departments to appoint persons to assistant, associate, and full professorships on a part-time basis, they would be able to staff their institutions with persons of diverse interests and specialties whom they could perhaps not afford to employ on a full-time basis. In large departments these persons could supplement the traditional offerings, and in small departments which are not scheduled for substantial growth they could provide some of the necessary breadth. At senior levels, the university could select outstanding persons of proven accomplishment at salaries roughly comparable to, or less than, those now paid to lecturers and instructors. More imaginative research appointments for women might also be made along these lines.

Full provision needs to be made for opportunities for part-time faculty to shift to full-time status when the individual and the department agree that such a change would be desirable.

Similarly, tenure should be available to part-time professors, just as it is to full-time professors, and the same standard should be used in determining qualifications for promotion. Anything less would create a category of second-class citizens. Committee obligations, student advising, and the other duties associated with professorial appointments would be apportioned to part-time faculty members roughly on the basis of the full-time equivalent position; thus, for example, a half-time associate professor would have half the number of student advisers that a full-time associate professor had.

Obviously men as well as women might be interested in these part-time appointments and should be eligible for them. Departments should be cautious, however, about permitting large numbers of their members to be on part-time appointments, and they should look with some skepticism upon persons who want continuing part-time appointments in order to devote more time to remunerative activities for other institutions or businesses. These difficulties should be construed not as insurmountable but merely as requiring some additional consideration before a part-time professorial appointment is made.

Maternity leave. The appointment of women in significant numbers to faculties must involve a policy concerning pregnancy and maternity leave. Most universities currently have no such policy, and many administrators, when queried, reply that none is necessary. The principal reason why none seems necessary is that women have never been on these faculties in substantial numbers. Typically, a woman faculty member either manages to have her baby in midsummer or simply loses her appointment when she takes time off to have the baby. Not all women have been as fortunate as Millicent McIntosh, who was debating whether to accept the position of headmistress of the Brearley School in New York City. Her aunt, M. Carey Thomas, the illustrious president of Bryn Mawr, is supposed to have advised her, "Take it, you can have your babies in the summer." Mrs. McIntosh accepted the advice and went on to have five children and to become president of Barnard College. In short, academic women who become pregnant must handle this part of their life as they do all other parts — they must pretend to be as much like men as possible and not permit this event to interfere with the regular performance of their duties.

No university should be exploited by women professors who keep having children and expecting the university to pay them while they are on maternity leave. A more rational policy than the present one ought to be developed, so that pregnancy, of itself, does not discriminate against a woman scholar. It would seem that guaranteeing a woman a maximum of two 16-week maternity leaves, with pay, during her academic career would not bankrupt most colleges or universities. This would in effect be a one-semester leave with pay, twice in a woman's life. Additional pregnancies would be the woman's own financial responsibility.

Tenure. In many institutions the hurdles that must be run in order to achieve tenure are considerable. It is now standard in many fields to receive a Ph.D. when one is in one's late twenties. If the new Ph.D. accepts a teaching appointment at the assistant professor level, then ordinarily within 6 or 7 years the tenure decision is made. In many universities this means that the dissertation must have been converted to a publishable manuscript, and that some other scholarly research, ideally another book, has been completed. This 6- or 7-year period coincides with a woman's childbearing years, and, if one assumes that the couple wants two children, both are ordinarily born before a woman is 35. Therefore, the greatest pressures both for scholarly publication and for domestic performance coalesce in these years between the ages of 28 and 35.

One way of handling this difficulty is to grant women assistant professors an automatic 1-year extension, before the tenure decision is made, for each pregnancy they have, up to a maximum of two, during their nontenure years. This addition of 1 or 2 years before they are subjected to the scrutiny of their colleagues for the tenure decision would give them some additional time to complete the scholarly work necessary to justify promotion. Should they prefer that the tenure decision be made earlier, this could be done.

Husbands and wives on the same faculty. Another policy that colleges and universities would do well to adopt is one that permits husband and wife to serve on the same faculty. Twenty percent of the wives of junior faculty members at one prestigious university have Ph.D.'s, yet none is a member of the faculty. At a large Midwestern university throughout the 1930's,

1940's, and 1950's, one faculty wife published over two dozen articles and one book and coauthored two other books with her husband, yet was never permitted to become a member of the department, despite a research record superior to that of all but two members of the department. Obviously, having both husband and wife on the faculty can lead to some awkward circumstances, particularly if both are junior members of the same department and only one promotion can be made. The other frequently cited difficult case is that in which one spouse is a tenured member of the department and the other is up for promotion. The supporters of nepotism rules cite such cases with great alacrity, and they are absolutely right in pointing to the possibilities for hard feeling that can develop within a department. Nonetheless, the case is rarely made for the advantages of having two members of a family employed at the same institution. In this era of considerable faculty mobility and declining institutional loyalty, one way of insuring faculty support is to employ both husband and wife in positions commensurate with their ability and trainings. A husband and wife who both enjoy their work will be much less inclined than a single individual to heed the siren call of another university. In those fields in which collaboration is essential to research, husbands and wives are often much more effective as a team than either would be alone, hence the university is brought distinction by having both members on its faculty.

Although the problems should not be minimized and any department thinking of hiring such a husband-and-wife team should examine the situation carefully, any university rule which explicitly forbids such a practice should be abolished. Departments and senior faculty members should be strong enough to say starkly that only one spouse will be hired because only one is really wanted or needed, rather than dragging out a university regulation that officially prohibits the practice. The proportion of women Ph.D.'s who are married is increasing, and the nepotism question will become more acute.

Day care centers. A great boon to women faculty members with children would be the establishment of university day care centers. In these days of constricted university budgets this recommendation is perhaps the most expensive of all to implement, but it does deserve careful consideration. On those many campuses which now have nursery schools in connection with

their School of Education programs for training nursery and primary school teachers, it would probably not be very difficult to convert these laboratory schools, which now function for the convenience of the School of Education, to all-day centers. For mothers to have a place where they can leave their children, confident that they will be well cared for, would be a tremendous help. Ideally these centers should be open to all employees and students of the university with preference in admission given to children of women attached to the university. Thus the women graduate students who have children would have a real chance to finish the work for their degrees despite their maternal responsibilities. Similarly, women employed by the university in food services and custodial capacities would have a much better place to leave their children than is frequently now the case.

A less ambitious aid than a day care center would be a placement service for domestic workers maintained by the university for the use of women faculty, administrators, students, and employees. Most universities have an extensive employment office in which they screen applicants for various jobs in the university. If this office would also supply names and references for persons willing to do cleaning, housekeeping, or babysitting, this would be a tremendous help to women working at the university. Astin found in her study of women receiving Ph.D.'s (2, p. 101) that the difficulty of finding adequate domestic help was their single greatest problem.

Curriculum changes. A recommendation less directly tied to insuring the full participation of scholarly women in the university life, but nonetheless related to it, concerns the curriculum. Departments within the university should be encouraged to review their departmental offerings to be sure that women's experience is given adequate treatment. English courses in biography, for example, might well cover women subjects as well as men. Anthropology courses might give considerable attention to male and female sex roles in various cultures. Courses in American social history could probably do better by the experience of American women in the 19th century than the usual hasty reference to the Seneca Falls convention and the suffragette movement. Much greater sophistication is needed to deal appropriately with women's historical experience; the particular psychological and cultural factors affecting women at a given time are poorly understood. In this connection the professional associations, such as the American Historical Association or the American Psychological Association, can be of genuine service by sponsoring sessions at their conventions on questions of this kind, so that historians and psychologists can become aware not only of the issues but also of what some of their colleagues are doing about them.

Continuous review. Finally, most colleges and universities would benefit from appointing a senior administrator, or establishing a committee, to keep under continuous review the status of women on their own campus. This would in effect be an individual or a group lobbying effort for the cause of women at that institution. The administrator or committee would be concerned with matters such as faculty salaries, making sure that women and men received equal compensation for equivalent services. On most campuses some change needs to be made if women are to have truly equal access to the opportunities of the institution, and change usually does not come, in a university or any other institution, simply on the basis of goodwill. Some steps needs to be taken to assure that the needed alterations will take place, and these are not likely to be taken unless some person or group recognizes that the responsibility for change is theirs.

Generally a university does not create a lobby within itself in order to create change. In fact, too often administrations are forced to modify policies as a result of lobbies within the university that the administration did not foster. Unlike many other constituencies within the university community, women undergraduates (and to a lesser degree women graduate students) have not yet pushed for the cause of women on their own campus. Many women scholars on the faculty have not done so either, although such activity is now being initiated on some campuses, chiefly among the younger women faculty members and among women teaching assistants and graduate students.

The frequently drawn analogy between the status of blacks and of women in this society is perhaps least appropriate here. There is indeed much historic similarity between the two groups, particularly in regard to the way in which their respective heritages have been ignored, the patronizing manner in which both are treated, the economic discrimination both suffer, the inability of both to "pass" as members of the dominant race or sex, and, finally, the reluctance of some of the successful members of both groups to assist younger and more militant members to attain more satisfactory situations. In two critical areas, however, the analogy does not hold, and both of these are germane to the academic situation. One is the reluctance of young women, unlike young blacks, to band together to push for their own causes, and the other is the vastly more complicated relationship that women have with their so-called oppressors, males, than blacks have with whites. Unlike blacks, who can indeed develop a separatist mode of life, women as a group cannot. In the core of their lives they are deeply involved with men (whereas blacks are not inevitably tied to whites), and the nature of that bond is such that, for many women, an overt attack upon the male establishment is not possible. A major goal of the rapidly developing militant feminist groups is to increase women's sensitivity to their plight in this society. To do this many rely heavily upon informal conversations of women in small groups in which an effort is made to build a group solidarity. The hope is that these closer ties with other women will help "emancipate" women from their dependence — economic, social, and psychic — upon men.

A Rare Opportunity

So far the radical feminists have been must successful among women in their twenties and thirties, not yet among undergraduates. This laggardness in feminine militancy on the campuses gives university administrations an opportunity to act to improve the status of women on their campuses before being confronted with demands — an opportunity of a kind that is rare these days. Difficult as it is for an academic institution to gird for change when danger is not imminent, the present moment is a time when universities can assume the leadership they have so rarely exhibited in these years of confrontation politics.

NOTES

1. Alice Rossi reported these figures and other related data to the general business meeting of the American Sociological Association on 3 September 1969. They were summarized in a mimeographed document, "Status of Women in Graduate Departments of Sociology: 1968-69," circulated by the Women's Caucus of the American Sociological Association; for excerpts, see *Science* 166, 356 (1969).

2. H. S. Astin, *The Woman Doctorate in America: Origins, Career, and Family* (Russell Sage Foundation, New York, 1969).

3. R. J. Simon, S. M. Clark, K. Galway, *Soc. Probl.* 13, 221 (1967).

4. L. R. Harmon, "High School Ability Patterns. A Backward Look from the Doctorate," *Sci. Manpower Rep. No. 6* (Office of Scientific Personnel, National Research Council, Washington, D.C., 1965); *Careers of PhD's, Academic v. Nonacademic, A Second Report on Follow-ups of Doctorate Cohorts, 1935-69.* (National Academy of Sciences, Washington, D.C., 1968).

5. E. Keniston and K. Keniston, *Amer. Scholar* 33, 355 (1964).

6. M. Horner, *Psychol. Today* 3, 36 (1969); *ibid.*, p. 61.

7. Reported in *New York Times*, 5 March 1967.

fifty-three

The Myth of the Egalitarian Family: Familial Roles and the Professionally Employed Wife

MARGARET M. POLOMA and T. NEAL GARLAND

The existence of the egalitarian family in American society has been assumed by family researchers and writers — an assumption that remains to be verified and may well be an erroneous one.[1] It is argued that a wife is no longer the property of her husband, she has the right to both vote and to run for public office, she can pursue a higher education, and she can become economically self sufficient through employment outside the home. A wife is assumed to have the same rights as her husband — and maybe then some! Admittedly she has a *different* role from that of her husband's, but no one except a militant feminist would question her *equality!*

This *difference* is well documented in the sociological literature; the question of *equality* is more difficult to resolve. In 1955 Parsons and Bales suggested that the adult feminine role was firmly anchored in the internal affairs of the family, while the adult male role is "primarily anchored in the occupational world." They further stated:

> Even if, and it seems possible, it should come about that the average married woman had some kind of job, it seems most unlikely that this relative balance would be upset; that either the roles would be reversed, or through qualitative differentiation in these respects completely erased. (Parons & Bales, 1955:15)

While we are indeed approaching the day when the average married woman has some kind of a job, we are *not* witnessing any dramatic increase in the prestige of the feminine role nor

Paper presented at the 65th annual meeting of the American Sociological Association, September, 1970. Printed by permission.

any reversal of male-female roles in the family. Blood and Wolfe (1960) have shown certain differences in the division of labor in families where the wife is employed outside the home, but there is no indication that the overall "relative balance" has been upset.

Nor is there any evidence that the woman herself has any inclination to disturb the traditional balance; the roles remain very sex segregated (Safilios-Rothschild, 1969). In a study of high school seniors, for example, Turner (1964) reported [much like Empey's (1958) earlier findings] that by and large women chose to add a special role to obtain extrinsic rewards, rather than substitute career involvement for the traditional homemaker role. He further comments: "In adding this role they leave the extrinsic reward of material living entirely in its traditional place, as a function of the husband's efforts. But so long as they accept this traditional assignment, women cannot reap the intrinsic rewards of accomplishment that their husbands will in association with extrinsic returns." More recently Angrist (1970) reported that only about one half of her female college-age respondents expected to work if their husbands' earnings sufficed. Clearly among the student group, traditional feminine roles are salient.

The importance of the role of wife and mother for the American woman is further verified in studies done on working women. Hartley (1960) found in her interviews with working mothers that these women saw their work as an "aspect of their nurturant function." Gainful employment was viewed as another way of serving the family and as an added woman's duty, not as a substitute for family obligations. Tropman's (1968) married social workers perceived their work an an extension of the traditional feminine role of "service" — serving the community much in the same way the woman is serving her family. Once more the anchor is firmly caught on the traditional feminine role of wife and mother.

The studies cited suggest that the traditional feminine role of a wife and mother, who is responsive to the will of her husband and the needs of her children, is not threatened by a married woman's employment outside the home. Paradoxically it may well be that the modern role of an employed married woman may be used to *strengthen* the traditional role of a wife and mother.

In an attempt to further explore the possibility of the continued separate but not-so-equal role of the married woman in America, a study was conducted of women who were perceived to be among the most emancipated (at least in economic terms) — the highly educated married professional woman. Our sample consisted of fifty three (53) women actively practicing in the fields of law, medicine or academia and their husbands. It was reasoned that each of these professions required an initial commitment of either earning a law degree, fulfilling the requirements of a Ph.D., or pursuing the long years of medical training — a commitment which could lead to conflict between the traditional and modern roles. Moreover, all are high status professions in which a wife could have a rank equal to or higher than that of her spouse, which was presumed most likely to insure an egalitarian family.

The data were gathered through the use of semi-structured interviews held in the respondents' homes. The female interviewer talked with the husbands while the male researcher simultaneously interviewed the wives. All interviews were tape recorded and lasted on an average between 1¾ to 2½ hours.

The data presented in this paper are largely from the wives' responses (although where pertinent, information on the husband is also given).[2]

Family Power Structure in the Dual Profession Family

Structurally the contemporary American family consists of the statuses of the husband-father, the wife-mother, and the children, with the husband-father status being the dominant one. As Parsons and Bales (1955) have pointed out, it is the occupational status of the person occupying the husband-father status from which the entire family derives its socio-economic position in the larger society. A number of writers have discussed the severe strain placed upon the self-image of the person occupying the husband-father status when he is unable to be the main provider for the family — even when his "failure" is due to forces beyond his control.[3] The question which arises in connection with the present study is "what happens when the traditional structure of statuses and roles within the family face potential disruption due to the professional activities of the wife?"

Based on the accompanying role prescriptions for those occupying the statuses of wife-mother or husband-father, family types can be arranged from the traditional patriarchy to the deviant matriarchy. The data collected from 53 dual profession couples allows four types to emerge: (1) the traditional patriarchy, (2) the neo-traditional patriarchy, (3) the egalitarian family, and (4) the matriarchy. The distribution of the number of cases found in each category may be seen in Table 1.

Table 1 / Distribution of Family Types

Family Type	Number of Families
Traditional	20
Neo-Traditional	27
Egalitarian	1
Matriarchal	5
Reluctant (3)	
Resigned (2)	

The traditional patriarchy is characterized by typical sex-segregated roles with the husband as family protector and provider and the wife as homemaker. In the neo-traditional family (representative of the majority of our respondents) the status of provider remains the predominant male role with the wife in a "helping" economic position. The wife continues to be *responsible* for the traditional homemaking role, with her husband possibly *assisting* her. In only one instance was a couple truly egalitarian in *sharing* both the duties and rights of the husband-father and the wife-mother roles. In another five cases the wife was de facto the breadwinner of the family with her income larger than that of her husband. In these cases of matriarchy, two were apparently satisfactorily resigned to being the dominant member of the family while the other three wives wanted a reversal toward either a neo-traditional or traditional family. (In one case, the husband's income had been on the upswing for the last couple of years and the family appeared to be moving toward the neo-traditional pattern.) In the matriarchy the wife plays the major economic role but the husband in no case perceived himself as *sharing* the homemaker role (although he may assist his wife with feminine tasks). Consideration will be given to each of these family types, with a special section on those cases in which the wife's achievement, education, income, and/or occupational status is greater than that of her husband's.

The Traditional Family:
The Male Provider and the Female Homemaker

Despite popular sociological talk about the American egalitarian family, its existence remains to be proven (Safilios-Rothschild, 1969). Lopata's (1965) research suggests that in reality the traditional family form may be very much with us. Married woman are quick to define the "breadwinning" role as the most salient element in the male role while the task of being a "mother" is conceived to be the most important element in the female role. The traditional family described here is characterized by, for the most part, a complete separation of family tasks on the basis of sex, with the headship of the family belonging undisputedly to the husband. (By no means is this to insinuate that the husband is a despot! In the traditional family both the husband and the wife assert that the *legitimate* power of family headship is to be found in the status of husband-father.)

Studies attempting to measure the distribution of power within the family reveal that the working wife in the United States has more influence in economic matters than her non-employed sister (Blood and Wolfe, 1960; Heer, 1957). These same studies demonstrate, however, that the working-class wife has more power than the middle-class woman. This has been explained by pointing out two facts: (1) the income difference between the working-class husband and his wife is less than for the middle-class husband and his wife and (2) the need for the wife's income is presumably greater in the working class than in the middle class. Keeping this in mind, it is not surprising that twenty (20) of our dual profession couples were classified as being *traditional* in family type. Table 2 breaks down the distribution according to the wife's occupation, whether or not she is involved in a second career (i.e., entering her profession only after the children were older), and whether or not she is employed on a full-time basis. As can be seen from the table, wives involved in traditional marriages were likely to be second career women and/or not employed on a full time basis. In all except one case, the husband's education was either equal to or greater than his wife's. In all except one other case the husband was better known in his profession than his spouse was in hers, and in all cases he was clearly seen as the "breadwinner" of the family.[4]

A woman professor, married to a physician, (Case #27) pro-

Table 2 / Occupational Involvement of Traditional Wives

Occupation	Second Career		Full time Employment	
	Yes	No	Yes	No
Law (6)	1	5	2	4
Medicine (8)	0	8	1*	7
Academia (6)	5	1*	4	2

*Both of these cases represented a modified career with an interruption of more than ten years while the children were younger.

vides a typical illustration of the traditional family.[5] When Dr. and Mrs. W's children were younger, Mrs. W. was not employed (although she held a graduate degree in social work). She was awarded her Ph.D. when her youngest child was 17 years of age, and she now holds a full-time position at the city's leading university. She described her career as being "really and truly secondary in my book" — secondary to caring for the needs of the family. When asked about the degree of consideration she would give to her career if her husband were to receive a good job offer out of town, she responded:

> I wouldn't give any consideration to my position. (WOULD YOU LOOK FOR ANOTHER JOB IN A DIFFERENT CITY IF YOU WERE TO LEAVE THE AREA?] Probably. I can't imagine not being able to find something that I would enjoy in my line of work, and I don't think that I would enjoy doing nothing. I've had a taste of that. What I'm saying, really, is that what I'm doing is out of pure choice, which makes it a great pleasure. I don't have to work for the usual reasons. I suppose I have to work because it is what I *like to do.* (27-W)

The respondent viewed her husband's unqualified approval as essential to what she was doing:

> I know I wouldn't do it if my husband didn't want me to work. You'd have to have a pretty darn good reason for working if your husband didn't want you to. I can't imagine being married to some one who didn't want me to do what I wanted to do. Even thoug my career is clearly secondary, I don't feel cheated in any wa: because I want it this way. If I didn't want it this way, I thinl the marriage institution as we know it, and as we say it is in fact, in our society would be disrupted and that my marriage wouldn't be a successful one. (27-W)

She saw her husband as the head of the household asserting, "I think it has to be this way; and if a woman is bucking this all the time, I think something is wrong." She carefully pointed out that her income was not used to provide for the family's needs: "I just use my income for whatever I want — mostly I have invested it. It is never used for living expenses — not for my needs or my family's needs or household needs."

She prided herself in "holding down two jobs" explaining:

> I run a household, and a very full household, with marketing and not as much help as I had when the children were small. There are a lot of household responsibilities that I carry now, and my house wouldn't be run any better if I weren't working. And I have a full-time job, which for many men, is all they do.

When asked about her husband's assistance in making her work easier, she responded:

> He is very insistent about the help situation; he doesn't want me to have any household responsibilities. He feels I do too much on the outside for that. He's very protective of me as a human being, and I suppose in this way (by having me employ domestic help) he is showing his support.

While the physical care of the home is managed by hired help, this wife still maintains sole responsibility for hiring and firing the help and for performing any of the tasks not completed by the domestic employee. When the children pressed with their responsibilities, she did not work.

The traditional family is thus characterized by four main features:

1) The wife's career is equivalent to a "hobby" (a couple of women actually used this term) or viewed on a par with their neighbor's volunteer work.[6]
2) The husband is clearly the status giving and income earning member of the couple, with the wife's income not being used for family needs.
3) The wife's principle role is that of wife and mother and homemaker.
4) Hired domestic help generally takes care of the bulk of the routine household chores, with the wife caring for the remainder of the feminine tasks (e.g. entertaining, cooking, marketing, etc.)

The Neo-Traditional Family:
Husband and Wife of Equal Professional Status

In the neo-traditional family, the husband and wife could objectively be seen as sharing the breadwinning role in the family. While in all cases the husband's income was greater than the wife's, the wife was also earning a salary for full time or nearly full time professional activity as an attorney, a physician or a university professor. The question arises, what happens to the family roles when the male is not the uncontested 'status-giving' and "income-earning' member of the family and shares this central role with his wife.[7] Twenty seven (27) of the fifty three cases were classified as neo-traditional, including three couples where the husband was occupying an obviously temporary position as a graduate or professional student.

The neo-traditional couples differed from the traditional ones in two interrelated ways: (1) in most cases, the wife's income was needed and utilized to maintain the family's present standard of living and (2) the wife's professional activity assumed a certain importance in any decision the family makes, particularly around the issues of moving to another city and vacation time. It is quite probable that the reason her career assumes an importance is precisely because her income is needed for the family's increased comfort. This does not necessarily mean that both incomes are put into one pot (although in some cases this is the working arrangement), but more often that the wife's income is reserved for luxuries, such as an expensive family vacation, sending the children to private schools, for an elaborate interior decoration of the home, or to maintain the family's country home. While in the traditional couples, the wife could stop working tomorrow and her income would not be greatly missed (in fact, it sometimes cost the husband money for his wife to work in terms of increased taxes), in most neo-traditional couples this is not the case.[8] In one extreme case of two college professors, the husband viewed his wife's Ph.D. as an investment and strongly urged her to work full time even though she personally would have preferred to be working only on a part-time basis to enable her to spend more time with her children (#04). In most instances, however, it must be emphasized that the woman was under no strong pressure to work. The main benefit of her employment was cited as her being a more interesting and more content person than when she is not employed, with the income being a most pleasant fringe benefit.

Two young college professors provide a good case example. When asked how her husband felt about her professional involvement, the wife responded:

> I am probably more sensitive to creating possible trouble for him than he is. But it is clear to both of us that it just doesn't make any sense to make a move that would involve a loss in opportunity for me also. We could no longer manage without my salary. And we both feel that we wouldn't be happy over time if I was not working — and I think he feels that even more strongly than I do. I imagine I could survive if for one reason or another I wasn't working, but I don't think I would like it. (06-W)

She made it quite clear that her career had been retarded by marriage (due to the time of marriage, she was unable to obtain her Ph.D. from the Ivy League university she was then attending, later being awarded a degree from a less prestigious institution), but she felt that her husband's careeer mobility had to come first. When asked how she felt about this, she responded, "Well, certainly the marginal difference is not sufficient to say I'll scrap the husband and child. That's what the mix is (career, husband and child). And on the whole, the mix is certainly attractive."

In terms of the division of labor in the home, this couple is much more egalitarian than most others in our sample; but the *responsibility* for child care rests with the wife. Most of the housecleaning is taken care of by a full-time domestic and the husband takes care of cooking all the family meals. When asked whether the wife regarded the children as primarily her responsibility she replied:

> Yes. He (husband) takes more responsibility for her than a lot of other fathers would, but she is still primarily my responsibility. I am the one who figures out when she is sick, when she ought to go to the pediatrician, when she ought to take a nap, and takes care of keeping track when she didn't have her egg in the morning. (06 W)

Child care provides the clearest example of the lack of a sense of *true sharing* of domestic responsibilities. The husband may "help out," but both husband and wife view it to be the woman's responsibility to shop for children's clothes, take the children to the pediatrician, keep in touch with the teacher, arrange for baby sitters and housekeepers, and finally to cancel her own appointments if a conflict of schedules occurred with her work and her husband's work at a time the sitter didn't show up. Of our 45 couples who had at least one child, only one couple (#42) viewed the responsibility of childrearing to be a *shared* one by both mother and father.

With few exceptions, the wife also considers herself and is considered by the husband to be in charge of the home. Most women have hired domestic help to take care of the bulk of the housecleaning, with the remaining tasks frequently performed by the woman herself. A woman pediatrician with two children married to a pathologist represents the case in point. When asked whether her husband helps around the house, her response was:

> He does a lot. I don't ask him to clean up the living room or to wash the diapers — I have a maid to clean. It's the little things that are most important. If I am tired, he will take the baby. . . And he is not at all demanding. If I am busy, he doesn't mind having a TV dinner for supper. (18-W)

Those few cases in which the husband comes closer to sharing the household tasks with his wife still bear witness to the fact that the domestic chores of the home are thought of as the woman's *responsibility*. The wife of a young college professor who herself also teaches college pointed out that her husband does a good deal of the housework, including the vacuuming and cleaning. When asked whether he has ever voiced any feelings about this, she responded:

> Oh, once in a while he will get a little huffy about it — mostly when other people are around. A lot of my friends don't work, so their wives wait on them hand and foot. So once in a while, he feels put upon. He is very much worse about not doing things when other people are here. When no one is here, he will do absolutely anything. But he is sensitive and wants to put out the typical male image. (46-W)

In another case of two young physicians both still in advanced stages of training, this 'put upon' feeling led the husband to abandon the original agreement that the household tasks would be shared. The husband commented:

My wife does everything. I just stopped doing things. I don't really remember why I stopped. I think it was a feeling that she has always done somewhat better than I did in the classroom phase of the work and it wasn't necessary for her to study as much as I did. [HAS SHE EVER COMPLAINED ABOUT THIS?] No. When she complains, she complains that she is not capable of doing a good job. She feels she is not doing what she ought to as a female, a wife and a mother — this sort of thing. It is very convenient for me; she has two roles and I have one. (30-H)

The wife's response concurred with her husband's:

I used to want him to do more to help me out. I used to think that that was the way things were going to have to be. It just didn't work out. There isn't much cleaning for me — and he just didn't like doing it. Things like dishes, I don't like doing them either. But it is a lot easier for me to do them for him. I think I used to worry that I didn't have time to do the dishes. I think now it is demonstrated that there is time or the dishes can go undone for now. You have to be more flexible about it. (30-W)

Unlike with the traditional couples, the wife's professional activities are viewed as significantly providing for the family's economic well being. Yet both husband and wife assert that the husband is the primary breadwinner. One very successful woman physician married to an equally successful husband commented:

I think of my husband as the major breadwinner, and yet our salaries are not that far apart. I think of him as the boss of the family, and earning the most money . . . and I would not want to be making more than he makes or even to be making the same amount. I am very happy just the way it is. [COULD YOU GIVE A REASON FOR THIS?] I don't know. I am very happy to be able to contribute anything that I make to the family pot, but I am happy that he is the main breadwinner. Maybe this is the way it is supposed to be. (38-W)

Probably the biggest difference between the neo-traditional and traditional families *cannot* be seen in terms of marital role expectations. As with the traditional families, the wife is expected and expects to see that the home is run smoothly, that her husband's needs are met, and that the children are cared for. The husband is expected and expects to be the main provider and status giver. He does not expect his wife to work if she does not want to. The career is *her choice.* By the same token, he will *assist* his wife with her domestic role tasks if there is little or no domestic help and if he has no strong personal objections to performing such tasks.[9]

Where the traditional and egalitarian families *do differ* noticeably is with respect to the importance of the wife's career in making family decisions. While the traditional couples asserted that the wife's profession would be a small factor (if indeed it figured at all) in deciding either to move or not to move from the city, neo-traditional couples felt they would give the wife's career varying degrees of consideration. Two of the younger couples still asserted that they would not move unless both had acceptable positions, but couples who had been in their fields of professional endeavor for longer periods of time were less idealistic. Most women had made a conscious decision to place the husband's career above their own and to follow him wherever he went. The only point of consideration would be whether the wife could find some suitable professional activities in due time.[10]

Cases of Feminine Excellence

While the neo-traditional family differed from the traditional in use of the wife's income for the family and to the extent that her career is considered in making family decisions, the roles continue to be largely sex segregated. The husband is still considered the main breadwinner and the wife retains her power over the internal operations of the family. If there are children, the wife holds prime responsibility for them; it is she who secures the domestic help, is responsible for the smooth operation of the home, and does the planning for entertaining. The husband in return may help his wife with these tasks and tries not to put other unnecessary demands upon her. But there is no perceived *sharing* of roles — only a helping of each other. The husband is chiefly the provider while the wife is primarily the homemaker. What happens, however, when the wife's career performance in some way excels her husband's? Analysis of our interviews with the 53 couples in our sample found this to be the case in fourteen (14) cases based upon the following considerations: education, occupational status, public or professional recognition, and/or income. Table 3 lists each of the cases of feminine excellence and its corresponding family type. Each of these will be considered separately in an attempt to learn its possible importance for the maintenance of traditional family norms.

Table 3 / Distribution of Cases of Female Career Excellence

Source	Case Number	Family Type
Achievement (1)	#32	Traditional
Education Alone (4)	#05	Neo-traditional
	#12	Neo-traditional
	#23	Neo-traditional
	#31	Traditional
Income Alone (2)	#07	Reluctant Matriarchy
	#03	Reluctant Matriarchy
Income, Education, and Achievement (2)	#25	Reluctant Matriarchy
	#53	Resigned Matriarchy
Income and Education (1)	#37	Resigned Matriarchy
Physician Status (4)	#48	Traditional
	#50	Neo-traditional
	#51	Neo-traditional
	#52	Traditional

In three cases the achievement of the wife was clearly greater than that of her husband. Only in one case, however, was this public achievement *not* combined with other variables. In case #32 the husband was unquestionably the breadwinner and provider, in spite of the wife's reknown. This family was clearly characterized as traditional, with the woman taking full responsibility for the homemaking tasks while the husband was the sole supporter of the family. The wife noted:

> We live on his income. We have never lived on my income. I have always felt very strongly that a man should feel masculine, and I don't think he is going to feel masculine if every time he says 'no, I don't think you should buy that,' I go out and buy it with my own money. I have always been terribly careful to not do anything in that way to make him feel that he is not masculine. (32-W)

In six cases, the educational level of the wife was greater than that of her husband, two of which were combined with other variable differences. As in the case of public or professional recognition, a difference in education alone does not necessarily alter the traditional male-female roles. Take for example our most extreme case of a man with a high school degree and his highly successful attorney wife (case #23). While he most clearly saw himself as the breadwinner, his wife viewed herself as "economically independent and able to take care of myself." The husband is a self-made millionnaire so that even his wife's very substantial salary could not come close to his annual income. While she was not willing to see her husband in the unqualified role of family breadwinner, she did emphasize that he was the head of the house and this was the way both of them wanted it. This couple saw the wife as the homemaker, with a traditional division of labor in existence — the husband took care of the yard work while the wife was in complete control inside the home and had primary responsibility for the care of the children.

A difference in education alone appears to have little effect upon the family type of dual professional couples, with three respondents being characterized as neo-traditional and the fourth fitting into the traditional typology.

During the course of our interviews with physician couples, several respondents asserted that there would be an insurmountable problem when a woman physician is married to a non-physician. This "problem" was attributed to the difference in status between physicians and occupants of most other professions. Four couples were interviewed where the professional dichotomies were: (1) physician-business executive (#50); (2) physician-public service employee (#51); (3) physician-college professor (#52); and (4) physician-psychologist (#48). In no way, however, was this supposed difference in status found to change the traditional balance in the family. The husband in all four cases saw himself, was seen by the wife, and was in fact the main provider. In two cases the wife's career was a very secondary interest as described in the traditional families. In the remaining two cases, neo-traditional traits were observed. One couple came very close to being egalitarian in terms of the importance of the wife's career (but not in terms of a division of labor or in terms of the uses of the wife's income). This husband, when offered a promotion and a transfer out of town, refused the company's offer saying: "Unlike other husbands, I have a doctor and her patients to consider." While he realizes that this refusal may deter further career opportunities, he is extremely proud of his wife's accomplishments. (It was he who financed her way through college, graduate school, and now medical school and apparently views the medical career as much his as hers.) But as in the other traditional and neo-traditional cases, in no way was there a reversal of roles. The wife expressed it in the following way:

> The care of the home is definitely my responsibility. The maintenance — replacing screws and nails and painting — is his or a shared concern. But I feel that it is definitely my job to see that the place gets cleaned. And if the cleaning woman doesn't come, I am the one who does it. I do think that sometimes he could help a little more than he does, but it is my responsibility. I don't see it as something he *should* do. I just think it would be nice if he sometimes did help me more. But it is my responsibility to do it as part of my role as a housewife. (50-W)

It is important to emphasize, however, that in none of these cases was the income of the wife greater than that of her husband. If this physician status were coupled with a higher income, a much different picture might emerge.

The studies on the power relations in the American family have demonstrated that the wife's earning power may be a definite factor in shifting the balance of power away from the husband (Blood and Wolfe, 1960; Heer, 1957). While education and achievement differences are important, our respondents had little fear of the husband's traditional role being jeopardized unless the wife's income exceeded his. Most men who were asked about their reaction to their wives' earning more than they, responded to this hypothetical situation with "it would be great; there would be more to spend." The wives, however, were more aware of what it might do to disrupt traditional sex roles.

A number of women clearly stated that they would cut down on their work rather than let their income exceed that of their husbands. When asked how she would feel at the prospect of making more money than her husband, a physician married to a college professor stated emphatically:

> I wouldn't feel that it would be good for our marriage at all. The only way that I would ever let that happen would be if we were in dire need. And if it were possible for me to increase my income (and he were unable to increase his), then I might let this happen.

Psychologically it would upset the roles. There is enough difficulty in this kind of marriage without dirupting these roles. (52-W)

Of our sample, three wives having the same education as their husbands earned a larger salary and two others had both a higher education and earned the greater income.[11] All of these families were classified as matriarchal.

While in the neo-traditional family (where the income was supplemental to the male breadwinner), we saw some "helping" with female domestic roles, the cases in which the wife's income exceeded her husband's revealed little such assistance. While the husband was not able to assert himself as the sole breadwinner and main economic provider, nor was he willing to assume any extensive helping or sharing role with domestic tasks. In a very real sense, the husband was without a clearly defined status in the family.

In three cases, the wife clearly wanted her husband to retain (or wished he could assume) his status of provider and status giver. If he was unable to provide in the manner in which she felt was necessary, she was resentful of his incompetence and sometimes ambivalent about her own success. A highly successful woman professor married to a husband of lesser academic rank asserted that she would like to forsake the career for a better family life. "I think the career would be something I would like to try after the children were grown — or at least I would prefer working on a lower level." (25-W) Both husband and wife acknowledged that this was mere wishful thinking because the family needed her income to maintain their present standard of living.[12]

When the wife's income is greater than her husband's, (unlike differences in education or status ranking alone), the husband's role in the family is clearly threatened. It is significant that no wife *wanted* to earn more than her husband, but some in fact did in order to meet the family's needs.

Summary and Conclusion

American society has designated the role of the breadwinner and status giver to the male, while the female's role revolves around homemaking tasks. The fact that a woman may also assume an additional role of working in a profession has been the subject of countless books and articles. Little attempt, however, has been made to analyze the impact of the wife's assumption of the professional role on the marriage and the family.

In analyzing the responses of 53 dual-profession couples, it becomes quite apparent that *the assumption of a professional role by the wife does not mean a dramatic change in family roles.* In only one case did we find the dual-profession insuring an egalitarian family. This case (#42) consists of two professors who made a conscious effort to *share* both the breadwinning and homemaking roles. In all other cases, the wife was responsible for the traditional feminine tasks while her husband (with the exception of the matriarchal type) being responsible for providing the family with status and income. Our data yield no indication that either men or women desire to see an equal *sharing of* both masculine and feminine role tasks in the family. The wives (so long as their husbands were able to provide adequately) preferred not to *have to* work in the same ways their husbands did, leaving the provider role and its corresponding rights and duties as his domain. In return they accepted their prime responsibilities to be in the area of homemaking and child care.[13]

French and Raven (1968) distinguished five types of power; coercive, reward, expert, legitimate, and referent. With respect to the first four categories, the husband's hold has weakened to varying degrees in the American family, leading sociologists to herald the birth of the egalitarian family. They neglect to note, however, that referent power continues to insure the existence of the traditional and neo-traditional family types. *Wives are constrained by their own idea of ideal feminine roles.* They are very concerned about their possible infringement on their husbands' provider role and they are unwilling or unable to relinquish their traditional feminine role.[14]

This fact inevitably lessens a wife and mother's opportunities for success in her profession for at least two major reasons: (1) she must channel her energies in two directions (home and profession) whereas her husband's very success in his family role is contingent on his professional success; and (2) since her career is not a primary concern of the family, her lack of mobility and bargaining power causes professional success to be even more difficult to achieve. Only a truly egalitarian family will allow the highly educated married woman the freedom necessary for planned career success — a family form which appears to be the exception rather than the rule in American society.

NOTES

This paper is based on a study carried out with the assistance of the Lena Lake Forrest Fellowship granted by the Business and Professional Women's Foundation, Washington, D.C.

1. Safilios-Rothschild (1969) suggests that the egalitarian family may be a myth perpetuated by the secondary source of family textbooks and not supported by actual research. She notes, ". . . the myth that the American family is equalitarian was probably born as an ideal congruent with major American values and has been perpetuated despite all research evidence to the contrary. Neither decision making nor the division of labor in the family has been found to be equalitarian, nor has the conception of marital roles by married people been reported as companionate or equal in any sense."

2. For a discussion of male attitudes and an analysis of the male responses see T. Neal Garland, "The Better Half?: The Male in the Dual Profession Family." Paper presented at the American Sociological Association Meetings, Washington, D.C., August, 1970.

3. Perhaps one of the clearest examples of the importance of the bread-winning role for the male in American society can be illustrated by the black family, where stability appears to be very much linked with the husband's ability to perform his role as provider. For further discussion, see Clark (1965); Moynihan (1965); Rainwater and Yancey (1967); Billingsley (1968); and Frazier (1939).

4. Three cases classified as "traditional" will be further discussed in a later special section. In these cases the husband had completed fewer years of formal education than his wife, was less known in his profession than his wife in hers, or held a less prestigious occupational status. Yet all three cases were clearly traditionally patriarchal as described here.

5. Case numbers are used throughout this paper to enable the reader to distinguish between and among different responses.

6. The one exception was an attorney (#32) who had begun her career on a volunteer staff and eventually was promoted to a very prestigious position. The wife viewed her work as an important career, but her husband refused to regard her efforts as anything more than voluntary community service.

7. Even for a position of equal prestige, it was common for the husband to receive a larger salary. One couple (#42) reported that the university refused to give both an equal salary (in spite of relatively similar qualifications) because "it was too much money to give to one family." There were five couples in the sample where the wife earned a greater income; these are considered as special cases and were classified as matriarchal.

8. In three case the wife's income was purely superfluous in the

same manner as the traditional cases. In two of these cases, (#19 and #38), the woman was over 30 years of age when she married and her career pattern was well established before marriage. In the third case (#40) the couple apparently shifted toward a neo-traditional set up after the children were in college and the wife simultaneously achieved a good deal of career success. It should also be pointed out that the wife is nearly 15 years younger than her husband and is reaching the peak of her career as her husband is nearing retirement. It has only been within the last few years that the wife's profession has assumed much significance to the family.

9. The use of the wife's income and the husband's ability to be the sole provider seems to be related to whether or not he will even assist his wife with the household tasks. Recently after a class discussion of sex roles a student commented, "I do a lot of housework on Saturdays while my wife washes and irons. She works all week and needs the help. But I would not do it if her working wasn't necessary to send our boy through college. If she was working just because she wanted to, she would have to take care of the house by herself." We found this same attitude voiced by one of the husbands in our sample who was presently a Ph.D. candidate and his wife was an attorney. He planned to discontinue helping with household tasks once he earned his degree and secured a position. A number of families reported that the husband helped out with domestic tasks early in the marriage (presumably when her income was greatly needed), but as time continued, he withdrew his help.

10. One couple was in the process of shifting from the idealistic notion of an equal importance of both careers to the more realistic position of one career's being more important during the time of the interview. A year prior to the interview, the husband had turned down a high status and lucrative position because the wife refused to interrupt her career. Recently, however, she learned that she would not receive tenure nor would her contract be renewed. With a certain bitterness she acknowledged that she would not dare to stand in her husband's career plans again if she wanted their marriage to last. She felt she would have to be more realistic about her career goals and would follow him wherever he received his next position. For a further discussion on the importance of the husband's career over his wife's profession, see M. Poloma and T. N. Garland, "Jobs or Careers? The Case of the Professionally Employed Woman"; International Journal of Comparative Sociology; Fall, 1971 (Forthcoming).

11. Strictly speaking, the student husbands and professional wives should be included in this special category, but these cases are very transitional and a traditional family type was apparent. For example, one husband took some of the domestic work upon himself because his wife was gone most of the day (earning a living for both

of them). But he clearly felt that she would take over all of the domestic tasks once he got his degree and became the breadwinner. In another case, however, a medical school student supported by his wife (who was a professor) left the domestic responsibilities largely to her. He reasoned that she was home more than he was and welcomed the household tasks as a break from her work. Both of these students fully realized that their student status was temporary.

12. It should be noted that four out of the five families classified as "matriarchal" were black. In two cases recent economic opportunities opening for the black husband appeared to insure a closing of the gap between the husband and wife income, which may well yield the desired traditional or neo-traditional family form. In two other cases (one due to the husband's lack of education and in the other to poor career planning) the income differences are not likely to close.

13. This distinction between "helping" and "sharing" of tasks was recently pointed out in "Are You Ready for Liberation: An Introductory Course in Libthing" in *Mademoiselle* (February, 1970). The quiz asked: "What's wrong with this statement? 'My husband is a liberated man. He helps me around the house.' " The answer was that if he were truly liberated, he would be *sharing* rather than *helping*. Feminists are well aware of the fact that the egalitarian family is a myth, but they are less willing to take note that many women are aware of this lack of egality but want the situation to continue as is in the family.

14. It is not clear whether the wife wants her husband to assume a sharing role as far as domestic work is concerned and he is not willing *or* whether the husband is willing (especially in many neo-traditional families) but the wife is reluctant to share the feminine role with her husband. No female respondent felt that her husband *should* do more to help her out, although a few wished that their husbands *would* do more. One or two husbands claimed that they were willing to assume more of a responsibility for domestic tasks, but that their wives would not let them. Whatever the reason, the domestic work remains the wife's *responsibilty* even when the wife is the prime breadwinner.

REFERENCES

Angrist, Shirley S., "Changes in Women's Work Aspirations During College (Or Work Does Not Equal Career)." Paper presented at the Ohio Valley Sociological Society annual meeting, Akron, Ohio, May 1970

Billingsley, Andrew, Black Families in White America. New Jersey: Prentice Hall, 1968

Blood, Robert O. and Wolfe, Donald M., Husbands and Wives. The Free Press of Glencoe, 1960.

Clark, Kenneth B., Dark Ghetto. New York: Harper and Row, 1965.

Empey, Lamar T., "Role Expectations of Young Women Regarding Marriage and a Career." Marriage and Family Living 20: 152-155, 1958.

Frazier, E. Franklin, The Negro Family in the United States. The University of Chicago Press, 1939.

French, John and Raven, Bertram, "The Bases of Social Power." Pp. 259-268 in Darian Cartwright and Alvin Zander, eds. Group Dynamics. New York: Harper and Row, 1968.

Hartley, Ruth, "Some Implications of Current Changes in Sex Role Patterns." Merrill-Palmer Quarterly: 153-164, 1960.

Haug, Marie R. and Sussman, Marvin B., "The Second Career — Variant of a Sociological Concept." Journal of Gerontology 22 (October): 439-444, 1967.

Heer, David M., "The Measurement and Bases of Family Power: An Overview." Marriage and Family Living 25, 1963. "Dominance and the Working Wife." Social Forces 36: 347-352, 1957.

Lopata, Helena Znaniecki, "The Secondary Features of a Primary Relationship." Human Organization 24 (Summer): 116-123, 1965.

Moynihan, Daniel P., The Negro Family: The Case for National Action. Washington, D.C.: U.S. Department of Labor, Office of Planning and Research, 1965.

Parsons, Talcott and Bales, Robert E., "The American Family." Family Socialization and Interaction Process. Glencoe, Ill.: The Free Press, 1955.

Rainwater, Lee and Yancy, William L.,The Moynihan Report and the Politics of Controversy. Cambridge, Mass.: M.I.T. Press, 1967.

Riesman, David, "Some Continuities and Discontinuities in the Education of Women." Pp. 324-348 in David Riesman, Abundance for What? and Other Essays. Garden City, New York: Doubleday and Co., 1964.

Safilios-Rothschild, Constantina, "Marital Expectations and Marital Experience: Why Such a Discrepancy." Paper read at the ICOFA meetings in Rennes, France, April 3-7, 1969.

Tropman, John E., "The Married Professional Social Worker." Journal of Marriage and the Family 30 (November): 661-665, 1968.

Turner, Ralph, "Some Aspects of Women's Ambition." American Journal of Sociology 70: 271-285, 1964.

Index